The Organizational Ombudsman

Origins, Roles, and Operations
A Legal Guide

Charles L. Howard

Cover design by ABA Publishing.

The materials contained herein represent the opinions and views of the author and/or the editors, and should not be construed to be the views or opinions of the law firms or companies with whom such persons are in partnership with, associated with, or employed by, nor of the Section of Dispute Resolution of the American Bar Association unless adopted pursuant to the bylaws of the Association.

Nothing contained in this book is to be considered as the rendering of legal advice for specific cases, and readers are responsible for obtaining such advice from their own legal counsel. This book and materials contained herein are intended for educational and informational purposes only.

© 2010 American Bar Association. All rights reserved. No part of this publication may be reproduced, stored in a retrieval system, or transmitted in any form or by any means, electronic, mechanical, photocopying, recording, or otherwise, without the prior written permission of the publisher. For permission contact the ABA Copyrights & Contracts Department, copyright@americanbar.org or via fax at (312) 988-6030.

16 15 14 13 12   9 8 7 6 5 4

Cataloging-in-Publication data is on file with the Library of Congress

The Organizational Ombudsman: Origins, Roles, and Operations—A Legal Guide / Howard, Charles L.

Discounts are available for books ordered in bulk. Special consideration is given to state bars, CLE programs, and other bar-related organizations. Inquire at Book Publishing, ABA Publishing, American Bar Association, 321 North Clark Street, Chicago, Illinois 60654.

www.ShopABA.org

Dedication

To Joan

who encouraged me to write this book and
whose love and understanding made it possible to do so.

To Phil Gerbino —
With great admiration
and appreciation for having
been able to work with
you.
Clark Hull

Contents

Dedication iii

Acknowledgments xiii

About the Author xv

Preface xvii

Introduction xxiii

Chapter 1
What Is an Organizational Ombuds? 1
Part I: A Short History of the Ombudsman Role 1
   A. Origins in Sweden 2
   B. Expansion in Scandinavia 4
   C. Expansion Beyond Scandinavia 5
      1. Ombudsman Programs Transition to Universities . . 10
      2. Ombudsman Programs Transition to Corporations . 15
      3. Impact of the Defense Industry Initiative 17
      4. Ombudsman Associations 20
      5. Ombudsman Programs in the Federal
         Government 21
   D. American Bar Association Resolutions 24
Part II: Essential Characteristics of an Organizational
Ombuds Program 27
   A. 1969 ABA Resolution and the Spread of Ombuds
      Programs 27
   B. Evolution of Codes of Ethics and Standards of
      Practice of Ombuds Associations 30
   C. 2001 American Bar Association Resolution 37
   D. 2004 American Bar Association Resolution 42
   E. Agreement and Disagreement on Key Principles of
      Organizational Ombuds Programs 44
   F. IOA Best Practices Recommendations 72
Part III: What Does an Organizational Ombuds Do? 75

v

Chapter 2
Why Should Organizations Create Ombuds Programs? .. 79
Part I—The Forces of Change 86
   A. Demographics 86
      1. Immigration 87
      2. Diversity 89
      3. Impact on Educational Institutions 89
      4. Impact in Other Countries 91
      5. Increase in the Role of Women in the Workforce .. 92
      6. Other Demographic Trends: Generational Change and Talent Shortage 93
      7. Impact of Demographic Changes 94
   B. Technology and Globalization 95
      1. Growth of the Information Technology Sector 98
      2. Increased Need for Knowledge Workers 98
      3. Emergence of the Virtual Workspace 99
      4. Emergence of the Global Workforce 101
      5. Globalization of Universities 102
   C. Globalization and the Multinational Corporation 104
      1. Growth of Multinational Corporations 105
      2. Globalization of Multinational Corporations 106
      3. The Need for a Global Corporate Ethics 108
      4. World Recession—Impact on Globalization 112
      5. Impact of the Forces of Change 113
Part II—Legal and Regulatory Pressures on Organizations ... 115
   A. Criminal Liability 117
      1. Early Development of Criminal Liability for Organizations 117
      2. United States Sentencing Guidelines for Organizations 119
      3. Development of Ethics and Compliance Programs 122
      4. 2004 Revisions to the Organizational Sentencing Guidelines 122
      5. Criminal Liability Provisions of the Sarbanes-Oxley Act of 2002 124
      6. Prosecution Guidelines 125
   B. Corporate Governance and Government Regulation .. 126
      1. *In re Caremark* 126
      2. Federal Agency Reporting Incentives 128

　　　　3. USA Patriot Act 128
　　　　4. Sarbanes-Oxley Act of 2002 129
　　　　5. SEC and Stock Exchange and Association
　　　　　　Requirements 129
　　　　6. Best Practices Recommended by Business
　　　　　　Groups 131
　　C. Employment Law 132
　　　　1. Title VII Cases 133
　　　　2. Title IX Cases 137
　　　　3. Mandatory Discrimination and Harassment
　　　　　　Training Programs 139
　　　　4. Spread of Whistle-blower Laws 139
Part III—Insufficiency of Current Best Practices 141
　　A. Necessity of Current Best Practices 142
　　B. Ethics Officers, HR, and Compliance Programs 144
　　　　1. Limits on the Promise of Confidentiality 144
　　　　2. The Risks of Strict Enforcement 145
　　C. Whistle-blower Laws and Policies 147
　　　　1. Limitations on the Effectiveness of Whistle-
　　　　　　blower Laws and Policies 147
　　　　2. Data on the Effectiveness of Whistle-blower Laws .149
　　　　3. Why Whistle-blower Policies Fail to Address the
　　　　　　Concerns of an Individual 151
　　　　4. American Recovery and Reinvestment Act of 2009 156
　　D. Hotlines and Ethics Survey Data 157
　　　　1. Reasons for Creating Hotlines 158
　　　　2. Features of Hotline Services 160
　　　　3. Limitations on Hotline Effectiveness 161
Part IV—Ombuds Programs 170
　　A. Ombuds Structure Is Important 171
　　B. An Organizational Ombuds Fills Gaps 177
　　C. Reported Effectiveness of Ombuds Programs 184
Part V—Conclusion: Why Create an Ombuds Program? 187

Chapter 3
How Can Ombuds' Confidentiality Be Protected? 189
Part I—Imputed Notice 193
　　A. Basic Principles of Imputed Notice 193
　　B. General Principles of Agency Law 195
　　C. Cases Relevant to Imputed Notice 197

D. IOA and the 2004 ABA Resolution 212
E. Imputed Notice—Conclusion 218
Part II—Legal Bases for Ombuds Confidentiality 220
   A. Common-Law Privilege 221
      1. Background on Development of Federal
         Testimonial Privileges 221
      2. Development of the Ombuds Privilege 227
      3. Subsequent Cases Citing the *Carman* Decision ...239
      4. Subsequent Cases Recognizing an Ombuds
         Privilege 243
      5. An Ombuds Privilege Belongs to the Ombuds 244
      6. Observations on the Recognition of an
         Ombudsman Privilege 245
   B. Program Conditions of Use—Implied Contract of
     Confidentiality 249
   C. Other Bases for Confidentiality 255
      1. *Garstang* and the California Constitutional Right of
         Privacy 256
      2. State Statutes—Generally 259
      3. Uniform Mediation Act 263
      4. Administrative Dispute Resolution Act 264
      5. Federal Mediation Privilege 269
      6. A Court's Inherent Authority to Regulate Discovery 271
      7. Arbitration 273
Part III—Documentation 277
   A. Ombuds Charter 278
   B. Ombuds Contract 283
   C. Position Descriptions 285
   D. Documentation Publicizing the Ombuds Office 285
      1. Brochures and Web Sites 286
      2. Other Ombuds Office Publicity Information 289
      3. Organizational Information 290
   E. Documentation of Ombuds Operations 290
      1. Policies and Procedures 291
      2. Case Files—Preservation and Destruction 292
   F. Trend Reports 295
   G. Measures of Effectiveness 297
Part IV—Protecting Confidentiality in Litigation 300
   A. What to Avoid Doing 301
   B. Independent Counsel for the Ombuds Office 305
   C. Motions 307

Chapter 4
What Else Would Be Helpful for an Organizational Ombuds to Know? 311
Part I: Overview of Litigation Discovery Tools and Remedies, including the Fundamentals of Electronic Discovery 315
    A. Introduction to Discovery Rules in Civil Actions 315
    B. Discovery Methods 316
        1. Depositions 316
        2. Interrogatories 317
        3. Requests for Production and Inspection 319
        4. Requests for Admission 320
    C. Scope of Discovery 321
        1. In General 321
        2. Privileges 322
    D. Discovery Remedies 324
        1. Protective Orders 324
        2. Motion to Compel Discovery 325
        3. Sanctions for Failure to Comply with Discovery Order 326
        4. Assessment of Expenses for Failure to Admit 327
    E. Discovery of Electronically Stored Information 327
        1. Triggering the Duty to Preserve ESI 329
        2. Materials to Be Preserved (Scope of Discovery) .. 332
        3. How to Satisfy the Obligation to Preserve 335
        4. Consequences of Noncompliance 336
    F. Implications of Discovery Methods and e-Discovery for Ombuds' Practices 338
Part II: The Federal Arbitration Act, the Uniform Mediation Act, and the Mediation/Confidentiality Privilege 340
    A. Overview of ADR 340
    B. Arbitration Generally 340
    C. Federal Arbitration Act 343
    D. Mediation 345
        1. Mediation Process and Procedures Generally 345
        2. Mediation Privilege/Confidentiality 347
    E. Uniform Mediation Act 348
        1. Overview 348
        2. The UMA Mediation Privilege 349
    F. Implications of the Mediation Privilege for Ombuds' Practices 351

Part III: Imminent Threat of Serious Harm as an Exception to
  Confidentiality 354
  A. Background 354
  B. *Tarasoff v. Regents of University of California* 356
  C. Adoption of the Tarasoff Rule 359
  D. Implications for Ombuds 361
Part IV: Ombuds Confidentiality in Criminal Cases 364
  A. Background 364
  B. The Sixth Amendment Right to Confront and Cross-
    Examine 364
  C. The Sixth Amendment and Privilege Claims 367
  D. Implications for Ombuds 369
Part V: Federal Sentencing Guidelines for Organizations 372
  A. Background 372
  B. Basic Structure of the Sentencing Guidelines 374
  C. 2004 Amendments to the Sentencing Guidelines 379
  D. Implications for Ombuds 382
Part VI: The Clery Act 384
  A. Background 384
  B. Reporting Requirements 384
  C. Reporting Channels 386
  D. Implications for Ombuds 387
Part VII: Public Sector Ombuds—Records Retention and
  Freedom of Information Acts 389
  A. Introduction 389
  B. Records Preservation, Retention, and Destruction 390
  C. Access to Public Records 393
    1. Freedom of Information Act 393
    2. The Privacy Act 400
  D. Implications for Ombuds 401
  E. State FOIA Statutes 403
Part VIII: European Union Data Protection Directive and
  Subsequent Developments 406
  A. Introduction 406
  B. Overview of the EU Data Protection Directive 407
  C. History of Data Protection Law in Europe 409
  D. Summary of the Directive and Key Provisions 411
  E. Subsequent Developments and Issues Related to
    European Data Protection Directive 417
    1. Safe Harbor Agreement 418

     2. Whistle-blower Provisions of the U.S. Sarbanes-Oxley
        Act 420
   F. Implications for Ombuds 423
Part IX: Employment Laws and Cases 425
   A. Federal Employment Laws 425
   B. Selected Landmark Supreme Court Employment Law
      Cases 435
   C. Common Areas of State Employment Laws 437

Appendixes **439**

Appendix 1: 1969 ABA Resolution and Report 439

Appendix 2: 1971 ABA Resolution and Report 447

Appendix 3: The Ombudsman Association Code of Ethics and
   Standards of Practice (1995) 455

Appendix 4: Ethical Principles for University and College
   Ombudsmen 457

Appendix 5:
   A. International Ombudsman Association Code of
      Ethics 459
   B. International Ombudsman Association Standards of
      Practice (effective prior to October 2009) 460
   C. International Ombudsman Association Standards of
      Practice (effective October 2009) 460

Appendix 6: Standards for the Establishment and Operation of
   Ombuds Offices (ABA Policy Adopted August 2001) 468

Appendix 7: Standards for the Establishment and Operation of
   Ombuds Offices (ABA Policy Adopted February 2004) ...494

Appendix 8: The Ombudsman Association Standards of
   Practice, 1995 525

Appendix 9: The University and College Ombuds Association
   Standards of Practice, 2000 529

Appendix 10: The International Ombudsman Association Guidance
   for Best Practices and Commentary on the American Bar
   Association Standards for the Establishment and Operation of
   Ombuds Offices (Revised February 2004) 534

Appendix 11: IOA Best Practices—A Supplement to IOA's Standards of Practice (Version 3, October 13, 2009) 557

Appendix 12: American Recovery and Reinvestment Act of 2009, Section 1553, Protecting State and Local Government and Contractor Whistleblowers 571

Appendix 13: H.B. 3578, Introduced in Texas Legislature, 2007 581

Appendix 14: Additional Ombuds Examples 587

Acknowledgments

I am deeply indebted to many people for helping me learn about ombuds programs and for their assistance with this book. I would not have become involved with ombuds without Ann Bensinger, Tom Furtado, Pat Gnazzo, and George Wratney of United Technologies Corporation in the *Roy* case and in other cases thereafter. I was ably assisted in preparing the motion for a protective order in *Roy* by two associates, Linda Yoder and Leslie Davenport, who have long since been my partners at Shipman & Goodwin. Maria Gulluni, a former associate, helped me in one of my first writing efforts on ombuds issues—a booklet on ombuds confidentiality for the Ombudsman Association. Vaughan Finn and Lee Anne Duval have worked with me on various ombuds matters since then. Margaret Watson, Randy Williams, Arlene Redmond, Mary Rowe, Marsha Wagner, Ralph Hasson, Leander Dolphin, Lee Anne Duval, Wayne Blair, and Sue Murphy all provided helpful comments on drafts of various sections of this book. I also appreciate the many research projects undertaken by summer associates at Shipman & Goodwin in 2008, which were particularly helpful with the material presented in Chapters 2 and 4.

I have imposed on the time and assistance of many ombuds in collecting the examples included in Chapter 3 and Appendix 14. I thought it was important that all of these examples be real, but confidentiality requires me to present them anonymously. To mention them by name would undermine that confidentiality, but I want to thank them nevertheless. I believe that these stories are a powerful aspect of this book.

And, finally, I would not have been able to complete the research or the many tedious details involved in writing this book without the extremely able assistance of Harry Burgess, the librarian at Shipman & Goodwin, and my assistant, Terry Banister. They both have my most sincere appreciation.

Charles L. Howard

About the Author

Charles Howard is a partner with Shipman & Goodwin LLP, a Connecticut law firm, where he was chair of the Litigation Department from 1985 to 2000. He has served as independent counsel for ombudsman offices at major corporations, universities, research facilities, and other organizations throughout the United States for almost 20 years. He has written articles and been a frequent presenter on ombudsman issues at numerous bar association and professional association seminars.

In addition to his representation of ombudsman offices, Mr. Howard has more than 34 years of civil litigation experience in state and federal courts and has briefed and/or argued over 70 appeals. His practice has included business and intellectual property litigation, as well as the representation of municipal, quasi-public, and state governmental entities in a wide range of matters. He has been included in *Best Lawyers in America*® in the Commercial litigation practice area and has been recognized by *Law & Politics* as a "Connecticut Super Lawyer"® in the intellectual property litigation practice area.

Mr. Howard served on the Ad Hoc Advisory Group to the U.S. Sentencing Commission, which reviewed and recommended changes to the federal organizational sentencing guidelines in 2004. He also served for 10 years on the Connecticut Criminal Justice Commission.

Mr. Howard graduated from the Woodrow Wilson School of Public and International Affairs at Princeton University with honors and from the University of Virginia School of Law. He began his legal career as an Assistant Attorney General for then Attorney General John C. Danforth of Missouri. For more information on Mr. Howard, see http://www.shipmangoodwin.com/choward/.

Preface

My involvement with the world of ombuds began almost 20 years ago. As the chair of my law firm's litigation department, I had been part of a marketing "pitch" to a potential client. The first call I received from the general counsel's office was to serve as independent counsel for their ombudsman office (and I couldn't even pronounce "ombudsman" correctly), which was seeking to protect the confidentiality of its communications with an employee. We undertook the assignment with relish and, despite scant precedent on which to rely, filed a motion for a protective order in the federal court case. We asserted that the communications were privileged and that both the company and the employee were bound by an implied contract of confidentiality, which was the central defining characteristic of the program and the reason for its creation. Our motion was granted on both grounds based on the facts we presented, and only later did we realize that the court's ruling in that case was an important step in building the foundation for ombuds confidentiality.

In the years since that case, I have been privileged to continue to have an active litigation practice that has been unusually varied and interesting. It has included the representation of state and local governmental and quasi-governmental entities, complex business litigation, intellectual property matters, employee benefits litigation, and appeals. I have defended civil rights cases, conducted procurement fraud and ethics violation internal investigations, and served on the Ad Hoc Advisory Group to the U.S. Sentencing Commission that recommended revisions to the federal organizational sentencing guidelines in 2004. While completely serendipitous, this broad experience in other matters has been of great benefit to my representation of ombuds offices. These varied experiences have given me a peripheral vision of many different types of issues and a sense of the challenges of litigation in different areas of the law. During this same time, my representation of ombuds offices also expanded and became a national practice, giving me the opportunity to advise ombuds offices at major corporations, universities, and national laboratories throughout the country.

It was with this background and in this context that I decided to write this book.

First, as a lawyer who has represented organizational ombuds offices at major corporations and institutions for almost 20 years, I have seen how beneficial organizational ombudsman offices can be in providing guidance to people on how to resolve workplace disputes and on how to surface issues of misconduct in their organizations. Ombuds accomplish this by:

- providing information that an inquirer would not seek from other channels out of concerns about confidentiality or for fear of retaliation;
- providing an inquirer with options for reporting misconduct or resolving conflict and explaining how each option works;
- coaching an inquirer on how an issue may best be articulated; and
- generally serving as an off-the-record resource someone can use to seek guidance or advice.

Perhaps just as important, ombuds are available for extended or multiple conversations on an issue until an inquirer becomes comfortable with a particular approach. At the same time, organizational ombuds are able to provide trend reports and analysis on systemic issues to management that can be useful and that do not involve disclosure of confidential information from any particular inquirer. I have become convinced that these services are both valuable and increasingly necessary in large organizations and institutions where people come to work or learn, and I believe society will benefit if more organizations create organizational ombuds programs.

Second, there is no clear understanding of what an "ombuds" or "ombudsman" is. As the concept has been adapted and applied in various ways over the years, the original meaning has been obscured and new meanings have emerged in contemporary American society. As a result, there are several models—and a wide variation of practice within each model—so that today, neither those who create the programs nor the public have a clear understanding of what an *organizational ombuds* is and does. The lack of understanding about the variety of models is compounded by the undifferentiated use of the term "ombudsman" to apply to all of them. This confusion also affects the courts, where ombuds' claims of confidentiality and privilege are analyzed and decided, sometimes without an adequate factual record or a clear analysis of whether the particular program at issue deserves such protection. A ruling by a court based on a poorly conceived or operated program or based on an incomplete factual record can be compounded by subsequent court decisions that rely on a previous decision without either analyzing the factual disparities between the ombuds programs or paying close attention to the holding of the previous case. Accordingly, I offer information on the different types of ombuds programs and their origins to provide a clearer understanding of what is meant by an *organizational ombuds* program. My focus here is on organizational ombuds, and I hope that the discussion presented here will yield greater recognition of the need for organizational ombuds and that organizational ombuds will adhere to the best practices and the key principles underpinning such programs.

Third, I want to review the essential characteristics of an organizational ombuds program and explain how these components fit together to justify legal protection for the confidentiality of ombuds communications. It is the confidentiality of organizational ombuds communications that sets them apart from other formal communication channels, such as compliance officers, management or administration, and human resources personnel. It is the assurance of confidentiality that makes organizational ombuds such a valuable resource—people are willing to go to an ombuds with an issue they would not take to one of the formal channels. But confidentiality is not bestowed easily by courts. Thus, a primary goal of this book is to demonstrate why a properly organized organizational ombuds program justifies legal recognition for the confidentiality that is so essential to the efficacy of its work.

Fourth, I want to expand the peripheral vision of ombuds. Even though many ombuds are not lawyers, I believe it is important for ombuds to be able to view their profession in the legal context in which it necessarily operates. In other words, it is important for ombuds to understand the legal issues that shape and constrain their work. The battle over confidentiality is a hard one, because it goes against the grain of a fundamental concept of our system of justice: namely, that all evidence relevant to a dispute should be disclosed. In my experience, however, ombuds sometimes (and often quite understandably) are preoccupied with the internal processes of dispute resolution and fail to fully comprehend the larger legal environment in which their programs function. Thus, I have written this book as a legal guide, but I hope that ombuds will find the issues addressed here useful in their work and in dealing with their organizations.

And finally, but perhaps most important, I have written this book for those in organizations who create or interact with ombuds programs. With such a variety of ombuds programs and practices and no comprehensive explanation of why certain features are important and necessary or how all the pieces fit together, it is not easy for organizations to learn how to structure or operate an ombuds program to optimize its benefits and effectiveness. The general muddle of information about the ombudsman concept is exacerbated by the fact that there are always cost constraints that must be considered together with the competing interests of formal channels of communication within an organization, who may see the creation of an alternate and off-the-record channel of communication as unnecessary or a threat to their job functions and scope of responsibility. There are also concerns about an office becoming too independent or having information that may not be passed along to the formal channels for investigation and action. And finally, some of the concepts relied on by ombuds, such as their ownership of a privilege (rather than its belonging to an inquirer), run counter to assumptions based on prior experience in other contexts, such as the attorney-client privilege. If I am successful in this endeavor, however, the people who create and interact with ombuds programs will be better able to understand and support organizational ombuds' work.

Charles L. Howard
Hartford, Connecticut
August, 2009

The experience of the political ombudsman has demonstrated that he is a most useful tool to society. Nobody, including his initial detractors, wants to give him up. Yet society must be willing to accept him as a check on its accidental and intentional excesses. He can only be successful in his limited role if he is allowed to be; all the power in the world without support is of no consequence.

Ultimate justice obviously cannot be achieved on earth. The ombudsman is not the great panacea for social ill implied by much of the folklore. He has always been, and will continue to be, most effective in cases of petty dimension. Yet political society has found him to be truly indispensible. In all enterprise, justice *felt* is often justice *achieved*. The corporation, in our time, is a "dispenser of justice"—both actual and perceived.

> Isidore Silver, "The Corporate Ombudsman,"
> *Harvard Business Review* 77, 87 (May-June 1967)

Upon this point a page of history is worth a volume of logic.

> Oliver Wendell Holmes,
> *New York Trust Co. v. Eisner*,
> 256 U.S. 345, 349 (1921)

Introduction

The current pressures and demands on large corporations, universities, and other institutions are formidable. First and foremost, they need to survive, which means they are always mindful of costs and continually reexamining programs and operations to determine whether they are essential. They must also comply with a bewildering array of laws and regulations on virtually every aspect of their enterprise—requirements that can vary from jurisdiction to jurisdiction—wherever they operate. Not only are these organizations expected to comply with the law (and sometimes punished even if their employees act against the interests of the organization in breaking the law), they are expected to provide an ethical culture and common code of conduct for their workplaces that often, of necessity, must transcend national boundaries and ethnic cultures. They must do all of this with a diverse workforce that includes people drawn from developed and undeveloped countries around the world, who are able to work together because they are linked with an increasingly sophisticated web of electronic communication tools.

The pressures and demands on the people in these organizations and institutions are no less formidable. Gone are the days when one expected a lifetime of employment with a single employer. The need to prove current worth is ever present. The fear of loss of employment is never far from the surface, even for "knowledge" workers who have been in high demand. The technology that has facilitated global enterprise has another side—employees are expected to remain in constant contact with their organizations, and, increasingly, many are connected to their organizations only through technology and as consultants, rather than as employees.

With such pressure on both organizations and people, it is inevitable that conflict will arise and misconduct occur, as people and their organizations maneuver for advantage. Responding to these pressures and the need to comply with the law and provide an orderly and structured working environment, organizations have developed approaches and mechanisms to deal with the inevitable by-products of these pressures. As a general matter, management is expected to offer training on how to operate within the law and to supervise employees and other affiliated people. Particularized functions have also developed. Human resource (HR) departments deal with the everyday requirements of employee hiring, discipline, and discharge, and investigate claims of employment misconduct; compliance officers investigate reports of other types of misconduct; and a whole new industry has evolved to provide hotline services that employees may use anytime, day or night, to make a confidential report of misconduct. Moreover, because there are literally hundreds of whistle-blower laws at the state and federal levels, virtually all large organizations have promulgated their own policies that prohibit retaliation against people who report misconduct.

Despite these commendable efforts, however, reports of misconduct in our corporations and other organizations remain alarmingly high, and the fear of retaliation is unabated. One of the reasons is that many of the existing organizational responses are not responsive to the real-world predicaments people occasionally find themselves in. Consider the following examples.

- An employee believes that a co-worker is cheating the organization, but he is reluctant to share his concerns with the supervisor because he knows the supervisor is having an affair with that same co-worker. He does not want anyone to question why he can't report his belief to the supervisor, but he does want to raise the issue of cheating. Where can he turn?
- What do workers do when local management is engaged in an improper side business but none of the workers know whether it is sanctioned or supported by others higher in the organization and they have no real connection with upper management?
- What does a woman do when she is called in to her manager's office in the foreign country in which they work and is informed that he is aware that she is pregnant and unmarried and told (consistent with the customs of that country but not with company policy) that she must be married before the baby arrives or she must find another job?

- Where does a post-doctoral researcher or a medical resident go when she is being harassed by the nationally known and highly regarded principal investigator or doctor with whom she works and who has the ability to make or break her career?
- A department chair is struggling to deal with two valued members of the department who cannot get along. If he reports the problem through official channels, he risks revealing his inability to resolve the conflict, and he could damage his reputation as well as that of his feuding colleagues. What can he do?
- Where does the probationary or new employee go to report a problem or discuss a concern when the person is not sure that he has all the facts, and the possibility of being wrong could put his job at risk?
- Where does a person go when she, after going through the proper channels to raise an issue, still believes that the decision made is wrong or contrary to policy?
- How can someone raise concerns about the conduct of a senior official who is highly regarded but who also has a reputation for punishing those who challenge him?

These are all real situations. These, and many more like them, are presented in Chapter 3 and Appendix 14 to show why some people need a way to discuss issues in a confidential, off-the-record manner before acting, even though they know the organization's policies require them to act. These types of situations are not well addressed by the current suite of mechanisms for many reasons. Some people are not sure of themselves or confident that what they observe is true. Others are afraid to take on entrenched power. Some just need to talk things through with someone to get a sense of what the options are and what will happen before they are willing to take any action. Then there are those people who believe that—despite whatever the organization may say about retaliation—if they come forward they will be ostracized and retaliated against by their friends and co-workers if not by others in the organization.

An organizational ombuds program is designed to help address these types of situations. The organizational ombuds is an independent, neutral, confidential, and informal resource made available to employees (and sometimes others) to discuss issues, get information, and help them find ways to report their concerns. The organizational ombuds is, however, only one variation of many types of "ombudsman" programs, and one that has been transformed from the original "classical" ombudsman, a public official first established in Sweden to investigate and prosecute official misconduct.

This book, therefore, is an extended discussion of the history, rationale, and legal underpinnings of the American organizational ombuds concept. For that reason, I have organized the main portion of the book around three important questions: (1) What is an organizational ombuds program? (2) Why should organizations create them? and, (3) If their confidentiality is essential to their function, how can ombuds' confidentiality be protected? In the fourth chapter, I present additional information to serve as a resource for ombuds on several related subjects. To provide an overview for this discussion, I should elaborate on my purposes for each chapter.

In the first chapter, I address *what* an organizational ombuds program is. This chapter includes the background on the origins of the ombuds concept and how the significant differences in the types of ombuds programs evolved in the United States. While I hope this is interesting and helps the reader understand the forces that pushed the evolution of the ombuds concept from the governmental official who both investigated and prosecuted misconduct to the private mediator model who does not even undertake investigations, my objective in presenting this history is much more purposeful. Part one of the first chapter demonstrates that the organizational dysfunction, whether in universities, corporations, or government, that gave rise to the adoption of the ombudsman concept in American institutions has existed for at least the last 40 years and has involved matters of significant national purpose and policy. One of the planks in the platform on which confidentiality is defended requires demonstrating the importance of just such national policies. My hope is that the material presented in the first part of this chapter can be used to provide understanding and support for the importance in establishing ombuds programs.

In the second part of the first chapter, I review in detail the development of the essential characteristics of an organizational ombuds program and how both ombudsman organizations and the American Bar Association have dealt with these principles. This part does not make for easy reading, but it is important to understand how the key principles on which ombuds programs are created interrelate. This exercise is also critical to understanding why the focus of this book is only on organizational ombuds. By not focusing on readability in this section, my goal has been to present the material here in a format that will facilitate future reference for information relating to those key principles. In the third part of the first chapter, I give a brief overview of what organizational ombuds actually do. My hope is that, together, these three sections of the first chapter provide a basis to understand what an organizational ombuds is as a predicate to considering why organizations may wish to create such programs and how confidentiality can be protected, the subjects of the next two chapters.

In the second chapter, I explain *why* a properly constituted organizational ombuds program should be an essential component in the current work or university environment, frequently characterized by large—and often multinational—organizations, cultural diversity, intense competition, governmental regulation, and with the need for global standards of conduct. In my view, this requires looking first at how our society is changing due to various forces such as demographics, technology, and globalization and the pressure that these changes have exerted on our organizations. I have presented much statistical information in this section as a means to add substance to my point that significant and serious change is occurring and that such change is itself exerting significant pressure on our institutions.

Against this backdrop, I then examine the pressures on our organizations that have come from another direction—the law. The developments in criminal law for organizations, government regulation, corporate governance standards, and employment law have all converged with a common set of expectations. Our laws require organizations to be accountable for the actions of their employees and agents and to comply with the law in all ways and in every jurisdiction. Moreover, organizations themselves are now required to investigate all credible allegations of misconduct and to take corrective action and report it where the allegations have merit.

The ways in which organizations have responded to these pressures, however, has left a gap that an organizational ombuds program can help fill. The discussion of why an organization should create an ombuds program is greatly informed by the fact that surveys and other evidence repeatedly demonstrate that a significant percentage of people will not raise conflict or misconduct issues out of fear of retaliation or because they are not sure they are correct in the perceptions of misconduct. People need the protection of first having an off-the-record conversation with a real person instead of reporting to an impersonal hotline by e-mail or telephone, where the recipient may not have any real sense of their situation or their workplace culture.

The third chapter addresses *how* ombuds' confidentiality is protected. I try to do this in two ways. First, the principal discussion in this chapter focuses almost exclusively on cases and legal concepts, but an understanding here is important both for ombuds and those with whom they deal. I begin with an analysis of why knowledge of an issue or claim by an ombuds should not be imputed notice to the organization, and then proceed to the legal grounds on which a claim of confidentiality can be based. It is here that one can see why the key principles and assumptions underlying ombuds programs are necessary. I also present various bases on which ombuds confidentiality can be protected. My experience is that some organizations that have considered an ombuds program have concluded that communications are not privileged and have not gone further in the analysis of how confidentiality can be protected. No privilege, however—not even the attorney-client privilege—is absolute, and thus the difficulties in asserting a privilege should not cause one to forfeit the opportunity to structure and operate a program so that a privilege could be asserted (especially with the benefit of information presented in the first chapter). Yet, with no federal or state statute that creates a privilege for ombuds (at least not yet), there are other ways to protect confidentiality. These other bases rely on previously recognized principles of law, sometimes applied in a new way. This can be and has been done in many cases, but it requires close attention to detail—the power of bad precedent is formidable. I also include practice points and important information on the types of documentation that are important in establishing an organizational ombuds program, as well as some litigation considerations to keep in mind when a challenge is made to ombuds confidentiality.

The second way I try to demonstrate how confidentiality can be protected is the inclusion of numerous real but, in keeping with the principles of ombuds' confidentiality, anonymously presented examples of cases that ombuds have dealt with to illustrate why people go to ombuds and how ombuds help people to raise an issue to the organization or resolve a conflict or problem. The real-life examples presented in Chapter 3 and Appendix 14 came from many sources, not just from clients that I have represented. As many of these examples demonstrate, the fact that communications with an organizational ombuds are confidential and that one can have repeated and extended conversations with an ombuds on a topic are important aspects of the role they serve.

Finally, in the fourth chapter, I address specifically a variety of legal issues that touch upon or affect the work of ombuds. As with some of the earlier material, this chapter is meant more for reference than for general reading. The book as a whole is intended to be a legal guide and, while I know that many ombuds are not lawyers, I hope that these additional topics will serve as a resource guide for non-lawyer ombuds if additional information is needed or desired on a particular topic. All ombuds will hopefully benefit from a broader understanding of these issues. For the same reason, I have included several documents in the appendices that I believe may be helpful for ombuds and those with whom they work to have readily available for reference. As programs continue to expand and new legal issues arise, there will undoubtedly be a need to present additional material to address those issues.

What Is an Organizational Ombuds?

The Evolution of Organizational Ombuds as an Independent, Neutral, Confidential, Informal, and Alternate Resource

PART I: A SHORT HISTORY OF THE OMBUDSMAN ROLE

The main problem with the term *ombudsman* is that it does not a have a clear meaning. It has many meanings and is used interchangeably to refer to many different kinds of programs, despite the fact that the role of an ombudsman in one context can be quite different from that in another context. This book, however, was written to address only one kind of ombudsman, the organizational ombudsman,[1] which is a comparatively new variation of the position.

Relatively little changed in the role of an ombudsman from the time of its appearance in Sweden in the eighteenth century through its adoption by governments all over the world, including some in the United States, be-

---

1. The original term was *ombudsman*, and I use that term in referring to the development of the role and its introduction to the world of American government, universities, and corporate organizations. Thereafter, I often use the simpler term *ombuds* to refer to current organizational ombudsman programs.

ginning in the 1960s. The original ombudsman was a public official who investigated and, in some cases, even prosecuted allegations of misfeasance and malfeasance (wrongdoing) by other governmental officials. But the subsequent adaptation of this concept to universities and corporations in America drastically reshaped the way in which the ombudsman operates in nongovernmental organizations and produced a new variety of ombudsman: the organizational ombudsman. The result is an office that is very effective in helping people in private corporations, universities, and other organizations—including some governmental agencies—resolve disputes and report misconduct. While much of the original purpose of the office remains the same, the private sector's need to protect confidentiality in the absence of statutory protection changed both the primary emphasis of the office and how organizational ombudsmen operate compared to their governmental cousins. The history of this evolution is important to understanding differences in ombudsman programs and why organizational ombudsman programs are structured the way they are. This history is also critical to the examination in later chapters of various legal issues related to organizational ombudsmen and the confidentiality they seek.

A. Origins in Sweden

Leading scholars on the origins of ombudsman programs have credited King Charles XII of Sweden with appointing the first ombudsman.[2]

As described in an article on the history of ombudsmen in which Professor Gerald Caiden was the lead author, the appointment of a

---

2. *See* Alfred Bexelius, *The Origin, Nature, and Functions of the Civil and Military Ombudsmen in Sweden*, ANNALS AM. ACAD. POL. & SOC. SCI. 10, 10–11 (1968) (Alfred Bexelius was then the incumbent ombudsman in Sweden); Gerald E. Caiden, *The Institution of Ombudsman*, *in* INTERNATIONAL HANDBOOK OF THE OMBUDSMAN: EVOLUTION AND FUNCTION 3, 9 (Gerald E. Caiden ed., 1983); Donald C. Rowat, *The Parliamentary Ombudsman: Should the Scandinavian Scheme Be Transplanted?*, 28 INT'L REV. ADMIN. SCI. 399 (1962). Governmental complaint-handling systems go back even further, though without a direct connection to ombudsmen:

> Ancient Egyptian kings had complaint officers in their court. Moses appointed grievance officers to deal with complaining Hebrews. During the Roman Republic, two censors both scrutinized administrative actions and received complaints alleging maladministration. The Control Yuan in the Han Dynasty in China undertook similar activities. In the Middle

Chancellor of Justice in 1713 came about as a result of the Swedish king's concern over maintaining authority over his kingdom:

> In 1709, Charles XII was forced to flee to Turkey after Russia defeated Sweden. There he came to know the Turkish office of chief justice which ensured that officials followed Islamic Law. He thereupon ordered the creation of an office to be headed by his highest ombudsman to ensure that Swedish officials followed the law and fulfilled their obligations. The word "ombudsman" was derived from medieval Germanic tribes which applied the term to a third party whose task was to collect fines from remorseful culprit families to give to the aggrieved families of victims. In time, it came to refer to any kind of agent.[3]

A parliamentary form of government in Sweden followed the death of Charles XII in 1718, and, beginning in 1739, the parliament (Riksdag) compelled the office of the Chancellor of Justice to report to it. From 1766 until the Riksdag was supplanted by an absolute monarchy in 1772, the Riksdag even appointed the Chancellor of Justice.[4]

Sweden's defeat by Russia in 1809 led to the restoration of a parliamentary government and the enactment of a new constitution. The constitution of 1809 provided for a "Justitieombudsman"[5] whose function was to "supervise the observance of laws and statutes."[6] He was

---

Ages, intermediaries between rulers and ruled, administrators and administered were common in government, church, and business organizations. Absolute monarchs of the emerging nation-states appointed special representatives or agents or officials to see that public officials obeyed the law, carried out their instructions, and generally behaved themselves.

Caiden, *supra*, at 9 (footnote omitted).

3. Caiden, *supra* note 2, at 9–10 (footnote omitted). *See also* WALTER GELLHORN, OMBUDSMEN & OTHERS: CITIZENS' PROTECTORS IN NINE COUNTRIES 194–95 (1967).

4. Caiden, *supra* note 2, at 10.

5. Shirley A. Wiegand, *A Just and Lasting Peace: Supplanting Mediation with the Ombuds Model*, 12 OHIO ST. J. ON DISP. RESOL. 95, 97 (1996).

6. Caiden, *supra* note 2, at 13.

elected by and reported to the Riksdag and was required to be a person of known legal ability and outstanding integrity. He not only could investigate allegations of official wrongdoing but was authorized to prosecute officials who "committed an unlawful act or neglected to perform official duties properly."[7] In the ensuing years, the role became less prosecutorial and more that of a "citizen-defender."[8] Sweden created an additional ombudsman office during World War I with responsibility for supervising military authorities and in 1968 consolidated the two ombudsman offices.[9]

B. Expansion in Scandinavia

It took more than a century from the 1809 Swedish constitution for the ombudsman concept to expand beyond Sweden, but the idea was incorporated into a new Finnish constitution in 1919. Although the office of the Chancellor of Justice (formerly the Office of the Attorney General) had existed in Finland as part of the executive branch of government to serve as prosecutor and guardian against illegal activity, an ombudsman position under the control of the legislature was created in the 1919 constitution. The Chancellor of Justice and the ombudsman had overlapping jurisdictions, but the Finnish parliament adamantly preserved the prerogatives of its own ombudsman to investigate complaints of official misconduct.[10] By 1933, the Finnish ombudsman had also assumed more of an investigative—and less of a prosecutorial—role and was given sole responsibility for investigating military and prison complaints.[11]

The third country to create an ombudsman office was Norway, which created a military ombudsman in 1952 and later added a general ombudsman in 1962.[12] Denmark followed suit in 1955, when an ombudsman was appointed with somewhat different powers and a different scope of responsibility. For example, the Danish ombudsman did not have jurisdiction over the judiciary.[13] The Danish ombudsman also differed

---

7. Caiden, *supra* note 2, at 10.
8. *Id.*
9. *Id.*
10. *Id.*
11. *Id.*
12. *Id.* at 10–11. *See also* GELLHORN, *supra* note 3, at 154–57.
13. Caiden, *supra* note 2, at 10. *See also* Henry J. Abraham, *A People's Watchdog Against Abuse of Power*, 20 PUB. ADMIN. REV. 152, 152–53 (1960).

from the previous Scandinavian models in that it had no authority to prosecute officials for misconduct.[14]

Despite the variations among the Swedish, Norwegian, Finnish, and Danish ombudsmen offices, Professor Donald Rowat observed that, as they existed in the 1960s, they all had similar "competence and practices":

> All of them can receive and investigate any written complaint, which can be submitted in a sealed envelope without reference to any superior authority. All can initiate investigations and make inspections, without first having received a specific complaint. All can call upon government agencies to give reports and all have the power to demand departmental records. All are appointed by Parliament, are entirely independent of the executive, and report annually to a special committee of the House. All can comment critically on official actions in their annual reports, and all can make a report on an urgent matter at any time.[15]

Two of the powers of these governmental ombudsman offices—the authority to investigate and the charge to issue public reports—are areas that were transformed and essentially eliminated as the role of organizational ombudsman subsequently developed.

C. Expansion Beyond Scandinavia

By the end of the first century and a half after the ombudsman concept was first institutionally created, ombudsman offices remained a practice limited to the Scandinavian countries, and even there they existed only as part of the government. Following this incubation period, however, the expansion of classical ombudsman offices was rapid. Beginning with the creation of a military ombudsman in 1957 in the Federal Republic of Germany and then a national ombudsman in New Zealand in 1962, the ombudsman idea expanded globally in the 1960s and 1970s to countries, cities, and other governmental bodies all over the world, including provinces in Canada and states in the United States.[16]

---

14. Caiden, *supra* note 2, at 10. *See also* GELLHORN, *supra* note 3, at 5–18. *See* Rowat, *supra* note 2, at 400–01, for a discussion of the roles and authority of the Swedish, Norwegian, and Danish ombudsmen.

15. Rowat, *supra* note 2, at 400.

16. Caiden, *supra* note 2, at 10–11. Hawaii, in 1969, became the first state in the United States to create a governmental ombudsman. *Id.*

One of the first attempts to introduce the ombudsman concept to the United States was by Professor Kenneth Culp Davis, a leading expert on administrative law in the 1950s and 1960s. In a 1961 *University of Pennsylvania Law Review* article, he stated that he had spent the previous year traveling the world looking for "new ideas for solving problems about the administrative process," and that the large idea that he found most interesting was the Scandinavian ombudsman:

> When a bureaucrat irritates you, or delays too long, or requires too much red tape, or denies what you want, you can quickly and easily get relief, if you are entitled to it, by merely writing to the Ombudsman. If the bureaucrat is wrong, the Ombudsman may publically reprimand him. If the governmental system is out of gear, the Ombudsman may recommend that it be set right, and his view is likely to prevail. This is what happens in such places as Utopia and Scandinavia. The institution of the Ombudsman works exceedingly well, especially in Denmark. Maybe the general idea is one that we Americans ought to explore. . . . *The idea, coupled with American ingenuity to adapt it to our institutions, may have considerable potentiality for our various governments, federal, state, and local.*[17]

The observations of Professor Davis were prophetic—American ingenuity did indeed adapt the idea to its institutions, beginning with various levels of government. The spread of the ombudsman idea was also aided by the writings and involvement of three other prominent law professors later in the 1960s: Donald C. Rowat,[18] Stanley Anderson,[19] and, to an even greater extent, Walter Gellhorn, as well as the

---

17. Kenneth Culp Davis, *Ombudsmen in America: Officers to Criticize Administrative Action*, 109 U. PENN. L. REV. 1057–58 (1961) (emphasis added) (footnote call number omitted). Professor Davis credits Professor Walter Gellhorn with "provid[ing] leadership in American thinking about the potentialities of an Ombudsman in America." *Id.* at 1058 & n.7. At least one source credits the article by Henry J. Abraham, *supra* note 13, with first raising the ombuds issue in the United States, but the primary focus of Abraham's article was on the Danish Parliamentary Commissioner. David R. Anderson & Diane M. Stockton, *Federal Ombudsmen: An Underused Resource*, 5 ADMIN. L.J. 275, 279 n.6 (1991).

18. *See, e.g.*, Rowat, *supra* note 2.

19. *See, e.g.*, STANLEY V. ANDERSON, OMBUDSMAN PAPERS: AMERICAN EXPERIENCE AND PROPOSALS (1969).

speaking and writings of the Swedish, Norwegian, and Danish ombudsmen.[20] Congress even attempted to create a federal ombudsman in the United States. Although that effort failed,[21] Professor Gellhorn's work continued to exert a great influence. His two books on ombudsmen were widely read and were highlighted in a *Time* magazine article in December 1966 that reported on the significant public attention being given to the ombudsman concept at a time when *Time* said that the word "ombudsman" did not even appear in the *Webster's Unabridged Dictionary*.[22]

By 1967, Professor Gellhorn had drafted a widely circulated model bill to create a public ombuds office. His work was also influential in the publication of *The Ombudsman or Citizen's Defender: A Modern Institution,* in the *Annals of the American Academy of Political and Social Science* in May 1968.[23] By 1969, Professor Gellhorn had persuaded the American Bar Association to adopt a resolution calling on state and local governments to give "consideration to the establishment of an ombudsman authorized to inquire into all administrative action and to make public criticism."[24] The 1969 ABA Resolution identified 12 essential characteristics of an ombudsman:

1. authority of the ombudsman to criticize all agencies, officials, and public employees except courts and their personnel, leg-

---

20. *See* Caiden, *supra* note 2, at 11 & n.24. Walter Gellhorn, a law professor at Columbia University, was quite active in the United States, publishing WHEN AMERICANS COMPLAIN: GOVERNMENTAL GRIEVANCE PROCEDURES in 1966 and OMBUDSMEN AND OTHERS: CITIZENS' PROTECTORS IN NINE COUNTRIES in 1967, both of which argued for the creation of public ombudsman offices. *See also* Wiegand, *supra* note 5, at 102–03.

21. Wiegand, *supra* note 5, at 103–04.

22. *See* Donald C. Rowat, *Preface to the Second Edition* of THE OMBUDSMAN— CITIZEN'S DEFENDER, at xii (Donald C. Rowat ed., 2d ed. 1968). Professor Rowat noted that the burgeoning interest in ombudsmen had led to what he termed "Ombudsmania." *Id.* He also reported that after the article was published on December 2, 1966, *Time* received letters from the publishers of other dictionaries indicating that "ombudsman" did appear in their works. *Id.*

23. Roy V. Peel, *Preface to* Symposium, *The Ombudsman or Citizen's Defender: A Modern Institution*, 377 ANNALS AM. ACAD. POL. & SOC. SCI., at ix–x (1968).

24. ABA Sec. Admin. Law, Rep. on Establishment of Ombudsman, *in* ABA 94 ABA REP. 265 (1969) [hereinafter the 1969 ABA RESOLUTION]. The 1969 ABA RESOLUTION and the accompanying Report are reprinted in Appendix 1.

islative bodies and their personnel, and the chief executive and his personal staff;
2. independence of the ombudsman from control by any other officer, except for his responsibility to the legislative body;
3. appointment by the executive with confirmation by a designated proportion of the legislative body, preferably more than a majority, such as two-thirds;[25]
4. independence of the ombudsman through a long term, not less than five years, with freedom from removal except for cause, determined by more than a majority of the legislative body, such as two-thirds;
5. a high salary equivalent to that of a designated top officer;
6. freedom of the ombudsman to employ his own assistants and to delegate to them, without restraints of civil service and classification acts;
7. freedom of the ombudsman to investigate any act or failure to act by any agency, official, or public employee;
8. access of the ombudsman to all public records he finds relevant to an investigation;
9. authority to inquire into legality, fairness, correctness of findings, motivation, adequacy of reasons, efficiency, and procedural propriety of any action or inaction by any agency, official, or public employee;
10. discretionary power to determine what complaints to investigate and to determine what criticisms to make or to publicize;
11. opportunity for any agency, official, or public employee criticized by the ombudsman to have advance notice of the criticism and to publish with the criticism an answering statement; and
12. immunity of the ombudsman and his staff from civil liability on account of official action.[26]

---

25. A resolution adopted by the American Bar Association in 1971 revised this element to read: "(3) appointment by the legislative body or appointment by the executive with confirmation by a designated proportion of the legislative body, preferably more than a majority, such as two-thirds." ABA Sec. Admin. Law, Rep. on Establishment of Ombudsman, 96 ABA REP. 749 (1971) [hereinafter the 1971 ABA RESOLUTION]. The 1971 ABA RESOLUTION also urged the federal government to enact ombudsman programs. The 1971 ABA RESOLUTION and the accompanying Report are reprinted in Appendix 2.

26. 1969 ABA RESOLUTION, *supra* note 24, at 265. *See* Appendix 1 at 440.

These characteristics thus placed a premium on independence (nos. 2 and 4), unfettered discretion and freedom to investigate and criticize (nos. 1, 6, 7, and 9), and protection from devaluation (no. 5) and retribution (no. 12).

Professor Gellhorn's model bill and the 1969 ABA Resolution were the inspiration for the subsequent enactment of numerous municipal and state ombudsman offices. As envisioned by Professors Davis and Gellhorn, the ombudsman was a public official—not a private employee—still very much in the Scandinavian tradition. This type of ombudsman, often referred to as the "classical ombudsman" model, is an independent government official and conducts investigations on matters of public interest to remedy injustice. By 1980, 25 states had adopted some aspect of the classical ombudsman function.[27]

The structure of ombudsman offices created by states, especially those created in the late 1960s and early 1970s, remained relatively true to their Scandinavian precursors and the 12 characteristics of an ombudsman embodied in the 1969 ABA Resolution and Professor Gellhorn's model bill. Yet, changes had begun to occur. The ombudsman was developing as:

> an agent of government, supervising and prosecuting wrongdoing. He protects the citizenry against arbitrary or unreasonable governmental agency actions, even though such actions may be legal. The essential characteristics of an ombuds office are present to varying degrees: independence, expertise, impartiality, accessibility and powers of persuasion rather than control. But all of the state models exempt the actions of key elected officials, and four of them exempt the courts, from the ombuds' investigative power. Although legally established, it cannot be said that these offices are truly external to the administration of state governments . . . .[28]

When American ingenuity adapted the concept for county and municipal governments, however, the variations became more pro-

---

27. Wiegand, *supra* note 5, at 105 & n.50. *See also* ADMIN. CONFERENCE OF THE U.S., THE OMBUDSMAN: A PRIMER FOR FEDERAL AGENCIES 3 (1991).

28. Wiegand, *supra* note 5, at 108. Professor Wiegand provides a more complete analysis of the ombudsman schemes in Hawaii, Iowa, Nebraska, Alaska, and Arizona at 106–08.

nounced, as local institutions responded to "particularized needs."[29] Private organizations also started creating ombudsmen. Ombudsman programs were created, for example, to respond to problems with prisons, nursing homes,[30] and newspapers, among many other purposes.[31] These extensions led to compromises in many ways, including impartiality and non-advocacy, as organizations experimented with the creation of ombudsman programs in a wide variety of settings.[32]

1. Ombudsman Programs Transition to Universities

The popularity of the ombudsman idea led to interest in the concept as one with the potential to help even nongovernmental entities respond to the social upheaval that characterized the mid-1960s. By that time, American society was in turmoil, and virtually all public and private institutions were under attack. The civil rights movement had sparked widely publicized demonstrations and public unrest. The war in Vietnam added fuel to the fires of discontent. These forces and the social upheaval they wrought combined with the coming of age of the post–World War II "baby boom" generation to create conditions where independent and neutral parties were needed to mediate disputes. And nowhere was this more necessary than on college and university campuses. It is not surprising, then, that the ombudsman concept was quickly adapted to the university setting.

Eastern Montana College is credited with appointing the first college ombudsman in the United States in 1966, but the first ombudsman program at a major university was created at Michigan State University in 1967.[33] Carolyn Stieber, the longtime ombudsman at Michigan State University, described the conditions there and at many other universities at that time:

---

29. *Id.* at 105.
30. *Id.* at 108–09. *See also* Mildred Mailick, *The Ombudsman in Health Care Institutions in the United States, in* INTERNATIONAL HANDBOOK OF THE OMBUDSMAN, *supra* note 2, at 121, 121–28 (discussing ombudsman programs for patients in nursing homes and in acute, short-term care facilities, such as hospitals).
31. Rowat, *supra* note 22, at xv–xvi.
32. *See generally* ANDERSON, *supra* note 19; Carolyn Stieber, *57 Varieties: Has the Ombudsman Concept Become Diluted?*, 16 NEGOTIATION J. 49, at 52–55 (2000).
33. Carolyn Stieber, *Resolving Campus Disputes—Notes of a University Ombudsman*, 37 ARB. J. 5, 7 (1982).

1967 was a different world in many ways. The concept in loco parentis was in its terminal stages. Virtually every campus of any size was traumatized by repeated demonstrations against the Vietnam War. A military draft was in effect. In 1968 disorder spilled over to the streets of Chicago at the Democratic National Convention, undoubtedly influencing the presidential election. Yellow ribbons belonged only to a corny song; military recruiters came on campus at their peril. . . . Recurrent political protests, which involved faculty as well as students, were joined to other complaints about bureaucratic indifference and professorial casualness toward teaching responsibilities. . . . There was a generalized sense that no one cared about major, much less minor, injustices, system glitches, organizational errors, or unclear rules and regulations with arbitrary if not capricious enforcement. . . .

Police were often called upon to clear out buildings and arrest demonstrators or escort people into buildings, picking their way over shards of broken glass. . . . (At the same time) Universities were still experiencing rapid growth; no one thought that strenuous recruitment efforts and sophisticated marketing strategies would later be needed in a search for warm bodies. There was money then. The word "Budget" did not have all the connotations of uncertainty, if not mystery, which now attach to that term. However, top administrators often were attempting to assert more centralized control over burgeoning campuses while faculty, historically anxious about protecting their prerogatives, had no great enthusiasm for the notion. . . .[34]

---

34. William C. Warters, The History of Campus Mediation Systems: Research and Practice 7 [hereinafter Warters, *History*] (unpublished monograph on file with author) (quoting Carolyn Stieber, *Perspectives on the Profession: Past, Present, Future, in* UCI OMBUDSMAN: THE JOURNAL 1991, www.ombuds.uci.edu/cal_caucus_journals.shtml (follow "UCI: Ombudsman: The Journal 1991" hyperlink) (last visited July 21, 2009)). *See generally* Tim Griffin, *The Evolution of the Role of Ombudsperson on University and College Campuses*, THE FOURTH R, (Nat'l Ass'n for Mediation in Educ.), Feb.–Mar. 1995, www.campus-adr.org/Main_Library/Articles/Griffin.html (last visited July 21, 2009); William C. Warters, *The Emergence of Campus Mediation Systems: History in the Making*, 2 CONFLICT MGMT. IN HIGHER EDUC. (2001), www.campus-adr.org/cmher/ReportArticles/Edition2_1/Warters2_1a.html [hereinafter Warters, *Emergence*].

In 1969 there was enough interest in the ombudsman idea for a conference to be convened titled "The Ombudsman in Higher Education: Advocate or Subversive Bureaucrat?"[35] When the National Guard shot and killed students during a demonstration at Kent State University in 1970, President Nixon appointed a Commission on Campus Unrest. The commission report approvingly noted that one of the dispute resolution mechanisms used by universities included an ombudsman. The commission recommended that universities give special attention to grievance procedures as part of the reform of university governance.[36] Apart from the informal airing of grievances, the report observed that "[s]everal kinds of formal grievance procedures have been tried on campuses across the country."[37] While the commission stated that the most common form of formal procedure was a grievance committee, it also listed major drawbacks to such an approach: "polarization of their members, a tendency to handle grievances on the basis of politics instead of merit, and the slowness with which they respond."[38] Grievance petitioning procedures, used elsewhere, were described as another option but also presented a less than adequate solution. A third approach reported by the commission was "the so-called ombudsman method."[39] As described by the report:

> The ombudsman is an individual who acts as a mediator and fact-finder for students, faculty members, and administrators. To be successful, the ombudsman must have both great autonomy and the support of the university president. He must not be penalized by the college administration if his findings and recommendations embarrass university leaders.[40]

While the report stopped short of recommending any particular approach on the grounds that the circumstances at each institution

---

35. Warters, *History*, *supra* note 34, at 1.
36. REPORT OF THE PRESIDENT'S COMMISSION ON CAMPUS UNREST, COLLEGE AND UNIVERSITY REPORTS, Special Edition, Sept. 29, 1970, at 6/30; Wiegand, *supra* note 5, at 113–14.
37. REPORT OF THE PRESIDENT'S COMMISSION ON CAMPUS UNREST, *supra* note 36, at 6/32.
38. *Id.*
39. *Id.*
40. *Id.* at 6/32–6/33.

would vary, it did urge some action: "We can only urge that each university recognize the necessity of establishing such procedures and the vital new channels of communication which they require."[41]

The concept of a campus ombudsman received further attention the following year, when it was included as a recommendation for colleges and universities in a report issued by the Carnegie Corporation's Commission on Higher Education. This influential report recommended that colleges and universities appoint:

> an individual or agency to inform members of the campus of the appropriate agency to hear their individual complaints and suggestions, and to assist them in being heard; ombudsman or hearing committees composed of faculty, students, and administrators can serve this function. When the complaints are responded to, both the response and the rationale behind it should be widely known.[42]

The report also recommended using ombudsmen to "respond *informally* to faculty, student and administrator complaints"[43] rather than as a formal channel for investigations and dispute resolution, for which the report recommended hearing officers. In particular, the report recommended that "[T]he ombudsman [appointed by a committee of faculty, students, and administrators] would independently attempt to resolve both academic and nonacademic grievances, as well as help individuals to use existing avenues for redress of grievances."[44]

By 1971, 69 colleges or universities had appointed an ombudsman,[45] and the role of an ombudsman in a private institution was beginning to take shape. Among the institutions to create ombudsman programs during this period were public universities in California.[46]

---

41. *Id.* at 6/33.

42. CARNEGIE COMM'N ON HIGHER EDUC., DISSENT AND DISRUPTION: PROPOSALS FOR CONSIDERATION BY THE CAMPUS 64 (1971).

43. Wiegand, *supra* note 5, at 114 (emphasis added).

44. DISSENT AND DISRUPTION: PROPOSALS FOR CONSIDERATION BY THE CAMPUS, *supra* note 42, at 97.

45. Warters, *History*, *supra* note 34, at 1.

46. *See* Donald C. Rowat & Geoffrey Wallace, *The Campus Ombudsman in North America*, *in* INTERNATIONAL HANDBOOK OF THE OMBUDSMAN: EVOLUTION AND FUNCTION, *supra* note 2, at 151, 154–56.

With so many ombudsman programs located in California, it is not surprising that the California Caucus of College and University Ombuds was established in 1973, and it began to hold annual meetings at the Asilomar Conference Center.[47] The number of ombudsman programs at colleges and universities may have been as high as 190 in the 1970s, but there were still at least 100 such offices in 1982.[48] By 1985, the University and College Ombuds Association (UCOA) had been organized.[49]

A number of the university offices were created and functioned like ombudsman offices but were not called ombudsman offices. As the ombudsman concept spread and was identified as such, many of these other offices became the ombudsman office. For example, one of the early offices was at Massachusetts Institute of Technology (MIT), which was begun in 1973 with the appointment of Dr. Mary Rowe as a "special assistant" to the president and chancellor. Only later was the office characterized as "ombudsperson." Similar actions were taken elsewhere, with the appointment of persons to be an "alternative communications channel," a "troubleshooter," "assistant to the chairman," or "dean of university relations," but the common denominator in these positions was that they were expected to be impartial, independent, and confidential, and to resolve disputes informally. Some of these offices were later renamed as "ombudsmen" without necessarily referring to the international classical ombudsman role. This evolution and coalescence of function is important to the development of the current organizational model because it underscores how powerfully the needs of organizations in the twentieth century shaped the organizational model of ombudsman programs.

The social forces that led to the creation of campus ombudsman programs thus transformed the ombudsman role in the university setting compared to its classical antecedent. Campus ombudsmen were used primarily to "mediate between groups of demonstrators and the college/university administration."[50] This naturally led to a more proactive role in attempting to anticipate and prevent conflict rather than just mediate it. The ombudsmen at some institutions were "charged

---

47. Warters, *History, supra* note 34, at 1.
48. Wiegand, *supra* note 5, at 115.
49. Warters, *History, supra* note 34, at 2.
50. Griffin, *supra* note 34, at ¶ 4.

with bringing students' concerns to the appropriate campus administrators so that an institutional response could be devised and group demonstrations forestalled."[51] In keeping with the recommendations of the Carnegie Commission report, they were an *informal* resource that could help resolve issues and direct people to the proper dispute resolution resources, rather than an officer whose mandate included authority to conduct his own investigations and then issue reports with findings on allegations of misconduct.

The role of the campus ombudsman continued to evolve even after the tumultuous period of the 1960s and 1970s. In addition to adopting a proactive role in identifying areas of conflict (as opposed to merely mediating conflict and disputes after they arose), there were two additional ways in which the role evolved that are significant to the current position of organizational ombudsmen.[52] First, the focus of many of the ombudsman programs' efforts shifted over time from dealing with groups to dealing with individuals (although a few of them, even in the beginning, had dealt with individuals rather than groups). Thus, the role evolved from one in which the ombuds dealt with conflict between students as a whole and the institution to one that dealt with conflict between individuals and the institution or among individuals.[53] Second, the constituencies served by narrowly focused ombuds offices expanded. Rather than dealing only with the concerns of students or faculty and the administration, most ombudsmen in the 1970s and 1980s increasingly came to serve all components of the university community, including staff.[54]

2. Ombudsman Programs Transition to Corporations

Professor Gellhorn's books on ombudsmen also influenced the creation of ombudsman programs at corporations. One of the early works inspired by Gellhorn was an article in the May-June 1967 issue of the *Harvard Business Review* by Isidore Silver, "The Corporate Ombudsman." Silver argued that the modern corporation had evolved to the point that it was "a socially responsible institution" and that it was "in the long-range interest of the corporation to seek mechanisms to ef-

---

51. *Id.*
52. Griffin, *supra* note 34, at ¶¶ 4–6.
53. *Id.* at ¶ 7.
54. *Id.* at ¶ 8.

fect employee justice."[55] Silver noted what he described as a "communications gap" at companies that resulted in organizational conflict, which the ombudsman could address by working *with* management but not as part of management, and operating in a more informal manner.[56] Silver's conception of the authority and function of the ombudsman, however, was still very much in the classical model: he envisioned the ombudsman conducting investigations (though he asserted it should be in a "nonadversary" setting), interpreting company policy, recommending decisions, and creating a body of precedent.[57] He dismissed fears that that an ombudsman would be unduly intrusive into the work of the company or that the office would be too expensive. Rather, he saw the ombudsman as the "embodiment of the corporate conscience," useful in the imperfect world in which we live:

> Ultimate justice obviously cannot be achieved on earth. The ombudsman is not the great panacea for social ill implied by much of the folklore. He has always been, and will continue to be, most effective in cases of petty dimension. Yet the political society has found him to be truly indispensible. In all enterprise, justice *felt* is often justice *achieved*. The corporation, in our time, is a "dispenser of justice"—both actual and perceived.[58]

Professor Anderson, in his 1969 book, *Ombudsman Papers: American Experience and Proposals*,[59] also noted the applicability of ombudsmen to corporations. He referred to both campus ombudsmen and the ombudsmen for corporations as "ombudsman-like institutions" and called for greater exploration of other contexts in which this concept could be adapted. Regardless of the setting, however, he was clear that he believed that the "standards for an Ombudsman require him to be independent, impartial, expert, accessible, informed, and

---

55. Isidore Silver, *The Corporate Ombudsman*, Harv. Bus. Rev., May-June 1967, at 77, 78.
56. *See id.* at 78–79, 82–83, 85–87.
57. *Id.* at 82–84.
58. *Id.* at 87.
59. Anderson, *supra* note 19.

empowered only to express an opinion."[60] Another early advocate for an ombudsman was Professor J. H. Foegen of Winona State College in Wisconsin. In an article he wrote in 1972, he asserted that a neutral full-time ombudsman "appointed from the community by unions and management, could make many grievance procedures work better."[61] As envisioned by Foegen, the three qualifications most needed by such an ombudsman were availability, neutrality, and power (in the sense of backing by senior management).[62] Professor Foegen's proposal appears not to have found wide acceptance.

Even though the ombudsman concept did not spread as rapidly during the 1960s and 1970s among corporations as it did among colleges and universities, a number of corporations spontaneously evolved ombudsman-like offices (under various names). These offices were expected to help resolve concerns impartially and informally and work for systems change. The "spontaneous" creation of internal, impartial problem-solving offices in various corporations demonstrated that there was also a business need for such a function. By 1982, enough companies had created programs that a small group convened at MIT at the urging of Dr. Rowe of MIT and Lee Robbins of the Wharton School of Finance to begin the formation of an ombuds organization. Word of the formation of this group led to the discovery of more such offices, many of which had developed independently, in a wide variety of institutions. The first corporate ombudsman conference was held in Falmouth, Massachusetts, in 1984 with 30 attendees who came from international organizations, government agencies, corporations, and academic institutions. By 1985, the Corporate Ombudsman Association was formally organized.[63]

3. Impact of the Defense Industry Initiative

The 1980s were a difficult time for corporations. Just as colleges and universities had been in turmoil in the late 1960s and early 1970s, corporations found that they were being criticized during the 1980s

---

60. *Id.* at 58.
61. J. H. Foegen, *An Ombudsman as Complement to the Grievance Procedure*, LAB. L.J., May 1972, at 289.
62. *Id.* at 293.
63. The Corporate Ombudsman Association was not formally incorporated, however, until July 1986.

for having inadequate internal control and reporting mechanisms. Widespread allegations of corporate misconduct and the highly publicized findings of actual misconduct in several investigations during the 1980s caused many people to see corporations in an unfavorable light. The insider-trading prosecutions, savings and loan crisis, junk bond scandals, major antitrust investigations, and defense-contracting scandals are but a few of the major public investigations and scandals that characterized that era. Sexual harassment and race discrimination also were matters of concern. Public perception of business was seen as being at a low point. In comments made in a speech, the chairman of Johnson & Johnson noted in 1987 that "[a] recent *New York Times* poll said that only one-third of Americans believe that business does an excellent or even pretty good job of behaving ethically. A Harris poll says 82 percent of Americans believe business is primarily motivated by greed."[64] In the defense-contracting arena, in particular, the facts were even more startling and justified public concern:

> As of May 1985, 131 separate investigations were pending against 45 of the [Department of Defense's] 100 largest contractors. These involved such issues as defective pricing, cost and labor mischarging, product substitution, subcontractor kickbacks, and false claims. From June 1983 to April 1985, 12 separate investigations were instituted against one major contractor alone.[65]

To help the government respond to the crisis in the management of defense contacting, President Reagan appointed David Packard to chair the President's Blue Ribbon Commission on Defense Management (the Packard Commission). In its interim report, the Packard Commission recognized the limits of governmental regulation and called on defense contractors to undertake greater measures themselves to mitigate misconduct:

---

64. Victor Futter, *An Answer to the Public Perception of Corporations: A Corporate Ombudsperson?*, 46 BUS. LAW 29, 30 (1990). Futter lists 21 major "corporate disasters" that occurred in the preceding few years. *Id.* at 32–35.

65. PRESIDENT'S BLUE RIBBON COMM'N ON DEF. MGMT., CONDUCT AND ACCOUNTABILITY: A REPORT TO THE PRESIDENT 1 n.2 (1986) (also known and hereinafter referred to as the PACKARD COMMISSION REPORT). *See also* Victor Futter, *supra* note 64, at 32–35, for a list of other corporate scandals and investigations.

To assure that their houses are in order, defense contractors must promulgate and vigilantly enforce codes of ethics that address the unique problems and procedures incident to defense procurement. They must also develop and implement internal controls to monitor these codes of ethics and sensitive aspects of contract compliance.[66]

Following the issuance of the interim report, and without waiting for the completion of the final report, 18 of the largest American defense contractors met in the spring of 1986 and formed the Defense Industry Initiative on Business Ethics and Conduct (DII). The DII represented a pledge by those companies (and the number has since grown substantially) to implement policies, procedures, and programs in six areas: codes of ethics, ethics training, internal reporting of alleged misconduct, self-governance systems to monitor compliance and procedures to voluntarily disclose violations, attendance at best practices forums, and accountability to the public.

These DII principles were favorably received by the Packard Commission and were even included as an appendix in the final report that was issued later in 1986. DII Principle 3, Corporate Responsibility to Employees, is especially relevant to the development of ombudsman programs, since some ombudsman programs were created as a result of this recommendation:

Every company must ensure that employees have the opportunity to fulfill their responsibility to preserve the integrity of the code and their honor system. Employees should be free to report suspected violations of the code to the company without fear of retribution for such reporting.

To encourage the surfacing of problems, normal management channels should be supplemented by a confidential reporting mechanism.

It is critical that companies create and maintain an environment of openness where disclosures are accepted and expected. Employees must believe that to raise a concern or report misconduct is expected, accepted, and protected behavior, not the exception. This removes any legitimate rationale for employees

---

66. PRESIDENT'S BLUE RIBBON COMM'N ON DEF. MGMT., AN INTERIM REPORT TO THE PRESIDENT 21 (1986) [hereinafter INTERIM REPORT].

to delay reporting alleged violations or for former employees to allege past offenses by former employers or associates.

To receive and investigate employee allegations of violations of the corporate code of business ethics and conduct, defense contractors can use a contract review board, *an ombudsman,* a corporate ethics or compliance office or other similar mechanism.

In general, the companies accept the broadest responsibility to create an environment in which free, open and timely reporting of any suspected violations becomes the felt responsibility of every employee.[67]

4. Ombudsman Associations

Whether because of the corporate scandals, DII, or a general concern for better corporate self-government, the number of corporate ombudsman programs greatly expanded at this time. Mary Rowe, the MIT ombudsman and one of the co-founders of the Corporate Ombudsman Association, reported in 1987 that at least 50 new ombudsman programs had been created in North America during the preceding two years and that the total number of corporate ombudsman offices had risen to an estimated 200.[68]

Despite the popularity of the concept, there was still widespread confusion about what was meant by an ombudsman. Even as late as 1987, Dr. Rowe reported that there was "no universally accepted definition of an intra-corporate ombudsman."[69] She also described practices and structures that reflected a wide variety of embodiments of the ombuds concept. For example, while impartiality had generally been perceived as a core principle for ombudsmen from the earliest classical programs, Rowe stated that only about half of the companies with ombuds offices had "designated their practitioners as neutrals."[70] Yet, despite the variation in form, there was increasing agreement on the purpose of such offices. She summarized the goals of ombudsmen thus: to "foster and support fair and proper communications and processes" and "to deal

---

67. PACKARD COMMISSION REPORT, *supra* note 65, at 43 (emphasis added).
68. Mary P. Rowe, *The Corporate Ombudsman: An Overview and Analysis,* NEGOTIATION J., Apr. 1997, at 127.
69. *Id.*
70. *Id.* at 128 & *passim.*

with *people* as individuals, and with *problems* as systematically as possible."[71] She categorized the principal functions of the ombudsman as "dealing with feelings," "giving and receiving information on a one-to-one basis," "counseling and problem-solving to help the manager or employee help him- or herself," "shuttle diplomacy," "mediation," "investigation," "adjudication or arbitration," and "upward feedback."[72]

In 1992, the Corporate Ombudsman Association (COA) changed its name to The Ombudsman Association (TOA), in part because its constituency included college and university ombudsmen, as well as both government and international organizational ombudsmen. Many of these university, governmental, and interventional ombuds were already members of COA, and their practices were increasingly seen as similar to those in the corporate world. One of the initial undertakings of COA/TOA was to develop an ombudsman code of ethics and standards of practice as a way to define the essential characteristics and functions of a corporate ombudsman. This was considered both appropriate and necessary, given the various responsibilities and structures that were being employed. At the same time, an effort was made to expand and regularize training and mentoring programs. In this effort, and in companion undertakings by UCOA to articulate its essential ethical principles, the contours of the organizational ombudsman as an independent, neutral, confidential, and informal resource began to emerge.[73]

5. Ombudsman Programs in the Federal Government

With ombudsmen becoming more common in state and local governments, colleges, universities, and corporations, it was only natural that the ombudsman concept would once again exert an influence on the

---

71. *Id.* at 129, 130.

72. *Id.* at 130–32.

73. For a complete discussion of the essential characteristics of an organizational ombuds, see Chapter 1, Part II at 27 to 75. See Appendix 3 at 455 for the initial Code of Ethics and Standards of Practice of The Ombudsman Association and Appendix 4 at 447 for the Statement of Ethical Principles by the University and College Ombudsman Association. See Appendix 5 at 459 for the Code of Ethics and the Standards of Practice developed by the International Ombudsman Association, an organization that resulted from the merger of The Ombudsman Association and the University and College Ombudsman Association in 2005. Appendix 5 also contains the Standards of Practice effective prior to October 2009 as well as the Standards of Practice that became effective October 2009.

federal government. A 1971 ABA Resolution had recommended that the federal government consider implementing ombuds schemes,[74] but a bill in Congress to create a federal ombudsman failed shortly thereafter. In an article in 1998, D. Leah Meltzer reviewed the origins of ombuds in federal agencies and presented several case studies on how they functioned.[75] According to Meltzer:

> Beginning in the late seventies, federal executive agencies began establishing workplace ombuds programs as well. In 1977, the Smithsonian Institution established a workplace ombuds. In 1985, the United States Information Agency (USIA) briefly established an ombuds program. In 1988, the ombuds was reestablished for the Voice of America, the international broadcasting division of USIA. In 1987, the U.S. Secret Service established a pilot ombudsman program. Toward the end of the same year, Congress directed the U.S. Department of State to establish an "Ombudsman for Civil Service Employees." Into the nineties, other federal agencies have continued to experiment with the ombuds concept.[76]

In 1990, the Administrative Conference of the United States recommended that "all government agencies that interact frequently with the public consider establishing an ombudsman service to deal with grievances from the public."[77] This recommendation was publicized in *The Ombudsman: A Primer for Federal Agencies*, published in 1991.[78] A law review article the same year reviewed the limited number of ombudsman programs in federal agencies and concluded that the experience to date was "enough to promote or support the view that, as a rule, federal departments and agencies administering pro-

---

74. 1971 ABA Resolution, *supra* note 25.
75. D. Leah Meltzer, *The Federal Workplace Ombuds*, 13 Ohio St. J. on Disp. Resol. 549, *passim* (1998).
76. *Id.* at 556–57 (footnotes omitted).
77. Admin. Conference of the U.S., *supra* note 27, at 1; *see also id.* at 13–14 (reprinting *Recommendation 90-2: The Ombudsman in Federal Agencies (adopted June 7, 1990)*); Wiegand, *supra* note 5, at 110 & n.83.
78. Admin. Conference of the U.S., *supra* note 27, at 13–14.

grams that serve or directly affect large numbers of the public, should have an effective ombudsman program."[79]

The move toward creating more federal agency ombudsman programs took another step forward in 1996 with the reenactment of the Administrative Dispute Resolution Act (ADRA), which was intended to foster the greater use of alternative dispute resolution (ADR) mechanisms by federal agencies. The federal government, like academic institutions and business organizations, had begun to emphasize the role of mediation and ADR in resolving workplace conflict and as a way to avoid costly litigation. Not only did the ADRA define "alternative means of dispute resolution" to include an ombuds,[80] it also contained provisions to help protect the confidentiality of "dispute resolution communication[s]."[81]

The ADRA, in some ways, marked the coming of age of the organizational ombuds model in that it implicitly recognized that the form of ombudsman that had been reintroduced into government service was not the prosecutorial/investigative formal channel of Scandinavian origin, but rather a distinct, informal, meditative, and confidential channel that later came to be known as an organizational ombuds. But even with this progress, the problems created by a wide variation in ombuds structure and practice elsewhere also have persisted in governmental programs; as recently as 2001, the Government Account-

---

79. Anderson & Stockton, *supra* note 17, at 277. *See generally* Harold J. Krent, *Federal Agency Ombuds: The Costs, Benefits, and Countenance of Confidentiality*, 52 ADMIN. L. REV. 17 (2000).

80. 5 U.S.C. § 571(3) (2007) (defining "alternative means of dispute resolution" as "any procedure that is used to resolve issues in controversy, including, but not limited to, conciliation, facilitation, mediation, factfinding, minitrials, arbitration, and use of ombuds, or any combination thereof").

81. 5 U.S.C. § 571(5). The definition provides that a:

> 'dispute resolution communication' means any oral or written communication prepared for the purposes of a dispute resolution proceeding, including any memoranda, notes or work product of the neutral, parties or nonparty participant; except that a written agreement to enter into a dispute resolution proceeding, or a final written agreement or arbitral award reached as a result of a dispute resolution proceeding, is not a dispute resolution communication.

Id. See 5 U.S.C. § 574 for the provisions relating to the protection of confidentiality; *see also* Chapter 3 for a more complete discussion of the ADRA.

ing Office reported a variety of ombudsman models and practices among federal agency ombudsmen.[82]

Nevertheless, federal agency ombuds have continued to move toward a consensus on the role of an organizational ombuds in much the same way as have ombuds in the private sector. In May 2006, the Coalition of Federal Ombudsmen (CFO) and the Federal Interagency ADR Working Group Steering Committee adopted *A Guide for Federal Employee Ombuds*.[83] Further demonstrating the perseverance of the ombuds concept in the federal government, the CFO issued in February 2009 a comprehensive guide for the establishment of ombuds offices that, though directed to federal agencies, is broadly applicable.[84]

D. American Bar Association Resolutions

The lack of any universally applicable definition of an ombudsman, compounded by the growth of ombuds programs of different types in academia, corporations, and in the government, led to another set of resolutions[85] on the essential characteristics of ombudsmen by the American Bar Association in 2001 and 2004 in an attempt to clarify how such programs should be established and function. Ombudsmen from many organizations and types of programs came together over the course of many meetings to help draft these resolutions. The preamble of the 2001 ABA Resolution acknowledged that:

> [a]s a result of the various types of offices and the proliferation of different processes by which the offices operate, indi-

---

82. U.S. GENERAL ACCOUNTING OFFICE, HUMAN CAPITAL: THE ROLE OF OMBUDSMEN IN DISPUTE RESOLUTION 14–18, 33 (2001).

83. AMERICAN BAR ASS'N, A GUIDE FOR FEDERAL EMPLOYEE OMBUDS—A SUPPLEMENT TO AND ANNOTATION OF THE STANDARDS FOR THE ESTABLISHMENT AND OPERATIONS OF OMBUDS OFFICES (2006), *available at* http://www.usdoj.gov/adr/pdf/final_ombuds.pdf (last visited April 21, 2009).

84. COALITION OF FEDERAL OMBUDSMEN, A UNIFIED MODEL FOR DEVELOPING AN OMBUDSMAN FUNCTION (2009), *available at* http://www.federalombuds.ed.gov/pdfs/FederalOmbudsGuide.pdf (last visited July 22, 2009).

85. *See* AMERICAN BAR ASS'N, STANDARDS FOR THE ESTABLISHMENT AND OPERATION OF OMBUDS OFFICES (2001) [hereinafter 2001 ABA RESOLUTION] (a copy of which is reprinted in Appendix 6 at 468, together with the accompanying Report); AMERICAN BAR ASS'N, STANDARDS FOR THE ESTABLISHMENT AND OPERATION OF OMBUDS OFFICES (revised Feb. 2004) [hereinafter 2004 ABA RESOLUTION] (a copy of which is reprinted in Appendix 7 at 494, together with the accompanying Report).

viduals who come to the ombuds office for assistance may not know what to expect, and the offices may be established in ways that compromise their effectiveness. These standards were developed to provide advice and guidance on the structure and operation of ombuds offices so that ombuds may better fulfill their functions and so that individuals who avail themselves of their aid may do so with greater confidence in the integrity of the process.[86]

The 2001 ABA Resolution was a significant step forward for the ombudsman profession. It not only set forth basic criteria on the establishment and operations of ombuds offices generally,[87] it also outlined what should be an ombud's basic qualifications. Other provisions addressed issues such as appropriate limitations on ombuds' authority and their removal from office.[88] Two other aspects of the resolution are also of particular significance.

First, it distilled the essential characteristics of *all* modern ombuds programs—independence, impartiality, and confidentiality—in both the classical ombudsman programs and the new variants in academia, business, and government. The resolution provided substance to the meaning of these principles in the descriptive text of the resolution as well as in the accompanying report.[89]

Second, it provided the first workable method of describing the types of ombuds programs and set forth the essential characteristics of each type. The three main types recognized included "classical ombuds" (independent government officials, frequently with the power to issue subpoenas, who conduct investigations and issue reports), "advocate ombuds" (independent advocates for a designated constituency), and "organizational ombuds." The 2001 ABA Resolution's use of the term "organizational ombuds" quickly became the standard term for the type of ombudsman that it described as follows:

---

86. 2001 ABA RESOLUTION, *supra* note 85, at 2–3. *See* Appendix 6 at 471–72.
87. The 2001 ABA Resolution uses the term "ombuds" in place of other terms, such as "ombudsman" or "ombudsperson," that had been used.
88. 2001 ABA RESOLUTION, *supra* note 85, at 6–7. *See* Appendix 6 at 474–76.
89. *Id.* at 5–7; *id.* at 16–21. See Appendix 6 at 473–74; 484–89.

An organizational ombuds facilitates fair and equitable resolutions of concerns that arise within the entity. In addition to and in clarification of the standards contained in Paragraphs A-F,[90] an organizational ombuds should:

(1) be authorized to undertake inquiries and function by informal processes as specified by the charter
(2) be authorized to conduct independent and impartial inquiries into matters within the prescribed jurisdiction of the office
(3) be authorized to issue reports
(4) be authorized to advocate for change within the entity.[91]

These attributes of an organizational ombuds were not altered in the revisions of the 2004 ABA Resolution,[92] but that resolution did eliminate the "Classical" ombuds category, replacing it with separate descriptions of "Legislative Ombuds" and "Executive Ombuds" to describe two variants of the public-sector ombuds programs. While the classifications of the two types of classical ombuds programs have not been widely embraced following the 2004 ABA Resolution, a consensus has gradually emerged that organizational ombuds programs are different both from public-sector programs, which have a mandate to conduct investigations and issue reports on governmental malfeasance or agency matters, and from advocate ombuds, who advocate for their constituency, rather than serve as neutrals.

Notwithstanding the growing consensus on the essential characteristics in the evolution of the organizational ombuds, it is notable that there was no legislation to clarify the types of programs or address the impact of a variety of legal issues, including confidentiality

---

90. These are the provisions that relate to the establishment and operations of ombuds offices; qualifications of ombuds; independence, impartiality, and confidentiality; limitations on authority; and removal from office. *Id.* at 3–7. *See* Appendix 6 at 472–75.

91. 2001 ABA RESOLUTION, *supra* note 85, at 8–9. *See* Appendix 6 at 476.

92. The 2004 ABA Resolution did, however, make changes to Section D, "Limitations on the Ombuds's Authority," and it filled in the provisions in Section F, "Notice," which had been left blank in the 2001 ABA Resolution. *Compare* 2001 ABA RESOLUTION 6–7 *with* 2004 ABA RESOLUTION 4–6. These changes are explored in greater detail in Part II of this chapter at 42–44 and in Chapter 3 at 212–18.

and testimonial privilege, with each type of program. And while the 2001 and 2004 ABA Resolutions provided helpful guidance in sorting out the various types of programs, they were more descriptive of the types of programs already in existence—programs that had been created to respond to a multiplicity of needs, with varying expectations as to the role and effectiveness of an ombuds—rather than a driving force in the creation of new programs. Accordingly, to better understand essential characteristics of an organization ombuds program, we need to take a closer look at the development of the key principles upon which they are based.

PART II: ESSENTIAL CHARACTERISTICS OF AN ORGANIZATIONAL OMBUDS PROGRAM

When the American Bar Association articulated the 12 essential characteristics of an ombudsman in the 1969 ABA Resolution, crafted under the direction of Professor Gellhorn, there was no contemplation of what we would now consider to be an organizational ombudsman.[93] It is therefore not surprising that the principal focus of the 12 essential characteristics was on independence. What may be surprising to current organizational ombuds, however, is that there was no reference either to neutrality or to confidentiality. There also was no reference to "informal" resolution practices that do not include management decision-making. Accordingly, to understand the current role and function of an organizational ombuds, it is necessary first to explore how a consensus on the key principles for an organizational ombuds—independence, impartiality, confidentiality, and informality—developed, especially through the evolution of ombuds' codes of ethics and standards of practice, and then to discuss in more detail just what is meant by the essential characteristics of an organizational ombuds program.

A. *1969 ABA Resolution and the Spread of Ombuds Programs*

Neutrality, or perhaps impartiality, has undoubtedly always been assumed to be inherent in the nature of an ombuds office. The 1969

---

93. *See* Silver, *supra* note 55. (Silver was an early advocate for the creation of corporate ombudsmen, but his conception of what the role would be differs from what is currently understood to be an organizational ombuds.)

ABA Resolution did not mention neutrality, but it also probably assumed that the ombuds would be widely respected, since it required that he or she be confirmed by two-thirds of a legislative body and thus could not be too partisan. Nevertheless, the concept of neutrality was not addressed explicitly, in contrast to other characteristics that were specifically described. Likewise, there appears to have been no expectation that the work of the ombudsman would be confidential. It was understood that ombudsmen would conduct fact-finding investigations, and the resolution stated that an ombudsman should have discretion on what criticisms he or she would make or publicize. In fact, one of the characteristics articulated in the 1969 ABA Resolution was that the "agency, official, or public employee criticized by the ombudsman [would] have advance notice of the criticism and [the opportunity] to publish with the criticism an answering statement."[94]

By the time of the 2001 ABA Resolution, however, a consensus had developed that the essential characteristics of an ombuds, and those of an organizational program in particular, were independence, impartiality, *and confidentiality*.[95] The emphasis on confidentiality for organizational ombuds was undoubtedly influenced by the differences in the way ombuds functioned in private organizations in contrast to governmental agencies. In other words, because private ombuds had a role different from public ombuds, they needed to be structured differently. Ombuds in nongovernmental settings typically have not conducted public investigations (for instance, they have no power to compel testimony) or issued investigative reports, in contrast to governmental or classical ombudsmen. While both types of ombuds are now and have always been concerned with addressing specific instances of maladministration and systemic change generally, most of the work of organizational ombuds has focused on mediation techniques and attempting to resolve the concerns of or disputes among individuals.[96] In mediation and other forms of alternative dispute resolution, confidentiality had long been seen as a critical element of the process, because only with the assurance of confidentiality will the parties reveal their real concerns and goals. The mediator, privy to the claims and hopes of both sides, can then begin to try to find common ground or a

---

94. 1969 ABA Resolution, *supra* note 24, at 265. *See* Appendix 1 at 440.
95. 2001 ABA Resolution, *supra* note 85, at 3. *See* Appendix 6 at 472.
96. *See* Rowe, *supra* note 68, at 127, 129–30.

means to resolve the dispute. Because so much of what organizational ombuds now do closely resembles this type of mediation, application of similar process confidentiality to organizational ombuds was a natural development.

The lessons learned by defense contractors and others in the 1980s added yet another force driving the need for confidentiality: with the recognition that many people fear loss of relationships and retribution, confidentiality was seen as necessary to encourage employees and others to come forward with their concerns about misconduct in their organizations. The programs created in response to the Packard Commission report and the Defense Industry Initiative (DII) attempted to be responsive to this issue. When the first organizational sentencing guidelines were promulgated by the United States Sentencing Commission in 1991 (building upon the work by the Packard Commission and DII), the need to address the fear of retribution was again recognized. One of the criteria for an "effective program to prevent and detect violations of law" under the Organizational Sentencing Guidelines (Sentencing Guidelines) was "having in place and publicizing a reporting system whereby employees and other agents could report criminal conduct by others within the organization *without fear of retribution*."[97]

Both of these reasons for confidentiality in the private sector, in turn, influenced the perception of other essential characteristics of organizational ombuds programs. In other words, what organizational ombuds did and how they did it was strongly influenced by what was required to protect confidentiality. In contrast to classical ombuds programs that were created by a government (generally through legislation) and that either did not emphasize the need for confidentiality or had confidentiality addressed in the enabling legislation, private ombuds programs perceived that confidentiality was critical to their mission but were bereft of legislative protection and thus were forced to defend their claim of confidentiality on the basis of traditional legal principles.

---

97. U.S. SENTENCING COMMISSION, GUIDELINES MANUAL § 8A.1.2 application note 3(k)(5) (1994) (emphasis added), *superseded by the promulgation of* U.S. SENTENCING COMMISSION, GUIDELINES MANUAL, § 8B.2.1 (Nov. 2004) [hereinafter U.S.S.G. MANUAL].

B. Evolution of Codes of Ethics and Standards of Practice of Ombuds Associations

Early attempts to articulate the principles on which organizational ombuds programs operated reflected awareness of the need for confidentiality but only as one operating principle, and not even the primary one. For example, the Ethical Principles for University and College Ombudsmen, developed by the University and College Ombudsman Association (UCOA) in the mid-1980s, began with the statement that "[a]n ombudsman should be guided by the following principles: objectivity, independence, accessibility, confidentiality and justice; justice is pre-eminent."[98]

The first Code of Ethics adopted by the Corporate Ombudsman Association (COA) in 1986 did not expressly address independence, but it did emphasize the need for confidentiality. In fact, of the four statements in that version of the Code of Ethics, two specifically addressed confidentiality:

I. The Ombudsman, as a designated neutral, has the responsibility of maintaining strict confidentiality concerning matters that are brought to his/her attention. The only exception, at the sole discretion of the ombudsman, is the instance of threat to the physical safety of others[99] and/or threat to company assets. This duty to warn, however, shall be initiated only after the ombudsman has strongly counseled with the client involved to encourage the client to personally come forth. In the event the client still refuses, the ombudsman has an obligation to notify the client of the intended breach of confidentiality in this situation. Even then, the ombudsman has the responsibility and obligation to discuss the situation only with those who have a need to know.

II. The ombudsman has the responsibility to insure that any records or files pertaining to confidential discussions with clients are safe from

---

98. Univ. & Coll. Ombudsman Ass'n, Ethical Principles for University and College Ombudsmen. *See* Appendix 4 at 457.

99. This exception was drawn from the ruling in *Tarasoff v. Regents of University of California*, 131 Cal. Rptr. 14, 551 P.2d 334 (1976). *See infra* Chapter 4 at 354.

inspection at all time by other employees, including management at all levels.[100]

After the Corporate Ombudsman Association changed its name in 1992 to The Ombudsman Association, the Code of Ethics was revised. The revisions incorporated much of the prior language but gave additional emphasis to the principle of confidentiality by claiming "strict confidentiality," by simplifying the exception to confidentiality, and by making it clear that ombuds should not testify in any formal judicial or administrative hearing. The initial TOA Code of Ethics (Appendix 3), in its entirety, stated:

> The ombudsman, as a designated neutral, has the responsibility of maintaining strict confidentiality concerning matters that are brought to his/her attention unless given permission to do otherwise. The only exceptions, at the sole discretion of the ombudsman, are where there appears to be imminent threat of serious harm.
>
> The ombudsman must take all reasonable steps to protect any records and files pertaining to confidential discussions from inspection by all other persons, including management.
>
> The ombudsman should not testify in any formal judicial or administrative hearing about concerns brought to his/her attention.
>
> When making recommendations, the ombudsman has the responsibility to suggest actions or policies that will be equitable to all parties.[101]

While this Code of Ethics, like its predecessor, gave voice to the principles of neutrality and confidentiality (and, in fact, linked confidentiality to neutrality in the same way), the code was silent on two other principles that generally are recognized today as essential to an organizational ombuds: independence and informality.

Independence and informality, however, were recognized as significant enough to be included in the first version of the Standards of Practice adopted by TOA in the early 1990s. In this version of the

---

100. CORPORATE OMBUDSMAN ASS'N, CODE OF ETHICS (1986).
101. THE OMBUDSMAN ASS'N, CODE OF ETHICS (undated). *See* Appendix 3 at 455.

Standards of Practice, the principle of confidentiality remains paramount—so much so that, for the first time, ombuds claimed that their communications are privileged.[102] The complete text of the Standards of Practice provided as follows:

Standards of Practice

We adhere to The Ombudsman Association Code of Ethics.

We base our practice on confidentiality.

We assert that there is a privilege with respect to communications with the ombudsman and we resist testifying in any formal process inside or outside the organization.

We exercise discretion whether to act upon a concern of an individual contacting the office. An ombudsman may initiate action on a problem he or she perceives directly.

We are designated neutrals and remain independent of ordinary line and staff structures. We serve no additional role (within an organization where we serve as ombudsman) which would compromise this neutrality.

We remain an informal and off-the-record resource. Formal investigations—for the purpose of adjudication—should be done by others. In the event that an ombudsman accepts a request to conduct a formal investigation, a memo should be written to file noting this action as an exception to the ombudsman role. Such investigations should not be considered privileged.

We foster communication about the philosophy and function of the ombudsman's office with the people we serve.

We provide feedback on trends, issues, policies and practices without breaching confidentiality or anonymity. We identify new problems and we provide support for responsible systems change.

We keep professionally current and competent by pursuing continuing education and training relevant to the ombudsman profession.

---

102. These Standards of Practice are also reprinted in Appendix 3. The claim of privilege stems from court rulings, beginning in 1990, in which communications with an organizational ombuds were held to be confidential and privileged. For a discussion on the development of the law on ombuds confidentiality and privilege, Chapter 3, Part II, beginning at page 220.

We will endeavor to be worthy of the trust placed in us.[103]

This first version of the TOA Standards of Practice was codified and revised in 1995.[104] The 1995 TOA Standards of Practice represents a significant milestone for organizational ombuds in that it marks the first comprehensive effort to document what are now recognized as the essential functions of an organizational ombudsman. The emphasis on confidentiality was carried over from the previous version of the Standards of Practice, but the provisions were even more detailed:

2. We base our practice on confidentiality.
   2.1 An ombudsman should not use the names of individuals or mention their employers without express permission.
   2.2 During the problem-solving process an ombudsman may make known information as long as the identity of the individual contacting the office is not compromised.
   2.3 Any data that we prepare should be scrutinized carefully to safeguard the identity of each individual whose concerns are represented.
   2.4 Publicity about our office conveys the confidential nature of our work
3. We assert that there is privilege with respect to communications with the ombudsman and we resist testifying in any formal process inside or outside the organization.
   3.1 Communications between an ombudsman and others (made while the ombudsman is serving in that capacity) are considered privileged. Others cannot waive this privilege.
   3.2 We do not serve in any additional function in the organization which would undermine the privileged nature of our work (such as compliance of officer, arbitrator, etc.)
   3.3 An ombudsman keeps no case records on behalf of the organization. If an ombudsman finds case notes necessary to manage the work, the ombudsman should establish and

---

103. THE OMBUDSMAN ASS'N, STANDARDS OF PRACTICE (undated). *See* Appendix 3 at 456.
104. The 1995 TOA Standards of Practice are reprinted in Appendix 8.

follow a consistent and standard practice for the destruction of any such written notes.

3.4 When necessary, the ombudsman's office will seek judicial protection for staff and records of the office. It may be necessary to seek representation by separate legal counsel to protect the privilege of the office.[105]

The 1995 TOA Standards of Practice retained and slightly expanded provisions relating to neutrality and independence.[106] Likewise, these standards reiterated the notion from the previous standards that ombuds were an "informal and off-the-record resource."[107] This linkage of informality, confidentiality, and neutrality was especially evident in a new provision in the 1995 TOA Standards of Practice that for the first time explicitly addressed the question of whether communications with an ombudsman would be imputed notice to an organization:

6.1 We do not act as an agent for the organization and we do not accept notice on behalf of the organization. We do always refer individuals to the appropriate place where formal notice can be made.

Even as the 1995 TOA Standards of Practice continued the emphasis on confidentiality and tried to specify just what this meant and how it related to independence, neutrality, and informality, the

---

105. THE OMBUDSMAN ASS'N, STANDARDS OF PRACTICE (1995) [hereinafter 1995 TOA STANDARDS OF PRACTICE]. *See* Appendix 8 at 525–26.

106. Sections 5 and 5.1, for example, state:

> 5. We are designated neutrals and remain independent of ordinary line and staff structures. We serve no additional role (within an organization where we serve as ombudsmen) which could compromise this neutrality.
> 5.1 An ombudsman strives for objectivity and impartiality.

Id.

107. Section 6 states:

> 6. We remain an informal and off-the-record resource. Formal investigations—for the purpose of adjudication—should be done by others. In the event that an ombudsman accepts a request to conduct a formal investigation, a memo should be written to file noting this action as an exception to the ombudsman role. Such investigations should not be considered privileged.

Id.

standards nevertheless reflected an uncertainty over the limits of confidentiality. In both the Scandinavian ombudsman models and the 1969 ABA Resolution, an essential function of the "classical" ombudsman was conducting investigations. As the ombudsman concept moved further away from its classical roots and was applied to American universities and corporations, there was an expectation in some quarters that this function would continue. Consequently, ombudsmen were still on occasion being called upon to conduct formal investigations. At the same time, however, there was a growing realization that conducting any such "formal investigation"—meaning an investigation for the purpose of determining facts or adjudicating an issue—violated the principles of neutrality (having no other role in the organization) and informality, and was increasingly inconsistent with the alternative dispute resolution function of ombuds. Similarly, ombudsmen realized that conducting investigations was likely to undermine their attempts to claim privilege or otherwise protect confidentiality. As a result, the language used in the 1995 TOA Standards of Practice reflects an effort to describe what organizational ombuds do as something other than investigations (by, for example, using terms such as "the problem-solving process" (§ 2.2) and "an informal and off-the-record resource" (§ 6.)), while at the same time articulating a separate procedure (creating a memo to the file) for any formal investigation the ombudsman is called upon to conduct. The standards state that no claim of privilege would extend to such investigations by ombudsmen.[108]

The most significant accomplishment of the 1995 TOA Standards of Practice is that it brought together in one place an expression of the essential characteristics of an organizational ombudsman. Not only did it provide a glossary that provided definitions for what the standards meant by "confidential," "independent," "neutrality," and "privilege,"[109] it also provided a succinct statement of the mission of ombuds in the introductory paragraph:

---

108. See Chapter 3 at 193 for a discussion on imputed notice. While this procedure may help the ombuds document activities that are not considered confidential or privileged, it does not address the need of the entity and the ombuds to make it clear to potential inquirers that the ombuds has no authority to accept notice of claims to avoid notice to the ombuds being imputed to the entity.

109. See Appendix 8 at 527.

> The mission of the organizational ombudsman is to provide a confidential, neutral and informal process which facilitates fair and equitable resolutions to concerns that arise in the organization. In performing this mission, the ombudsman serves as an information and communications resource, upward feedback channel, advisor, dispute resolution expert and change agent.

This description of the essential purpose of an organizational ombudsman still has currency.

Since a large number of the college and university ombuds during the 1990s were members of TOA as well as UCOA (leading eventually to their combination in 2005 to form the International Ombudsman Association), TOA's efforts to express common principles prompted UCOA to do likewise. The UCOA Standards of Practice, adopted in 2000,[110] reflected many of the same themes as those of TOA, but they differed in at least two significant ways. First, they were more clearly organized in accordance with the major principles (independence, impartiality/neutrality, confidentiality, informality, access to services, and professional competence), a construct that has largely survived to the present. As in the earlier UCOA Statement of Ethical Principles, confidentiality was not given primacy. Even more important, however, was the way that the UCOA Standards dealt with the issue of investigations. While the 1995 TOA Standards of Practice permitted such investigations (albeit with the dubious requirement of writing a memorandum to the file), the later UCOA Standards explicitly stated that such formal investigations should be conducted by others. The clarity of this practice limitation, however, was undercut by language that permitted ombuds to "informally investigate" and to "conduct informal fact finding," but the UCOA provisions on "informality" were clearly an advance over the corresponding TOA provisions:

> 4. Informality
>   The Ombuds functions on an informal basis by such means as: listening, providing and receiving information, reframing issues, developing options, referral, third-party intervention, shuttle diplomacy, mediation, and systems change.

---

110. The 2000 UCOA STANDARDS OF PRACTICE are reprinted in Appendix 9.

4.1 The Ombuds does not take an active role in any formal institutional investigative or adjudicative procedures. The Ombuds may informally investigate or otherwise examine alleged procedural irregularities of a formal process and allegations about alleged acts, omissions, improprieties and/or broader systemic problems.

4.2 The Ombuds supplements, but does not replace, any steps required in formal internal or external procedures. Use of the Ombuds office is not a required step in any grievance process or organizational policy.

4.3 The Ombuds hears, considers, and as appropriate, pursues resolution of the concerns, issues, perceptions, interpretations, facts, and/or allegations of inappropriate acts, omissions, or improprieties presented by individuals.

4.4 The Ombuds may conduct informal fact finding when appropriate.

4.5 When a formal investigation is requested, the Ombuds refers individuals to the appropriate offices or persons.[111]

While there is no evidence that this emphasis on informality was directly linked to the Carnegie Commission Report that spawned the initial growth of academic ombudsman programs, the informality contemplated by these standards is entirely consistent with the recommendations in that report.[112]

C. 2001 American Bar Association Resolution

The provisions of the 2000 UCOA Standards of Practice—and indeed, their very adoption—was influenced by the fact that representatives from TOA and UCOA were engaged at that time in a new endeavor with the American Bar Association to adopt a resolution on the establishment and operation of ombuds offices. It had been almost 30 years since the ABA had last addressed the ombudsman topic, and that was limited to governmental ombudsmen. In the interim, ombuds programs had multiplied and diversified. This renewed ABA effort, spearheaded by Ellen Waxman and Sharan Levine, the chairs of the Ombuds Com-

---

111. UCOA STANDARDS OF PRACTICE, *supra* note 110. *See* Appendix 9 at 532.
112. *See supra* notes 41 & 42.

mittee of the ABA Section of Dispute Resolution and the Ombuds Committee of the ABA Section of Administrative Law and Regulatory Practice, involved participants from numerous other groups. Comments were received on draft proposals from ombuds in all types of organizations, including governments at the federal, state, and local level, academic institutions, and private-sector and nonprofit organizations. Moreover, in addition to the input of the Dispute Resolution and Administrative Law and Regulatory Practice Sections of the ABA, other ABA bodies were involved, including the Commission on Legal Problems of the Elderly, the Section of Business Law, the Senior Lawyer Division, and the Government and Public Sector Division. And finally, the proposed resolution, as is the case with all ABA resolutions, was presented to the ABA House of Delegates, a representative body with delegates from every state, for final adoption.

As noted in Part I, the 2001 ABA Resolution that came out of this process[113] is especially noteworthy. Perhaps its most significant impact was the formal recognition of the need for a "publically available written policy (the 'charter') that clearly sets forth the role and jurisdiction of the ombuds" and includes certain authorized functions of the ombuds.[114] While a charter or terms of reference, as it was sometimes called, had previously been considered good practice, the 2001 ABA Resolution lent support to the proposition that such a charter should be a key requirement for the establishment of an ombuds office.

In addition, the 2001 ABA Resolution provided a new conceptual framework in which to view the various types of ombuds programs. It not only classified ombuds programs by type but articulated the essential characteristics of all ombuds types. This was no small accomplishment because, by 2001, in addition to organizational ombuds programs, there were ombuds programs organized strictly in the classical tradition (to serve a public investigatory function), and other programs that had been created to become advocates for particular constituents (such as for nursing homes, prisons, or newspaper readers). Aside from the name "ombudsman," many of these programs had little in common.

---

113. 2001 ABA RESOLUTION and Report, *supra* note 85. *See* Appendix 6 at 468.
114. 2001 ABA RESOLUTION, *supra* note 85, at 3. *See* Appendix 6 at 472.

Even though the 2001 ABA Resolution rejected the "one size fits all" approach to the definition of an ombuds in favor of a classification by type, it failed to address some particularly hard questions stemming from the different types of programs. Indeed, on the issue of notice (meaning whether information about a legal issue given to or known by an ombuds is imputed to the entity for which it operates), it took a pass entirely, explicitly stating: "These standards do not address the issue whether a communication to the ombuds will be deemed notice to anyone else including any entity in or for which the ombuds acts. Important legal rights and liabilities may be affected by the notice issue."[115] On the issue of confidentiality, the 2001 ABA Resolution helpfully stated that confidentiality was an essential characteristic of ombuds, but unfortunately it left unaddressed the limits of that confidentiality and whether any communications with an ombuds could be privileged. Confidentiality was bundled together with independence and impartiality in one section dealing with all three principles:

Independence, Impartiality, and Confidentiality

C. To ensure the effective operation of an ombuds, an entity should authorize the ombuds to operate consistently with the following essential characteristics. Entities that have established ombuds offices that lack appropriate safeguards to maintain these characteristics should take prompt steps to remedy any such deficiency.

(1) *Independence*. The ombuds is and appears to be free from interference in the legitimate performance of duties and independent from control, limitation, or a penalty imposed for retaliatory purposes by an official of the appointing entity or by a person who may be the subject of a complaint or inquiry.

In assessing whether an ombuds is independent in structure, function, and appearance, the following factors are important: whether anyone subject to the ombuds jurisdiction or anyone directly responsible for a person under the ombuds jurisdiction (a) can control or limit the ombuds performance of assigned duties or (b) can, for retaliatory purposes, (1) eliminate the office, (2) remove the ombuds, or (3) reduce the budget or resources of the office.

---

115. *Id.* at 7. *See* Appendix 6 at 473–74.

(2) *Impartiality in Conducting Inquiries and Investigations.* The ombuds conducts inquiries and investigations in an impartial manner, free from initial bias and conflicts of interest. Impartiality does not preclude the ombuds from developing an interest in securing changes that are deemed necessary as a result of the process, nor from otherwise being an advocate on behalf of a designated constituency. The ombuds may become an advocate within the entity for change where the process demonstrates a need for it.

(3) *Confidentiality.* An ombuds does not disclose and is not required to disclose any information provided in confidence, except to address an imminent risk of serious harm. Records pertaining to a complaint, inquiry, or investigation are confidential and not subject to disclosure outside of the ombuds office. An ombuds does not reveal the identity of a complainant without that person's express consent. An ombuds may, however, at the ombuds discretion disclose non-confidential information and may disclose confidential information so long as doing so does not reveal its source. An ombuds should discuss any exceptions to the ombuds maintaining confidentiality with the source of the information.[116]

Both the 1995 TOA Standards of Practice and the 2000 UCOA Standards of Practice had given more detailed guidance on these points.

Even with these shortcomings, the 2001 ABA Resolution was significant not only for stating what an ombuds must do but also because it expressly addressed what an ombuds should *not* do. In the paragraph following the one quoted above, it specified "Limitations on the Ombuds Authority":

---

116. *Id.* at 5–7. Footnote 3 to the 2001 ABA Resolution, which appears at this point, provides:

> A classical ombuds should not be required to discuss confidentiality with government officials and employees when applying this paragraph to the extent that an applicable statute makes clear that such an individual may not withhold information from the ombuds and that such a person has no reasonable expectation of confidentiality with respect to anything that person provides to the ombuds.

Id. at 6 n.3

D. An ombuds should not, nor should an entity expect or authorize an ombuds to:

(1) make, change or set aside a law, policy, or administrative decision

(2) make binding decisions or determine rights

(3) directly compel an entity or any person to implement the ombuds recommendations

(4) conduct an investigation that substitutes for administrative or judicial proceedings

(5) accept jurisdiction over an issue that is currently pending in a legal forum unless all parties and the presiding officer in that action explicitly consent

(6) address any issue arising under a collective bargaining agreement or which falls within the purview of any existing federal, state, or local labor or employment law, rule, or regulation, unless the ombuds is authorized to do so by the collective bargaining agreement or unless the collective bargaining representative and the employing entity jointly agree to allow the ombuds to do so, or if there is no collective bargaining representative, the employer specifically authorizes the ombuds to do so, or

(7) act in an manner inconsistent with the grant of and limitations on the jurisdiction of the office when discharging the duties of the office of ombuds.[117]

The 2001 ABA Resolution thus is consistent with the 2000 UCOA Standards of Practice in providing that ombuds should not conduct investigations that substitute "for administrative or judicial proceedings," but it went a step further in addressing the scope of ombuds authority in the context of collective bargaining and labor relations.[118] This issue had not previously been addressed either by UCOA or TOA in their Codes of Ethics or Standards of Practice, and the result demonstrated the ABA's conclusion that the labor and employment laws trumped any organizational ombuds mandate.

---

117. *Id.* at 6–7. See Appendix 6 at 474–75.
118. See Chapter 2 at 132 and Chapter 4 at 425 for a more complete discussion of significant employment decisions by the U.S. Supreme Court and a listing of labor and employment laws that may impact the work of ombuds.

D. 2004 American Bar Association Resolution

Some of the hard questions left on the table by the 2001 ABA Resolution were addressed three years later in another ABA Resolution that was intended to build upon the earlier effort.[119] The 2004 ABA Resolution and the issues it addressed were significantly influenced by the participation of the ABA Section of Individual Rights and Responsibilities (which included lawyers who typically represented plaintiffs in employment disputes). This group had not officially participated in the development of the 2001 ABA Resolution, but by 2004 had asserted themselves and thus had to be dealt with in order to reach agreement on such issues as limitations on ombuds' authority in the context of collective bargaining, notice, and confidentiality. The resulting resolution has drawn criticism and rebuke from TOA and UCOA (and their successor organization, the IOA).[120] A more detailed discussion of the implications of this resolution on the issue of imputed notice is reserved for later,[121] but it is important here to mention the important aspects of the 2004 ABA Resolution and the IOA response to it.

First, and not to be overlooked, it reaffirmed and restated much of the good work of the 2001 ABA Resolution on the essential characteristics of an ombuds. And, while not relevant for the present purposes, it also added further clarity to the classification of types of ombuds by eliminating the "classical" ombuds category, replacing it with separate descriptions for "legislative ombuds" and "executive ombuds."

Second, it deleted a clause from the subsection in "Limitations on the Ombuds's Authority" that had appeared in the 2001 ABA Resolution and which had indicated that an ombuds could address issues arising under a collective-bargaining agreement when the collective-

---

119. See *supra* note 85 & Appendix 7 at 494 for the 2004 ABA RESOLUTION and Report.

120. *See* Appendix 10 at 534 for the INTERNATIONAL OMBUDSMAN ASSOCIATION (IOA), GUIDANCE FOR BEST PRACTICES AND COMMENTARY ON THE AMERICAN BAR ASSOCIATION STANDARDS FOR THE ESTABLISHMENT AND OPERATION OF OMBUDS OFFICES (Revised Feb. 2004) [hereinafter IOA GUIDANCE AND COMMENTARY]. This IOA Guidance and Commentary was adopted by IOA on March 14, 2006, and contains the resolution adopted by the boards of directors of both TOA and UCOA in August 2004, noting that the 2004 ABA Resolution departs from their standards of practice and reaffirming their commitment to their own standards.

121. *See, e.g.*, Chapter 3 at 212–18.

bargaining representative and the employing entity agreed to so authorize the ombuds.[122] Instead, a new footnote was added at the end of the revised subparagraph D(6):

> Under these Standards, the employer may authorize an ombuds to address issues of labor or employment law only if the entity has expressly provided the ombuds with the confidentiality specified in Paragraph C(3). An ombuds program as envisioned by these Standards supplements and does not substitute for other procedures and remedies necessary to meet the duty of employers to protect the legal rights of both employers and employees.[123]

The third major change made by the 2004 ABA Resolution is that it added an entirely new provision dealing with notice, to replace the language in the 2001 ABA Resolution that declined to address the issue. These new notice provisions, which would under some circumstances impute notice to an organization based on communications to an ombuds, have been the most problematic for ombuds and are analyzed in detail in Chapter 3.[124]

In August 2004, the boards of directors of TOA and UCOA each adopted a resolution reaffirming their own Standards of Practice and taking issue with provisions in the 2004 ABA Resolution:

> RESOLVED: The Ombudsman Association and The University and College Ombuds Association note the Resolution

---

122. Paragraph D(6) of the 2001 ABA Resolution provided that an ombuds should not, nor should the entity authorize an ombuds to:

> address any issue arising under a collective bargaining agreement or which falls within the purview of any existing federal, state, or local labor or employment law, rule, or regulation, unless *the ombuds is authorized to do so by the collective bargaining agreement or unless the collective bargaining representative and the employing entity jointly agree to allow the ombuds to do so, or if* there is no collective bargaining representative, the employer specifically authorizes the ombuds to do so . . . .

2001 ABA RESOLUTION, *supra* note 85, at 7. The 2004 ABA Resolution deleted the language above that appears in italics. *See* Appendices 6 & 7 at 475 & 500.
123. 2004 ABA RESOLUTION, *supra* note 85, at 4 n.4. *See* Appendix 7 at 500.
124. See the discussion of imputed notice in Chapter 3 at 193.

adopted by the American Bar Association House of Delegates on February 9, 2004, on Standards for the Establishment and Operation of Ombuds Offices. The ABA Resolution significantly departs—in provisions including but not limited to confidentiality and notice—from the Standards of Practice adopted by The Ombudsman Association and The University and College Ombuds Association, which were derived from the best practices of organizational ombuds based on many years of collective experience. The Ombudsman Association and The University and College Ombuds Association therefore reaffirm their Standards of Practice.[125]

In the decade leading up to the 2004 ABA Resolution, the practices of academic ombuds and those of corporate and even some governmental ombuds had coalesced around the principles of independence, neutrality, informality, and confidentiality. The earlier efforts of TOA to articulate a Code of Ethics and Standards of Practice had influenced those developed by UCOA, and representatives of both organizations had come together to participate in the 2001 and 2004 ABA Resolution process. Even though they had differences in organizational emphasis and structure, both organizations realized that it was in their interest to join forces, which they accomplished with their merger in 2005 and the creation of the International Ombudsman Association (IOA).

E. Agreement and Disagreement on Key Principles of Organizational Ombuds Programs

The combination of TOA and UCOA created an opportunity for organizational ombuds to formulate a common code of ethics and standards of practice. In a sense, this effort brought together the latest thinking on what an organizational ombuds should and should not be and how organizational ombuds should operate. There were two significant products of this effort. The first was a carefully considered critical response to the 2004 ABA Resolution, and the second was a revised Code of Ethics and Standards of Practice.

---

125. IOA GUIDANCE AND COMMENTARY, *supra* note 120, at 3. *See* Appendix 10 at 534. *See also* Appendix 11 at 557 for IOA Best Practices. Version 3, Oct. 13, 2009.

The IOA elaborated on the position adopted by its predecessor organizations by approving a document, "Guidance for Best Practices and Commentary on the American Bar Association Standards for the Establishment and Operation of Ombuds Offices, Revised February 2004" (IOA Guidance and Commentary), setting forth its position in rebuttal to the employment law and notice provisions of the 2004 ABA Resolution.[126]

On the employment law and collective bargaining issues addressed by the ABA in Paragraph D(6), the IOA Guidance and Commentary emphasized four recommendations that recognized the primacy of the collective bargaining process and the need to inform people about legal rights, but stopped short of taking the position, as the 2004 ABA Resolution had done, that an ombuds has no role in these areas:

- The ombuds charter, and, where possible, any relevant collective bargaining agreement, should define the involvement of the ombuds with union employees and with issues that arise under the collective bargaining agreement. For those ombuds whose scope of services includes union employees, the ombuds should defer to the union process any issue covered by the CBA [collective bargaining agreement] unless otherwise agreed to by the union, the entity, and the persons involved.
- The ombuds should always inform covered employees about the union process when providing assistance on an issue that might be covered by the CBA.

* * *

- Ombuds should function in a way that addresses concern for preserving the legal rights of visitors. An ombuds should present and if appropriate discuss an appropriate range of options available to the visitor from the very informal to the most formal. Formal options may include ways to put management on notice of an issue, referrals to rights-based elements of the organization's conflict resolution system, or the provision of information about seeking external legal advice (for example, providing contact information to the local bar association's attorney referral service).

---

126. *See supra* notes 120, 125.

- When the ombuds works with the visitor to address issues that may involve other formal alternatives (under law, rules, or regulations), it should be made clear to the visitor that an informal approach does not automatically exclude the visitor's later participation in more formal options. The ombuds should remind the visitor to keep in mind possible time limits and their potential impact on the visitor's more formal options. The ombuds should not provide legal advice, but should suggest alternatives that make the visitor aware of the possible need to seek legal advice.[127]

On the issue of notice, the IOA rejected the provisions in the 2004 ABA Resolution and, in place of the complicated procedures advocated by the ABA, recommended a straightforward rule: the IOA's position is that what someone may say to an ombuds is confidential and not notice to the entity, but what an ombuds communicates to an entity point of contact may be deemed notice to the entity.[128]

In addition, the IOA adopted a revised Code of Ethics and Standards of Practice built upon the principles of independence, neutrality, confidentiality, and informality articulated by the preceding codes and standards and by the ABA Resolutions.[129] For all their differences, the IOA Code of Ethics and the ABA Resolutions and Reports are, nevertheless, remarkably consistent in providing guidance to organizational ombuds and in describing the proper functioning of organizational ombuds programs. The following compilation of the provisions of each of these important documents by on a principle-by-principle basis demonstrates the widespread acceptance of these principles and the implications flowing from them. An awareness of what is encompassed by each of these core principles is the foundation for the discussion pre-

---

127. *Id.* at 7–9.
128. As mentioned above, see Chapter 3 at 212 for a more complete discussion on this point. The IOA Best Practices were revised in October 2009. *See* Appendix 11. These Best Practices, which correspond to particular sections of the IOA Standards of Practice, are presented below as the last item under each principle and following the 2006 IOA Guidance for Best Practices and Response to 2004 ABA Resolution, the full text of which appears in Appendix 10.
129. INT'L OMBUDSMAN ASS'N, CODE OF ETHICS (undated) [hereinafter IOA CODE OF ETHICS]; INT'L OMBUDSMAN ASS'N, STANDARDS OF PRACTICE (undated) [hereinafter IOA STANDARDS OF PRACTICE]; *see* Appendix 5 at 459 for the IOA CODE OF ETHICS and STANDARDS OF PRACTICE.

sented in the next chapter on why organizational ombuds programs are effective in addressing the needs that arise out of the scope and diversity of our society and the legal pressures on current businesses and academic institutions.

INDEPENDENCE

- *IOA Code of Ethics*:
  The Ombudsman is independent in structure, function, and appearance to the highest degree possible within the organization.[130]

- *IOA Standards of Practice*:
  1.1 The Ombudsman Office and the Ombudsman are independent from other organizational entities.
  1.2 The Ombudsman holds no other position within the organization which might compromise independence.
  1.3 The Ombudsman exercises sole discretion over whether or how to act regarding an individual's concern, a trend or concerns of multiple individuals over time. The Ombudsman may also initiate action on a concern identified through the Ombudsman's direct observation.
  1.4 The Ombudsman has access to all information and all individuals in the organization, as permitted by law.
  1.5 The Ombudsman has authority to select Ombudsman Office staff and manage Ombudsman Office budget and operations.[131]

- *2001 and 2004 ABA Resolutions*:
  Independence. The ombuds is and appears to be free from interference in the legitimate performance of duties and independent from control, limitation, or a penalty imposed for retaliatory purposes by an official of the appointing entity or by a person who may be the subject of a complaint or inquiry.

  In assessing whether an ombuds is independent in structure, function, and appearance, the following factors are important: whether anyone subject to the ombuds jurisdiction or anyone directly responsible for a person under the ombuds jurisdiction (a) can control or limit the ombuds performance of assigned

---

130. IOA CODE OF ETHICS, *supra* note 129. *See* Appendix 5 at 459.
131. IOA STANDARDS OF PRACTICE, *supra* note 129 at 1. *See* Appendix 5 at 460–61.

duties or (b) can, for retaliatory purposes, (1) eliminate the office, (2) remove the ombuds, or reduce the budget or resources of the office.

REMOVAL FROM OFFICE

E. The charter that establishes the office of the ombuds should also provide for the discipline or removal of the ombuds from office for good cause by means of a fair process.[132]

- *2004 ABA Report*:[133]
  1. Independence in structure, function, and appearance

  To be credible and effective, the office of the ombuds is independent in its structure, function, and appearance. Independence means that the ombuds is free from interference in the legitimate performance of duties and independent from control, limitation, or a penalty imposed for retaliatory purposes by an official of the appointing entity or by a person who may be the subject of a complaint or inquiry. In assessing whether an ombuds is independent, the following factors are important: whether anyone subject to the ombuds's jurisdiction or anyone directly responsible for a person under the ombuds's jurisdiction (a) can control or limit the ombuds's performance of duties, or (b) can, for retaliatory purposes, (1) eliminate the office, (2) remove the ombuds, or (3) reduce the office's budget or resources.

  Historically, ombuds were created in parliamentary systems and were established in the constitution or by statute, appointed by the legislative body, and had a guarantee of independence from the control of any other officer, except for responsibility to the legislative body. This structure remains a model for ensuring independence for legislative ombuds, and a number of states have followed it. In more recent times, however, executive ombuds had been created by public officials without legislation, by regulation or decree, and by private entities. Ensuring the independence of

---

132. 2001 ABA RESOLUTION, *supra* note 85, at 5; 2004 ABA RESOLUTION, *supra* note 85, at 3. *See* Appendices 6 & 7 at 473 & 498.
133. Similar language appears in the 2001 ABA Report.

ombuds is equally important in these instances but will require other measures.[134]

Great care has to be exercised in establishing the ombuds structure to ensure that the independence described in the resolution is, in fact, achieved. Choosing which of these approaches are appropriate will depend on the environment. The instrument used to establish independence should be the strongest available and should guarantee the independence from control by any other person.

The 12 essential characteristics of the 1969 ABA Resolution continue to serve as the model for an ombuds reporting to the legislative branch of government who is authorized to investigate administrative action, help provide legislative oversight, and offer criticism of agencies from an external

---

134. Footnote 11 to the 2004 ABA Report, which appears at this point, provides as follows:

> In the United States since the late 1960s, a number of other ways have been developed to ensure independence. Examples of approaches that contribute to an ombuds's independence include: establishment of the office through a formal act of a legislature or official governing body of an organization; establishment outside the entity over which the ombuds has jurisdiction; a direct reporting relationship to a legislative body, the official governing body of an organization or the chief executive; designation as a neutral who is unaligned and objective; a broadly defined jurisdiction not limited to one part of the entity or one subject matter; appointment or removal of the ombuds free of influence from potential subjects of a complaint or inquiry; a set term of office; no reporting relationship to someone with assigned duties that conflict with the ombuds's role; no assignment of duties other than that of the ombuds function; specifically allocated budget and sufficient resources to perform the function; freedom to appoint, direct, and remove staff; sufficient stature in the organization to be taken seriously by senior officials; placement in an organization at the highest possible level and at least above the heads of units likely to generate the most complaints; discretion to initiate and pursue complaints and inquiries; access to and resources for independent legal advice and counsel; prohibition of disciplinary actions against the ombuds for performing the duties of the office; removal only for cause; provision of an employment contract that the ombuds will receive a significant severance provision if terminated without good cause.

2004 ABA RESOLUTION, *supra* note 85, at 13 n.11. *See* Appendix 7 at 512.

perspective. While there are a number of potential avenues of achieving independence, experience on the state and local level has demonstrated rather consistently that unless there is a structural independence for these ombuds akin to the 1969 Resolution, that independence will not be accomplished and the office will not be able to function as envisioned in the resolution and the accompanying standards.

Structuring independence for ombuds who serve inside organizations requires similar care. These elements should be in the charter. The ombuds position should be explicitly defined and established as a matter of organizational policy, authorized at the highest levels of the organization; the ombuds should have access to the chief executive officer, senior officers, and the oversight body or board of directors of the organization; the ombuds should also have access to all information within the organization, except as restricted by law; and the ombuds should have access to resources for independent legal advice and counsel.

The standards, recognizing that currently there are ombuds who have not achieved this goal, urge and anticipate that these variations will be eliminated over time.[135]

- *IOA Guidance for Best Practices and Response to 2004 ABA Resolution*:[136]
  Each entity that establishes an organizational ombuds office should ensure that the office has a charter that affirms the essential characteristics of the ombuds function—independence, impartiality, and confidentiality—that govern the role in which the ombuds receives complaints, works to resolve particular issues informally, and makes recommendations for the general improvement of the organization. The charter should also specify and define the ombuds' scope of practice and limitations on the ombuds' authority, qualifications to be an ombuds, office structure, procedures,

---

135. 2004 ABA RESOLUTION, *supra* note 85, at 12–13. *See* Appendix 7 at 512–13.
136. The full text is attached at Appendix 10. Only selected recommendations are included here.

confidentiality, and an understanding about the ombuds office not accepting notice on behalf of the entity.[137]

- *October 2009 IOA Best Practices:*
  The director of the Ombudsman Office should report directly to the highest level of the organization (such as board of directors, CEO, agency head, etc.) in a manner independent of ordinary line and staff functions.

  The director of the Ombudsman Office should have terms of employment that indicate that his or her stature in the organization is not subordinate to senior officials.

  The Ombudsman should be able to function independently from control, limitation, or interference imposed by any official in the entity.

  The Ombudsman should be protected from retaliation (such as elimination of the office or the Ombudsman, or reduction of the Ombudsman budget or other resources) by any person who may be the subject of a complaint or inquiry.

  The Ombudsman should have a set and renewable term, or should be removable only for neglect of duty, misconduct, or medical incapacity, and only by means of a fair process and procedure.

  The Ombudsman should obtain assurance from the organization at the outset, and apart from any particular dispute, of access to outside legal counsel at his or her own discretion.

  The expense of outside counsel should be covered by the organization and included in the overall budget for the Ombudsman Office. The Ombudsman should have an understanding with the organization that the Ombudsman is not required to inform the organization when it communicates with or accesses outside counsel.

  The purpose of outside legal counsel should be to enhance the Ombudsman's ability to practice according to the Standards of Practice. The Ombudsman should consider how outside counsel may assist in a variety of situations, including when the entity and the

---

137. IOA GUIDANCE AND COMMENTARY, *supra* note 120, at 5. *See* Appendix 10 at 539–40.

Ombudsman need to strategize how best to handle a discovery request made of the Ombudsman, or when the Ombudsman and the entity could benefit from consultation with outside counsel regarding how best to establish and operate the office so as to ensure the integrity of function, and to protect the Ombudsman. . . .

The Ombudsman should bring to the attention of the appropriate office those policies, programs, procedures or practices which may be problematic for the organization or which negatively affect people's health, safety or rights.

The Ombudsman should issue periodic reports summarizing activities, problem areas identified, and recommendations for systemic change. Ombudsman Office materials (websites, brochures, etc.) should state that all such reporting is conducted in a manner that protects the identity of individuals and does not place the organization on notice. . . .

The Ombudsman Office must be provided with sufficient resources to operate an independent and effective program. These resources include adequate space, equipment, staffing, staff development, and the production and distribution of informational materials.

The independence of the Ombudsman Office may be supported by having the selection and evaluation of the Ombudsman, as well as the establishment of an appropriate level of funding, be determined by or in consultation with committees representative of various institutional constituencies.[138]

NEUTRALITY AND IMPARTIALITY

- *IOA Code of Ethics*:
  The Ombudsman, as a designated neutral, remains unaligned and impartial. The Ombudsman does not engage in any situation which could create a conflict of interest.[139]

---

138. IOA Best Practices, A Supplement to IOA's Standards of Practice, Version 3, Oct. 13, 2009 (hereinafter referred to as October 2009 IOA Best Practices), *available at* http://www.ombudsassociation.org/standards/IOA_Best_Practices_Version3_101309.pdf (last visited November 2, 2009); Appendix 11 at 558–60

139. IOA CODE OF ETHICS, *supra* note 129. *See* Appendix 5 at 460.

- *IOA Standards of Practice*:
  2.1 The Ombudsman is neutral, impartial, and unaligned.
  2.2 The Ombudsman strives for impartiality, fairness and objectivity in the treatment of people and the consideration of issues. The Ombudsman advocates for fair and equitably administered processes and does not advocate on behalf of any individual within the organization.
  2.3 The Ombudsman is a designated neutral reporting to the highest possible level of the organization and operating independent of ordinary line and staff structures. The Ombudsman should not report to nor be structurally affiliated with any compliance function of the organization.
  2.4 The Ombudsman serves in no additional role within the organization which would compromise the Ombudsman's neutrality. The Ombudsman should not be aligned with any formal or informal associations within the organization in a way that might create actual or perceived conflicts of interest for the Ombudsman. The Ombudsman should have no personal interest or stake in, and incur no gain or loss from, the outcome of an issue.
  2.5 The Ombudsman has a responsibility to consider the legitimate concerns and interests of all individuals affected by the matter under consideration.
  2.6 The Ombudsman helps develop a range of responsible options to resolve problems and facilitate discussion to identify the best options.[140]

- *2001 and 2004 ABA Resolutions*:
  Impartiality in Conducting Inquiries and Investigations. The ombuds conducts inquiries and investigations in an impartial manner, free from initial bias and conflicts of interest. Impartiality does not preclude the ombuds from developing an interest in securing changes that are deemed necessary as a result of the process, nor from otherwise being an advocate on behalf of a designated constituency. The ombuds may become an advo-

---

140. IOA STANDARDS OF PRACTICE, *supra* note 129, as revised October 2009. *See* Appendix 5 at 461.

cate within the entity for change where the process demonstrates a need for it.[141]

- *2001 and 2004 ABA Reports*:
  2. Impartiality in conducting inquiries and investigations[142]

  The ombuds' structural independence is the foundation upon which the ombuds' impartiality is built. If the ombuds is independent from line management and does not have administrative or other obligations or functions, the ombuds can act in an impartial manner.

  Acting in an impartial manner, as a threshold matter, means that the ombuds is free from initial bias and conflicts of interest in conducting inquiries and investigations. Acting in an impartial manner also requires that the ombuds be authorized to gather facts from relevant sources and apply relevant policies, guidelines, and laws, considering the rights and interests of all affected parties within the jurisdiction, to identify appropriate actions to address or resolve the issue.

  The ombuds conducts inquiries and investigations in an impartial manner. An ombuds may determine that a complaint is without merit and close the inquiry or investigation without further action. If the ombuds finds that the complaint has merit, he or she makes recommendations to the entity or seeks resolution for a fair outcome. Impartiality does not, however, preclude the ombuds from developing an interest in securing the changes that are deemed necessary where the process demonstrates a need for change, nor from otherwise being an advocate on behalf of a designated constituency.[143] The ombuds therefore has the authority to become an advocate for change where the results of the inquiry or investigation demonstrate the need for such change. For example, where an ombuds identifies a sys-

---

141. 2001 ABA RESOLUTION, *supra* note 85, at 5–6; 2004 ABA RESOLUTION, *supra* note 85 at 3. *See* Appendices 6 & 7 at 474 & 498–99

142. As stated above, the characteristics of ombuds offices described in the 2001 and 2004 ABA Resolutions were designed to be applicable to all types of ombuds, including those that conduct investigations, hence the inclusion of a reference to investigations in this text.

143. *See* text accompanying *supra* note 142. For the same reason, references to advocacy on behalf of a constituent group are included in this text.

temic problem, it would be appropriate for the ombuds to advocate for changes to correct the problem. An advocate ombuds may initiate action and therefore serve as an advocate on behalf of a designated population with respect to a broad range of issues and on specific matters when the individual or group is found to be aggrieved. But, when determining the facts, the ombuds must act impartially.[144]

- *October 2009 IOA Best Practices*:

    See [IOA Standards of Practice] Section 1.2.

    All members of the specified community served by the Ombudsman may voluntarily seek services from the Ombudsman Office and will be treated with respect and dignity. The Ombudsman should assure access impartially, including to people with disabilities, people who need language interpreters, or people whose work hours require flexibility in scheduling appointment times.

    The organization should assure that all specified members of the organization have the right to consult with the Ombudsman, and retaliation for exercising that right will not be tolerated. . . .

    The Ombudsman should have direct access to the board of directors (or other oversight body as appropriate). See [IOA Standards of Practice] Sections 1.1 and 1.2.

    While the Ombudsman should be an internal position, it should not report to, nor have the appearance of reporting to, any compliance office or function or the organization.

    The Charter or Terms of Reference for the Ombudsman Office should state specifically that the Ombudsman does not serve as an agent of notice for the organization. . . .

    See [IOA Standards of Practice] Sections 1.2, 4.4, and 4.5.

    Except in the administrative capacity as manager of the Ombudsman Office, the Ombudsman should not participate in formal management functions or serve in any other role that poses an actual

---

144. 2001 ABA RESOLUTION, *supra* note 85, at 19; 2004 ABA RESOLUTION, *supra* note 85, at 14. *See* Appendices 6 & 7 at 486–87 & 513–14.

conflict of interest or creates the perception of one. For example, an Ombudsman ought not conduct formal investigations; serve in a position or role that is designated by the organization as a place to receive notice on behalf of the organization; serve as a voting member on a search committee (other than for Ombudsman staff); handle formal appeals of management actions; keep case records on behalf of the organization; or be charged in any way to make, change, enforce or set aside a law, rule or management decision.

If possible, the Ombudsman should hold only one position in the organization.

If the Ombudsman does hold another role within the organization, the different roles should be structured so that they are as separate and distinct as possible. The Ombudsman should not provide Ombudsman services to people whom the Ombudsman — in the other role — serves, manages, reports to, teaches, advises, or evaluates, in order to avoid partiality or perceptions of conflict of interest. The Ombudsman should provide Ombudsman services in a location that is different from the location in which the Ombudsman, in the other role, works, teaches, counsels, etc., to clarify the distinctions between roles, and to assure confidentiality and off-the-record informality of the Ombudsman communications. The Ombudsman's support staff (people who take messages or receive visitors, for example) for the Ombudsman role should be separate and distinct from the support staff in any other role. The Ombudsman should continually call attention to the role in which he or she is acting at any given time, and repeatedly educate members of the organization about the principles in the Ombudsman Office's Charter. The Ombudsman should attempt to provide alternatives for people and situations in which the Ombudsman cannot serve as Ombudsman due to actual or perceived conflicts of interest. . . .

An Ombudsman should help the visitor explore and assess an appropriate range of options, from the very informal to the most formal. Formal options may include ways to put management on notice of an issue, referrals to rights-based elements of the organization's conflict resolution system, or the provision of information about the possibility of seeking external resources or assistance. The Ombudsman should never provide legal advice.

When the Ombudsman works with the visitor to address issues that may involve formal alternatives (under laws, policies, rules, or regulations), the Ombudsman should make clear to the visitor that an informal approach does not automatically exclude the visitor's later participation in more formal options, but that the visitor should keep in mind possible time limits and their potential impact on the visitor's formal options. See [IOA Standards of Practice] Section 4.4.

The impartiality of the Ombudsman Office may be supported by consultation with various organizational constituencies regarding the Ombudsman Office's effectiveness.[145]

CONFIDENTIALITY

- *IOA Code of Ethics*:
  The Ombudsman holds all communications with those seeking assistance in strict confidence, and does not disclose confidential communications unless given permission to do so. The only exception to this privilege of confidentiality is where there appears to be imminent risk of serious harm.[146]

- *IOA Standards of Practice*:
  3.1 The Ombudsman holds all communications with those seeking assistance in strict confidence and takes all reasonable steps to safeguard confidentiality, including the following: The Ombudsman does not reveal, and must not be required to reveal, the identity of any individual contacting the Ombudsman Office, nor does the Ombudsman reveal information provided in confidence that could lead to the identification of any individual contacting the Ombudsman Office, without that individual's express permission, given in the course of informal discussions with the Ombudsman; the Ombudsman takes specific action related to an individual's issue only with the individual's express permission and only to the extent permitted, and even then at the sole discretion of the Ombudsman, unless such action can be taken in a way that safeguards the identity of the individual contacting the Ombudsman Office.

---

145. October 2009 IOA Best Practices, *supra* note 138, Appendix 11 at 560–63.
146. 2001 IOA CODE OF ETHICS, *supra* note 129. *See* Appendix 5 at 460.

The only exception to this privilege of confidentiality is where there appears to be imminent risk of serious harm, and where there is no other reasonable option. Whether this risk exists is a determination to be made by the Ombudsman.

3.2 Communications between the Ombudsman and others (made while the Ombudsman is serving in that capacity) are considered privileged. The privilege belongs to the Ombudsman and the Ombudsman Office, rather than to any party to an issue. Others cannot waive this privilege.

3.3 The Ombudsman does not testify in any formal process inside the organization and resists testifying in any formal process outside of the organization regarding a visitor's contact with the Ombudsman or confidential information communicated to the Ombudsman, even if given permission or requested to do so. The Ombudsman may, however, provide general, non-confidential information about the Ombudsman Office or the Ombudsman profession.

3.4 If the Ombudsman pursues an issue systemically (e.g., provides feedback on trends, issues, policies and practices) the Ombudsman does so in a way that safeguards the identity of individuals.

3.5 The Ombudsman keeps no records containing identifying information on behalf the organization.

3.6 The Ombudsman maintains information (e.g., notes, phone messages, appointment calendars) in a secure location and manner, protected from inspection by others (including management), and has a consistent and standard practice for the destruction of such information.

3.7 The Ombudsman prepares any data and/or reports in a manner that protects confidentiality.

3.8 Communications made to the ombudsman are not notice to the organization. The Ombudsman neither acts as agent for, nor accepts notice on behalf of, the origination and shall not serve in a position or role that is designated by the organization as a place to receive notice on behalf of the organization.

However, the Ombudsman may refer individuals to the appropriate place where formal notice can be made.[147]

- *2001 and 2004 ABA Resolutions*:
  Confidentiality. An ombuds does not disclose and is not required to disclose any information provided in confidence, except to address an imminent risk of serious harm. Records pertaining to a complaint, inquiry, or investigation are confidential and not subject to disclosure outside the ombuds office. An ombuds does not reveal the identity of a complainant without that person's express consent. An ombuds may, however, at the ombuds discretion, disclose non-confidential information and may disclose confidential information so long as doing so does not reveal its source. An ombuds should discuss any exceptions to the ombuds maintaining confidentiality with the source of the information.[148]

- *2001 and 2004 ABA Reports*:
  3. Confidentiality

  Confidentiality is an essential characteristic of ombuds that permits the process to work effectively. Confidentiality promotes disclosure from reluctant complainants, elicits candid discussions by all parties, and provides an increased level of protection against retaliation to or by any party. Confidentiality is a further factor that distinguishes ombuds from others who receive and consider complaints, such as elected officials, human resource personnel, government officials, and ethics officers.

  Confidentiality extends to all communications with the ombuds and to all notes and records maintained by the ombuds in the performance of assigned duties. It begins when a communication is initiated with the ombuds to schedule an appointment or make a complaint or inquiry. Confidentiality may apply to the source of the communications and to the content of the communications.

---

147. IOA STANDARDS OF PRACTICE, *supra* note 129, as revised October 2009. *See* Appendix 5 at 465–66

148. 2001 ABA RESOLUTION, *supra* note 85, at 6; 2004 ABA RESOLUTION, *supra* note 85, at 3–4. *See* Appendices 6 & 7 at 474 & 499.

Individuals may not want the ombuds to disclose their identity but may want the ombuds to act on the information presented. Therefore, an ombuds does not reveal the identity of a complainant without that person's consent. The ombuds may, however, disclose confidential information as long as doing so does not compromise the identity of the person who supplied it. It should be emphasized that the decision whether or not to disclose this information belongs to the ombuds, and it would not be appropriate for anyone to demand that the ombuds disclose such information, except as required by statute. To the extent that an ombuds may not maintain confidentiality, the ombuds should discuss those exceptions with individuals who communicate with the office.

The authorizing entity should allow the ombuds to keep confidential the identity of persons who communicate with the ombuds and information provided in confidence. The authorizing entity should not seek information relating to the identity of complainants nor seek access to the ombuds's notes and records.

Providing for confidentiality and protection from subpoena in a statute is particularly important because, where statutes have not provided confidentiality, state courts have not consistently recognized an ombuds privilege nor granted protective orders to preserve the confidentiality of communications made to an ombuds. One federal district court, *Shabazz v. Scurr,* 662 F. Supp. 90 (S.D. Iowa 1987), recognized a limited privilege under federal law for an ombuds with a state statutory privilege. The only federal circuit court to have addressed the issue, *Carman v. McDonnell Douglas Corp.*, 114 F.3d 790 (8th Cir. 1997), failed to recognize an ombuds privilege.[149]

---

149. The Reports overlooked several other cases in which federal courts had recognized an ombuds privilege and failed to explain that the holding in the *Carman* case was that the claimed privilege was denied because the company, which sought protection for an ombuds office that had been eliminated by the time the case came to court, failed to offer any evidence to demonstrate entitlement to a privilege. For a more complete discussion of this issue, see Chapter 3.

Short of explicit statutory authority, ombuds offices should adopt written policies that provide the fullest confidentiality within the law, and the entities that establish ombuds offices should expressly provide the ombuds with the fullest confidentiality specified in the standards. These policies should be publically available, broadly disseminated, and widely publicized. Several existing model ombuds acts and policies of ombuds organizations address confidentiality.

An ombuds will rarely, if ever, be privy to something that no one else knows. Therefore, providing confidentiality protection to the ombuds allows the ombuds to perform the assigned duties while at the same time, society continues to have access to the underlying facts. As evidenced by the statutes and policies that have been developed, there may be instances in which other, competing societal interests dictate that the ombuds must disclose some information. If an individual speaks about intending [to cause] harm to himself or herself or others, an entity may require an ombuds to disclose this information. Moreover, an ombuds may be compelled by protective service laws or professional reporting requirements to report suspected abuse.[150]

- *October 2009 IOA Best Practices:*

The Ombudsman publicizes the confidential nature of Ombudsman work.

The Ombudsman Office should be situated in an appropriate location to protect the privacy of visitors to the office.

When an individual gives the Ombudsman permission to reveal his or her identity, disclose information, or act on his or her concerns, such permission must be given at the time that the Ombudsman is engaged in the informal conflict resolution process, not as part of a formal process.

---

150. 2001 ABA RESOLUTION, *supra* note 85, at 20–21; 2004 ABA RESOLUTION, *supra* note 85, at 14–15. *See* Appendices 6 & 7 at 487–89 & 514–16.

The Ombudsman Office Charter for each organization should specify what types of events rise to the level of "imminent risk of serious harm." The Ombudsman may negotiate with the organization to be exempt, based on Ombudsman confidentiality, from some mandates that require reporting by other employees. Best practice is to interpret "imminent risk of serious harm" as narrowly as possible — for example, imminent risk to human life. . . .

The confidentiality privilege is critical to making the Ombudsman Office a place where people can raise any issue, including an alleged violation of statute, regulation, rule, policy, or ethical standard.

IOA asserts that communications made to the Ombudsman do not constitute "notice" to the organization. No one, including the employing entity, should consider the Ombudsman Office to be agent of notice (that is, an office that receives formal notice on behalf of the organization) and no one, including the entity, should seek information about communications to the Ombudsman Office.

The nature and role of confidentiality should be explained to the visitor, who should understand that the Ombudsman claims the privilege for the office and that it is not the visitor's privilege to waive. Whenever possible, this information should be communicated prior to discussing the concerns brought by the visitor.

Visitors should understand that as a condition for accepting and benefiting from the Ombudsman Office services, they have the obligation to support the Ombudsman claim of privilege and not to attempt to breach this claim.

The Ombudsman should emphasize in office materials and with the management of the organization:

- that the ability to have confidential communications that do not constitute "notice" to the organization is essential to the effective functioning of an Ombudsman Office and distinguishes the Ombudsman from formal reporting channels;
- that it is the "off-the-record" aspects of the office that lead people who use the Ombudsman to do so before taking any official or formal action;

- that the Ombudsman Office enables people to come forward with an issue when they might otherwise be afraid to do so or when they fear retaliation from managers or peers;

- that only by offering the security of confidentiality can the Ombudsman facilitate organizational responsibility and accountability, which are at the heart of provisions contained in the U.S. Sentencing Guidelines and the Sarbanes-Oxley Act that call for mechanisms of confidential reporting and/or guidance;

- that where issues cannot be confidentially raised, they may not be raised at all, thereby depriving the organization of an opportunity to address issues and rectify misconduct that has not yet surfaced through other channels. . . .

The IOA Board has asked the IOA Standing Committee on Professional Ethics, Standards, and Best Practices to review the language and interpretation of [IOA Standards of Practice Section] 3.3. Please look for updates in the near future.

See [IOA Standards of Practice] Section 4 on informality. . . .

Ombudsman materials should state that any Ombudsman reporting of trends, or communication of recommendations for systemic change, is done in a manner that protects the identity of individuals. . . .

The Ombudsman record-keeping systems and/or database should be independent of the organization's technology system, with access allowed only to Ombudsman Office personnel. The Ombudsman Office should also be secure to protect private information and records. The office should develop and implement processes and procedures to regularly purge information that could identify individual visitors to the office. Records such as phone bills, which may indicate with whom the office has communicated, should be made available only to the Ombudsman Office staff. The Ombudsman should take all reasonable steps to protect the confidentiality of any temporary notes or documents, such as locking file drawers and offices, and exercising extreme vigilance if any notes are carried from one place to another. . . .

Except in the administrative capacity as manager of the Ombudsman Office, the Ombudsman is never an agent of notice (that is, an officer who receives notice for the organization), and communications to the Ombudsman Office never constitute notice to the organization.

If a visitor wishes to make a record, or put the organization "on notice," the Ombudsman can provide information about how to do so.

Best practice is for the organization to receive allegations of wrongdoing directly from a complainant or witness, and not indirectly through the Ombudsman.

If the visitor is reluctant to make a formal report to the organization, the Ombudsman can work with the visitor to address the reasons the visitor resists reporting, or to work with the organization to make formal reporting channels more accessible.

If the visitor gives the Ombudsman permission to discuss a concern with a manager, and if the concern may involve some allegation of wrongdoing, the Ombudsman should pass on information only in general terms (without specifying names, dates, or events). If the Ombudsman does pass on allegations of wrongdoing, the Ombudsman should emphasize the he or she has not confirmed the accuracy of the allegations. It is not appropriate for the organization to take any adverse action on the basis of information reported informally through the Ombudsman. The Ombudsman may coach the manager on how to make reporting channels more accessible or how to gather information himself or herself.

An ombudsman may place the organization on "notice" when the ombudsman evaluates the circumstances and specifically elects to place the organization on notice by identifying an appropriate point of contact within the organization and communicating to that point of contact specific information which the ombudsman expressly intends to share for the purpose of placing the organization on notice of a specific concern or specific situation. If an ombudsman makes such an intentional notice communication, confidentiality is waived only with regard to the specific communication made with the point of contact for purposes of the notice communication. It is the conversation between the ombudsman and the appropriate point of contact within the organization that constitutes notice and not the conversation between the Ombudsman and the visitor. Thus, under no circumstances, is the original communication to the ombudsman part of the notice communication.

All ombudsman offices should have a well-defined and generally available procedure detailing the limited circumstances and the processes under which the Ombudsman may provide notice. If the ombudsman elects to place the organization on notice under the conditions above, the Oombudsman should follow the protocol of the particular Ombudsman office regarding this unusual action. The protocols should include specific steps so that it is clear that the Ombudsman made an intentional decision to make a notice disclosure.[151]

INFORMALITY AND OTHER STANDARDS

- *IOA Code of Ethics*:
  The Ombudsman, as an informal resource, does not participate in any formal adjudicative or administrative procedure related to concerns brought to his or her attention.[152]

- *IOA Standards of Practice*:
  4.1 The Ombudsman functions on an informal basis by such means as: listening, providing and receiving information, identifying and reframing issues, developing a range of responsible options, and—with permission and at Ombuds discretion—engaging in informal third-party intervention. When possible, the Ombudsman helps people develop new ways to solve problems themselves.
  4.2 The Ombudsman as an informal and off-the-record resource pursues resolution of concerns and looks into procedural irregularities and/or broader systemic problems when appropriate.
  4.3 The Ombudsman does not make binding decisions, mandate policies, or formally adjudicate issues for the organization.

---

151. October 2009 IOA Best Practices, supra note 138, *See* Appendix 11 at 563–68.
152. 2001 IOA CODE OF ETHICS, *supra* note 129. *See* Appendix 5 at 460.

4.4 The Ombudsman supplements, but does not replace, any formal channels. Use of the Ombudsman Office is voluntary, and is not a required step in any grievance process or organizational policy.

4.5 The Ombudsman does not participate in any formal investigative or adjudicative procedures. Formal investigations should be conducted by others. When a formal investigation is requested, the Ombudsman refers individuals to the appropriate offices or individual.

4.6 The Ombudsman identifies trends, issues and concerns about policies and procedures, including potential future issues and concerns, without breaching confidentiality or anonymity, and provides recommendations for responsibly addressing them.

4.7 The Ombudsman acts in accordance with the IOA Code of Ethics and Standards of Practice, keeps professionally current by pursuing continuing education, and provides opportunities for staff to pursue professional training.

4.8 The Ombudsman endeavors to be worthy of the trust placed in the Ombudsman Office.[153]

- *2001 and 2004 ABA Resolutions*:

    LIMITATIONS ON THE OMBUDS AUTHORITY

D. An ombuds should not, nor should an entity expect or authorize an ombuds to:

(1) make, change or set aside a law, policy, or administrative decision

(2) make binding decisions or determine rights

(3) directly compel an entity or any person to implement the ombuds recommendations

(4) conduct an investigation that substitutes for administrative or judicial proceedings

(5) accept jurisdiction over an issue that is currently pending in a legal forum unless all parties and the presiding officer in that action explicitly consent

---

153. IOA STANDARDS OF PRACTICE, *supra* note 129, as revised October 2009. *See* Appendix 5 at 465–66.

(6) address any issue arising under a collective bargaining agreement or which falls within the purview of any existing federal, state, or local labor or employment law, rule, or regulation, unless the ombuds is authorized to do so by the collective bargaining agreement or unless the collective bargaining representative and the employing entity jointly agree to allow the ombuds to do so, or, if there is no collective bargaining representative, the employer specifically authorizes the ombuds to do so,[154] or

(7) act in an manner inconsistent with the grant of and limitations on the jurisdiction of the office when discharging the duties of the office of ombuds.[155]

- *2001 ABA Report*:[156]

Section D. Limitations on the ombuds authority

An ombuds works outside of line management structure and has no direct power to compel any decision. The office is established by the charter with the stature to engender trust and to help resolve complaints at the most appropriate level of the entity. To ensure the ombuds's independence, impartiality, and confidentiality, it is necessary to establish certain limitations on the ombuds's authority.

An ombuds should not, nor should an entity expect or authorize an ombuds to, make, change, or set aside a law, policy or administrative/managerial decision, or directly compel an entity or any person to make those changes. While an ombuds may expedite and facilitate the resolution of a complaint and recommend individual and systemic changes, an ombuds cannot compel an entity to implement the recommendations.

---

154. *See supra* note 122. The 2004 ABA Resolution eliminated this clause and added an explanatory footnote.

155. 2001 ABA RESOLUTION, *supra* note 85, at 6–7; 2004 ABA RESOLUTION, *supra* note 85, at 4. *See* Appendices 6 & 7 at 474–75 & 499–500.

156. The 2004 ABA Report contains similar language, with the exception of the references to collective bargaining, where some changes were made to conform to the changes in the 2004 ABA Resolution.

It is essential that an ombuds operate by fair procedures, which means that the actions taken will likely vary with the nature of the concern and that care must be taken to protect the rights of those who may be affected by the actions of ombuds. Furthermore, since due process rights could well be implicated, it would not be appropriate for the ombuds's review to serve as the final determination for any disciplinary activity or civil action, nor as a determination of a violation of law or policy. An ombuds's inquiry or investigation does not substitute for an administrative or judicial proceeding. In an administrative or judicial proceeding, the deciding official should not consider the ombuds's review or recommendations to be controlling. Rather, the deciding official must conduct a de novo examination of the matter.

Moreover, it would not be appropriate for the ombuds to act as an appellate forum when a complainant is dissatisfied with the results in a formal adjudicatory or administrative proceeding. Thus, an ombuds should not take up a specific issue that is pending in a legal forum without the concurrence of the parties and the presiding officer. It may, however, be fully appropriate for an ombuds to inquire into matters that are related to a controversy that is in litigation as long as he or she is not the subject of the suit.

Further, an ombuds should not address, nor should an entity expect or authorize an ombuds to address, any issue that is the subject of a collective bargaining agreement or that arises under labor or employment law. Even where an employee is not covered by a collective bargaining agreement, the involvement of ombuds in matters that fall within the purview of labor or employment laws raises sensitive issues that may implicate the rights and liabilities of the parties under those laws, such as the issue of notice mentioned in Section F of the Standards. Accordingly, the Standards contemplate that an employer, in establishing an ombuds office, should consider its overall policies for maintaining compliance with those laws, and determine in that light whether to authorize the ombuds to address those matters. The entity should do so only if the ombuds office meets the three essential characteristics of independence, impartiality, and confidentiality. This recommendation is not intended to suggest, however, that a policy of authorizing an ombuds to address labor or employment-related matters should be suspect or disfavored practice. Involvement in such matters is a role typically performed by organizational ombuds, and the growing reliance on ombuds at institutions across the country is largely attributable to the broad satisfaction with ombuds's fulfillment of that role on the part of both management and the affected employees. Thus, the language in the Standards indicating that an employer should specifically authorize an ombuds to address labor- or employment-related matters does not require any detailed or ponderous recitals. Rather, it should be read as simply a particularized application of the generalized expectation in Section A of the Standards, that jurisdiction of an ombuds office should be identified in its charter.

Finally, an ombuds should not act in a manner inconsistent with the grant and limitations on the jurisdiction of the office when discharging the duties of the office of ombuds.[157]

- *IOA Guidance for Best Practices and Response to 2004 ABA Resolution*:

The ombuds charter and, where possible, any relevant collective bargaining agreement should define the involvement of an ombuds with union employees and with issues that arise under the collective bargaining agreement. For those ombuds whose scope of services includes union employees, the ombuds should defer to the union process any issue covered by the CBA [collective bargaining agreement] unless otherwise agreed to by the union, the entity, and the persons involved.

The ombuds should always inform covered employees about the union process when providing assistance on an issue that might be covered by the CBA.

Ombuds should function in a way that addresses concern for preserving the legal rights of visitors. An ombuds should present and, if appropriate, discuss a range of options available to the visitor, from the very informal to the most formal. Formal options may include ways to put management on no-

---

157. 2001 ABA RESOLUTION, *supra* note 85, at 15–16. *See* Appendix 6 at 489–90.

tice of an issue, referrals to rights-based elements of the organization's conflict resolution system, or the provision of information about seeking external legal advice (for example, providing contact information to the local bar association's attorney referral service).

When the ombuds attempts to address issues that may involve other formal alternatives (under law, rules, or regulations), it should be made clear to the visitor that an informal approach does not automatically exclude the visitor's later participation in more formal options. However, the ombuds should tell the visitor to be aware of possible time limits and their potential impact on more formal options. The ombuds should not provide legal advice, but should suggest alternatives that make the visitor aware of the possible need to seek such advice.[158]

- *October 2009 IOA Best Practices:*
  The Ombudsman should work with the organization to encourage it to provide its constituents with a variety of effective formal (rights-based) and informal (confidential and interest-based) options for surfacing and resolving concerns. All options should be well established and clearly and regularly communicated to the entire organization.

  As the visitor may wish to consult with additional resources and services, such as the employee assistance program, human resources, or the benefits office, the Ombudsman should describe resources that might be appropriate to the visitor's presenting circumstances. See [IOA Standards of Practice] Section 2.6

  The Ombudsman may consider issues, perceptions, interpretations, information, and concerns about inappropriate acts, omissions, or improprieties presented by individuals or groups.

  Ombudsman functions include informal third-party intervention, such as shuttle diplomacy, facilitating communication, and informal mediation, which is voluntary and may or may not produce a written agreement.

---

158. IOA GUIDANCE AND COMMENTARY, *supra* note 120, at 7–9. *See* Appendix 10 at 542 & 544.

Any documents or written agreements resulting from informal processes should not be maintained by or within the Ombudsman Office.

The Ombudsman uses a flexible approach with regard to concerns brought to the Ombudsman Office; options are tailored to individual circumstances. . . .

The Ombudsman should not participate in formal management functions. See [IOA Standards of Practice] Section 2.4. . . .

For most entities, it is the combination of informal services and formal grievance procedures, embodied in a conflict management system, that provides the appropriate range of options to allow for early identification and resolution of potential legal issues or concerns. The Ombudsman should give visitors information about the entity's formal procedures and remedies whenever appropriate. While a visitor may choose to explore informal options for a wide variety of reasons, the Ombudsman should remind the visitor to keep in mind possible time limits and their potential impact on the visitor's formal options. See [IOA Standards of Practice] Section 2.6.

The Ombudsman Charter or Terms of Reference should define the role, if any, of the Ombudsman in relation to employees and issues covered by collective bargaining agreements (CBAs). This role definition should also, where possible, be incorporated in CBAs, and should include a statement that although the CBA permits the Ombudsman to function in these defined ways, the Ombudsman nevertheless retains the authority to decline to be involved. (See [IOA Standards of Practice] Section 1.3.) The union and management may also enter into an ad hoc agreement permitting an Ombudsman to handle an issue. . . .

The Ombudsman may be requested or required to speak with public officials, in a private or public setting, about the functions of the Ombudsman Office, or about trends published in a written report. If so, the Ombudsman should still observe the confidentiality standards as stated in [IOA Standards of Practice Sections] 3.1 and 3.3. . . .

> The Ombudsman should be particularly careful to maintain neutrality when making recommendations for system change.[159]

As this compilation demonstrates, a consensus has developed on the meaning of each of the core characteristics of an organizational ombuds program. As the practice of organizational ombuds has evolved from the investigative/prosecutorial role of the Scandinavian model, the primacy of confidentiality as an operating principle has emerged. With other non-confidential avenues available for reporting misconduct or conflict, the confidentiality of the ombuds office has become the defining characteristic of an organizational ombuds and sets an organizational ombuds apart from the other, more formal channels of communication. Although the principles of independence, neutrality, and informality are important for their own sake in supporting the work of the organizational ombuds, they are also the key to confidentiality. As discussed further in Chapter 3, if an ombuds program does not operate in accordance with these other principles, the ability to make the legal case for confidentiality is seriously undermined.

F. IOA Best Practices Recommendations

In the area in which the principles in the ABA Resolutions diverge from those articulated by IOA—when notice should be imputed to an organization—IOA has adopted a series of additional recommendations for organizational ombuds that minimize these differences. These recommendations, which also set forth the best practices for organizational ombuds, are important to bear in mind in evaluating the potential benefits of an organizational ombuds program. While many of the Best Practices in the 2006 10A Guidance for Best Practices and Response to the 2004 ABA Resolution were included in the October 2009 revisions to the IOA Best Practices, there are additional recommendations that bear repeating. They are as follows:

- The nature and role of confidentiality should be explained to the visitor, who should understand that the ombuds claims the privilege for the office and that it is not the visitor's privilege to waive.

---

159. October 2009 IOA Best Practices, *supra* note 137, Appendix 11 at 568–70.

- In most situations where notice to the organization may be appropriate, the ombuds helps direct the visitor to the proper point of contact. It is only in rare instances that the ombuds may take action, at his or her discretion, directly to place the organization on notice of an allegation of wrongdoing, such as in the rare event that the visitor to the ombuds office is not able or not willing to do so himself or herself.
- An ombuds may also place the organization on notice in the unusual situation in which the ombuds perceives an imminent risk of serious harm. However, even in this instance, the original communication to the ombuds is not part of the notice communication.
- Every ombuds office should have a well-defined and generally available procedure detailing the limited circumstances and processes under which the ombuds may provide notice, and this protocol should be strictly followed when the ombuds takes the unusual action of placing the organization on notice.
- In circumstances where the ombuds places the organization on notice, it may or may not be appropriate to seek permission from or to inform the original source(s) of the information.

* * * *

- It is extremely important for the ombuds to demonstrate consistent practice when discussing with visitors the potential impact and limits of "notice" to the organization. The ombuds should ensure that all visitors, at the very least, have access to materials that explain the ombuds role and limits in relation to notice in detail. In addition, the ombuds should develop criteria (specific to the environment and needs of the ombuds's own organization) for a consistent approach to providing information about notice, where and when relevant. Failure to demonstrate consistency of practice in this regard may expose the ombuds to the need to discuss ombuds conversations on a case-by-case basis relevant to determining whether the visitor adequately understood the options and the notice implications.
- ABA Standards Section F(1)(a)–(f), which lists appropriate communications with persons who contact the ombuds of-

fice, should be published on the ombuds office Web site, in the ombuds office brochures, and in the entity's charter for the ombuds office, so that this information is generally and publicly available.
- The decision on which, if any, items on the list should be communicated directly to the visitor should be left to the discretion of the ombuds, who will make the decision based on the overall circumstances and the criteria developed within the ombuds' own organization (consistent with these guidelines).
- When necessary or appropriate, the ombuds should clarify how an ombuds program "fits" with other systems and services by explaining to visitors that:
  a. The visitor may have important legal rights that may be involved with the visitor's issue, and important time limits and other factors may be involved.
  b. The ombuds program is not a substitute for a lawyer or other professional who might represent the visitor's rights, and the visitor may wish to consult with these other services separately.
  c. The visitor may wish to consult with additional resources and services (e.g., an employee assistance program) that the ombuds may suggest if they might be appropriate given the visitor's presenting circumstances.

* * *

- Ombuds materials (Web sites, brochures, etc.) should state that ombuds do report trends and advocate for systemic change when appropriate, but that they do so in a manner that protects the identity of individuals.
- Ombuds materials that make reference to ombuds disclosure when there is "an imminent risk of serious harm" should always state that the decision to make such disclosure rests solely with the obuds.[160]

With this understanding of the essential characteristics and best practices for an organizational ombuds office, we should take a brief

---

160. IOA GUIDANCE AND COMMENTARY, *supra* note 120, at 14–17. *See* Appendix 10 at 551–55.

look at what an organizational ombuds does in his or her organization before examining why an organization may find it appropriate to create such an office.

PART III: WHAT DOES AN ORGANIZATIONAL OMBUDS DO?

It is important to describe the principles of independence, neutrality, confidentiality, and informality by which organizational ombuds operate, but doing so does not really explain what an ombuds does. A brief look at what organizational ombuds actually do in their organizations, however, will help give context and meaning to the next two chapters on why organizations may want to create these programs and how to protect confidentiality.

In general, the work of an organizational ombuds can be distilled into three broad categories: communications and outreach, issue resolution, and identification of areas for systemic change. and issue prevention. The work of an ombuds varies on a daily basis, depending on the calls or visits of inquirers, and in some situations these inquiries demand all of the emotional, analytical, creative, and political skills of the ombuds in helping an individual find an acceptable way to resolve or report an issue. While I am attempting here to summarize only the general types of activities of ombuds, in Chapter 3 and Appendix 14 I have presented many actual examples of cases handled by ombuds to illustrate why an individual often perceives that a confidential resource is necessary and how an ombuds can provide assistance to an inquirer.

The communications and outreach activities of ombuds offices are premised on the notion that the usefulness of the office requires that people know about it and understand how it operates. Accordingly, ombuds usually meet with all new hires or people new to the organization and explain the role, functions, and limitations of the office. They also periodically meet with employee and other groups to provide refresher information on the office. This type of activity can be especially important in large, multi-location organizations. As one might expect, part of the communications and outreach function is the creation of information pieces—including brochures, Web sites with FAQs (Frequently Asked Questions), and other relevant information, newsletter features, posters, etc.—that can provide basic information about the office.[161]

The potential benefit of the ombuds' communications and outreach role of ombuds offices, however, can be much greater than just focusing on the role of the ombuds office. Many offices provide periodic training sessions generally available to employees or other groups on techniques for resolving workplace disputes, workplace civility, and sensitivity to issues of cultural differences and diversity. As trained mediators and facilitators, they are frequently called upon for such speaking opportunities and can be a valuable additional resource for the organization's human resources personnel. In addition, many of the Web sites have valuable resource information on topics that employees or others can access, such as how to have a difficult conversation with a supervisor or co-worker.

Most of the everyday work of an ombuds, however, is involved in issue resolution and serving as a resource for employees, members of a university community, or other constituents to obtain information. This can be done in person or by telephone, but ombuds eschew communication by e-mail for confidentiality reasons. When necessary, ombuds make themselves available for after hours calls or off-premises meetings to support the confidentiality of their role. Usually they deal with people individually for similar confidentiality reasons, though they have served quite effectively in mediations between co-workers or between employees and supervisors, or in the context of group facilitation. In each of these settings, ombuds first explain the role and limitations of their office to make sure that the inquirer is aware that it is a confidential and off-the-record resource, that it does not serve as an advocate for either the organization or the inquirer, and that it is not a place for providing notice of claims against the organization.

With the preliminary introduction to the office out of the way, the primary role of the ombuds is to listen to the concerns of an inquirer. Many times all that is sought is information, but the inquirer is not willing to be visible or identified as the person making the request (such as questions about the requirement for drug testing or the availability of maternity or paternity benefits). In these situations, an ombuds can obtain the relevant information from other sources in the organization and then pass it along to the inquirer. Because ombuds are of-

---

161. More information on documentation for an ombuds office is provided in the third part of Chapter 3.

ten called upon to help obtain this type of information or other information on the organization's policies and procedures, it is important that they be given full access to information in their organizations without being called upon to explain why they want it or who they want it for.

Once an ombuds has listened to the concerns of an inquirer, the real work often begins. Sometimes it involves helping the inquirer sort through a jumble of concerns to find the ones that really matter. Sometimes it involves coaching the inquirer on how to express the concern, and helping him or her to understand others' perspectives or to appreciate the limits of what others or the organization can do. In almost all cases, the ombuds, as a person knowledgeable about both conflict management and the organization's compliance policies and resources, works with the inquirer to create and evaluate options for addressing the inquirer's issue. Ombuds sometimes will work with an inquirer over an extended period, involving many conversations, as they continue to search for an option with which the inquirer is comfortable. If the issue involves some misconduct, the ombuds will often help identify a way acceptable to the inquirer that the issue can be brought forward, even if the inquirer's identity is not disclosed. There are other times when, at the request and with the consent of the inquirer, the ombuds agrees to be the person to bring an issue forward. If the ombuds believes that there may be an imminent risk of serious harm, he or she must also make a disclosure to a formal channel but informs the inquirer (when possible) that a disclosure will be made, and then tries to limit the disclosure to the information necessary to prevent the harm while preserving to the extent possible the confidentiality of the source's identity. In each of these situations where the ombuds is the person providing notice of an issue to the organization, he or she typically explains to the inquirer that although what the inquirer says to the ombuds is confidential, what the ombuds then discloses to the organization will not be confidential.

In meeting or speaking with people on how their concerns can be addressed, the ombuds has the benefit of being a real, visible, and accessible person who is knowledgeable about the formal channels available in the organization; but just as important, the ombuds is a person knowledgeable about the culture, personalities, and informal folkways of the organization. This is in contrast to being an unknown and remote service representative at a company providing anonymous call services to many companies. Many ombuds transition to the ombuds position from other positions in the organization after many years of experience, and it is this deep insight into how things really work that can make them particularly effective.

The third element of an ombuds's role is a critical one: supporting issue prevention and systemic change. As a result of working daily with a wide variety of inquirers throughout the organization (and a surprisingly large percentage of inquirers come from the middle and upper ranks as opposed to the "rank and file"), an ombuds frequently is in a position to observe systemic problems and provide early warnings. Without breaching confidentiality or disclosing information that could be tracked to a particular inquirer, an ombuds provides trend reports on the nature and types of issues handled by the ombuds office and can bring to the attention of senior managers, or even boards, areas where some system change may be appropriate. This can be of great benefit to the organization, as it is not uncommon that existing channels of upward feedback have limitations. While an ombuds does not participate in any policy or management decision-making, consistent with the guiding principles of independence and neutrality, the ombuds can be a valuable listening post, complementing or adding to information coming to senior management from other sources. As such, the ombuds can identify to appropriate stakeholders issues or systemic change opportunities as they become apparent.

With this overview of what organizational ombuds have become and what they do, let us now look at why they are an important resource for organizations.

Why Should Organizations Create Ombuds Programs?

A Confidential Resource Helps People Resolve Conflict and Report Misconduct

Organizational ombuds programs in the United States usually have been created to respond to particular societal needs: bureaucratic and inflexible government, student riots and campus unrest, and business scandals demonstrating a failure of corporate responsibility and governance. Even the first official ombudsman, created by King Charles XII of Sweden, was in response to a specific need: to ensure that government officials performed their duties in the king's absence.[1] The confusion and misunderstanding over the role of an ombudsman have been caused, in large part, by the fact that so many different kinds of ombudsmen have been created ad hoc to respond to so many specific problems both in government and elsewhere.

Looking beyond the rationale used to create an ombuds program in a particular situation, however, I believe that there are two fundamental aspects of the American outlook that have also propelled the spread of ombuds programs in the United States: a faith in the value of checks and balances and a core belief that both people and insti-

---

1. Donald C. Rowat, *The Parliamentary Ombudsman: Should the Scandinavian Scheme Be Transplanted?*, 28 INT'L REV. ADMIN. SCI. 399 (1962).

tutions should behave properly (combined with a sense of what "proper" behavior is). As the scale and complexity of modern society and organizations have increased, with the attendant increase in laws, bureaucracy, and regulation, ombuds programs have been a way to provide a check on institutional power to correct injustice or to assist the surfacing and resolution of issues that would otherwise be blocked or ignored.

The fundamental principle that institutional power should be counterbalanced lies deep in the American psyche and, no doubt, has been influenced by the system of checks and balances embodied in the Constitution that created our federal government. One of the reasons for the success and perseverance of the ombudsman concept in America, however, is that we also believe that in our private institutions, as in our government, a system of checks and balances is important to make organizations more responsible and less susceptible to abuse. This allocation of power is also evident, for example, in the differing roles and responsibilities of executive officers, boards of directors, and shareholders.

While an organizational ombuds does not have organizational *power*, as is the case with a board of directors or the branches of our government, he or she does have the ability to check and inform organizational power. The freedom from management responsibility, combined with the everyday process of speaking with people from any and all levels or locations of the organization, give the ombuds a unique perspective on how the organization is performing and what problems it and its people face. Where an ombuds is established as a confidential resource for people, the ombuds will hear of conflict and allegations of misconduct that otherwise would not have been reported. If the ombuds also has access to the highest levels of an organization, he or she can help bring the existence of these issues to the attention of senior management (while still preserving confidentiality) to help the organization correct unfairness or wrongdoing in specific cases. The ombuds can also raise issues that may repeatedly cause concern or conflict or where systemic change may be appropriate to help an organization prevent issues from recurring. The ombuds office is thus an institutional response to curb wrongdoing or unethical behavior, a facilitator of appropriate conduct by both individuals and the organization itself, and an agent for promoting systemic change where necessary. Of course, the operation of the ombuds office is also subject to significant checks and balances: it is generally an appointed position, and it has no policy or decision-making authority. Its influence derives from its integrity, persuasion, and ability to provide an alternate channel for information to flow to policy makers.

The societal challenges that prompted the creation of so many organizational ombuds programs in the past have not abated. There are remarkable parallels in both the corporate and the university sectors between the conditions that gave rise to the modern organizational ombuds concept and those present today. Consider for a moment the similarities between the war in Vietnam and the current entanglements in Iraq and Afghanistan, or the parallels between the financial (remember junk bonds and the savings and loan disasters?) and procurement scandals of the 1980s with the accounting and auditing scandals of the late 1990s and the early 2000s. Indeed, the financial crisis on Wall Street that began in the fall of 2008, the worst since the Great Depression, will undoubtedly be investigated and reveal inappropriate conduct at all levels.[2] When academic freedom combines with the youth and diversity of large student populations, the non-hierarchical structure of universities (with tenured faculty), and the absence of a unifying force of the profit motive (and the attendant incentives and discipline), conflict in large universities may be even more intractable than in corporations. Stated simply, there is no reason to expect that the societal forces that disrupted and compromised our significant private institutions in the recent past will not continue to do so for the foreseeable future. The need for institutional checks and balances to support ethical conduct has not abated.

---

2. *See* George J. Terwilliger III, *The Financial Crisis*, NAT'L L.J., Dec. 1, 2008, at 12, for a discussion of the investigations that have begun into various aspects of the financial crisis of 2008. Another example is the reported settlement by Northop Grumman Corp. in April 2009 (based on conduct alleged to have occurred between 1995 and 2002). In what *The Wall Street Journal* called "the largest ever of a so-called whistleblower case alleging military-procurement fraud," Northrop agreed to pay $325 million to settle the suit, which was settled simultaneously with Northrop's claim against the government in a contract dispute and without admitting any wrongdoing. The article is *available at* http://online.wsj.com/article/SB123871451033784579.html?mod+dist_smartbrief (last visited July 13, 2009).

The scope and influence of our private institutions has increased, if anything, during the past quarter century. In the Preface to *Global Inc,*, Bruce Mazlish of MIT wrote in 2003 that:

> [i]t is startling to realize that, as reported by the UN (another factor in globalization?), *of the 100 largest economies in the world, 53 are multinationals [corporations], which means that they are larger and wealthier on this index than 120-130 of the remaining nation-states. Their power and effect are almost incalculable in regards not only to the economy but to politics, society, and culture. They have an impact on practically every sphere of modern life, from policy making in regard to the environment and international security; from problems of identity and community; and from the future of work to the future of the nation-state.*[3]

Universities, likewise, are big business. Fareed Zakaria has written that higher education is America's "best industry":

> In no other field is the United States' advantage so overwhelming. A 2006 report from the London-based Center for European Reform points out that the United States invests 2.6 percent of its GDP in higher education, compared with 1.2 percent in Europe and 1.1 percent in Japan. Depending on which study you look at, the United States, with five percent of the world's population, has either seven or eight of the world's top ten universities and either 48 percent or 68 percent of the top 50. The situation in the sciences is particularly striking. In India, universities graduate between 35 and 50 Ph.D.'s in computer science each year; in the United States, the figure is 1,000. A list of where the world's 1,000 best computer scientists were educated shows that the top ten schools were all American.[4]

The prominence of American universities as major industrial organizations is also demonstrated by the number of large institutions and the size of their budgets. Data compiled by the National Center for Education Statistics reflects that in the United States in 2005, 280

---

3. MEDARD GABEL & HENRY BRUNER, GLOBAL INC.: AN ATLAS OF THE MULTINATIONAL CORPORATION, at vi (2003) (emphasis added).
4. Fareed Zakaria, *The Future of American Power: How America Can Survive the Rise of the Rest*, 87 FOREIGN AFFAIRS 18, 31–32 (2008).

universities had more than 15,000 students; of those 280, 120 had approximately 24,000 or more.[5] While total budget information for these institutions is difficult to ascertain, reported information on expenditures underscores the point that they are big business: institutions with more than 15,000 students enrolled in 2005 each had average annual total expenses and deductions of almost $539 million.[6] The University of Pennsylvania reported the highest total expenses (almost $4 billion), with numerous other institutions spending well in excess of $1 billion annually.[7]

The ever-present societal pressures on these large organizations would be hard enough to deal with even if there were not also more fundamental change occurring in modern society; but significant structural change is all around us. Part I of this chapter describes some of the forces of change that have been transforming—and will continue to transform—American society and two of its most important types of institutions, corporations and universities. Fundamental demographic changes, together with technological change and the increasing globalization of the world,[8] will continue to create pressures on these

---

5. National Center for Education Statistics, Table 226: Selected statistics for degree-granting institutions enrolling more than 15,000 students in 2005, Selected years 1990 through 2006, *available at* http://nces.ed.gov/programs/digest/d07/tables/dt07_226.asp (2007) (last visited July 13, 2009), and Table 225: Enrollment of the 120 largest degree-granting college and university campuses, by selected characteristics and institution, Fall 2005, *available at* http://nces.ed.gov/programs/digest/d07/tables/dt07_225.asp (2007) (last visited Apr. 28, 2009).

6. *Id.*, Table 226.

7. *Id.*

8. While my research into the fundamental forces producing change in our private institutions independently focused on demographic, technological, and globalization trends, I am indebted to the insights of two sources in particular. The first is *Workforce 2020: Work and Workers in the 21st Century*, by Richard W. Judy & Carol D'Amico, published by the Hudson Institute in 1999. This is the sequel to the 1987 study by the Hudson Institute, *Workforce 2000*, which presciently anticipated much of the workplace change that occurred in the 1990s. The second is *The 21st Century at Work: Forces Shaping the Future Workforce and Workplace in the United States*, by Lynn A. Karoly & Constantin W.A. Panis, a research report prepared in 2004 by the Employment and Labor division of the RAND Corporation for the U.S. Department of Labor. The clarity of their presentation and, as will be seen, much of their data provided great assistance in the writing of this book.

institutions, and as a result, both generate conflict and create the need for common ethical principles. Part I also takes a close look at the scope and power of multinational corporations and their need to have corporate cultures that transcend national boundaries and local customs. Paradoxically, the pressure caused by these changes on people and institutions has been increased by the attempts by government and organizations to eliminate misconduct and impose formal legal obligations to curb abuse.

Part II of this chapter chronicles the pressures on organizations from a different direction: the law. Legal developments that have resulted in increased criminal exposure for organizations for misconduct of their employees, along with developments in corporate governance and employment law, have increased the pressure on our institutions to comply with the law and more—to act ethically on a global scale—and not to tolerate misconduct by employees or agents. Our collective thinking has produced a variety of structures (e.g., compliance and ethics officers, human relations and equal employment opportunity personnel) and policies (e.g., whistle-blower and non-retaliation policies and laws) to address these problems. As good and necessary as those responses have been, the evidence, however, demonstrates that the most common responses have been incomplete.

Part III discusses some of the shortcomings of the institutional responses that have been developed and presents data on their inability either to substantially reduce the level of misconduct in large organizations or to meaningfully increase the reporting of it. The structures and policies that have been recognized as best practices are premised on the assumption that people will come forward and that the law will protect them. Yet there are flaws in this model. First, if the certain consequence of reporting misconduct is that a complete investigation will be conducted and offenders disciplined, at least some of the people who might want to report misconduct will not be so confident of their information or position as to risk all by speaking out, even if they were not involved in the wrongdoing. Second, in America and many other cultures, people are indoctrinated from an early age not to be a "snitch," and these lessons are often brutally reinforced with peer pressure. As a result, many people do not want to be a "rat," or the person who complains, because they fear retaliation or shunning by co-workers or the organization. This is particularly true where a whistle-blower does not receive any direct benefit from reporting, so the lack of benefit is almost always outweighed by the risk of retaliation. And finally, it is both a fact and common knowledge that whistle-blowers, regardless of the law, suffer adverse consequences from their reporting activity. Retaliation can be inflicted or experienced in innumerable ways, and many of them are too subtle, fleeting, or insidious for the law to address adequately. Even where legal protection is available, it offers little solace when it comes only after the damage is done or when vindication cannot undo the damage or mend relationships with co-workers. Moreover, just the process of seeking legal vindication can result in further retaliation by peers, if not by managers and supervisors, and it can take years for a case to proceed through the courts.

Once we recognize that some of the barriers to reporting are not easily addressed by laws or policies, it is easy to see why organizations need confidential places where people can go to air their concerns or questions and discuss how they might then report or resolve them without setting in motion the cumbersome apparatus of formal investigations or dispute resolution channels. These barriers include the fears of a person who may be new to the organization (or even to American society) that she may be wrong or does not know the whole story and does not know where to go, what to do, or what will happen if she does come forward, or the fears of someone who works from home or who sees himself as only an insignificant cog in an institution that employs tens (or hundreds) of thousands of people. Despite the progress that has been made to date, there is still a need for a confidential and proactive resource for those associated with large institutions to address these fears. Such a confidential resource does not replace those organizational functions (such as compliance or HR) that have management responsibilities to deal with employee disputes or wrongdoing, but a confidential resource can be a valuable supplement that helps get people to the channels that can then take appropriate action.

Part IV, the final section, presents an explanation of how a properly established organizational ombuds program addresses these gaps and can be a critical component of an organization's effort to minimize workplace conflict and comply with ethical and legal requirements. Many organizations have already taken this step, but the reasons for creating an ombuds office have additional weight and urgency in light of the pressures—from the changing pressures of demography, technology, and globalization described in Part I and the pressures for more responsible organizational behavior described in Part II—that are and will be impacting our institutions.

PART I—THE FORCES OF CHANGE

As the old saying goes, the one constant is change. And yet there are periods when the forces driving change are greater than at other times. These forces may arise suddenly, as in new technological developments, or may be the result of a more gradual acceleration of trends. Occasionally, however, the interaction of a variety of forces produces fundamental and structural change. In the past few years, we have begun to experience the effects of just such a fundamental shift, but the effects of three forces in particular—demographic changes in the United States (and indeed, throughout the world), technology that has allowed information and knowledge to transform the way we work and live, and the resulting globalization of many aspects of our lives—set the stage for a reexamination of the institutional pressures in our private organizations. While books describing the forces of change and the resulting impact on society, such as *The World Is Flat*, by Thomas Friedman, to take just one example, are legion and provide greater detail and background on these phenomena, the goal here is to highlight some of the relevant information to illustrate the point that fundamental change is occurring. The key point is that while we may not be able to precisely predict the future, we do know *now*, based on information that is presently available to us, that transformational demographic, technological, and globalization forces are collectively exerting increasing amounts of stress on our institutions, creating the need for more effective responses.

A. Demographics

Current and projected demographic trends forecast a far more racially and ethnically diverse population, not just in our cities but throughout the United States. The data show a workforce that will increasingly have more older workers, more women, and more non-white groups than it did in the past. Unions will continue to shrink in relation to the size of the workforce and in overall influence. Hispanics and Asians have been and will continue to represent ever-larger percentages of the American population, a fact that will be reflected both in the enrollment at our universities and in the workplace. Many different cultures will be present in significant numbers, and while the ethnic and racial differences will blur with increasing intermarriage and social mixing, these differences will remain a significant fact of life. Our institutions, which are inextricably part of the societies in which they operate, will need to encourage and empower this racial and cultural pluralism; but to do so, they will need mechanisms that deal with the conflict and concerns that will inevitably arise as the established order and newcomers, with different expectations and cultural perspectives, adjust to dealing with each other.

1. Immigration

The single most significant force in this demographic shift has been immigration. This will come as no surprise to anyone who has followed the national immigration debate for the past several years, but the very scope of this issue may not be fully appreciated. At the height of the previous period of greatest immigration into the United States, the 60 years between 1860 and 1920, the proportion of foreign-born residents in the United States varied between 13 percent and 15 percent.[9] Due to the enactment of restrictive laws (the Immigration Act of 1924, for example), a worldwide economic depression, and the second World War, the percentage of immigrants in the U.S. population fell from a twentieth-century peak of 14.7 percent (in 1910) to just 4.7 percent by 1970.[10] However, with the enactment of the Immigration and Nationality Act in 1965 as an outgrowth of the civil rights movement, a new round of immigration began, the effects of which will equal or exceed that of all earlier periods of high immigration and which we are only now beginning to recognize.[11] Consider the following facts:

- "Almost 5 million immigrants came to the United States during the 1970s—the highest level of immigration, in both absolute and relative terms, since the early decades of the twentieth century . . . . The number of immigrants who arrived in the

---

9. Jeffrey S. Passel & D'Vera Cohn, *U.S. Population Projections: 2005–2050*, at 2 (Pew Research Center, Feb. 11, 2008).

10. *Id.* at 6.

11. NEW FACES IN NEW PLACES: THE CHANGING GEOGRAPHY OF AMERICAN IMMIGRATION 1 (Douglas S. Massey ed., 2008).

1980s exceeded that of the 1970s, and both numbers were surpassed by arrivals in the 1990s."[12]
- "By 2000, there were over 30 million foreign-born persons in the United States, almost one-third of whom arrived in the prior decade. Adding together these immigrants and their children (the second generation), more than 60 million people—*or one in five Americans*—have recent roots in other countries."[13]
- "If current trends continue, the population of the United States will rise to 438 million in 2050, from 296 million in 2005, and *82 percent of the increase will be due to immigrants arriving from 2005 to 2050 and their U.S.-born descendants. . . .*"[14]
- The result is an unprecedented number of foreign-born persons who will be an unprecedentedly large portion of our overall population: *"[b]y 2025, the immigrant, or foreign-born, share of the population will surpass the peak during the last great wave of immigration a century ago."*[15]

The impact of this round of immigration means they are settling not just in the traditional gateway cities, but in relatively homogeneous communities throughout the country where their presence is a new experience.[16] And, while the global economic recession that began in 2008 has had an arresting effect on the world's migration patterns,[17] the fact remains that many of those who have migrated will not be returning to their home countries.

---

12. *Id.*
13. *Id.* at 2 (emphasis added).
14. Jeffrey S. Passel & D'Vera Cohn, *U.S. Population Projections: 2005–2050, supra* note 9, at i (emphasis added).
15. *Id.* (emphasis added). *See also* Ginger Thompson, *Remade in America, The Newest Immigrants and Their Impact: Where Education and Assimilation Collide*, N.Y. TIMES, Mar. 15, 2009, at 1 (This is the first of a multipart series on the impact of immigrants on American society and institutions. While this article focuses on the impact on schools, it contains much other data on the scope of immigration and, in particular, where various immigrant groups have located.).
16. *See, e.g.*, Part I, "Emerging Patterns of Immigrant Settlement," *in* NEW FACES IN NEW PLACES: THE CHANGING GEOGRAPHY OF AMERICAN IMMIGRATION (Douglas S. Massey ed.), *passim*; Connor Dougherty & Miriam Jordan, *Surge in U.S. Hispanic Population Driven by Births, Not Immigration*, WALL ST. J., May 1, 2008, at A3.
17. Patrick Barta & Joel Millman, *The Great U-Turn*, WALL ST. J., June 6–7, 2009, at A1 and A10.

2. Diversity

The diversifying impact of this immigration on our overall population is transforming America. Based on current trends, there will be a profound change in the ethnic and racial mix of the U.S. population. In 1950, 90 percent of the population in the United States was white.[18] By 2005, non-Hispanic whites constituted only 67 percent of the population.[19] By 2050, they are projected to be only 47 percent of the population—a dramatic change by any standard.[20] The change in composition will largely come from two sources: Hispanics and Asians. This segment of the population is expected to triple over the next 50 years.[21] Indeed, Hispanics are projected to increase from approximately 14 percent of the population in 2005 to 29 percent by 2050. Asians are projected to increase from 5 percent of the population in 2005 to 9 percent by 2050.[22] Meanwhile, the black population is projected to increase by less than a percentage point, from 12.8 percent in 2005 to 13.4 percent in 2050.[23]

The effect of this population shift is already being felt everywhere, but in some places it is already quite pronounced. In California and (if not now, then soon) Texas, non-Hispanic whites are already in the minority.[24] The 2000 census revealed that 18 percent of Americans spoke a language other than English at home[25]—a number that will undoubtedly go up in the next census.

3. Impact on Educational Institutions

This change is also beginning to work its way through our institutions of higher education. The United States is the preferred destination for

---

18. ANDRÉS TAPIA, BEYOND BEST PRACTICES: NEW STRATEGIES FOR DIVERSITY BREAKTHROUGHS (Hewitt Assoc., 2008), *available at* http://www.hewittassociates.com/_MetaBasicCMAssetCache_/Assets/Articles/2008/Beyond_Best_Practices.pdf (last visited July 13, 2009).
19. Passel & Cohn, *supra* note 9, at 1.
20. *Id.*
21. TAPIA, *supra* note 18.
22. Passel & Cohn, *supra* note 9, at 9.
23. *Id.*
24. *Making Diversity Count—The Census 2000 Toolkit*, Report by the Society for Human Resource Management, *available at* http://www.shrm.org/diversity/census2000/ (last visited Sept. 21, 2004).
25. *Id.* at 1–2.

foreign students, "taking in 30 percent of the total number of foreign students globally, and its collaborations between business and educational institutions are unmatched anywhere in the world."[26] Immigration is a major advantage of the United States today, and this is particularly evident in the interrelationships among immigration, the presence of foreign students in our universities, and business innovation:

> Without immigration, the United States' GDP growth over the last quarter century would have been the same as Europeans. Foreign students and immigrants account for 50 percent of the science researchers in the country and in 2006 received 40 percent of the doctorates in science and engineering and 65 percent of the doctorates in computer science. By 2010, foreign students will get more than 50 percent of all Ph.D.'s awarded in every subject in the United States. In the sciences, that figure will be closer to 75 percent. Half of all Silicon Valley start-ups have one founder who is an immigrant or a first-generation American. *In short, the United States' potential new burst of productivity, its edge in nanotechnology and biotechnology, its ability to invent the future—all rest on its immigration policies. If the United States can keep the people it educates in the country, the innovation will happen there. If they go back home, the innovation will travel with them.*[27]

Other statistics confirm the increasing diversity of our universities. In 1976, even after several years of a significant affirmative action push, the average student body at a college or university had a total minority population of around 15 percent.[28] The comparable per-

---

26. Zakaria, *supra* note 4, at 32.

27. *Id.* at 35 (emphasis added). *See also* Matt Richtel, *Remade in America, The Newest Immigrants and Their Impact: A Google Whiz Searches for His Place on Earth*, N.Y. TIMES, Apr. 12, 2009, at 1 (This is another installment of the series referred to at ch. 2, note 15, *supra*, and focuses on the impact of immigrants on high-tech industries in general and Google in particular.).

28. IES, National Center for Education Statistics, Fast Facts, http://nces.ed.gov/fastfacts/display.asp?id=98. Similar figures are also available from IES, National Center for Educational Statistics, Table 216: Total fall enrollment in degree-granting institutions, by race/ethnicity, sex, attendance status, and level of student:

centage for minority students in 2005 was about 31 percent.[29] Further illustrating this point, the number of bachelor's degrees conferred on African-Americans increased by 150 percent between 2003 and 2008, reflecting a 26 percent annual increase.[30] Although the increase in minority population in colleges and universities represents increases in virtually every segment of ethnicity, the Hispanic population represents the most striking increases, rising from only 3.5 percent in 1976 to 10.8 percent in 2005.[31] During this same period, the average percentage of African-American students rose from 9.4 percent to 12.7 percent, and the average percentage for Asian/Pacific Islander students rose from 1.8 percent to 6.5 percent.[32]

4. Impact in Other Countries

These trends are not just occurring in the United States. Even though, in absolute numbers, the United States has a larger foreign-born population than other countries, other countries, on a relative basis, are experiencing similar if not greater effects. In contrast to the 12 percent of the American population that was foreign-born in 2005, 20 percent of the population in Australia and 19 percent of the population in Canada were foreign-born.[33] Data from the United Nations for the year 2000 indicates that:

> 175 million people worldwide live in a country other than where they were born. Although this number is less than 3 percent of the world's population, the number of migrants has more than doubled since 1975. The majority (60 percent) of these migrants live in the developed world (41 million in North America,

---

Selected years, 1976 through 2005 (2007), *available at* http://nces.ed.gov/Programs/digest/d07/tables/dt07_216.asp (last visited July 26, 2009); and from Andy Guess, *40 Years of Change in the Student Body*, INSIDE HIGHER ED. (2007), *available at* http://www.insidehighered.com/news/2007/04/09/cirp (last visited July 6, 2009).

29. IES Fast Facts, *supra* note 28.

30. Victor M. H. Borden, *Top 100 Undergraduate Degree Producers—Interpreting the Data*, DIVERSE ONLINE, June 12, 2008, *available at* http://www.diverseeducation.com/artman/publish/printer_11265.shtml (last visited Apr. 28, 2009).

31. *Id.*

32. *Id.*

33. Passel & Cohn, *supra* note 9, at 8.

for example), so that about 1 in 10 persons living in developed countries is a migrant.[34]

These figures do not include the 16 million people that are classified as refugees.[35]

5. Increase in the Role of Women in the Workforce

Immigration is not the only force changing who we are and who is in the workplace. In 1950, only 34 percent of women over the age of 16 were in the workforce. By 2002, that percentage had increased to 60 percent.[36] In 1950, women accounted for only 29 percent of the total workforce,[37] but that percentage is expected to increase to 48 percent by 2010.[38]

Women may even constitute a majority of the workforce sooner than predicted, as the job losses associated with the recession that began in 2008 have fallen disproportionately on men, who represent most of the workforce in the most distressed industries, such as manufacturing and construction.[39] Even more significant in terms of the potential impact on workplace dynamics is the fact that the percentage of working women with children under six years old has risen from 18.6 percent in 1960 to 53.4 percent in 1985 to 64 percent in 1999.[40] Not only are more women in the workforce, the positions held by women are also changing. The percentage of women in professional and managerial positions has increased since 1977 from 24 percent to 39 percent.[41] With women outnumbering men in obtaining bachelor's and master's degrees and earning nearly 40 percent of the doctorate

---

34. KAROLY & PANIS, *supra* note 8, at 146.
35. *Id.*
36. *Id.* at 24.
37. JUDY & D'AMICO, *supra* note 8, at 53.
38. KAROLY & PANIS, *supra* note 8, at 24.
39. Catherine Rampell, *As Layoffs Surge, Women May Pass Men in Job Force*, N.Y. TIMES, Feb. 6, 2009, at A1. *See also* Pew Research Center, *America's Changing Workforce—Recession Turns a Graying Office Grayer* at 26, Sept. 3, 2009, *available at* http://pewsocialtrends.org/pubs/742/americas-changing-work-force (last visited Sept. 4, 2009).
40. JUDY & D'AMICO, *supra* note 8, at 53.
41. JAMES O'TOOLE & EDWARD E. LAWLER III, THE NEW AMERICAN WORKPLACE 94 (2006).

degrees,[42] the influence of women on the workplace—and in leadership positions—will continue to increase.

The combined impact of women and minorities is profound. The U.S. Bureau of Labor Statistics reported that by 2008, 70 percent of the new labor force entrants will be women and minorities.[43]

6. Other Demographic Trends: Generational Change and Talent Shortage

Two other trends that are also reshaping the American workforce deserve mention. First, and no surprise to those of us in the baby-boom generation, is the fact that the workforce itself is aging, resulting in significant changes in the age distribution of workers. The Bureau of Labor Statistics reports that by 2010 there will be a 29 percent increase in workers in the 45–64 age group and a 14 percent increase in the over-65 age group, but a 1 percent decline in workers in the 18–44 age group.[44] Thus, in addition to having many new population groups joining the workforce, a significant portion of the existing workforce is aging and is likely to remain at work (often in senior positions) even as it reaches ages at which people traditionally would have left the workforce. The 2008-2009 economic recession will only exacerbate this trend. The continued presence of older workers will almost certainly frustrate younger workers who will be looking for promotional opportunities.

Second, the need for workers will outstrip the supply. We have already experienced a decrease in the growth rate of the workforce from

---

42. *Id.*

43. NANCY R. LOCKWOOD, WORKPLACE DIVERSITY: LEVERAGING THE POWER OF DIFFERENCE FOR COMPETITIVE ADVANTAGE 3 (Society of Human Resource Management) (2005).

44. Hewitt Associates, *Timely Topic Survey—Results: Preparing for the Workplace of Tomorrow*, at 1 (Feb. 2004), *available at* http://www.hewittassociates.com/_MetaBasicCMAssetCache_/Assets/Articles/workforce_tomorrow.pdf; *see also* Clare Ansberry, *Elderly Emerge as a New Class of Workers—and the Jobless*, WALL ST. J., Feb. 23, 2009, at 1 ("The growing numbers reflect, in part, an increase in the number of older workers. The percentage of people 65 and older who are in the workforce rose to 16.8% at year end, from 11.9% a decade earlier. Among people 75 and older, the increase was even greater—to 7.3%, from 4.7%."). *See also* Pew Research Center, *supra* note 39 (observing that the workplace is graying both because older workers remain at work and because younger workers are delaying entry into the workforce).

2.6 percent annual increases in the 1970s to a projected 1.1 percent by 2010.[45] The projection is that this rate will drop even further, to just 0.4 percent between 2010 and 2020 and to 0.3 percent in the decade thereafter.[46] The impact of these trends is that "in the next 10 years, 32 million jobs will be vacated and 20 million new jobs created (52 million jobs will need to be filled). However, projected labor force availability will be only 29 million, leaving a 23 million job gap."[47] As a result, there will be a demand for new workers, and with the technological changes described below, this demand will have global implications.

7. Impact of Demographic Changes

What does all this mean? Simply stated, there will be many more new people in our colleges and universities and in the workplace, with a greater potential for misunderstandings and conflict. The sheer size of the new population groups means that many people will not have had previous experience with their new work environments or their new positions, while others will have to work with people from cultures with which they are unfamiliar.[48] The interaction of the new entrants with aging co-workers, whose outlook and values were largely shaped in earlier and simpler times, is necessarily going to put a premium on managing this diverse group and creating a common institutional culture.[49]

---

45. KAROLY & PANIS, *supra* note 8, at 17.
46. *Id.*
47. Hewitt Associates, *supra* note 44, at 1.
48. The difficulty in dealing with divergent cultures is illustrated in a *Wall Street Journal* report on the problems encountered by Nomura Holdings, Inc., a Japanese securities firm that acquired the international operations of Lehman Brothers. *See* Alison Tudor, *Nomura Stumbles in New Global Push*, WALL ST. J., July 29, 2009 at A1 & A12 (In a training session for former Lehman Brothers employees, employees were separated by gender, and the women, including Harvard graduates, were instructed on "how to wear their hair, serve tea and choose their wardrobe according to the season." . . . "They told women joining from Lehman to remove highlights from their hair, to wear sleeves no shorter than midbicep and avoid brightly colored clothing, according to several people who joined from Lehman." In addition, "Nomura's human-resources department changed some women's email addresses to their married names, from their maiden names, without asking which names they used professionally, according to the people who joined from Lehman.").
49. I have found two books to be helpful in understanding the legacy and influence of ethic diversity on the development of American society. In an older work, *Ethnic America; A History* (Basic Books, Inc., 1981), Thomas Sowell de-

All of this will be occurring in an environment in which there will be an overall shortage of skilled and quality workers or students and, at least in the short term, economic dislocation, resulting in intense competition for the most capable people. While the population generally, and hence the workforce in particular, is always changing, the current demographic changes are significant precisely because they are so extensive and different in kind. In essence, the result will be a fundamental redefinition of who we are and how we interact with one another.

B. Technology and Globalization

Even for people who came of age 30 or more years ago, it is hard to remember what life was like without the communications technology of today. Photocopiers, fax machines, computers, voicemail, the Internet, cell phones, e-mail, and PDAs were each transformational technologies. My intent here is not to present a comprehensive analysis of all technological change, but rather to illustrate how communications technology has affected and will continue to impact our major institutions. It has made work location less significant, because as long as one is connected to the Internet, much of the knowledge work can be—and is now being—performed from home, from locations scattered across the world, or even on a part-time basis by contract workers. The extreme interconnectivity of our information systems, however, has given rise to yet another paradox in modern society: while this communications technology allows us to be connected with others in our institutions on virtually a 24/7 basis, the physical separation that this connectivity permits often means that an increasing segment of the population feels less connected to and invested in the fabric and cultures of the institutions in which they operate. With much of the communication and contact confined to e-mail and voicemail—and especially in light of the demographic changes described in the earlier section—the potential for alienation and conflict is significant.

---

scribes the history of several of the ethnic groups that came to the United States in terms of what it was like for them when they left their home country, how they came to the United States, and how they assimilated. In a more recent book by Malcolm Gladwell, *Outliers: The Story of Success* (Little, Brown & Co., 2008), the author explores a variety of factors, including ethnic background and the timing of one's birth, on the ability to succeed.

The great advances in communications technology are the result of ever-accelerating computer chip capacity,[50] the incredible reduction in the cost of processing power, and vast increases in computer storage capacity and the capacity of bandwidth made possible by fiber-optic cables.[51] Even with an awareness of how rapid and profound this change has been, the statistics nevertheless give us pause:

- Although the personal computer (PC) did not exist until the 1980s and the World Wide Web was not introduced until 1989,[52] by 1996 40 percent of American households owned a computer, and that figure is expected to rise to 90 percent by 2010.[53]
- The number of Internet domain hosts grew from just under 6 million in 1995 to almost 110 million by 2001.[54] By the end of the first quarter of 2009, that number had grown to nearly 183 million; and even though the rate of growth had slowed in the fourth quarter of 2008, the number of new registrations by the end of the first quarter of 2009 represented a 12 percent growth over the first quarter of 2008.[55] Approximately 90,000 domain names are purchased each day as thousands of other names expire.[56]
- The capacity of fiber-optic cables increased a thousandfold in the 10 years prior to 2004, largely due to wavelength division multiplexing (WDM), and WDM is projected to be available to homes in the United States by 2010.[57]
- In 2003 it was determined that the number of e-mail communications sent in a day in the United States was almost equal to

---

50. Gordon Moore, co-founder of Intel, predicted in 1965 that the transistor density of integrated circuits would roughly double every 18 months—a prediction that has largely proven to be correct. *See* KAROLY & PANIS, *supra* note 8, at 81–82.
51. *Id.* at 81–83.
52. *Id.* at 84.
53. JUDY & D'AMICO, *supra* note 8, at 18–19.
54. KAROLY & PANIS, *supra* note 8, at 85.
55. *6 The Domain Name Industry Brief No. 2* at 2 (June 2009), VeriSign, Inc., *available at* http://www.verisign.com/domain-name-services/domain-information-center/domain-name-resources/domain-name-report-june09.pdf (last visited July 27, 2009).
56. Benjamin D. Silbert, *Trademark law, ICANN, Domain Name Expiration*, 36 AIPLA Q.J. 311, 313 (2008).
57. KAROLY & PANIS, *supra* note 8, at 91.

the number of pieces of mail delivered by the United States Postal Service in a year.[58]
- *By August 2008, an estimated 210 billion e-mails were being sent every day.*[59]

As staggering as some of these statistics are, it is sobering to recognize that in some areas of technology, the United States is lagging behind other countries. For example:

most of the rest of the industrialized world—and a good part of the non-industrialized world as well—has better cell-phone service than the United States. Computer connectivity is faster and cheaper across the rest of the industrialized world, from Canada to France to Japan, and the United States now stands 16th in the world in broadband penetration per capita.[60]

Nevertheless, the implications of this revolution have been so profound that whole industries have arisen to manufacture, sell, and service technology products. With each technological development, the pace of further development appears to accelerate, and we are now able to communicate and do business on a global scale, with communication costs a fraction of what they had been in earlier eras.[61] Indeed, "[b]y the late 1990s, the marginal cost of communicating globally via the Internet had plunged to zero for most users."[62] And that was almost 10 years ago.

---

58. THE SEDONA PRINCIPLES, BEST PRACTICES RECOMMENDATIONS & PRINCIPLES FOR ADDRESSING ELECTRONIC DOCUMENT PRODUCTION, 2005 ANNOT. VERSION 4 (Jonathan M. Redgrave ed., 2005), *available at* http://www.thesedonaconference.org/content/miscFiles/7_05TSP.pdf.

59. Heinz Tschabitsher, About.com, *How Many Emails Are Sent Every Day?*, *available at* http://email.about.com/od/emailtrivia/f/emails_per_day.htm (last visited Jan. 13, 2009) ("183 billion messages per day means more than 2 million emails are sent every second. About 70% to 72% of them might be span and viruses. The genuine emails are sent by around 1.3 billion email users."). For an analysis of the impact of this volume of data on the legal system, see George L. Paul & Jason R. Baron, *Information Inflation: Can the Legal System Adapt?*, 13 RICH. J.L. & TECH. 10 (2007), *available at* http://law.richmond.edu/jolt/v13i3/article10.pdf (last visited Apr. 28, 2009).

60. Zakaria, *supra* note 4, at 39.

61. JUDY & D'AMICO, *supra* note 8, at 22.

62. *Id.*

1. Growth of the Information Technology Sector

One of the most immediate consequences of this communications revolution has been the rapid expansion of the Information Technology (IT) sector of the economy. Current data are hard to obtain, but the trends reflected in available data indicate that if anything, these trends have accelerated rather than abated. For instance, between 1991 and 2001, the IT sector grew at a rate more than five times that of overall occupational growth and is "estimated to have contributed about one-third of all output growth between 1995 and 1999."[63] Even in non-IT fields, the widespread use of computer technology has resulted in an overall increase in the skill level required of workers, as routine manual and non-analytic jobs are losing ground to jobs that require "nonroutine cognitive analytic (problem-solving) and interactive (communication) skills."[64]

2. Increased Need for Knowledge Workers

All of this has put a premium on the so-called "knowledge workers":

> As a result of these trends, an increased emphasis is being placed on knowledge as the key source of comparative advantage for businesses and their employees in the twenty-first century economy. (citations omitted) While the concepts of knowledge workers, knowledge organizations, and knowledge management have taken on a variety of meanings, at the core, knowledge embodies another economic input that combines with capital, labor, or natural resources to produce goods and services. In this context, knowledge is more than just technology but embodies understanding of markets, customers, suppliers, business processes, best practices, and other invisible assets of the organization.[65]

With the increasing importance of such knowledge workers, there is a corresponding increase in wage stratification between higher-skill workers and those without the education or skill to meet the new demands of the workplace.[66] People who dropped out of high

---

63. KAROLY & PANIS, *supra* note 8, at 100.
64. *Id.* at 109.
65. *Id.* at 188–89.
66. *Id.* at 112–15.

school or who have only a high school diploma experienced a decline in real wages from 1973 to 2001 of 18.5 percent and 4.1 percent, respectively, whereas those with a college or advanced degree experienced an increase in real wages of 15.9 percent and 19.5 percent, respectively.[67]

3. Emergence of the Virtual Workspace

The combined effect of the demand for capable knowledge workers, virtually no marginal cost of communications, and technology advancements around the globe is that "the physical location of the workforce is increasingly less relevant."[68] This permits more flexibility and less full-time or long-term commitment to (and from) workers, increasing numbers of whom are considered "contingent" workers: people with temporary, part-time, or contract employment instead of full-time employment.[69] There has also been an increase in people who work from home. A few statistics help illustrate these points:

- "Part-time work accounts for something like 13 percent of total employment in the United States, and 68 percent of part-timers are women."[70]
- Independent contractors were 7.4 percent of the workforce in 2005 and were employed by 62 percent of the *Fortune* 1000 companies, according to one survey.[71]
- According to a prominent national employment law firm, "Whatever its genesis, one fact is clear: based on a February 2003 study, 22 percent of the workforce in 2002 was comprised of free agents, temporary employees or self-employed workers; by February 2003, that number increased to 28 percent and the expected rate by 2010 is 36 percent."[72] There is nothing to suggest that this trend will not continue.

---

67. *Id.* at 112.
68. *Id.* at 139.
69. O'TOOLE & LAWLER, *supra* note 41, at 75.
70. *Id.* at 77.
71. *Id.*
72. LITTLER MENDELSON, P.C., STRATEGIC INITIATIVES FOR THE CHANGING WORKFORCE, 2004–2005, at 20 (2004).

- As of 2004, almost one in 10 workers had an alternative or flexible work arrangement. *If part-time and self-employed workers are considered, this figure increases to 1 in 4 workers in a "nonstandard work arrangement."*[73]
- In a survey in 2000, 41 percent of workers indicated that they could do their job by telecommuting if they had access to a telephone, fax machine, and an Internet connection.[74] That number would certainly be higher today.
- The separation between home and work is increasingly becoming blurred, as mobile technology permits people to receive e-mail on their telephones and to send and receive message at all hours. In a 2002 survey, "23 percent of Americans reported that working at home after hours is expected of them and 19 percent reported that they have received job-related e-mails at home."[75]
- "As of 2001, data collected by the BLS [Bureau of Labor Statistics] indicated that nearly 20 million workers, or 15 percent of the workforce, usually did some work at home (at least one day a week) as part of their primary job . . . ."[76]
- *"Using a broader definition of off-site work, about four out of five workers either work off site themselves or work with others who work at a distance."*[77]
- In a 2005 survey, 57 percent of employees in *Fortune* 1000 companies have "flex-location policies that include work from home."[78]
- According to WorldatWork, an association for HR professionals, *an estimated 100 million U.S. workers will "telework" by 2010.*[79]

It is difficult to fully integrate employees who work remotely. In a survey for a 2008 study by the American Management Association titled

---

73. KAROLY & PANIS, *supra* note 8, at 192 (emphasis added).
74. *Id.* at 195.
75. O'TOOLE & LAWLER, *supra* note 41, at 95.
76. KAROLY & PANIS, *supra* note 8, at 120
77. *Id.* (emphasis added) (citation omitted).
78. O'TOOLE & LAWLER, *supra* note 41, at 95.
79. Josephine Rossi, *Telework Increases*, Bnet Business Network, *available at* http://findarticles.com/p/articles/mi_qa5366/is_200704/ai_n21287869 (last visited Apr. 28, 2009) (emphasis added).

Cultivating Effective Corporate Cultures, only 34 percent of the responding organizations indicated that they provided "'training and development for employees who work remotely' to a high or very high extent, only 23 percent said that 'succession planning includes remote leaders' to such an extent, and just 16 percent said their companies provide 'team-building opportunities designed for remote employees' to a high or very high extent."[80]

4. Emergence of the Global Workforce

The changes in communications technology that have allowed people to work from home and given both employers and employees greater flexibility have also had a global impact: they have enabled companies to outsource work to other parts of the world. Some estimate that between 400,000 and 500,000 additional computer-related jobs migrated abroad by 2003 or 2004, and projections are for that number to increase to 3.3 million by 2015.[81] The estimated cost savings to U.S. companies from creating back-office operations in low-cost countries can be as significant as 30–40 percent.[82] The rapid rise of call centers and software development companies in India are two cases in point. The domestic economic impact of the globalization made possible by communications technology is no less significant. Indeed, even as international trade grew from less than 10 percent of the U.S. economy to more than 20 percent from 1960 to 2000, the increase in services-related exports outpaced the increases from merchandise exports:[83] "[s]ince 1980, services have gone from 18 percent of all U.S. export activity to 30 percent."[84]

In addition to outsourcing certain ancillary functions like call centers to other parts of the world, many companies have responded to the need for high-end knowledge workers and the ready availability of talent on a global scale by creating global work teams to work on important projects. Even where global work teams are not used, the

---

80. AMERICAN MGMT. ASS'N, CULTIVATING EFFECTIVE CORPORATE CULTURES, A GLOBAL STUDY OF CHALLENGES AND STRATEGIES, CURRENT TRENDS AND FUTURE POSSIBILITIES 2008–2018, at 57 (2008).
81. KAROLY & PANIS, *supra* note 8, at 141.
82. *Id.* at 140.
83. *Id.* at 132.
84. *Id.* at 133.

workforce is being profoundly affected by the global competition for talent. Indeed, in a report based on a study by Hewitt Associates in 2004, it was estimated that in the next decade, "75 percent of new workers will likely be from Asia, while North America and Europe will have 3 percent of the world's new labor force."[85]

5. Globalization of Universities

Globalization pressures and communications technology have also had a major impact on American universities, enabling them to create new programs in other countries and permitting their students to study abroad. In late 2008, for example, Duke University announced plans to expand its programs in India. To accommodate two new masters degree programs in business administration in which students would rotate through India, Duke "plans to employ an India-based faculty, open two new research centers, and bring some of the university's environmental studies, global health and public policy programs there . . . ."[86] Were it not for limitations imposed by Indian law that restrict foreign institutions from creating separate degree-granting institutions there, the involvement by American universities would be even greater. As it is, in just India alone, more than 100 foreign institutions now offer programs, with Carnegie-Mellon, Columbia Business School, and California State University–Long Beach among them.[87]

According to an Open Doors study, 40 different United States campuses during the 2005–2006 school year had more than 1,000 students each to whom they awarded academic credit for study abroad.[88] These colleges and universities were primarily large research institutions.[89] Of these schools, New York University sent the greatest number of students abroad, with a total of 2,809.[90] Michigan State University and the University of Texas at Austin sent the second and third most

---

85. NANCY R. LOCKWOOD, WORKPLACE DIVERSITY: LEVERAGING THE POWER OF DIFFERENCE FOR COMPETITIVE ADVANTAGE (Soc'y for Human Resources Mgmt., 2005).
86. Geeta Anand & Brittany Hite, *Duke Expands India Offerings as U.S. Schools Seek Foothold,* WALL ST. J., Oct. 16, 2008, at A10.
87. *Id.*
88. Open Doors 2007, *American Students Studying Abroad at Record Levels: Up 8.5%, available at* http://opendoors.iienetwork.org/?p=113744 (last visited Apr. 28, 2009).
89. *Id.*
90. *Id.*

students, with over 2,000 each. However, it is not just large universities that are sending their students abroad; 18 smaller degree-granting institutions reported sending more than 80 percent of their student body abroad in the 2005–2006 school year.[91]

If universities are establishing more study-abroad programs, it is because more students want to go abroad to study. Over the last decade, the number of American students choosing to study abroad has steadily increased.[92] During this period, the number of American students receiving academic credit for their study abroad has increased by 150 percent,[93] from approximately 76,000 students during the 1993–1994 school year[94] to over 223,534 students during the 2005–2006 school year.[95] Indeed, the number for the 2005–2006 year itself represented an 8.5 percent increase over the previous year.[96]

The most popular destinations for study abroad have also changed, reflecting greater awareness of global opportunities. Increasingly, students are choosing to study in Latin America, Asia, Oceania (i.e., Australia, New Zealand, and South Pacific Islands), and Africa rather than Europe.[97] Of the students studying abroad during the 2005–2006 school year, Europe hosted only 52 percent [98] compared to 63 percent a decade ago.[99] These changes reflect both evolving student preferences and increasing international opportunities.[100]

---

91. *Id.* More recent data is not substantially different. *See* Education Life Supp., N.Y. TIMES, July 26, 2009 at 10–11.

92. Inst. of Int'l Ed., Open Doors, Table 26: Profile of U.S. Study Abroad Students, 1993/94–2001/02, *available at* http://opendoors.iienetwork.org/?p=35977 (last visited July 26, 2009); Inst. of Int'l Ed., Open Doors 2007, Table 24: Profile of U.S. Study Abroad Students, 1995/96–2005/06, *available at* http://opendoors.iienetwork.org/?p=113282 (last visited Apr. 28, 2009).

93. Open Doors 2007, *supra* note 88.

94. Open Doors, Table 26, *supra* note 92.

95. Open Doors 2007, Table 24, *supra* note 92.

96. Inst. of Int'l Ed., Open Doors 2007, Figure 8C: Top 20 Leading Destinations of U.S. Study Abroad Students, 2004/05 & 2005/06, *available at* http://opendoors.iienetwork.org/?p=113274 (last visited Apr. 28, 2009).

97. Carl U. Zachrisson, *New Study Abroad Destinations: Trends and Emerging Opportunities*, *available at* http://www.aifsfoundation.org/pdf/Destinations.pdf (last visited July 26, 2009).

98. Open Doors 2007, Figure 8C, *supra* note 96.

99. Zachrisson, *supra* note 97.

100. *Id.*

More Americans may be studying abroad than ever before, but foreign students still want to study in the United States. Although the world economic recession has slowed the rate of applications compared to previous years, foreign student applications for graduate school admission overall rose 4 percent in 2009.[101] In comparison, applications rose 6 percent in 2008 and 12 percent in 2006.[102] Even with an overall increase in the rate of applications, the countries from which those applications are made changed fairly dramatically:

> The [Council of Graduate Schools] survey of U.S. institutions, which fielded more than 400,000 applications in all, showed growth of applications from China along with the Middle East and Turkey up 16 percent and 20 percent, respectively. But applications from India and South Korea fell 9 percent and 7 percent, respectively.[103]

If these trends continue, they will have a substantial impact on American universities that have come to rely on this influx of foreign students, particularly in the sciences.[104]

C. Globalization and the Multinational Corporation

If, as some assert, globalization is "measured by the flow of goods, services, money, people and ideas across borders,"[105] the demographic and technological changes described above have helped usher in a truly global era. Besides more diverse people working together in the global workforce in increasingly different ways, the sheer volume of work with international implications has shown phenomenal growth: even five years ago, "[w]orld trade ha[d] increased in volume by more than 25 times since 1950. Measured in dollar value, the increase is an even more dramatic 90 times"[106] And nowhere has the impact of this globalization been greater than on multinational corporations, which have been expected not only to deliver economic value to their share-

---

101. Mitra Kalita, *Foreign Applications to U.S. Graduate Schools Slow*, WALL ST. J., Apr. 7, 2009, at A4.
102. *Id.*
103. *Id.*
104. *Id.*
105. GABEL & BRUNER, *supra* note 3, at 12.
106. *Id.*

holders but also to bridge the cultural, economic, and political divides that exist among nations.

1. Growth of Multinational Corporations

The globalization "niche"[107] occupied by multinational corporations today is a relatively new one, but the existence of multinational corporations as a business vehicle is not new. Companies such as the English and the Dutch East India Companies, along with Hudson's Bay Company, were formed in the 1600s. By 1700 there were approximately 1,000 such companies in existence. By 1900 the total number of multinational corporations had increased only to approximately 3,000; and while growth accelerated after 1900, the growth rate was quite slow—by 1970 there were still only around 7,000 multinational corporations in the world.[108] Soon thereafter, however, explosive growth occurred: by 1990 the number had grown to approximately 30,000, and by 2000 the number of multinational corporations in the world was more than 63,000.[109]

More important than the sheer number of multinational corporations in existence is the power and influence they have acquired. An analysis of the world's 100 largest economies in 2003 concluded that 53 of them were multinational corporations, "which means that they are larger and wealthier on this index than 120–130 of the remaining nation-states."[110] Related statistics give even more definition to the dominant role of these organizations:

> With more than 63,000 multinational enterprises and 821,000 foreign subsidiaries, multinational corporations directly employ about 90 million people (more than 20 million are in the developing world), pay more than $1.5 trillion in wages, contribute 25 percent of the gross world product, and pay more than $1.2 trillion in taxes to the governments of the world—as well as produce much of the goods and services that have raised global standards of living. *Out of the 63,000 multinational corporations in the world, the 1,000 largest account for 80 percent of world industrial output.* The *Fortune* Global 500 alone had more

---
107. *Id.*
108. *Id.* at 2–3.
109. *Id.*
110. *Id.* at vi.

than $45 trillion in assets, $14 trillion in revenues, $667 billion in profits, and about 47 million employees in 2000.[111]

2. Globalization of Multinational Corporations

As powerful as multinational corporations have been, they themselves have also been the victims of globalization. In the early 1960s, almost 60 percent of the world's 500 largest corporations were U.S. companies; by 1999, that number was only 36 percent.[112] Thirty-three percent of the companies on the *Fortune* 500 list in 1980 no longer existed as separate companies by 1990, and by 1995 "another 40 percent were gone."[113] Likewise, while in 1980 most of the 500 largest multinational corporations were either American or European, by 2005 about one-third had headquarters in Asia or Latin America.[114] In 2005, 24 of the 25 largest initial public stock offerings were held in countries other than the United States.[115] In 2008, 62 of the *Fortune* 500 largest firms were from Brazil, Russia, India, and China—twice the number that had been on the 2003 list.[116]

A few specific examples help to illustrate the impact of globalization on corporations. In 2007, Halliburton, a Houston, Texas, energy services company that had business interests throughout the world, moved its corporate headquarters to Dubai. In 2008 Anheuser-Busch, the maker of Budweiser, the largest-selling beer in America, was acquired by a Belgian-Brazilian conglomerate.[117] And finally, Lenovo, a Chinese company, purchased the personal-computer business of IBM in 2005 for $1.75 billion. Although this deal gave Lenovo the right to continue to use the IBM name on PCs it manufactured for the next five years, confidence in the Lenovo brand had increased to the point that it made the transition to its own brand name two years early.[118] To

---

111. *Id.* at 7 (emphasis added).
112. *Id.* at 8.
113. LEVIATHANS: MULTINATIONAL CORPORATIONS AND THE NEW GLOBAL HISTORY 3 (Alfred D. Chandler, Jr. & Bruce Mazlish eds., 2005).
114. *Id.* at 8.
115. Zakaria, *supra* note 4, at 36.
116. *A Bigger World: A Special Report on Globalisation*, ECONOMIST, Sept. 20, 2008, at 3, *available at* http://www.economist.com/specialreports/displaystory.cfm?story_id=12080751 (last visited July 26, 2009).
117. *Id.*
118. *Id.*

assist it in the transition from a large Chinese company to a truly global one, Lenovo took the challenge of globalization further than just hiring experienced international managers. As reported in *The Economist*, the chairman of Lenovo, Yang Yuanqing, described his company's approach:

> "We are proud of our Chinese roots," says Mr. Yang, but "we no longer want to be positioned as a Chinese company." So the firm has no headquarters; the meetings rotate among its bases around the world. Its development teams are made up of people in several centres around the world, often working together virtually. The firm's global marketing department is in Bangalore.
>
> A huge effort has been made to integrate the different cultures within the firm. "In all situations assume good intentions; be intentional about understanding others and being understood; respect cultural differences," reads one of many tip sheets issued by the firm to promote "effective teamwork across cultures." Mr. Yang even moved his family to live in North Carolina to allow him to learn more about American culture and to improve his already respectable command of English, the language of global business.[119]

Meanwhile, IBM, the company that sold the PC business to Lenovo, is taking its own steps to deal with globalization. In the fall of 2008, it had 73,000 employees in India, compared with only 2,000 10 years ago, and planned to increase its revenues from global markets to 30 percent from the current 18 percent within five years.[120] While it has retained its world headquarters in the United States, it has moved its chief procurement officer and the head of its emerging markets to China.[121] As a result of this focus on the international labor pool, by the beginning of 2009, "[f]oreign workers accounted for 71 percent of Big Blue's nearly 400,000 employees . . . up from about 65 percent in 2006."[122] The layoff of nearly 5,000 workers in the United States in

---

119. *Id.* at 3–4.
120. *Id.* at 4.
121. *Id.* at 13.
122. William M. Bulkeley, *IBM to Cut U.S. Jobs, Expand in India*, WALL ST. J., Mar. 26, 2009, at B1.

early 2009, combined with the transfer of jobs and work to India,[123] will continue this trend.

3. The Need for a Global Corporate Ethics

With globalization exerting such overwhelming pressures on major corporations that exercise such a huge influence on total world economic output and depend on people and operations throughout the world, one of their most critical challenges is how to harness this diversity and disparity into a common and effective enterprise. The challenge is not only one of economics; it is also one of business ethics. The *AMA/HRI Business Ethics Survey* in 2005 identified business ethics as one of the top three issues that businesses must deal with and predicted that globalization would be "the number one business ethics driver by the year 2015."[124] As explained by *The Economist*, the reasons are clear even for companies from emerging markets:

> [A] globally integrated company needs a single culture, and that the best way to foster this is to make the highest ethics anywhere in the firm the norm for everyone, wherever they are working. Anything less tends to corrode the culture.
>
> A globally integrated firm cannot allow corrupt practices by employees in some countries and not others, so it must outlaw them everywhere. On the other hand, it cannot enforce religious practices and holidays, or different ways of life, so it must preach tolerance. One investment bank, for example, is extending its lesbian, gay, bisexual, and transgender network to its Indian operations over the opposition of its local boss.[125]

Ben W. Heineman Jr., general counsel of General Electric for over 15 years, is equally clear in his advice: multinational corporations that aspire to high performance and high integrity must create a culture of adherence to global ethical standards:

---

123. *Id.*
124. AMERICAN MGMT. ASS'N/HUMAN RESOURCE INST., THE ETHICAL ENTERPRISE: DOING THE RIGHT THINGS IN THE RIGHT WAYS, TODAY AND TOMORROW; A GLOBAL STUDY OF BUSINESS ETHICS 2005–2015, 10 (2006).
125. *In Praise of the Stateless Multinational,* ECONOMIST, Sept. 20, 2008, at 20, *available at* http://www.economist.com/opinion/displaystory.cfm?story_id=12263150 (last visited July 26, 2009).

[T]he high-performance-with-high-integrity culture must be strong and unyielding everywhere in the world. The core principles and practices that create that culture, therefore, also must also be uniform and universal across different business lines, different markets, and different regions. True, the transnational company must always be sensitive to local conditions. But variation on these fundamental cultural issues is hypocritical and confuses people. It is antithetical to integrity. It risks creating a cancer that can metastasize across the company, eating away at the culture.[126]

Even apart from the most celebrated failures of corporate ethics by Enron, Tyco, WorldCom, Adelphia, Société Générale, and Arthur Anderson, Heineman cites the impact of this failure in the past decade on once-heralded CEOs who were fired or forced out early because of integrity issues: "Hank Greenberg at AIG (company accounting), Frank Raines at Fannie Mae (company accounting), Peter Dolan at Bristol-Myers Squibb (failure to inform board), Phil Condit (procurement scandals) and Henry Stonecipher (employee relationship) at Boeing, John Browne at BP (safety practices, and Klaus Kleinfeld at Siemans (widespread improper payments) . . . ."[127]

---

126. BEN W. HEINEMAN JR., HIGH PERFORMANCE WITH HIGH INTEGRITY: MEMO TO THE CEO 27 (2008).
127. *Id.* at 18. A similar list of companies appears in "Bad Apples or Bad Barrel?" in the May/June 2007 edition of *The Conference Board Review* by John. C. Bogle, in which he identified corporations that restated earnings or were involved in settlements with the Securities and Exchange Commission. These included Adelphia, American Int'l Group, Avon, Boeing, Bristol-Myers Squibb, Cendant, Ceridian, Citibank, Coca-Cola, Computer Associates, Conesco, Critical Path, Dynergy, Enron, Fannie Mae, Fleming Cos., Freddie Mac, Gateway, GemStar-TV Guide Int'l, General Electric, Global Crossing, Halliburton, Hanover Compressor, HBO, McKesson-Robbins, HealthSouth, Homestore, Household Int'l, Informix, Interpublic, Kimberly-Clark, Kmart, Kodak, Krispy Kreme, Legato Systems, Lernout & Hauspie, Lucent Technologies, Marsh McClennan, MBIA, Merrill Lynch, MGIC, MicroStrategy, Microsoft, Network Associates, Oxford Health Plans, Peregrine Systems, PNC Financial Services, Qwest Communications, Raytheon Corp, Reliant Resources/Energy, Rite-Aid, Royal Dutch Petroleum, Safety Kleen Corp., Shell Transport Co., Silicon Graphics, Spiegel, Sunbeam, Symbol Technologies, Time-Warner, Trump Hotels & Casino Resorts, Tyco, Warnaco Group, Waste Management, and WorldCom. *Id.* at 16. This list, which includes some of the most well-known corporations, illustrates the point that problematic corporate activity, like weeds, can flourish almost anywhere.

There is a consensus that protecting a corporate brand from taint arising out of corruption and scandals is one of the most important issues for corporate management. In the 2003-2004 Major Issues Survey of North American companies by The Human Resource Institute of the American Management Association, "ethics in business" was one of the top three issues (out of 120) in terms of the impact of workforce management.[128] Even more significant was the reason why:

> . . . businesses view ethics as having a big impact on their brands and reputations as well as on customer trust and investor confidence. In other words, business ethics isn't only about "doing the right thing" or even avoiding the kind of scandals that can utterly devastate a company. It's about good business.[129]

This conclusion is corroborated by an international survey in 2002 by the World Bank Institute in which 87 percent of the respondents said that they pay attention to the social behavior of businesses in their countries.[130]

Aside from the impact on customers and investors, perceptions about ethical practices can also have a big impact on employee recruitment and retention. A global survey of senior executives by Booz Allen Hamilton and Aspen Institute in 2004 "found that 61 percent of respondents said that employee recruitment and retention is strongly affected by organizational values and is important to business strategy."[131] With the demand for high-quality value workers forecast to outstrip the supply, the importance of ethics on employee motivation and retention cannot be overstated.

The concern by corporations about how they are perceived by the public and their employees is well founded. As the failures recited by Heineman and others attest, many corporations are not seen as living up to high ethical standards, regardless of what they may say about themselves. In a 2004 World Economic Forum opinion poll of 19,000 respondents from 20 nations, only 7 percent of the respondents said

---

128. THE ETHICAL ENTERPRISE, *supra* note 124, at vi.
129. *Id.*
130. *Id.* at 7.
131. *Id.* at 9.

that they had "a lot" of trust in global companies, and only 35 percent said that they had "some" trust in them.[132] Research on employee attitudes confirms that employees also are skeptical of corporate business ethics. In *The New American Workplace*, James O'Toole and Edward E. Lawlor III cite to research conducted for their book by Jeffrey Pfeffer:

> ". . . over the past couple of decades most organizations in the U.S. have moved systematically to more market-like, distant, and transactional relationships with their people." Executives at many American corporations clearly believe that they have benefited from this choice in terms of greater organizational flexibility, innovation, and competitiveness. But as Pfeffer documents, their choice has also carried some costs for corporations. He cites surveys showing low levels of trust, engagement, and commitment among American workers: fewer than 40 percent say they trust their company to keep its promises, 67 percent say they do not identify with or feel motivated to achieve their company's goals, 50 percent say they feel disconnected from their employers, and 25 percent say they are showing up just to collect a paycheck. Only 30 percent of the companies that participated in the 2005 Society for Human Resource Management benefits survey had communities that provided significant help to employees in need . . . .[133]

The distrust and alienation of employees articulated by Jeffrey Pfeffer is corroborated by a 2003 Conference Board survey of more than 80 ethics, HR, and legal officers, which found that "almost 5 percent of their companies promoted good workers who fell short of the firm's ethical values, 22 percent 'tolerated' those workers, more than a quarter said they coached them, and only 8 percent said they were fired."[134]

---

132. *Id.* at 10.
133. O'TOOLE & LAWLER, *supra* note 41, at 137.
134. THE ETHICAL ENTERPRISE, *supra* note 124, at 7; *see also* GARRY G. MATHIASON ET AL., THE CRITICAL ROLE OF TRUST BETWEEN EMPLOYEES AND EMPLOYERS IN THE DEVELOPMENT OF WORKPLACE LAW 6–8 (2003).

4. World Recession—Impact on Globalization

There is no question that the world economic situation has changed since 2008. As posed by *The Economist*, the question is:

> But is globalization really ending? The world's economies are certainly slowing fast. And the speed and scale of this recession are raising doubts about the assumption that had underpinned the drive to integrate the world markets. At the end of 2008 the IMF [International Monetary Fund] said that the world economy would grow 2.2 percent in 2009, less than half the rate in 2007. Now it thinks growth will be just 0.5 percent this year, the lowest for 60 years. Even that may be optimistic; in the last quarter of 2008, some economies shrank at annualized rates of over 10 percent.[135]

While "economic slowdown is not deglobalization,"[136] and poor countries are still growing faster than rich ones, this economic recession has affected world trade, foreign investment, and jobs—all in ways that vary, depending on the country and its vulnerabilities. Of these effects, the impact on employment lags but is related to decreases in trade and investment:

> The International Labour Organisation forecasts that unemployment worldwide will rise by around 30m above 2007's level in 2009. Most of that will be the result of recession, not deglobalization, but some will be attributable to the fall in trade (exporting companies will lay off workers) and some to declining investment (if expansion plans are cut, new jobs will not be created).
>
> Deglobalization will have a dire impact on migrants. In the past decade, more people have been moving voluntarily than ever before; now some are going home.[137]

---

135. *Turning Their Backs on the World*, ECONOMIST, Feb. 19, 2009, at 59, *available at* http://www.economist.com/world/international/displaystory.cfm?story_id=13145370 (last visited July 26, 2009).

136. *Id.*

137. *Id.* at 60.

Nevertheless, world support for international trade remained strong as recently as 2007 and provides at least a residual base of support for the globalizing power of world trade.[138]

5. Impact of the Forces of Change

While it is still too early to tell what the long-term impact will be of the recession that began in 2008, it is clear that demographic, technological, and globalization forces have introduced dramatic change into the workplace in the United States and in our major organizations. Moreover, these changes will not be undone even with the slowing economies; many of the demographic changes have already occurred, and a decrease in migration patterns will not fundamentally alter them. Likewise, the technological advances that have enabled a global workforce will not be undone. If anything, economic pressures from the recession will drive organizations to further economize by making greater use of part-time and contingent workers and global work teams. These forces of change will undoubtedly continue.

What has changed and may continue to be exacerbated by world recession is organizations' willingness to spend money to support ethics programs, as well as attitudes and perspectives of employees toward their employers. The world recession has had an impact on the ethics programs of major companies, and they have looked to cut costs in all "non-essential" areas, including ethics programs and training. In an article in the *Christian Science Monitor*, Michael Hoffman, the executive director of Bentley University's Center for Business Ethics, was quoted as stating: "In a time where the economy is bad and corporations are struggling to survive, there is more temptation to cut corners and step over the ethical line than there is in other times."[139] Moreover:

> There's some statistical evidence to back this up. Workplace misconduct tends to increase by at least 11 percent during pe-

---

138. *Id.* ("A poll in 2007 by the Pew Global Attitudes Project found that majorities in 47 countries saw international trade as good for them; majorities in 41 of 46 welcomed multinational firms; in 39 out of the 47, most felt better off with a free market. In more than half the countries where changes could be tracked, support for free markets was rising.").

139. G. Jeffrey MacDonald, *Are Ethics too Expensive?*, CHRISTIAN SCIENCE MONITOR, June 14, 2009, at 30.

riods of turmoil, including times of layoffs and budget cuts, according to a 2008 report by the Ethics Resource Center in Arlington, Va.

Also, 46 percent of executives expect fraud levels in their organizations to increase this year, according to a Compliance Week/Deloitte survey of 249 public companies in December. Only 3.6 percent expected it to go down.[140]

Thus, at a time when additional resources are most needed to deal with the dislocations and pressures caused by the recession, virtually all organizations have been compelled to reduce budgets and cut costs in order to survive.

From the employee perspective, the impact is even more dire. "The long-standing assumption of long-term attachment between an employee and a single firm has broken down and a new form of transitory employment relationship has taken its place."[141] In this new employment relationship, employees are at greater risk and have less security in the face of increasing demands by their employers for greater flexibility and creativity.[142] In one of the few worldwide surveys to have been conducted since the onslaught of the recession, "the World Economic Forum found that 62 percent of respondents in 20 countries said they trusted companies less or a lot less now."[143] This will only increase pressure on organizations to find a way to connect a uniform global ethical standard with diverse and dispersed employees (including those who are not even "employees") who are more willing to leave or change jobs than ever before, less connected to or invested in the culture of the organization, and (with good reason) skeptical about whether any ethical principles espoused by management are in fact a meaningful part of the organization's practices. Organizations will also have to anticipate that, whether due to fear of retaliation or just losing a job, employees during a recession are less willing to come forward with concerns over inappropriate conduct. Organizations are not alone

---

140. *Id.*
141. Katherine V. W. Stone, *Procedural Justice in the Boundaryless Workplace: The Tension Between Due Process and Public Policy*, 80 NOTRE DAME L. REV. 501, at 503 (2005).
142. *Id.* at 503–07.
143. *Turning Their Backs on the World, supra* note 135, at 60.

in worrying how to maintain high ethical standards in this environment. Governments also have responded to this situation by enacting laws and regulations to try to make organizations act in lawful and ethical ways.

PART II—LEGAL AND REGULATORY PRESSURES ON ORGANIZATIONS

Analyzing the forces of change—demographics, technology, and globalization—looks at just one aspect of the context in which our large institutions must function. As surely as our organizations are being shaped by these forces, they are also being shaped by pressures from legal and regulatory requirements. The starting point for analysis on these issues, however, is to understand that "[t]here is no international or global legal structure or code that governs multinational corporate behavior, nor is there a global enforcement or judicial system to deal with lawbreakers or decide on guilt or innocence. There are national laws and courts."[144] While the patchwork of national laws is frequently incomplete and inconsistent, there are occasionally situations in which the national laws and courts of one jurisdiction impose requirements that are directly incompatible with those of another jurisdiction.[145]

The same principle applies even when the focus is limited to the United States, because organizations have had requirements imposed on them from a wide variety of sources, including acts of Congress, court decisions, regulation by federal agencies, and legislation or regulation by states and state agencies. While the body of law that most impacts our organizations and their compliance activities comes from federal law, there are important state laws or state law principles dealing with corporate governance, whistle-blowers, and employees that have had a significant impact on organizations. Taken as a whole, this

---

144. GABEL & BRUNER, *supra* note 3, at 136; *see also* Emily Layzer Sherwood, *In the Absence of Governing Law, International Financial Institutions Create Their Own Ethics Programs*, ETHIKOS & CORP. CONDUCT Q., Mar./Apr. 2006, at 12.

145. The requirements of the Sarbanes-Oxley Act of 2002 that publically traded companies have a mechanism for "confidential, anonymous" reporting of accounting and auditing misconduct (Section 301) is an example. There have been difficulties in reconciling this requirement with the requirements of the European Union Data Privacy Directive. *See* Chapter 4 at 406 for a more complete discussion of the EU Data Privacy Directive.

body of American law has been in the vanguard in developing many of the legal structures that have found acceptance in major organizations. Given the size and economic importance of the United States, this body of law has affected virtually every global institution.

From the excesses of the Gilded Age through the Great Depression, to the procurement and stock scandals of more recent times, American legislators and regulators have moved inexorably to impose ever greater and more detailed government regulation on organizations in an attempt to foster greater corporate compliance and accountability. President Theodore Roosevelt's trust-busting crusade and the establishment of the Securities and Exchange Commission in the years after the stock market crash in 1929 are just two of the better-known examples of this movement. Even as the breadth and depth of regulation increased over the next 80 years, it has not prevented corporate scandals and excesses. An investment scandal involving Bernard Madoff, a former chairman of NASDAQ, became public in late 2008 and allegedly involved over $50 billion, which may make it the largest swindle in the history of the United States.[146] Undoubtedly, similar misconduct will be uncovered in connection with the near-collapse of the financial markets in the fall of 2008, and all of this will lead to even more government regulation in an attempt to achieve greater corporate accountability.

Significant efforts, however, have been made over the past quarter century to compel or entice organizations to operate in ethical and lawful ways. Much of the legal environment in which organizations function today is the result of developments in three areas in particular: criminal law, corporate governance, and labor and employment law. As the law has evolved in each of these areas, it has exerted additional pressures on organizations, and consequently, organizations have had to respond accordingly. Structures and practices such as ethics or compliance offices, required ethics training programs, corporate codes of conduct, hotlines, intolerance of discrimination and abusive employment practices, and aggressive investigation of allegations of misconduct are now widely accepted as standard operating procedure. Before turning to the evidence that suggests that even these responses are incomplete and inadequately responsive, we need to review a few

---

146. Stephen Greenspan, *Why We Keep Falling for Financial Scams*, WALL ST. J., Jan. 3–4, 2009, at W1. *See also* Terwilliger, *supra* note 2.

of the most significant developments in criminal law, corporate governance and regulatory requirements, and employment law.

A. Criminal Liability

1. Early Development of Criminal Liability for Organizations

The fate of Arthur Anderson, which was one of the world's largest accounting firms, has generally made people aware that corporations can be prosecuted criminally, but one cannot understand the world in which modern American organizations operate without a somewhat deeper understanding of their exposure to criminal liability for actions taken by their employees. Much of American law today is rooted in English common law made by courts on a case-by-case basis. One example of this influence is the notion from English common law that a principal (such as a company or other institution) may be held liable for the conduct of agents (such as employees or others) acting on its behalf. This doctrine of respondeat superior was developed under English common law to impose *civil* liability on a corporation for the acts of its employees that were intended to benefit the corporation, as long as the employees were acting within the scope of their employment.[147] American courts, however, took this idea one step further and applied it to create corporate *criminal* liability. The seminal 1909 decision by the United States Supreme Court in *New York Central & Hudson Railroad v. United States*[148] clearly established the principle that a corporation could be found guilty of a crime intended to benefit the corporation based on acts of employees acting within the scope of their employment. While this core principle has since been further refined, the basic rule of corporate criminal liability for acts of its employees can be simply stated:

> [A] corporation is liable under federal law for the criminal misdeeds of its agents acting within the actual or apparent scope of their employment or authority if the agents intend,

---

147. HON. JED. S. RAKOFF ET AL., CORPORATE SENTENCING GUIDELINES: COMPLIANCE AND MITIGATION § 1.02[1] n.5, at 1–5 (1996).

148. New York Central & Hudson River R.R. v. United States, 212 U.S. 481 (1909).

at least in part, to benefit the corporation, even though their actions may be contrary to corporate policy or express corporate order.[149]

Despite the expansive scope of potential corporate criminal liability, federal prosecution of corporations remained at fairly minimal levels for most of the twentieth century. Beginning in the 1970s and 1980s, however, corporate scandals (some of which were described in Chapter 1) began to reshape the criminal liability landscape for corporations. With the enactment of the Foreign Corrupt Practices Act (FCPA) in 1977, as a result of disclosures stemming from the Watergate investigation that revealed a history of bribery of foreign officials,[150] corporations began to come under greater scrutiny. The FCPA prohibited bribery of foreign governmental officials and required companies to create and maintain accurate books and financial records as well as to establish internal controls.[151] As a result, some companies began to develop compliance programs and codes of conduct that prohibited bribery.[152] Indeed, the FCPA has continued to remain a potent threat: as of the end of May 2009, at least 120 companies were under investigation by the Department of Justice for possible violations, a 20 percent increase over the previous year.[153] Since December 2008, settlements with the government over bribery allegations have included $800 million with Siemens AG and $579 million with Kellogg Brown

---

149. Report of the Ad Hoc Advisory Group on the Organizational Sentencing Guidelines 8 (Oct. 7, 2003), *available at* http://www.ussc.gov/corp/advgrprprpt/AG_FINAL.pdf (last visited April 28, 2009). *See* Melissa Ku & Lee Pepper, *Corporate Criminal Liability*, 45 AM. CRIM. L. REV. 275 (2008) for a good summary of the evolution and current status of corporate criminal liability.

150. Rebecca Walker, *The Evolution of the Law of Corporate Compliance in the United States: a Brief Overview*, in PLI, Corporate Law and Practice Course Handbook Series, No. B-1661, 19 at 23–24 (2008).

151. *Id*. at 24. *See* Foreign Corrupt Practices Act, Pub. L. No. 95-213, 91 Stat. 1494 (1977) (amended by the Foreign Corrupt Practices Act Amendments of 1988, Pub. L. No. 100-418, 102 Stat. 1415 and the International Anti-Bribery and Fair Competition Act of 1998, Pub. L. No. 105-366, 112 Stat. 3302, §§ 3, 4, and codified at 15 U.S.C. § 78dd). The 1998 amendments to the FCPA greatly expanded its reach over foreign entities.

152. Walker, *supra* note 150, at 24.

153. Dionne Searcey, *U.S. Cracks Down on Corporate Bribes,* WALL ST. J., May 26, 2009, at A1.

& Root LLC and its former parent company, Halliburton Co.[154]

The penalties for a corporate criminal conviction were substantially increased by the enactment of the Criminal Fine Enforcement Act of 1984.[155] The greatly increased fine levels in this and subsequent legislation (including consideration of fines based on the defendant's gain or the victim's loss) coincided with the much-publicized securities fraud and procurement fraud scandals of the 1980s to increase the visibility of corporations as potential criminal targets. The securities fraud scandals led to the passage of the Insider Trading and Securities Fraud Enforcement Act of 1988, which, among other things, requires broker-dealers to establish compliance programs to prevent insider trading.[156] The procurement fraud scandals led to the formation of the Defense Industry Initiative (DII), as described in Chapter 1,[157] and the DII principles, in turn, were the precursor to the Sentencing Guidelines.

2. United States Sentencing Guidelines for Organizations

The Sentencing Guidelines have been described as a "watershed event" in the evolution of corporate compliance programs.[158] Their importance lies not in their application to corporations after conviction but in the way they caused organizations to take action in advance of criminal investigation. Many organizations created compliance programs in the hope that prosecutors would not prosecute the organization itself for a crime if its employees were suspected of committing illegal acts, or, if the organization were criminally charged, it would receive a lower penalty.

The Sentencing Guidelines, both for individual criminal defendants and for organizations, came about as the result of Congress's concern in the 1980s over the disparity in criminal sentencing by federal judges, who previously had wide discretion in imposing sentences. The Sentencing Reform Act, passed by Congress in 1984, created the

---

154. *Id.* at A4.
155. Criminal Fine Enforcement Act of 1984, Pub. L. No. 98-596, 98 Stat. 3134.
156. Insider Trading and Securities Fraud Enforcement Act of 1988, Pub. L. No. 100-704, 102 Stat. 4677 (codified at 15 U.S.C. § 78u).
157. *See* Chapter 1 at 17–20.
158. Walker, *supra* note 150, at 25.

United States Sentencing Commission (USSC, or the Sentencing Commission)[159] and specifically charged it with creating guidelines to make criminal sentencing more uniform among federal judges. The USSC first turned its attention to the manner in which individuals convicted of a crime were sentenced, and subsequently proposed sentencing guidelines for individuals to Congress in 1987. It did not develop sentencing guidelines for organizations[160] until 1991, and these became effective in November 1991.[161]

The approach to criminal sentencing for organizations adopted by the Sentencing Commission and approved by Congress involved what has become known as the "carrot and stick" approach. The guidelines created incentives for responsible corporate behavior, but also provided for a scalable penalty for criminal conduct based on a variety of factors, including the severity of the offense, the organization's previous record, the level at which the misconduct occurred, and whether the organization responded by reporting the misconduct to the government and otherwise taking corrective action:

> The "carrot and stick approach" grew out of the Sentencing Commission's acceptance of three propositions. First and foremost, the Sentencing Commission recognized that the *respondeat superior* principles of liability did not adequately respond to gradations in organizational culpability . . . . Second, the Sentencing Commission came to believe that organizations could "hold out the promise of fewer violations in the first instance and greater detection and remediation of offenses when

---

159. Sentencing Reform Act of 1984, Pub. L. No. 98-473, 98 Stat. 1837 (1984) (codified in scattered sections of 18 U.S.C. and 28 U.S.C.).

160. *See* U.S. Sentencing Comm'n Guidelines Manual § 8A.1.1, App. Note 1 (An "organization" does not include an individual person but does include "among other entities, corporations, partnerships, unions, unincorporated organizations, governments and political subdivisions thereof, and non-profit organizations.") (hereinafter U.S.S.G. Manual).

161. *See* Ilene H. Nagel & Winthrop M. Swenson, *The Federal Sentencing Guidelines for Corporations: Their Development, Theoretical Underpinnings, and Some Thoughts About Their Future*, 71 WASH. U. L.Q. 205 (1993) for a detailed history of the development of the organizational sentencing guidelines. The authors were a member of the U.S. Sentencing Commission and its deputy general counsel. For a general overview of the Sentencing Guidelines, *see* Chapter 4 at 372.

they occur" through the following: internal discipline; reformation of standard operating procedures, auditing standards, and the organizational culture; and the institution of compliance programs. Finally, the Sentencing Commission concluded that it could create incentives for responsible organizational actors to foster crime control by the creation of a mandatory guidelines penalty structure that rewarded responsible organizational behavior by mitigating punishment and sanctioned truly culpable organizations. The Sentencing Commission structured its framework to create a model for the good "corporate" citizen, use[d] the model to make organizational sentencing fair and predictable, and ultimately employ[ed] the model to create incentives for organizations to take steps to deter crime.[162]

The implementation of these principles resulted in a structure that involved assigning organizations a "culpability score" starting at five, but adjusted upwards to 10 or more or downwards to zero, based on various factors. The lower the score, the better; and each score had a corresponding multiplier for a minimum and maximum fine range. This fine-range multiplier was applied to the highest of (1) the statutory penalty for the violation involved, (2) the victim's loss, or (3) the defendant's gain from the criminal conduct, in order to determine the amount of the fine that would be imposed. The highest maximum multiplier (4.0) was more than 80 times greater than the lowest minimum (0.05), so that large organizations with many employees had a great incentive to take steps to try to minimize their culpability score to prepare for the possibility (or even probability) that actions of their employees might someday involve criminal conduct.

One such step (worth a deduction of three points from the culpability score) was for organizations to create an "effective program to prevent and detect violations of law" prior to any criminal conduct. In the Commentary to the Sentencing Guidelines, the Sentencing Com-

---

162. Report of the Ad Hoc Advisory Group on the Organizational Sentencing Guidelines, *supra* note 149, at 14–15 (quoting Winthrop M. Swenson, *The Organizational Guidelines' "Carrot and Stick" Philosophy, and Their Focus on "Effective" Compliance*, *reprinted in* U.S. SENTENCING COMM'N, MATERIALS FOR PROGRAM ON CORPORATE CRIME IN AMERICA: STRENGTHENING THE "GOOD CITIZEN" CORPORATION 1 (Sept. 7, 1995)).

mission delineated seven steps that would be considered part of any such effective program even though compliance with those steps had not prevented the criminal conduct at issue. Indeed, much of what has since come to define corporate compliance programs stems from efforts to develop "effective programs to prevent and detect violations of law" to earn the three-point reduction in a potential culpability score.

3. Development of Ethics and Compliance Programs

The existence and function of many ethics or compliance programs are a direct result of the promulgation of the organizational Sentencing Guidelines. In an article chronicling the impact of the first 10 years of the organizational Sentencing Guidelines,[163] Jeffrey M. Kaplan noted that that the Ethics Officer Association (EOA), a trade association, was formed in 1992 with only 12 members. "Its growth over the coming years is often seen as a measure of the business community's embrace of the Guidelines' proactive approach to corporate compliance."[164] By 2001, the EOA had 760 members, and a similar trade association for health-care compliance officers, the Health Care Compliance Association, had more than 2,700 members.[165]

4. 2004 Revisions to the Organizational Sentencing Guidelines

As influential as the 1991 Sentencing Guidelines were, by 2001 there was a perception that even more might be done to increase their effectiveness. In 2002, the Sentencing Commission appointed an advisory group to review the effectiveness of the Sentencing Guidelines and to make recommendations to the Sentencing Commission for any proposed revisions. The Ad Hoc Advisory Group undertook its study over the next 18 months, just as the corporate scandals involving Enron, Worldcom, Tyco International, and Adelphia Communications were unfolding, and just after Congress had enacted the Sarbanes-Oxley

---

163. Jeffrey M. Kaplan, *The Sentencing Guidelines: The First Ten Years*, ETHIKOS & CORP. CONDUCT Q., Nov./Dec. 2001, at 1.
164. *Id.* at 2.
165. *Id.* at 10. For additional background on the reasons for and development of compliance programs, see CORPORATE LEGAL COMPLIANCE HANDBOOK, 2D ED., Chapter 1, General Principles Behind a Compliance Program, at 1-1 *et seq.*, Frederick Z. Banks & Theodore L. Banks eds. (Aspen Publishers, 2007), 2008 Supp.

Act of 2002 (SOX). The final report of the Ad Hoc Advisory Group was sent to the Sentencing Commission in October 2003 and included recommendations for revisions to the Sentencing Guidelines that were largely accepted by the Sentencing Commission in May 2004 and forwarded to Congress. They became effective in November 2004.[166]

The Sentencing Guidelines, as amended in 2004, not only incorporated the seven steps from the Commentary into the Sentencing Guidelines (which had the force of law), they were substantially revised to describe the essential components necessary to meet a new standard labeled an "effective compliance and ethics program."[167] While the overall structure of the Sentencing Guidelines for culpability scores and minimum and maximum multipliers remained the same, the revised guidelines specifically required organizations to exercise due diligence to prevent and detect criminal conduct as well as to promote "an organizational culture that encourages ethical conduct and a commitment to compliance with the law"[168] to be eligible for a three-point deduction in the culpability score. Among the significant changes was a provision that compliance activities be adjusted based on a risk assessment of the organization, an issue not addressed specifically in the 1991 Sentencing Guidelines, and another that imposed specific compliance responsibilities on an organization's board of directors and high-level management.

In January 2005, shortly after the revised Sentencing Guidelines had become effective, the U.S. Supreme Court issued a decision in companion cases challenging the constitutionality of the Sentencing Guidelines that that had been briefed and argued on an expedited basis in light of its significant potential impact. In *United States v. Booker*,[169] the Court held, by different 5-4 majorities (with Justice Breyer as the swing vote), that although the Sentencing Guidelines were an unconstitutional violation of the Sixth Amendment (because they permitted a judge to consider facts in sentencing that had not been submitted to a jury), the appropriate remedy was to make them advisory rather than to invalidate them entirely. Despite the importance of the *Booker* decision on constitutional scholarship, it has not substantially

---

166. U.S.S.G. Manual, *supra* note 160, at § 8B.2.1.
167. *Id.*
168. *Id.* §§ 8B2.1(a), (b).
169. United States v. Booker, 543 U.S. 220 (2005).

changed the impact of the Sentencing Guidelines on organizations, because federal judges are still required to consider them.[170]

5. Criminal Liability Provisions of the Sarbanes-Oxley Act of 2002

The Sarbanes-Oxley Act of 2002 (SOX),[171] enacted just as the Ad Hoc Advisory Committee was beginning its review of the 1991 Sentencing Guidelines, not only created regulatory requirements for companies issuing publically traded stock listed on stock exchanges, it also created criminal penalties that reinforce the need for these companies to have effective compliance programs. One provision requires a company's chief executive officer and chief financial officer to certify that financial reports filed with the Securities and Exchange Commission (SEC) fully comply with "the requirements of section 13(a) or 15(d) of the Securities Exchange Act . . . and that the information contained in the periodic report fairly presents, in all material respects, the financial condition and results of operations of the [company]."[172] Executives who make such certifications knowing that the statements do not meet the statutory requirements are subject to up to 10 years' imprisonment, or 20 years' imprisonment if they acted willfully.[173] In addition, Section 1107 of the act provided that anyone who knowingly, and with the intent to retaliate, takes "any action harmful to any person, including interference with the lawful employment or livelihood of any person, for providing to a law enforcement officer any truthful information relating to the commission or possible commission" of a federal crime was also subject to a fine and up to 10 years' imprisonment.[174] The provisions of Section 1107 apply more broadly than just to publically traded companies; they apply to contractors, subcontractors, and agents of those companies.[175] Moreover, this section applies to more than just financial issues; it makes it a crime to retaliate against employees who report violations of *any* federal stat-

---

170. Walker, *supra* note 150, at 31 n.41.
171. Pub. L. No. 107-204, 116 Stat. 745 (2002).
172. *Id.* § 302.
173. 18 U.S.C. § 1350(c) (2006).
174. 18 U.S.C. § 1513(e) (2006).
175. Marcia P. Miceli, Janet P. Near & Terry Morehead Dworkin, Whistle-blowing in Organizations 159 (2008).

ute to law enforcement officials.[176]

6. Prosecution Guidelines

Organizations were provided with additional incentives to adopt effective compliance programs through a series of memoranda issued by Deputy Attorneys General of the United States that gave direction to federal prosecutors on when and how they should prosecute organizations. The first of these memoranda, "Bringing Criminal Charges Against Corporations," was issued in June 1999 by then Deputy Attorney General Eric Holder and became known as the Holder Memo.[177] In 2003, it was revised and reissued as "Principles of Federal Prosecution of Business Organizations" by then Deputy Attorney General Larry D. Thompson[178] (the Thompson Memo), which in turn was again revised and reissued in 2006 by the then Deputy Attorney General Paul J. McNulty (the McNulty Memo).[179] And finally, even the McNulty Memo was replaced in August 2008 with a new articulation of the "Principles of Federal Prosecution of Business Organizations."[180] These memoranda were premised on the government's position that organizations can be prosecuted for the criminal acts of their officers, directors, and other agents. As most recently stated in the McNulty Memo, prosecutors are instructed to consider a variety of factors in determining whether an organization will be criminally charged for miscon-

---

176. *Id.* at 160.

177. Memorandum from the Deputy Attorney General on Bringing Criminal Charges Against Corporations (June 16, 1999), *available at* http://www.usdoj.gov/criminal/fraud/docs/reports/1999/chargingcorps.html (last visited Mar. 18, 2009).

178. Memorandum from Larry D. Thompson, Deputy Attorney General, on Principles of Federal Prosecution of Business Organizations (Jan. 20, 2003), *available at* http://www.usdoj.gov/dag/cftf/business_organizations.pdf (last visited Apr. 28, 2009).

179. Memorandum from Paul J. McNulty, Deputy Attorney General, on Principles of Federal Prosecution of Business Organizations (Dec. 2006), *available at* http://www.usdoj.gov/dag/speeches/2006/mcnulty_memo.pdf (last visited Apr. 29, 2009).

180. Principles of Federal Prosecution of Business Organizations, Title 9, Chapter 9-28.00, *available at* http://searchjustice.usdoj.gov/search?q=cache:aJ5x-AEJohwJ:www.usdoj.gov/opa/documents/corp-charging-guidelines.pdf+Principles+of+Federal+Prosecution+of+Business+Organizations&site=default_collection&client=default_frontend&access=p&ie=iso-8859-1&output=xml_no_dtd&proxystylesheet=default_frontend&oe=UTF-8.

duct. Because prosecutors in the United States have discretion whether to charge organizations for misconduct committed by their agents, the factors that prosecutors are directed to consider in making these decisions are thus extremely important. Among these factors are "the adequacy of the corporation's pre-existing compliance program" and "the corporation's remedial actions, including efforts to implement an effective corporate compliance program or to improve an existing one . . . ."[181] The McNulty Memo also provides guidance on how these assessments should be made.

The potential for criminal prosecution, even for organizations, is a powerful motivating force. The development of guiding principles for criminal prosecution of organizations, however, has not been the only source of pressure on organizations; similar developments have occurred in the world of government regulation.

B. Corporate Governance and Government Regulation

1. *In re Caremark*

As noted at the beginning of this chapter, corporations and other organizations are subject to law and regulation from a variety of sources, and there is often interplay between state and federal law. A prominent example of this interaction is the opinion rendered by a chancery court in Delaware in 1996, *In re Caremark Int'l Inc. Derivative Litigation*.[182] In *Caremark*, shareholders brought suit against the directors of the company to recover approximately $250 million that the company was compelled to pay in fines and reimbursements after pleading guilty to a felony charge for making illegal payments to doctors. When the parties in the suit reached a settlement and submitted it to the court for approval, the chancellor (court) approved the settlement but in dicta (statements made by the court but that are not, strictly speaking, necessary for the decision of the case) commented on the obligations of company directors and made specific reference to the 1991 Sentencing Guidelines. In this decision, which has been cited widely as articulating a standard for corporate directors' liability, the chancellor observed that a director's obligation:

includes a duty to attempt in good faith to assure that a corpo-

181. *Id.* at 4.
182. *In re* Caremark Int'l Inc. Derivative Litig., 698 A.2d 959 (Del. Ch. 1996).

rate information and reporting system, which the board concludes is adequate, exists, and that the failure to do so under some circumstances may, in theory at least, render a director liable for losses caused by non-compliance with the applicable legal standards.[183]

The standard expressed by the chancery court in *Caremark* was subsequently approved by the Delaware Supreme Court in another shareholder derivative suit in 2006. In *Stone v. Ritter*,[184] shareholders appealed the lower court's dismissal of their complaint, which conceded that the company's directors neither knew nor should have known that violations of law were occurring, but alleged that the directors "utterly failed to implement any sort of statutorily required monitoring, reporting or information controls that would have enabled them to learn of problems requiring their attention."[185] Although the court in *Stone v. Ritter* affirmed the dismissal of the complaint, it nevertheless stated:

> We hold that *Caremark* articulates the necessary conditions predicate for director oversight liability: (a) the directors utterly failed to implement any reporting or information system or controls; *or* (b) having implemented such a system or controls, consciously failed to monitor or oversee its operations thus disabling themselves from being informed of risks or problems requiring their attention. In either case, imposition of liability requires showing that the directors knew that they were not discharging their fiduciary obligations.[186]

Since so many large and multinational corporations are incorporated under the laws of Delaware, and Delaware is widely seen as a leading state on law governing corporations, these cases have significantly reinforced the notion that companies have a duty to maintain an effective compliance program.

2. Federal Agency Reporting Incentives

183. *Id.* at 970.
184. 911 A.2d 362 (2006).
185. *Id.* at 364.
186. *Id.* at 370; *see* Jeffrey M. Kaplan, *Stone v. Ritter: Implications for Directors and Compliance Programs*, ETHIKOS AND CORP. CONDUCT Q. 1, January/February 2007.

The Sentencing Guidelines also influenced the creation of compliance and reporting incentives by various federal agencies. The report of the Ad Hoc Advisory Group on the Organizational Sentencing Guidelines cited to regulations adopted by the Environmental Protection Agency, the Department of Health and Human Services, and the State Department that closely tracked the seven elements of an effective compliance program that had been articulated in the 1991 Sentencing Guidelines.[187]

In a more recent development, the Civilian Agency Acquisition and Defense Acquisition Regulation Councils adopted rules that became effective at the end of 2007 that impose compliance program requirements on federal government contractors receiving awards in excess of $5 million.[188] These contractors must establish an "ongoing" business ethics and conduct program as well as an internal control system (including internal reporting mechanisms, such as a hotline) within 90 days of the award.[189]

3. USA Patriot Act

While the decisions in cases such as *Caremark* and *Stone v. Ritter*, along with the various regulatory schemes, created incentives for organizations to establish compliance programs, other federal legislation and regulatory developments were more direct: they required certain classes of organizations to take action. The requirements of the Insider Trading and Securities Fraud Enforcement Act of 1988 were augmented in 2001 by the passage of the Uniting and Strengthening America by Providing Appropriate Tools Required to Intercept and

---

187. Report of the Ad Hoc Advisory Group on the Organizational Sentencing Guidelines, *supra* note 149, at 33–34. The Department of Health and Human Services' Office of Inspector General has issued voluntary disclosure guidance documents *available at* http://oig.hhs.gov/fraud/complianceguidance.asp (last visited March 15, 2009). *See also, e.g.,* the "Incentives for Self-Policing: Discovery, Disclosure, Correction and Preventions of Violations" promulgated by the U.S. Environmental Protection Agency, 65 Fed. Reg. No. 70 at 19,618 (April 11, 2000), *available at* http://www.epa.gov/compliance/resources/policies/incentives/auditing/auditpolicy51100.pdf (last visited March 20, 2009); and Department of Defense Voluntary Disclosure Program, IGDPH 5505.50, as revised Feb. 7, 1996.

188. FAR 52-203-23, 72 Fed. Reg. 65,868 (Nov. 23, 2007).

189. *See* Walker, *supra* note 150, at 21–22.

Obstruct Terrorism Act (the USA PATRIOT Act) following the September 11, 2001, attack on the United States.[190] The USA PATRIOT Act requires financial institutions (which were broadly defined) to establish compliance programs to ensure adherence with federal anti-money-laundering laws. Not only did the act impose very specific requirements (such as the establishment of internal policies, procedures, and controls; the designation of a responsible compliance officer; mandatory employee training; and independent auditing requirements), the implementing regulations issued by the Treasury Department are even more detailed.[191]

4. Sarbanes-Oxley Act of 2002

The Sarbanes-Oxley Act of 2002 (SOX) contains several provisions, in addition to the sections dealing with criminal liability described above, that reinforce the need for compliance programs. One such provision, Section 406, requires issuers of securities to disclose whether they have adopted a code of ethics for their senior management, and if not, to explain why not. Another provision, Section 806, created a civil cause of action to protect whistle-blowers from retaliation. And finally, Section 301 of SOX requires the national securities exchanges and associations to prohibit the listing of securities for companies whose audit committees did not establish certain procedures relating to audits and the handling of complaints concerning accounting or auditing matters. One of the specific areas that Section 301 requires audit committees to address was the establishment of procedures for "the confidential, anonymous submission by employees . . . of concerns regarding questionable accounting or auditing matters."[192]

5. SEC and Stock Exchange and Association Requirements

Oversight for the implementation of most of these SOX provisions is vested in the SEC, which subsequently issued rules for the national securities exchanges and associations.[193] In November 2003, the SEC

---

190. Pub. L. No. 107-56 § 352(a) (2001).
191. 31 U.S.C. § 5318(h)(1) (2003); *see* Walker, *supra* note 150, at 40.
192. Pub. L. No. 107-204, § 301, 116 Stat. 745, 789 (codified as amended at 15 U.S.C.S. § 78j-1 (2002)).

approved corporate governance rules that had been proposed by the New York Stock Exchange (NYSE) and NASDAQ to comply with SOX and the SEC rules.[194] The rules adopted by the NYSE require listed companies to "adopt and disclose corporate governance guidelines" and to "adopt and disclose a code of business conduct and ethics for directors, officers and employees, and promptly disclose any waivers of the code for directors and executive officers."[195] The NASDAQ rules[196] require that NASDAQ-listed companies have codes of ethics meeting the requirements of SOX Section 406(c) and the implementing SEC regulations, and that such codes "contain an enforcement mechanism, protection for reporting persons, clear and objective standards for compliance, and a fair process to determine violations. . . ."[197]

For a brief period, from late 2003 until early 2005, at least nine consent orders were issued by the SEC to financial firms that included a provision for an ombudsman.[198] While this requirement was apparently discontinued, it revealed that the SEC recognized that some additional mechanisms were appropriate to help people come forward with issues of concern.

6. Best Practices Recommended by Business Groups

---

193. Listing Standards Relating to Audit Committees, Rule10A-3, SEC Release No. 34-47654 (April 1, 2003).
194. NASD and NYSE Rulemaking: Relating to Corporate Governance, SEC Release No. 34-48745 (Nov. 4, 2003).
195. NYSE Listed Company Manual, §§ 303A.9, 303A.10 (2005); *see also* American Stock Exchange Company Guide, § 807 (2008).
196. Nasdaq Rule 5610.
197. Walker, *supra* note 150, at 42.
198. The language used in most of the orders appears to have misconstrued the role of an organizational ombuds. The orders required the companies to "establish a corporate ombudsman to whom [Company] employees may convey concerns about [Company] business matters that they believe implicate matters of ethics or questionable practices. [Company] shall establish procedures to investigate matters brought to the attention of the ombudsman. . . . [Company] shall also review matters to the extent relating to fund business brought to the attention of the ombudsman." *E.g.*, Consent Order issued to Banc of America Capital Management, Feb. 9, 2005 at 27, *available at* http://www.sec.gov/litigation/admin/33-8538.htm (last visited March 18, 2009).

The principles underlying these requirements for compliance programs and corporate governance have been broadly endorsed by the business associations. One of the recommendations contained in a report titled *Principles of Corporate Governance*, issued in May 2002 by The Business Roundtable, was that:

> [a] corporation should have a code of conduct with effective reporting and enforcement mechanisms. Employees should have a means of alerting management and the board to potential misconduct without fear of retribution, and violations of the code should be addressed promptly and effectively.[199]

The Conference Board Commission on Public Trust and Private Enterprise issued similar recommendations as "best practices" in a report the following year:

> Among the practices that boards should consider for establishing an ethical corporate culture are:
>
> 2. Tools and processes
>   a. Programs to ensure that employees understand, apply and adhere to the company's code of ethics;
>   b. Processes that encourage and make it safe for employees to raise ethical issues and report possible ethical violations;
>   c. Processes for prompt investigation of complaints and prompt disposition, including discipline and corrective action, if necessary; and
>   d. Processes to measure and track employees' adherence to the company's ethical requirements and to assess the ethical performance of the company as a whole.[200]

These recommendations are not just limited to the United States. The Organisation for Economic Co-operation and Development (OCED), an international organization of 30 member countries (including the United States) committed to the development of democracy and the

---

199. BUSINESS ROUNDTABLE, PRINCIPLES OF CORPORATE GOVERNANCE 10 (2002).
200. CONFERENCE BD. COMM'N ON PUB. TRUST AND PRIVATE ENTER., FINDINGS AND RECOMMENDATIONS 32 (2003).

market economy around the world, also recognized this need when it published its *OECD Principles of Corporate Governance* in 2004.[201] Principle IV E provides that "[s]takeholders, including individual employees and their representative bodies, should be able to freely communicate their concerns about illegal or unethical practices to the board and their rights should not be compromised for doing this."[202]

Thus, the effect of these developments in corporate governance and government regulation strike a note similar to what has occurred in criminal law: organizations must have or create effective programs to help them comply with the law. As a result, not only does the law require organizations to have such programs, many of their own policies do so as well.

C. Employment Law

A discussion of the pressures on organizations to comply with legal obligations would not be complete without a review of the develop-

---

201. ORG. FOR ECON. COOPERATION AND DEV., OECD PRINCIPLES OF CORPORATE GOVERNANCE 17 (2001), *available at* http://www.oecd.org/document/49/0,3343,en_2649_34813_31530865_1_1_1_37439,00.html (last visited April 15, 2009).

202. *Id.* at 21. The Annotations to the *OECD Principles of Corporate Governance* elaborate on this principle: "Unethical and illegal practices by corporate officers may not only violate the rights of stakeholders but also be to the detriment of the company and its shareholders in terms of reputation effects and an increasing risk of future financial liabilities. It is therefore to the advantage of the company and its shareholders to establish procedures and safe-harbours for complaints by employees, either personally or through their representative bodies, and others outside the company, concerning illegal and unethical behavior. In many countries the board is encouraged by laws and or principles to protect these individuals and representative bodies and to give them confidential direct access to someone independent of the board, often a member of an audit or an ethics committee. Some companies have established an ombudsman to deal with complaints. Several regulators have also established confidential phone and e-mail facilities to receive allegations. While in certain countries representative employee bodies undertake the tasks of conveying concerns to the company, individual employees should not be precluded from, or be less protected when, acting alone. When there is an inadequate response to a complaint regarding contravention of the law, the *OECD Guidelines for Multinational Enterprises* encourage them to report their *bona fide* complaint to the competent public authorities. The company should refrain from discriminatory or disciplinary actions against such employees or bodies." *Id.* at 47–48.

ments in employment law, since many of the same principles have had parallel development in the employment law arena. In particular, the U.S. Supreme Court has issued several opinions in harassment, discrimination, and retaliation cases that employ similar agency principles and give employers protection if employees fail to follow compliance programs. In addition, almost all large employers now have training programs on compliance with employment laws,[203] and whistle-blower protection laws have proliferated at both the state and federal levels.

1. Title VII Cases

In 1986, the U.S. Supreme Court decided *Meritor Savings Bank v. Vinson*,[204] a landmark "hostile environment" sexual harassment case brought under Title VII of the Civil Rights Act of 1964, which makes it "an unlawful employment practice for an employer . . . to discriminate against any individual with respect to his compensation, terms, conditions, or privileges of employment, because of such individual's race, color, religion, sex, or national origin."[205] The Court held that such a case could be brought under Title VII, but stated that it would look to general principles of agency law in determining when employers would be liable for sexual harassment actions by supervisors.

The Supreme Court also relied on agency principles in subsequently deciding two cases, *Burlington Industries, Inc. v. Ellerth*[206] and *Faragher v. City of Boca Raton*,[207] whose opinions were released on the same day in 1998. In these cases, the Court refused to draw a distinction between the quid pro quo type of discrimination and hostile environment discrimination, relying instead on agency law principles to hold that an employer could be held vicariously liable "to a victimized employee for an actionable hostile environment created by a supervisor with immediate (or successively higher) authority over the employee."[208] The Court also created an affirmative defense that the employer could use, but only if the supervisor's harassment did

---

203. These programs are mandated by some states, including Connecticut, Maine, and California.
204. Meritor Sav. Bank, FSB v. Vinson, 477 U.S. 57, 72 (1986).
205. 42 U.S.C. § 2000e-2(a)(1) (2006).
206. Burlington Indus., Inc. v. Ellerth, 524 U.S. 742, 765 (1998).
207. Faragher v. City of Boca Raton, 524 U.S. 775, 792 (1998).
208. *Ellerth, supra* note 206, 524 U.S. at 765.

not result in any tangible employment action against the employee.

> The defense comprises two necessary elements: (a) that the employer exercised reasonable care to prevent and correct promptly any sexually harassing behavior, and (b) that the plaintiff employee unreasonably failed to take advantage of any preventive or corrective opportunities provided by the employer to avoid harm otherwise. While proof that an employer had promulgated an anti-harassment policy with complaint procedure is not necessary in every instance as a matter of law, the need for a stated policy suitable to the employment circumstances may appropriately be addressed in any case when litigating the first element of the defense. And while proof that an employee failed to fulfill the corresponding obligation of reasonable care to avoid harm is not limited to showing any unreasonable failure to use any complaint procedure provided by the employer, a demonstration of such failure will normally suffice to satisfy the employer's burden under the second element of the defense.[209]

If organizations did not previously have anti-harassment policies and complaint mechanisms, these opinions were a great incentive to create them. The Court's decisions in *Faragher* and *Ellerth* thus had "the unusual effect of eliciting praise from all sides."[210] Employers were pleased that they could create effective sexual harassment compliance policies that should shield them from liability, and employee advocates praised the imposition of vicarious liability on employers and the fact that employers had the burden of proof on the affirmative defense that was created.[211]

The Supreme Court decided another Title VII employment discrimination case the following year in which it observed that the agency principles articulated and relied on in its earlier decisions conflicted with the goal under Title VII for employers to implement antidiscrimination programs. In *Kolstad v. American Dental Association*,[212] the

---

209. *Id.*
210. Martha F. Davis, *Court Clarifies Sexual Harassment Tests*, NAT'L L. J., Aug. 10, 1998, at B10.
211. *Id.*

Court resolved that conflict in favor of providing an incentive for employers to develop effective employment compliance programs. The Court held that "in the punitive damages context, an employer may not be vicariously liable for the discriminatory employment decisions of managerial agents where these decisions are contrary to the employer's good-faith efforts to comply with Title VII."[213] (Internal quotations omitted.) Thus, the clear effect of the *Faragher*, *Ellerth*, and *Kostad* line of cases is to reinforce the need of employers to have effective compliance antidiscrimination and harassment policies and procedures.[214]

In subsequent decisions, the Supreme Court ruled in favor of allowing retaliation claims to be brought by employees. One of the most significant of these cases was *Burlington Northern & Santa Fe Railway Co. v. White*,[215] a case decided in 2006 in which the Court broadly construed the anti-retaliation provision of Title VII[216] to include any action—not limited to compensation, terms, conditions, or privileges of employment—that "might well have dissuaded a reasonable worker from making or supporting a charge of discrimination."[217] Statistics collected by the Equal Employment Opportunity Commission reflect an almost 20 percent spike in allegations of retaliatory discrimination in the year following the *Burlington Northern* decision.[218] And during

---

212. Kolstad v. Am. Dental Ass'n, 527 U.S. 526, 545 (1999).
213. *Id.*
214. *See* Rebecca S. Walker, *What We Can Learn About Effective Compliance Policies From Recent Employment Discrimination Cases*, ETHIKOS & CORP. CONDUCT Q., June-July 2000, at 4.
215. Burlington Northern & Santa Fe Ry. Co. v. White, 548 U.S. 53, 68 (2006).
216. Pub. L. No. 88-352, § 704(a)(1964) (current version at 42 U.S.C. § 2000e-3(a)(2009)), which provides: "It shall be an unlawful employment practice for an employer to discriminate against any of his employees or applicants for employment . . . because he has opposed any practice made an unlawful employment practice by this [subchapter], or because he has made a charge, testified, assisted, or participated in any manner in an investigation, proceeding, or hearing under this [chapter]."
217. *Burlington Northern*, *supra* note 215, 548 U.S. at 68; *see also* Crawford v. Metro. Gov't of Nashville and Davidson County, 129 S. Ct. 846, 853 (2009) (Alito, J., concurring) (citing statistics from the U.S. Equal Opportunity Employment Commission and noting that retaliation charges filed with the EEOC doubled between 1997 and 2007).

the Court's 2007-2008 term, two more decisions were rendered that favored employees' bringing retaliation suits. In *Gomez-Perez v. Potter*,[219] the Court ruled that federal employees could assert a claim of retaliation under the Age Discrimination in Employment Act.[220] In *CBOCS West v. Humphries*,[221] the Court held that a claim of retaliation, as well as claims of race discrimination, could be brought under Section 1981 of the Civil Rights Act of 1866.[222]

Another case decided by the Supreme Court in the 2008-2009 term with important implications is *Crawford v. Metropolitan Government of Nashville and Davidson Cty.*,[223] which involved a claim of retaliation for cooperation with an employer investigation of another employee's harassment claim. In a unanimous ruling, the Supreme Court held that the protection under the "opposition" clause of Title VII's anti-retaliation provision, 42 U.S.C. § 2000e-3(a)(1), "extends to an employee who speaks out about discrimination not on her own initiative, but in answering questions during an employer's internal investigation."[224] Justice Souter, writing the Court's majority opinion, noted that *Ellerth-Faragher* rulings created a "strong inducement" to employers to "ferret out and put a stop to any discriminatory activity in their operations as a way to break the circuit of imputed liability."[225] Thus, it concluded that its holding in *Crawford* was necessary to support the *Ellerth-Faragher* enforcement scheme.

> If it were clear law that an employee who reported discrimination in answering an employer's questions could be penalized with no remedy, prudent employees would have a good reason to keep quiet about Title VII offenses against themselves or against others. This is no imaginary horrible given the documented indications that "[f]ear of retaliation is the

---

218. Marcia Coyle, *Court Looks at Scope of a Title VII Shield*, NAT'L L. J., Oct. 6, 2008, at 1.
219. Gomez-Perez v. Potter, 128 S. Ct. 1931, 1935 (2008).
220. Age Discrimination in Employment Act of 1967 (ADEA), 88 Stat. 74 (codified as amended, 29 U.S.C. § 633a(a) (2009)).
221. CBOCS West, Inc. v. Humphries, 128 S. Ct. 1951, 1954 (2008).
222. *Id.*
223. *Crawford, supra* note 217, 129 S. Ct. at 849.
224. *Id.*
225. *Id.* at 852.

leading reason why people stay silent instead of voicing their concerns about bias and discrimination." Brake, Retaliation, 90 *Minn. L. Rev.* 18, 20 (2005); *see also id.* at 37 and n. 58 (compiling studies).[226]

The Supreme Court, however, has not uniformly rendered decisions favorable to retaliation claims. In *Garcetti v. Ceballos*,[227] the plaintiff's claim was that as a public employee (a prosecutor) he spoke out to his supervisors about what he thought were serious misrepresentations in another prosecutor's affidavit and that he subsequently suffered retaliation in violation of his free speech rights under the First Amendment to the Constitution. In a 5-4 decision that applies to an estimated 20 million public employees, the court stated that the First Amendment does not protect "every statement a public employee makes in the course of doing his or her job."[228] Rather, the court held that "when public employees make statements pursuant to their official duties, the employees are not speaking as citizens for First Amendment purposes, and the Constitution does not insulate their communication from employer discipline."[229] The minority opinion of Justice Souter criticized the majority for striking the wrong balance among the competing interests and, in particular, noted vagaries of protection from the "patchwork" of whistle-blower laws.[230]

2. Title IX Cases

The Supreme Court has made it harder for a plaintiff to prevail on a discrimination claim for the acts of teachers in school systems under Title IX than under Title VII. Title IX of the Education Amendments of 1972 provides in relevant part that a person cannot "be subjected to discrimination under any education program or activity receiving Federal financial assistance."[231] In *Gebster v. Lago Vista Independent School District*,[232] the plaintiffs were a high school girl and her parents who brought suit against their school district alleging that it was

---

226. *Id.*
227. Garcetti v. Ceballos, 547 U.S. 410, 413–15 (2006).
228. *Id.* at 426.
229. *Id.* at 421.
230. *Id.* at 427–45, *e.g.*, 439–42.
231. 20 U.S.C. § 1681(a) (2007).
232. Gebser v. Lago Vista Indep. Sch. Dist., 524 U.S. 274, 278–79 (1998).

responsible for sexual harassment of the student by one of her teachers. In part because the basis for a lawsuit under Title IX was created by the courts rather than contained in the legislation, and because of the differing language and structure of Title IX and Title VII, the Court did not find the school system responsible. Although the Court articulated a more restrictive standard for Title IX actions than in the Title VII context, school systems were not entirely removed from potential liability: "We conclude that damages may not be recovered [for the sexual harassment of a student by one of her teachers] unless an official of the school district who at a minimum has authority to institute corrective measures on the district's behalf has actual notice of, and is deliberately indifferent to, the teacher's misconduct."[233]

In 2005, however, the Supreme Court permitted a plaintiff to bring a lawsuit for retaliation under Title IX even though the statute did not contain an express provision barring retaliation. In *Jackson v. Birmingham Board of Education*,[234] the Court in a 5-4 decision held that a male coach of a girls' basketball team whose employment was terminated because of complaints that the girls' team was underfunded had an implied cause of action for retaliation. The Court expressly found that even though such a remedy was not contained in the statute, it was necessary to encourage enforcement of Title IX:

> If recipients [of federal funds] were permitted to retaliate freely, individuals who witness discrimination would be loathe to report it, and all manner of Title IX violations might go unremedied as a result. Reporting incidents of discrimination is integral to Title IX enforcement and would be discouraged if retaliation against those who report went unpunished. Indeed, if retaliation were not prohibited, Title IX's enforcement scheme would unravel.[235]

Moreover, the remedy afforded by Title IX is not the only potential basis for liability. In January 2009, the Supreme Court ruled that Title IX does not preclude a civil rights claim also being brought under 42 U.S.C. § 1983 for gender discrimination in schools.[236]

---

233. *Id.* at 277.
234. Jackson v. Birmingham Bd. of Educ., 544 U.S. 167, 171 (2005).
235. *Id.* at 180 (citation omitted).
236. Fitzgerald v. Barnstable School Comm., 129 S. Ct. 788, 792 (2009).

3. Mandatory Discrimination and Harassment Training Programs

In addition to the development of case law, two other developments in employment law are also important. The first is the emerging requirement that employers have mandatory discrimination and harassment training programs. California, Connecticut, and Maine already mandate such programs for certain employers, and such programs have become standard procedure in most large organizations. These programs serve the same purpose in the employment context as other types of ethics and compliance training that companies have been encouraged or required to conduct under the Sentencing Guidelines.

4. Spread of Whistle-blower Laws

The second noteworthy trend has been the proliferation of whistle-blower statutes. Aside from the whistle-blower protections in SOX (Sections 806 and 1107) discussed above, there are literally hundreds of whistle-blower statutes in federal and state law.[237]

At the federal level, one of the earliest and most prominent and successful statutes is the False Claims Act (FCA), which dates back to the Civil War era.[238] The FCA represents one model of whistle-blower statutes in that it creates a financial incentive for the whistle-blower to report misconduct. Most of the federal statutes, however, do not create such a financial incentive to report misconduct, but rather represent attempts to protect whistle-blowers in specific areas (such as specific environmental protection statutes) or specific types of reporting.[239] For example, in 1978 Congress passed the Civil Service Reform Act of 1978 (CSRA), which contained a general whistle-blower protection

---

237. C. FRED ALFORD, WHISTLEBLOWERS: BROKEN LIVES AND ORGANIZATIONAL POWER (Cornell Univ. Pr., 2001); *see also* Elletta Sangrey Callahan & Terry Morehead Dworkin, *The State of Whistleblower Protection*, 38 AM. BUS. L. J. 99, 100 (2000); DANIEL P. WESTMAN & NANCY M. MODESITT, WHISTLEBLOWING: THE LAW OF RETALIATORY DISCHARGE 10–12 (Bureau of Nat'l Affairs, Inc., 2d ed., 2005).

238. 31 U.S.C. § 3729 (2007).

239. *See* ALFORD, *supra* note 237, at 107–08; David Culp, *Whistleblowers: Corporate Anarchists or Heros? Toward a Judicial Perspective*, 13 HOFSTRA LAB. L. J. 109, 120–21 (1995).

provision designed to prevent "retaliation for 'disclosure of information which the employee reasonably believes evidences' fraud, waste, or abuse of authority."[240] Because of concerns over effective enforcement of the CSRA, it was amended in 1989 by the Whistle-blower Protection Act.[241] Even with this amendment, there are still concerns about both its coverage and effectiveness.[242]

Despite whatever concerns there may have been on the effectiveness of whistle-blower laws, the federal emphasis on them remains strong. One example is Congress's passage of the Notification and Federal Employee Antidiscrimination and Retaliation Act of 2002 (the NO FEAR Act).[243] This act contains requirements for federal agencies to track and report on whistle-blower cases, retaliation disciplinary actions taken, settlement amounts paid for whistle-blower claims, and whistle-blower policies developed by the agency in response to whistle-blower cases.

Another example is the whistle-blower provisions in the American Recovery and Reinvestment Act of 2009, the legislation enacted in the first month of the Obama administration to deal with the economic recession.[244] This legislation, which may contain possibly the most extensive federal whistle-blower provisions to date, in effect prohibits reprisals by anyone in any entity receiving any of the massive distribution of federal funds under that act, including state and local governments, against anyone who makes whistle-blower complaints as provided in the act. Moreover, the act creates a detailed administrative framework for the processing of any such complaints.

At the state level, some sort of whistle-blower statute exists in every state, most of which bar retaliation for whistle-blowing activities rather than create a financial incentive for reporting misconduct. In addition, the courts in many states have recognized a common-law cause of action for whistle-blowers as a public policy exception to the

---

240. ALFORD, *supra* note 237, at 108 (quoting 5 U.S.C. § 2302(b)(8) (2007)).
241. 5 U.S.C. § 1221 (2000).
242. *See* discussion in Part III of this chapter at 149; *see also* Culp, *supra* note 239, at 122.
243. Pub. L. No. 107-174, 116 Stat. 566, 566–67 (2002).
244. American Recovery and Reinvestment Act of 2009, Pub. L. No. 111-5, 123 Stat. 115, § 1553 (2009). *See* Appendix 12 at 572.

employment-at-will doctrine.[245] Apart from the statutory protection for whistle-blowers, the concept that employees should be protected if they disclose organizational misconduct has been a principal motive for many regulatory and compliance initiatives. Virtually all corporate codes of conduct and ethical standards bar retaliation against whistle-blowers. Indeed, an emphasis on not retaliating against whistle-blowers was one of the concepts embedded in the original seven steps of the 1991 Sentencing Guidelines' Commentary and was carried over into the 2004 revisions of the Sentencing Guidelines.[246] Accordingly, there is wide consensus that a person disclosing misconduct should not suffer retaliation for doing so.

PART III—INSUFFICIENCY OF CURRENT BEST PRACTICES

In Part I, we examined the forces that are changing the demographics, technology, and scope of large institutions. These forces have been inexorably transforming who we are and how we work; and while they have enabled us to be far more connected to the larger world, paradoxically, they have resulted in our being less commited to the institutions with which we are affiliated. In Part II, we looked at pres-

---

245. Callahan & Dworkin, *supra* note 237, at 99–100 n.3, Appendix A (collecting both state whistle-blower statutes and listing states recognizing such public policy exceptions); *see also* Geoffrey Christopher Rapp, *Beyond Protection: Invigorating Incentives for Sarbanes-Oxley Corporate and Securities Fraud Whistleblowers*, 87 B.U. L. Rev. 91, 139–43 (2007); Westman & Modesitt, *supra* note 237, *passim*.

246. The 1991 U.S.S.G. Manual provided: "The organization must take reasonable steps to achieve compliance with its standards, e.g., by utilizing monitoring and auditing systems reasonably designed to detect criminal conduct by its employees and other agents and by having in place and publicizing a reporting system whereby employees and agents could report criminal conduct by others within the organization *without fear of retribution*." U.S.S.G. Manual § 8A.1.2 cmt. N.3(k)(5) (1991). As revised in 2004, the corresponding provision reads: (5) The organization shall take reasonable steps—(A) to ensure that the organization's compliance and ethics program is followed, including monitoring and auditing to detect criminal conduct; (B) to evaluate periodically the effectiveness of the organization's compliance and ethics program; and (C) to have and publicize a system, which may include mechanisms that allow for anonymity or confidentiality, whereby the organization's employees and agents may report or seek guidance regarding potential or actual criminal conduct *without fear of retribution*. U.S.S.G. Manual § 8B.2.1 (2004) (emphasis added).

sures on our institutions coming from the law. Here we saw that the trends and recent developments in criminal liability for organizations, corporate governance, and employment law have converged to the same end. These forces have exerted pressures and imposed mandates on organizations operating in the United States not only to act lawfully but also to adhere to ethical standards, which need to be implemented on a transnational basis to be effective.

A. Necessity of Current Best Practices

The responses by corporations and other organizations to these pressures include many components—some undertaken because they are required by law or regulators and some undertaken voluntarily. Certain of these "best practices" relate to management practices, such as the inclusion of independent directors on the board of directors, executive compensation, transparency of transactions and corporate decision-making, and the like, and are outside the scope of this book. Yet actions such as these clearly have an effect on everything that follows. One of the key findings of the U.S. Sentencing Commission's Ad Hoc Advisory Group and others who have studied these issues is that the "tone at the top" is one of the most significant factors affecting the overall ethical environment of an organization.[247] Other steps, such as whistle-blower statutes and policies, the creation of codes of conduct, development of compliance programs, expanded roles for human resources personnel (and creation of the role of compliance or ethics officer) to investigate allegations of misconduct by employees

---

247. Report of the Ad Hoc Advisory Group on the Organizational Sentencing Guidelines, *supra* note 149, at 52–69; HEINEMAN, *supra* note 126, at 28–36; *see also* DELOITTE & TOUCHE USA LLP, LEADERSHIP COUNTS: DELOITTE & TOUCHE USA 2007 ETHICS & WORKPLACE SURVEY RESULTS 3 (2007) ("Clearly leadership counts. . . . As the findings from the survey clearly reveal, the role of management and direct supervisors is critical in fostering an ethical workplace environment. As such, an overwhelming majority of survey respondents cite management and direct supervisors' behaviors—more than written credos and codes of conduct—as the top factors that help promote an ethical workplace. Specifically, when asked to identify the top factors for promoting an ethical workplace, 77% of working adults cite either the behavior of management, or of direct supervisors, as setting the tone for ethical behavior."); KPMG FORENSIC, KPMG LLP, INTEGRITY SURVEY 2008–2009 9 (2008) ("The 'tone at the top' is often cited as a determining factor in creating a high-integrity organization.").

or others, and institution of hotlines or helplines, have also been considered best practices.

All of the steps in this latter category are, or should be, components of an "effective compliance and ethics program," and not just because they are necessary for credit under the Sentencing Guidelines; they also make sense if an organization truly wants to operate in a global environment and to preserve its reputation for operating legally and ethically. But, just as the Sentencing Guidelines were revised in 2004 to require ongoing risk assessment,[248] the effectiveness of these steps should be examined periodically not only for what they do, but also for what may be missing. It is this last point that lies at the core of this chapter, because while the existing governmental and institutional responses are good and appropriate, something is missing: a meaningful confidential mechanism for employees to use to make inquiries and to discuss their concerns.

The focus of much of the compliance activity to date, including codes of ethics and organizational non-retaliation policies, has been to encourage employees to report misconduct to their supervisors or the appropriate compliance or HR officer, who can then investigate and report the findings. Management can then decide on such issues as punishment for the wrongdoers, reporting (to higher management, law enforcement, or regulators), and whether changes should be made in the organization's structure or operations to prevent a recurrence. The assumption underlying these policies, as well as most whistleblower laws, is that people will report misconduct, and that an organization's policies or the law will protect them when they do.

This assumption, however, is flawed and discredited by experience.[249] Likewise, the widespread use of hotlines has not achieved the results desired. If the past experience with these mechanisms has been disappointing, their effectiveness is not likely to improve in the future, especially in light of the workplace changes described in Part I. To understand why, we need to take a closer look at these mechanisms, together with the results of the business surveys and other data over

---

248. U.S.S.G. Manual § 8B.2.1(b)(5) (2004).
249. *See, e.g.*, L. Camille Hebert, *Why Don't "Reasonable Women" Complain about Sexual Harassment?*, 82 IND. L. J. 711, 734–43 (2007); Mary Rowe, Linda Wilcox & Howard Gadlin, *Dealing with—or Reporting "Unacceptable" Behavior (with additional thoughts about the "Bystander Effect")*, 2 J. INTL. OMBUDSMAN ASS'N 1, 52 (2009).

the past decade that confirm that something else is needed to enable employees and others to come forward.

B. Ethics Officers, HR, and Compliance Programs

1. Limits on the Promise of Confidentiality

Compliance and HR officers are responsible for ensuring compliance with the law and company polices in the organization's normal operations and its employment practices. As such, under generally recognized agency principles (the same principles recognized by the Supreme Court in *Faragher*, *Ellerth,* and *Kolstad*), they are clearly agents of their employer for such matters as receiving notice of illegal acts or other misconduct, conducting investigations, and recommending remedial steps (including employee discipline); reporting to law enforcement or regulatory authorities; and recommending or making operational changes. They cannot promise employees that communications with them are confidential, because agency law principles impute their knowledge of misconduct to the organization as a whole, placing the organization on notice of the misconduct, and, much like "tag, you're it," they are compelled by their job function to act on what they hear and learn. As Patrick J. Gnazzo and George R. Wratney, the former vice president of business practices and corporate ombudsman, respectively, at United Technologies Corporation, put it:

> You did the right thing. You created an ethics program for your organization built around a workable and enforceable code of behavior for employees. You appointed compliance or ethics officers to administer the program, and you built a structure to receive employee allegations and feedback.
>
> Have you done enough? No.
>
> Here's a simple truth: A certain number of your employees will not raise issues to management unless they are promised confidentiality throughout the process, including in any potential litigation. Under current law, your ethics program cannot guarantee that protection. Consequently, you will not hear some things that you should.[250]

---

250. Patrick J. Gnazzo & George R. Wratney, *Are You Serious About Ethics? For Companies that Can't Guarantee Confidentiality, the Answer Is No*, CONFERENCE BOARD REVIEW, July/August 2003.

While compliance and HR officers can indicate that they will try to preserve an employee's request for confidentiality as long as possible or until they must disclose it, this necessarily limits their ability to serve the segment of the population that will not come forward without an assurance of confidentiality.

2. The Risks of Strict Enforcement

Along with the growth in the number of compliance programs and compliance or ethics officers since 1991, the role and function have matured; there is now a better understanding of how matters should be investigated, what records should be kept, who should be informed, what punishment should be administered, etc. But more and better compliance programs can inhibit reporting precisely because they are now more effective than ever. Mary Rowe, Ph.D., and Corinne Bendersky, both of the Massachusetts Institute of Technology, in a 2002 paper, "Workplace Justice, Zero Tolerance, and Zero Barriers," drew on social science research to describe this process as follows:

> Individual employees and managers need to have choices about how they will address conflict and report misconduct. A single channel system that emphasizes only one approach to dispute resolution will fail to address many conflicts. This is especially likely to occur when people are unwilling to come forward because they lack confidence that the organization will take any action or, conversely, because they fear the organization at the other extreme, and they become fearful.
>
> We call these two barriers to individual action "Type 1" and "Type 2" errors. Type 1 errors occur when individuals fail to report misconduct because they do not think the employer is serious about proscribing it. In other words, Type 1 errors result from not pushing hard enough to stop unacceptable behavior. Type 2 errors occur when an employer appears too draconian and individuals will therefore not come forward in a timely way, or perhaps at all, because of the perceived consequences of doing so. Type 2 errors result from pushing too hard to stop unacceptable behavior.
>
> Imagine an example: The employer is committed to zero tolerance. It therefore sets up mandatory reporting, investigat-

ing, and discipline for certain types of misconduct, and it trains everyone to report the smallest infringement. The workplace learns that various kinds of misconduct will be seriously punished if proven. (We assume the best case here, that there is appropriate due process.) Type 1 errors have been addressed—the failure to report misconduct because people think the employer is not serious about proscribing bad behavior. All seems to be going well—but then the employer learns that some people do not report the offenses and problems that they actually observe, suspect, or even endure. *In our experience more than half of the observers of bad behavior do not act, or come forward, in a timely way if an employer pushes too hard.*

Many factors explain why [this may be so]. . . . An excellent employee in these circumstances may fear being seen as a frivolous, mischievous, supersensitive, or deceitful complainer. In some cases, employees may fear explicit retaliation for having blown the whistle on peers or, especially, supervisors. *In other words, an organizational culture that is hierarchical and oriented toward punishment may, ironically, inhibit the willingness to act or to come forward.*[251]

This research on zero tolerance policies in the work setting is consistent with analyses of zero tolerance policies in other settings, such as school discipline, as not achieving the intended purposes.[252] And even where a desired result is achieved, the problem is not eliminated, as demonstrated in an analysis of strict drug enforcement policies in the military which showed that zero tolerance drug policies have a deterrent effect but they do not eliminate all drug use.[253]

---

251. Mary Rowe & Corinne Bendersky, *Workplace Justice, Zero Tolerance, and Zero Barriers*, in NEGOTIATION AND CHANGE 6–7 (Thomas Kochran & Richard Lock eds., Cornell Univ. Pr. 2002), *available at* http://web.mit.edu/ombuds/publications/zero_zero.pdf (last visited March 15, 2009) (emphasis added; internal citations omitted).

252. *See, e.g.*, CECIL R. REYNOLDS ET AL., ARE ZERO TOLERANCE POLICIES EFFECTIVE IN THE SCHOOLS? AN EVIDENTIARY REVIEW AND RECOMMENDATIONS, *passim* (Am. Psychol. Ass'n Zero Tolerance Task Force, 2006), *available at* http://www.apa.org/ed/cpse/zttfreport.pdf (last visited March 9, 2009).

253. Stephen L. Mehay & Rosalie Liccardo Pacula, *The Effectiveness of Workplace Drug Prevention Policies: Does 'Zero Tolerance' Work?* 21 (Nat'l Bureau of Econ. Research, Working Paper No. 7383, 1999), *available at* http://www.nber.org/

Regardless of whether an organization adopts a zero tolerance policy, one of the lessons of this research is that strict enforcement of policies can have an inhibiting effect on some people coming forward. Supervisors, together with compliance and HR officers who administer compliance programs and company policies, should realize that the very nature of their role operates as a barrier to such reporting—and that the more "effective" they are, the greater this barrier can become. Some people need another route in order to come forward.

C. Whistle-blower Laws and Policies

There are innumerable whistle-blower laws in the United States—some at the federal level and some at the state level (with at least some statutes in every state); some serve a general purpose (meaning that they purportedly protect any whistle-blower), and some protect only certain types of whistle-blower activity or apply in only some situations; some create financial incentives for reporting and some do not; and finally, some make retaliation a criminal offense and some have civil penalties or remedies. Supplementing these laws are the policies of companies and other institutions that urge or require employees to report misconduct and that ban organizational retaliation if someone does come forward. With such a ubiquitous mechanism, one would think that whistle-blower statutes and policies would be quite effective. Unfortunately, the truth is just the opposite.

1. Limitations on the Effectiveness of Whistle-blower Laws and Policies

The reason whistle-blower laws and policies have limited effectiveness is rooted deeply in our common experiences: people are afraid to come forward, are not sure that they want to "get involved," or have learned, from their own or others' experiences, that people who do come forward are punished. Despite the law or company policies that urge reporting misconduct, it is well known that the people who do

---

papers/w7383 (last visited March 9, 2009) ("It is interesting to note that even the strictest workplace anti-drug program cannot eliminate illicit drug use among employees. Although drug participation rates in the military are low, they are not zero. This raises the question as to whether or not such strict anti-drug programs are worth their cost. The primary cost of zero tolerance is the cost of replacing terminated workers.").

come forward suffer retaliation, whether officially sanctioned or not. Of 300 whistle-blowers interviewed in depth by researchers for an article in 1999, 69 percent said that they had lost their jobs or were forced to retire as a result; 68 percent had their work more closely monitored by their supervisors; 64 percent received negative performance evaluations; and 64 percent also reported that they were blacklisted from getting another job in their field.[254] These are not trivial numbers. It is not surprising, therefore, that people generally perceive that bad things happen to people who "snitch": a December 2002 *Time*/CNN Survey/Harris Interactive poll that revealed that 57 percent of the public believed that whistle-blowers face negative consequences, such as being fired or treated poorly "most of the time," and *another* 30 percent believed that whistle-blowers had such consequences "some of the time."[255] The result is that 87 percent of the public perceived that whistle-blowers face retaliation some or most of the time.[256] Whether this perception is accurate, however, is beside the point. If people hold this view, it will influence what actions they will take.

The impact of being a whistle-blower is not limited to retaliation in the form of a lost job or poor treatment at work—there is a personal toll. The same 1999 study found that "[t]he most common fallout from their whistle-blowing involved: (a) severe depression or anxiety (84 percent), (b) feelings of isolation or powerlessness (84 percent), (c) distrust of others (78 percent), (d) declining physical health (69 percent), (e) severe financial decline (66 percent), and (f) problems with family relations (53 percent)."[257] These findings clearly indicate that

---

254. Joyce Rothschild & Terrance D. Miethe, *Whistle-Blower Disclosure and Management Retaliation: The Battle to Control Information about Organization Corruption*, 26 WORK AND OCCUPATIONS 107, 120 (1999); *see also* Alford, *supra* note 237, at 18; MICELI, NEAR & DWORKIN, *supra* note 175, *e.g.*, at 23–25 (critiquing the unreliability of reports concerning the incidence of whistle-blowing and retaliation).

255. The Conference Bd. Comm'n on Pub. Trust and Private Enter., *supra* note 200, at 23.

256. *Id.* The stories of retaliation are too numerous to recite here, *but see* Rothschild & Miethe, *supra* note 254, at 119. For more recent articles, *see, e.g.*, Jayne O'Donnell, *Blowing the Whistle Can Lead to Harsh Aftermath, Despite Law*, USA TODAY, Aug. 1, 2005, at B1; Tim Arango, *From a Whistle-Blower to a Target*, N.Y. TIMES, June 9, 2008, at C1; Andy Pasztor & Christopher Conkey, *FAA Whistleblower Intimidation Probed*, WALL ST. J., May 20, 2008, at A3.

257. Rothschild & Miethe, *supra* note 254, at 121.

the impact of whistle-blowing activity is not limited to the whistle-blower himself or herself; there are collateral consequences on the family and those economically dependent on the whistle-blower.

As if these consequences were not bad enough, the implication of taking action may even affect a supervisor of the employee involved. In a empirical study comparing pre-grievance and post-grievance data in the context of non-union labor arbitrations, an examination of the consequences of filing a grievance indicated that not only did the grievance filers themselves have "significantly higher turnover rates and significantly lower mean job performance ratings and mean promotion rates than non[grievance]filers in the post-grievance settlement period," their supervisors also had "significantly lower performance ratings, promotion rates, and work attendance rates, and significantly higher overall turnover rates than the supervisors of non-grievance filers in the post-grievance settlement period."[258] If these are the consequences to non-union employees and their supervisors who merely filed grievances, it stands to reason that the consequences to whistle-blowers and their supervisors would be just as severe if not more so. If the consequences *to supervisors* holds true for whistle-blower supervisors, it may help explain why the perception of retaliation for raising whistle-blower issues is so persistent and intractable.

2. Data on the Effectiveness of Whistle-blower Laws

Even with the widespread enactment of whistle-blower laws and policies and their necessity as a matter of public policy, their effectiveness is highly questionable, with the possible exception of statutes, such as the False Claims Act (FCA), that create financial incentives for reporting misconduct.[259] The reasons are many, but statistics on the success

---

258. David Lewin, *Symposium on Labor Arbitration Thirty Years After the Steelworkers Trilogy: Grievance Procedures in Nonunion Workplaces: An Empirical Analysis of Usage, Dynamics, and Outcomes*, 66 CHI.-KENT L. REV. 823, 841–42 (1990).

259. *See* Rapp, *supra* note 245, at 96–98. Because the FCA is focused on stopping efforts to defraud the government, it does not apply in other contexts. Still, the results are impressive in terms of money collected by the government: "Since 1986 the Fraud Section [of the U.S. Justice Department], along with U.S. Attorney's Offices, has obtained more the $20 billion in settlements and judgments" primarily from false claims cases. *See* http://www.usdoj.gov/civil/frauds/who_we_are.html (last visited April 28, 2009).

rate of whistle-blowers who prevail on their claims of retaliation bear this out. The Civil Service Reform Act, for example, which vested enforcement in an ineffective Office of Special Counsel, had the opposite of the intended effect: "retaliation increased, up to ninety percent of the employees lost their appeals, and whistle-blowing declined."[260] Even after it was amended in 1989 by the Whistle-blower Protection Act, this law "did not allow for damages, nor did it extend the limited statute of limitations. Again, the protection proved inadequate. Among other signs of failure, only one of the 120 appeals brought by whistle-blowers to the Federal Circuit Court of Appeals— the designated recipient—has been successful since 1984."[261] More recent statistics reflect that whistle-blowers had only two wins and 183 losses in the Federal Circuit from October 1994 to October 2007, leading some commentators and lawyers to call for a revision of the law that gives the Federal Circuit jurisdiction over such claims.[262]

Results at the administrative level for the whistle-blower provisions of SOX are no better. According to U.S. Department of Labor statistics, only 17 of approximately 1,300 SOX claims filed since 2002 with the Occupational Safety and Health Administration, the agency responsible for initial investigation of the complaints, have been found to have merit.[263] Another 841 cases were dismissed.[264] While reasons for the lack of success vary from the merits to procedural and technical issues,[265] the fact remains that there has been an astounding lack of success for whistle-blowers in the face of dramatic personal and workplace consequences.

---

260. Terry Morehead Dworkin, *SOX and Whistleblowing*, 105 U. MICH. L. REV. 1757, 1766 (2007).
261. *Id.*
262. Marcia Coyle, *Federal Circuit a "Hostile" Forum? Court's Sole Grip on Whistleblower Cases at Stake*, NAT'L L. J., Jan. 14, 2008, at 1.
263. Jennifer Levitz, *Whistleblowers Are Left Dangling*, WALL ST. J., Sept. 4, 2008, at A3; *see also* Teresa Baldas, *Employers Scoring in Whistleblower Actions*, NAT'L L. J., Oct. 29, 2007, at 4; and Michael Delikat, *Sarbanes-Oxley Whistleblower Update 2008*, *in* INTERNAL INVESTIGATIONS 2008: LEGAL ETHICAL & STRATEGIC ISSUES 157, 235–36 (Practicing Law Inst. 2008).
264. Levitz, *supra* note 263.
265. *Id.*; *see also* Baldas, *supra* note 263.

3. Why Whistle-blower Policies Fail to Address the Concerns of an Individual

Thus, while whistle-blower protections may make good policy sense from an organizational or legislative perspective, they are not responsive to the workplace reality of many individual employees. This is true in at least five critical respects.

First, employees may work for an organization, but the representative of that organization with whom they must deal is their boss:

> From the whistle-blower's perspective, organizations are particularistic. The organization is organized around men and women called bosses. One serves not an organization and not a purpose. One serves a boss. Organizations are, in other words, based on the principle of vassalage. . . .
>
> The organization is more feudal than we know. Power is decentralized, and power is personal, located in the figure of the boss.[266]

As we all know, this personal power can be exercised in ways that are perfectly legal but that nevertheless send a message to anyone who may have had the temerity to break ranks and come forward. The motivations for giving an employee the "cold shoulder," giving a good assignment to a co-worker, or closely monitoring an employee's work are extremely difficult, if not impossible, to link to retaliation for whistle-blowing. Nevertheless, this type of conduct does occur and serves as a very powerful punishment and deterrent to any future whistle-blowing by that employee *and* by other employees who witness the conduct.

Second, whistle-blower laws do not address another real issue from an employee's perspective: peer or co-worker retaliation. In the interviews of 300 whistle-blowers cited earlier, 69 percent reported that they were criticized or avoided by their co-workers.[267] The "fear of social ostracism" can have "a tremendous impact on its targets on both a psychological and physical level."[268] Unlike the retaliatory conduct of supervisors, this type of conduct can be and is meted out by

---

266. ALFORD, *supra* note 237, at 100–01.
267. Rothschild & Miethe, *supra* note 254, at 120.
268. Rapp, *supra* note 245, at 121.

anyone, regardless of position or power, but with no less impact on the targeted employee.[269] And since it is also almost impossible to prove under any circumstances, it is particularly immune to effective elimination by laws, company policies, or codes of conduct.

Third, the very concept of whistle-blowing is an anathema in certain areas of the world or for people from some cultures. In parts of Europe, for example, "anonymous mandatory denunciations smack of WW II and communist-era authoritarianism—neighbor spying on, and then denouncing, neighbor."[270] As described by one writer:

> In light of this history, some Europeans seem to have a visceral reaction against "snitching" to authorities, which can evoke the secret police denunciations that, for some of their countrymen, meant death in a concentration camp. As such, anonymous hotlines and mandatory reporting rules spark intense push-back from some employee populations in certain, but by no means all, European jurisdictions. Anonymity (whistle-blower staying anonymous while denouncing a named target) poses a special concern to some in Continental Europe because the cloak of anonymity is inherently untrustworthy and all but invites enemies to lodge some trumped-up denunciations out of spite. Ironically, given the conflict between this view and SOX, it is actually the *Europeans'* priorities here that champion two values we *Americans* see as associated with our justice system: due process and the presumption of innocence.[271]

These suspicions are not limited to Europeans; many other cultures, including some Asian cultures, are typically wary of such re-

---

269. *Id.*; *see also* Courtney J. Anderson DaCosta, Note, *Stitching Together the Patchwork: Burlington Northern's Lessons for State Whistleblower Law*, 96 GEO. L. J. 951, 973–74 (2008).

270. Donald C. Dowling, Jr., *Sarbanes-Oxley Whistleblower Hotlines Across Europe: Directions Through the Maze*, 42 INT'L LAW. 1, 12 (2008); *see also* Lori Tansey Martens & Amber Crowell, *Whistleblowing: A Global Perspective (Part I)*, ETHIKOS & CORP. CONDUCT Q., May-June 2002, at 6; Lori Tansey Martens & Amber Crowell, *Whistleblowing: A Global Perspective (Part II)*, ETHIKOS & CORP. CONDUCT Q., July-August 2002, at 9.

271. Dowling, *supra* note 270, at 12–13 (emphasis in original).

porting. With the convergence of global demographics in the workplace and in our institutions, it is a virtual certainty that people from some of these backgrounds are present in most large organizations and will fail or refuse to respond to any policy that encourages or mandates reporting.

Fourth, even when there is not a cultural aversion to whistle-blowing, it is sometimes hard for a whistle-blower to be taken seriously. The testimony of Harry Markopolos before the House of Representatives Financial Services Committee in February, 2009 is just one example of this problem. Mr. Markopolos, who had deciphered the Madoff Ponzi scheme, tried on several occasions to discuss the conclusions with staff of the SEC, only to be rebuffed because of interoffice rivalry or what he claimed was arrogant or ill-informed bureaucratic distain.[272] He finally discontinued his warnings because of fear of retribution.[273] And yet, from the perspective of an agency charged with investigating such reports, it is often hard to sort out what may be real from complaints that have no substance.

And finally, and most important, laws and policies do not provide the protection that they ostensibly promise, at least from an employee's point of view. "[M]ost legal protection for whistle-blowers is illusory; few whistle-blowers are protected from retaliatory actions because of numerous loopholes and special conditions of these laws and the major disadvantage that individual plaintiffs have against corporate defendants."[274] This is borne out by the statistics cited above. In part, this failure occurs because of the procedural safeguards built into our legal system, which, in a context such as whistle-blowing, heavily favor a corporate or institutional defendant. The costs and delay involved in seeking vindication are major handicaps that work against a potential whistle-blower. Despite this, however, the procedural advantages held by the organization:

---

272. Markopolos's testimony is *available at* http://financialservices.house.gov/markopolos020409.pdf (last visited March 20, 2009); *see also* Gregory Zuckerman & David Gauthier-Villars, *A Lonely Lament From a Whistle-Blower*, WALL ST. J., Feb. 3, 2009, at C3. *See also* Office of Investigations, U.S. Securities and Exchange Commssion, "Investigation of Failure of the SEC to Uncover Bernard Madoff's Ponzu Scheme—Public Version," Report No. 016-509 (August 2009).

273. Zuckerman & Gauthier-Villars, *supra* note 272.

274. ALFORD, *supra* note 237, at 109.

[are] not what bothers the whistle-blower most. What bothers the whistle-blower most is that the legal issues involved are almost always procedural. To many theorists of democracy this is the point. To the whistle-blower, this is the problem. "Whether I win or lose has nothing to do with what I did, whether I was right or wrong. No one cares about that. All they care about is that my boss followed the correct procedure in firing me."[275]

Even where the issue is not about termination, the procedural hurdles can be formidable for the uninitiated. Section 806 of SOX, for example, requires that complaints with the Department of Labor must be filed within 90 days "after a violation occurs."[276] It can be very hard for someone to digest what may have just happened, make the decision to complain, and then take action in such a short time frame, except for the most egregious conduct.[277]

In sum, the goal of laws and policies that encourage employee reporting are necessary and desirable, but they have limits constrained by human nature and procedural requirements. This was summed up in a September 2008 report by Thomas Devine and Tarek Maassarani for the Government Accountability Project, which describes "Your Rights on Paper" and then begins the section on "Your Rights in Reality" as follows:

> Unfortunately, there is little common ground between what is advertised and what you get. In practice, corporate whistle-

---

275. *Id.* at 111.
276. Sarbanes-Oxley Act of 2002 § 806, 18 U.S.C. § 1514A (2002); *see generally* Beverly H. Earle & Gerald A. Madek, *The Mirage of Whistleblower Protection Under Sarbanes-Oxley: A Proposal for Change*, 44 AM. BUS. L. J. 1 (2007).
277. On January 29, 2009, President Obama signed into law his first piece of legislation, the Lilly Ledbetter Fair Pay Act of 2009. Pub L. No. 111-2, 123 Stat. 5 (2009). This act, which amends Title VII of the Civil Rights Act of 1964, came about as a legislative reversal of a ruling by the U.S. Supreme Court in *Ledbetter v. Goodyear Tire & Rubber Co. Inc.*, 550 U.S. 618 (2007). In *Ledbetter*, the Court held that the statute of limitations for wage discrimination claims begins to run when the pay decision is made. This result was greatly criticized from a policy perspective, because the limitations period for bringing a discrimination claim could easily run before someone became aware that there was a pay differential. The act provides that that the limitation period runs, instead, from the issuance of the allegedly discriminatory paycheck.

blower law is a patchwork of inconsistent protections. With scattered exceptions, if you file a lawsuit you are sentencing yourself to an administrative process with unforgiving, short deadlines and a maze of bureaucratic procedures. Decisions are seldom issued in less than two to three years, and most statutes do not offer any chance for interim relief. When interim reinstatement is permitted, as under SOX, the employer may request that it be denied upon persuasive evidence that the employee would be dangerous or threatening back at work. And at the end of the process, you will have spent years and five or six figures for results that predictably rubberstamp whatever retaliation you challenged.[278]

Accordingly, many people are reluctant to have conversations with the "police" (HR and compliance officers) when they are unsure of themselves or do not want to become embroiled in the investigation that is sure to follow.

The more thorough the investigation is, or the more sure or strict the penalty, the more likely that the process will result in unreported matters. To the extent that both the law and organizational policy encourage reporting of misconduct and prohibit retaliation against someone for doing so, these avenues also fall short. Experience demonstrates that to come forward, one must risk substantial social, psychological, physical, and economic losses. No one is safe from these consequences. Indeed, one of the most important findings of whistle-blower researchers is that:

> [n]either gender, age, race, educational attainment, nor years on the job can save you from retaliation. . . . [E]ven people in supervisory positions and in their current position for over four years garner only a modest amount of insulation, and this is true if they report on less severe, nonsystemic abuses. The bottom line is that the larger and more systemic the abuse that is being exposed, the more intense will be the managerial effort to discredit and punish the whistle-blower.[279]

---

278. Thomas Devine & Tarek Maassarani, *Running the Gauntlet: The Campaign for Credible Corporate Whistleblower Rights*, Gov't Accountability Project, September 2008, *available at* http://www.whistleblower.org/doc/2008/rtgfinal.pdf (last visited April 29, 2009) (internal footnotes omitted).

279. Rothschild & Miethe, *supra* note 254, at 125.

Despite the laudable objectives of whistle-blower laws and policies, they fail to address real issues from the perspective of an individual faced with a decision on whether to report misconduct.

4. American Recovery and Reinvestment Act of 2009

The most recent whistle-blower statute created by Congress illustrates all of the problems with whistle-blower laws, despite its sweeping breadth and comprehensive structure.[280] This provision applies to the employee of any non-federal employer, including state and local governments, receiving "covered funds." It provides an opportunity for such employees to make a disclosure in the ordinary course of employment in a variety of ways, including to "the [newly created Recovery Accountability and Transparency] Board, an inspector general, the Comptroller General, a member of Congress, a State or Federal regulatory or law enforcement agency, a person with supervisory authority over the employee (or such other person working for the employer who has the authority to investigate, discover, or terminate misconduct), a court or grand jury, the head of a Federal agency, or their representatives. . . ."[281] Reprisals and retaliation are forbidden for people making reports that meet the articulated standard (gross mismanagement, a substantial and specific danger to public health or safety, abuse of authority or a violation of laws, rules, or regulations) with respect to covered funds, and such complaints are to be investigated by an agency inspector general within a specified time frame (but the deadlines are subject to extension upon agreement or certain findings).[282] The act requires that the inspector general's report, upon the completion of the investigation, be submitted to the whistle-blower but also to his employer, the head of the applicable federal agency, *and* the Recovery Accountability and Transparency Board. The employee is given the right to bring a civil ac-

---

280. American Recovery and Reinvestment Act of 2009 § 1553, Pub. L. No. 111-5, 123 Stat. 115 (2009). A copy of section 1553, "Protecting State and Local Government and Contractor Whistleblowers," is reprinted in Appendix 12.

281. *Id.* at § 1553(a). The Board to which reference is made is the Recovery Accountability and Transparency Board, created pursuant to section 1521 of the act.

282. *Id.* at § 1553(b).

tion in some circumstances, and the law specifies the burden of proof and presumptions that apply.[283]

While the act thus allows a whistle-blower to keep his job, the risks he confronts are formidable. He has to be sure that his complaint meets the required standard, and while he may have the statutory benefit to protect himself from official retaliation, he runs the risk that his report may put both his employer and all of his co-workers in jeopardy. At the very least, a whistle-blower complaint places his employer in a position where it must defend itself, with huge consequences to everyone associated with the company if it fails to do so.

As this brief summary of some of the provisions of Section 1553 demonstrates, it clearly represents an attempt by Congress to add teeth to whistle-blower protection for reports of misuse of federal money. It creates an elaborate administrative process, but it requires whistle-blower complaints to meet a certain standard and assumes the availability of several reporting channels (such as members of Congress and the head of a federal agency) that, from the perspective of an employee, will likely be viewed as remote and intimidating. Moreover, the act is replete with the type of procedural requirements that, in and of themselves, frustrate and impede whistle-blowers. The likely consequences of either being correct in the complaint or being incorrect are very great from the perspective of the employee who is concerned that something may be wrong.

In stark contrast, the act contains no provisions that encourage or require a confidential mechanism to be made available to employees who might want to discuss their concern before going forward with it or who need guidance on where to file a complaint or on what will happen once they fire up the investigative machinery. There is also nothing that provides guidance to an employee who wants to raise an issue but who does *not* want to be the whistle-blower, even with all of the act's protections.

D. *Hotlines and Ethics Survey Data*

One of the most widely adopted compliance practices has been the creation of hotlines or helplines, as they are sometimes called. Hotlines

---

283. *Id.* at § 1553(d). It is interesting, however, that the right of appeal is vested in the federal court of appeals in the circuit in which the reprisal is alleged to have occurred, rather than in the Federal Circuit. §1553. *See* Coyle, *supra* note 262.

usually are toll-free numbers that someone can call any time, day or night, and either leave a message or speak with someone to report misconduct. Because a caller is not required to identify himself or herself, hotlines are promoted as a way to raise an issue confidentially and anonymously. The information provided is then routed to the appropriate office inside the organization for a follow-up investigation or action. Thus, the information almost always finds its way directly to the compliance officer, the HR representative, or the organization's lawyers.

1. Reasons for Creating Hotlines

The use of hotlines greatly increased along with the development of other elements of compliance programs in the aftermath of the 1991 Sentencing Guidelines. One of the original seven components of an "effective program to prevent and detect violations of law" was that an "organization must take reasonable steps to achieve compliance with its standards" by, among other things, "having in place and publicizing a reporting system *whereby employees and other agents could report criminal conduct by others within the organization without fear of retribution.*"[284]

The perceived need for such a reporting channel was reinforced by some of the subsequent surveys and studies of misconduct reporting. For example, a 1997 study sponsored by the American Society of Chartered Life Underwriters & Chartered Financial Consultants and the Ethics Officer Association reported that a majority of workers felt "a substantial amount of pressure on the job" (60 percent) and "some pressure to act unethically or illegally on the job (56 percent)," but that "[v]ery few respondents 'reported to company authority (ex. HR, audit, legal) (4 percent overall), and this percentage did not significantly vary by company size.'"[285]

---

284. U.S.S.G. Manual § 8A1.2 cmt. n.3(k) (1991) (emphasis added).
285. Edward S. Petry et al., *Sources and Consequences of Workplace Pressure: Increasing the Risk of Unethical and Illegal Business Practices*, 99 Bus. & Soc'y Rev. 25, 25–30 (1997). Interestingly, however, this study also stated that "[w]orkers who took no action did not do so because of fear. Only 6% explained their action by saying that they 'didn't want to risk position/job.'" This finding is contrary to much of the other available survey data.

In 2000, the Ethics Resource Center conducted a National Business Ethics Survey and compared its findings to the survey findings of the 1994 Ethics in American Business survey. The new survey found that employees appeared more willing to report misconduct in 2000 than they had been earlier, but that "two in five employees still do not report the misconduct they observe."[286] This survey found that "[r]oughly one in three employees feel that management will view them as troublemakers for reporting misconduct or other ethics concerns" and that the same percentage "fear that co-workers will see them as snitches for such reporting."[287] Moreover, 42 percent reported that they were not satisfied with action taken on previously reported misconduct, and 74 percent of those believed that they would be seen as troublemakers by management if they made similar reports in the future.[288] With this kind of data being reported generally, it is not surprising that concern over how to encourage reporting and how to discourage retaliation for reporting still existed in 2002, when SOX was enacted, and in 2004, when the Sentencing Guidelines were revised.

If there had been any doubt about whether an organization should have a confidential and anonymous reporting mechanism before SOX and the Sentencing Guidelines, these two federal enactments should have eliminated it. Even though the application of SOX was limited to companies that had publicly traded stock listed on the stock exchanges and associations, the requirement in Section 301 that companies have "confidential, anonymous" mechanisms for reporting accounting and auditing fraud quickly became recognized as standard practice by most organizations regardless of whether they were directly subject to SOX. The 2004 revision to the Sentencing Guidelines was to the same effect. While it took a less mandatory approach, it broadened the application of a confidential and anonymous mechanism to apply to employees reporting as well as seeking guidance:

> (5) The organization shall take reasonable steps—
> . . . .

---

286. JOSHUA JOSEPH, ETHICS RESOURCE CENTER'S 2000 NATIONAL BUSINESS ETHICS SURVEY VOLUME I: HOW EMPLOYEES PERCEIVE ETHICS AT WORK 21 (Ethics Resource Center, 2000).
287. *Id.* at xi; *see also id.* at 24–25.
288. *Id.* at xi, 25.

(C) to have and publicize a system, *which may include mechanisms that allow for anonymity or confidentiality,* whereby the organization's employees and agents may report or seek guidance regarding potential or actual criminal conduct *without fear of retaliation.*[289]

The confidential and anonymous reporting mechanisms brought about by the development of compliance systems generally, and SOX and the Sentencing Guidelines in particular, have made hotlines big business. Many companies and organizations administer their own hotline, with the information frequently going to legal, compliance, or HR, but many organizations—particularly large ones—have outsourced this activity to vendors.

2. Features of Hotline Services

As of 2004 there were at least 35 national companies offering hotline services, but information on them is carefully guarded.[290] The four largest hotline vendors, however, service most of the major multinational corporations. One of these vendors, Global Compliance Services, had as many as 1,450 clients by 2006, including nearly half of the *Fortune* 100 companies and nearly a third of the *Fortune* 1,000 companies. All of the programs are marketed as compliant with SOX and other federal requirements and as a cost-effective way to protect an organization's reputation. The hotline companies essentially provide an organization with a turnkey system that can be implemented with complete support in terms of roll-out training, publicity materials, and call handling, as well as ongoing training and the development of policies.

The better programs also permit Web reporting, and all of the companies offer sophisticated case-reporting and management services. For multinational organizations, these services include toll-free international calls, translators or interpreters in multiple languages, and secure data facilities. The people who receive the calls or Internet messages are employed by the hotline company and work out of its facilities, and thus generally handle inquiries for multiple clients. Rep-

---

289. U.S.S.G. Manual § 8B.2.1(b)(5)(C) (2004) (emphasis added).
290. MICELI, NEAR & DWORKIN, *supra* note 175, at 158.

resentatives receiving the calls have inquiry protocols prescreened and approved by the client that they use in taking information from an inquirer. When the contact takes place by phone, the information sought is the usual "who, what, when, and where" type. In these situations, the inquirer can decide whether to remain anonymous. When the inquiry comes from the Web, a completed questionnaire is used to generate a call report. In some of the better programs, a personal PIN (personal identification number) can also be given to an inquirer so that he or she can call back later to get a report on action taken or to respond to follow-up questions to further the investigation.

From a management perspective, the service and functionality of hotlines—especially in the context of a global enterprise—are impressive. One of the most useful tools for management coming out of this process is a report that can be generated. Because all of the inquiry information is logged as data, a client can tailor the type of report it wants. Reports can detail each kind of allegation or violation at each level in each division or facility of the organization and can track the aging and resolution of all inquiries. In the end, the reports produce a complete audit trail.

3. Limitations on Hotline Effectiveness

With all of these features and functionality, one would think that hotlines, like whistle-blower laws, would be extremely successful. Unfortunately, much as with whistle-blower laws, the effectiveness of hotlines has been disappointing.

One of the limitations on the effectiveness of hotlines is the byproduct of an intentional design feature: information from the hotlines almost always goes to a formal reporting channel. While this in many cases is exactly what an organization wants, it also limits the willingness of many to use a hotline. A good illustration of this point comes from an August 2007 report of the U.S. Government Accountability Office (GAO) on the Securities and Exchange Commission. In this report, "Securities and Exchange Commission—Steps Being Taken to Make Examination Program More Risk-Based and Transparent," the GAO studied the SEC's examination procedures following the mutual fund trading scandals of 2003. The report noted that the SEC established an examination hotline in 2006 "where registrants can call or e-mail anonymously to ask questions about their specific examinations or other issues, lodge complaints, or make comments" and that "[t]o preserve anonymity of the registrants, OCIE [the SEC's Office of Compliance Inspections and Examinations] does not keep a formal log of calls and e-mails to share with OCIE management although staff take notes on the calls."[291] Despite these precautions, however, the GAO found that some industry participants were still reluctant to use the hotline out of "concern about the independence of the staff that operate the hotline, because . . .OCIE's hotline is staffed by attorneys in the OCIE's Office of the Chief Counsel."[292] In particular the GAO noted that:

> [i]n contrast to the OCIE, NASD [National Association of Securities Dealers] has created an Office of the Ombudsman to receive and address concerns and complaints, whether anonymous or not, from any source concerning the operations, enforcement, or other activities of NASD. The Office of the Ombudsman is an independent office within the NASD that reports directly to the Board of Directors. As part of its responsibilities, the Office of the Ombudsman also provides summary information on the development of trends based on complaints, which may support resulting system change. By locating the hotline in an office or division that is independent of OCIE, OCIE could lessen registrants' concern about the independence of that staff who operate the hotline and thus encourage greater use of it.[293]

The GAO, therefore, recommended that the SEC consider "relocating the hotline to an independent office, such as an ombudsman function, within the agency or within a division or office outside the OCIE."[294]

Another major limitation on hotlines comes from blunt commentary by Gary Edwards: hotlines are not working because "outsourcing them acknowledges—without repairing—a lack of trust in the corpo-

---

291. U.S. Gov't Accountability Office, Securities and Exchange Commission: Steps Being Taken to Make Examination Program More Risk-Based and Transparent 26 (2007), *available at* http://www.gao.gov/new.items/d071053.pdf (last visited April 15, 2009).
 292. *Id.* at 28–29.
 293. *Id.* at 29.
 294. *Id.* at 31.

rate culture." Edwards's perspective is significant because it is informed by a long career of involvement with ethics and compliance issues: he helped create one of the first compliance offices at McDonnell-Douglas Corporation in the 1980s following a procurement fraud scandal and then helped draft the Defense Industry Initiative (DII) before becoming the executive director of the Ethics Resource Center for the first half of the 1990s.[295] According to Edwards, one of the main reasons hotlines are not working is that they are managed by outside vendors. Based on a survey undertaken by his current company, Ethos International:

> 58 percent of companies take this approach. . . . This dampens reporting within a company—at least compared with hotlines that are managed in in-house ethics offices. "Nearly two-thirds (65 percent) of outside contractors used by respondents heard from less than 1 percent of employees in the twelve months prior to the survey. By contrast, half of the ethics officers heard from 1–5 percent of employees, and another 17 percent of ethics offices hear from 5–10 percent of employees during the same period." He concludes from this that "employees are more likely to report misconduct to, or seek ethics advice from, a company's ethics office rather than a vendor."[296]

Direct information on the utilization of hotlines is rarely disclosed by the very third-party vendors that Edwards criticized companies for using, but cross-industry information presented in 2007 by one of the hotline vendors, Global Compliance, is revealing. Using 2006 data, it reported that, based on weighted averages across all industry sectors, the percent of employees using hotlines to make reports was 1.73 percent.[297] The reports that were made, however, dealt very infrequently (only 1.74 percent) with the accounting, auditing, or financial report-

---

295. Andrew Singer, *Corporate Ethics Has Taken a Wrong Turn, Says Former ERC Chief*, ETHIKOS & CORP. CONDUCT Q., July-Aug. 2008, at 1 (citing an interview with Gary Edwards and an article by him, *Compliance, Ethics, and Corporate Culture: A Call to Action for Board Leadership*, DIRECTORS MONTHLY, December 2007, at 1).

296. *Id.* at 4 (citing the same article by Edwards).

297. Dennis Muse, *Help for Your Helplines*, *in* ADVANCED CORPORATE COMPLIANCE WORKSHOP 2007 505, 517 (PLI Corporate Law and Practice Handbook Series, B-1623, 2007).

ing issues that were a prime motivation for SOX. Rather, almost 75 percent of the reports dealt with employment issues (human relations, administration, and compensation—54.63 percent, and diversity, equal opportunity, and workplace respect—12.38 percent).[298] Almost 49 percent of the users wished to remain anonymous, while 51 percent were willing to be named.[299] And finally, almost 90 percent of the reports involved follow-ups (investigations) without additional information; only slightly more than 10 percent involved follow-ups with additional information.[300]

The data indicating that hotline usage is concentrated in employment-related issues and that hotlines are rarely used for the type of accounting and auditing fraud contemplated by SOX is not unusual. The overall utilization rate reported by Global Compliance is higher but consistent with experience that has been reported elsewhere. In its *2007 Corporate Governance and Compliance Hotline Benchmarking Report*, the Security Executive Council reported, based on its survey of over 650 companies, that the aggregate reporting rate for all industry sectors was 8.27 reports per 1,000 employees in 2006—still less than 1 percent.[301] On a related issue, a 2007 survey by Language & Culture World Wide reported that most (65 percent) of the respondents indicated that "misconduct appeared to be reported less often by international employees than by domestic employees."[302] And while 67 percent of respondents from the Language & Culture 2007 World

---

298. *Id.* at 518; *see also* MARTIN T. BIEGELMAN, BUILDING A WORLD-CLASS COMPLIANCE PROGRAM 95 (John Wiley & Sons, Inc., 2008) (citing the experience of Patrick Gnazzo, senior vice president, business practices and chief compliance officer at CA, Inc. [formerly known as Computer Associates] that most of the calls received by the hotline at CA were employment-related).
299. Muse, *supra* note 297, at 519.
300. *Id.* at 520.
301. SECURITY EXECUTIVE COUNCIL, 2007 CORPORATE GOVERNANCE AND COMPLIANCE HOTLINE BENCHMARKING REPORT: A REPORT TO SECURITY EXECUTIVE COUNCIL MEMBERSHIP 11 (2007) [hereinafter HOTLINE BENCHMARKING REPORT].
302. LANGUAGE & CULTURE WORLDWIDE, LLC, 2007 SURVEY REPORT, GLOBAL ETHICS & COMPLIANCE PROGRAMS BEST PRACTICES & BENCHMARKING: ETHICS COMPLIANCE 14 (2007). Note that the survey indicated that respondent companies believed that the three top reasons for the apparent underreporting by international employees were: "Cultural differences regarding what is considered misconduct"; "Fear [of] retaliation from supervisor or manager"; and "Don't trust that the report will be kept confidential." *Id.*

Wide survey indicated that they have an anonymous e-mail reporting mechanism available to international employees and 92 percent have hotlines available to international employees, the use of these avenues is limited: 31 percent described use of the e-mail service by international employees as "limited or nonexistent," with 45 percent of the respondents reporting that usage is increasing slightly. For the hotlines, 42 percent of the respondents reported that usage by international employees was "limited or nonexistent," and 39 percent said that the number of hotline calls was increasing slightly.[303] This undoubtedly is a result, at least in part, of the antipathy in some cultures to anonymous reporting, as discussed above in the context of whistle-blower laws.[304] Moreover, the use (or lack of use) of hotlines highlights the predicament of many worldwide organizations, because while the use of hotlines is strongly encouraged or mandated in the United States, they create problems in complying with laws in other jurisdictions, such as the European Union Data Protection Directive.[305]

More recent data confirm the conclusion that while hotlines may be required by law and considered best practices, they have not found favor with their intended audience: employees or others who were perceived to need a confidential or anonymous reporting channel. One of the key findings of the 2007 National Business Ethics Survey (NBES) undertaken by the Ethics Resource Center was that "[e]mployees are not using established hotlines to report. Regardless of the type of behavior observed, the 2007 NBES found that employees prefer to talk with a person with whom they already have a relationship."[306] This finding is not limited to just the business world. In a similar ethics study of government in 2007, the Ethics Resource Center reported that:

> only 1 percent of reports are made using a whistle-blower hotline. Whistle-blower hotlines have received a great deal of legislative and regulatory attention; however, they are the re-

---

303. *Id.* at 15.
304. Dowling, *supra* note 270.
305. *Id.*; *see also* Carrie J. DiSanto & Brian Hengesbaugh, *U.S. Helplines Raise EU Privacy Concerns*, ETHIKOS & CORP. CONDUCT Q., Sept./Oct. 2005 at 1.
306. ETHICS RESOURCE CENTER, NATIONAL BUSINESS ETHICS SURVEY: AN INSIDE VIEW OF PRIVATE SECTOR ETHICS 3 (2007); *see also id.* at 18.

porting choice *less than 1 percent* of the time for observations of the following kinds of misconduct:

- Abusive or intimidating behavior;
- Putting one's own interests ahead of the organization's;
- Alteration of documents;
- Using competitor's inside information;
- Alteration of financial records;
- Lying to customers, vendors, or the public;
- Misreporting of hours worked; and
- Environmental violations.[307]

The 2007 NBES, along with findings from the KPMG Integrity Survey (2008-2009),[308] reinforce the conclusion that the accomplishments of compliance programs to date are to be commended, but also that the existing vehicles that purportedly are available for confidential and anonymous communication are insufficient.

The Private Sector NBES, for example, concluded that the most effective way to reduce ethics risks for an organization is to have an "enterprise-wide cultural approach" and that companies that take such an approach "reduce misconduct by three-fourths and virtually eliminate retaliation at all levels."[309] Likewise, the survey suggested that "[w]ell-implemented formal ethics and compliance programs dramatically increase reporting of observed misconduct and also help decrease the rate of misconduct."[310] On the issue of reporting, in particular, it was encouraging that, in contrast to the low use of hotlines (3 percent), most people prefer to speak with someone "with whom they already have a relationship" including their supervisor (43 percent) and higher management (34 percent).[311] But in the face of these positive developments, the survey revealed continuing issues of concern:

---

307. ETHICS RESOURCE CENTER, NATIONAL GOVERNMENT ETHICS SURVEY 7 (2007) (emphasis in the original).
308. KPMG FORENSIC, *supra* note 247. This is the third such survey by KPMG. Similar surveys were completed in both 2000 and 2005–2006.
309. ETHICS RESOURCE CENTER, *supra* note 463, at ix.
310. *Id.*
311. *Id.* at 3.

- There is still "a disturbingly high percentage of workers witnessing misconduct at work. . . . [M]ore than half (56 percent) of employees surveyed had personally observed violations of company ethics standards, policy, or the law. The misconduct rate has increased steadily since 2003, returning in 2007 to pre-SOX levels."[312]
- "More than two in five employees (42 percent) who witnessed misconduct [in the previous year] . . . did not report it through any channels. This is nearly as high as it was in 2000, and, looking more closely at the 58 percent who did report, many did not report *every* incidence of misconduct they observed."[313]
- "The reasons employees cite most often for staying silent about their observations of misconduct have virtually remained the same over time—a strong sense of futility and fear. More than half (54 percent) of the employees who witnessed but did not report misconduct believed that reporting would not lead to corrective action. More than a third (36 percent) of non-reporters feared retaliation from at least one source."[314]
- *For those who chose to try to resolve an issue themselves rather than reporting it to an official channel,* "[t]wo in five of these employees did not report because they would have had to report the misconduct to the person involved, and one in four were not aware of any mechanism to report anonymously."[315]
- And finally, *"the 2007 NBES found that only 9 percent of U.S. employees believe their company has a strong ethical culture. And, the percentage of employees that identified their companies as having a weak or weak-leaning ethical culture has been steadily rising since 2003.* Just under 50 percent of employees said their employers have a weak or weak-leaning ethical culture in 2007—almost identical to the levels in 2000. The increase . . . is most evident in the Peer Commitment component, where *39 percent of employees responded that their*

---

312. Reille Miller Gabriel, *No Improvement in Ethics Risk Landscape, ERC Survey Finds*, ETHIKOS & CORP. CONDUCT Q., Jan./Feb. 2008 at 1-2 (emphasis in original).
313. *Id.* at 1-2.
314. *Id.* at 2.
315. ETHICS RESOURCE CENTER, *supra* note 306, at 3 (emphasis added).

> *peers are not committed to ethics in 2007, compared with 34 percent in 2005 and 25 percent in 2000.*"[316]

These NBES findings are corroborated by the findings of the 2008-2009 KPMG Integrity Survey, both with respect to positive accomplishments of compliance programs and the ways in which current compliance efforts fall short. The KPMG survey found that "ethics and compliance programs continue to have a favorable impact on employee perceptions and behaviors across the board" and that strong programs make a difference.[317] It also found that most employees (81 percent) indicated that they would be inclined to notify their supervisor or another manager if they observed a violation of their organization's standards of conduct and that they felt comfortable seeking advice from supervisors (79 percent) and peers or colleagues (75 percent) on "doing the right thing."[318] More than half believed that a report would be handled confidentially (64 percent) and that they would be protected from retaliation (53 percent).[319] But the KPMG survey also revealed reasons for continued concern about the effectiveness of current efforts:

- "The prevalence of misconduct remains high. Nearly three out of four employees (74 percent) report that they have personally observed or have firsthand knowledge of wrongdoing within their organizations during the previous 12 months. This figure is largely unchanged from our findings in the years 2005 and 2000."[320]
- "The nature of misconduct remains serious. Nearly half of the employees (46 percent) reported that what they observed could cause 'a significant loss of public trust if discovered.' This figure not only remains on par with previous years at the national level, it peaks at 60 percent for employees working in the banking and finance industry."[321]

---

316. Gabriel, *supra* note 312, at 3, 15 (emphasis added).
317. KPMG Forensic, *supra* note 247, at iii.
318. *Id.* at 7–8.
319. *Id.* at 8.
320. *Id.* at iii.
321. *Id.*

- The root causes of conduct were identified as "pressure to 'do whatever it takes' to meet business targets" (59 percent); the belief that employees "will be rewarded for results, not the means to achieve them" (52 percent); a belief "that the code of conduct is not taken seriously" (51 percent); lack of familiarity with standards or lack of resources (51 percent and 50 percent, respectively); "fear of losing their jobs if they do not meet targets" (49 percent); and a belief that "policies or procedures are easy to bypass or override" (47 percent).[322]
- *As with previous years, "the functions that are primarily charged with taking action in response to alleged misconduct (i.e., legal, internal audit, and board and audit committee functions) were cited among the least likely channels employees would feel comfortable using to report allegations."*[323]
- *"While whistle-blower mechanisms are gaining traction, there remains a risk that boards and senior management may not hear from employees about fraud and misconduct risks until it is too late. More than half (57 percent) of the respondents reported that they would feel comfortable using a hotline to report misconduct, which is up from 40 percent. . . [in the 2000 survey]. However, only half (53 percent) believed they would be protected from retaliation, and even fewer (39 percent) believed that they would be satisfied with the outcome if they reported misconduct to management."*[324]

Some of the points above are emphasized because they demonstrate that, even with the "additional traction" of whistle-blower mechanisms, hotlines, and compliance efforts, a significant segment of the employee population is not comfortable using them. One of the conclusions drawn by the Ethics Resource Center from the 2007 NBES is that organizations should:

Recognize that your hotline statistics are telling only part of the story. The research demonstrates that whistle-blower hotlines and formal internal control mechanisms are impor-

---

322. *Id.* at 6.
323. *Id.* at 7 (emphasis added).
324. *Id.* at iii (emphasis added).

tant, but they provide an incomplete picture of the amount of conduct occurring.[325]

Fear of retaliation remains a major impediment to reporting, and peer retaliation is particularly pernicious and hard to combat. The increasing numbers of employees who reported that their peers were not committed to ethical standards is especially problematic in this regard. Moreover, while the KPMG survey appears not to have asked the question, the 2007 NBES found that reporting issues are particularly troublesome when the misconduct involves one's supervisor. In the face of this data, which is the most current available, it is worth referring back to two changes that were made in 2004 to the Sentencing Guidelines. First, organizations with "effective compliance and ethics programs" should have and publicize "a system, which may include mechanisms that allow for anonymity and confidentiality whereby the organization's employees and agents may report or seek guidance regarding potential or actual criminal conduct without fear of retaliation."[326] And second, organizations should periodically evaluate the effectiveness of their compliance and ethics program.[327] We have just undertaken such an evaluation of current compliance programs, and it is clear that the most prevalent confidential and anonymous mechanisms are not as effective as they can and should be.

PART IV—OMBUDS PROGRAMS

There is broad consensus, derived from both legal requirements and common experience, that organizations need confidential and anonymous channels of communication for people. Since data show that many people do not or will not use the usual present suite of mechanisms—in which heavy reliance is made on compliance officers, whistle-blower policies, and hotlines—we must conclude that these alone are not sufficient. The key point here is not that these other mechanisms should be eliminated; they should not. They are important features that need to remain in place. Rather, the key point is that something else is also needed, especially in light of the extent and

---

325. ETHICS RESOURCE CENTER, *supra* note 306, at 26.
326. U.S.S.G. Manual § 8B.2.1(b)(5)(C) (2004).
327. *Id.* at § 8B.2.1(b)(5)(B).

type of hotline usage discussed above. A comprehensive program to resolve workplace conflict and help people report misconduct must include a variety of communication channels.[328] As Patrick Gnazzo, the former chief compliance officer at both United Technologies Corporation and at CA, Inc., has indicated:

> A well-communicated hotline, a strong independent audit committee, a professionally staffed human resources department, an ombudsperson program, and an effective compliance program are all key elements for successful communication of compliance issues. . . .[329]

The same reasoning was evident in Congress's passage of The American Red Cross Governance Modernization Act of 2007, which, among other governance changes to the National Red Cross following the disaster of Hurricane Katrina, required that organization to create an ombudsman program.[330] Because ombuds programs can fill gaps unmet by the other mechanisms, organizations should consider an ombuds program as a confidential and anonymous way for employees and others to seek guidance and ultimately help them report their concerns.

A. Ombuds Structure Is Important

As discussed in Chapter 1, a wide variety of ombuds programs currently exists. At present, the term "ombuds" or "ombudsman" can mean virtually anything, from special interest advocates to offices that

---

328. *See* Ralph Hasson, *Providing Oversight to Comprehensive Systems*, 2 J. INT'L OMBUDSMAN ASS'N 1, 9, 23–26 (2009) (describing the roles and reporting arrangements for various elements, including an ombuds, in a comprehensive management system for an organization).

329. BIEGELMAN, *supra* note 298, at 102.

330. American National Red Cross Governance Modernization Act of 2007, Pub. L. No. 110-26, 121 Stat. 103; *see also* AMERICAN RED CROSS, AMERICAN RED CROSS GOVERNANCE FOR THE 21ST CENTURY: A REPORT OF THE BOARD OF GOVERNORS 101 (2006), *available at* http://6l3zyr.redcross.org/static/file_cont5765_lang0_2202.pdf (last visited March 20, 2009) (reviewing whistle-blower processes and the internal audit function (at 89–100) and recommending that the Red Cross consider establishing an ombudsman position).

function according to the classical investigator/prosecutor model. In referring to an organizational ombuds, I mean an ombuds that practices in accordance with the Code of Ethics and Standards of Practice of the International Ombudsman Association. The essential characteristics of such an office—that it is independent, neutral, confidential, informal, and an alternate channel of communication—are at the core of why a properly structured and operated organizational ombuds program reaches people not reached by other methods.[331]

Before discussing the advantages of an ombuds program, however, it is important to examine the structural requirements and prerequisites for an organizational ombuds office, because, in this context, structure is especially important.

First and foremost, an ombuds office should be an "alternate" mechanism. It cannot and should not be seen as a replacement for any of the formal compliance channels. Those mechanisms remain necessary for an organization because they serve essential business functions, and they are an effective reporting channel for many people. An ombuds office is designed to supplement them, not replace them; with coaching from an ombuds, many people become comfortable using those channels and can use them more effectively. An ombuds office's great benefit, however, is to be available to people who do not know what to do or who will not discuss or report their concerns to their supervisor, compliance officer, HR, or a hotline. It is also available to people who want more guidance rather than to just file a report. Some people just need to talk through their issue with someone else. For others, it takes some time to get comfortable with the notion of making a report or starting an investigation. Especially in light of the diversity and varied cultural backgrounds of people in our organizations, alternative options are needed. No one solution can respond effectively to all situations, but having an alternate and risk-free channel facilitates the work of a formal channel. "[S]tatistics indicate that when there are multiple reporting channels in place, including an ombuds

---

331. It is precisely because an "organizational ombuds" program must have this profile of characteristics that efforts of the International Ombudsman Association to develop a certification protocol, both for offices and for ombuds, are so critical. Indeed, the very characteristics that make the office such a desirable addition to compliance programs also make it harder for organizations to incorporate their activities into existing structures or evaluate their work in traditional ways.

function, the formal channels can be more efficient."[332] Indeed, the CEO of Global Compliance, one of the leading hotline companies, has stated: "As a best practice, Global Compliance counsels our clients to implement multiple vehicles and channels for the reporting of business misconduct or noncompliance."[333]

In addition to being an alternate channel, an ombuds office should be purely voluntary. Its effectiveness as a place to seek guidance confidentially depends on people deciding that they want to use it, not being required to do so. It should be a place where someone can ask questions or explore reporting or conflict resolution options without running the risk that by doing so, they are initiating the investigatory machinery or coming to the attention of their bosses or their colleagues. In this sense, one of the most significant functions of an organizational ombuds office is that it provides people with information about policies, reporting options, and processes. An organizational ombuds can also provide valuable coaching and role-playing exercises so that an inquirer can sort out the relevant from the irrelevant, understand the situation from the perspective of other side, or hear what the limitations may be on management and others.

Confidentiality is the defining characteristic of organizational ombuds programs. Without the ability to have confidential conversations with inquirers, an ombuds program would be no different from or better than the formal communication channels.

As we saw in Part II, courts have used traditional agency law principles to decide when an organization should be held responsible for the actions of its agents.[334] Thus, if an ombuds office serves as an agent of management or has management responsibilities, then statements made to an ombuds, along with other information learned by an ombuds, risk being imputed to the organization and cannot be kept confidential.[335] This is why compliance and HR officers, which are

---

332. Jonathan E. McBride & James S. Hostetler, *Board Champions for the Ombudsman,* NACD-DIRECTORS MONTHLY, May 2008 at 16.
333. *Id.* at 17 (quoting Dennis Muse, CEO of Global Compliance, Inc.).
334. *See* Chapter 3, Part I, at 193.
335. This is analogous to and consistent with guidance provided by the U.S. Equal Employment Opportunity Commission (EEOC) in its publication, *Enforcement Guidance: Vicarious Employer Liability for Unlawful Harassment by Supervisors* [hereinafter EEOC ENFORCEMENT GUIDANCE] (1999), *available at* http://

formal communication channels, can never promise real confidentiality.[336] This point also explains why an organizational ombuds office should never be seen as a reporting channel for allegations of misconduct. Rather, the ombuds's principal reason for existence is that it can help people resolve workplace conflict informally and help those who would not otherwise report misconduct find a way to do so. An ombuds office provides a confidential and safe place for an inquirer to go *before* he or she reports it to an official channel. The premise, borne out by experience, is that some people will not report an issue until they are first comfortable with their understanding of how the process works or until they have talked it through with someone. An ombuds office thus provides guidance to inquirers on how to make a report, where reports can be made, and what likely will happen. In some situations,

---

www.eeoc.gov/policy/docs/harassment.html (last visited April 30, 2009), in which the EEOC recommends an informational phone line for anonymous discussion in order to avoid the conflict between an employee's desire for confidentiality and an employer's duty to prevent and correct harassment. EEOC ENFORCEMENT GUIDANCE at 12 n.67 ("Employers may hesitate to set up such a phone line due to concern that it may create a duty to investigate anonymous complaints, even if based on mere rumor. To avoid any confusion as to whether an anonymous complaint through such a phone line triggers an investigation, the employer should make clear that the person who takes the calls is not a management official and can only answer questions and provide information. An investigation will proceed only if a complaint is made through the internal complaint process or if management otherwise learns about alleged harassment.") This is discussed in greater detail in the next chapter. Likewise, the court in substantially similar companion cases involving IBM's procurement ombudsman program rejected IBM's claim of attorney client privilege and work product protection for investigations undertaken by the ombuds at the direction of an assistant general counsel. Accounting Principals, Inc. v. Manpower, Inc., 2009 U.S. Dist. LEXIS 66428 (N.D. Okla., July 28, 2009) and Pinstripe, Inc. v. Manpower, Inc. 2009 U.S. Dist. LEXIS 66430 (N.D. Okla., July 28, 2009). In both cases the court noted that although the IBM Web site had described the ombudsman office as "an objective and impartial organization [that] assists in resolving procurement-related concerns and issues," the investigation that the ombudsman office undertook was directed by an assistant general counsel and that "[i]t appears that IBM's legal office co-opted the Ombudsman investigation because IBM now claims that the impartial and neutral Ombudsman was actually working as part of IBM's legal defense team in preparing for litigation." *Accounting Principals, Inc., supra* at *17–*18 and nn. 6 & 7; *Pinstripe, Inc., supra* at *16–*18 nn. 6 & 7.

336. *See* Gnazzo & Wratney, *supra* note 250.

that information is enough to provide the inquirer with a better understanding of the process and a better focus on the issue. In other situations, the ombuds works with an inquirer to find a way to raise the issue with the organization while protecting the identity of the inquirer. Only when an inquirer and the ombuds agree that it makes sense to do so will the ombuds actually report the alleged misconduct, except in the rare situation where he or she determines that the situation presents an imminent threat of serious harm.

Some organizations have been resistant to the notion that an ombuds has no independent duty to report information to the organization unless he or she determines that it presents an imminent threat. There are several responses to this concern. First, as a practical matter, effective ombuds almost always can find ways to bring an issue to the attention of the proper channels, even though the identity of the person raising the issue may not be disclosed in that process. At the very least, an ombuds can strategize with an inquirer on how best to send an anonymous communication to a formal channel. Second, people go to an ombuds on many occasions to *get* information, not necessarily to report something. Even though other channels may exist to obtain this information, some people prefer that even a request for information remain confidential.[337] Third, data indicate that at present, not all issues are brought forward through the existing mechanisms. If a program such as an ombuds office helps increase the amount of reporting, it should not be condemned because it cannot make assurances that every instance will be reported; some misconduct would otherwise never have been reported in any event. And finally, organizations cannot have it both ways; if an organization wants an alternative channel of communication that employees will use and that does not put the organization on notice of issues, it cannot be a mandatory reporting channel.

The concepts of confidentiality and not being a notice channel are, therefore, critically interdependent. By not being a notice channel and not performing other management functions, the ombuds office can avoid the impact of having its knowledge imputed to the organization; and it is the assurance of confidentiality that enables an organizational ombuds office to effectively address the inherent limitations of other compliance mechanisms. In other words, not being a notice

---

337. *See* George Wratney, *Ah! The Power of Data*, OMBUDSMAN NEWS, First ed. 2001, at 1–2.

channel is what makes confidentiality possible for an ombuds office. For these reasons, a properly structured ombuds office should not be organizationally subordinate to compliance or HR functions or have the responsibility, as those channels do, to report to management and investigate specific allegations of misconduct.

In order to maintain confidentiality and not be construed as a notice channel, an ombuds office must be both independent and neutral. Structural independence and neutrality can be achieved either within the organization or by contracting with an outside entity to perform ombuds services. If the office is placed outside the organization and staffed by non-employees, the critical aspects of independence and neutrality undoubtedly can be addressed in the services contract. If the office is located within the organization and staffed by employees, it is even more imperative that the structural and operational independence of the office be both well-documented in a charter and publicized.[338] Regardless of which model is used, however, an organization contemplating the creation of an ombuds office should recognize that the office is most effective when staffed with people who can present options or discuss issues with an understanding of how things really work at that organization. This also offers a great advantage compared to a hotline program. Without some personal presence (which over time can develop a reputation for credibility and confidentiality), an ombuds office becomes little more than another form of hotline.

The structural neutrality of the ombuds office is important not only to support a claim of confidentiality, but also for long-term effectiveness. Since an ombuds regularly interacts with both inquirers and management representatives, an effective program must be widely perceived as promoting a fair process, rather than advocating for either management or employee issues. The neutrality of the office, though, should not be mistaken for passivity. Indeed, one of the great advantages of ombuds offices over hotlines is that in most cases, they know the identity of their inquirers. This permits an ombuds to have multiple contacts with an inquirer and even to initiate contact in order to continue exploring options, to make sure that all questions have been answered, or until ombuds and inquirer settle on an acceptable way to bring an issue to a formal channel for investigation.[339]

---

338. *See* Appendix 10, p.5 at 539.
339. *See* Chapter 3 and Appendix 14 (examples of how ombuds handle issues presented).

B. An Organizational Ombuds Fills Gaps

With these considerations in mind, what does an ombuds office add to an organization? The most significant gap in current approaches to compliance is that, as demonstrated in Part III, a large segment of people will not use hotlines or make reports directly to their supervisors or existing formal channels.[340] The low incidence of reporting by way of hotlines confirms the fact that while hotlines can serve as a channel for confidential and anonymous reporting and offer organizations robust activity reports, these systems are not widely used. Statistics on utilization vary by organization and effectiveness of the incumbent ombuds, but data demonstrate that the utilization of organizational ombuds programs is typically much higher than hotline usage. Jan Schonauer, the ombuds at Alliance Bernstein in 2006, has reported that utilization of the ombuds office at her company in its first year was 2.7 percent but that studies in the 1990s "pegged the typical response rate at organizations between 4 percent and 8 percent," with utilization at the 4 percent level probably closer to normal.[341] Other studies report utilization in the 3–6 percent range.[342] A survey in 2003 by The Ombudsman Association revealed that average utilization in the government and corporate sectors was 5 percent, with a slightly smaller utilization (4 percent) in the academic sector.[343] Regardless of which of these numbers is the most accurate, they are a

---

340. In both the KPMG 2008-2009 Integrity Survey, *supra* note 247, at 8, and in the Ethics Resource Center 2007 National Business Ethics Survey, *supra* note 286, at 3, employees reported that they were more confident in raising issues with a supervisor, peer, or someone with whom they already had a relationship than with a hotline. These findings are important in that they underscore the advantages of having a knowledgeable person with whom one can speak, but they do not support the conclusion that supervisors should be the only other communication channel besides compliance and HR. Such an approach would be particularly ill-suited to situations involving concerns with supervisors.

341. Singer, *supra* note 295, at 13; *see also* Andrew Singer, *Ombuds Office Helps Coca-Cola Bottler Avoid Explosions*, ETHIKOS & CORP. CONDUCT Q., Nov./Dec. 2005 at 11–12 (utilization at MIT was on the order of 8–10%, but at Coca-Cola it was 2–4%).

342. *See* Richard Starr, Randy Williams & Arlene Redmond, *When Formal Channels Aren't Enough: the Advantages of an Ombuds Program*, ACC DOCKET, Oct. 2006 at 83.

343. TOA Survey Data, Spring 2003, on file with the author.

multiple of the hotline usage rates. Moreover, in considering these rates, it is important to remember that the ombuds utilization rates typically are for ombuds programs at organizations that also have hotlines, compliance officers, and HR operations that people could use if they preferred.

In addition to utilization data, another measure of effectiveness for ombuds programs is what people have said they would do in the absence of a program. One organization's internal survey posed just this question, and the results confirm why an ombuds program should be a necessary complement to the other formal channels:

- 28 to 35 percent would not have brought up their issues at all;
- 13–25 percent would not have brought them up as quickly; and
- 8–10 percent would have left the company.[344]

For an organization with tens of thousands of employees, students, or affiliated people, the potential financial impact of these results is quite significant. Just the cost savings from not having to replace employees who would otherwise would have left may in some cases justify the cost of an ombuds program. Likewise, a consultant on ombuds

---

344. *Id.* Retention of employees represents a significant opportunity for cost savings for virtually all large organizations. An article on hiring and employee retention at the Big Four accounting firms in *The Economist*, for example, reported that the Big Four firms collectively "employ some 500,000 people around the world" and that "[t}heir product is their employees' knowledge and their distribution channels are the relationships between their staff and clients," but that "the sheer numbers they employ can still make them feel like sausage factories." The article went on to state:

> Retaining good people is the biggest challenge. Turnover rates at the Big Four have historically been high—roughly 15–20% leave each year, compared with as few as 5% in some other industries. The cost of this is "astronomical," says Jim Wall, Deloitte's managing director of human resources. **Mr. Wall reckons that every percentage-point drop in annual turnover rates equates to a saving of $400m–500m.**

Accounting for Good People, ECONOMIST, July 19, 2007, *available at* http://www.economist.com/business/displaystory.dfm?story_id=E1_JVDSPNN (last visited April 30, 2009) (emphasis added).

program performance metrics, John Zinsser of Pacifica Human Communications, LLC, has calculated that the average return on investment for each dollar invested in an ombuds program was $14, without including any potential cost savings from legal fees if an employee resorted to litigation to address his or her issue.[345]

In addition to reaching a population segment that will not use other channels for compliance purposes, an organizational ombuds program addresses another significant problem: at present there is little correlation between the typically articulated purpose for a hotline program and how it is, in fact, most commonly used. Most organizations decided to create hotline programs because of the mandates or incentives of the Sentencing Guidelines, SOX, and the general perception that hotlines are an indispensible component of any properly structured compliance program. While those perceptions are correct, it is important to keep in mind that, as reported by Global Compliance, only 1.74 percent of the issues raised (by less than 2 percent of the employee base) dealt with accounting, auditing, or financial reporting issues.[346] On this data, it is hard to make a strong case that hotlines provide an effective mechanism for reporting on fraud and compliance issues, particularly when ethics survey data still reflect large amounts of unreported misconduct and deep fears of retaliation. On the other hand, the same data reflect that hotlines are used most often for employment-related issues, much to the frustration of compliance officers.[347] There are no widespread surveys to confirm that these percentages are universal or would apply in all situations, but it is clear from broad experience with different types of organizations that the vast majority of concerns conveyed to hotlines are employment rather than compliance issues, and that very few involve the type of conduct that compliance officers are charged with investigating. More important, because of the very nature of the employment-related issues that are most prevalent, they do not fit the "incident reporting and investigation" model on which hotlines are based. Instead, these types of issues are more naturally suited to coaching and mediation. They often are the types of issues that are best addressed in personal discus-

---

345. McBride & Hostetler, *supra* note 332, at 17.
346. Muse, *supra* note 297, at 518.
347. *Id.*; MICELI, NEAR, & DWORKIN, *supra* note 175, at 174; *see also* HOTLINE BENCHMARKING REPORT, *supra* note 301, at 13, 17, 21, 25, 29, 33, 37, 41, and 45.

sions and often in multiple sessions. The experience of ombuds is that in many cases, a person's real issue is not expressed until after several conversations, during which the inquirer is testing and evaluating the ombuds to see if confidentiality is maintained and the ombuds can be trusted. This distinction between a "report" and the opportunity for continued discussion is especially important in light of widespread concern over potential damage to peer relationships and fear of retaliation revealed by the national ethics and integrity surveys. In this context, having a knowledgeable individual available for extended or multiple discussions is an approach much more likely to be effective in addressing the employment-related concerns currently being expressed to hotline services.

The direct benefit of an ombuds program does not just accrue to employees. Because ombuds can have confidential discussions with people throughout the organization, they are ideally situated to know what really is going on in the organization. While they do not reveal the substance of those discussions, an integral part of their work is to identify systemic issues or trends and to pass along that information to the organization's management. In this sense, the ombuds can help their organization make structural or systemic changes.

An organizational ombuds program is thus more than just another variation of a hotline approach; it has a much broader focus and more time and tools to bring to bear on people's concerns—for the benefit of those people as well as for the organization. Not only does an ombuds program supplement the compliance function by serving as a resource for people who need or want guidance on how to report misconduct, it supplements the human resource function as an effective alternative dispute mechanism to help resolve work-related disputes and avoid employment litigation. Even though developments in employment law have pressured organizations to develop effective employment practices policies and reporting mechanisms, the role of an ombuds program in helping to eliminate employment litigation or resolve conflict in an organization has not been fully appreciated by the corporate compliance community. The advantages of reducing employment litigation, however, are substantial.[348] "As noted in a recent article ap-

---

348. For a discussion on how an ombuds program can become an effective part of a workplace conflict resolution system, *see* KARL A. SLAIKEU & RALPH H. HASSON, CONTROLLING THE COSTS OF CONFLICT: HOW TO DESIGN A SYSTEM FOR YOUR ORGANIZATION (Jossey-Bass Publishers, 1998).

pearing in *Business Week*, in 2005 and 2006, retaliation claims represented 30 percent of all charges individuals filed with the Equal Employment Opportunity Commission, an increase from about 20 percent 10 years ago."[349] This number will undoubtedly increase over time in light of the Supreme Court's ruling in *Burlington Northern & Santa Fe Railway Co v. White*.[350]

Employment lawsuits afford successful plaintiffs a much higher recovery, on average, than other types of claims.[351] In a 2005 study conducted by the National Center for State Courts, the civil trial litigation dockets of 46 counties were examined.[352] The survey found that of the counties reviewed, the median award granted to a prevailing plaintiff in an employment discrimination jury trial was $226,177,[353] and this was based only on cases in state courts. The same study also surveyed the median punitive awards, and the median punitive award for plaintiffs in employment discrimination lawsuits was found to be $350,000—notably higher than the average of $82,644 for contract claims overall.[354] The high cost of employment lawsuits is confirmed by data collected by Jury Verdict Research, an Internet-based company, which maintains a nationwide database of plaintiff and defendant verdicts and settlement for personal injury claims.[355] According to their calculations, the median compensatory award in employment cases rose 18 percent in 2003 to reach $250,000.[356] Jury Verdict Research has also analyzed compensatory awards by sector.[357] Their find-

---

349. MICELI, NEAR & DWORKIN, *supra* note 175, at 196.
350. *See Burlington Northern*, *supra* note 215, and accompanying discussion.
351. Robert C. LaFountain & Neal B. Kauder, *An Empirical Overview of Civil Trial Litigation*, CASELOAD HIGHLIGHTS: EXAMINING THE WORK OF STATE COURTS (Nat'l Center for State Courts, Williamsburg, Va.), Feb. 2005, at 1.
352. *Id.*
353. *Id.*
354. *Id.*
355. Jury Verdict Research, *available at* http://www.juryverdictresearch.com/About_JVR/about_jvr.html (last visited July 20, 2009).
356. Charles Krugel, *How Much Money Does an Employment Dispute Cost & What's a Business' Likelihood of Getting into an Employment Related Dispute?*, http://www.evancarmichael.com/Human-Resources/762/How-Much-Money-Does-an-Employment-Dispute-Cost—Whats-A-Business-Likelihood-of-Getting-Into-an-Employment-Related-Dispute.html (last visited March 30, 2009).
357. *Id.*

ings reflect an overall average award of $581,000 from 1998 to 2004.[358] These awards varied among industries, with an average of $900,000 in manufacturing and high-tech sectors, $486,000 in service and retail sectors, and $445,000 in transportation sectors.[359]

These figures are for the average verdict amounts for a successful plaintiff and do not include the costs of litigation defense. While data on average defense costs is elusive and figures are often cited without evident explanation, an article citing Jury Verdict Research data has reported that for an employer who has provided anti-discrimination training to its employees (which presumably lowers the risk or severity of misconduct), the cost of litigating an employment case is approximately $155,000, and the cost of settling is $85,000.[360] In contrast, for an employer who has not provided such training, the cost of litigation is about $960,500 and the cost of settling about $304,000.[361] With potential costs such as these, systems that help resolve workplace conflict and provide guidance on reporting options quickly become cost-effective if the incidence of employment litigation is reduced.[362]

Effective organizational ombuds offices help reduce litigation costs by working to resolve employment and interpersonal conflict disputes before they become lawsuits with such techniques as effective listening, coaching, facilitated discussions, mediation, and references to formal channels. To take just one example, the 2007 Annual Report of the Office of the Ombuds at Eaton Corporation reported that the office "focuses on working with an inquirer to identify and evaluate options and methods for issue resolution at the closest level of control in a non-threatening and cooperative way."[363] It was able to accomplish this by developing an action plan with an inquirer in 92.5 percent of its cases involving coaching (55 percent), facilitation (17 percent), references to formal channels (22.5 percent), mediation (1 percent) and other techniques (5.5 percent).[364]

---

358. *Id.*
359. *Id.*
360. *Id.*
361. *Id.*
362. *See* SLAIKEU & HASSON, *supra* note 348, at 14–15 (reporting a decrease in outside litigation expenses for three companies of between 50% and 80% where conflict management systems, including ombuds, have been instituted).
363. OFFICE OF THE OMBUDS, EATON CORP., ANNUAL REPORT 2007 6 (2008) (on file with the author).
364. *Id.*

Because of these techniques, another important aspect of an ombuds office is that it typically is used by employees at *all* levels of an organization. Thus, it fills a need for those other than just the stereotypical "victimized" employee in the lower wage scales. One of the surprising facts about ombuds use is that a large percentage of the people who go to ombuds offices are managers or the more senior people in an organization. The same Eaton 2007 Annual Report reflects, for example, that, based on 2006 user demographics, 9 percent of its inquirers were managers or supervisors, 20 percent were nonsupervisory technical or professional employees, and 19 percent were senior managers or executives.[365] The inference to be drawn from this data is that even those people well-placed in an organization and with knowledge of their reporting options still prefer having a confidential avenue to discuss their options before taking action. Indeed, in some ways it is more important for them because they have more to lose, and to the organization their loss has more impact than does the departure of a lower-level employee.

Several organizations with large numbers of engineering, technical, scientific, or professional personnel report that a third or more of their inquiries come from people with managerial responsibilities looking for informal and off-the-record suggestions on how to deal with personnel issues for which they have management responsibility. Ombuds indicate that managers are unwilling to take these issues to *their* supervisors or discuss them with HR out of concern that doing so might affect their own performance evaluations. By discussing options and coaching, an ombuds can thus assist in training such an inquirer to make better management decisions. This illustrates one of the reasons why an ombuds office is ideally suited to organizations in technical or professional environments, including hospitals and law, financial, and accounting firms.[366] In these types of organizations, highly trained people are acting under great pressure in areas that can

---

365. *Id.* at 4; *see also* AMERICAN EXPRESS OFFICE OF THE OMBUDSPERSONS, OFF THE RECORD: 2008 ANNUAL REPORT 3 (2008) (reflecting that 31% of its inquiries came from Band 35 or above (management employees) (on file with the author) and 16% from Band 30 or above).

366. *See* Sara Thacker, *Where Are the Ombuds? The Hidden Potential of Law Firm Ombuds*, THE INDEPENDENT VOICE (Newsletter of the Int'l Ombudsman Ass'n) 2006, at 8; Vaughan Finn, *The Hospital Ombudsman: A Missed Opportunity?*, NORTHEAST NETWORK HEALTHCARE REVIEW, 2004 Issue No. 1 (Dec. 30, 2003); HCPro,

have important consequences if illegal or bad behavior occurs. Moreover, in each of these environments, there is a hierarchical structure that necessarily inhibits coming forward with an issue for fear of compromising one's future prospects.

C. Reported Effectiveness of Ombuds Programs

The reported effectiveness of ombuds programs, from the perspective of the users, stands in stark contrast to the survey evidence on hotlines. In addition to the survey evidence that some people would not have brought an issue forward or would not have done so as quickly without the ombuds office, and that some would have left the organization rather than do so, satisfaction surveys demonstrate that effective ombuds programs are appreciated by their users. For example, survey results reported in the 2006 Annual Report of the American Express Office of the Ombudspersons were that 97 percent of respondents indicated generally that they would consider using the office if the need arose. Of people who had actually used the office, 97 percent reported that the office met or exceeded their expectations for timeliness, 97 percent for respectfulness, 96 percent for confidentiality, and 88 percent for usefulness. Ninety-one percent of prior users responded that they would use the office again.[367] Another report on an ombuds program indicated that "90 percent (or more) of constituents know about the ombuds program, would use it if they needed it and would recommend it to others."[368]

Inc., 19 *Medical Staff Briefing* 4, 6 (2009) (discussing the use of an ombuds program to help hospitals manage leadership conflict in compliance with the standard LD.02.04.01 issued by the Joint Commission). Indeed, in April 2009, the Minority Corporate Counsel Association issued a report, *Sustaining Pathways to Diversity: The Next Steps in Understanding and Increasing Diversity & Inclusion in Large Law Firms (2009)*, *available at* http://www.mcca.com/_data/global/images/Research/5298%20MCCA%20Pathways%20final%20version%202009.pdf (last visited April 30, 2009), which included the recommendation that "[l]aw firms should create an ombudsperson role for their workplaces, so that attorneys who want to discuss their experiences have a well-trained and well-informed person to whom they can turn for guidance." *Id.* at 38.

367. AMERICAN EXPRESS OFFICE OF THE OMBUDSPERSONS, 2006 ANNUAL REPORT 4 (2006).

368. Starr, Williams & Redmond, *supra* note 342, at 83; *see also* Frank Fowlie, *A Blueprint for the Evaluation of an Ombudsman's Office: A Study of the ICANN Office of the Ombudsman* (November 2008) (Ph.D. thesis, Latrobe University),

Comments from senior leaders of organizations that have created organizational programs report that the programs are a vital complement to their existing compliance and ADR efforts. For example, Steven Norman, corporate secretary of American Express Company, made this comment about the American Express ombuds office:

> According to the current American Express Corporate Ombudsman, the Ombudsman's Office [as of 2005] has provided assistance to more than 27,000 people since it opened. All employee groups use the Office, from associates to senior leaders. It's led to nipping problems in the bud and lowering cynicism about the Company's commitment to resolving employee issues. Every fall, we get a report card as a company in the form of an Employee Value Survey; the integrity scores have risen steadily. The Ombuds program has contributed to these results. It is a useful program which can be measured and has tangible benefits.[369]

Endorsements from other inside counsel with responsibility for compliance functions are similar. Mark Manley, senior vice president, deputy general counsel, and chief compliance officer at AllianceBernstein has stated:

> The ombudsman is a completely neutral, confidential, informal and independent resource for employees who are initially

---

available at http://www.icann.org/ombudsman/blueprint-for-evaluation-of-an-ombudsman-nov08.pdf (last visited April 30, 2009) (evaluating the effectiveness of an ombuds office).

369. *The Ombudsman and the Corporate Secretary*, CORP. SEC'Y & GOVERNANCE PROF'L, Jan. 2005, at 1; *see also* Andrew Singer, *Do You Know Me? I'm the American Express Ombudsperson*, ETHIKOS & CORP. CONDUCT Q., Sept./Oct. 2005, at 12. For other articles on the benefits of ombuds programs, *see generally* Starr, Williams & Redmond, *supra* note 342, at 66; Gnazzo & Wratney, *supra* note 250; Arlene Redmond & Randy Williams, *Benefits of an Ombuds Program to Corporate Governance*, NACD-DIRECTORS MONTHLY, Nov. 2003, at 15–16; BNA, INC., OMBUDSMAN PROGRAMS: REDUCING RISK AND STIRRING GROWTH THROUGH COMMUNICATION: WORKFORCE STRATEGIES, Feb. 2006; and Arlene Redmond & Randy Williams, *The Organizational Ombuds: Complementing the Ethics Office*, ETHIKOS & CORP. CONDUCT Q., Sept./Oct. 2003, at 10.

uncomfortable going to a formal channel, who do not know where to take an issue or how to take it forward, who do not understand the implications of an issue, or who want to remain anonymous. The ombuds helps these employees generate options to resolve their issue, and helps ensure that issues are brought to the most appropriate resource at Alliance. That saves us all time and effort and helps all of us to be smarter and more efficient. The ombuds acts as a communications channel between an employee and formal channels. She can provide employees with information that may answer their questions about policies and procedures. . . and acts as a listening post.[370]

John B. Phillips, vice president and deputy general counsel at Coca-Cola Enterprises, Inc., has made similar comments:

Since its inception in 2001, the ombuds office at Coca-Cola Enterprises has played a significant role in helping our company be proactive in identifying employment risks and taking appropriate action to mitigate those risks. Although our ombuds acts in an appropriately confidential manner, the informal relationship existing between the ombuds office and our legal department provides a mechanism for routinely talking about recurring problems, possible hotspots, and developing trends within the company. The ombuds office complements our ethics and compliance hotline and our solutions (ADR) program as a "heads up" tool in our risk mitigation strategy for dealing quickly and effectively with employment concerns.[371]

From a management perspective, an effective ombuds program not only serves as a resource to assist people in resolving workplace conflicts and as a referral source to the official notice channels, it also can offer senior leaders insights into the well-being of the organiza-

---

370. Redmond & Williams, *supra* note 369, at 70; *see also* Andrew Singer, *AllianceBernstein Invests in New Ombuds Office*, ETHIKOS & CORP. CONDUCT Q., May/June 2006, at 12.

371. *Id.* at 78. *See also* Singer, *Ombuds Office Helps Coca-Cola Bottler Avoid Explosions, supra* note 341, at 11.

tion. Senior leaders in an organization can benefit from periodic "trend" reports from an ombuds on the types of issues and problems that the ombuds is dealing with in the organization. These reports, which do not reveal identities of ombuds' inquirers or confidences from any conversation with an inquirer, can be useful to management by highlighting emerging issues and systemic or recurring problems. It is not unusual for systemic problems to affect formal reporting channels that otherwise would be the primary information channel to senior management. With an effective ombuds program as an alternate "listening post" with insight into whether the other systems are functioning as intended, a senior leader is in a better position to rely on the fact that problems and concerns are being reported and dealt with before they explode.

PART V—CONCLUSION: WHY CREATE AN OMBUDS PROGRAM?

As we have seen, the forces of change on American organizations include pressures exerted by changing demographics, information technology, and globalization. As a result, there is a greater potential than ever for organizational conflict and personal disengagement at a time when the need for global cooperation within an organization and uniform global standards is an imperative. Managing such a diverse population in any organization would be challenge enough, but the demographic, technological, and globalization forces compelling change are not the only source of pressure on our organizations. In the absence of a single global legal structure, the many sources of law and regulation in the United States and elsewhere have converged to exert their own pressure and to reinforce the need for organizations to have uniformly high ethical and compliance programs wherever they operate. Developments in the law have resulted in higher standards for criminal liability and corporate governance, and in greater liability for improper employment practices.

How Can Ombuds' Confidentiality Be Protected? 3

What an Organization and Its Ombuds Should Know to Establish an Ombuds Program and to Defend Its Confidentiality

Chapter 2 explained why organizations should have confidential channels to help people resolve issues and report misconduct in their organizations. It also explained why the current best-practice responses to compliance have limitations that a properly designed organizational ombuds program can supplement by being a confidential and off-the-record resource.

Claiming to be confidential, however, does not make it so. Confidentiality is protected by law only in situations where, as a matter of public policy as determined by a legislature or a court, the benefit of confidentiality is perceived to be more important than the benefits of full disclosure of potentially relevant information. There are many reasons why this is true with respect to ombuds communications, but at present no federal statute guarantees the confidentiality of ombuds communications as such.[1] Like-

---

1. However, as discussed in Part II of this chapter at 264 and in Chapter 4 at 397, The Administrative Dispute Resolution Act of 1996,

wise, no state has a shield law that specifically makes communications with an organizational ombuds confidential. Even with a statute, however, absolute confidentiality cannot be guaranteed, because there may be other strong public policy reasons—like a claim of fraud or a constitutional right to confront one's accusers in the criminal context—to which confidentiality would have to yield in some circumstances.[2] In the absence of specific legislation protecting the confidentiality of ombuds communications, protection must rest on the application of other legal principles. This means that ombuds ultimately will have to go to court in most situations to counter a party who tries legally to compel the disclosure of communications or information that an ombuds claims are confidential, and a court then becomes the ultimate arbiter of whether confidentiality will be protected.

In addition to the usual limitations inherent in the litigation process, an ombuds office's assertion of confidentiality is made more difficult because most judges are not familiar with organizational ombuds programs. Moreover, judges are compelled by the law to approach a dispute over confidentiality with a strong presumption in favor of full disclosure of communications that may be relevant to a dispute because of long-standing and widely held legal assumptions and principles.

Despite these obstacles, however, there are ways that ombuds and their organizations can assert and protect confidentiality. While none of these approaches provides as much protection as a statute, ombuds programs nevertheless have successfully defended against attempts to breach confidentiality. To achieve this result, however, an ombuds program should be both structured and operated in a manner consistent with the key principles for organizational ombuds programs and be able to defend its claim of confidentiality with prompt responses from both counsel for the organization and counsel for the ombuds office. In most cases, this involves the timely filing of a motion for a protective order or to preclude the ombuds from being compelled to make disclosure of confidential communications.

Pub. L. No. 101-552, 104 Stat. 2736 (1990), does include communications within the definition of "alternative means of dispute resolution" and provides a process for a court to use in determining whether confidentiality should be preserved.

2. *See* the discussion in Chapter 4 at 364–72 on the constitutional limits of testimonial privilege.

While some ombuds programs have been successful in asserting confidentiality in court based on traditional legal theories, others have not. These latter cases usually have failed because of a flawed structure, misguided activities, or because the court was not given adequate documentation to justify an order to protect ombuds' confidentiality. The power of this bad precedent presents yet another obstacle to ombuds, because with the plethora of types of ombuds programs and scant awareness or analysis of the differences among them, some courts have relied on this precedent in their rulings without fully examining the substantive differences in programs or the differences between the procedural posture of the case before them and that of the precedent on which they rely.

The lesson from this record is not that confidentiality cannot be protected; it is that to do so, an organization and its ombuds office must work together to make sure that the program is properly structured, that it operates in a manner consistent with the preservation of confidentiality, and that when a challenge is made to the ombuds' confidentiality, adequate documentation and legal support for the ombuds position are provided to the court. When this has occurred, courts usually have recognized ombuds' confidentiality.

This chapter provides information and practice tips on how to protect confidentiality. It is divided into four parts, and each of these areas represents an important element of the framework for an ombuds' claim of confidentiality.

Part I contains a detailed discussion of the concept of imputed notice. The assertion that communications with an ombuds should not be imputed to the organization underlies all of the legal theories that have been used to protect confidentiality. This part explains why communications with an ombuds should not be considered notice to the organization and provides legal authority to support this assertion.

Part II then addresses each of the legal principles that have been used to date to protect ombuds confidentiality. Included here is information on an ombuds privilege and an implied contract defense on the issue of confidentiality, along with other bases upon which an ombuds can assert confidentiality: constitutional protection (in California), state and federal statutes dealing with the confidentiality of alternative dispute resolution and privilege for mediation communications, arbitration provisions to addresss confidentiality, and the inherent power of the court to supervise the discovery of relevant information. Relevant case law is presented here as well.

Part III addresses essential points for documentation of the establishment of organizational ombuds programs and for their operation. The burden of demonstrating that confidentiality should be protected rests upon the party claiming it (the ombuds office), and the ombuds office must have documentation to prove to a court that it is properly established and operated and thus deserving of protection against compelled disclosure of confidential communications. Accordingly, there is a premium on documenting a structure based on the principles of independence, neutrality, informality, and confidentiality. Correspondingly, if a program does not adhere to standard practices that support the claim of confidentiality, a court likely will conclude that, despite how the program may have been initially structured, it was managed in a way that does not merit protection of confidentiality.

Part IV, the final section of this chapter, contains some suggestions on litigation practices to ensure that a claim of confidentiality is presented in the strongest way possible. Even with good programs that have adequate documentation and that operate appropriately, when a challenge is raised to confidentiality, there are precautions that an ombuds office and its organization should take to make sure that the claim is properly presented to a court without being compromised.

Throughout the chapter, in boxes interspersed with the text, and in Appendix 14, specific examples are presented on how organizational ombuds have dealt with issues by virtue of being a confidential resource. These are real—not hypothetical—examples, and an effort has been made to make them representative of the types of matters with which ombuds deal. They have been drawn from many different programs both in corporations and universities. Consistent with the underlying principle of confidentiality of organizational ombuds, however, the facts are presented in generic language, and neither the organization nor the source of the example is disclosed. These examples illustrate the way in which issues are presented to organizational ombuds, how an ombuds' creativity or perseverance can resolve an issue or assist it in being reported to a formal channel for corrective action, and how the unique window on an organization that an ombuds has can be used to provide guidance on trends for the betterment of the organization.

PART I—IMPUTED NOTICE

As discussed in Chapter 2, structure matters in creating organizational ombuds programs. To overcome a presumption in favor of full disclosure of potentially relevant communications, an organizational ombuds must be able to articulate not only why its confidentiality should be protected, but also why doing so does not offend other established legal principles. Nowhere is this more important than on the issue of whether an ombuds's knowledge of something should be imputed to the organization. This section, therefore, explains why organizational ombuds are not a channel for giving notice of claims to their organizations. It also provides ombuds offices and their organizations with legal authority to use in defending against a claim that information that the ombuds was told or knew should be imputed to the organization for which the ombuds works. Without this most fundamental step, all that follows is for naught.

The concern over whether communications with an ombuds constitute imputed notice of claims against an organization arises most frequently in discrimination and harassment cases, where a court may find that an organization is liable because certain individuals within the organization knew or should have known of the allegedly illegal conduct. Another reason for this concern is found in criminal statutes that hold organizations liable for crimes committed by their agents if the agents were acting within the scope of their employment or authority or the agents intended to benefit the organization. Organizations may be held liable where certain individuals who were employees of or agents for the organization knew or should have known of the criminal activity.

A. Basic Principles of Imputed Notice

It is not possible here to identify every circumstance or factor under state and federal law that has resulted in a decision that notice of a claim may be imputed to an organization. It is possible and useful, however, to distill from reported cases those circumstances generally in which knowledge of an individual is imputed to and considered to constitute notice to an organization, thereby rendering the organization potentially liable for a claim. Basic principles, derived from opinions of the U.S. Supreme Court and other well-established law, include the following:

- Managers, supervisors, and other "high-echelon officials" of the organization who have actual knowledge of the complaint or discriminatory/harassing conduct impute notice to the employer;[3]
- Managers, supervisors, and other officials of the organization who have "substantial authority and discretion to make decisions concerning the [complainant's] or [accused's] employment" impute notice to the employer;[4]
- Persons within the organization whose job functions and responsibilities require them to investigate and report complaints of illegality or discrimination/harassment (e.g., senior corporate officers, directors, human resource personnel, and compliance officers) impute notice to the employer.
- Generally, if a "co-worker has knowledge of a . . . complaint, but that co-worker lacks authority to counsel, investigate, suspend, or fire the accused . . . or to change the conditions of the [complainant's] employment, the co-worker's inaction does not spark employer liability *unless that co-worker has an official or strong de facto duty to act as a conduit to management for complaints about work conditions*."[5]
- "In cases of peer sexual harassment, it remains an 'open' question [under Title IX] as to whether knowledge of the discrimination by a classroom instructor constitutes knowledge by the funding recipient. In such cases, however, knowledge by an assistant principal, a Title IX coordinator, an affirmative action officer or dean, and a university lawyer ('an official respon-

---

3. *See, e.g.*, Faragher v. City of Boca Raton, 524 U.S. 775, 789 (1998) (discrimination claims by employees against employers under Title VII); Gebser v. Lago Vista Indep. Sch. Dist., 524 U.S. 274, 290 (1998) (discrimination claims by students against schools under Title IX). *See* U.S. Equal Employment Opportunity Commission (EEOC), ENFORCEMENT GUIDANCE: VICARIOUS EMPLOYER LIABILITY FOR UNLAWFUL HARASSMENT BY SUPERVISORS [hereinafter EEOC ENFORCEMENT GUIDANCE] (1999), *available at* http://www.eeoc.gov/policy/docs/harassment.html (last visited April 30, 2009).

4. Torres v. Pisano, 116 F.3d 625, 637 (2d Cir. 1997).

5. *Id.* (internal quotation omitted) (citing RESTATEMENT (SECOND) OF THE LAW OF AGENCY § 275 (1958) (emphasis in original)).

> **Actual Ombuds Example**
>
> **Policy clarification wanted but fear of asking**
>
> The organization had a drug-testing policy for safety-sensitive positions. An employee came to the ombuds to ask whether he would have to take the drug test if notified to do so. He said that he objected to the drug test on principle, not because he had any fear of the results. He was afraid to ask for a clarification of the policy, however, because that may mark him as a "dangerous druggie" or cause him to lose his sensitive duty status or even his job.
>
> The ombuds reviewed the policy with the inquirer. Among other options presented by the ombuds was the possibility that the ombuds could make an inquiry of the director in charge without naming any employee to see if there were any exceptions or "wiggle room" in the policy. That was the option selected by the inquirer. When the ombuds made the inquiry, the answer was that no exceptions were permitted because the test was required by federal policies. When this information was communicated back to the inquirer, he understood and very much appreciated the chance to raise the issue without being the person identified with doing so.

sible for fielding sexual harassment complaints'), all have been deemed sufficient." (Internal citations omitted.)[6]

B. General Principles of Agency Law

In deciding whether notice of a claim should be imputed to an organization, many courts frequently cite to the *Restatement (Second) of the Law of Agency*, published by the American Law Institute (ALI).[7] The

---

    6. Snethen v. Bd. of Pub. Educ. for the City of Savannah and the County of Chatham, 2008 U.S. Dist. LEXIS 22788 (S.D. Ga., Savannah Div., March 24, 2008) at *8 n.4, *quoting* S.S. v. Alexander, 177 P 3d 724, 737–38 (Wash. App. Div. 1, 2008).

    7. The American Law Institute published the RESTATEMENT (THIRD) OF THE LAW OF AGENCY IN 2005, though the RESTATEMENT (SECOND) OF THE LAW OF AGENCY (1958) remains most widely cited. *See* Sections 5.01–5.04 of the RESTATEMENT (THIRD) OF THE LAW OF AGENCY (2005) for the current articulation of these principles, which continue to emphasize the scope of the agent's real and apparent authority and the nature of the agent's duties.

Restatement represents a codified summary of legal principles dealing with agency issues developed through common law. Chapter 8 of this Restatement deals with the liability of a principal (in this case, the organization) to third persons and focuses on "Notice through Agent." Two sections are particularly relevant to this analysis. Section 268 sets forth the General Rule. It states in relevant part:

(1) Unless the notifier has notice that the agent has an interest adverse to the principal, a notification given to an agent is notice to the principal if it is given:
 (a) to an agent *authorized* to receive it;
 (b) to an agent *apparently authorized* to receive it;
 (c) to an agent authorized to conduct a transaction, with respect to matters connected with it as to which notice is usually given to such an agent, *unless the one giving the notification has notice that the agent is not authorized* to receive it. . . .
(2) The rules as to the giving of notification to an agent apply to the giving of notification by an agent.[8]

A related provision in the Restatement is Section 275 ("Agent Having Duty to Reveal Knowledge"):

Except where the agent is acting adversely to the principal or where knowledge as distinguished from reason to know is important, the principal is affected by the knowledge which an agent has a duty to disclose to the principal or another agent of the principal to the same extent as if the principal had the information.[9]

The significance of these provisions is that they make the question of whether notice is imputed turn on whether the agent (the ombuds) has a *duty* to disclose his or her knowledge *or* on whether the agent is *held out* to others as an *official channel* or as one having "*apparent*" authority to receive notice on behalf of the organization. Likewise, whether the agent is *not authorized* to receive notice can be impor-

---

8. RESTATEMENT (SECOND) OF THE LAW OF AGENCY § 268 (1958) (emphasis added).
9. *Id.* § 275 (1958).

tant. An ombuds program that complies with the IOA Code of Ethics and Standards of Practice is independent and has no other management responsibilities (hence, no duty) and publicizes its independence and the fact that it is not a notice channel (hence, an express disclaimer of authority to receive notice as well as no apparent authority to receive notice). The importance of these points, however, cannot be overstated: ombuds programs must publicize the fact that they were created as an alternate or supplemental channel of communication, and they do *not* serve as agents for an organization for purposes of receiving notice of claims.

Organizations that group the ombuds office with all of the other reporting channels or that indicate that an ombuds office is available for "reporting" claims or misconduct may face a claim that the ombuds office had real or apparent authority to act on behalf of the organization and thus enable someone to successfully claim that statements to an ombuds should be imputed to the organization.

C. Cases Relevant to Imputed Notice

Only a few known cases have directly ruled on the issue of whether communications with an ombuds should be imputed to an organization. There are other cases, however, in which courts have respected a request that a complaint of harassment or discrimination be kept confidential, sometimes even when it has been made to a supervisor. While this latter group of cases does not address directly the issue of ombuds notice, they are helpful because they show that courts have, on occasion, given effect to a condition of confidentiality imposed by an employee in a statement to a potential agent of the organization. A properly structured ombuds program is essentially this circumstance in reverse: an individual should be prevented from claiming that notice is imputed to an organization where the person communicated with an ombuds program that publicly describes itself as independent, only a supplemental communication channel, and *not* as an office authorized to receive notice of claims. Even though a manager's nondisclosure of information relating to a claim of illegality would probably violate the anti-discrimination and non-retaliation policies of most organizations, these cases also illustrate the point that a victim is not required by law to come forward with a claim. Thus, where there is a clearly articulated and publicized policy that communications with an ombuds office are confidential and off-the-record, consistent with a structure that makes the office an independent and alternate channel of communication, there are strong legal grounds to assert that an individual who communicated with the ombuds did not put the organization on notice of a claim.

Relevant cases on the issue of imputed notice include the following:

***Karibian v. Columbia University,* 812 F. Supp. 413 (S.D.N.Y. 1993),** *rev'd on other grounds,* **14 F.3d 773 (2d Cir. 1994),** *cert. denied,* **512 U.S. 1213 (1994)**

This is a sexual harassment case in which the plaintiff had a sexual relationship with her superior (Urban). In September 1988, she consulted about it with a member of the Columbia University Sexual Harassment Panel and also with an employee of the university's Office of Equal Opportunity and Affirmative Action (EOAA), two channels that Columbia's policies stated were entirely confidential and which did not conduct investigations or take action against an allegedly offending party. The plaintiff admitted that she was aware of that policy and specifically requested that there not be an investigation in these conversations. She subsequently met with a higher-level supervisor and complained about sexual harassment, at which point the matter was promptly investigated and disciplinary action taken against Urban. In response to her claim that the university should be liable under a hostile environment theory because it had imputed knowledge of the ongoing relationship after she met with the Sexual Harassment Panel and the EOAA, the court stated:

> The information which certain Columbia employees learned in September 1988 was obtained in the course of consultations which were intended to be completely confidential. It cannot be said that this was "knowledge" on the part of Columbia of the kind that gave Columbia the duty to inquire and take remedial action. Plaintiff chose these confidential procedures instead of availing herself of the right, offered by the University, to file a grievance and initiate an investigation leading to a possible remedy against Urban. Columbia could hardly be expected to act against Urban as a result of the confidential communications of September 1988.[10]

---

10. Karibian v. Columbia Univ., 812 F. Supp. 413, 417 (S.D.N.Y. 1993).

> **Actual Ombuds Example**
>
> **A desire to protect others but an uncertainty over whether the problem continues**
>
> A female employee had filed a formal complaint about male employee's sexual harassment of her, including his inappropriate touching of her. The male employee was reprimanded and moved to another location. The female employee was given coaching and additional protection, including an escort to her car at the end of work.
>
> The female employee sometime later came to the ombuds because she believed that the male employee, in his new work location, was engaged in the same conduct with another female employee, but the suspected conduct did not involve her and she had no direct proof. She also did not want to be identified in any complaint, but she indicated that she was trying to protect other women from what she had gone through. After discussing various options with the ombuds about how this issue could be addressed, the female employee permitted the ombuds to contact HR to advise them that a person who wished to remain anonymous had concerns—but no direct proof—about sexual harassment by the male employee.
>
> HR conducted its own investigation and concluded that the male employee was, in fact, sexually harassing another female employee. His employment was subsequently terminated.

Faragher v. City of Boca Raton, 111 F.3d 1530 (11th Cir. 1997) (en banc), *rev'd on other grounds*, 524 U.S. 775 (1998)

The Eleventh Circuit Court of Appeals accepted the district court's finding on the issue of direct liability for hostile work environment—that the plaintiff's complaints to her immediate supervisor (Gordon) should not be imputed to the city because he did not rank as higher management. On the issue of indirect liability, however, the appeals court held that the trial court erred in finding the city liable because of Gordon's knowledge: "Gordon did not receive that information as the City's agent; he received it as a friend held in high repute by his colleagues."[11] The U.S. Supreme Court did not reach this issue in its opinion, as it reversed the Eleventh Circuit on other grounds and reinstated the judgment from the district court.[12]

Torres v. Pisano, 116 F. 3d 625 (2d Cir. 1997), cert. denied, 522 U.S. 997 (1997)

This case, cited by the U.S. Supreme Court in *Faragher*, considered whether written and verbal complaints to the plaintiff's indirect supervisor (Pisano) about sexual and racially harassing behavior by her direct supervisor gave rise to imputed knowledge on the part of New York University, their employer. The Court noted that the plaintiff on several occasions requested Pisano to keep her complaints about her supervisor confidential. Only later, and after a meeting with a higher-level officer of the university, were her complaints investigated and she was given a transfer. While the Court *did* impute Pisano's knowledge of her complaints to the university, it held that the university did *not* breach its duty to remedy the harassment because of her requests for confidentiality: "On these facts, it must be said as a matter of law that Pisano behaved reasonably in honoring Torres' request for confidentiality and in failing to act immediately to end the harassment. Accordingly, while NYU is liable for Pisano's actions, Pisano did not breach his duty to protect Torres from further harassment."[13]

Sims v. Med. Ctr. of Baton Rouge, Inc., 1997 WL 436258 (E.D. La. Aug. 1, 1997)

The district court in the Eastern District of Louisiana relied on *Torres* to hold that the defendant hospital (Lakeside) did not have notice of the plaintiff's claims of sexual harassment. Although the plaintiff reported the incidents to her supervisor, who reported them to the HR director, the plaintiff told the HR director that she did not want to file a complaint and she denied his requests to initiate a formal investigation. The HR director did not investigate the claims because of her "request for confidentiality and privacy." Noting that the plaintiff's complaints occurred over only four days, the court found that as a

---

11. Faragher v. City of Boca Raton, 111 F. 3d 1530, 1538 n.9 (11th Cir. 1997) (en banc), *rev'd on other grounds*, 524 U.S. 775.
12. 524 U.S. at 810.
13. *Torres,* 116 F.3d at 639.

matter of law the supervisor acted reasonably in protecting the plaintiff's privacy: "The bottom line is that Sims could not request confidentiality and then berate Lakeside for complying with her own wishes."[14]

Hooker v. United Parcel Services, 77 F. Supp. 2d 753 (S.D. W. Va. 1999)

The district court in *Hooker* found that UPS had an effective policy in place to prevent sexual harassment and that the company took prompt action both to investigate the plaintiff's allegations against her supervisor (Wentz) and to discipline him once it received the complaint in her lawsuit. Citing *Torres,* however, the court held that because the plaintiff's comments about Wentz's behavior to her part-time supervisor were made with the request that he keep them private and not report them to a higher authority, the part-time supervisor did not breach his duty to remedy the harassment.[15] Accordingly, the court granted the UPS motion for summary judgment based on the affirmative defense recognized in *Faragher* and *Ellerth*.

Chambers v. Wal-Mart Stores, Inc., 1998 U.S. Dist. LEXIS 22698 (N.D. Ga. July 17, 1998)

In this hostile work environment sexual harassment case, the plaintiff inquired of the store manager what would happen if someone in management had done something wrong, but she did not disclose the identity of the other person involved or the nature of the improper conduct. The store manager responded that such conduct would, under the circumstances she described, be the other person's word against hers. Because this case was decided after the Supreme Court had decided *Faragher,* the court analyzed whether the plaintiff had properly complained to higher management and whether higher management failed to act, based on the test articulated in *Faragher*. The court indicated that it was undisputed that she had asked the store manager "to retain her complaint in confidence, as she had spoken to him as a friend, not as a member of management; and she had not yet made a decision as

---

14. Sims v. Med. Ctr. of Baton Rouge, Inc., 1997 WL 436258 at *5 (E.D. La. Aug. 1, 1997).

15. Hooker v. United Parcel Services, Inc., 77 F. Supp. 2d 753, 757–58 (S.D. W.Va. 1999).

to whether she wanted to pursue the matter further."¹⁶ Relying on the Eleventh Circuit's opinion in *Faragher* that was reversed on other grounds by the U.S. Supreme Court, the court in *Chambers* ruled that "notice to a manager does not constitute notice to management when the complainant asks the manager as a friend, albeit a member of management, to keep the information confidential."[17]

Elezovic v. Ford Motor Co., 472 Mich. 408 (2005)

The Michigan Supreme Court in 2005 cited the opinion in *Hooker* and the Eleventh Circuit opinion in *Faragher* in holding that the plaintiff's claim that she told two low-level supervisors of the improper activity of another person did not constitute imputed notice of her claim to the defendant employer. In particular, the court noted:

> It must be recalled that, if an employee is sexually harassed in the workplace, it is that employee's choice whether to pursue the matter. In other words, the victim of harassment "owns the right" whether to notify the company and start the process of investigation. Until the employee takes appropriate steps to start the process, it has not started. . . . Thus, when an employee requests confidentiality in discussing workplace harassment, and the request for confidentiality is honored, such a request is properly considered a waiver of the right to give notice.[18]

Palomo v. The Trustees of Columbia Univ., 2005 U.S. Dist. LEXIS 14428 (S.D.N.Y. July 20, 2005)

The plaintiffs alleged hostile work environment, constructive discharge, and retaliation for acts of their supervisor (Hanabury). The court held that they had not alleged sufficient facts on the hostile work environment and constructive discharge claims. With respect

---

16. Chambers v. Wal-Mart Stores, Inc., 1998 U.S. Dist. LEXIS 22698 at *17 (N.D. Ga. July 17, 1998).

17. *Id.*

18. Elezovic v. Ford Motor Co., 697 N.W.2d 851, 861–62 (2005). The court also observed at n.25, however, that "[a]n employer, of course, remains free to discipline a supervisor for failing to report a sexual harassment complaint to the proper persons as required by the employer's policy. But, that is a different issue, and it does not mean that a confidential report of sexual harassment to a supervisor constitutes notice to the employer." *Id. But see* EEOC ENFORCEMENT GUIDANCE, *supra* note 3.

> **Actual Ombuds Example**
>
> **Make him stop but don't disclose that I brought it up**
>
> A manager made a comment in front of several employees that the area where they worked "smelled like a whorehouse." An employee brought this issue to the ombuds but was not willing to take it to other management or HR because of concerns that the manager who made the comment would retaliate against the employee.
>
> After discussing various options to address the issue, the employee gave the ombuds permission to disclose the comment but not the employee's identity to HR. When HR was informed of the comment, it conducted an investigation and confirmed from several sources that the comment had been made. The manager was disciplined and HR provided additional harassment training to the entire unit.

to the retaliation claim, the court rejected the claim that the plaintiffs were subjected to retaliation for having gone to the Columbia Ombuds Office. The court found that the supervisor's only knowledge of their complaints to the Ombuds Office came after the plaintiffs had submitted their resignations. Thus, they did not present "a material issue of fact concerning whether Hanabury knew of their participation in a protected activity, assuming the complaints to the Ombuds Office constituted protected activity, prior to their announcements of their decisions to leave Columbia."[19]

Grother v. Union Pacific Railroad Co., 2006 U.S. Dist. LEXIS 38415 (S.D. Texas, Houston Div., June 9, 2006)

The court refused to impute to the company knowledge of claims allegedly given to an ombuds, stating:

> . . . the record shows that when Fryar evaluated Grother in late 2002 and Bishop finished the evaluation before January 2, 2003, they did not know of Grother's complaint to the ombudsman. "If an employer is unaware of an employee's protected conduct at the time of the adverse employment action,

---

19. Palomo v. Trustees of Columbia Univ., 2005 U.S. Dist. LEXIS 14428 at *66 (S.D.N.Y. July 20, 2005).

the employer plainly could not have retaliated against the employee based on that conduct."[20]

Webb v. Merck & Co., Inc., 450 F. Supp. 2d 582 (E.D. Pa. 2006)

While not, strictly speaking, a case involving imputed notice, *Webb* is instructive because the court found that an employee's reports to an *ombuds office that was created to investigate allegations of race discrimination* constituted "protected activity" under Title VII. An imputed notice analysis, therefore, is not necessary where the function of the ombuds is to conduct investigations, and communications with such an office constitute direct notice. Thus, the court in *Webb* denied the company's motion for summary judgment on the plaintiff's claim that the company retaliated against him by suspending him after he complained to the ombudsman. In particular, the court found that the Merck ombudsman reported to the company's chief ethics officer and had responsibility to investigate cases of race discrimination, to "'hear any work-related issues or concerns of employees' and to 'work[] with management to try to resolve employee issues or concerns.'"[21] The evidence considered by the court included the fact that the plaintiff (Green) "reported" discriminatory remarks by his supervisor to the ombudsman (Johnson) and that while Green did not tell Murphy that he had gone to the ombudsman, he alleged that everyone knew he had done so because he was seen leaving the office and because he had told others that he had done so. The court concluded: "From this evidence, a jury could reasonably determine that when Green complained to Johnson, he was acting in a good faith belief that his right to be free from discrimination was violated. Therefore, Green's complaints to Johnson are sufficient to establish that he engaged in a protected activity under Title VII." (Internal citation omitted.)[22]

---

20. Grother v. Union Pac. R.R. Co., 2006 U.S. Dist. LEXIS 38415 at *39 (S.D. Texas, Houston Div., June 9, 2006). Note that it is not clear from the record whether the Union Pacific Railroad Ombuds Office was an organizational ombuds program that complied with the IOA Code of Ethics and Standards of Practice.

21. Webb v. Merck & Co., Inc., 450 F. Supp. 2d 582, 589 n.6 (E.D. Pa. 2006).

22. *Id.* at 601. *See also* Byra-Grzegorczyk v. Bristol-Myers Squibb Co., 572 F. Supp. 2d 233, 249 (D. Conn. 2008), in which the court, based on similar facts, also found that internal complaints to the company's ombuds constituted "protected activity." The opinion in *Byra-Grzegorczyk* provides no insight into the type of ombuds office that existed at Bristol-Myers Squibb.

Cotrone v. Marquette University, 2007 U.S. Dist. LEXIS 41930 (E.D. Wis. June 8, 2007)

In *Cotrone*, the court recognized the confidentiality of employees' communications with the ombuds notwithstanding the fact that the ombuds subsequently communicated the substance of those issues to the plaintiff's supervisor. In particular, when three of the 20 employees supervised by the plaintiff complained separately to the university ombuds about the plaintiff's management style, the ombuds brought the substance of those complaints to the plaintiff's supervisor without disclosing the identity of any of the complainants, and the supervisor then discussed those issues with the plaintiff. The court noted that the mission of the ombuds office at Marquette was "to provide a confidential . . . resource to facilitate resolutions to workplace concerns."[23] In concluding that the plaintiff had not presented any evidence from which a jury could conclude that he was constructively discharged or suffered from a hostile work environment, the court found that "plaintiff shows only that three employees used the well-established university ombuds process to criticize him. Further, by keeping the process confidential, defendant did no more than follow the ombuds process's rules. . . . And, as discussed, based on the ombuds rules, he had no right to communicate with employees who used the ombuds process in the first place."[24]

Dudley Thompson v. The Coca Cola Company, 497 F. Supp. 2d 80 (D. Mass. 2007), *affirmed*, 522 F.3d 168 (1st Cir. 2008)

This case illustrates how the issue of notice can be clouded by a lack of precision in how the word "report" is used. In granting summary judgment for the defendant company on the plaintiff's claims of discriminatory discharge and hostile work environment, the district court noted:

> It is undisputed that Defendant has a comprehensive anti-discrimination and workplace dispute resolution system, which provides employees with several avenues for reporting incidents. These avenues include a toll-free phone number to *report* issues

---

23. Cotrone v. Marquette Univ., 2007 U.S. Dist. LEXIS 41930 at *2 (E.D. Wis. June 8, 2007).
24. *Id.* at *8–9.

> ### Actual Ombuds Example
>
> **Averting a class-action lawsuit**
>
> Several African-American employees came to the ombuds office as a group to express frustration with their manager, who they felt continuously treated them inappropriately. They thought he was discriminating against them on the basis of their race and said that they were willing to file suit against the organization and the manager.
>
> The ombuds reminded the employees that the ombuds office was neither an office of notice for claims against the organization nor a place to provide them with legal advice on any claims they may or may not have but, instead, an office where they could have confidential discussions to see if there might be an informal way to resolve their concerns. They said they wanted to speak confidentially. After a few meetings with the ombuds, during which a variety of options were discussed, they gave permission for the ombuds to contact the manager, share their concerns, and request that he meet with them as a group in a meeting facilitated by the ombuds.
>
> When the ombuds spoke with the manager, he immediately expressed his own frustration at his inability to communicate effectively with this group of employees. It appeared to the ombuds that the manager was experiencing his own insecurities, and he clearly welcomed the opportunity to vent in a safe and confidential setting. At the manager's request, the ombuds coached the manager on active listening and effective communication techniques. The manager then began implementing these new listening and communication skills as he communicated with the employees he supervised, including the African-American group. Communication between the manager and his employees markedly improved and no facilitated meeting was ever needed. This manager contacted the ombuds on his own initiative thereafter when he felt stuck and needed to discuss options on how he might handle a situation. As a result, the manager continued to build better relations with the employees and to improve his own communication skills.

of concern, as well as the opportunity for a confidential consultation with an ombudsman.[25]

Note that here, the district court's opinion made a distinction between the toll-free number "to report issues of concern" and the ombuds office ("for a confidential consultation"). However, when the First Circuit affirmed the summary judgment granted by the district court, it found that the plaintiff never reported the allegedly discriminatory remarks of his supervisor to anyone. The court quoted the above language from the district court and then stated: "Thompson concedes that he never made or attempted to report any alleged incidents until after he was terminated."[26] Thus, while the district court recognized the distinction that that the toll-free number was available to "report" issues of concern and that the ombudsman was available for a confidential consultation, the First Circuit opinion conflated the two points.

Norden v. Samper, 503 F. Supp. 2d 130 (D.D.C. 2007)

The plaintiff asserted a claim against the acting secretary of the Smithsonian Institute for failure to accommodate her handicap under the Rehabilitation Act of 1973, and the court considered whether the ombudsman had been designated as a party to whom a claim should be made. The court held that the plaintiff's alleged discussion with an ombudsman on her need for accommodation did not satisfy the specific regulatory requirement that notice of a claim be given to the EEO Counselor:

> This argument is also unavailing. In order to satisfy the exhaustion requirement, an employee must contact an EEO Counselor. *See* 29 *C.F.R. § 1614.105(a).* There is no dispute that none of the individuals who Dr. Norden contacted before April 2003 . . .was designated as an EEO Counselor. Informal efforts to resolve employment disputes outside the EEO process do not satisfy the requirements of § 1614.105(a).[27]

---

25. Dudley v. The Coca Cola Co., 497 F. Supp. 2d. 80, 84 (D. Mass. 2007) (emphasis added).

26. Dudley v. The Coca Cola Co., 522 F.3d 168, 180–81 (1st Cir. 2008).

27. Norden v. Samper, 503 F. Supp. 2d 130, 147 (D.D.C. 2007). Note that it is not clear whether the ombuds program at the Smithsonian Institution was an organizational ombuds program that complies with the IOA Code of Ethics and Standards of Practice.

208 CHAPTER 3

***S.S. v. Alexander*, 177 P.3d 724 (Wash. App. Div. 1, 2008)**
The court in this Title IX discrimination case imputed to the university defendant knowledge of claims made to the university ombuds (and other university officials) by a female student against a varsity football player at the University of Washington. In doing so, the court found that the ombuds was an "appropriate person" under Title IX who was aware of the discrimination and who then failed to act reasonably. This decision by the State of Washington Court of Appeals, however, well illustrates the point that where an organizational ombuds office is not appropriately established and operated, it will be deemed to be a notice channel for its institution.

The facts cited by the court in *S.S. v. Alexander* are so problematic that they merit extended discussion. A female student who held a campus job as an assistant equipment manager for the varsity football team became involved in a consensual sexual relationship in the fall of her freshman year with Alexander, one of the star players on the team. As a result of increasingly demeaning actions by Alexander, the plaintiff broke off the relationship. She alleged that five days later he pushed his way into her room, removed her clothing, and had intercourse with her against her will and despite her verbal protest. The plaintiff did not report this to anyone at that time. The following summer she told an assistant coach that she had been sexually assaulted. She subsequently reported the assault to the equipment manager, the associate athletic director, and also to his supervisor (Tuite) and the assistant athletic director. None of these people advised her of her options for reporting the assault to a formal channel. Tuite spoke with the plaintiff and advised the plaintiff that Tuite would arrange for counseling sessions and that something would be done. When the plaintiff subsequently did not hear back from Tuite, she went to Tuite and said that she wanted to file a police report. Tuite again did not give her options for reporting but specifically told her to wait because Tuite was working on a solution.

Tuite contacted the athletic director and the Title IX coordinator, who then met with the university ombuds to determine how to proceed. Collectively, they decided that the ombuds would conduct a mediation between the plaintiff and Alexander. In footnote 4 of the court's opinion, the court specifically noted the authority of the ombuds office: "The ombudsman is charged with the *authority* to receive complaints from students with regard to 'alleged inequities,' to seek to resolve such inequities and 'recommend to the President redress when the Ombudsman believes that an individual has been improperly treated and when the Ombudsman has been unable to resolve the matter.'"[28]

By the time the ombuds met with the plaintiff for the mediation, the ombuds had already met with Alexander, and she reported to the plaintiff that he had said that he was sorry and had cried when she spoke with him. The ombuds met with the plaintiff twice more before the mediation at which the plaintiff, Tuite, Alexander, and the ombuds were present. The court specifically noted that up to this point, no one had conducted any investigation of the alleged rape, despite detailed accounts of it, and that no one gave the plaintiff other options for reporting the incident. Moreover, the court pointed out that despite the plaintiff's request that Alexander be suspended, *Tuite and the ombuds decided* that he would undergo counseling and community service.[29] When the plaintiff subsequently complained first to the ombuds and then to Tuite about the outcome of the mediation, they still did not advise her of other reporting options. And finally, as evidence of even more outrageous conduct by the ombuds, the court stated that the ombuds made the plaintiff fill out a form indicating that the plaintiff had spoken with Alexander and was satisfied with his response and considered the matter closed.[30]

The key issue with respect to the plaintiff's Title IX claim was whether an "appropriate person" was aware of the discrimination and then failed to reasonably respond. The court cited a leading Supreme Court case for the proposition that an "appropriate person" is "at a minimum an official of the recipient entity with *authority to take corrective action to end the discrimination*" and that this is a fact question.[31] The court held that the assistant coach and the equipment manager were not "appropriate persons" because their duties were "more akin to a classroom instructor" (and thus were not appropriate persons for receiving notice), but the ombuds, the Title IX coordinator, the athletic director, assistant athletic director Tuite, and the associate athletic director were held to be "appropriate persons."[32]

---

28. S.S. v. Alexander, 177 P.3d at 730 n.4 (emphasis added).
29. *Id.* at 730–31.
30. *Id.*
31. *Id.* at 737 (emphasis added).
32. *Id.* at 738.

Actual Ombuds Example

The ombuds helps the student and helps preserve evidence of wrongdoing

A student employee came to the ombuds office to describe a situation she did not know how to handle. She wanted to discuss the matter confidentially with the ombuds before taking any action.

The problem arose in connection with her job in the campus housing office. Her manager told her when she started work that his mother was sick and could not afford food or medicine, so he wanted to add six hours each week to her timesheet and assured her that she would still be paid for the eight hours a week that she in fact worked but that she would give him back the extra money so he could give it to his mother. The student agreed, and they operated under this arrangement for several months. When she received her W-2 form, however, she realized that not only would she owe taxes on the extra money, her earnings were so high that she would no longer be eligible for her scholarship.

The ombuds advised the student to turn herself in to the dean's office, but also offered options on how to deal with the misconduct of the manager. The ombuds was aware of the need to preserve evidence, an issue that had not occurred to the student. They agreed that, before the student went to the dean, the ombuds and the student would go to the senior vice president in charge of student life. Because of the ombuds' knowledge of the university, the ombuds felt that going to the most senior level first was the best way to proceed and was able to arrange for such a meeting. The senior vice president immediately arranged for HR and security to gather the necessary information in a professional and discreet manner before alerting the manager involved. The ombuds had been concerned that a less thorough or easily noticed investigation might have been done if the matter had been reported at a lower level.

Only after this was accomplished did the student report the incident to the dean and deal with her own situation. Since the university had already obtained the incriminating documentation on the manager, there was no risk that he could destroy the

> evidence or flee. He was subsequently confronted, arrested, and later terminated from employment. The student's assistance led to some leniency in terms of disciplinary action by the university and the financial aid office helped her explore other sources of financial aid, but her W-2 form was not changed and she was ineligible for her scholarship for the following year.

While the holding that notice to the ombuds should be imputed to the university is problematic as a general proposition, the facts considered by the court in this case compel such a conclusion. The ombuds program in *S.S. v. Alexander*, however, is readily distinguishable from ombuds programs created and functioning in accordance with the IOA Code of Ethics and Standards of Practice. For example:

- The University of Washington ombuds program appears to have been improperly structured from the beginning, having expressly been given the authority to receive complaints;
- It appears to have had management functions and participated in the management decision to require the plaintiff to go to mediation;
- Based on the facts found by the court, it appears to have colluded with the athletic department administrators and the Title IX compliance officer to put the interests of the football team ahead of those of the plaintiff;
- None of the formal channels, or even the ombuds, advised the plaintiff of other options to report the incident;
- No one investigated her complaint; and
- The mediation appears to have been a sham, both in what occurred in the mediation and in compelling the plaintiff to report that it was successfully concluded.

For these reasons, any attempt by a party to cite the *S.S. v. Alexander* case for the proposition that an ombuds should be consider an agent of notice or an "appropriate person" under Title IX should be countered with the factual differences between the program considered by the court there and a properly structured ombuds program.[33]

D. IOA and the 2004 ABA Resolution

This review of the basic principles of imputed notice and agency law on imputed notice, together with the case law, provide a context in which to look more closely at the positions on imputed notice taken by the IOA and in the 2004 ABA Resolution.

The IOA Standards of Practice specifically disclaim ombuds as an agent of notice. Section 3.8 of the IOA Standards of Practice provides:

> Communications made to the Ombuds are not notice to the organization. The Ombuds neither acts as agent for, nor accepts notice on behalf of, the organization. However, the Ombuds may refer individuals to the appropriate place where formal notice can be made.[34]

The provisions in Paragraph F the 2004 ABA Resolution, however, take a somewhat different position: it provides that if an ombuds

---

33. The University of Washington is not alone in vesting the ombuds with authority to receive complaints and participate in investigations. In another recent case, *Herndon v. College of the Mainland,* 2009 U.S. Dist. LEXIS 12425 (S.D. Texas, Galveston Div., Feb. 13, 2009), the court cited the sexual harassment policy of the defendant, which provided that a student filing a sexual harassment complaint would have an initial conference with the college ombudsman and that the "College Ombudsman or designee shall coordinate an appropriate investigation, which ordinarily shall be completed within seven days of the receipt of the complaint." *Id.* at *14. Herndon failed to file a complaint as required by the policy, but the court nevertheless denied the college's motion for summary judgment on the issue of sexual harassment. The court observed: "Moreover, a complainant's failure to follow a formal sexual harassment complaint procedure is not dispositive in a Title IX case. '[U]nder *Gebser* and its progeny, an aggrieved student or employee need not follow the institution's official route for reporting sexual harassment. She must merely report to someone with authority to take corrective measures.' *Crandell v. N.Y. College of Osteopathic Med.,* 87 F. Supp. 2d 304, 321 (S.D.N.Y. 2000)." *Id.* at *69–70. The lesson in cases like *S.S. v. Alexander* and *Herndon* is to structure the ombuds program so that it does not have either actual or apparent authority to receive notice, investigate, or participate in taking corrective actions.

34. INTERNATIONAL OMBUDSMAN ASSOCIATION, STANDARDS OF PRACTICE, 3.8. *See* Appendix 5 at 460 (IOA Standards of Practice in effect prior to October 2009); *see also* Appendix 5 at 463 (Standards of Practice effective October 2009).

functions in accordance with the "Independence, Impartiality, and Confidentiality" provisions of Paragraph C of the Resolution, the ombuds should not be deemed an agent of the entity for notice purposes, but that if an ombuds communicates with the entity, communications with the ombuds can be, in some circumstances, imputed to the entity.[35] The issue of imputed notice in the context of an ombuds communicating with the entity, however, is an issue that was never addressed in any iteration of the Ombuds Association's Codes of Ethics or Standards of Practice. The 2004 ABA Resolution sought to address the issue of notice left unaddressed in the 2001 ABA Resolution and in the association's standards of practice and has been recognized for reinforcing the notion that ombuds, as a supplement to formal communication channels rather than a formal channel itself, should not in most cases be seen as imputing notice to the organization.[36] Unfortunately, the solution it articulates is vague and confusing, does not comport with the general principles of agency law presented above, and ultimately is unworkable.

Paragraph F, "Notice," of the 2004 ABA Resolution has three subsections.[37] The first addresses an ombuds's need to supply accurate information about the office and is often referred to by ombuds as the "Miranda warnings." The practices of many organizational ombuds have largely adopted these provisions, except where they implicate the subsequent subparagraphs to which most organizational ombuds have taken exception, and thus the provisions in this section are largely not in dispute. These warnings serve to make sure at the beginning of an ombuds communication that both the ombuds and the inquirer are proceeding with the same understanding of the role of the ombuds and the confidential nature of the communications. The second subparagraph, however, addresses the particularly thorny question of when an *ombuds's* communication with others in an entity should be considered notice. The final subparagraph attempts to summarize when notice is imputed

---

35. AMERICAN BAR ASS'N, STANDARDS FOR THE ESTABLISHMENT AND OPERATION OF OMBUDS OFFICES (revised Feb. 2004) [hereinafter 2004 ABA RESOLUTION]. *See* Appendix 7 at 501–02.

36. *See* Katherine A. Welch, *Note: No Notice Is Good News: Notice Under the New Ombuds Standards for the Establishment and Operation of Ombuds Offices*, 2005 J. DISP. RESOL. 193 (2005).

37. 2004 ABA RESOLUTION, *supra* note 35. *See* Appendix 7 at 500–02.

to an entity from communications with an ombuds and when it is not. Paragraph F, together with its footnotes, reads as follows:

NOTICE

F. An ombuds is intended to supplement, not replace, formal procedures.* Therefore:
(1) An ombuds should provide the following information in a general and publicly available manner and inform people who contact the ombuds for help or advice that—
   (a) the ombuds will not voluntarily disclose to anyone outside the ombuds office, including the entity in which the ombuds acts, any information the person provides in confidence or the person's identity unless necessary to address an imminent risk of serious harm or with the person's express consent
   (b) important rights may be affected by when formal action is initiated and by and when the entity is informed of the allegedly inappropriate or wrongful behavior or conduct
   (c) communications to the ombuds may not constitute notice to the entity unless the ombuds communicates with representatives of the entity as described in Paragraph 2
   (d) working with the ombuds may address the problem or concern effectively, but may not protect the rights of either the person contacting the office or the entity in which the ombuds operates**
   (e) the ombuds is not, and is not a substitute for, anyone's lawyer, representative or counselor, and
   (f) the person may wish to consult a lawyer or other appropriate resource with respect to those rights.
(2) If the ombuds communicates*** with representatives of the entity concerning an allegation of a violation, then—

---

* An ombuds program as envisioned by these Standards supplements and does not substitute for the need of an entity to establish formal procedures that may be necessary to *protect legal rights* and to address allegedly inappropriate or wrongful behavior or conduct.

** The notice requirements of Paragraph F do not supersede or change the advocacy responsibilities of an Advocate Ombuds.

*** Under these standards, any such communication is subject to Paragraph C(3).

(a) a communication that reveals the facts of
  (i) a specific allegation and the identity of the complainant or
  (ii) allegations by multiple complainants that may reflect related behavior or conduct that is either inappropriate or wrongful should be regarded as providing notice to the entity of the alleged violation and the complainants should be advised that the ombuds communicated their allegations to the entity; but otherwise,
(b) whether or not the communication constitutes notice to the entity is a question that should be determined by the facts of the communication.
(3) If an ombuds functions in accordance with Paragraph C, "Independence, Impartiality, and Confidentiality," of these standards, then—
  (a) no one, including the entity in which the ombuds operates, should deem the ombuds to be an agent of any person or entity, other than the office of the ombuds, for purposes of receiving notice of alleged violations, and
  (b) communications made to the ombuds should not be imputed to anyone else, including the entity in which the ombuds acts, unless the ombuds communicates with representatives of the entity, in which case Paragraph 2 applies.

One of the reasons that subsection 2 of Paragraph F is problematic is that it uses terms that are unclear and difficult to apply. For example, subsection (2) begins with a reference to a communication between the ombuds and the entity "concerning an allegation of a violation." A subsequent provision in subsection (2) makes reference to "allegations by multiple complainants that may reflect related behavior or conduct that is either inappropriate or wrongful." As drafted, it is not at all clear what is meant by a "violation" as opposed to "conduct that is either inappropriate or wrongful." From an ombuds perspective, this subsection appears to assume that an ombuds determines what behavior is a violation, inappropriate, or wrongful. Such decisions are not typically within the province of an ombuds; an ombuds may disclose facts to the entity, but the determination of whether the actions are a violation, inappropriate, or wrongful is the responsibility of the entity.

A more serious problem with the imputed notice provisions of Paragraph F is that, if the ombuds makes disclosures to the entity as described in subsections (a)(i) and (ii), those communications can be read as imputing notice to the entity of what is communicated to the ombuds by an inquirer.[38] If the ombuds office has been created as an independent and neutral office, there no reason that this result is required based on either the general principles of notice and agency law or case law.

Finally, the provisions of the 2004 ABA Resolution are highly impractical, hard to apply, and make it virtually impossible for both the entity and the ombuds to really know when the entity has been placed on notice. Consequently, the 2004 ABA Resolution was a laudable but ultimately flawed attempt to wrestle with the difficult issues of notice and confidentiality, arguably influenced more by lawyers representing the interests of their clients in employment cases than by a coherent attempt to help develop the law. In responding to this resolution, however, the IOA developed a more workable and legally consistent response to the issue of notice to the entity based on communications from an ombuds. In doing so, the IOA in effect side-stepped the issue of imputed notice. Their response provides a much clearer and more workable rule: what an inquirer says to the ombuds is not considered notice to the entity, but if the ombuds then speaks with a formal channel of the entity about an issue, the entity is on notice of what the ombuds communicates to it, not what may have been communicated to the ombuds.

[A] communication to the ombuds *never constitutes notice to the organization.* As ombuds office administrative manager,

---

38. This is because of the provisions in subsection (3)(b): "communications made *to the ombuds* should not be imputed to anyone else, including the entity in which the ombuds acts *unless* the ombuds communicates with representatives of the entity *in which case Paragraph 2 applies.*" (Emphasis added.) Paragraph 2 states that a disclosure made by the ombuds to the entity under the circumstances described in subsections (i) and (ii) "should be regarded as providing notice to the entity *of the alleged violation* and complainants should be advised that the ombuds communicated their allegations to the entity. . . ." (Emphasis added.)

> **Actual Ombuds Example**
>
> **Issue raised but identity of inquirer protected**
>
> An employee came to the ombuds with a concern that a co-worker had been repeatedly using the Internet at work to review adult content videos and other inappropriate materials. While this activity was clearly prohibited by the organization's policies, the person coming to the ombuds just wanted it stopped and did not want to be identified as the source of the complaint.
>
> After discussing various options on how to raise this issue, *the employee permitted the ombuds to disclose to management the name of the co-worker and the nature of the concern.* HR investigated the conduct, determined that the co-worker had violated policy, and the co-worker was disciplined. The identity of the worker who came to the ombuds was never recorded. HR also used this occasion as an opportunity to send a reminder on the Internet policy to all employees and urged them to notify their managers or HR if they had concerns. At the same time, HR reminded employees that the ombuds office was available if they wanted to protect their anonymity or discuss a matter confidentially.

the lead ombuds may be responsible for receiving notice about wrongful behavior of any ombuds office staff member whom the lead ombuds supervises. Except in this ombuds's administrative capacity as manager of the ombuds office, the ombuds is never an agent of notice or a designated point of contact to accept formal claims or concerns. A communication between an ombuds and an organization's point of contact may serve as notice under some circumstances, as explained below, but the scope of that notice is limited strictly to the substance of the communication between the ombuds and the point of contact, and *never* includes any communications between the visitor and the ombuds.[39]

---

39. INTERNATIONAL OMBUDSMAN ASSOCIATION (IOA), GUIDANCE FOR BEST PRACTICES AND COMMENTARY ON THE AMERICAN BAR ASSOCIATION STANDARDS FOR THE ESTABLISHMENT AND OPERATION OF OMBUDS OFFICES (Revised Feb. 2004) [hereinafter IOA GUIDANCE AND COMMENTARY] (emphasis in the original). *See* Appendix 10 at 549. *See also* IOA Best Practices, A Supplement to IOA's Standards of Practice Version 3, Oct. 13, 2009 (herinafter October 2009 IOA Best Practices) at 5–9, Appendix 11 at 557.

While this rule eliminates the vagaries of the provisions of the 2004 ABA Resolution and creates a bright-line rule that can be easily applied by the ombuds and communicated to inquirers, it also serves as a caution to ombuds in communicating with a formal channel about an issue. This should not present problems for ombuds, however; they should be able to structure any communications with formal channels of the entity with this rule in mind—not disclosing information that is not necessary or that the ombuds does not have permission to disclose. Indeed, the IOA Response enhances the ability of ombuds to assist their inquirers by making limited or partial disclosures to the organization when given permission to do so while protecting the identity and other aspects of the inquirer's communication with them. Likewise, from the organization's perspective, the IOA Response is clear and workable: the entity is on notice and obligated to act only on what the ombuds says to the formal channel, not on information that was not communicated to it.

E. Imputed Notice—Conclusion

As the discussion and case law cited above illustrate, a person can decide whether to place an organization on notice of any claims he or she may have. When the plaintiff has elected to make those complaints in confidence and with the request that no investigation be conducted, courts either have not imputed notice of those claims to the organization or have held that the organization did not breach any duty to eliminate the harassment or discrimination. Of course, as noted by the court in *Elezovic*,[40] an employer remains free to adopt policies that would discipline any supervisor or manager who did not report a claim that he or she learned about, and many organizations in fact have such policies. Thus, when an individual chooses to speak confidentially with an ombuds under a program that is created specifically as a confidential and off-the-record channel, and the ombuds office publicizes the fact that it is not authorized to receive notice of claims on behalf of the organization, the promise of confidentiality should

---

40. Elezovic v. Ford Motor Co., 472 Mich. 408, 427 (2005). *See also* EEOC Enforcement Guidance, *supra* note 3, in which the EEOC may impute notice to an employer if a management representative is aware of harassment but which would permit anonymous calls to a phone line if it is clear that the person taking the calls is not part of management.

not result in imputed notice to the organization. Where the ombuds, with the permission of the inquirer or under an exception to confidentiality, communicates with the organization, the better rule is that what the ombuds communicates to the organization—not what may have been communicated to the ombuds—places the organization on notice. In this circumstance, the ombuds becomes the notice giver, and the organization is on notice of only what is communicated *by* the ombuds; imputed notice of what was communicated *to* the ombuds is inappropriate.

Imputed Notice Practice Tips

To prevent communications with an ombuds office from being imputed to its organization, the organization and the ombuds office should take the following steps:

1. Create and publicize the ombuds office as an alternate and confidential resource that supplements, but does not replace, existing compliance and formal reporting channels.
2. Create the ombuds office so that it has structural independence and is not subservient to one of the existing reporting channels, such as HR or compliance, so that potential inquirers will not be misled as to the apparent authority of the ombuds office. This information should be publicized and made available to all employees or other constituents.
3. In all of the documentation evidencing the creation and publicizing the existence of the program, expressly state that communications with the ombuds are considered confidential and off the record, and that the ombuds office is not part of management and not authorized to receive notice of claims against the organization.
4. Monitor the way in which the ombuds interacts with the formal channels so that the ombuds office does not, in fact, become an extension of those offices or participate in making management decisions, conducting investigations, or have other management responsibilities.
5. Make sure that the ombuds and inquirers understand that, even though communications with the ombuds do not constitute imputed notice to the organization, if an inquirer and the ombuds agree on an option that involves an ombuds

communicating an issue to a management agent, that communication may be giving the organization notice of a claim.[41] For this reason, an ombuds should agree to undertake this action only after careful consideration and only with the express permission of the inquirer. In making such a communication, the ombuds should convey only the information that is necessary and authorized. The organization, therefore, is placed on notice of only what the ombuds communicates to the management representative, not everything that may have been communicated to the ombuds by the inquirer.
6. A formal channel should not expect ombuds to confirm or deny that any particular person consulted with the ombuds office.
7. A formal channel should not expect or ask an ombuds to discuss confidential communications with people with whom the ombuds may have spoken.
8. A formal channel should not inquire of people who come to them whether they have spoken with the ombuds office or what may have been communicated with the ombuds.

PART II—LEGAL BASES FOR OMBUDS CONFIDENTIALITY

Organizational ombuds and their organizations assert that ombuds communications should be protected from compelled disclosure. Although there are statutes that recognize the confidentiality of certain types of communications, including in some situations ombuds communications, most of the present development in this area of the law as applied to ombuds has been on a case-by-case basis in the courts. There are various legal grounds upon which this claim can be based, including privilege, contract, constitutional protection, statutory protections, arbitration procedures, and a court's inherent power to control discovery. The development of the case law in this area began with a federal court applying a state statutory scheme that included a testimonial privilege to an issue before it. Since then, the case law has

---

41. *See* IOA GUIDANCE AND COMMENTARY, *supra* note 39. Appendix 10 at 547–54. *See also* Appendix 11 at 561–68.

grown to include the recognition of a common-law privilege and other bases to protect the confidentiality of ombuds communications.

While court rulings on the claim of privilege initially were favorable, a case decided in 1997 by the Eighth Circuit, *Carman v. McDonnell Douglas Corporation*,[42] rejected a claim of ombuds privilege based on a record inadequate to support the claim. In some subsequent cases, courts have rejected a claim of ombuds privilege based on the fact that the *Carman* court did not recognize an ombudsman privilege, even where the privilege claim at issue was adequately supported by the factual record. Despite these rulings, however, other courts have recognized an ombuds claim of privilege. While ombuds may continue to assert privilege as a basis for protecting confidentiality, given the uncertainty involved and the disfavor with which courts view claims of privilege generally, ombuds and their organizations should also be prepared to structure their programs so that other bases for confidentiality can also be asserted.

A. Common-Law Privilege

1. Background on Development of Federal Testimonial Privileges

Federal courts and the courts of some—but not all—states are authorized by court rules or state law to recognize new testimonial privileges through the development of common law. Federal Rule of Evidence 501 is perhaps the clearest and most well known of these provisions. It states in relevant part, "[e]xcept as otherwise required by the Constitution of the United States or provided by Act of Congress or in rules prescribed by the Supreme Court pursuant to statutory authority, the privilege of a witness . . . shall be governed by the principles of the common law as they may be interpreted by the courts of the United States in the light of reason and experience."

Federal Rule of Evidence 501 was created by Congress in 1974 when Congress rejected a set of proposed privilege rules that would have recognized nine specifically articulated privileges. The proposed privilege rules had been drafted by the Judicial Conference Advisory Committee on Rules of Evidence and had been approved by both the

---

42. Carman v. McDonnell Douglas Corp., 114 F.3d 790 (8th Cir. 1997).

> **Actual Ombuds Example**
>
> **Access to all levels of the organization**
>
> A person whose employment had been terminated after 28 years of service contacted the ombuds office with concerns that his termination was unfair and unjustified. His attempts to appeal to HR and management had been unsuccessful and he was prepared to take his case to an attorney and the media.
>
> The ombuds discussed options with the former employee that he had not yet considered. He decided that the option he wanted to pursue was writing a letter directly to the CEO of the company. The ombuds served as a sounding board for the former employee as he crafted the letter. The ombuds also facilitated getting the letter directly to the CEO.
>
> The CEO responded to the letter with a phone call to and an in-depth conversation with the former employee. The termination was not overturned, but the process of talking to the ombuds and the CEO satisfied many of the concerns the former employee had expressed and allowed him to move forward with a better feeling toward the organization. It also had the effect of avoiding the potential expense and embarrassment of a lawsuit and media involvement.

Judicial Conference of the United States and the U.S. Supreme Court. As the Supreme Court stated in *Trammel v. United States*:

> In rejecting the proposed Rules and enacting Rule 501, Congress manifested an affirmative intention not to freeze the law of privilege. Its purpose rather was to "provide the courts with the flexibility to develop rules of privilege on a case-by-case basis," 120 Cong. Rec. 40891 (1974) (statement of Rep. Hungate), and to leave the door open to change. See also S. Rep. No. 93-1277, p. 11 (1974); H. R. Rep. No. 93-650, p. 8 (1973).[43]

While Rule 501 evinced a determination by Congress that privileges develop on a case-by case basis, it did not change the judicial

---

43. Trammel v. United States, 445 U.S. 40, 47 (1980).

reluctance to recognize new privileges. This bias against recognizing new privileges was evident the same year that Rule 501 was adopted, when the U.S. Supreme Court decided one of its most important cases on the issue of privilege, *United States v. Nixon*,[44] a case in which former President Nixon asserted an absolute privilege for the executive branch that would have enabled him not to comply with a third-party subpoena issued to him by the district court to produce certain records. In rejecting the President's claim of absolute privilege and then trying to find the proper balance between the competing interests of the presidency and the criminal justice system, the Court observed that "[t]he very integrity of the judicial system and public confidence in the system depend on full disclosure of all the facts, within the framework of the rules of evidence."[45] The Supreme Court then articulated its bedrock principles:

> Only recently the Court restated the ancient proposition of law, albeit in the context of a grand jury inquiry rather than at trial, "that 'the public . . . has a right to every man's evidence,' except for those persons protected by a constitutional, common-law, or statutory privilege . . . . The privileges referred to by the Court are designed to protect weighty and legitimate competing interests. Thus, the *Fifth Amendment to the Constitution* provides that no man "shall be compelled in any criminal case to be a witness against himself." And, generally, an attorney or a priest may not be required to disclose what has been revealed in professional confidence. These and other interests are recognized in law by privileges against forced disclosure, established in the Constitution, by statute or at common law. Whatever their origins, these exceptions to the demand for every man's evidence are not lightly created nor expansively construed, for they are in derogation of the search for the truth.[46]

Guided by these core principles, the Supreme Court in *Nixon* held that the President's "generalized interest in confidentiality" could not

---

44. United States v. Nixon, 418 U.S. 683 (1974).
45. *Id.* at 709.
46. *Id.* at 709–10 (internal citations and footnote omitted).

prevail over the "demonstrated, specific need for evidence in a pending criminal trial."[47]

In two other significant cases decided by the Supreme Court in the period following *Nixon,* the Court demonstrated a similar disinclination to recognize new privileges. In *Trammel v. United States,* the Court held that a man could not prevent his spouse from testifying. Instead, the Court held that the privilege against adverse spousal testimony belongs to the witness spouse, who can be neither compelled to testify nor prevented from testifying.[48] In addition, the Court in 1990 rejected a claim of privilege against compelled disclosure of peer-review materials in a case involving a denial of tenure at the University of Pennsylvania.[49] The opinions in both of these cases indicated that claims of privilege should be "strictly construed."[50] As stated by the Court in *University of Pennsylvania,* quoting *Trammel,* "We do not create and apply an evidentiary privilege unless it 'promotes sufficiently important interests to outweigh the need for probative evidence . . . .'"[51]

Despite its reluctance to recognize new privileges, the Supreme Court did exactly that in a case decided in 1996. In *Jaffee v. Redmond,*[52] the Court recognized a psychotherapist-patient privilege pursuant to Federal Rule of Evidence 501 that it applied in the context of the plaintiff's communications with a licensed social worker. The Court began its analysis by citing *United States v. Bryan*[53] and *United States v. Nixon*[54] for the proposition that "[f]or more than three centuries it has now been recognized as a fundamental maxim that the public . . . has a right to every man's evidence."[55] It then drew from *Trammel* the standard that had to be met in order to justify an exception to this general rule:

---

47. *Id.* at 713.
48. Trammel v. United States, *supra* note 43, at 53.
49. Univ. of Pa. v. EEOC, 493 U.S. 182 (1990).
50. *Id.* at 189; *Trammel, supra* note 43, at 50.
51. *Univ. of Pa., supra* note 49, at 189 (emphasis added).
52. Jaffee v. Redmond, 518 U.S. 1 (1996).
53. United States v. Bryan, 339 U.S. 323, 331 (1950).
54. United States v. Nixon, 418 U.S. 683, 709 (1974).
55. *Jaffee, supra* note 52, at 9 (internal quotation marks omitted).

> **Actual Ombuds Example**
>
> **An ombuds's cultural awareness helps the organization avoid a badly timed decision**
>
> The ombuds learned that a global restructuring announcement would be made across a region on a particular day. As part of the announcement, there would be many layoffs and the plan was to tell affected employees about their severance pay and last work day when the announcement was made. For one country in the region, however, the day scheduled for the announcement was the eve of a major holiday. That country's market was considered strategic from the company's perspective, and there was a great potential for a public backlash against the company if such an announcement were made on the eve of the holiday.
>
> The ombuds expressed his concern about the timing of the announcement to the senior management. Management was unaware of the issue and subsequently decided to defer the announcement by a week.

Exceptions from the general rule disfavoring testimonial privileges may be justified, however, by a 'public good transcending the normally predominant principle of utilizing all rational means for ascertaining the truth.'"[56]

And finally, the Court cited its prior decision in *Upjohn v. United States*,[57] in which it had defined the contours of the attorney-client privilege in the corporate setting, for the proposition that "an asserted privilege must 'also serve public ends.'"[58]

Using this analytical framework, the Court cited the widespread recognition of a psychotherapist-patient privilege in all of the states and reasoned that recognition of a privilege in federal court is warranted where the relationship is "rooted in the imperative need for confidence and trust"; where the privilege serves "public ends"; and where the likely evidentiary benefit that would result from the denial

---

56. *Id.* (citing *Trammel,* 445 U.S. at 50).
57. Upjohn Co. v. United States, 449 U.S. 383, 389 (1981).
58. *Jaffee, supra* note 52, at 11.

of the privilege would be modest because without the privilege, communications would be "chilled," and much of the sought-after communications would not come into being.[59]

The Court in *Jaffee* balanced the general interests of the public in fostering unfettered communication in the particular relationship at issue there against the general interests in the search for truth in litigation. It refused to undergo a balancing analysis specific to the case before it. The Court noted that:

> [I]f the purpose of the privilege is to be served, the participants in the confidential conversation "must be able to predict with some degree of certainty whether particular discussions will be protected. An uncertain privilege, or one which purports to be certain but results in widely varying applications by the courts, is little better than no privilege at all.[60]

Aside from its refusal to engage in a balancing of competing interests, the Supreme Court's analysis in *Jaffee* is similar to the long-recognized and well-established four-part analysis that had been formulated by a leading expert on evidence, Professor Wigmore. Under the "Wigmore test," the factors to be considered to determine whether a privilege should be recognized include the following:

(1) the communication must be one made in the belief that it will not be disclosed;
(2) confidentiality must be essential to the maintenance of the relationship between the parties;
(3) the relationship should be one that society considers worthy of being fostered; and
(4) the injury to the relationship incurred by disclosure must be greater than the benefit gained in the correct disposal of the litigation.[61]

These four criteria had been considered by courts prior to *Jaffee* in deciding whether to recognize a common-law privilege under Rule

---

59. *Id.* at 10–12.
60. *Id.* at 18 (citing Upjohn Co. v. United States, 449 U.S. 383, 393 (1981)).
61. *In re* Doe v. United States, 711 F. 2d 1187 (2d Cir. 1983) (citing 8 WIGMORE, EVIDENCE § 2285, at 527 (McNaughton, rev. 1961)).

501. *See In re* Doe, 711 F.2d 1187, 1192 (2d Cir. 1983); *see also* Somer v. Johnson, M.D.P.A., 704 F.2d 1473, 1479 n.6 (11th Cir. 1983); *In re* Grand Jury Investigation, 918 F.2d 374, 383–84 (3d Cir. 1990); Caesar v. Mountanos, 542 F.2d 1064, 1068 n.13 (9th Cir. 1976); Garner v. Wolfinbarger, 430 F.2d 1093, 1100 (5th Cir. 1970), *cert. denied sub nom.* Garner v. First American Life Ins. Co., 401 U.S. 974 (1971).

With this background, let us turn to the development of case law on an ombudsman privilege.

2. Development of the Ombuds Privilege

Shabazz v. Scurr, **662 F. Supp. 90 (S.D. Iowa 1987)**

Shabazz is the first reported case in which a federal court recognized a common-law bar to disclosure by an ombuds. In *Shabazz*, the office of an Iowa prison ombuds sought to prevent a former employee from testifying about events he witnessed during a prison riot. Iowa state law authorized the office to keep the identities of the complainants and witnesses secret and specifically provided that members of that office could not be compelled to testify about matters within the scope of their official duties. Although this state law scheme was not binding on the federal court, the court nevertheless was persuaded that confidentiality was critically important to the effectiveness of that ombuds office and exercised its authority under Federal Rule of Evidence 501—nine years before the U.S. Supreme Court decided *Jaffee*—to apply the state testimonial immunity law to recognize a privilege in federal court. The court made three specific findings to support its ruling. First, it found that the complaints received by the ombudsman "are privileged because such confidentiality is necessary to ensure that complaints will be made."[62] The court was concerned that the assurances of confidentiality contained in the state statute would be threatened or undermined if they could not be protected in federal court. Second, the court agreed with the argument that confidentiality was needed for informal dispute resolution:

> Courts have a special interest in protecting the office's problem-solving function. . . . While informal dispute resolution is seldom protected by privileges, other rules of evidence such

---

62. Shabazz v. Scurr, 662 F. Supp. 90, 92 (S.D. Iowa 1987).

as the exclusion of settlement discussions and plea bargain statements reflect "the public policy favoring the compromise and settlement of disputes." (*Fed. R. Evid. 408* advisory committee note.)[63]

And third, the court noted that the privilege recognized applied only to protect communications to the prison ombudsman; it did not preclude "the plaintiffs from using other means to prove the existence of facts communicated to him."[64] Thus, what was *said* to an ombudsman was privileged; the underlying facts were not.

Under these circumstances, and quite significantly, the court expressly found that the privilege belonged to the office itself, rather than to any particular individual who had occupied the office.[65] The

---

Actual Ombuds Example

Limited disclosure solves the problem and protects the informant

An employee came to the ombuds to report that he suspected that one of the subcontractors working on plant renovations at the facility where he worked was not doing the work to code. The employee felt that this should be brought to the attention of the company for safety reasons but because he was a union member in the same trade as the subcontractor, he was unwilling to be the one to raise the issue with a formal channel. He was certain that he would suffer retaliation by other members of the union if it became known that he had been the person who reported the issue.

After discussing various options, the employee agreed to permit the ombuds to contact the facility manager to advise him that it would be advisable to have an inspection of the construction work by the local building inspector, but no other information was revealed. The manager arranged for the inspection, which uncovered the defective work, and the company required the subcontractor to correct it. Since the inspection appeared to be a routine inspection by the building inspector, the identity of the employee who came to the ombuds office was protected.

---

63. *Id.*
64. *Id.* at 93.
65. *Id.* at 92.

office itself, therefore, rather than the particular ombuds to whom a communication was made or the individual who had the communication with the ombuds, had standing (the legal right) to assert the privilege in court.

Roy v. United Technologies Corp., Civil H-89-680 (JAC) (granting motion for a protective order); *Kientzy v. McDonnell Douglas Corp.*, 113 F.R.D. 570 (E.D. Mo. 1991); and *Acord v. Alyeska Pipeline Service Co.*, U.S. Dep't of Labor Case No. 95-TSC-4 (Oct. 4, 1995)

While the federal court in *Shabazz* was merely asked to apply a state statutory testimonial immunity scheme in federal court, the court in *Roy v. United Technologies Corp.* (UTC) had to go much further to protect the confidentiality of ombuds' communications.[66] In *Roy*, District Judge Cabranes[67] granted the ombuds's motion for a protective order to limit inquiries about confidential communications at a deposition of the ombuds. Although court's ruling is available only in a transcript of the court hearing, rather than as a published decision, *Roy* is the seminal case recognizing both a federal common-law privilege for ombuds and as authority for an implied contract basis for protecting the confidentiality of ombuds' communications.

The facts in *Roy* were straightforward: Roy sued UTC for discrimination on the basis of his age, race, and national origin. While employed at UTC, he had consulted with the ombuds office. When he later sought to depose the person with whom he had dealt in order to obtain information from those confidential communications, the ombuds office moved for a protective order to preclude the parties from deposing her. In particular, the office of the ombudsman asserted two grounds for its motion for a protective order, one of which was that the federal court should recognize, under federal common law, a testimonial privilege that would bar the compelled disclosure of the confidential communications.[68] The ombuds argued that Federal Rule

---

66. Civil H-89-680 (JAC) (D. Conn.), transcript of May 29, 1990 proceedings (Roy Transcript) at 22, on file with the author.
67. Judge Cabranes now sits on the Second Circuit Court of Appeals.
68. The Office of the Ombudsman also asserted that disclosure was barred by the existence of an implied contract. *See infra* at 250.

of Evidence 501 and the reasoning of the court in *Shabazz* allowed the court to recognize such a privilege.[69]

In considering the claim by the office of the ombudsman for recognition of a federal common-law privilege for ombuds, the court noted that "the burden is on the party claiming the privilege to establish those facts that are the essential elements of the privileged relationship."[70] It also accepted the analytical framework of the Wigmore test, which had previously been recognized by the Second Circuit Court of Appeals in *In re Doe*.[71]

In addition to citing Federal Rule of Evidence 501, the Wigmore test, and the ruling by the court in *Shabazz*, the UTC Office of the Ombudsman provided the court with an extensive affidavit of the ombuds, together with attached supporting documentation, that addressed each of the elements of the Wigmore test. In considering this factual record, the court made findings that supported its recognition of the claim of privilege. As to the first factor, the court found that the office of the ombudsman had taken "extensive precautions," including the use of an 800 number, to ensure confidentiality.[72] The ombuds's affidavit set forth that and other confidentiality precautions in great detail. The court found that the ombuds had proved the second element, that confidentiality was essential to the relationship, with documentation demonstrating that confidentiality was the very purpose for establishing the office and that confidentiality "is generally understood to be a defining characteristic of an ombudsman."[73] The third element, the societal worth of the relationship, was satisfied by the presentation of facts to show that UTC, as a defense contractor, had adopted its ombuds program in response to a general recognition that such programs are necessary to encourage the reporting of waste and fraud and the informal resolution of disputes.[74] In this regard, the affidavit and supporting documentation of the ombuds recited the history

---

69. Roy Transcript, *supra* note 66.
70. *Id.* at 24, *citing In re* Grand Jury Subpoena, 750 F. 2d 223, 224 (2d Cir. 1964).
71. Roy Transcript, *supra* note 66, at 24–25 (citing *In re* Doe, 711 F.2d 1187, 1193 (2d Cir. 1983), which had cited to the Wigmore test, *see supra* note 61). Note that *Roy* was also decided before the Supreme Court's decision in *Jaffee*.
72. *Id.*
73. *Id.*
74. *Id.* at 26.

of procurement fraud scandals generally leading to the formation of the Defense Industry Initiative, of which UTC was an original member, and the recommendations of the Packard Commission.[75] Indeed, the UTC Office of the Ombudsman was created as a direct consequence of those recommendations. And finally, the ombuds demonstrated that its interest in confidentiality outweighed the plaintiff's interest in discovery on the facts of the case.[76] In connection with this last point, the ombuds reiterated the court's observation in *Shabazz*, namely that the privilege protected only the communications with the ombuds and did not preclude a party from proving any underlying facts by other means.

The court in *Roy* concluded its analysis by finding that, "[g]iven the ombudsman's procedures to ensure confidentiality and its announcements of these safeguards, plaintiff must have been aware that his own communications with it would be confidential."[77] The court also emphasized that, because the ombuds had not revealed its information to any party, including UTC, the plaintiff was not placed under any greater burden than the defendant.[78] And finally, in recognizing the ombuds's claim of privilege under Rule 501, the court emphasized that its ruling was based on the specific facts of the case before it.[79]

Other courts applied the ruling from *Roy* in subsequent cases. Less than a year after the ruling in *Roy*, the U.S. District Court for the Eastern District of Missouri relied on it to hold that confidential communications made to an ombuds were protected from disclosure.[80] In that case, *Kientzy v. McDonnell Douglas Corp.*, the plaintiff had consulted the ombuds office at McDonnell Douglas before her employment was terminated.[81] She then sued the company, alleging that her employment was terminated on account of her gender, and she sought to depose the ombuds with whom she had consulted.[82] The ombuds moved for a protective order.[83] As the *Roy* court had

---

75. *See* Chapter 1 at 17–20.
76. Roy Transcript, *supra* note 66, at 26.
77. *Id.*
78. *Id.*
79. *Id.* at 24.
80. Kientzy v. McDonnell Douglas Corp., 133 F.R.D. 570 (E.D. Mo. 1991).
81. *Id.* at 571
82. *Id.*
83. *Id.*

> **Actual Ombuds Example**
>
> **An alert from the ombuds helps the organization avoid committing illegal acts**
>
> Information was conveyed to the ombuds that the organization may have been skirting the law in hiring foreign nationals, but the source of this information was unwilling to come forward directly or to permit disclosure of his identity. The inquirer was willing, however, to permit the ombuds to alert the COO of the organization that this type of activity might be occurring.
>
> With the alert from the ombuds, policies and procedures were tightened to eliminate the potential for misconduct. In the process, the COO was able to reinforce to those responsible for hiring what the law and the organization required and that violations would not be tolerated.
>
> No further concerns on this issue have been brought to the ombuds.

done, the court in *Kientzy* held that the *In re Doe* factors (the Wigmore test) were satisfied and determined that Federal Rule of Evidence 501 protected the ombuds's communications from disclosure.[84] After *Kientzy* was decided, other courts, both state and federal, also found a common-law privilege for the ombuds.[85] Federal administrative case law also recognized this common-law privilege. An administrative law judge for the Department of Labor recognized a privilege for ombuds in *Acord v. Alyeska Pipeline Service Co.*[86] After citing Rule 501, *Roy*, *Shabazz*, and *Kientzy*, the judge recited the four *In re Doe* factors for consideration.[87] With respect to the third

---

84. *Id.* at 572–73.
85. *See also, e.g.*, McMillan v. The Upjohn Co., Case No. 1:92:CV:826 (W.D. Mich. March 8, 1995) (court granted the ombuds's petition for a protective order to prevent the parties from deposing the ombuds about communications by Upjohn employees other than the plaintiff, on the grounds that Fed. R. Evid. 501 and policy interests favor the creation of a privilege); Kozlowski v. The Upjohn Co., File No. 94-5431-NZ (Mich. Cir. Ct. Aug. 16, 1995) (court granted ombuds's motion for a protective order and found that a common-law privilege for ombuds exists and belongs to the ombuds, as opposed to the employees who seek the ombuds's help).
86. U.S. Dep't of Labor Case No. 95-TSC-4 (Oct. 4, 1995).
87. *Id.* at 3. The judge did not recite the facts of the case.

factor, that there is a societal interest in maintaining the confidentiality of the ombuds program, the judge stated:

> Complainant argues that the *Kientzy* rationale does not apply here because Alyeska is not similarly situated to McDonnell Douglas inasmuch as Alyeska does not produce military products for the United States, or contract with the government for the purposes of producing a product, but rather "is simply a consortium of oil companies for the purpose of maintaining and operating the Trans Alaska Pipeline." However, an ombudsman program which improves work conditions by facilitating the resolution of disputes with management, and encouraging the reporting of safety and environmental concerns, thus promoting the safe and efficient transportation of an American-produced oil supply, is also important to society. Moreover, effective ombudsman programs that address concerns of employees, protect whistleblowers and minimize their need are also important to society. Accordingly, it is determined that Alyeska's ombudsman program as depicted by Alyeska has a definite societal benefit that is worth protecting.[88]

The judge concluded that the existence of an ombuds privilege warranted the issuance of an order protecting Alyeska's ombuds from discovery.[89]

Carman v. McDonnell Douglas Corp., 114 F.3d 790 (8th Cir. 1997)

Carman v. McDonnell Douglas Corp. was the first federal court of appeals decision on the issue of an ombuds privilege, and it is the case most frequently cited for not recognizing such a privilege. As such, it merits extended discussion. Although the way in which this claim was presented to the court was deeply flawed and the opinion has been relied on by other courts, the actual holding of the court was limited: that the record before the court did not support recognition of an ombuds privilege. This ruling is entirely justified and appropriate based on the

---

88. *Id.* at 4.
89. *Id.* at 7.

record that was, in fact, before the court. However, the decision in this case, along with various comments made by the court in *dicta*, serve as an important reminder to organizations and ombuds offices that they must be prepared to prove how their programs function and why confidentiality is important.

The ombuds program involved in *Carman* was the same one that had been considered by the court in *Kientzy*, but there was a significant difference: even though the *Carman* court's opinion makes no reference to it, the McDonnell Douglas ombuds program was no longer in existence by the time of this decision.[90] Perhaps as a result of the elimination of the program, the ombuds office was not separately represented in this dispute. Compounding the absence of an advocate representing the interests of the ombuds office was the fact that counsel for the company appears not to have been knowledgeable on the history and nuances of the ombuds privilege and utterly failed to make a presentation to the district court or to the court of appeals that would justify the recognition of any privilege, much less an ombuds privilege.[91] Whatever the reason, it is clear that neither the ombuds office nor the company provided the court with *any* evidentiary record to support the claim of privilege, such as the one considered by the court in *Roy*. Even if that had been done, however, comments by the court of appeals suggest that the basic structure of the ombuds program at issue probably should not have been accorded a testimonial privilege.

The way in which the ombuds privilege issue arose in *Carman* is especially important, and some of this information cannot be gleaned from the opinion itself:

> While not fully apparent from the decision, the appellate record reveals that in response to the plaintiff's request to produce documents, McDonnell Douglas objected to the production of documents from the ombuds on the grounds that they were "immune from discovery" because the ombuds' activities were considered confidential. This objection was overruled [by the District Court]. In a subsequent motion for reconsideration filed by McDonnell Douglas, the company [only] cited two unre-

---

90. Jeffrey M. Kaplan, *Federal Appeals Court Rejects Ombudsman's Privilege*, 11 ETHIKOS AND CORP. CONDUCT Q. No. 2 at 4, 5 (Sept./Oct. 1997).

91. Charles L. Howard & George R. Wratney, *In the Aftermath of the* Carman *Decision, Ombuds 'Privilege' Still Has Validity*, 12 ETHIKOS AND CORP. CONDUCT Q. No. 6 at 9 (May/June 1999).

ported orders from the same federal district court involving the McDonnell Douglas ombuds program in which the privilege had been recognized. The district court reconsidered its prior ruling and, without [providing] any analysis on the issue, ordered that McDonnell Douglas did not have to produce the ombuds' documents.

Thus, the record before the appeals court in Carman reveals no facts (by testimony, affidavit, or otherwise) concerning the ombuds office, how it operated or why confidentiality was important.[92]

Indeed, the appeals court expressly stated that the company had not presented any evidence on important aspects of the claimed privilege, such as the importance of the relationship that the privilege would serve or the importance of confidentiality and its implications on an employee's willingness to come forward, or on the office's relationship with management.[93] Although the company made an argument based on the role of an ombuds office as an alternative dispute mechanism, the record is entirely devoid of any reference to other important societal interests, such as those articulated in *Roy*, based on the President's Blue Ribbon Commission on Procurement Fraud (the Packard Commission), or other benefits of the office to a company such as McDonnell Douglas, which also was a major defense contractor, based on principles articulated in the Defense Industry Initiative.

The court's holding in *Carman* was that this lack of evidence defeated the claim of privilege that had been asserted. The court began its analysis by citing the Supreme Court's ruling in *Trammel* that the burden of establishing a privilege is on the party claiming it and concluded by stating:

> To justify the creation of a privilege, McDonnell Douglas must first establish that society benefits in some significant way from the particular brand of confidentiality that the privilege affords. Only then can a court decide whether the advantages of the proposed privilege overcome the strong presumption in favor of disclosure of all relevant information. The creation of a

---

92. *Id.* at 10 (emphasis added).
93. *Carman*, 114 F. 3d at 793–94.

wholly new evidentiary privilege is a big step. This record does not convince us that we should take it.[94]

The *Carman* court's holding, therefore, was not that there could never be an ombuds privilege; it was that the facts in the case before it did not justify recognition of a privilege.

The court in *Carman* made observations about the program at McDonnell Douglas and articulated assumptions about the way in which ombuds programs operate (even though there was no evidence before the court) that reveal issues that were important to the court and that should be addressed by ombuds programs wishing to assert a privilege in order to distinguish themselves from the program in *Carman*. First, the court noted that the ombudsman at McDonnell Douglas was a vice president of the company and that the "corporate ombudsman is paid by the corporation and lacks the structural independence that characterizes government ombudsmen."[95] As discussed above, as a corporate vice president, the ombuds was an officer of the company and thus, from either an actual or apparent authority perspective, part of management. If the issue had been raised (and it appears not to have been raised directly), a court would likely have deemed the ombuds an agent for notice of claims under these circumstances. Moreover, even if the ombuds were not a company officer, the court was not persuaded that the office was structurally independent of management.

Second, the comments and assumptions by the *Carman* court in dicta highlight areas that any claim of privilege should address in order to prevail. Some of the observations by the court are on issues that

---

94. *Id.* at 794 (emphasis added).

95. *Id.* at 793 and n.1. Note also that management responsibilities for ombuds are inconsistent with the IOA Code of Ethics and Standards of Practice. For the same reason, ombuds offices should not conduct investigations for management. The lack of structural independence and the fact that an ombuds investigation was co-opted by the legal department were factors relied on by a court in rejecting a company's claim that the investigation was not subject to disclosure under the attorney-client privilege and attorney work product doctrine, despite a description of the ombudsman office on the company's Web site as an "objective and impartial organization." Accounting Principals, Inc. v. Manpower, Inc., 2009 U.S. Dist. LEXIS 66428 (N.D. Okla., July 28, 2009) at 17–*18 and nn. 6 & 7 and Pinstripe, Inc. v. Manpower, Inc., 2009 U.S. Dist. LEXIS 66430 (N.D. Okla., July 28, 2009) at *16–*18 nn. 6 & 7.

> ### Actual Ombuds Example
>
> #### Where does a vice president go with concerns about the president?
>
> The ombuds of a multinational organization received a call from a regional vice president with concerns about an international region president. The inquirer expressed concerns that the regional president was acting strangely and making improper comments about people at an offsite meeting where over a dozen other vice president–level organization officials were present, together with several outside counsel, professionals, and other consultants to the organization. The inquirer was concerned that the regional president could have a drug problem, as the strange behavior had been evident for at least the preceding few months. The vice president making the call, however, was also obviously concerned that he may be wrong and was worried about the possible impact on his own career.
>
> The ombuds discussed various ways this issue could be surfaced and investigated. The inquirer gave the ombuds permission to convey information about the regional president's conduct (but not the inquirer's identity) at the off-site meeting to the top levels of the organization at its international headquarters. When this information was relayed to the president of the entire organization and the head of HR, they instigated an investigation almost immediately by having many of the attendees of the offsite meeting interviewed. The regional president was also interviewed. As a result of this investigation, they made the decision to remove the regional president from his position and announced that he was relocating back to the organization headquarters. He retired from the organization not long thereafter.

should have been addressed in documentation supporting the claim of privilege, but others reflect the court's fundamental misunderstanding of how properly structured ombuds offices function. With no evidence before the court to prove otherwise, it is clear that these assumptions played a role in the court's aversion to the asserted privilege claim. The comments by the court include the following:

- There was no evidence that the ombuds program is successful in serving as an alternative dispute mechanism or that it helps resolve workplace disputes before litigation;[96]
- There was no context in which to evaluate the significance of statistics concerning the number of communications the ombudsman office had received;[97]
- There was no compelling argument that "most of the advantages afforded by the ombudsman method would be lost without the privilege";[98]
- The court thought that even without a privilege, ombuds would still "have much to offer employees in the way of confidentiality, for they are still able to promise to keep employee communications confidential from management," and "an ombudsman will still be able to promise confidentiality in most circumstances even with no privilege";[99]
- With no factual basis apparent from the record, the court assumed that when a employee goes to an ombudsman, "his greatest concern is not likely to be that the statement will someday be revealed in civil discovery";[100]
- And finally, the court articulated a remarkable series of assumptions (again, in the absence of any evidence) that show that it did not understand how varied the assistance of an ombuds office can be, that there is also a need for a confidential source of guidance or information (as opposed to merely having a place to file a complaint), or that an employee may have concerns over possible retaliation by the organization or peers that may cause him or her to want confidentiality:

> An employee either will or will not have a meritorious complaint. If he does not and is aware that he does not, he is no more likely to share the frivolousness of his complaint with a company ombudsman than he is with a court. If he has a meritorious complaint that he would prefer not to litigate, then he will generally feel that he

---

96. *Carman,* 114 F.3d at 793.
97. *Id.*
98. *Id.*
99. *Id.* at 793–94.
100. *Id.* at 794.

has nothing to hide and will be undeterred by the prospect of civil discovery from sharing the nature of the complaint with the ombudsman. The dim prospect that the employee's complaint might someday surface in an unrelated case strikes us as an unlikely deterrent.[101]

Thus, while *Carman* placed a cloud on an ombuds's ability to claim a testimonial privilege, the court's opinion serves as a useful guide in articulating several issues that should be addressed by ombuds in seeking recognition of an ombudsman privilege.

3. Subsequent Cases Citing the *Carman* Decision

One of the unfortunate consequences of the *Carman* decision is that it has been cited by subsequent courts, sometimes without a careful analysis of its holding or procedural differences. For example, this has been done in connection with rulings on other claims of privilege: *Carman* was cited by the Third Circuit Court of Appeals in denying a claim of privilege based on Pennsylvania statutes that made certain communications dealing with child abuse confidential[102] and by the Court of Appeals for the Ninth Circuit in granting a claim of privilege for an Employee Assistance Program.[103] A similarly summary reference was made by the district court for the District of Columbia in denying a claim of a privilege for settlement communications.[104] In rejecting a

---

101. *Id.*
102. Pearson v. Miller, 211 F. 3d 57, 67 (3d Cir. 2000) (The court stated that ". . . with very limited exceptions, federal courts have generally declined to grant requests for new privileges . . . ; Carman v. McDonnell Douglas Corp. (rejecting a corporate ombudsman privilege and stating that 'the creation of a wholly new evidentiary privilege is a big step') . . .").
103. Oleszko v. State Comp. Ins. Fund, 243 F.3d 1154, 1156 (9th Cir. 2001) ("The contrary cases on which *Oleszko* relies are easily distinguished. In *Carman v. McDonnell Douglas Corp.*, 114 F.3d 790 (8th Cir. 1997), the Eighth Circuit held that communications to an ombudsman employed to resolve workplace disputes without litigation were not protected by the psychotherapist-patient privilege. *Id.* at 791. The court concluded that the resolution of workplace disputes prior to litigation was not a sufficiently important interest to justify creation of a new evidentiary privilege. *Id.* at 793.").
104. *In re* Subpoena Issued to Com. Fut. Trading Comm'n, 2005 U.S. Dist. LEXIS 9074 (D.D.C. April 28, 2005) at *19 (". . . courts in recent years have declined to recognize a privilege for . . . corporate ombudsman records, Carman v. McDonnell Douglas Corp. . . .").

claim for a medical peer review privilege, the Fourth and Eleventh Circuits cited *Carman* for the proposition that the issue of whether to recognize a privilege under Federal Rule of Evidence 501 is a mixed question of law and fact that courts of appeal review *de novo*.[105]

Carman was also cited by the Tenth Circuit Court of Appeals in an unpublished opinion in *Miller v. Regents of the University of Colorado*,[106] affirming a summary judgment and various discovery orders of the district court. One of the discovery orders at issue in *Miller* was a magistrate judge's denial of a motion for sanctions in connection with the destruction of certain documents by the university's office of the ombudsman. Citing *Shabazz* and *Kientzy*, the magistrate judge had recognized an ombudsman privilege that the ombudsman had asserted.[107] On the plaintiff's appeal from the summary judgment granted by the district court, the appeals court affirmed and held that the discovery limitations imposed by the district court were not an abuse of discretion and did not affect the substantial rights of the parties. On the issue of whether the district court had properly recognized the ombudsman privilege, the appeals court stated:

> For the same reason [it would not have saved the plaintiff's claims from summary judgment for the university], we affirm the district court's ruling regarding the ombudsman privilege. It is clear that neither Colorado law nor federal law, including the decisions of this circuit, recognize an ombudsman privilege. Other federal courts have gone both ways on the issue. *Compare Carman v. McDonnell Douglas Corp., 114 F.3d 790, 793–94 (8th Cir. 1997)* (concluding complaints registered with a corporate ombudsman office were not privileged) *with Shabazz v. Scurr, 662 F. Supp. 90, 92 (S. D. Iowa 1987)* (concluding communications received by prison ombudsman were

---

105. Virmani v. Novant Health Inc., 259 F.3d 284, 287 (4th Cir. 2001); Adkins v. Christi, 488 F.3d 1324, 1327 (11th Cir. 2007).

106. Miller v. Regents of the Univ. of Colo., 188 F.3d 518 (10th Cir 1999), unpublished opinion may be found at 1999 U.S. App. LEXIS 16712. (The opinion contains the following notation: "Rules of the Tenth Circuit Court of Appeals may limit citation to unpublished opinions. Please refer to the rules of the United States Court of Appeals for this circuit.")

107. Miller v. Regents of the Univ. of Colo., Civ. A. No. 95-S-2929, U.S. Dist. Ct. for the District of Colorado, Order dated July 2, 1996.

privileged). We find it unnecessary to address the issue here because the district court's ruling does not affect the substantial rights of the parties.[108]

Especially since the Tenth Circuit expressly stated that it did not need to reach the issue of an ombuds privilege and it affirmed the discovery orders of the district court, the court's statements on the nonexistence of an ombudsman privilege are dicta and not binding in subsequent cases.[109] Nevertheless, the court's characterization of the holding in *Carman*—like some of the other cases mentioned above—is misleading, as the holding of the court in *Carman* was that the record there did not support the claim of privilege.

Despite the ambiguities in the court's language in *Miller,* it too has been cited in subsequent cases in support of a refusal to recognize an ombudsman privilege. In *Solorzano v. Shell Chemical Co.*,[110] for example, a magistrate judge was faced with an issue of whether to compel production of documents from the Shell RESOLVE program, an ombuds office. As with *Carman*, the issue came to the court without an adequate factual record and without separate representation for the ombuds office.[111] In analyzing the issue, the court in *Solorzano* first considered whether a Louisiana statute granting confidentiality to written and oral communications in mediation should apply to the case, but rejected the application of the state statute on the ground that the federal law of privilege applies in federal court even where there are pendent state law claims.[112] The court then turned to the question of

---

108. Miller v. Regents of the Univ. of Colo., *supra* note 106, at *42.

109. Moreover, the opinion was unpublished, and Tenth Circuit rules limit subsequent reliance on it.

110. Solorzano v. Shell Chem. Co., 2000 U.S. Dist. LEXIS 12072 (E.D. La. Aug. 14, 2000).

111. Counsel for the ombuds office was notified of the dispute at the last minute and only after the motion for a protective order had been filed by the company. Counsel for the ombuds office responded immediately with a letter to the court citing four unpublished decisions recognizing an ombudsman privilege and requesting permission to address the issue with briefs and affidavits. Without responding to this request, the court issued its ruling.

112. On the issue of the applicability of Federal Rules of Evidence in cases where there are also state law claims, *see* Folb v. Motion Picture Ind. Pension & Health Plans, 16 F. Supp. 2d 1164, 1168–72 (N.D. Cal. 1998).

> **Actual Ombuds Example**
>
> **Help me understand**
>
> The ombuds received a call from a U.S.-based expatriate executive asking for help in understanding the culture in China. The caller told the ombuds that he was not having much success or cooperation in his new organization and felt like it was due to his lack of understanding of the norms and culture of the country. Because the caller was new to the organization, he was unwilling to raise these concerns through any of the formal channels and was afraid that his failure to understand the culture would adversely affect his evaluation.
>
> The ombuds was able to provide the caller with helpful information about local practices, background, and cultural norms in China. The ombuds was also able to suggest a Web site and other resources that have extensive information about doing business in China and the cultural norms and practices in the area. The executive was pleased to be able to obtain this guidance without going through formal channels. Without it, the caller would have continued to struggle with living and working in his new environment or disclose his difficulties to higher management.

whether there is a federal statutory or common-law privilege. Notwithstanding the fact that four unpublished decisions recognizing an ombudsman privilege had been provided to the court, the magistrate judge rejected the claim of privilege, citing both *Carman* and *Miller*:

> Shell has not pointed out the existence of any such legal privilege, beyond the assertion of it in the Resolve Program documents, and the Court's own research has located none. *See Miller v. Regents of the Univ. of Colo., 188 F.3d 518, 1999 WL 506520,* at *15 (10th Cir. July 19, 1999) (federal law does not recognize ombudsman's privilege) (unpubl. opin. avail. on Westlaw); *Carman v. McDonnell Douglas Corp., 114 F.3d 790, 795 (8th Cir. 1997)* (same).[113]

Aside from the references to *Carman* and *Miller*, the court engaged in no analysis of the ombudsman issue. Yet, because no supporting

---

113. Solorzano v. Shell Chem. Co., *supra* note 110, at *12.

documentary record other than the program documents were submitted to the court, any attempt to analyze the claim with regard to the four elements of the Wigmore test would have been impossible.

4. Subsequent Cases Recognizing an Ombuds Privilege

Despite the rulings in *Carman, Miller,* and *Solorzano,* other courts have recognized an ombudsman privilege and granted motions for protective orders to prevent compelled discovery of ombuds communications.

In *Van Martin v. United Technologies Corp.*,[114] a magistrate judge had granted a motion for a protective order before the decision in *Carman,* based on submissions made by the UTC ombudsman and an analysis of the four factors from the Wigmore test. The district court subsequently granted the company's summary judgment motion, and the plaintiff appealed. One of the principal issues on appeal was whether the motion for a protective order to preclude discovery from the ombudsman should have been granted. In contrast to *Carman,* the UTC Ombudsman Office appeared in the case with independent counsel and received permission to brief the issue of the ombudsman privilege and the trial court's ruling on the motion for a protective order. While the appeal was pending, the Eighth Circuit issued its decision in *Carman,* and the parties filed additional briefs addressing the implications of that decision to the case on appeal, as the ombuds privilege issue was one of the major issues. While it was good for ombuds programs that the Eleventh Circuit affirmed the trial court's decision, unfortunately it did so without a published opinion.[115]

A motion for a protective order was also granted by a magistrate judge on behalf of the UTC Office of the Ombudsman in another case in the Southern District of Florida in 1998.[116] In *Leslie v. United Technologies Corp.*, the court granted the motion for a protective order without specifically articulating the basis, other than to state that ad-

---

114. Van Martin v. United Technologies Corp., Case No. 95-8389-CIV-Ungaro Benages (S.D. Fla.) (Order on Motion for Protective Order, July 16, 1996).
115. Van Martin v. United Technologies Corp., 141 F.3d 1188 (11th Cir. 1998).
116. Leslie v. United Technologies Corp., Case No. 97-8212-CIV-Gold (S.D. Fla.) (Omnibus Order, Dec. 2, 1998).

equate grounds for granting the motion were contained in the memorandum filed by the office of the ombudsman.[117]

A year later, another magistrate judge granted a motion for a protective order with respect to a different ombuds program, the American Express Office of the Ombudsperson, citing *Kientzy, Van Martin,* and *Leslie,* and specifically finding that the four factors of the Wigmore test necessary for the recognition of an ombudsman privilege had been established.[118]

5. An Ombuds Privilege Belongs to the Ombuds

An important issue in cases concerning an ombuds privilege is who "owns" or can invoke the claim or privilege—and, even more important, who can waive its protections. This issue usually occurs in a situation in which counsel wants to depose or obtain information from an ombuds, is faced with a claim of ombuds privilege for the first time, and assumes that the ombuds privilege, like the attorney-client privilege, belongs to the "client" and attempts to waive it the client's behalf.[119] Ombuds, however, have taken the position that they, not an inquirer, own the privilege and only they can waive it.[120]

Beginning with the court in *Shabazz,* courts have permitted an office to assert and claim the ombuds privilege. In *Shabazz,* the current incumbent of the office was asserting the privilege to prevent the

---

117. *Id.,* Omnibus Order at 6; *see also* Howard & Wratney, *supra* note 91.

118. Smith v. American Express Co., Case No. 98-7206-CIV-Jordan (S.D. Fla.) (Order, Jan. 3, 2000).

119. There appears to be a paradox in this recurring fact pattern. Because ombuds typically excel in listening skills and in providing useful advice for the people with whom they work, they are often perceived by their inquirers as the only people who have ever listened to them or taken their concerns seriously. Consequently, the inquirers tend to view ombuds as validating witnesses for their issues or concerns. Thus, it appears that the motivation for someone seeking discovery from the ombuds is often based on the premise that "if only the bad organization would let the ombuds testify, he or she would prove that I am right." Based on my experience, if the testimony of ombuds were permitted, it would often neither validate the merits of the plaintiff's claim nor condemn the actions of the organization.

120. Under the IOA Standards of Practice, *see* Appendix 5 at 465, an ombuds would waive privilege only where there is an imminent threat of serious harm. *See also* Chapter 4 at 354–63 for a discussion of the cases on which this principle is based.

testimony of a former ombuds. Similarly, in *Roy,* the court permitted the office to assert the privilege in the face of a direct challenge by the person who was seeking disclosure of his communications with the ombuds. In *Kozlowski v. The Upjohn Co.*,[121] the court specifically found that the privilege belongs to the ombuds office rather than to employees coming to the ombuds office for help.

Arguments that the ombuds privilege should be controlled by an inquirer are misplaced. The essence of the attorney-client relationship is that the attorney is the *representative of and acting on behalf of* the client. Promoting candor in communications between attorney and client to support that relationship thus serves those ends. By contrast, an ombuds does not act as anyone's agent. Core principles require that organizational ombuds be independent and neutral. Their goal is to serve as a resource and to promote fair process.[122] Where they are properly structured, they do not serve as an agent to receive notice of claims for their organizations, and have no other role. Moreover, one of their central functions is to help resolve organizational conflict and disputes.[123] For these reasons, the proper analogy is that ombuds are like mediators, and it is widely recognized in many statutes that mediators themselves are entitled to assert a mediator privilege, even in the face of attempts by a party to the mediation to compel disclosure.[124] Similarly, it is important to protect a *process* and to ensure that others in the future will be able to use it, so that the analysis cannot be limited to a focus only on the ombuds and the inquirer in the dispute; the programmatic goals and future users must also be considered.

6. Observations on the Recognition of an Ombudsman Privilege

Since the flurry of cases in the late 1990s and early 2000s, there have been other cases in which ombuds offices have filed motions to protect ombuds communications on the basis of privilege, as well as on other grounds. In some cases, a motion for a protective order or a

---

121. Kozlowski v. The Upjohn Co., *supra* note 85.
122. INTERNATIONAL OMBUDSMAN ASSOCIATION [IOA] CODE OF ETHICS; IOA STANDARDS OF PRACTICE. *See* Appendix 5 at 460.
123. *Id.*
124. *Id.*

motion in limine[125] has been granted—sometimes without further explanation. In other instances, the court remained unconvinced that a privilege is appropriate.

Despite this mixed record, a strong argument can be made for the recognition of an ombuds privilege. As discussed in Chapter 1, the history of ombuds programs in the United States, whether in the corporate, university, or governmental context, demonstrates that they were frequently created because of significant social problems and to address important national issues recognized by presidential and other national commissions. Moreover, as shown in Chapter 2, ombuds pro-

---

Actual Ombuds Example

The ombuds can provide assistance to a manager without breaching confidentiality

Several employees in a country other than the United States came to the ombuds to express concern about a new country manager for their organization. He was an expatriate American, and his communication style and approach were different from and clashed with their local culture. To the locals, he was "rough, rude and loud." They also found him unapproachable. That country's team morale started to fall and absenteeism spiked.

Before any action was taken on the concerns expressed by the several employees, the country manager himself also contacted the ombuds office, asking for help and guidance on how to become a better leader in that culture. Without revealing that any employees had raised concerns about him, the ombuds was able to provide suggestions to the manager, such as changing his style of communication and advising him on how to participate in various activities to better understand the local culture.

---

125. Non-lawyers may wish to consult Chapter 4 at beginning at 315 for a discussion of litigation procedure generally. In general, a motion for a protective order is a motion made to the court in while the parties are engaged in the discovery process (learning facts from the other parties) and seeks to restrict or impose conditions on the discovery. A motion in limine is typically a motion that is made just before a trial begins to obtain a ruling from the court on the admissibility of evidence, including the testimony of a witness.

grams are responsive to the problems arising from the pressures transforming our society as well as to the requirements imposed by law to have better compliance systems and to provide people with a confidential and anonymous resource. There is widespread recognition that organizations should have confidential and anonymous mechanisms. It is the confidentiality of the ombuds office that makes it different from other channels. Ombuds programs, therefore, should not assume that they cannot meet the burden of proving that it is appropriate to recognize an ombudsman privilege.

Given the uncertainties inherent in the process of seeking court recognition of a testimonial privilege,[126] it is understandable that ombuds have also relied on contract and other theories as additional means to protect confidentiality (discussed in the next section). Although Section IV of this chapter addresses in greater detail various aspects of discovery, including motions for protective orders or motions in limine for ombuds, the history of previous attempts to assert an ombudsman privilege yields several important practice tips.

Ombudsman Privilege Practice Tips

1. To support the ombuds's claim of independence and the critical point that an ombuds's knowledge should not be imputed to the organization, an ombuds office should have counsel separate from counsel representing the organization. Moreover, the ombuds's counsel should take primary responsibility for the preparation and filing of an appropriate motion to assert privilege or confidentiality, which, of course, should be coordinated with counsel for the organization and supported by the organization.

2. If there is any lesson that is crystal-clear in the aftermath of *Carman*, it is that any attempt to seek recognition of a privilege is futile without a substantial factual record to present to the court. This can be done through affidavits or declarations with attached documentation or though an evidentiary hearing, but it is essential. Courts have made it clear that the burden is on the party claiming a privilege to prove facts that support it.

---

126. As recognized by the court in *Jaffee*, an uncertain privilege is "little better than no privilege at all." 518 U.S. 1 at 18.

3. Both the factual record to be presented to the court and the accompanying memoranda of law need to address the elements considered by the court in *Jaffee,* in the Wigmore test, or the test applicable to the jurisdiction in which the dispute is pending. In addition, these filings should address the issues and misconceptions expressed by the court in *Carman.* One of the most important of these elements is the demonstration of important public purposes that would be served by such a privilege. While the substantial benefits of an ombuds office to address workplace conflict and as an ADR mechanism are important and should be emphasized, there are additional important public policies that can be articulated, as evidenced in such developments as the DII, the Packard Commission recommendations, the Federal Sentencing Guidelines, the Report of the President's Commission on Campus Unrest, the report of the Carnegie Commission on Higher Education, the Sarbanes-Oxley Act of 2002, various standards for corporate governance, and decisions from cases involving employment claims.[127] Many ombuds programs were in fact created directly as a result of these considerations.

4. Organizations and their ombuds offices should understand that a claim of privilege is but one means to protect confidentiality. In other words, the ombuds's goal is to protect confidentiality, not necessarily the recognition of a privilege per se. Virtually every privilege has its limits, and none is absolute.[128] In some situations it may not be possible to assert a claim of privilege, as, for example, in a state court in a state that does not permit its courts to recognize common-law privileges. Accordingly, the assertion of a privilege should almost never be the only basis used by an ombuds office to protect confidentiality, and neither the organization nor the ombuds office should fail to preserve the confidentiality of ombuds communications just because a court may not recognize a privilege. Experience has

---

127. These matters are discussed more fully in Chapters 1 and 2.
128. See Chapter 4 at 364 for a discussion on the constitutional right to confront accusers.

shown that even though a court may be reluctant to protect confidentiality by giving recognition to a testimonial privilege, the evidence and argument presented to the court in support of the privilege claim is usually considered by a judge in deciding whether to protect confidentiality on some other basis.

5. Even with the recognition of a privilege, a claim of confidentiality is not absolute. Communications otherwise protected by the attorney-client privilege are subject to disclosure in some circumstances, such as the crime-fraud exception, and an ombuds privilege would also be subject to similar limitations. An ombuds privilege would also have to yield to constitutional rights in the criminal prosecutions. However, where there are challenges to ombuds confidentiality in these contexts, there are also methodologies that can be adapted from other contexts to limit the disclosure to the court or only to the extent necessary.[129]

B. Program Conditions of Use—Implied Contract of Confidentiality

In many of the cases in which ombuds' confidentiality has been protected, beginning with *Roy*, the ombuds office has, in addition to asserting an ombuds privilege, asserted that confidentiality should be protected on the basis of an implied contract.[130] Courts rarely have separately analyzed the implied contract argument; instead, they have either granted or denied a motion without further elaboration. However, asserting an implied contract basis for confidentiality has become more important over the years in light of courts' citation to *Carman* as authority for not recognizing a privilege. At the same time,

---

129. These issues are addressed elsewhere. *See* Chapter 4 at 364.

130. Unlike mediation, ombuds programs eschew the use of express written agreements to enforce confidentiality. This is in keeping with the principles of both confidentiality and informality articulated in the IOA Code of Ethics and Standards of Practice. *See* Appendix 5 at 459. Avoiding the use of such written agreements is also consistent with the fact that one of the principal reasons ombuds programs exist is to serve as a resource for people who fear that their concerns will be disclosed or that they will suffer retaliation.

some ombuds offices have begun applying the principles of an implied contract claim in their program documentation to more clearly articulate that communications with it are confidential and that, by using the program, a visitor agrees not to call upon the ombuds to produce records or to testify concerning any confidential communications in any subsequent legal or administrative proceeding. As a result, there appears to have been fewer challenges to the confidentiality of programs that have done so.

In *Roy*, the ombuds office asserted in more general terms an implied contract theory as an alternate ground upon which the court could protect the confidentiality of ombuds communications. The ombuds office supplied the court with documentation that made it clear that confidentiality was the defining characteristic of the program and was the aspect of the program that made it different from all other communication channels at UTC. This documentation also demonstrated the extensive efforts made by UTC to publicize the confidentiality of the ombudsman office. In considering the second element of the Wigmore test, the court stated: "The second element, that confidentiality must be essential to the relationship, is provided by the fact that confidentiality—and the candor it engenders—was the purpose for establishing an ombudsman's office at UTC and is generally understood to be a defining characteristic of an ombudsman."[131] The court also found that "[g]iven the ombudsman's procedures to ensure confidentiality and its announcements of those safeguards, plaintiff must have been aware that his own communications with it would be confidential."[132] Accordingly, the court, while again limiting its holding to the particular facts and circumstances before it, found that "[a] separate and independent basis for the Court's ruling here in favor of the movant is provided by the theory of implied contract persuasively asserted by the movant in her papers."[133]

Depending on the circumstances, there are two distinct types of implied contract that can be asserted by an ombuds program: an *implied in fact*[134] contract and an *implied in law* contract. An *implied in fact* contract is a contract in the ordinary sense of the term and con-

---

131. Roy Transcript, *supra* note 66, at 25.
132. *Id.* at 26.
133. *Id.* at 27.
134. To enable the reader to more clearly follow the ensuing discussion, the different contract terms are indicated in italics.

> **Actual Ombuds Example**
>
> **A need for information without revealing who asked for it**
>
> An employee came to the ombuds office because he was concerned that, with several job functions being outsourced, he could be displaced or offered a job at another location. Since this was a result of a company-wide reengineering initiative, any such displaced employee would be eligible for severance benefits. The employee was unwilling to go through formal channels for obvious reasons to find out "what constituted a comparable job" and asked the ombuds if that inquiry could be made without revealing his identity.
>
> The ombuds was able to speak with HR on a generic basis without revealing the identity of the employee and then provide the employee with the information requested. The ombuds was also able to direct the employee to the company's Web site for additional information.

tains all the elements of an *express* contract in terms of its legal significance.[135] General contract law recognizes and enforces *implied in fact* contracts to the same degree as *express* contracts.[136] However, *implied in law* contracts, or, as they are sometimes called, "quasi-contracts" or "constructive contracts," are not really contracts at all. Rather, they are a judicial construct developed to prevent unjust enrichment or benefit despite the parties' lack of agreement.[137]

These two kinds of implied contracts are broadly recognized, including by the *Restatement (Second) of the Law of Contracts*, a distillation of generally accepted common-law principles drawn from many jurisdictions. While these Restatement principles are recognized by most courts, an ombuds program and its organization should nevertheless research the law in the applicable jurisdiction to locate and also cite cases that support these principles.

The enforceability of contracts generally requires that the parties to the contract prove their mutual assent to the terms of the agree-

---

135. RESTATEMENT (SECOND) OF THE LAW OF CONTRACTS § 4 (1979); 17A AM. JUR. 2D *Contracts* § 15 (2004).
136. 17A AM. JUR. 2D *Contracts* § 12 (2004).
137. RESTATEMENT (SECOND) OF THE LAW OF CONTRACTS § 4 cmt. b (1979).

ment; in other words, there must have been a "meeting of the minds" on certain terms.[138] The only difference between an *express* contract and an *implied in fact* contract is the manner in which this assent to the contract's terms has been manifested.[139] Parties to an *express* contract establish assent and indicate intent to agree simply by verbal or written statements. Assent to an *implied in fact* contract, however, is inferred from the conduct of the parties and all surrounding circumstances which, evaluated objectively, establish the existence of an agreement.[140] As contracts generally are viewed on an *objective* basis, courts do not normally consider whether a particular individual *subjectively* intended for his or her conduct to indicate assent. Rather, the critical question is whether a reasonable person would fairly conclude, from the conduct of the parties and the surrounding circumstances, that the parties intended to be bound to an agreement.[141] The essential elements of an *implied in fact* contract, therefore, remain identical to requirements of an *express* contract—the parties must manifest mutual assent to the agreement; but, because the agreement in the *implied in fact* context may not have been not stated orally or reduced to writing, the agreement is implied from the conduct of the parties and the surrounding facts.

Applying this concept to the context of an ombuds program, an ombuds office should be able to prove the existence of an *implied in fact* contract that communications with the ombuds were confidential and that an ombuds should not be compelled to furnish documents or testify in formal proceedings concerning those confidential communications. For example, an implied in fact contract would likely be recognized where the ombuds office can prove that: (1) the ombuds office was specifically created as an alternate channel for confidential communications; (2) the ombuds office consistently stated that communications with the ombuds are confidential and that the ombuds office was created with the express understanding (or on the condition) that communications with the ombuds are confidential and that ombuds should not be called as witnesses or compelled to disclose documents concerning those confidential communications in legal or formal pro-

---

138. 17A AM. JUR. 2D *Contracts* § 19 (2004).
139. RESTATEMENT (SECOND) OF THE LAW OF CONTRACTS § 4 cmt. a (1979).
140. 17A AM. JUR. 2D *Contracts* § 12 (2004).
141. *Id.* § 31 (2004).

ceedings; (3) the ombuds office widely publicized its policies of confidentiality, its resistance to testifying in any formal proceeding with respect to these confidential communications (even when requested to do so), and that the office does not and is not authorized to receive notice of any claim or complaint on behalf of the organization; (4) people communicating with the ombuds were aware of, or reasonably should have been aware of, these program features; and (5) the ombuds office relies on these program features, including the implied assent of inquirers to these terms, in providing assistance. Under these circumstances, the conduct of an inquirer and the ombuds demonstrate that there was an agreement or understanding that communications were confidential and that the ombuds will not testify or produce documents concerning those confidential communications, even if the inquirer later requests that he or she do so.

The second type of implied contract is a contract *implied in law*. This is not actually a contract in the normal sense, meaning the parties did not actually agree or intend to agree on any terms, and their conduct, even viewed objectively, does not suggest agreement to those terms. Rather, in a contract *implied in law*, a court determines that a party is bound by certain terms for reasons of justice. In this sense, a contact *implied in law* is a form of restitution to prevent one party from unjust enrichment.[142] Indeed, recognition of an *implied in law* contract will often directly conflict with the intent of one or more parties, but courts nevertheless deem the contract a necessary equitable measure to avoid an unfair result.

This type of *implied in law* contract argument may be available to an ombuds office if the evidence shows that one party (which, in all likelihood, will be an inquirer who later seeks to compel disclosure from an ombuds) disclaims any knowledge of or agreement to the confidentiality policies of an ombuds office. Yet, the office may be able to demonstrate that its confidentiality policies were in existence, were widely publicized, and have been successfully used and relied on by many other inquirers, and that it would be unfair to the program if one inquirer were able to destroy the office's ability to keep all communications confidential. The claim of inequity or unjust benefit may be further demonstrated by showing that compelling an ombuds to disclose confidential communications, after an inquirer has received

---

142. RESTATEMENT (SECOND) OF THE LAW OF CONTRACTS § 4 (1979).

the benefit of being able to use the office in confidence, undermines the basic principles of the ombuds program and its reason for existence. Thus, it would be unfair for someone to gain the benefit of a confidential resource and then destroy that confidentiality for other people or potential users in the future.

Use of the implied contract theory as a means to establish the confidentiality of the ombuds office has been resisted occasionally by employment counsel, who want to avoid asserting any claim that could undermine the employment-at-will doctrine.[143] However, the concept of an implied contract is almost universally recognized, and even in the employment context, this concept has been widely applied—for example, to establish an implied covenant of good faith and fair dealing. Applying this concept to the ombuds office, therefore, does not create new law, it only applies existing law to benefit the organization and the ombuds office. Moreover, it is ideally suited to this context, because it relates to a program that is offered to employees or other people in the organization as a purely voluntary and alternate channel of communications. It does not create substantive employee rights or alter any conditions of employment precisely because the ombuds program is an independent resource with no management or decision-making responsibilities. Thus, asserting that the program is made available to people in the organization subject to certain terms and conditions assists both the ombuds office and the organization articulate the policy basis on which the ombuds program is made available. It is not unreasonable to expect that people who use it under those circumstances be bound by that policy. Although reliance on this theory was in the past considered a potential argument to supplement a claim of privilege, making this argument is strongly advised in the aftermath of the *Carman* decision and with appropriate program documentation.

Implied Contract Practice Tips

1. Documentation concerning the ombuds office should expressly state that communications with the ombuds are made

---

143. The employment-at-will doctrine gives employers the right to hire and discharge employees for any or no reason. It also gives employees the right to resign or quit without notice. Frequently, employee handbooks containing various employment policies expressly state that nothing contained therein creates a contract of employment.

with the express understanding (or on the condition) that they are and will remain confidential. The program description may also want to state that people who use the office do so with the understanding that they will not call upon the ombuds in subsequent legal or formal proceedings to serve as witnesses or to disclose information concerning confidential communications. And finally, this documentation may address specifically the claim that the ombuds office, rather than the individual inquirer, retains the right to waive confidentiality, and that it will only do so under circumstances permitted by the IOA Code of Ethics and Standards of Practice (i.e., where there is an imminent threat of serious harm).
2. It is always a good idea to include in documents describing the ombuds office language that indicates that confidentiality is essential to the work of the ombuds. The documentation should also be clear that the ombuds office is an independent, neutral, and confidential channel, and that it is not a place to give the organization notice of claims.
3. Without making any inquiry as to whether a plaintiff may have used the ombuds office or inquiring into the substance of any confidential communications, it is desirable to elicit from the plaintiff (or the party seeking disclosure of the ombuds communications) that he or she was aware of the confidential nature of those communications and had seen, or had access to, information that describes the office as confidential and indicates that use of it is with the understanding that communications are confidential and ombuds should not be called as witnesses or asked to produce other evidence with respect to these communications.
4. Being able to support an implied contractual basis for confidentiality is important, because not all disputes will arise in federal court or a jurisdiction in which a court has the ability to recognize a common-law privilege.

C. Other Bases for Confidentiality

There are at least four other legal bases that ombuds may be able to use to protect confidentiality: constitutional assurances of privacy, statutory provisions (particularly mediation statutes), general court supervision over the scope of discovery, and arbitration procedural requirements.

1. *Garstang* and the California Constitutional Right of Privacy

In the most sweeping opinion to date on the confidentiality of ombuds' communications, a California court of appeals in *Garstang v. The Superior Court of Los Angeles County* held in 1995 that communications made during mediation sessions conducted by an ombuds are protected by a state constitutional qualified privilege.[144] When the plaintiff in *Garstang* attempted to depose her co-workers about statements made in mediation sessions with the ombuds, her co-workers refused to answer on the basis that their statements were privileged under the California Evidence Code and because the California constitutional right of privacy protected communications with the ombuds from disclosure.

The plaintiff's motion to compel responses to these questions reached the state appellate court, which held that there is a qualified privilege based on the California constitutional right of privacy that bars the disclosure of communications made before an ombuds who is mediating an employee dispute. In arriving at this decision, the appellate court first rejected the claim of a privilege based on the California Evidence Code.[145] In California, courts are not authorized to recognize privileges under common law, as federal courts can do under Federal Rule of Evidence 501, and the mediation privilege created by the Evidence Code required (at the time) that parties to the mediation execute a writing, which had not been done.[146] Thus, a statutory privilege was not applicable.

---

144. Garstang v. Super. Ct. of Los Angeles County, 39 Cal. App. 4th 526 (Cal. Ct. App. 1995).

145. *Id.* at 532.

146. This section of the California Evidence Code, § 1152.5, was later amended to delete the writing requirement. *See Garstang*, 39 Cal. App. 4th at 532 n.3, and the current version of this provision of the Evidence Code, CAL. EVID. CODE § 1119 (2008), discussed at 260–61. Note also that, in keeping with the principles of confidentiality and informality, organizational ombuds do not require parties to execute written agreements prior to entering into mediation sessions. *See* the discussion on the provisions of the Uniform Mediation Act at 263–64.

> ### Actual Ombuds Example
>
> #### Ombuds arranges for an anonymous call to a formal channel
>
> Multiple employees on a regional sales team had been talking among themselves about the disrespectful, abusive, unsupportive behavior of their mutual supervisor. The employees all worked in different states and were connected only by way of a virtual network, so that their interaction with each other, their supervisor, and potential resources was entirely by phone and e-mail. They expressed great fear of retribution from the supervisor if they spoke up. They also did not trust other resources in the organization. With frustration mounting and many of them finding it increasingly difficult to focus on their jobs, a representative of the employees contacted the ombuds in search of a way to anonymously raise their concerns,
>
> After listening to the concerns expressed and understanding what the employees had already attempted to do to resolve the problem, the ombuds discussed various options. The option selected was for the ombuds to contact HR to arrange for an anonymous telephone call between a regional HR director and some of the employees. The understanding was that the ombuds would coordinate the conference call and that four employees would participate in it with the HR director but that the employees would not identify themselves. The ombuds coordinated the call and once all participants were connected, the ombuds dropped off so as not to be part of a formal, but unusual, teleconference.
>
> As a result of the conversation, an investigation was begun into the leadership behavior of the supervisor in question. In the end, the supervisor was switched to a non-leadership role in the organization.

The court then addressed the issue of the constitutional right of privacy. Here, the court found a qualified privilege based on Article I, section 1 of the California constitution, which states: "All people are by nature free and independent and have inalienable rights. Among these are enjoying and defending life and liberty, acquiring, possessing and protecting property, and pursuing and obtaining safety, happiness, and privacy."

While the constitutional right recognized in *Garstang* is of limited use in other jurisdictions because it is specifically based on the California constitution, there are three aspects of the court's decision that nevertheless should be noted. First, the court based its decision on the record that had been placed before the court, which the court found demonstrated that the ombuds had made a commitment to confidentiality.[147] This underscores the lesson from *Carman*[148] that there is no substitute for placing an adequate factual record before the court in connection with a claim of privilege. Second, the court cited *Kientzy*[149] and analyzed the claim of privilege based on the four factors of the Wigmore test, as the court in *Kientzy* had done. These are factors central to any confidentiality analysis. Being able to address these factors, regardless of the basis for a claim of confidentiality, is always a good idea. And finally, the court cited to both the widespread publicity concerning the confidentiality aspects of the ombuds program and parties' reliance on that confidentiality:

> The record reveals that every Caltech employee, including Garstang, was made aware of Hasenfeld's status as an ombudsperson, of Caltech's pledge of confidentiality, and that Caltech guaranteed the independence of the ombudsman office. Under these circumstances, and in the absence of evidence indicating that Caltech breached its confidentiality pledge and/or its guaranty that the ombudsman would be independent, we must uphold the trial court's implied findings that Hasenfeld was acting in her capacity as an ombudsperson at the time she attempted to resolve Garstang's workplace dispute; that the individuals participating in the Hasenfeld meetings (including Garstang) did so believing that their communications would not be disclosed; and that the ombudsman's office is independent of all Caltech's structures.[150]

---

147. *Garstang, supra* note 144, at 534–35.
148. Carman v. McDonnell Douglas Corp., 114 F. 3d 790 (8th Cir. 1997).
149. Kientzy v. McDonnell Douglas Corp., 133 F.R.D. 570 (E.D. Mo. 1991).
150. *Garstang, supra* note 144, at 536.

While it does not appear that a claim of an implied contract of confidentiality was asserted in *Garstang,* and these findings by the court were made in connection with recognizing a constitutional right of privacy, they also would be directly relevant to a claim of an implied contract of confidentiality had that claim also been asserted. The reasoning of the court is also applicable to claims of privilege under mediation statutes that do not require a written agreement to mediate, as well as to claims based on a common-law mediation privilege.

Because of *Garstang's* reliance on *Kientzy*, which was undermined by the court's ruling in *Carman,* there were concerns as to whether *Garstang* remains good law. In 2004, a California appellate court refused to apply the *Garstang* ruling to a claim by a retired California Superior Court judge that statements made during a hearing conducted by an employment termination hearing were privileged.[151] However, another decision by the California Court of Appeals in 2007 relied on both *Garstang* and the analysis of the factors articulated in *Kientzy* to find that investigative records maintained by a state long-term care ombudsman were confidential and privileged from disclosure under the California constitutional right of privacy.[152]

2. State Statutes—Generally

The first—and to date the only—statutory shield law specifically for organizational ombuds was introduced in Texas in 2007.[153] Although it passed the Texas House of Representatives without any negative votes, it ultimately died in the Texas Senate in the last few days of the legislative session. Thus, there are no state statutes that specifically provide that ombuds communications are confidential. Yet, virtually all states have statutes—often in the mediation or alternative dispute resolution context—that protect the confidentiality of certain communications and that may be applicable to ombuds communications.[154]

---

151. Saeta v. Super. Ct. of Los Angeles County, 117 Cal. App. 4th 261 (Cal. Ct. App. 2004).

152. Ombudsman Servs. of Northern Cal. v. Super. Ct. of Placer County, 154 Cal. App. 4th 1233 (Cal. Ct. App. 2007). Note that a long-term care ombudsman is an advocate ombuds, not an organizational ombuds.

153. A copy of H.B. 3578 can be found in Appendix 12.

154. In the Prefatory Note to the Uniform Mediation Act, the National Conference of Commissions on Uniform State Laws commented in 2001 that "[v]irtually

Protection of discussions in the course of alternative dispute resolution and settlement negotiations has already influenced those courts that have found a privilege for ombuds communications.[155]

Texas and California are two states with mediation statutes that are broadly applicable. In Texas, for example, Texas Civil Practice and Remedies § 154.073(a) (2007) provides that, subject to certain provisions in other subsections, "a communication relating to the subject matter of any civil or criminal dispute made by a participant in an alternative dispute resolution procedure, *whether before or after the institution of formal judicial proceedings*, is confidential, is not subject to disclosure, and may not be used as evidence against the participant in any judicial or administrative proceeding." Subsection (b) provides that "[a]ny record made at an alternative dispute resolution procedure is confidential, and the participants or the third party facilitating the procedure may not be required to testify in any proceedings relating to or arising out of the matter in dispute or be subject to process requiring disclosure of confidential information or data relating to or arising out of the matter in dispute."[156]

Sections 1115–1128 of the California Evidence Code also provide broad protection for the confidentiality of mediation communications.[157] Section 1119 provides:

Except as otherwise provided in this chapter:

---

all state legislatures have recognized the necessity of protecting mediation confidentiality to encourage the effective use of mediation to resolve disputes. Indeed, state legislatures have enacted more than 250 mediation privilege statutes." Prefatory Note at 2.

155. For example, the *Kientzy* court recognized that a successful ombuds program resolves problems informally and more quickly than court actions, and that the utility of the program is founded on the confidentiality of its communications. *See* 133 F.R.D. 570. Similarly, a Michigan state court noted that ombuds serve a dispute resolution function, which is preferable to the utilization of judicial processes. *See* Wagner v. Upjohn Co., No. A91-2156CL (Mich. Cir. Ct., Apr. 22, 1992).

156. TEX. CIV. PRAC. & REM. § 154.073(a) & (b) (2009) (emphasis added).

157. A mediation privilege based on a prior version of this statute was asserted in *Garstang* but held not to be applicable, as it required a writing to evince the agreement to the mediation. The statute was later amended to eliminate this requirement and is now is codified as CAL. EVID. CODE § 1119.

(a) No evidence of anything said or any admission made for the purpose of, in the course of, or pursuant to, a mediation[158] or a mediation consultation is admissible or subject to discovery, and the disclosure of the evidence shall not be compelled, in any arbitration, administrative adjudication, civil action, or other noncriminal proceeding in which, pursuant to law, testimony can be compelled to be given.

(b) No writing, as defined in Section 250, that is prepared for the purpose of, in the course of, or pursuant to, a mediation or a mediation consultation, is admissible or subject to discovery, and the disclosure of the writing shall not be compelled, in any arbitration, administrative adjudication, civil action, or other noncriminal proceeding in which, pursuant to law, testimony can be compelled to be given.

(c) All communications, negotiations, or settlement discussions by and between participants in the course of a mediation or a mediation consultation shall remain confidential.[159]

Furthermore, under Section 1127, a court may award attorney's fees and costs to a mediator against a party who subpoenas or attempts to compel a mediator to testify regarding protected matters.[160]

Of course, not everything an ombuds does is mediation, but some of the statutes, such as those in Texas and California, are broadly worded and may provide a basis for asserting ombuds confidentiality under some circumstances. As virtually every state has some form of mediation protection statute, it is important for ombuds, their organizations, and their counsel to review the state statutes that may be applicable to

---

158. "Mediation," "mediator," and "mediation consultation" are broadly defined in CAL. EVID. CODE § 1115. For example, subsection (a) provides defines "mediation" as "a process in which a neutral person or persons facilitate communication between the disputants to assist them in reaching a mutually acceptable agreement." Subsection (b) provides that "'mediator' means a neutral person who conducts a mediation. 'Mediator' includes any person designated by a mediator either to assist in the mediation or to communicate with the participants in preparation for a mediation."

159. CAL. EVID. CODE § 1119 (2009).

160. CAL. EVID. CODE § 1127 (2009).

> **Actual Ombuds Example**
>
> **Saving a life and saving a career**
>
> A graduate student and her faculty advisor developed an intimate relationship. After several months, the graduate student tried to break off the relationship, but the faculty advisor threatened to prevent the student from graduating. In addition, the faculty advisor had planned an out-of-state trip and was demanding that the student share his hotel room. It was at this point that the graduate student contacted the ombuds office. She said she was on the verge of taking her own life.
>
> In light of the student's fragile condition, the ombuds concluded that there was an imminent threat of serious harm and made limited disclosures to get the student access to mental health counseling. After her condition stabilized, the ombuds discussed options she might use to deal with her advisor. The option selected was to give the ombuds permission to contact the administration about the advisor. Since there had been other complaints about that advisor, the ombuds was able to indicate that concerns had been expressed by students generally, though no other details were provided.
>
> The administration conducted its own investigation and determined that there was merit to the concerns raised. As a result, the faculty member was stripped of all advisor assignments. Since all of his advisees were reassigned to other advisors, neither this graduate student nor any of the other students who had complained were singled out. Once this episode was behind her, the student went on to graduate and is now a highly respected scholar in her field.

their jurisdiction to determine if they might apply to communications with an ombuds program.[161]

---

161. For a good discussion of the difficulties in asserting confidentiality for mediation under state and federal law, *see* Ellen E. Deason, *Predictable Mediation Confidentiality in the U.S. Federal System*, 17 OHIO ST. J. ON DISP. RESOL. 239 (2002).

3. Uniform Mediation Act[162]

Ombuds offices in states that have adopted the Uniform Mediation Act (UMA) may be able to use its provisions to help assert their claim of confidentiality. The UMA, approved by the National Conference of Commissioners on Uniform State Laws in 2001, and amended in 2003, has already been enacted as law in 11 jurisdictions and may provide protection in more jurisdictions as it becomes enacted elsewhere.[163]

Section 2 of the UMA broadly defines "mediation," "mediator," and "mediator communication." Section 4 contains the provisions creating a privilege against disclosure of mediation communications and makes them not subject to discovery. Section 3 articulates various "triggering" events or mechanisms by which the provisions of the UMA become applicable. The Official Comments to Section 3(a) state that "[s]ection 3(a) sets forth three conditions, the satisfaction of any one of which will trigger the application of the Act."[164] This triggering requirement is necessary because the many different forms, contexts, and practices of mediation and other methods of dispute resolution make it sometimes difficult to know with certainty whether one is engaged in a mediation or some other dispute resolution or prevention process that employs mediation and related principles.[165] One such circumstance is where "the mediation parties use as a mediator an

---

162. The Uniform Mediation Act (hereinafter UMA) is *available at* http://www.law.upenn.edu/bll/archives/ulc/mediat/2003finaldraft.htm (last visited April 28, 2009). *See* Chapter 4 at 348 for a more complete discussion of mediation and the UMA.

163. As of February 2009, the Uniform Mediation Act has been adopted by the District of Columbia (D.C. CODE §§ 16-4201 to 16-4213), Idaho (IDAHO CODE §§ 9-801 to 9-814), Illinois (710 ILCS 35/11 to 35/99), Iowa (IOWA CODE ANN. §§ 679C.101 to 679C.115), Nebraska (NEB. REV. STAT. §§ 25-2930 to 25-2942), New Jersey (N.J. STAT. ANN. 2A:23C-1 to 2A:23C-13), Ohio (Ohio R.C. §§ 2710.01 to 2710.10), South Dakota (S.D. Codified Laws, §§ 19-13A-1 to 19-13A-15), Utah (Utah Code Ann. 78-31c-101 to 78-31c-114), Vermont (VT. STAT. ANN. tit.12, §§ 5711 to 5723), and Washington (West's WASH. REV. CODE ANN. §§ 7.07.010 to 7.07.904). *See* http://www.nccusl.org/Update/uniformact_factsheets/uniformacts-fs-uma2001.asp.

164. UMA § 3(a), *supra* note 162.

165. *Uniform Mediation Act Symposium: Uniform Mediation Act,* 2003 J. DISP. RESOL. 1 at 21, *citing to* Ellen J. Waxman & Howard Gadlin, *Ombudsmen: a Buffer Between Institutions, Individuals,* 4 DISP. RESOL. MAG. 21 (1998) (describing functions of ombuds, which at times include mediation concepts and skills).

individual who holds himself or herself out as a mediator or the mediation is provided by a person that holds itself out as providing mediation."[166] The applicability of the provisions of the UMA to ombuds programs is specifically addressed in the Reporter's Notes to Section 3(a) addressing the triggering mechanisms:

> Mediations can be conducted by ombuds practitioners. *See* Standards for the Establishment and Operation of Ombuds Offices (August 2001).[167] If such a mediation is conducted pursuant to one of these triggering mechanisms, such as a written agreement under Section 3(a)(2), it will be protected under the terms of the Act. There is no intent by the Drafters to exclude or include mediations conducted by an ombuds a priori. The terms of the Act determine applicability, not a mediator's formal title.[168]

Since the "holding out" provisions in Section 3(a)(3) are also an appropriate triggering mechanism, ombuds programs that provide mediation services should publicize that fact in brochures and elsewhere. Where that is done, the UMA should be able to be used by ombuds to protect the confidentiality of mediation communications.

4. Administrative Dispute Resolution Act[169]

In an attempt to encourage federal agencies to make greater use of alternative dispute resolution (ADR) techniques, Congress passed the Administrative Dispute Resolution Act (ADRA) in 1990.[170] While

---

166. UMA § 3(a)(3), *supra* note 162.

167. AMERICAN BAR ASS'N, STANDARDS FOR THE ESTABLISHMENT AND OPERATION OF OMBUDS OFFICES (2001) [hereinafter 2001 ABA RESOLUTION]. *See* Appendix 6 at 468.

168. While Section 3(a)(2) is a triggering mechanism based on a written agreement, Section 3(a)(3) is a triggering mechanism that is not based on a writing. It provides that the act applies if "the mediation parties use as a mediator an individual who holds himself or herself out as a mediator or the mediation is provided by a person that holds itself out as providing mediation."

169. See Chapter 4 at 397–98 for additional comments on the Alternative Dispute Resolution Act as it relates to the federal Freedom of Information Act, 5 U.S.C. § 552 (2007).

170. Administrative Dispute Resolution Act of 1996, Pub. L. No. 101-552, 104 Stat. 2736 (1990).

it encouraged the use of ADR techniques, it did not mandate their use, and it resolved the conflict between confidentiality in the ADR process and required public disclosure under the federal Freedom of Information Act (FOIA) by permitting the FOIA to trump the ADRA: the 1990 act included a provision, codified as 5 U.S.C. § 574(j), that specifically provided that the provisions of the ADRA were "not to be considered a statute exempting disclosure under section 552(b)(3) of this title" (the FOIA disclosure provision).[171] As originally enacted, the ADRA had a sunset provision allowing it to expire on October 1, 1995.

The ADRA, however, was reauthorized in 1996,[172] and in this process it was amended to include a specific reference to the use of ombuds as a means of alternative dispute resolution. In particular, an amendment was added in 1996 to include a reference to the "use of ombuds" so that the definition of "alternative means of dispute resolution" now "means any procedure that is used to resolve issues in controversy, including, but not limited to conciliation, facilitation, mediation, factfinding, minitrials, arbitration, and *use of ombuds*, or any combination thereof."[173]

In addition, the 1996 act added a new provision that provided that ADRA confidentiality trumped disclosure required by the FOIA. This new provision (codified as 5 U.S.C. § 574(j)) specifically provides that "[a] dispute resolution communication which is between a neutral and a party and which may not be disclosed under this section shall also be exempt from disclosure under section 552(b)(3)."[174] The remainder of the confidentiality provisions, codified at 5 U.S.C. § 574,

---

171. *See* Mark H. Grunewald, *The Freedom of Information Act and Confidentiality Under the Administrative Dispute Resolution Act*, a report prepared for the consideration of the Administrative Conference of the United States, April 1995; *see also* Lisa B. Bingham & Charles R. Wise, *The Administrative Dispute Resolution Act of 1990: How Do We Evaluate Its Success?*, J. PUB. RES. & THEORY 383–414 (July 1996).

172. Pub. L. No. 104-320, 110 Stat. 3870 (1996).

173. This provision is codified at 5 U.S.C. § 571 (3) (2009) (emphasis added). Section 571 contains definitions of other important terms such as "dispute resolution communication," "dispute resolution proceeding," "in confidence," "issue in controversy," and "neutral." *See* Chapter 4 at 397–98 for more discussion on the importance of these definitions.

174. 5 U.S.C. § 574(j).

address several other important aspects of confidentiality. This section[175] provides the general rule that a neutral in a dispute resolution proceeding should not voluntarily disclose or be compelled to dis-

---

175. 5 U.S.C. § 574 provides as follows:
§ 574
(a) Except as provided in subsections (d) and (e), a neutral in a dispute resolution proceeding shall not voluntarily disclose or through discovery or compulsory process be required to disclose any dispute resolution communication or any communication provided in confidence to the neutral, unless—
(b) A party to a dispute resolution proceeding shall not voluntarily disclose or though discovery or compulsory process be required to disclose any dispute resolution communication, unless—
  (1) the communication was prepared by the party seeking disclosure;
  (2) all parties to the dispute resolution proceeding consent in writing;
  (3) the dispute resolution communication has already been made public;
  (4) the dispute resolution communication is required by statute to be made public;
  (5) a court determines that such testimony or disclosure is necessary to—
    (A) prevent a manifest injustice;
    (B) help establish a violation of law; or
    (C) prevent harm to the public health and safety, of sufficient magnitude in the particular case to outweigh the integrity of dispute resolution proceedings in general by reducing the confidence of parties in future cases that their communications will remain confidential;
  (6) the dispute resolution communication is relevant to determining the existence or meaning of an agreement or award that resulted from the dispute resolution proceeding or the enforcement of such an agreement or award; or
  (7) except for dispute resolution communications generated by the neutral, the dispute resolution communication was provided to or was available to all parties to the dispute resolution proceeding.
(c) Any dispute resolution communication that is disclosed in violation of subsection (a) or (b), shall not be admissible in any proceeding relating to the issues in controversy with respect to which the communication was made.
(d) (1) The parties may agree to alternative confidential procedures for disclosures by a neutral. Upon such agreement the parties shall inform the neutral before the commencement of the dispute resolution proceeding of any modifications to the provisions of subsection (a) that will govern the

close any dispute resolution communication or any communication provided in confidence to the neutral unless certain conditions are met; that this same protection applies also to litigation discovery; that disclosures in violation of these provisions are not admissible in evidence; and that where there is a challenge to confidentiality, subsections (a) and (b) require a court to make findings reflecting "manifest injustice" or a significant need for the information before compelling disclosure. The inclusion of this high standard underscores the importance of preserving the confidentiality of ombuds and other ADR communications to the extent possible.

---

confidentiality of the dispute resolution proceeding. If the parties do not so inform the neutral, subsection (a) shall apply.

(2) To qualify for the exemption established under subsection (j), an alternative confidential procedure under this subsection may not provide for less disclosure than the confidential procedures otherwise provided under this section.

(e) If a demand for disclosure, by way of discovery request or other legal process, is made upon a neutral regarding a dispute resolution communication, the neutral shall make reasonable efforts to notify the parties and any affected nonparty participants of the demand. Any party or affected nonparty participant who receives such notice and within 15 calendar days does not offer to defend a refusal of the neutral to disclose the requested information shall have waived any objection to such disclosure.

(f) Nothing in this section shall prevent the discovery or admissibility of any evidence that is otherwise discoverable, merely because the evidence was presented in the course of a dispute resolution proceeding.

(g) Subsections (a) and (b) shall have no effect on the information and data that are necessary to document an agreement reached or order issued pursuant to a dispute resolution proceeding.

(h) Subsections (a) and (b) shall not prevent the gathering of information for research or educational purposes, in cooperation with other agencies, governmental entities, or dispute resolution programs, so long as the parties and the specific issues in controversy are not identifiable.

(i) Subsections (a) and (b) shall not prevent use of a dispute resolution communication to resolve a dispute between the neutral in a dispute resolution proceeding and a party to or participant in such proceeding, so long as such dispute resolution communication is disclosed only to the extent necessary to resolve such dispute.

(j) A dispute resolution communication which is between a neutral and a party and which may not be disclosed under this section shall also be exempt from disclosure under section 552(b)(3).

Even with the additional protection provided by the 1996 amendments, the ADRA does not provide absolute protection for the confidentiality of communications that come within the purview of the act. There are only two known cases construing the confidentiality provisions of the ADRA (5 U.S.C. § 574), and the courts in those cases found that it was either inapplicable or did not prevent compelling disclosure of otherwise confidential information in connection with grand jury criminal proceedings.[176] Nevertheless, the ADRA does provide confidentiality protection for federal agency ombuds whose activities may be covered by the act.[177]

The important public policy implications of the ADRA that recognize the need for confidentiality in ADR communications is underscored by the fact that the ADRA was again amended in 1998[178] to require U.S. district courts to adopt local rules to encourage the use of alternative dispute resolution processes. The provisions of the 1998 act do not apply to ombuds, but the provisions in this act, just like those in the previous ADR acts passed by Congress, reflect recognition of the important public policy that mediation is to be encouraged and mediation communications should remain confidential. These provisions may also be cited in support of ombuds' claims of confidentiality to show the strength of and wide support for that policy.[179]

---

176. *In re* Grand Jury Proceedings Dated December 17, 1996, 148 F.3d 487 293 (5th Cir. 1998) and United States v. Edwards, 83 F. Supp. 2d 723, 728 (M.D. La. 1999). A third case, *In re* Anonymous, 283 F.3d 627 (4th Cir. 2002) (per curiam) applied the "manifest injustice" standard from § 574 to permit limited disclosure of confidential information from a successful mediation in a dispute over whether discipline sanctions should be imposed for disclosures made in a dispute over litigation expenses between a lawyer and a client.

177. For a good discussion of the limitations of the ADRA, even with the 1996 amendments, *see* Harold J. Krent, *Federal Agency Ombuds: The Costs, Benefits, and Countenance of Confidentiality*, 52 ADMIN. L. REV. 17 (2000).

178. Alternative Dispute Resolution Act of 1998, Pub. L. No. 105-315, 112 Stat. 2993 (1998).

179. Citing the ADRA of 1998, the court in *Fields-D'Arpino v. Restaurant Assoc., Inc.*, 39 F. Supp. 2d 412 (1999), granted a motion disqualifying a law firm from serving as counsel for a party. ("With the heavy caseloads shouldered today by federal and state courts alike, mediation provides a vital alternative to litigation. The benefits of mediation include its cost-effectiveness, speed and adaptability. Successful mediation, however, depends upon the perception and existence of mutual fairness throughout the mediation process. In this regard, courts have

> **Actual Ombuds Example**
>
> **A systemic issue identified by the ombuds leads to better policies**
>
> In separate communications with the ombuds, several employees reported that they were confused by various written and oral warnings they had received. Often employees were surprised when they were told that the verbal warning stage was over and a written warning had been issued.
>
> The ombuds identified this employee confusion as an issue in the ombuds mid-year trend report. As a result, HR reviewed its warning policies. The review resulted in revisions to the applicable procedures to simplify the process and to more clearly define and articulate when each type of warning should be given. As a result, instances of confusion were significantly reduced.

5. Federal Mediation Privilege

In ways very similar to the recognition of an ombuds privilege, some federal courts have recognized a federal common-law mediation privilege. The leading case on this issue is *Folb v. Motion Picture Industry Pension & Health Plans*.[180] In *Folb*, the district court considered a challenge to an order by a magistrate judge concerning the production of a mediation brief and related correspondence from a mediation in which the parties had participated. The plaintiff asserted that the materials were protected from disclosure by Federal Rule of Evidence 408[181]

---

implicitly recognized that maintaining expectations of confidentiality is critical (citing cases). Congress's view on the importance of alternative dispute resolution, and the need for confidentiality, is equally clear. The Alternative Dispute Resolution Act of 1998 requires each federal district court to authorize, by local rule, the use of alternative dispute resolution processes in all civil actions. *See 28 U.S.C. § 651*. The Act requires that ADR processes be confidential and prohibits disclosure of confidential dispute resolution communications, though it does not make mediation communications privileged. *See 28 U.S.C. § 652(d))*." 39 F. Supp. 2d at 417–18.

180. Folb v. Motion Picture Ind. Pension & Health Plans, 16 F. Supp. 2d 1164 (C.D. Cal. 1998), *aff'd without published opinion*, 216 F.3d 1082 (9th Cir. 2000).

181. Federal Rule of Evidence 408 provides that settlement offers and offers to compromise a claim are generally not admissible evidence.

and by Section 1119 of the California Evidence Code. The district court sustained the magistrate judge's order denying a motion to compel but did so on different grounds. Whereas the magistrate judge had applied the mediation privilege provisions of Section 1119 "as a matter of comity because it is consistent with federal interests,"[182] the district court held that any determination of privilege must proceed on the basis of Federal Rule of Evidence 501 and the factors used by the U.S. Supreme Court in *Jaffee v. Redmond*.[183]

In a long and thoughtful opinion, the court then reviewed the factors considered by the Court in *Jaffee*: (1) whether, in the context of mediation, there is a need for confidence and trust (the court concluded that "the proposed blanket mediation privilege is rooted in the imperative need for confidence and trust among participants");[184] (2) whether a new privilege "would serve a public good sufficiently important to justify creating an exception to the 'general rule disfavoring testimonial privileges'"[185] (the court found that it did);[186] (3) whether there was any evidentiary benefit to be gained from refusing to recognize a privilege (the court found that the reasoning on this issue from *Jaffee* also applied to mediation);[187] and (4) whether recognition of a privilege was supported by a "consistent body of state legislative and judicial decisions" (the court found that a privilege was supported by state law, since "every state in the Union, with the exception of Delaware, has adopted a mediation privilege of one type or another.").[188]

Courts in other jurisdictions have cited, and in some cases relied on, the holding of *Folb* concerning a federal common-law mediation privilege, though there also has been criticism of the decision.[189] While

---

182. Folb v. Motion Picture Ind. Pension & Health Plans, *supra* note 180, at 1170.
183. Jaffee v. Redmond, 518 U.S. 1 (1996).
184. *Folb, supra* note 180, at 1176.
185. *Id.*
186. *Id.* at 1177.
187. *Id.* at 1177–78.
188. *Id.* at 1179.
189. *See* Sampson v. School Dist. of Lancaster, 2008 U.S. Dist. LEXIS 91421 (E.D. Pa. Nov. 5, 2008) (in which a common-law mediation privilege was asserted but the case was decided on other grounds. The court's opinion, nevertheless, recites the cases in which a privilege has been recognized but also quotes from *Molina v. Lexmark Int'l, Inc.*, 2008 U.S. Dist. LEXIS 83014 (C.D. Cal. Sept. 30, 2008): "The existence of a federal common law mediation privilege is not nearly as

the existence of this asserted federal privilege, like the ombuds privilege, also lacks universal endorsement, the court's analysis in *Folb*, together with those cases that have followed it, are useful in supporting a claim that, where ombuds are engaged in services that are in the nature of mediation, a mediation privilege may also protect confidential communications from compelled disclosure.[190]

6. A Court's Inherent Authority to Regulate Discovery

Another—and often overlooked—potential basis on which to protect the confidentiality of ombuds communications is a court's inherent authority to determine the proper scope of discovery. Virtually all courts have rules or statutes that give them this authority. An example of such a rule is the one applicable to federal courts, which gives the court the authority to issue "any order which justice requires to protect a party or a person from annoyance, embarrassment, oppression, or undue burden or expense."[191] This authority includes the discretion to determine whether the information sought is relevant, and, if relevant, whether the probative value of the information is outweighed by any prejudicial effect.[192]

Because invoking the court's inherent authority necessarily implicates the exercise of judicial discretion, the predictability of the success of this argument—along with the ability to rely on it—is limited. But this ground should not be overlooked. It may be especially useful where the party seeking disclosure was not a party that used the ombuds office. Moreover, arguments can be made to convince a court that information sought from an ombuds is irrelevant or, even if relevant, its value is outweighed by the harm caused by breaching the promise of confidentiality, including the following:[193]

---

well established as [the defendant] suggests it is. No circuit court has ever adopted or applied such a privilege; indeed, both the Ninth and the Fourth Circuits have expressly declined to consider whether such a privilege exists (citing cases)." 2008 U.S. Dist. LEXIS 91421 at *18–19.

190. *See* Deason, *supra* note 161.
191. FED. R. CIV. P. 26(c).
192. *See, e.g.,* FED. R. EVID., art. IV (Relevancy and Its Limits).
193. *See, e.g.,* Miller v. Regents of the Univ. of Colo., 1999 U.S. App. LEXIS 16712 at *35 (10th Cir 1999) (finding that a district court did not abuse its discretion in barring the deposition of the university's ombudsman, where summary judgment was granted in favor of the university, because the granting of a protec-

- Since the ombuds usually has had no involvement in the issue in dispute other than to have had some discussions about the matter with one of the parties after it arose, any statements to the ombuds are hearsay and are not evidence of the underlying facts;
- Any testimony of the ombuds would be a "needless disclosure" relating to facts that can be proved from other sources of information;
- The plaintiff cannot demonstrate a particularized need for the ombuds to reveal confidential communications with the party seeking to compel disclosure or anyone else (e.g., the testimony is not necessary to establish any essential facts of a claim or defense, particularly on the issue of notice to the organization, because ombuds expressly do not serve as a notice channel, or because the organization was otherwise given notice of a claim);
- Ombuds do not conduct investigations and thus make no determination of the truth of what may have been told to them; and
- Many people have used the program in reliance on its promise of confidentiality, and the failure of the court to protect the confidentiality provisions of the ombuds program risks vitiating the program for others.[194]

Even though asking a court to protect ombuds' confidentiality on the basis of its inherent authority appears to be a weaker argument than the other grounds cited above, this basis has great practical advantages. Each of the other legal grounds requires a court to make factual findings or rule as a matter of law that confidentiality is protected by a privilege, statute, or implied contract, but a court in this context has broad discretion—and therefore more comfort—to make a finding that discovery from the ombuds is irrelevant or not necessary. Limitations on the scope of discovery typically are reversible only for an abuse of discretion; as a result, a court may prefer to make

tive order to preclude the deposition of an ombudsman "does not affect the substantial rights of the parties").

194. It is particularly important to have an adequate factual record before the court to make this last argument, since it only makes sense if the confidentiality feature of the office has been widely publicized and the organization can demonstrate reliance on or widespread recognition of that confidentiality.

a ruling on this ground to minimize the risk of being overturned on appeal. Making a strong showing on the other bases of confidentiality thus can have a spillover benefit on this argument if the court concludes that confidentiality should be protected but has reservations about making the ruling on the other grounds. Experience confirms that there have been instances in which, even with an adequate record presented on the other bases for protecting ombuds confidentiality, a court has been reluctant to grant protection on those bases but has nevertheless granted a motion for a protective order (or denied a motion to compel) by articulating that the court did not find the information sought to be relevant or that sufficient information was available elsewhere.

7. Arbitration

A final means of protecting confidentiality arises in circumstances in which an organization requires employees' disputes with it to be resolved through arbitration. Arbitration of employment disputes in nonunion settings was rare prior to 1991, but such a requirement has become increasingly common as a result of decisions by the U.S. Su-

---

Actual Ombuds Example

Better communication results in more transparency and trust

The ombuds received a call claiming that a third-party vendor was charging for services that had not been provided. The caller was concerned that the vendor was defrauding the organization's insurance company.

The ombuds discussed the various options with the caller and the caller decided to let the ombuds take the issue forward to the local HR manager. The ombuds disclosed only that there may be questions with billing from the identified vendor. The manager reacted quickly and worked with the controller and the vendor to initiate a comprehensive audit to investigate this claim and take corrective action where appropriate. The result was that changes were made to make the process more transparent and timely. The organization and the vendor also started a regular audit process to verify services to the employees who use the service.

preme Court, beginning in 1991.[195] In that year, the Court ruled in *Gilmer v. Interstate/Johnson Lane Corp.*[196] that an employer could require an employee to submit a claim against the employer for age discrimination to binding arbitration. In the period following *Gilmer*, almost 10 percent of non-union employers instituted arbitration systems.[197] In 1998, the Court held that even in the union context, a negotiated waiver of the right to go to court in favor of arbitration was enforceable if the waiver was "clear and unmistakable."[198] That trend toward arbitration of workplace claims continued and accelerated after the Supreme Court decided *Circuit City Stores v. Adams*[199] in 2001. *Circuit City* held that the Federal Arbitration Act[200] was applicable to most employment arbitration agreements. And most recently, the Supreme Court held in April 2009 that a provision in a collective bargaining agreement that clearly and unmistakably requires union members to arbitrate Age Discrimination in Employment Act (ADEA) claims is enforceable as a matter of federal law.[201] Consequently, where an organization has adopted such an approach to the resolution of employment disputes and has an ombuds office, many of the issues of privilege and confidentiality that would otherwise go to court will be resolved by arbitrators.

The use of arbitration presents both a challenge and an opportunity for organizations and their ombuds offices to protect the confidentiality of ombuds office communications. The challenge lies in the fact that the purpose of the arbitration requirement is to promote the speedy resolution of these disputes at a lower cost to all parties. As a

---

195. Katherine V. W. Stone, *Competing and Complementary Rule Systems: Civil Procedure and ADR: Procedural Justice in the Boundaryless Workplace; The Tension Between Due Process and Public Policy*, 80 NOTRE DAME L. REV. 501 (2005). *See also* the discussion of the Federal Arbitration Act in Chapter 4 at 343.
196. Gilmer v. Interstate/Johnson Lane Corp., 500 U.S. 20 (1991).
197. Stone, *supra* note 195, at 639–40.
198. Wright v. Universal Maritime Serv. Corp., 525 U.S. 70, 80 (1998).
199. Circuit City v. Adams, 532 U.S. 105 (2001).
200. Federal Arbitration Act, 9 U.S.C. §§ 1–16 (2000).
201. 14 Penn Plaza LLC v. Pyett, 129 S. Ct. 1456 (2009). *See also* Smith v. ServiceMaster, 2009 U.S. Dist. LEXIS 44269 (M.D. Tenn., Nashville Div., May 22, 2009) (court recognized that continued employment would be sufficient to compel an employee to arbitrate employment claims under the Federal Arbitration Act under the employer's program but found that the employer did not demonstrate that the plaintiff was aware of the existence of the program at issue).

result, arbitrators—rather than courts—not only decide the cases (render the awards), they also decide disputes between the parties over what information should be disclosed in the arbitration pre-hearing "discovery." While many arbitrators are able lawyers, the arbitration system is not well adapted to the briefing and resolution of what may be seen as novel and complex assertions of confidentiality. Just as is the case with most judges, there is a great deal of misunderstanding about ombuds programs, and many arbitrators are not likely to have encountered ombuds confidentiality issues before. In addition, the ability to challenge an arbitrator's ruling, especially a preliminary discovery ruling, in a subsequent court proceeding is extremely limited. For these reasons, where an organization with an ombuds program also provides for arbitration of employment disputes, it needs to address the issue of ombuds' confidentiality in the rules under which arbitrations are conducted.

The difficulties in dealing with ombuds' confidentiality in the arbitration setting also furnishes an opportunity to include provisions in the arbitration rules that require arbitrators to honor ombuds confidentiality. Indeed, the essence of arbitration is an agreement between the parties that a dispute be resolved in accordance with certain procedures.[202] When an employer requires arbitration of workplace claims, the rules must be fair and fairly administered; but there is no reason why these procedural rules cannot direct an arbitrator to recognize an ombuds's claim of confidentiality and/or privilege in order to protect confidential communications with the ombuds office from compelled disclosure.[203] With such rules to supplement other programmatic documentation of the ombuds office as an independent, neutral, confidential, and alternative channel of communication, everyone in the organization is given fair notice that ombuds are not proper witnesses in arbitration proceedings with respect to confidential communications. There is more predictability in the resulting rulings of arbitrators (as they are compelled to follow the rules under which the matter is submitted to them for arbitration). The consistency of application of

---

202. For a more complete discussion of arbitration, *see* Chapter 4 at 340.

203. As with some of the other bases for confidentiality described above, all that should be protected here is evidence of confidential communications. Imputed notice should not be an issue, and in virtually all other situations, there should be other ways for the parties to prove any underlying facts that may be in dispute.

the rules further enhances everyone's ability to rely on ombuds' confidentiality.[204] In the absence of such a provision in the arbitration rules, however, it is unlikely that ombuds' confidentiality will be reliably recognized in arbitration proceedings.

Other Grounds for Confidentiality Practice Tips

1. Ombuds programs should determine whether any of their activities can fairly be described as mediation or a type of alternative dispute resolution process. In almost all cases, the answer will be yes. If so, the program literature should make references to mediation or alternative dispute resolution in describing what the ombuds do. It is also a good idea to document that one of the important goals in the creation of the ombuds program was to lessen organizational conflict and provide a way of mediating disputes that arise in the workplace or the organization.
2. Organizations and ombuds should be familiar with mediation statutes and court rulings that may be applicable in their jurisdiction.
3. If a state or federal statute, such as the Alternative Dispute Mediation Act, may be applicable, some reference to it may be appropriate in the program documentation.
4. Being able to articulate bases other than an ombuds or mediation privilege is important, because not all disputes will arise in federal court, and the courts of many states, such as California, do not permit courts to recognize common-law privilege.
5. Even where an ombuds program can assert that its communications should be found to be confidential on the basis of an ombuds or mediation privilege, an implied contract, or under some other statutory protection, an ombuds of-

---

204. Organizations that provide for arbitration of employment disputes and that may wish to consider adding a procedural rule as recommended here should also be aware of a limitation of such a rule. Congress, in passing the American Recovery and Reinvestment Act of 2009, specifically provided that a waiver of rights and remedies in predispute arbitration agreements do not foreclose whistleblower actions under the act. American Recovery and Reinvestment Act of 2009, Pub. L. No. 111-5, 123 Stat. 115, § 1553(d) (2009). *See* Appendix 12 at 578.

fice should assert that the court has the inherent authority to control discovery and that compelled disclosure of confidential communications from the ombuds office is not warranted.
6. If an organization requires arbitration of a workplace dispute, it should include a provision in the arbitration procedural rules that directs arbitrators to recognize the confidentiality of ombuds communications.

PART III—DOCUMENTATION

The law is clear that the burden is on the party seeking to assert confidentiality to prove an entitlement to it. Consequently, proper documentation on the establishment of the office and the way it functions is the evidentiary foundation upon which ombuds' claims of confidentiality are built. The law is also clear on the issue of imputed notice—that notice can be imputed if there is either *actual* authority or *apparent* authority to to receive notice of claims. Accordingly, if an organization and its ombuds office want to assert that the office is not an agent of the organization for receiving notice of claims, they must be prepared with the necessary proof on this issue as well. Evidence here must show that the other information on the creation and operation of the office was widely disseminated to people in the organization to prove that they knew or should have known that the office is not an authorized channel for notice of claims.

The best time to ensure that the documentation contains the necessary provisions is when the office is created.[205] Even when this has been done, the task is not complete; it is important that the message be reinforced periodically with additional materials or publicity. If the necessary documentation was not prepared at the time the program was created, it should be done as soon as possible and before there is any litigation challenging the confidentiality of the office. When litigation does arise, it is too late at that point to prepare and disseminate material that can

---

205. A useful guide for universities is *Nuts and Bolts: Establishing and Operating a College or University Ombuds Office,* available at the IOA Web site. This guide also discusses ombuds functions and skills, as well as qualities that ombuds should exhibit. *See* http://www.ombudsassociation.org/members/documents/NutsandBolts102308.pdf (last visited April 28, 2009).

> **Actual Ombuds Example**
>
> **Religious concerns of a new employee can be accommodated**
>
> A new hospital tech employee was required, as part of her orientation, to scrub into an operating room to observe a surgery. She subsequently learned that the scrub uniform she would have to wear included pants. Her religious tenets prohibited her from wearing pants—normally she wore long uniform skirts that did not interfere with her work. She came to the ombuds because, as a new employee, she felt vulnerable and did not want to cause a problem. Confidentiality was important because she wanted to discuss available options before taking any action with a supervisor or the hospital itself.
>
> After speaking with the ombuds, she gave the ombuds permission to make inquiries in other areas of the hospital, including surgery, the intensive care unit, and the hospital laundry. The ombuds learned that disposable (and sterile) long sleeve skirt-like garments were used for patients in the ICU. The ombuds was also able to arrange for the tech (whose identity still had not been disclosed) to wear that garment in the operating room, provided that she wore regular scrubs under it. That solution satisfied everyone, and the problem was resolved.

have a significant impact on whether confidentiality will be protected in that case. Moreover, just the process of collecting documentation that may already have been prepared for use in a motion can be time-consuming and difficult if it has not been regularly kept.

A. *Ombuds Charter*

Many organizational ombuds programs had used "terms of reference" or charters before 2001 in much the same way that classical ombuds programs had used terms of reference to set forth the powers and responsibilities of the office. The need for a charter for an ombuds office, however, was first widely articulated in the 2001 ABA

Resolution.[206] Section A of the resolution, which was unchanged by the 2004 ABA Resolution,[207] directs that an "entity undertaking to establish an ombuds should do so pursuant to a legislative enactment or publicly available written policy (the 'charter') which clearly sets forth the jurisdiction of the ombuds" and what the ombuds is authorized to do. This recommendation has been endorsed by the International Ombudsman Association (IOA) in the Preamble to its Standards of Practice and as one of its "best practices."[208] The IOA Guidance and Commentary specifically cites to the 12-page report accompanying the 2004 ABA Resolution and recommends that:

> [e]ach entity that establishes an organizational ombuds office should ensure that the office has a charter that affirms the essential characteristics of the ombuds function—independence, impartiality, and confidentiality—that govern the role in which the ombuds receives complaints, works to resolve particular issues informally, and makes recommendations for the general improvement of the organization. The charter should also specify and define the ombuds' scope of practice and limitations on the ombuds' authority; qualifications to be an ombuds; office structure; procedures; confidentiality; and an understanding about the ombuds office not accepting notice on behalf of the entity.[209]

The recommendation that an ombuds office have a charter is a very good one. A charter provides the opportunity for the organization and the ombuds office to articulate in one place all of the core features of the office and to state what is and what is *not* the authority of the office. At a minimum, a charter should deal with all of the ele-

---

206. 2001 ABA Resolution, *supra* note 167, at 3. *See* Appendix 6 at 468.

207. 2004 ABA Resolution, *supra* note 35, at 2. *See* Appendix 7 at 494.

208. *See* IOA Standards of Practice and Appendix 5 at 460; IOA GUIDANCE AND COMMENTARY and Appendix 10 at 534; October 2009 IOA Best Practices, *supra* note 39 and Appendix 11 at 557. Note that the IOA GUIDANCE AND COMMENTARY and the October 2009 IOA Best Practices also recommend that the entity and the organization specifically address the ombuds role in connection with any matters that may be covered by collective bargaining agreements.

209. *Id. See also* the October 2009 IOA Best Practices, *supra* note 39 and Appendix 11 at 557.

ments referenced in the IOA recommendation. A charter also gives an organization and its ombuds office the opportunity to craft a document that would be good evidence to present to a court to help the court understand what an ombuds is, why the office was created, and how it supplements other functions of the organization and serves important public policies.

A well-drafted charter thus serves an important role as a foundation document for the program and as perhaps the most important piece of evidence in any challenge to confidentiality. With these dual goals in mind, a useful framework for a charter includes the following:

- The reasons for creating the office and the important public interests and public policies to be served by it;
- The responsibilities of the office and what it is not authorized to do;
- The standards by which the office will operate, including specific provisions on confidentiality, independence, neutrality, and informality, including a reference that the office's practices are in accordance with the Code of Ethics and Standards of Practice of the International Ombudsman Association;
- The qualifications for the ombuds and to whom they report; and
- Important operational provisions or limitations.

All of these elements are important, but one of the most important requirements is that the charter set forth the structural elements that support the claim of independence. Not only should the charter indicate that the ombuds is not an agent of the organization for notice purposes, it should reflect the structural aspects of the office that prove that it is, in fact, an independent office. Demonstrating independence is relatively straightforward if the ombuds office is created through a services contract with a third party, as described below. However, where ombuds personnel also are employees of the organization, documentation of structural independence is critical, because it is not unusual for someone to assert that an ombuds office cannot be independent and still be employees of the organization.[210] Creating and document-

---

210. One of the points made by the court in *Carman* was that the ombudsman at McDonnell Douglas "is paid by the corporation and lacks the structural independence that characterizes government ombudsmen." *See supra* note 93.

ing a formal structure that embodies independence of the office can effectively rebut this claim. Accordingly, the structural elements of independence should include facts such as where the ombuds office is located organizationally, to whom it reports in the organization, and that it has the authority to retain independent counsel if deems it appropriate to do so.

As indicated in the IOA Standards of Practice,[211] the best practice is that the office report to the "highest level possible of the organization." Ideally, this means that the ombuds should report directly to the CEO or a senior leader with overall organizational responsibility, but exactly what that reporting relationship is may vary depending on the organization. Equally important, however, is the admonition in the Standards of Practice that the reporting relationship not place the ombuds office, either in fact or in appearance, subservient to any compliance function. This would normally include any one of the other formal channels in the organization, such as HR, legal, or compliance.[212] To do that would create a risk that the office will be seen as just a part of those functions. Regardless of the direct reporting relationship, the ombuds office should, in virtually all cases, be given access (a "dotted line" relationship) to the organization's board of directors, board of trustees, or other governing authority, so that in the rare instance that an ombuds deems it necessary in a particular situation (such as misconduct at the most senior levels), he or she can communicate directly with the governing authority.

A second critical purpose of the charter is to articulate why creating the ombuds office serves important public policies. As the discussion of the case law on privilege demonstrates, a privilege is not recognized unless an important public purpose is served by the requested confidentiality. Thus, an organization should discuss, determine, and then articu-

---

211. Section 2.3 of the IOA Standards of Practice provides: "The Ombudsman is a designated neutral reporting to the highest possible level of the organization and operating independent of ordinary line and staff structures. The Ombudsman should not report to or be structurally affiliated with any compliance function of the organization." *See* Appendix 5 at 464.

212. To prevail on the claim that information provided to the ombuds is not considered imputed notice to the organization, the organization and the ombuds office must always be concerned with both the *reality* of a reporting relationship and the *appearance* of a reporting relationship, since *apparent* authority can also be used as a basis of imputing notice to an organization.

late how it sees the ombuds office serving various important public policies. For example, the charter could describe a purpose for creating an ombuds program as an attempt to complement the organization's other compliance activities and comply with the U.S. Sentencing Guidelines by providing a confidential and anonymous mechanism for people to seek guidance on how to report potential violations of law. Likewise, it could indicate that the ombuds office is an important component in the organization's efforts to promote the highest standards of corporate governance, or assist employees and others to use alternative dispute resolution techniques and mediation to deal with workplace disputes and improve the quality of worklife and organizational culture. Where an ombuds office was created as a consequence of (whether or not it was required by) litigation, an SEC enforcement action, or the like, some reference to those circumstances can be made in the charter to demonstrate that a serious effort has been made to address whatever were actual or perceived past deficiencies.

A third important element of a charter is a reference to and incorporation of the IOA Code of Ethics and Standards of Practice as governing the work of the ombuds office. This is best accomplished by indicating that members of the office are members of the International Ombudsman Association and adhere to its Code of Ethics and Standards of Practice. The charter can then refer to where those documents can be downloaded or accessed, either on the IOA Web site or on the ombuds office Web site. If there are limitations on how those rules are to be applied, that should also be set forth. Referencing the IOA Code and Standards, however, has significant benefits. First, doing so permits the organization and the office to incorporate by reference very detailed information about the principles, structure, and operation of the organization without needing to repeat all of those provisions. Second, doing so indicates that the rules and operating procedures that the office uses, along with its claim of confidentiality, are derived from the collective experience and best practices of the other leading organizations that have created such offices and the leading professional association for organizational ombuds. And third, by making the charter publicly available, it serves notice to the community that this is the way it works. Having these references enables the ombuds office to cite to the provisions both in the charter and in the IOA Code of Ethics and Standards of Practice in any pleadings that may be filed in connection with a claim of confidentiality.

B. Ombuds Contract

A charter is important for an ombuds office to demonstrate structural independence where the office is staffed with people employed by the organization. For all of the same reasons, charters are important for ombuds programs staffed by third-party contract ombuds, and the charters in this context should contain similar provisions. The use of a third-party ombuds, however, raises other issues that must be addressed in an agreement between the service provider and the organization. The need for a service agreement presents another opportunity to create a document that serves both operational and evidentiary purposes. At the very least, an ombuds service contract should incorporate or "wrap around" the charter so that it complements the charter.

Not every issue relating to a contract ombuds program, however, is suitable for the charter, so some form or separate agreement will be necessary in most cases to document the agreement between the organization and the service provider on many issues, such as staffing, the form of the ombuds organization (individual, company, LLC, etc.), insurance, billing and accounting, and information systems, that would not typically be included in a charter but are nevertheless important and may be relevant to a dispute in court. Thus, in drafting such an agreement, all parties should recognize that it, too, has evidentiary purposes and that it, too, likely will have to be introduced into evidence in a court proceeding if a challenge is made to confidentially. Important issues that should be addressed in such an agreement include the following:

- Scope of services
- Duties
- Status as an independent contractor
- Compliance with IOA Code of Ethics and Standards of Practice
- Compliance with the provisions of the charter
- Term
- Compensation and reimbursement of expenses

- Access to organization employees, facilities, and information without being compelled to disclose why or for whom
- Confidentiality
  - Ombuds confidentiality and exceptions to confidentiality
  - Organization proprietary information
- Reporting structure/notice provisions
- Hours
- Employees/subcontractors
- Right to counsel
- Indemnification/hold harmless provisions/defense
- Termination
- Whether rights under the agreement can be assigned to others.

While it is clear that an ombuds charter should be made available or accessible to everyone in the organization, there is no compelling need that the entire agreement with a third-party ombuds should be

---

Actual Ombuds Example

When the supervisor and HR are part of the perceived problem

A mid-level manager had concerns about how she was being treated by both her direct supervisor and her local HR representative. She felt that both were undermining her and not supporting her as she attempted to correct employee behaviors and improve the morale and production of the team she supervised. She felt very unsafe raising her concerns to anyone within the formal structure and reached out to the ombuds office so she could have confidential conversations there. She had repeated conversations with the ombuds regarding options and strategies.

Conversations with this manager continued over the course of approximately three months, after which time she had built up enough confidence and trust to reach out to her VP of HR with the assistance of the ombuds. As a result, a personal visit was made to her supervisor by the VP of HR, and changes were made in the HR department that addressed the concerns of the manager, as well as similar concerns of other employees that had surfaced through discussions with the ombuds.

publicized, though it is a good practice to describe some of the important terms in the agreement as a way of complementing the structural provisions in the charter. This could be accomplished, for example, by a response to a Frequently Asked Question, or in other provisions that describe how the program has been structured to ensure that the office remains independent.

C. Position Descriptions

A position description for an ombuds who is also an employee of the organization serves the same purpose as a services agreement for a third-party ombuds: it reinforces the organization's commitment to the structural independence of the ombuds office and supplements the provisions in the charter. It should address the same issues as the third-party contract, with the exception of issues such as status as an independent contractor and whether services can be subcontracted.[213] As with the third-party ombuds contract, a position description should be written in a manner consistent with the organization's approach to such agreements but with a view that it may also used as evidence in connection with a motion to establish ombuds confidentiality. It is a good practice to include provisions in the position description that ensure the ombuds access to information in other locations in the organization without being required to explain why or for whom the request is being made and that clearly articulate the confidentiality of the office. At a minimum, a position description should address all of the core principles of an organization ombuds and articulate the standards by which the ombuds is expected to operate, including when he or she is permitted to make an exception to confidentiality.

D. Documentation Publicizing the Ombuds Office

Publicizing the availability of the ombuds program is important, because even at the most basic level, the office cannot serve its intended purposes if no one knows about it. Publicity helps promote a clearer understanding of what the office is and can do, as well as what it *is not* and *cannot* do. Especially for large organizations, publicity on how the ombuds office operates should take a variety of forms: brochures; posters; Web sites that feature the charter, brochures, FAQs (frequently asked

---

213. IOA has previously prepared sample position descriptions.

questions), and contact information; videotape and other presentations at training sessions; internal newsletter and magazine articles about the office; business cards; and other related informative material. If an ombuds office does not communicate its existence and role in all or most of these ways, it should consider doing so. Regardless of how the availability and role of the office are publicized, however, it is important that the publicity convey a consistent theme on the core elements of the ombuds role: that it is neutral, confidential, independent, informal, and not a channel for placing the organization on notice of claims. Some forms of the publicity may present an opportunity to expand on these concepts or to present them in more detail, but virtually all of it should contain these essential elements. The failure to present a consistent message creates the risk that someone could assert that the role of the office is ambiguous or that, in consulting with the office, he or she relied on one set of materials (presumably the one without all of the critical elements) instead of other, more complete, materials.

1. Brochures and Web Sites

Most people learn about an ombuds office from brochures that are distributed throughout the organization and made available at training sessions or in public places where organizational literature is available. Brochures and Web site information should be prepared so that individuals reading the information can easily understand the principles upon which the ombuds office operates: independence, neutrality, confidentiality, and informality. It can also help avoid confusion and support the claim of confidentiality to explicitly state in easy-to-understand language what the ombuds office does and does not do. The information in a brochure or Web site should also reiterate or complement the important aspects of the office that are addressed in the charter. Thus, for example, references can be made to the office as a place where people may "seek guidance" on how to report misconduct. Likewise, references to "mediation" services of the ombuds office or its role in alternative dispute resolution may provide important supplemental documentation for a confidentiality or privilege claim. And finally, if an ombuds program wishes to assert an implied contract of confidentiality, language should be included in the brochure, on the Web site, and in other generally available information to specify that confidentiality is one of the conditions on which the program was established and is being made available.

Such programmatic information is necessary not only because it is important for legal issues such as imputed notice (actual and apparent authority), privilege, and implied contract claims of confidentiality; it is also necessary to respond to related concerns expressed in the 2004 ABA Resolution. The need for widespread publicity concerning the ombuds office is one of the standards articulated in the 2004 ABA Resolution on the Establishment and Creation of Ombuds Offices. The provisions in Section F(1) on the issue of notice[214] address both *how* notice is given ("in a general and publicly available manner" and in person to people who consult with the office) and *what* information should be conveyed about the office. There is little disagreement that basic programmatic information should be conveyed both in generally available information and in person to people who consult with an ombuds, but there is disagreement with the notice assumption embedded in Section F. Consequently, how the issues listed in Section F are presented is a more difficult issue.[215]

---

214. 2004 ABA Resolution, *supra* note 35, at 5. *See also* Appendix 7 at 500–02. Section F(1) provides that [a]n ombuds should provide the following information in a general and publicly available manner and inform people who contact the ombuds for help or advice that:

(a) the ombuds will not voluntarily disclose to anyone outside the ombuds office, including the entity in which the ombuds acts, any information the person provides in confidence or the person's identity unless necessary to address an imminent risk of serious harm or with the person's express consent;

(b) important rights may be affected by when formal action is initiated and by and when the entity is informed of the allegedly inappropriate or wrongful behavior conduct;

(c) communications to the ombuds may not constitute notice to the entity unless the ombuds communicates with the entity as described in paragraph 2;

(d) working with the ombuds may address the problem or concern effectively, but may not protect the rights of either the person contacting the office or the entity in which the ombuds operates;

(e) the ombuds is not, and is not a substitute for, anyone's lawyer, representative or counselor; and

(f) the person may wish to consult a lawyer or other appropriate resource with respect to those rights.

215. For a more complete discussion of disagreements with the notice assumptions in Section F, *see* Chapter 3 at 212–18.

Not dealing with these issues at all is not a good alternative, because there is no disagreement that most of the provisions in Section F also represent potentially important information about an ombuds office. On the other hand, listing all of the conditions enumerated in Section F and then trying to describe how the imputed notice assumptions in subsection 2 operate is highly impractical (even if one were to assume that ombuds agreed with those provisions and assumptions), whether in generally available information or in person. Particularly if the ombuds were to try to do this at the beginning of a conversation with each new inquirer, it would be extremely confusing and divert both the ombuds and the inquirer from the main focus of the conversation. Accordingly, the best compromise appears to be for an ombuds office to provide in person, and in Frequently Asked Questions or elsewhere on the ombuds Web site, a simplified version of the primary aspects of Section F of the 2004 ABA Resolution. This also helps reinforce the core principles of the ombuds office and would allow the ombuds to testify that, as standard procedure and without disclosing any confidential communication, the ombuds always informs inquirers that:

- The ombuds office has been created with the understanding that it is an independent, neutral, confidential resource for people who would like to obtain information, discussion options, or seek guidance on an issue;
- The ombuds will maintain confidentiality and will not voluntarily disclose to anyone outside the ombuds office any information the person provides in confidence or the person's identity unless necessary to address an imminent risk of serious harm or unless, in the course of discussions with the ombuds, a person grants consent to the ombuds to make a disclosure;[216]

---

216. Another failure of the 2004 ABA Resolution is that it does not address the issue of when a person may consent to disclosure. However, ombuds confidentiality would be meaningless if at any time after a dispute arose, a person could simply waive confidentiality. Accordingly, it is recommended that any provision relating to disclosure upon consent also indicate that any such consent be given at the time of the communications with an ombuds.

- Important legal rights may be affected when formal notice of a claim is given to the entity, but communications between the inquirer and the ombuds do not constitute notice of claims to the entity. If an ombuds is given permission to communicate with the entity and does so, however, what the ombuds says to the entity may constitute notice to the extent information is revealed; and
- Working with an ombuds may address a problem or concern effectively, but because an ombuds does not serve as anyone's lawyer, representative, or counselor, a person may wish to consult with a lawyer or other appropriate resource.

In addition to addressing the core principles of an ombuds office and the issues prompted by the 2004 ABA Resolution, brochures and other generally available information should contain contact information and reference the ombuds office Web site, where additional information, such as the IOA Code of Ethics and Standards of Practice, can be made available.

2. Other Ombuds Office Publicity Information

An ombuds charter typically is created only once; brochures and Web sites typically are created or revised periodically but still infrequently. If one of the goals of an ombuds office is to inform potential users what the office is and how it works, other forms of publicity should also be used to spread the word. Especially since most organizations have new people arriving constantly, and many employees may be working remotely or in locations physically removed from the ombuds office, other tools are needed to supplement information about the office. Some of these other ways to publicize the office include bulletin board posters, internal newsletter or magazine articles, presentations at training or other events, videos, letters to all new employees, and annual reports. Each of these mechanisms should repeat the core principles of the office. Copies of disseminated information should be retained in a central file in the ombuds office, with notations on how and when it was used, to be made available as supporting documentation in the event of a legal challenge to the office.

3. Organizational Information

It is not enough to look only at the material prepared by the ombuds office to determine if it is adequate. Information prepared elsewhere can also be problematic or supportive. This is particularly true with respect to an organization's code of conduct and the way it may use the word "confidential" with respect to other offices or functions. Accordingly, other company policies and documents should be reviewed to make sure that they are not inconsistent with the way in which the organization has positioned the ombuds office and to make good use of any opportunities to reinforce the office's role and limitations. If, for example, a description of the compliance office or the HR investigation procedures permit someone to make reports "in confidence," a question arises as to how that "confidentiality" is different or compares to the confidentiality of the ombuds office. Similarly, if references in those policies or in the organization's code of conduct permit someone to report misconduct to the ombuds office, the claim that information given to the ombuds should not be imputed to the organization is undermined. Yet, the claim that communications with the ombuds are confidential can be greatly enhanced if, for example, those same policies and the code of conduct present the ombuds office as an important aspect of the organization's efforts to provide an alternative channel of communication for people to seek guidance on company policies on reporting misconduct or their options for dealing with workplace disputes. As many of these types of documents are created outside of the ombuds office and may predate the creation of the ombuds office or be written by others without a clear understanding of the role of the ombuds office, a review of ombuds operational documentation must be accompanied by a review of documentation from outside the office, including documentation on other issues or policies, to assess their impact on the ombuds office and its claim of confidentiality.

E. Documentation of Ombuds Operations

Ombuds should not limit their efforts to documents that reflect the creation of the office and how it is publicized. It is important that the *operation* of the ombuds office be consistent with the core principles of organizational ombuds, and one of the best ways to prove this is for the ombuds office to document that it handles matters in a way that is consistent with the charter and the IOA Standards of Practice.

> **Actual Ombuds Example**
>
> **The ombuds as a knowledge resource in a pinch**
>
> A marketing middle manager was working with her boss under time constraints to prepare for a presentation to her boss's boss, a company vice president. In a rush to get the work done, her boss, who had not been with the company very long, told her to use a local vendor to accomplish one of the tasks necessary for the presentation. The manager knew that this vendor was not on the approved list of vendors but that the approved vendor would not be able to do the job in a timely manner. She also knew that the vendor suggested by her boss was a relative of his.
>
> Time was short and the manager was stuck in a quandary. She thought that using a non-approved vendor could result in penalties being assessed against her department, but the job needed to be done in a hurry. She didn't think her boss was intending to do anything wrong and did not want to get him in trouble, jeopardize her working relationship with him, or delay the work by reporting this through a formal channel for investigation. At the same time, she did not know him well and was uncertain how he would react if she confronted him with his mistake. Because she had heard that she could speak with the ombuds confidentially, she called the ombuds to discuss what she could do.
>
> Since the ombuds was intimately familiar with the company and its polices, the ombuds was able to help the manager quickly find the applicable policies and coach her on how to approach her boss to inform him of those policies. When the manager did that, her boss expressed appreciation for her effort to save him from a mistake. The ombuds was also able to direct the manager to higher levels in the company's procurement management to expedite approval of a vendor who could accomplish the task. Another vendor was located and the work was completed on schedule.

1. Policies and Procedures

Most ombuds offices, for example, avoid communicating with inquirers by e-mail on anything other than scheduling matters, since the confidentiality of e-mail communications cannot be assured. Yet at the same time, some use of e-mail is considered necessary, if for no other reason than to notify someone that the office does not communicate by e-mail. Consequently, ombuds frequently will have an automatic warning as part of their e-mail signature block to advise a recipient against the use of e-mail to convey confidential information. While this may be a simple example, it also illustrates the opportunity for ombuds to create documentation that reinforces the understanding of how they operate as a confidential resource and can be used as supporting evidence.

Many other aspects of the ombuds office can be documented in much the same way. Among the other types of documents that can be created to support the operation of the ombuds office and its claim of confidentiality are confidentiality agreements with staff and service providers and internal operating procedures dealing with such issues as e-mail, correspondence, and how long information is kept on a particular matter before it is destroyed. And while these types of documents can be supportive of an ombuds's claim of confidentiality, it is important to recognize that none is itself confidential, since confidentiality extends only to confidential communications. Therefore, in preparing these types of documents, care should be taken to make sure that the policies and procedures of the office are written in such a way that they can be used as supporting documentation in the event of a challenge to confidentiality.

2. Case Files—Preservation and Destruction

One of the most important operating practices of organizational ombuds, borne of their desire to promote confidentiality, has been that they typically make as few notes as possible in connection with communications with inquirers and that they then destroy all individually identifiable information as soon as possible, keeping only information that can be folded into aggregate statistics to track the type of issues handled by the office and to prepare trend reports. The assumption here is that the less documentation created and maintained, the easier it is to preserve confidentiality in practice. A companion assumption is that in the absence of any files or documents, an ombuds could testify only on the basis of his or her memory of any relevant communications, and that any such memory is necessarily limited without some documentary references to anchor it, especially in light of the volume of daily conversations that ombuds have. Furthermore, since ombuds are an alternate and supplemental communication channel and do not serve as agents of the organization to perform any mandatory business function, there is no obligation to preserve this information as a business record. Thus, a principal goal of most ombuds is to maintain as little documentation as possible on confidential communications for as short a time as possible to minimize the potential for discovery by others or a breach of confidentiality.

Translating these assumptions into practices that support confidentiality can be considerably more involved than merely shredding copies of notes at the conclusion of a matter. Ombuds need to design their paper record-keeping practices, as well as any computer or other electronically stored information (ESI) practices, in a way to promote and enhance their claim of confidentiality. For example, where paper files are still used, are intake forms labeled as confidential and not to be disclosed outside of the ombuds office? Do file-keeping practices, such as locked file cabinets and off-hours access to the ombuds office, support a claim of confidentiality? Who has access to the telephone bills of the ombuds office, and what precautions have been taken to protect the confidentiality of the telephone record of calls made to or by the ombuds?

Many ombuds, however, operate in large organizations and have long abandoned the days when they used only handwritten notes and file folders. The confidentiality issues raised by digital records are considerably more complex. Ombuds must remain connected to the electronic systems of their organization for e-mail and other purposes, but organizational policies invariably give information systems personnel, and possibly others, access to such information so that confidentiality through the organization e-mail cannot be guaranteed. Accordingly, most ombuds avoid using electronic messaging, such as e-mail or, in some newer technical environments, digital voice mail, for confidential communications. These media are used only to schedule appointments or to direct potential inquirers to telephone or visit the ombuds office; they are not used to communicate substantive information.

Similarly, electronic case records of the ombuds office should not be maintained on the organization's network server. Rather, ombuds can use local hard drives or other storage systems, confined to the ombuds office, to keep both case files and statistical information. To the extent that systems support is necessary to maintain even these systems, confidentiality agreements with support personnel can be used to document the fact that reasonable efforts have been made to maintain the confidentiality of ombuds communications and case information. And, of course, while deletion of electronic files is always more problematic than merely shredding paper files, ombuds should work with support personnel to develop systems to scrub their electronic files of unnecessary information at the conclusion of a matter.

There is an extremely important caveat to the practice of file destruction, regardless of whether the files are paper files or electronic: if the organization is involved in litigation or on reasonable notice that it will be involved in litigation, there is an obligation to halt routine file destruction of materials that may be relevant to that dispute. Beginning with changes to the Federal Rules of Civil Procedure in December 2006, the obligation to preserve electronically stored information in litigation has become more explicit, and court rulings have increasingly sanctioned parties for failure to maintain and produce documentation, including electronically stored information, relevant to a matter in dispute.[217] For this reason, it has become standard practice for organizations to send "litigation hold" memoranda to employees to alert them to the duty to preserve information identified in the memoranda so that ultimately it may be collected and produced to the opposing party in the lawsuit. Even though an ombuds office may have been structured as an independent office to assert confidentiality, once the office receives a litigation hold memorandum on a matter or becomes aware that a matter that it has worked on is now the subject of a lawsuit, the ombuds office must suspend its normal document and file destruction policy with respect to that material. Structural independence remains relevant to claims of confidentiality and privilege, but it is not sufficient to insulate the ombuds office, in the first instance, from a duty to comply with a litigation hold or to preserve any information it is holding at the time it becomes aware of the lawsuit. As

---

217. Non-lawyers may wish to refer to Chapter 4 at 327 for a general discussion on litigation and discovery, including "e-discovery" (discovery of electronically stored information), to learn more about this point.

discussed in Part IV, however, if such a situation occurs, the ombuds office should alert its counsel to this issue before producing such information, and work with its counsel to coordinate the filing of any motions for a protective order or production of the information either to the organization or an opposing party in the litigation.

The risk that confidential information can be the subject of a litigation hold underscores the need for policies and procedures that help ombuds create and maintain only necessary information, and that individually identifiable information should be kept only as long as necessary before being routinely destroyed.

F. Trend Reports

Organizational ombuds pledge to their inquirers that they will preserve the confidentiality of their identity, along with the substance of their communications, but one of the great values of the office to the organization is the ability to provide feedback to senior leaders on the nature of issues arising in the organization and any systemic problems observed by the ombuds. This is particularly valuable when the ombuds, because of confidentiality, has information from a variety of sources or on a variety of issues that, were they dealt with separately by formal channels, would not show the connection among seemingly disparate matters or reveal the true nature of the problem.

The challenge in tracking data for trend reports is to capture and present information that helps give guidance to the nature of issues, but without being so specific as to reveal the identity of an inquirer or the substance of his or her concern. Moreover, if data is not preserved at least initially, some patterns may not be detected. For example, if only the type of issue is preserved (say, racial harassment), but no record is kept of the division or facility at which this occurred, aggregated data may not be of much assistance to a senior manager. On the other hand, a trend report can be very helpful to management if it can be presented in a way that raises leadership issues at a particular facility without disclosing information that would, either by itself or with the addition of other information (such as the racial profile at that facility), be used to identify people who may have raised the issue.

A related challenge presented by the need to collect and present aggregate statistical data is that whatever information is presented in a trend report to management or others outside the ombuds office is no

> ### Actual Ombuds Example
>
> **First a test, and then the real issue**
>
> An ombuds who works outside of the United States received a call from an inquirer who lived in a Middle Eastern country and worked for a unit of the organization located in that country. The ombuds and the inquirer were of different nationalities and worked in different countries. The inquirer, who wished to remain anonymous, presented the ombuds with what appeared to be a relatively minor issue dealing with a business process within the organization. The ombuds was given permission to raise the issue, which the ombuds did. The issue was resolved and that appeared to be the end of the matter.
>
> Approximately three months later, the same inquirer called the ombuds again, but this time it was with a concern over what later was determined to be a major fraud. In the course of dealing with the inquirer on the second matter, the inquirer disclosed his identity and it came out that he had been the person who had raised the first issue. The inquirer indicated that while his real concern all along had been the fraud issue, he raised the first issue to test the ombuds office to make sure that his identity would be protected and to see if there would be any attempt by management to identify him and retaliate against him. He said that since the handling of the minor matter had shown that the ombuds office could be trusted to keep information confidential, he felt comfortable raising the fraud issue with the ombuds.
>
> After discussing options on how to deal with the fraud issue, the inquirer had a greater understanding of the process and indicated that he would be willing to disclose his identity to and meet with investigators for the organization. The fraud was investigated, uncovered, and resolved.

longer confidential under an ombuds privilege or confidentiality. This information may still be confidential and proprietary information of the organization, but it loses its entitlement to come within the scope of ombuds confidentiality because it is aggregate data rather than a record of confidential communications, and because it has been communicated outside of the ombuds office, thus giving the organization notice of the information conveyed. In light of these constraints, a few considerations should be kept in mind by ombuds preparing trend reports:

- Assume that the information contained in the trend report is or may be subject to disclosure.
- While data tracking that is internal to the ombuds office may be quite specific,[218] it may be advisable in trend reports not to be as specific either about the type of issue or the location (facility or organizational unit) in which the issue arose. This gives the ombuds the data to make connections that indicate systemic issues but also the ability to filter the information that is disclosed outside of the office to make sure that identities of inquirers or other confidential information is not disclosed or compromised.
- The ombuds should always be alert to the need to aggregate data and to consider whether, with the addition of some outside information, the reports presented would reveal the identity or the issues of an inquirer. Low volumes of incidents in particular categories or at particular locations are especially problematic and should be disclosed in trend reports only after careful consideration.
- Ombuds should consult regularly with senior management about the utility of the trend reports in an effort to try to improve ways to provide management with meaningful information that it can consider or act upon without compromising confidentiality.

G. Measures of Effectiveness

One of the most important but least developed areas of ombuds operations is collecting data to measure their effectiveness. Ombuds offices are not alone in this regard, as compliance offices, hotlines, and other resource channels face the same issue, but measuring effectiveness for ombuds is more difficult because of the strictures imposed by confidentiality and the need to preserve the identity of inquirers. It is also inherently difficult to measure the magnitude or cost of what was prevented by having an ombuds program precisely because the potential

---

218. The IOA has developed recommended data-tracking categories. These categories may be appropriate for collecting data but may be far too specific for reporting data out of the ombuds office. Ombuds offices and their organizations should consult with counsel to agree on what categories of data should be kept and reported.

adverse impact was avoided. Despite these difficulties, as the court in *Carman* revealed, preservation of confidentiality may depend on demonstrating that the office is effective in helping people resolve workplace disputes or report violations of law. Many different approaches have been taken to this issue,[219] and more work will be necessary going forward for the profession as a whole, but the importance of this point cannot be overemphasized: when confidentiality is challenged, an ombuds office should be prepared to prove to a court that it does, in fact, accomplish its purposes.

Documentation Practice Tips

1. It is important to document the reasons for creating an ombuds office, its structural independence, and how it operates.[220] There is also a need to prepare documentation to publicize the office and to demonstrate that it operates in accordance with its mission. Documents such as a charter, contracts, job descriptions, brochures, Web sites, operating polices and procedures, trend reports, and evidence of effectiveness are not themselves confidential and should be prepared with a view not only to their role in describing how the ombuds program operates but also with an understanding that they may become critical evidence to be used in court in the event of a challenge to ombuds confidentiality.

2. Many specific recommendations are included in the text above and need not be repeated here. At the very least, however, ombuds office documentation must reflect the

---

219. Some examples of ways to demonstrate effectiveness include surveys, statistics on what people would have done in the absence of an ombuds office, data on change prompted by inquiries to the ombuds office, and affidavits or declarations by senior management or other formal channels that testify to the important role of the ombuds office in supplementing other channels of communication or providing information that is used to help improve the organization. *See, e.g.,* Jonathan E. McBride & James S. Hostetler, *Board Champions for the Ombudsman,* NACD-DIRECTORS MONTHLY, May 2008 at 16; George Wratney, *Ah! The Power of Data,* OMBUDSMAN NEWS, First ed. 2001, at 1–2; and Richard Starr, Randy Williams, & Arlene Redmond, *When Formal Channels Aren't Enough: the Advantages of an Ombuds Program,* ACC DOCKET, Oct. 2006 at 83.

220. *See also* Charles L. Howard, *Documents: Suggestions on Their Creation, Maintenance, and Destruction,* OMBUDSMAN NEWS, Fall 2000, at 6–8.

core principles of organizational ombuds and provide support for a claim of confidentiality or privilege under the Wigmore or *Jaffee* tests used by courts in considering claims of confidentiality. Ombuds should maintain file copies of all such publicity, establishment, and operational documentation so that it can be used in appropriate pleadings in support of a motion to protect confidentiality.

3. Ombuds and their organizations should be mindful of how the ombuds office is described in information not prepared by the ombuds office and whether the description of other offices or services will create problems for or confusion with the ombuds office.

4. Many times there are related, or seemingly related, ombuds offices, such as offices for different campuses (or students, faculty, and staff) of the same university, or different subsidiaries or operating units of the same parent corporation. Where this is the case, the program documentation should be harmonized to minimize the risk that a person will claim confusion and attempt to use unclear or poor documentation from one program against another that appears to be related.

5. If, in a particular case, a claim of confidentiality is not recognized, ombuds office documentation should be examined and revised to clarify the nature of the office and how it operates and to differentiate the program going forward from the past.

6. Ombuds should inform inquirers in person, and state in generally available materials, that the office does not serve as an agent of the organization for receiving notice of claims and does not serve as the agent, lawyer, or representative of any inquirer. Other information addressed in the 2004 ABA Resolution can be included as indicated above.

7. Ombuds should create and maintain as little information as possible with respect to individual cases. Any information that is created should be destroyed at the earliest opportunity once it is no longer needed. Ombuds should work with information technology providers and the information services people in their organizations to make sure

that any electronically stored information is also being dealt with in accordance with ombuds principles.

8. Ombuds should not destroy information that is identified in a litigation hold or that is involved in a legal dispute. Once they are on notice of the need to preserve information, they will need to suspend any routine information destruction procedures that may apply to the information at issue. Ombuds should immediately notify their own counsel of this issue before any information is disclosed to the organization or elsewhere.

9. Ombuds should assume that any trend reports or other statistical information reported out of their office may become public. Accordingly, care should be taken not to reveal information that, either alone or in combination with information available elsewhere, can reveal the identity of inquirers or the nature of their inquiries with the ombuds office.

PART IV—PROTECTING CONFIDENTIALITY IN LITIGATION

A final aspect of how to preserve ombuds confidentiality arises when an organization is involved in litigation and there is an allegation that a person consulted with an ombuds, or, in some way, communications with an ombuds become an issue in the dispute. Almost invariably such a dispute involves a claim by the very individual who consulted with the ombuds. In some cases, the plaintiff's reason for wanting to implicate the ombuds is that the plaintiff now asserts that the organization knew or should have known what was communicated to the ombuds; in other cases, a plaintiff may claim that he or she suffered retaliation for speaking with an ombuds. In most cases, however, the attempt to compel disclosure from an ombuds is borne of the belief that the omsbuds, if only permitted to speak freely, would corroborate the claims being asserted by the plaintiff. In many cases, such a belief is contrary to what an ombuds would, in fact, testify if compelled to do so, but whatever the reason for wanting to involve the ombuds, the process of discovery in litigation will necessarily require action by the organization and/or the ombuds, or they risk waiving confidentiality. This is so because the discovery rules used by courts and the discovery tools available to a party in a lawsuit will, as a matter of course, permit a party to acquire information related to the claims in the suit—even irrelevant information—as long as the information is calculated to lead to the discovery of admissible evidence.[221] Thus, affirmative action will almost always be required to protect ombuds confidentiality.

Numerous practical suggestions on how to protect confidentiality have been made in the preceding three parts of this chapter, but additional precautions are necessary in the context of litigation. Specific strategy almost always depends on the facts in each case. Nevertheless, taking steps necessary to protect the confidentiality of ombuds communications once the litigation has commenced is almost always initially in the province of the organization and its counsel. At this stage of the case, it is not at all unusual for the ombuds not even to be aware that a lawsuit has been filed or to know that the ombuds office may be implicated in it even if the ombuds is aware of a lawsuit. After all, in most cases the lawsuit is against the organization (and possibly others), so it is the organization itself that retains counsel to defend it. It is at this critical juncture—before any involvement of the ombuds—that a claim of confidentiality can be irreparably compromised or substantially reinforced, so a few comments about initial litigation practices are appropriate.

A. What to Avoid Doing

Once a lawsuit is filed, lawyers for an organization get involved. This can be in-house counsel in the first instance or, depending on the circumstances, an organization may immediately involve counsel from an outside law firm to represent the organization. Regardless, there will almost invariably be an initial attempt to collect facts and documents to determine what the lawsuit is about and to make a preliminary assessment of the organization's potential liability and defenses. This process includes both collecting documents and interviewing people who may have been involved; and it has not been unusual, even at this early stage of the case, for an ombuds to be on the list of people from whom documents are expected (or to whom a "litigation hold" letter is issued). Especially if the organization's outside counsel is involved and not familiar with the workings of an ombuds office, the ombuds will not be seen as any different from

---

221. *See* Chapter 4 at 315 for a general discussion of the discovery process.

other employees of the organization who are expected to cooperate in the defense of the suit.

It is at this point that an ombuds's claim of confidentiality is most vulnerable, because neither the ombuds nor counsel for the ombuds is involved, and the organization's lawyers will likely take actions that they would normally take in any other case without being mindful of the impact of those actions on the ombuds office. For example, the lawyers for the organization may either fail to understand the claim of ombuds confidentiality or believe that, as the organization's counsel, any disclosure to them would be protected from further disclosure by the attorney-client privilege. As a result, ombuds on occasion have been denied the right to consult with separate and independent counsel representing just the ombuds office and have been compelled by their organizations to disclose confidential communications. Such action by an organization, however, risks destroying an ombuds's ability to claim confidentiality. When viewed from the perspective of a court in later assessing the merits of an ombuds's motion for a protective order, such an action appears fundamentally unfair: why should

---

Actual Ombuds Example

Effective mediation

A manager came to the ombuds with a long-standing conflict with a subordinate. The conflict between them was infecting the whole unit, and the manager had not been successful in dealing directly with the subordinate about the problems between them. The manager was concerned that this issue was going to adversely affect the manager's own evaluation because the manager's supervisor expected the problem to be handled without involvement by him.

After discussing various options on how this situation could be handled, the manager requested the ombuds to conduct a mediation between the manager and the subordinate. The subordinate agreed to the mediation. Two mediation sessions helped them each open up about their differences in a safe and confidential process. They were able to reach an agreement that resolved the conflict and increased the morale of their unit.

one party in a lawsuit (the organization) have access to that information, while the other side does not?[222] Moreover, compelling the ombuds to make disclosure to the organization's counsel vitiates the pledge of confidentiality and the other core principles that the office and the organization took great pains to document. The court in *Roy*, in ruling on the motion for a protective order and recognizing an ombuds privilege, expressly noted that since the ombuds had not revealed the information it claimed was confidential to any party, including the company, the plaintiff was not placed under any greater burden than the defendant.[223]

The better approach, and one entirely consistent with the obligations and objectives of the organization, is to notify the ombuds office that it must retain and not destroy any documentation currently in its possession and that at some point it may become necessary to disclose this confidential information or speak with organization counsel, but in the meantime the ombuds should alert independent counsel for the office. Once the ombuds office has conferred with its counsel, any further communications about required disclosure or court motions can be addressed between counsel for the organization and counsel for the ombuds office.

Another frequently encountered circumstance that has the potential for undercutting an ombuds's claim of confidentiality occurs in the course of depositions, particularly that of the plaintiff.[224] It is standard practice to depose a plaintiff in a lawsuit and, in the course of the examination, to inquire about all facts, documents, and communications that may be relevant or implicated in the lawsuit. Sometimes a seemingly innocuous question, like "What happened next?," can prompt an answer that discloses the fact that the plaintiff consulted with an ombuds or the substance of that communication. What the organization's lawyer does next can make a huge difference on the viability of an ombuds's confidentiality claim. If the lawyer proceeds

---

222. A similar situation can arise, unrelated to actions involving counsel, if compliance officers, HR representatives, or senior management compel an ombuds to make disclosure of confidential information in connection with an investigation.

223. Roy Transcript, *supra* note 66, at 26.

224. Similar problems can also arise in connection with the production of documents, but the issue most frequently arises and is best illustrated in the context of depositions.

to examine the witness on that communication and any related facts—as the lawyer would naturally do with respect to communications between the witness and virtually anyone else (except for the witness's lawyer)—a claim of confidentiality may be lost. It is just unfair and a breach of the pledge of confidentiality for one party to be able to inquire about confidential communications and then try to prevent the other party from doing likewise. On the other hand, the ombuds's claim of confidentiality is enhanced if the lawyer indicates, in an attempt to halt such an unprompted disclosure as soon as possible, that any communications between the witness and the ombuds office are considered by the organization and the ombuds office to be confidential and should not be disclosed. If appropriate, the organization's lawyer may want to indicate that he or she wishes to reserve the right to examine further on that point at some later time if the ombuds's confidentiality is not recognized by the court.

This issue also can arise in the context of inquiries by compliance officers, HR personnel, or senior management either in conducting investigations or in discussions. If, in speaking with a formal channel, a person mentions that he or she has spoken with an ombuds, the formal channel should immediately try to stop the person from making further disclosures and emphasize the following points:

- Communications with the ombuds are considered confidential and not notice to the organization; that the formal channel will not ask about the communications; and that the person should refrain from disclosing any ombuds communications to the formal channel or others.
- The ombuds office is made available to people with the express understanding that it is a voluntary program and that by using the ombuds office, a person is agreeing that any communications with an ombuds are confidential and that ombuds are not to be called as witnesses in legal or other proceedings with respect to confidential communications.
- If there are issues or concerns about which the person wants the organization to be aware, he or she may mention them now, regardless or what may have been communicated to an ombuds, as the formal channel is a proper place to give the organization notice of claims.

For these reasons, an organization's counsel and counsel for the ombuds office should communicate with each other as soon as it appears than an ombuds may be implicated in litigation to discuss how to avoid actions by the organization and its representatives that can vitiate or compromise an ombuds's claim of confidentiality before an ombuds has any direct involvement with it.

B. Independent Counsel for the Ombuds Office

One of the best ways to preserve ombuds confidentiality is for the organization to authorize the ombuds to retain counsel. Not only does having independent counsel demonstrate support for the independent structure of the office, it also helps avoid a claim that it is a conflict of interest for the same counsel to represent the organization and its "supposedly" independent ombuds office. Indeed, in one of the early cases involving an ombuds's assertion of a privilege for confidential communications, a motion for a protective order was filed by the organization on behalf of itself and the ombuds office. The motion was opposed, however, on the grounds that if the ombuds office were independent, as it was represented to be, the lawyer had a conflict of interest in representing both the organization and the ombuds. While that matter never resulted in a ruling (because the organization immediately retained independent counsel for the ombuds office), the point is a good one: if an organization wants to assert that the ombuds office is an independent, neutral, and confidential channel of communication, it should not be compelling ombuds to disclose those confidential communications to the same lawyer who has a fiduciary duty to represent the organization.

Aside from the benefit of having a lawyer knowledgeable on ombuds issues assist with the establishment and documentation of an ombuds program, there are other reasons specifically related to litigation that support retention of counsel to separately represent the interests of the ombuds office.

First, the independence of separate counsel for the ombuds office may enable him or her to informally resolve the conflict over information from the ombuds office. If a lawyer, other than the lawyer representing the organization, contacts the plaintiff's counsel to explain why discovery from the ombuds is not appropriate and to explain that the information sought has not even been disclosed to the organization, the message inherently has more credibility and less adversarial baggage than if the organization's counsel tried to deliver that message. Moreover, because the ultimate arbiter of confidentiality is usually a court, having independent counsel for the ombuds office appear in court and take the lead on a motion for a protective order impresses upon the court the importance the organization attaches to the office and its independence, neutrality, and confidentiality.

Second, an independent counsel for the ombuds office can have attorney-client-privileged communications on the issues involved in a case, including disclosure of the underlying confidential communications between the ombuds and the inquirer. With such information, the ombuds's lawyer can better assess what may be at stake in the litigation and formulate strategy recommendations for the ombuds office that also have important implications for the organization. Counsel for an ombuds under no circumstances would disclose to the organization or its counsel either confidential communications between the lawyer and the ombuds client or the underlying ombuds-inquirer communications; but the ombuds' lawyer, mindful of those communications, may be able to coordinate strategy with the organization's lawyers, under a common-interest privilege or otherwise, and decide how to respond to discovery requests that affect both the ombuds office and the organization, while still preserving the important confidentiality benefits of the ombuds office.

And finally, one of the areas where independent counsel for the ombuds office is most valuable is in representing ombuds in depositions. Because only communications with inquirers or follow-up communications are claimed to be confidential and privileged, there is often no way that an ombuds can avoid being deposed. Questions on the ombuds's background; training; general experience in the office; office policies, practices, procedures, and operations generally; publicity materials; and trends and reports are all fairly within the scope of proper examination. Thus, in most cases, an ombuds will have to be prepared for and defended in a deposition, and each of these areas of examination is fraught with difficulty for an ombuds in being able to respond to questions without disclosing confidential information. Without the ability to fully disclose to his or her own counsel the underlying communications and other issues that may be of concern, an ombuds will not be able to be fully prepared for the deposition. And during the deposition itself, the ombuds's lawyer can take the lead in asserting the basis for

Actual Ombuds Example

Confidential requests for information

Two situations that frequently involve confidential communications with an ombuds are in connection with internal job postings and post-employment restrictions on them.

The concern over internal job postings is that, despite many common policies that favor internal transfers and movement of employees, employees fear that their managers will react adversely if it becomes known that the employee is looking to transfer. There is a fear that the assignments, bonuses, etc., given by the current manager will be adversely affected by any signs of disloyalty. Ombuds are thus the sounding board for employees on how they can protect themselves in the process of searching for a new job inside the organization. This process often involves multiple conversations and suggestions for options for dealing with issues at various stages in the process.

The second persistent problem is employees who believe that they may have post-employment restrictions. Departing employees often do not have a copy of an agreement they may have signed when they began work but are reluctant to request a copy of the agreement. Ombuds have been able to advise HR that it is in management's best interests to routinely give a copy of such agreements to an employee upon departure and to coach an employee on how they may be able to ask for or get a copy of any such agreement if it is not given to them as a matter of course.

---

confidentiality, making objections, and, as appropriate, instructing the witness not to respond on the ground of privilege.

C. Motions

If a dispute over the production of testimony or documents from an ombuds cannot be resolved informally, the dispute invariably will require that one party or the other file a motion with the court, and the court will then determine whether the information should be produced or protected from disclosure. Depending on what the procedural posture of the case is at the time, this may involve a motion to compel,[225] a motion for protective order,[226] or a motion in limine.[227] If there is any clear and unequivocal message from Part II of this chapter, it is that the burden of establishing confidentiality—regardless of the form of the motion—rests on the party claiming confidentiality, and thus any such motion must be based on a factual record that is put before the court.

The time to prepare and file such motions can be short. In federal court, for example, a written objection to a subpoena compelling the production of documents must be made within 14 days of service of the subpoena or before the date of compliance, if that date is less than 14 days from the date of service.[228] In many jurisdictions, if an objection is going to be made to areas of testimony in a deposition, a motion must be made and ruled on before the deposition occurs. And because the rules vary on how much notice must be given before taking a deposition, the time to respond can be as short as a week or two.

Once alerted to the need for action, counsel for the ombuds must begin working on at least three fronts at the same time. First, it needs to prepare an appearance to be filed with the court to indicate that the ombuds office has separate counsel. In some jurisdictions, this may require a motion to the court for permission to appear and file a motion. Second, counsel for the ombuds must develop and prepare for submission to the court a factual record that meets the standards required by the case and various theories on which confidentiality is asserted. The factual record must represent admissible evidence introduced through affidavits, declarations, or testimony, and should be supported with authenticated documents. And finally, counsel should

---

225. A motion to compel would be appropriate, for example, if the plaintiff sought the information, and the ombuds and/or organization objected to the production so that the plaintiff would be required to seek a court order. In this situation, while the onus is on the plaintiff to file the motion, the burden of establishing confidentiality remains on those asserting it.

226. A motion for a protective order is necessary if the information is sought pursuant to a discovery method with which the court rules require compliance unless a court rules otherwise. An example of this situation would be a deposition that has been noticed and for which a subpoena has been issued to the ombuds.

227. A motion in limine is used to obtain a ruling in advance of trial on evidence that one party believes another party will seek to introduce at trial but which is claimed to be inadmissible evidence.

228. FED. R. CIV. P. 45(c)(2)(B).

prepare a motion and memorandum of law addressing the legal bases on which the office is asserting confidentiality in light of the factual record. As the confidentiality of ombuds communications is, in the first instance, the responsibility of the ombuds office, it should take the lead in preparing the memoranda of law and factual record to support the motion. Separate briefing by the organization in support of the motion or, at the very least, endorsement of the motion by the organization is critical. In order to have a chance at prevailing, a court must know that the organization believes that the office and the claim of confidentiality are important.

Litigation Practice Tips

1. An organization and its counsel should take care at the beginning of a case not to compel an ombuds to disclose either confidential communications or documents. Likewise, counsel for the organization should not elicit similar information from the plaintiff or others, even when it may be inadvertently volunteered in the course of a deposition. Once counsel for the organization is aware that an ombuds may become implicated in a case, the ombuds office should be advised to suspend any record destruction policies that may impact information relating to the case. If the ombuds has not previously retained independent counsel, it should be permitted to do so at this point.
2. Independent counsel for the ombuds can have attorney-client-privileged communications with the ombuds that include disclosure of the underlying ombuds-inquirer communications. Counsel for the ombuds may not disclose any of this information to the organization or counsel for the organization, but the ombuds counsel may work with counsel for the organization to develop a common strategy to protect the ombuds's confidentiality.
3. Independent counsel for the ombuds should take the lead in preparing both a factual record and a motion with a supporting legal memorandum in support of the ombuds's claim of confidentiality. Independent counsel should also take the lead role in preparing and defending any deposition of the ombuds.

4 What Else Would Be Helpful for an Organizational Ombuds to Know?

Reference Materials on Selected Topics

A principal purpose of this book is to serve as a legal guide for ombuds and those with whom they work on three critical questions: What is an organizational ombuds program? Why is it important? How can its claim of confidentiality be protected? Knowledge of the law or a legal background is helpful in understanding the answers to these questions, but since most ombuds are not lawyers, additional information is presented in this chapter to serve as resource materials for ombuds generally and non-lawyer ombuds in particular. Some of the additional material, such as the sections on litigation, discovery methods, and electronic discovery, provide more background to help non-lawyer ombuds understand the legal issues that have been presented in earlier chapters. Other topics, such as the Jeanne Clery Act or the European Union Data Protection Directive, were not discussed in the earlier chapters, or discussed only briefly, and so some additional research has been provided to help ombuds better understand how these issues impact what they do and to which they can refer if a particular issue arises.

The topics presented in this chapter, therefore, represent an attempt to provide additional resource material for ombuds. Each discussion is intended to stand alone and to provide a basic introduction to a topic. None is intended to serve as a complete or comprehensive treatment of an issue; and, as with any complex issue, legal advice may be necessary and will be based on the facts in each situation.

The topics, and my reasons for including them, include the following:

I. Overview of Litigation Discovery Tools and Remedies, including the Fundamentals of Electronic Discovery

For those who may be unfamiliar with litigation or the way in which a party obtains information from other parties in a lawsuit, this section discusses the role of discovery in a lawsuit and methods by which parties obtain information from other parties and non-parties. This area is highly relevant for ombuds, as the methods discussed are the ones that a party would use to seek information from an ombuds. Likewise, the methods by which ombuds and their counsel respond to those requests are also discussed. The discussion of electronic discovery is also highly relevant to ombuds, as it has the potential to substantially interfere with document destruction policies.

II. Alternative Dispute Resolution Methods, including the Federal Arbitration Act, the Uniform Mediation Act, and Mediation Privileges

Mediation and arbitration were discussed in Chapter 3 in connection with a possible basis for claiming confidentiality. This section provides additional information and more context on these subjects.

III. Imminent Threat of Serious Harm as an Exception to Confidentiality

The IOA Code of Ethics recognizes an exception to confidentiality where an ombuds determines that there is an imminent risk of serious harm. This section describes where that exception came from and how it has evolved to become a widely recognized exception to confidentiality in a variety of contexts. This discussion is also important for ombuds because it demonstrates that in some situations, the law—apart from any authorization under the IOA Code of Ethics—imposes a *duty* to disclose a confidential communication where an identifiable third party may be in danger.

IV. Ombuds Confidentiality in Criminal Cases

Ombuds rarely are confronted with matters that could result in their being called as a witness in a criminal case. Because a criminal case involves various constitutional rights, including the right to confront one's accusers, the bases for confidentiality in civil cases may be inadequate to prevent ombuds from being compelled to testify in criminal cases. Consequently, this section is intended to help ombuds better understand the limits of a privilege and the claim of confidentiality.

V. Federal Sentencing Guidelines for Organizations

The Sentencing Guidelines for Organizations have been referred to on many occasions in the earlier chapters. They have had a profound effect on the development of compliance programs and the push for organizations to operate legally and ethically, despite the fact that the Sentencing Guidelines themselves have infrequently been employed in determining a sentence for an organization that has been convicted of a crime. This section is intended to provide an overview and a more complete description of the mechanics of the Sentencing Guidelines.

VI. Jeanne Clery Act

An important issue for colleges and universities is the mandatory reporting of incidents of campus violence pursuant to the Jeanne Clery Act. Some university ombuds have had to resist attempts by administrators to compel ombuds who become aware of an allegation of violence to report it. The analysis presented here describes why ombuds should not be considered a mandatory reporting channel.

VII. Public Sector Ombuds—Records Retention and Freedom of Information

The federal Freedom of Information Act (FOIA) is referred to in Chapter 3 in connection with the discussion of the federal Alternative Dispute Resolution Act (ADRA). Yet every state also has some version of a freedom of information or open records act, and state FOIA statutes vary widely. While the ADRA contains confidentiality provisions that provide an exception to the federal FOIA, there are limits to the applicability of these provisions, and no known state FOIA cognate has provisions directly analogous to the ADRA. Since many ombuds are employed by governmental entities that are subject to the federal or a state FOIA law, some understanding of the difficult issues involved in this area is important. Using the federal FOIA as an example, this section discusses issues relating to records preservation and destruction. In addition, this section gives the statutory reference to the Freedom of Information act of each state.

VIII. European Union Data Protection Directive and Subsequent Developments

Ombuds in multinational organizations with operations in the European Union should be aware of the restrictions on the transfer of personal data under EU law. In many ways the provisions in the EU Data Protection Directive are in conflict with the business operations and scope of discovery—and e-discovery in particular—in the United States. A basic understanding of the issues here may be important as the law develops and multinational organizations adjust to competing pressures.

IX. Federal Employment Laws and Important Case Summaries

Most of the issues presented to organizations through hotlines, as well as through ombuds, involve employment-related issues. Accordingly, an ombuds should have an awareness and a working knowledge of the relevant statutes. Of necessity, the material presented here is abbreviated, but it should serve as a helpful guide and a ready reference.

PART I: OVERVIEW OF LITIGATION DISCOVERY TOOLS AND REMEDIES, INCLUDING THE FUNDAMENTALS OF ELECTRONIC DISCOVERY

A. Introduction to Discovery Rules in Civil Actions

Litigation discovery is the process by which parties in a lawsuit request or compel disclosure of information from one another that relates to the matter in dispute. Various discovery devices are discussed, along with the ways parties can resist. As courts decide whether discovery will be compelled, this section describes the types of sanctions that courts impose for discovery abuse or failure to respond.

The purpose of discovery is to enable parties to obtain evidence needed to evaluate and resolve their dispute.[1] Discovery helps the parties prepare their cases or defenses by allowing them to learn facts relevant to the case. It is also intended to expedite the disposition of a case and to encourage settlement by educating parties in advance of trial about the value of their claims and defenses.

Discovery in the federal courts is governed by Rules 26 to 37 of the Federal Rules of Civil Procedure (Federal Rules).[2] Discovery in state court actions may be governed by state statutes or court rules, though many states have adopted discovery provisions based on the Federal Rules.[3] Statutes or rules relating to discovery procedures generally are liberally construed by the courts in favor of disclosure to accomplish the purposes of discovery. Nevertheless, a trial court has discretion to keep the scope of discovery within certain bounds. For instance, where a demand for disclosure is unduly burdensome, lacks specificity, or seeks privileged information, a court may limit or reject the demand or deny a motion that the other party comply with the demand.

Parties may obtain discovery under the Federal Rules and corresponding state practice by one or more of the recognized discovery methods. These methods include depositions, interrogatories, production of documents or things for inspection, and requests for admission.[4]

---

1. 23 AM. JUR. 2D *Depositions and Discovery* § 1 (2007).
2. *See* FED. R. CIV. P. 26–37.
3. This chapter will focus on federal law and the Federal Rules. If in state court, consult the relevant case law and rules of procedure of that particular state.
4. The following discussion of discovery methods is necessarily abbreviated and is intended as an overview for the non-lawyer ombuds.

In federal court, before utilizing these methods, both parties must make certain initial disclosures—such as the names of individuals likely to have discoverable information that the disclosing party may use to support its claim—to the other side based on information reasonably available to them. Federal Rule 26(f) provides that the parties to a case must also schedule a pretrial conference to discuss the nature and basis of their claims and defenses, arrange for requisite initial disclosures, and develop a proposed discovery plan. A discovery plan outlines the parties' proposals concerning changes to the initial disclosure requirements, the subjects on which discovery may be needed, limitations that should be imposed on the scope of discovery, and any other orders that should be entered by the court under the Federal Rules authorizing the issuance of pretrial and protective orders.

B. Discovery Methods

1. Depositions

The Federal Rules authorize the taking of depositions for discovery purposes, as do similar state practice statutes and rules. Most depositions involve the taking of testimony in person in a question-and-answer format. Oral depositions are usually taken at the law office of one of the party's lawyers. The examining lawyer asks the witness questions related to the subject of the litigation and the witness's background. The witness (also called the deponent) is required to answer the questions under oath. Lawyers for the other parties and witness (if the deponent is not a party) are present and can make objections and cross-examine the witness. If appropriate, the deponent's lawyer can instruct the witness not to respond to a question on the grounds of privilege. A record of all questions, objections, and the deponent's testimony is made, usually by a court reporter, for later use in court or for discovery purposes. Depositions may also be taken upon written questions, though this process is rarely used.[5] Either deposition method may be used to take the testimony of any party or any other person (not necessarily a party), including an organization (through the organization's designated representative) or one of its officers or employees.

---

5. This process is less flexible and more cumbersome and thus is typically used where the witness being deposed is in another country or jurisdiction, and the party taking the deposition has to rely on lawyers in that jurisdiction, to conduct the deposition.

As with all discovery rules, courts interpret the rules regulating deposition procedures broadly, to favor the disclosure of information. Deposition testimony may be compelled if the information sought is reasonably calculated to lead to the discovery of admissible evidence, even where the questions posed may not themselves produce admissible evidence. Objections made at the time of the deposition as to the conduct of a party, manner of questioning, or evidence presented must be noted on the record of the deposition, but even if an objection is made, the witness typically must answer the question, with the testimony being taken subject to the objections.[6] Due to the general presumption in favor of disclosure, a motion for a protective order to preclude the taking of a deposition is often denied unless it can be shown that no questioning of the witness would be proper (or that questioning on certain categories of matters should be precluded) or that the taking of the deposition would be in bad faith or conducted in a way that would unreasonably harass, embarrass, or oppress the deponent or party. Although a motion for a protective order may sometimes be used in advance of a deposition to limit areas of questioning, those types of issues can also be raised in a motion following the deposition.

2. Interrogatories

Interrogatories are written questions submitted to an opposing party in a lawsuit during the discovery process. In federal court, they may be submitted as a set of no more than 25 questions, including subparts, unless the parties obtain permission to do otherwise. Any party may serve written interrogatories to be answered by the party served, or, if the party is an organization, by any officer or agent who must provide such information as is available to the party. Interrogatories may be directed only to parties (in other words, a party cannot send interrogatories to witnesses

---

6. The most significant exception is that where an answer would involve the disclosure of privileged information, the deponent is typically instructed by the deponent's lawyer not to answer on the grounds of privilege, such as attorney-client privilege. If the parties disagree over whether the claim of privilege is proper, one of three situations typically will occur: the parties may be able to locate a judge to rule on the issue and the parties then continue with the deposition; the deposition continues with the objection and instruction not to answer noted on the record, and the parties seek court resolution of the issue later; or the deposition is suspended, rather than completed, subject to a court ruling on the issue, at which point the deposition may continue.

who are not parties to the lawsuit) and may relate to any matter within the scope of discovery. The purposes of interrogatories include:

- obtaining relevant facts and evidence;
- securing information on where evidence can be found;
- obtaining admissions;
- narrowing the issues;
- identifying witnesses whose depositions should be taken;
- obtaining information on the existence and general nature of documents in preparation for filing a request for production; and
- ascertaining the contentions of an opposing party; and
- facilitating disposition of a case prior to trial.[7]

Interrogatories that inquire into the factual basis of a complaint are not objectionable on the grounds that they call for opinions or conclusions, but interrogatories that seek purely legal conclusions unrelated to the facts of the case are impermissible.

Each interrogatory must be answered separately and fully in writing under oath by the party receiving it, or by stating the reasons for objection.[8] A party receiving interrogatories may seek a protective order or serve objections if it believes that some or all of the interrogatories are objectionable. Grounds for objecting include burdensomeness, overbreadth, vagueness, questions seeking evidentiary details, and questions based on speculation. The trial court has discretion on what constitutes satisfactory responses to interrogatories. For example, a court may find it permissible for a party to restrict its answer to an ambiguous interrogatory if there is uncertainty as to the nature of the question posed. If a party has attempted in good faith to obtain an answer to an interrogatory but is unable to do so, the party must state under oath that it lacks sufficient knowledge to answer the question, setting forth in detail the efforts made to obtain the requested information.[9] Answers to interrogatories are not considered evidence until offered as such at trial, and may be excluded at trial if proven to be immaterial or irrelevant. Answers may be used as the admission of a

---

7. 23 AM. JUR. 2D *Depositions and Discovery* § 117 (2007).
8. *Id.* § 125.
9. *Id.* § 127.

party to certain facts, as well as to impeach or contradict witnesses by showing that the sworn answers differ from the testimony in court.[10]

3. Requests for Production and Inspection

Under the Federal Rules, any party may serve on any other party a request to produce and permit the inspection and copying of any designated documents or tangible things that constitute or contain discoverable matter in the possession or custody of that party.[11] Additionally, a party may request permission to enter upon designated land or other property in the possession of the other party for the purpose of inspection, as long as the matters sought are within the usual scope of discovery. Parties are entitled to inspect documents in the possession of other parties for the purpose of assisting in the preparation of their case for trial as long as the documents they seek are relevant to the subject matter of the litigation and otherwise within the scope of discovery. Such requests must set forth the items to be inspected, either by individual item or by category, describing each with reasonable particularity. Requests must also specify a reasonable time, place, and manner of making the inspection. Requests for production are often used with accompanying deposition notices and interrogatories.

The party upon whom a request for production and inspection is made may object to the request as unduly burdensome. In that case, the party must file a timely written objection to the request that specifies the parts objected to while permitting the remaining parts to be inspected. A party may not avoid compliance by using a system of records that conceals relevant records or makes it particularly difficult to identify or locate them. Conversely, a party does not have to search for records that could have no legitimate bearing on the issues of a case, and, upon filing the appropriate motion, can be protected from undue harassment or intrusions into its records.

Federal Rule 34 governs discovery of documents in possession of the parties themselves, while Federal Rule 45 concerns discovery of

---

10. "Impeachment" refers to the act of discrediting a witness at trial, as by catching the witness in a lie or inconsistent testimony, or by showing that the witness has been convicted of a crime.

11. Fed. R. Civ. P. 34(a)(1).

documents in the possession of persons or entities that are not parties to the lawsuit, known as "nonparties," through the issuance of subpoenas.[12] If a nonparty objects to an inspection request, it may serve a written objection that will halt discovery until a court order approves it. Furthermore, while requests for inspection upon parties are broad in order to promote the purposes of discovery, such requests upon nonparties are more limited to protect third persons from harassment, nuisance, or disclosure of confidential information.

4. Requests for Admission

A request for admission is a discovery procedure in which one party asks an opposing party to admit that certain facts are true. The Federal Rules and the court rules of many states permit a party to serve upon any other party a written request for the admission of the truth of any matters that relate to statements or opinions of fact, or of the application of law to fact, including the genuineness of particular documents.[13] The request must set forth the proper scope of discovery and must be for the purposes of the pending action only. Moreover, requests are limited to particular relevant facts so that they may be categorically admitted or denied without the need for explanation. The submission of a request for admission does not bind the requesting party to the truth of the facts contained in the answers even if it offers the answers in evidence, as it may offer more favorable evidence as well.[14] Requests for admission may relate to any or all of the issues in an action, even if such request presents a genuine issue for trial. Thus, requests for admission may relate to ultimate or central facts in dispute.

The Federal Rules provide that a matter is admitted unless, within 30 days after service of the request, the responding party serves the requesting party a written answer or objection.[15] If a party fails to respond in a timely manner to a request to admit, the matter is deemed admitted for purposes of the pending action. The responding party is not required to admit the truth of facts that are exclusively within the knowledge of the requesting party, nor does it have to obtain facts

---

12. 23 Am. Jur. 2d *Depositions and Discovery* § 147 (2007).
13. Fed. R. Civ. P. 36(a).
14. 23 Am. Jur. 2d *Depositions and Discovery* § 181 (2007).
15. Fed. R. Civ. P. 36(a).

upon which to make a response from a third party known to be hostile or interested in the outcome of the suit. The responding party may object to all or part of a request for admission that it feels is improper as to form or content, or due to a claimed privilege. Moreover, a court may grant a protective order to relieve a party of the duty to respond to a request for admission.

The requesting party may move for a court determination of the sufficiency of the answers or objections. A court may sustain an objection to a request and rule that the responding party has no duty to answer it, or may, if it determines that the objection is not justified, order that either the matter is admitted or that an amended answer be served.[16] Once a matter is admitted under Federal Rule 36, it is conclusively established for the purpose of the pending action, and no further proof of the admitted matter is required for trial or otherwise (such as a motion for summary judgment). Thus, once a matter is deemed admitted, the party bound by the admission cannot contradict it at trial. However, an admission is binding only upon the party to whom the request was directed and not on other parties in the lawsuit or a nonparty.

C. Scope of Discovery

1. In General

Under the Federal Rules, parties may generally obtain discovery regarding any matter, not privileged, that is relevant to the claim or defense of any party.[17] This includes the existence, description, nature, custody, condition, and location of any books, documents, or other tangible things, and the identity and location of persons with knowledge of any discoverable matter. If a party objects to a discovery request, a court will make the final determination as to its relevancy, balancing the need for disclosure with the countervailing need for privacy and freedom from undue hardship. Even if the discovery request appears irrelevant, there may still be good cause for authorizing it if it is relevant to the subject matter of the action. Moreover, discovery is permitted even for information that would not be admissible at

---

16. 23 AM. JUR. 2D *Depositions and Discovery* § 193 (2007).
17. FED. R. CIV. P. 26(b)(1).

trial if the information sought is reasonably calculated to lead to the discovery of admissible evidence. In other words, a party may discover information that, while inadmissible at trial, will have some likely effect on his case or will lead to the discovery of such information.

Discovery in federal courts is subject to the limitations imposed by the provisions of the Federal Rules governing scope. The scope of discovery is also subject to limitations imposed by the trial court to which the case has been assigned, which may alter the limits otherwise applicable under the Federal Rules on the number or length of depositions, the number of interrogatories, and the number of requests for admission of documents.[18] The trial court may also curb the use of discovery methods if it determines that the discovery sought is unreasonably cumulative, duplicative, or is obtainable from a source that is more convenient, less burdensome, or less expensive; the discovering party has had sufficient opportunity to obtain the sought information; or the burden of the proposed discovery outweighs its likely benefit, considering the amount in controversy, the needs of the case, the parties' resources, the importance of the proposed discovery in resolving the issues, and the importance of the issues at stake in the litigation.[19] A trial court will also consider the purpose of a discovery request in determining its validity. For instance, if a discovery request is used to delay bringing a case to trial or to harass or embarrass the other side, a court will likely deny such request. A court thus has the power to issue protective orders to regulate or prevent discovery, even where the information sought is within the designated scope of discovery.

2. Privileges

Under Rule 26(b) of the Federal Rules and similar state rules, a party may obtain discovery regarding any matter that is not privileged.[20] Courts apply the same rules of privilege to discovery as they do at trial, so testimonial privileges recognized by the law of evidence control.[21] Thus, a party cannot be forced to disclose privileged or confidential information which it cannot be compelled to testify on in court. In civil actions where state law governs the litigation, state law deter-

---

18. 23 AM. JUR. 2D *Depositions and Discovery* § 21 (2007).
19. *Id.*
20. FED. R. CIV. P. 26(b).
21. 23 AM. JUR. 2D *Depositions and Discovery* § 27 (2007).

mines the question of privilege: the Federal Rules of Evidence provide, in part, that "in civil actions and proceedings, with respect to an element of a claim or defense as to which State law supplies the rule of decision, the privilege of a witness [or] person . . . shall be determined in accordance with State law."[22] As discussed in Chapter 3, Federal Rule of Evidence 501 permits federal courts to recognize new privileges based "on the principles of common law as they may be interpreted by the courts of the United States in the light of reason and experience. As societal needs have changed, this flexible standard has accommodated additional privileges, such as the psychotherapist-patient privilege recognized by the Supreme Court in *Jaffe v. Redmond*.[23] States have recognized privileges, such as the marital communications privilege, the psychotherapist-patient privilege, the attorney-client privilege, and the cleric-congregant privilege. In some states, courts may recognize new privileges under common law in the same way that federal courts can; in other states, courts are permitted to recognize only privileges that are approved by the state's constitution or by the legislature.

A party objecting to discovery has the burden of establishing the existence of the privilege and must claim it expressly, describing the nature of the documents or communications it wishes to protect in a way that will not reveal the protected information itself. In assessing a claim of privilege, a court will often review not only the briefs and other documentation supporting the claim of privilege, but also the document or other information in dispute in the absence of the opposing party,[24] and either take out portions of the document that it deems privileged or issue a protective order with respect to the privileged parts of the document. Thus, a court may compel the production of matters that are claimed to be privileged so that it can assess the claim and may then compel the production of portions of a document, for example, that may not themselves be privileged, while protecting the rest of the document from disclosure. Although the right to object to

---

22. FED. R. EVID. 501. *See also* Solarzano v. Shell Chem. Co., 2000 U.S. Dist. LEXIS 12072 (E.D. La. Aug. 14, 2000) (federal law of privilege applies in federal court even as to pendant state law claims).

23. Jaffe v. Redmond, 518 U.S. 1 (1996). *See* Chapter 3 at 221 to 227 for a discussion of U.S. Supreme Court cases on recognizing testimonial privileges.

24. This process is referred to as an "in camera" review.

discovery on the grounds of privilege is not always lost simply because there has been disclosure, a privilege often is deemed waived if the information at issue is disclosed in unprotected ways during the discovery process.

D. Discovery Remedies

Federal Rule 37 and similar state statutes and rules establish a discretionary system by which courts may enforce compliance with discovery procedures through a variety of remedies and sanctions, including motions for a protective order, a motion to compel discovery, sanctions for failure to comply with a discovery order, and assessment of expenses for failure to admit.[25] The purposes of imposing sanctions under Federal Rule 37 include the need to ensure future compliance with discovery rules (deterrence), to punish past discovery failures, and to compensate the offended party for expenses incurred as a result of another party's failure to allow discovery. The decision on whether to grant a motion for a protective order or to impose sanctions, and, if so, which sanctions to impose, are within the sole discretion of the trial court. A court considers the totality of the circumstances surrounding the discovery issue or a failure to comply with discovery procedures, keeping in mind the constitutional requirements imposed by the Due Process Clause of the United States Constitution.[26]

1. Protective Orders

A court may issue a protective order regarding specified matters related to discovery, upon motion by a party or by the person from whom discovery is sought.[27] The party seeking the order bears the burden of demonstrating the requisite "good cause." Protective orders are issued for "good cause" when a party or person seeking the order can prove that justice requires that such an order be made to protect the party or person from annoyance, embarrassment, oppression, or

---

25. *See* Fed. R. Civ. P. 37.
26. The Due Process Clause of the U.S. Constitution limits the power of courts to dismiss an action without giving a party the opportunity for a hearing on the merits. *See* U.S. Const. amend. V ("No person shall be deprived of life, liberty, or property, without due process of law.").
27. Fed. R. Civ. P. 26(c).

undue burden or expense.[28] Factors that a court may consider in issuing a protective order include the purpose of the information sought, the effect that disclosure will have on the parties and on the trial, the nature of the objections urged by the party opposing disclosure, and the ability of the court to craft an alternative order that may grant partial disclosure.[29] Protective orders may provide that the disclosure not be made or be made only on specified terms and conditions or by certain methods, or that its scope be limited to certain matters if it is found that bad faith or harassment motivates the party seeking the discovery.[30]

Protective orders denying a party's right to take a deposition are hard to obtain. For instance, the fact that some information held by a witness may involve privileged information may not justify precluding a deposition entirely, as it may involve questioning on nonprivileged information. Likewise, a showing that harassment of a witness being deposed is more probable than not or that a proposed deponent may lack knowledge on the subject of the litigation does not suffice as a reason to prevent the deposition entirely. A court may issue a protective order against excessively long interrogatories that are shown to be an undue burden and an abuse of the discovery process, or interrogatories that seek irrelevant or incriminating answers. In the context of document production and inspection, a court may issue a protective order where a party can prove that the requested material is privileged or irrelevant to any issue in the lawsuit.

2. Motion to Compel Discovery

If a party fails to make a disclosure or produce information required by Federal Rule 26(a), the requesting party may apply for an order to compel the party to comply and for appropriate sanctions. Disclosure may be compelled for various reasons, such as if a deponent fails to answer a question asked in accordance with discovery rules; a party

---

28. 23 AM. JUR. 2D *Depositions and Discovery* § 61 (2007).
29. *Id.* § 64.
30. In addition, there are times that a party anticipates that another party is planning to introduce into evidence at the trial information produced in discovery that is objectionable or inadmissible. In these situations, parties often file "motions in limine" to obtain a ruling from the court before trial commences on whether the court will permit the introduction of such evidence.

fails to answer an interrogatory; or a party fails to permit inspection as requested.[31] A trial court has sole discretion whether to grant or deny a motion to compel discovery, recognizing that the parties are permitted to obtain discovery regarding any matter, not privileged, that is relevant to the subject matter of the litigation. In certain cases, a trial court may deny a motion to compel discovery if compliance would result in a violation of a recognized right of confidentiality. Furthermore, a court, in denying a motion to compel discovery, may also enter a protective order to protect the party from further discovery requests.

3. Sanctions for Failure to Comply with Discovery Order

If a deponent refuses to be sworn or to answer a question after being directed to do so by the court, the failure may be considered as contempt of that court.[32] If a party fails to obey an order to permit discovery or to participate in a pretrial conference to develop a discovery plan, a court may make such orders as are appropriate and equitable. For instance, a court may make an order staying further proceedings until the discovery order is obeyed; striking pleadings; asserting that the matters regarding which the order was made be taken as established; dismissing the action in part or in whole; or rendering judgment by default against the offending party.[33] The court has discretion on whether to impose a sanction and what the appropriate sanction may be in a given case, depending on the context of the particular facts. Such discretion is not unfettered, however, as the Due Process Clause of the Fifth Amendment to the Constitution limits the power of a court to dismiss an action without affording a party the opportunity for a hearing on the merits of its case. Thus, if a party establishes that

---

31. 23 AM. JUR. 2D *Depositions and Discovery* § 203 (2007).
32. FED. R. CIV. P. 37. There are two types of contempt—civil and criminal. Civil contempt is the failure to obey a court order that was issued for another party's benefit, sanctionable by fine or confinement until compliance with the order. BLACK'S LAW DICTIONARY 336 (8th ed. 2004). Criminal contempt is an act that obstructs justice or attacks the integrity of the court, and its sanctions are punitive in nature. *Id.*
33. 23 AM. JUR. 2D *Depositions and Discovery* § 210 (2007). Dismissal of an action and imposing a default judgment are drastic remedies that are appropriate only when the offending party's actions are due to willfulness, bad faith, or fault. *Id.* § 220.

its noncompliance was a result of inability rather than willfulness, bad faith, or fault, Federal Rule 37 is not construed to authorize dismissal of its case.

In crafting an equitable order for failure to comply, a court will consider the validity of the discovery order itself, the prejudice to the discovering party, the necessity to maintain the integrity of orders entered by the court, the deterrent effect of the sanction, and the principle that a party ought not to benefit from its refusal to permit discovery. Although willfulness may be required to justify the more drastic sanctions, simply failing to respond to discovery is sufficient to justify less severe sanctions.

4. Assessment of Expenses for Failure to Admit

The assessment of expenses is the only sanction available under the Federal Rules for a failure to comply with a request for admission. If a party fails to admit the truth of any matter or the genuineness of any document as requested, and if the requesting party proves the truth of the matter or the genuineness of the document, the requesting party may apply to the court for an order requiring the offending party to pay reasonable expenses, including attorney's fees, incurred in making that proof.[34] The court must make an order awarding reasonable expenses and fees unless it finds that the request was objectionable under Federal Rule 36(a), the admission sought was of no substantial importance, the party failing to admit reasonably believed that it might prevail on the matter, or there was another good reason for the failure to admit.

E. Discovery of Electronically Stored Information

Litigation is more expensive, time-consuming, and perilous today than ever before. A principal reason is the work required of the parties during the discovery phase, which occupies most of the time a case is pending before trial.[35] To compound the problem, additional problems and burdens have emerged in determining how to apply the tra-

---

34. FED. R. CIV. P. 37(c)(2).
35. An extremely high percentage of all federal court cases settle out of court. Thus, most of a litigator's time—and, accordingly, most of a client's expenses—are spent in discovery and pleadings (particularly in discovery) rather than at trial.

ditional scope and methods of discovery to electronically stored information (ESI). Today, over 90 percent of all information is created in an electronic format,[36] and much of it exists only in electronic form. ESI includes e-mail, Web pages, audio and video files, images, word-processing files, and nearly anything stored on a computing device, including servers, desktops, laptops, hard drives, flash drives, PDAs, MP3 players, and cell phones.[37] The cost of preserving, finding, and reviewing electronic information from these sources, in addition to preserving, finding, and reviewing the traditional paper and other documentary evidence, can be astronomical. The discovery of ESI, known as e-discovery, continues to be a source of considerable confusion and uncertainty for litigants and their lawyers, and ombuds are not immune from dealing with these issues.

To respond to changes caused by the explosion in communications and business information generated and stored electronically, the Supreme Court revised the Federal Rules on December 1, 2006, in an attempt to implement a degree of uniformity in e-discovery procedure. The Federal Rules, of course, apply only to federal court cases, though many states have adopted discovery provisions generally modeled on Federal Rules 26 to 37. Thus, the guidance offered by the revised Federal Rules has influenced, and undoubtedly will continue to influence, the development of rules for state courts. In fact, current proposed rules for e-discovery in some states follow closely the Federal Rules.[38]

---

36. THE SEDONA CONFERENCE, THE SEDONA PRINCIPLES: BEST PRACTICES RECOMMENDATIONS & PRINCIPLES FOR ADDRESSING ELECTRONIC DOCUMENT PRODUCTION 1 (2d ed. June 2007) (hereinafter THE SEDONA CONFERENCE), *available at* http://www.sedonaconference.com/content/miscFiles/TSC_PRINCP_2nd_ed_607.pdf (last visited April 28, 2009).

37. *Id.* Information is "electronic" if it exists within a medium that can be read only by a computer, which includes cache memory, magnetic disks, optical disks, and magnetic tapes. *Id.*

38. *See* NATIONAL CONFERENCE OF COMMISSIONERS ON UNIFORM STATE LAWS, UNIFORM LAW COMMISSION'S PROPOSED UNIFORM RULES RELATING TO DISCOVERY OF ELECTRONICALLY STORED INFORMATION (July 27–Aug. 3, 2007); RALPH C. LOSEY, E-DISCOVERY: CURRENT TRENDS AND CASES 106 (2008) ("Just like the Federal Rules, the proposed state rules have provisions requiring early discussion of e-discovery, protection from production of not-reasonably-accessible information with cost-shifting, privilege protection procedures, a default 'ordinarily maintained' or 'reasonably usable' production mode, and a safe harbor from sanctions for routine, good-faith destruction."); THE

Generally speaking, the new rules are based on the following principles:

- Parties and their counsel have a duty to familiarize themselves with where and how their ESI is stored;
- They must communicate with the other parties regarding the scope of preservation, the method of searching for responsive ESI, which sources are "reasonably accessible," and the form in which ESI will be produced; and
- They must learn to effectively convey to the court their disputes or objections to ESI discovery requests; and, while parties cannot possibly preserve all or every ESI ever created or stored, they must place a reasonable litigation hold on relevant and responsive information that they may need to produce.[39]

Courts already have begun to apply these rules, but because they are relatively new, we do not yet know whether they will adequately address all the issues raised by e-discovery. There are, however, critical elements of e-discovery that ombuds and their counsel should know about—what triggers the duty to preserve ESI, what materials must be preserved, how to satisfy an obligation to preserve, and what consequences exist in the event of noncompliance.

1. Triggering the Duty to Preserve ESI

The amendments to Federal Rule 26(f) state that the parties are obliged to address the issue of ESI early in a case. The revised rule, however, fails to provide guidance on what triggers this duty to preserve, what ESI must be preserved and in what form, and what steps to follow to preserve the ESI. Various statutes, such as Section 802 of the Sarbanes-Oxley Act of 2002, and regulations, such as those for the Equal Em-

---

SEDONA CONFERENCE, *supra* note 36, at 10 (noting that "[t]wo national initiatives are directed at promoting uniformity among the state trial courts . . . the Conference of Chief Justices . . . which has issued 'Guidelines for State Trial Courts on Discovery of Electronically Stored Information' . . . . [and] the Electronic Discovery Committee of the National Conference of Commissioners on Uniform Laws (NCCUSL).").

39. MOORE'S FEDERAL PRACTICE, E-DISCOVERY: THE NEWLY AMENDED FEDERAL RULES OF CIVIL PROCEDURE 30–31 (LexisNexis 2006).

ployment Opportunity Act, 29 C.F.R. § 1602.14, require the retention of records in specific contexts. Common law—rules and standards developed over time by courts—also establish a general duty to preserve evidence.

In addition to possible sanctions by a court for failure to preserve information that may be relevant, a party may be subject to a claim for damages under a theory known as "spoliation."[40] Under common law, a spoliation claim exists where a party had an obligation to preserve evidence at the time it was destroyed, the destruction transpired with a "culpable state of mind"—which includes intentional or willful destruction, destruction in bad faith, or gross negligence—and the destroyed evidence was relevant.[41] Some jurisdictions also recognize a tort of intentional spoliation of evidence, which exposes a defendant to liability if he or she had knowledge of a pending civil action, willfully or negligently destroyed evidence, and a plaintiff was unable to establish a claim without the destroyed evidence.[42] Courts in at least some jurisdictions permit a cause of action for negligent spoliation of evidence.[43] With a pre-existing, objective policy in place that addresses the retention of ESI in the ordinary course of business, organizations can show that they legitimately destroyed ESI by following reasonable standards. In fact, the U.S. Supreme Court has noted that the existence of a reasonable records and information management policy instituted in good faith ought to be considered in determining liability for evidence spoliation.[44]

The duty to preserve ESI has been discussed extensively in an influential series of decisions from the U.S. District Court for the South-

---

40. *See* West v. Goodyear Tire & Rubber Co., 167 F.3d 776, 779 (2d Cir. 1999) (defining spoliation as "the destruction or significant alteration of evidence, or the failure to preserve property for another's use as evidence in pending or reasonably foreseeable litigation").

41. Reilly v. Natwest Market Group Inc., 181 F.3d 253, 267 (2d Cir. 1999). If the evidence was destroyed willfully or intentionally, its relevance need not be proven. Byrnie v. Town of Cromwell, 243 F.3d 93, 107–112 (2d Cir. 2001).

42. *See, e.g.*, Nye v. CSX Transp., Inc., 437 F.3d 556 (6th Cir. 2006); J.S. Sweet Co. v. Sika Chem. Corp., 400 F.3d 1028 (7th Cir. 2005).

43. Residential Funding Corp. v. DeGeorge Fin. Corp., 306 F. 3d 99 (2d Cir 2002); Basso v. Boston Scientific Corp., 46 CONN. L. RPTR. No. 18, 642 (Conn. Super. Ct. Feb. 9, 2009).

44. Arthur Anderson LLP v. United States, 544 U.S. 696 (2005).

ern District of New York in *Zubulake v. UBS Warburg LLC*.[45] In *Zubulake IV*, the court held that the duty to preserve ESI arises "[o]nce a party reasonably anticipates litigation," at which time a party "must suspend its routine document retention/destruction policy and put in place a 'litigation hold' to ensure the preservation of relevant documents."[46] The rule articulated in this opinion has been widely cited and is often used to articulate when the duty to preserve information is triggered. The duty to preserve evidence, therefore, can arise at different times, depending on the case and the circumstances. Generally, the duty to preserve arises when a party is aware or should be aware that evidence in its possession, custody, or control is relevant to litigation or potential litigation.[47] Some courts have held that the duty arises once a party is on notice that such evidence may be used at trial;[48] some have held that the obligation may arise before the filing and service of a complaint;[49] and yet other courts have held that once a demand letter is sent, the parties should "reasonably anticipate" litigation, thus triggering the duty to preserve.[50] Some courts have even held that informal complaints made prior to the commencement of litigation trigger the duty to preserve,[51] while others have found the duty in informal

---

45. Zubulake v. UBS Warburg LLC, 217 F.R.D. 309, 312 (S.D.N.Y. 2003) (*Zubulake I*); Zubulake v. UBS Warburg LLC, 230 F.R.D. 290 (S.D.N.Y. 2003) (*Zubulake II*); Zubulake v. UBS Warburg LLC, 216 F.R.D. 280 (S.D.N.Y. 2003) (*Zubulake III*); Zubulake v. UBS Warburg LLC, 220 F.R.D. 212 (S.D.N.Y. 2003) (*Zubulake IV*); Zubulake v. UBS Warburg LLC, 229 F.R.D. 422 (S.D.N.Y. 2004) (*Zubulake V*).

46. *Zubulake IV, id.* at 218.

47. The definition of "control" has been construed broadly to include not only the legal right to obtain information, but also the practical ability to obtain documents from a nonparty.

48. Fujitsu Ltd. v. Federal Express Corp., 247 F.3d 423, 436 (2d Cir. 2001).

49. Silvestri v. General Motors Corp., 271 F.3d 583, 591 (4th Cir. 2001).

50. Consol. Aluminum Corp. v. Alcoa, Inc., 2006 WL 2583308 (M.D. La., July 19, 2006).

51. *See* Broccoli v. Echostar Commc'n Corp., 229 F.R.D. 506 (D. Md. 2005) (involving complaints made to supervisor in employment matter); *see also* Doe v. Norwalk Community College, 248 F.R.D. 372, 377 (D. Conn. 2007) (holding that duty to preserve arose during an initial pre-lawsuit meeting among employees of defendant to discuss the incident that ultimately gave rise to the lawsuit). *But see* Cache La Poudre Feeds, LLC v. Land O'Lakes, Inc., 244 F.R.D. 614, 623 (D. Colo., May 9, 2007) (holding that pre-litigation correspondence, if not explicit, is not enough to trigger a party's duty to preserve evidence).

situations, such as when a company is made aware of patent and licensing issues and begins to develop a strategy to address them.[52] The clear lesson from these cases is that potential litigants ought not to wait until the formal filing of a complaint to establish a strategy to make sure appropriate information is preserved.

The standard practice that is emerging for the preservation of ESI and other information is the preparation of a "litigation hold" letter or memorandum. This is a letter or memorandum that a lawyer sends to a client (or a potentially adverse party) to delineate what information must be preserved.[53] Often, in-house counsel will send a similar memorandum to selected employees in the organization who may have relevant information to alert them to preserve such information. In many situations, an ombuds will first learn of a potential dispute when in-house counsel includes the ombuds in the list of employees to whom such a litigation hold memorandum is sent. Because the duty to preserve goes beyond any requirements of internal retention policy in an organization, parties must take good-faith measures to suspend or alter features of information systems that might interfere with the preservation of ESI.[54] Ombuds are not exempt from this preservation obligation.

2. Materials to Be Preserved (Scope of Discovery)

ESI is inherently different from traditional paper documents in many ways, including its volume and ease of duplication; its persistence—for example, deleted e-mails and documents are not necessarily erased and can be recovered from the computer system in many cases; the ease of changing or altering it; the existence of metadata, which can give information about the creation, authors, and changes to documents, etc.; its potential to become unreadable due to the discarding or obsolescence of operating systems needed to read it; and ease of dispersion to multiple recipients.[55] In *Zubulake IV*, the court acknowledged the voluminous nature of ESI, noting that parties "need not preserve every shred of paper, every e-mail or electronic document,

---

52. Samsung Electronics Co., Ltd. v. Rambus, Inc., 439 F. Supp. 2d 524 (E.D. Va. 2006).
53. Litigation hold letters are discussed in greater detail *infra*.
54. THE SEDONA CONFERENCE, *supra* note 36, at 14.
55. *Id.* at 2–5.

and every backup tape, nor does the preservation obligation require freezing of all electronic documents and data, including e-mail."[56]

Similarly, amended Federal Rule 26(b)(2) limits the scope of production to what is "reasonably accessible," allowing a responding party to identify sources of information that are not reasonably accessible—that is, those that "cannot be retrieved without undue burden or cost."[57] Thus, whether an ESI source is reasonably accessible depends in large part on the costs and burdens involved in accessing and retrieving the information, determined on a case-by-case basis. E-mails, for instance, are generally discoverable, provided that the requesting party can show support for a claim that the e-mails exist and contain discoverable information. Additionally, it is reasonable to limit searches for e-mail messages to the accounts of key witnesses to the litigation. Courts will also allow discovery of electronic databases and computer hard drives due to their increased searchability and the ability to reveal active and deleted information.[58] Other ESI that is not reasonably accessible—including disaster recovery backup tapes, deleted information, and metadata in certain circumstances[59]—is generally not discoverable, absent a showing of good cause or special need. However, a party may be obligated to preserve ESI if the party "believes that the information on such sources is likely to be discoverable and not available from reasonably accessible sources."[60]

A responding party may object to a discovery request for ESI on various grounds, such as relevancy, undue expense or burden, privilege, an assertion that the request seeks cumulative or duplicative materials, and an assertion that an alternative, more convenient means to obtain information is available. In the context of privileged infor-

---

56. *Zubulake IV*, 220 F.R.D. at 217.

57. FED. R. CIV. P. 26(b)(2)(B).

58. One of the reasons the cost of e-discovery is so high is that the relevant information almost invariably must be retrieved from the vast quantities of data through the use of search terms, and the resulting culled data must then be reviewed to sort out privileged and responsive information.

59. The Sedona Principles recommend that parties routinely preserve metadata to protect against modification by others and so that a producing party can easily establish the authenticity of a document.

60. FED. R. CIV. P. 37(e).

mation, a responding party who inadvertently discloses such information may risk a waiver of the privilege.[61] Thus, a responding party may consider entering into a confidentiality agreement with the opposition, or preferably seek a court order, to maintain the privileged status of documents despite their disclosure.

The rules limiting the scope of discovery of ESI also apply to entities that are nonparties, or, in other words, people or entities that are not parties to a lawsuit. A nonparty's duty to preserve evidence is triggered when it is served with a subpoena or when it has a statutory or contractual duty to maintain certain information. A nonparty witness may be served a subpoena by any party to produce ESI. Thus, even if an ombuds office has not received a litigation hold letter or memorandum from opposing counsel or its own organization's counsel, it has a duty to preserve information from the time it receives notice of a subpoena.

The party serving the subpoena is obliged to avoid imposing undue burden or expense on a nonparty witness, and the court must ensure that a subpoena is reasonable, taking into account the relevance of the subpoenaed matter and the particularity and scope of its description. Overly broad ESI production requests directed to third parties can lead to sanctions under Federal Rule 45 and to liability under federal statutes protecting the privacy of electronic communications.

Production of employees' e-mail messages is routinely requested as part of discovery. Though an e-mail message may contain personal and private matters about an employee, it must be produced if otherwise discoverable and in accordance with a reasonable discovery request.[62]

---

61. The Federal Rules of Evidence were amended, effective September 2008, by the addition of new Federal Rule of Evidence 502, which specifically addresses the issue of inadvertent waiver of attorney-client-privileged information and attorney work product materials. The new rule sets forth circumstances in which the inadvertent production of privileged information will not constitute a waiver the of the attorney-client privilege or attorney work product protection.

62. *See, e.g.*, Strauss v. Microsoft Corp., 1995 U.S. Dist. LEXIS 7433, at *11–12 (S.D.N.Y. June 1, 1995) (holding that inappropriate e-mails of male supervisor were relevant to issue of whether gender played role in supervisor's decision not to promote female employee to higher position); Thompson v. U.S. Dep't of Housing and Urban Dev., 219 F.R.D. 93, 96 (D. Md. 2003) (holding that e-mails were subject to disclosure requirements and discovery request for production); Gale v. Levi Strauss & Co., 1999 U.S. Dist. LEXIS 9387, at *8–11 (N.D. Ga. April 26, 1999) (holding that e-mail provided evidence that plaintiff's supervisors had knowledge of and allowed plaintiff's uncompensated overtime work).

However, on a satisfactory showing, a court may issue a protective order to limit disclosure. In fact, protective orders should be in place to guard against any release of proprietary, confidential, or personal ESI accessible to the opposing party or its expert.[63] Courts have also held that an employee may have a reasonable expectation of privacy sufficient to protect communications against unconstitutional government intrusions. Despite this, no known court decision to date has recognized a privacy right of an employee to defeat a discovery request for employee e-mail messages as part of an employer's business records. Moreover, the presence of personal computers increases the probability that work-related information is created or stored in home personal computers, thus expanding the sources of ESI that are subject to discovery. For these reasons, it is a best practice for an ombuds office to explicitly advise employees who contact it not to communicate with it via e-mail. And, of course, an ombuds ought not to use his or her personal e-mail or computer to communicate with those employees.

3. How to Satisfy the Obligation to Preserve

Parties are responsible for finding and preserving relevant information, while their counsel is responsible for making sure that preservation takes place in the first case. Counsel must implement a litigation hold strategy, which involves becoming familiar with a client's data system by meeting with IT personnel and employees involved in the dispute; notifying all relevant parties of the need to preserve data for litigation; keeping in contact with these individuals throughout the discovery process to ensure that preservation is maintained; and eventually taking control of the data to protect any relevant ESI from being unintentionally destroyed. As the court in *Zubulake V* noted, once litigation is reasonably anticipated, "a party and her counsel must make certain that all sources of potentially relevant information are identified and placed 'on hold.'"[64]

The first step in the execution of a litigation hold strategy is an initial meeting between counsel and client where counsel becomes familiar with the client's information systems and retention policies, learns to what extent data is accessible, and becomes acquainted with

---

63. THE SEDONA CONFERENCE, *supra* note 36 at 52, cmt. 10.b.
64. *Zubulake V*, 229 F.R.D. at 432.

the client's methods of data storage and deletion.[65] Counsel also identifies employees that are likely to have relevant information—referred to as "key players"[66]—and meets with them to establish what documents they possess and how they manage those documents. Counsel also meets with IT personnel from the organization for help in determining the burden associated with producing the different forms of electronic data.

Counsel also will typically issue a comprehensive litigation hold letter, or memorandum, which identifies the information that must be preserved and the relevant time periods involved. The hold letter sets forth the standard for the scope of preservation, which requires a party to prevent spoliation once it is reasonably anticipated that the evidence will be sought in litigation. It also makes clear that normal deletion procedures should cease pending litigation. Significantly, the hold letter is forwarded to all employees who may have relevant information, which may include an ombuds.

Counsel should send follow-up reminders of the litigation hold and should monitor existing employees' preservation efforts. Monitoring compliance may involve counsel taking possession of backup tapes to avoid their unintentional destruction or retaining a third-party vendor to take possession and guarantee safe storage of information. Under Federal Rule 26(f), counsel on both sides of a case are required to meet and discuss preservation issues at the early "meet and confer" pretrial conference, including the scope of discovery and any potential claimed privileges. Follow-up litigation hold letters are then sent to clients to advise them of the narrowed scope of information to be preserved.

4. Consequences of Noncompliance

An aggrieved party may claim spoliation of evidence for "the destruction or significant alteration of evidence, or the failure to preserve property for another's use as evidence in pending or reasonably foreseeable litigation."[67] Thus, in addition to being liable under a claim for spoliation of evidence, courts may award sanctions against a party

---

65. Angelo A. Stio III & Marissa L. Quigley, *Getting a Grip on the Litigation Hold*, E-DISCOVERY: A SPECIAL PUBLICATION OF THE SECTION OF LITIGATION (2007), at 20.

66. *Zubulake IV*, 220 F.R.D. at 436.

67. West v. Goodyear Tire & Rubber Co., 167 F. 3d 776, 779 (2d Cir. 1999).

under their inherent authority or under Federal Rule 37. These can include entry of default judgment, an adverse inference charge, or monetary sanctions.[68] Entry of default judgment is the most severe sanction and is reserved for the most egregious forms of destruction of discovery, such as when the destruction has eradicated the other party's ability to litigate its claims. Monetary sanctions are usually imposed when the destruction of evidence is willful, such as when a party agrees to produce records despite knowing they have been destroyed. An adverse inference charge may also be imposed for the destruction of evidence. If an adverse inference sanction is imposed, the jury is instructed to assume that the destroyed document, if produced, would have been adverse to the party that destroyed it.[69]

Federal Rule 37(e) contains a good-faith exception providing that absent exceptional circumstances, a court may not impose sanctions on a party under the Federal Rules for failing to provide ESI lost as a result of the routine, good-faith operation of an electronic information system.[70] However, for this exception to apply, a party must actually have a routine system of purging ESI in place.[71] The Committee Notes to the Federal Rules describe "routine operation" as referring to the way that computer systems are "generally designed, programmed, and implemented to meet the party's technical and business needs."[72] The Committee Notes indicate that the good-faith operation of computer systems "may involve a party's intervention to modify or suspend certain features of that routine operation to prevent the loss of information, if that information is subject to a preservation obligation."[73] Thus, sanctions should be considered by the court only if it finds a clear

---

68. Stio & Quigley, *supra* note 65.
69. A notable distinction exists where the destruction of evidence is due to negligence—such as when a party destroys evidence pursuant to an existing retention policy after it knows or should have known of the litigation and the need to preserve it—rather than destruction that was willful, in bad faith, or due to fault. Where the destruction was due to negligence, an adverse inference may be drawn *only if* the requesting party can provide extrinsic evidence—evidence not before the court—that shows that the information was relevant and favorable to the requesting party.
70. FED. R. CIV. P. 37(e).
71. Doe v. Norwalk Community College, 248 F.R.D. 372 (D. Conn. 2007).
72. FED. R. CIV. P. 37(e), Notes of Advisory Committee on 2006 Amendments.
73. *Id.*

duty to preserve, a culpable failure to preserve relevant ESI—such as a knowing violation of the duty to preserve or a reckless disregard amounting to gross negligence—and a reasonable probability that the loss of evidence has materially prejudiced the other party.[74] Moreover, once a party reasonably determines that ESI in its control or custody may be relevant to pending or reasonably foreseeable litigation, the party must take reasonable steps to preserve the ESI, even if its records management program calls for its routine destruction.

F. Implications of Discovery Methods and e-Discovery for Ombuds' Practices

Regardless of any structural precautions to create independence, an organization's ombuds office will almost certainly have the same duty to preserve documents and ESI that any other employee or unit of the organization has once the ombuds is aware that litigation is reasonably anticipated. Accordingly, once the ombuds office receives a litigation hold letter or memorandum, it must suspend any routine document destruction policy that would be applicable to the matter in dispute.

While the duty to preserve information is clear, there are several grounds, as discussed above,[75] on which an ombuds and its organization can assert that any information or documents relating to confidential communications with an ombuds should not be disclosed or produced in litigation. Whether the organization and the ombuds office have sufficiently documented or implemented a program to satisfy the requirements for those grounds is a determination that the lawyers for the ombuds and the organization must assess based on the facts in the particular case. At the very least, however, a court's inherent authority to determine the proper scope of discovery represents a potential opportunity to protect the confidentiality of ombuds' communications,[76] though this depends on the exercise of judicial discre-

---

74. THE SEDONA CONFERENCE, *supra* note 36 at 70, Principle 14.
75. *See* Chapter 3 at beginning at 227.
76. *See* Miller v. Regents of the Univ. of Colo., 1999 U.S. App. LEXIS 16712 (10th Cir. 1999) (holding that a district court did not abuse its discretion in precluding the deposition of the university's ombudsman where summary judgment was granted in favor of the university, as the granting of a protective order barring the deposition did not affect the substantial rights of the parties).

tion. In support of the argument that information sought from an ombudsman is irrelevant or, if relevant, that its value is outweighed by the harm caused by breaching the promise of confidentiality, it can be argued that the testimony of an ombuds would be an unnecessary disclosure of information that is either irrelevant or available from other sources; the plaintiff cannot demonstrate any significant need for the ombuds to disclose confidential communications; and the ombuds do not conduct investigations and, therefore, make no determination of the truth of what may be told to them.

On an even more fundamental level, ombuds' practices should be informed by an awareness of the discovery methods and the manner in which courts treat the obligations to preserve and disclose documents and ESI. Two of the best ways to avoid having a court compel the production of confidential documents and ESI include not creating such information in the first place and, second, making sure that an ombuds adheres to a policy of routinely destroying confidential information as soon as it is no longer necessary. Not only are such practices good from a common-sense perspective, they also are consistent with the IOA Standards of Practice. The IOA Standards of Practice state that an ombuds keeps no records containing information on behalf of the organization, and that he or she maintains information—such as notes or phone messages—in a secure location and manner, protected from inspection by others, and has a consistent and standard practice for the destruction of such information.[77] Adhering to this standard represents a good-faith, routine document retention policy, which does not need to be interrupted under normal circumstances. However, to avoid potential sanctions against the organization, the standard practice for the destruction of the ombuds' information should be halted to the extent necessary if litigation is reasonably anticipated, or if the ombuds is requested or reasonably likely to be asked—in a litigation hold memorandum—to preserve and produce such information relevant to an anticipated or pending litigation.

---

77. Int'l Ombudsman Ass'n (IOA) Standards of Practice 3.5–3.6. *See* Appendix 5 at 466.

PART II: THE FEDERAL ARBITRATION ACT, THE UNIFORM MEDIATION ACT, AND THE MEDIATION/ CONFIDENTIALITY PRIVILEGE

A. Overview of ADR

For more than 30 years, there has been a trend in the United States toward using various types of alternative dispute resolution processes, rather than just the courts, to resolve disputes. This trend shows no signs of abating in light of the increasing costs of litigation. The recent developments in court rules to deal with discovery of electronically stored information—and the high costs associated with that process—will only accelerate efforts to use cheaper and more expeditious ways to resolve disputes.

Alternative dispute resolution (ADR) refers to a variety of practices that have been developed to resolve disputes by means other than traditional adversarial proceedings in a court before a judge. ADR practices are designed to manage and resolve disputes expeditiously, economically, and with minimal conflict.[78] ADR methods include arbitration, mediation, "arb-med" (hybrid of arbitration and mediation), negotiation, conciliation, minitrials, settlement conferences, "rent-a-judge," and ombuds.[79] Because arbitration and mediation are the two methods most relevant to the work of ombuds, they are the focus of this section.

B. Arbitration Generally

Arbitration is a method of ADR in which the parties to the dispute retain one or more neutral third parties to resolve their dispute and by whose decision they agree to be bound.[80] In arbitration, an arbitrator is selected by a process agreed to by the parties, and the selected arbitrator hears the case and then renders a decision (called an "award") within an agreed time period. The hearings are conducted by rules agreed to by the parties and can range from summary presentations to testimony of witnesses, either using or not using formal rules of evidence.

---

78. 4 AM. JUR. 2D *Alternative Dispute Resolution* § 1 (2007).
79. *See id.* §§ 8, 14–23.
80. BLACK'S LAW DICTIONARY 112–13 (8th ed. 2004). Note that arbitration can be voluntary or mandatory, and binding or non-binding.

The two principal forms of arbitration are private (or contractual) and judicial arbitration. Private arbitration, which is the most common form of ADR, generally involves an arbitration clause to a contract that stipulates that disputes arising from the contractual relationship must first be resolved through the process of arbitration. Less commonly, arbitration may be contractually stipulated in a submission agreement (an agreement signed after a dispute has arisen). In either case, if parties select arbitration, they may broadly agree to arbitrate without specifying a particular type of arbitration procedure, or they may tailor their arbitration agreement to use procedures particular to their needs and concerns.[81] Parties to a contractual arbitration clause have a great deal of control over the details of the arbitration, since private arbitration does not depend on the courts, except for enforcement.[82] For instance, a contract to arbitrate can limit the issues to be arbitrated. It can also set forth the elements of the arbitration process, ranging from restrictions on discovery to the selection of a proceeding more judicial in nature, involving procedures associated with conventional litigation.[83]

As described in Chapter 3,[84] the trend in favor of ADR generally has had a parallel development in the arbitration of employment disputes. In this setting, the employer typically establishes policies that set forth the procedures under which arbitration of employment-related disputes will be conducted, and the employees are deemed to have agreed to those procedures.

Parties to private arbitration also forego their right to an appeal to a court on substantive grounds except in very narrow or limited circumstances. For example, an award may be confirmed by a court or may be vacated for certain procedural reasons, such as where the award was procured by fraud or corruption, or where the arbitrator was found to be partial or had exceeded his or her authority. A court's involvement in private arbitration thus is typically limited to enforcing arbitration or matters dealing with enforcing the award.

Private arbitration also typically involves more limited discovery processes and evidentiary rules, unless otherwise provided by the par-

---

81. EDWARD BRUNET ET AL., ARBITRATION LAW IN AMERICA: A CRITICAL ASSESSMENT 3–4 (2006).
82. 4 AM. JUR. 2D *Alternative Dispute Resolution* § 9 (2007).
83. BRUNET, *supra* note 81, at 4.
84. *See* Chapter 3 at 273–76.

ties.[85] While some discovery is usually permitted, it usually is of a more limited nature in keeping with the cost constraints that motivate parties to use arbitration rather than litigation in the first place. And, as with a trial court's rulings on discovery motions, an arbitrator's rulings on discovery and, in particular, on issues such as privilege are subject to great deference. It is extremely difficult to obtain subsequent court review on an arbitrator's discovery rulings.

The second major type of arbitration is judicial, or court-annexed, arbitration. This is where arbitration is mandated by a statute or court rule and, consequently, differs from traditional private arbitration in a number of ways. For instance, a judicial arbitrator's award usually is binding only if the parties agree to make it binding; otherwise, the parties have the right to have a court look at the whole record, including the facts at issue and the arbitrator's award, and to have the court resolve the case in a separate proceeding without giving deference to the arbitrator's final decision.[86] Both types of arbitration are often faster and cheaper than litigation, and arbitral proceedings are most frequently conducted in private—not public—settings. As a result, arbitration hearings are usually confidential; the public is neither informed of the dispute nor allowed to be present at the hearing. Arbitrators are typically given the power to summon in writing any witnesses to appear at an arbitration hearing.

An arbitration hearing typically ends with a written award that does not contain a long opinion. The form of the award, like many other aspects of the arbitration, is also a matter for the parties to decide. An award can range from a short statement that simply indicates the decision (and, if appropriate, the dollar amount of the award) to one with a short statement of the reasoning.[87] Although the parties may agree that they want a longer statement of reasons for the award, in only a few contexts—such as in labor grievance arbitrations and maritime arbitrations—does an arbitrator write and publish an arbitration award. Accordingly, the custom of short, written awards that merely catalog the result of the arbitration, along with the private nature of

---

85. 4 AM. JUR. 2D *Alternative Dispute Resolution* § 10 (2007).

86. This type of judicial review is known as "de novo," which is defined by *Black's Law Dictionary* as "[a] court's nondeferential review of an administrative decision, [usually] through a review of the administrative record plus any additional evidence the parties present." BLACK'S LAW DICTIONARY 467 (8th ed. 2004).

87. 4 AM. JUR. 2D *Alternative Dispute Resolution* § 9 (2007).

arbitration hearings in general, facilitates confidentiality in private arbitration.[88]

C. Federal Arbitration Act

Most states have statutes that permit arbitration in various contexts. Organizations and ombuds programs that wish to avail themselves of those statutes will need to determine what, if any, impact they have on the work of ombuds and what their procedural requirements are. One of the most widely used arbitration provisions, however, is the Federal Arbitration Act (FAA), which applies to matters arising from commercial or maritime transactions.[89] State laws that disfavor the enforcement of arbitration agreements are preempted by the FAA, while those state laws that merely govern the procedures of arbitration but do not affect its enforcement are not. Consequently, the FAA does not prevent enforcement of arbitration agreements under rules different from those set forth in the FAA itself.

The FAA was passed by Congress in 1925 to make arbitration an equitable alternative to litigation to reduce the number of cases in the court system.[90] It was meant to enforce commercial and maritime agreements entered into by the parties. The FAA was designed to counter what was perceived to be the courts' traditional reluctance to enforce agreements to arbitrate and to place such agreements on the same footing as other contracts by allowing courts to invalidate arbitration agreements only for reasons that other contracts could be invalidated.[91] As such, the FAA is a matter of consent, not coercion, and parties are free to structure their arbitration agreements as they see fit. This includes, for example, limiting the issues to be arbitrated or specifying

---

88. *Id.* Some would argue, however, that such confidentiality comes with a price—namely, an attendant lack of transparency in arbitral proceedings. *Id.* (citing Richard C. Reuben, *Democracy and Dispute Resolution: The Problem of Arbitration*, 67 LAW & CONTEMP. PROB. 279, 301 (2004)). *See also* discussion of arbitration of employment cases in Chapter 3 at 273–76.

89. 4 AM. JUR. 2D *Alternative Dispute Resolution* § 27 (2007).

90. Federal Arbitration Act, 9 U.S.C. §§ 1–16 (2000).

91. *Id.* The Supreme Court has invalidated state court decisions where individual states refused to enforce arbitration clauses to the extent necessary to give those clauses the same enforceability as other contracts. *See, e.g., Allied-Bruce Terminix Cos. v. Dobson*, 513 U.S. 265 (1995).

the rules under which arbitration will be conducted.[92] As Congress intended the FAA to be applicable in both federal and state courts, pursuant to the Supremacy Clause of the U.S. Constitution,[93] the FAA thus trumps state statutes regulating arbitration agreements and invalidates such statutes where they are in conflict with the FAA.[94]

The key statutory provisions in the FAA are Sections 2 through 4. Section 2 establishes that an arbitration provision is "valid, irrevocable, and enforceable."[95] Section 2 also carves out a narrow exception to the general principle of arbitrability. It provides that state law may be invoked to invalidate an arbitration clause, but only on "such grounds as exist at law or in equity for the revocation of any contract."[96] This exception applies standard common-law contract defenses to arbitration agreements, such as fraud, duress, lack of consideration, lack of capacity, or unconscionability,[97] based on "a flaw in the formation of the agreement to arbitrate."[98]

Section 3 of the FAA provides that a court shall "stay" proceedings filed with the court where the issue should be resolved in arbitration,[99] thereby limiting the court's authority to resolve disputes where the contract contains an arbitration clause.[100] Section 4 allows a court

---

92. In fact, the FAA does not require parties to arbitrate where they have not agreed to do so, nor does it prevent parties who agree to arbitrate from excluding certain claims or issues from the scope of their arbitration agreement. Instead, the FAA merely requires courts to enforce arbitration clauses in accordance with their terms, as with any other privately negotiated contract. Additionally, it does not favor any particular set of procedural rules for arbitration. 4 AM. JUR. 2D *Alternative Dispute Resolution* § 27 (2007).

93. The Supremacy Clause establishes the Constitution, federal statutes, and U.S. treaties as the "supreme law of the land." U.S. CONST. art. VI, cl. 2. Therefore, both federal and state courts are required to uphold federal laws, even if a state statute conflicts with its federal counterpart.

94. Southland Corp. v. Keating, 465 U.S. 1 (1984).

95. 9 U.S.C. § 2 (2007).

96. *Id.*

97. "Unconscionability" refers to "[t]he principle that a court may refuse to enforce a contract that is unfair or oppressive because of procedural abuses during contract formation or because of overreaching contractual terms, [especially] terms that are unreasonably favorable to one party while precluding meaningful choice for the other party." BLACK'S LAW DICTIONARY 1560 (8th ed. 2004).

98. 9 U.S.C. § 2 (2007).

99. To "stay" is to postpone or halt a proceeding or judgment.

100. 9 U.S.C. § 3 (2007).

to compel arbitration.[101] It grants courts the authority to decide whether a claim goes to the "making" of the arbitration agreement, however, and if so, the claim may be decided by the court rather than through arbitration. Courts have consistently interpreted Section 4 in such a way as to require arbitration in nearly all cases brought under a contract containing an arbitration agreement, thus broadening the scope of claims subject to the FAA. For instance, in *Prima Paint Corp. v. Flood & Conklin Mfg.*,[102] the Supreme Court held that a claim of fraud in the inducement of a contract, which can invalidate the entire contract, should be resolved by arbitration. The Court reasoned that unless concern exists as to the "making" of the arbitration clause itself, Section 4 of the FAA mandates that the claim must be resolved by arbitration.[103] Thus, *Prima Paint* introduced the doctrine of separability, which severs arbitration clauses from the rest of the contract: where a claim does not attack the arbitration clause itself but rather the entire contract, then the claim must be resolved through arbitration rather than by a court; conversely, where a claim attacks the arbitration clause itself, the claim may be resolved by a court.

D. Mediation

1. Mediation Process and Procedures Generally

Mediation is a nonbinding and informal method of ADR in which a knowledgeable and neutral third party aids parties in the negotiation and voluntary settlement of a dispute. Mediation is an extension of the negotiating process, and a mediator serves as a facilitator of the negotiation between disputing parties. A mediator, unlike a judge or arbitrator, has no decision-making power. Therefore, the parties retain complete control over the dispute and its resolution. As mediation typically is nonbinding, parties do not waive their right to have their dispute resolved in court or by some other process.[104]

---

101. 9 U.S.C. § 4 (2007).
102. Prima Paint Corp. v. Flood & Conklin Mfg., 388 U.S. 395 (1967).
103. *Id.* at 403–04.
104. A major difference between arbitration and mediation is that arbitration is (typically) binding, while mediation is nonbinding. Significantly, when parties agree to binding arbitration, they waive their rights to litigate. Conversely, parties to non-binding mediation preserve their rights to have claims resolved in court if not resolved by agreement through the mediation.

The general purpose of mediation is to arrive at a mutually acceptable resolution at a low cost, in confidence, with privacy, and expeditiously. These aims require that the parties be involved early in the mediation process and remain engaged until its conclusion. Accordingly, the mediator's primary function is to aid the parties in reaching an agreement by identifying the issues, potential bases for agreement, and the consequences of not settling, and encouraging each party to acknowledge and accommodate the interests and concerns of the other party.[105] Legal rules of procedure and evidence do not apply, witnesses are not called, attorneys are often not present, no record is made, and mediation settlements need not be confined to legal remedies.

In its most common form, mediation involves the parties first crafting a written mediation agreement that outlines the scope and process of the mediation. A mediation agreement may be negotiated after a dispute arises, or it may be reached before any disputes materialize, such as in an employment contract. When a dispute arises that cannot be resolved by negotiations, parties will then effectuate such agreement and commence mediation. Alternatively, mediations may be conducted pursuant to a program that describes the process and procedures.

The parties typically choose a mediator by mutual agreement from a list available under the sponsoring program or approved by the applicable federal or state agency. In some situations, the agency will appoint a mediator. A mediator generally does not hold hearings or hear testimony or other evidence, and generally cannot compel the production of information.[106] Nor does a mediator file a report or make written recommendations. Instead, once the mediator explains the ground rules of the mediation, including its confidentiality, a standard mediation process involves the mediator receiving informal factual presentations in a conference setting with all parties present. After both sides present their view, each party typically meets individually with the mediator, and the mediator examines each party's position privately and confidentially. During these "caucus" sessions, the mediator attempts to find workable solutions to the dispute by identifying and addressing each party's interests and needs, keeping what he or she hears from each party strictly confidential unless permission to make a disclosure is specifically given. Finally, if and when an agree-

---

105. 4 AM. JUR. 2D *Alternative Dispute Resolution* § 16 (2007).
106. *Id.*

ment is reached, the mediator will often hold a final joint session to verify the terms of settlement and will draft—or have the parties draft—a final written and binding settlement agreement.[107]

2. Mediation Privilege/Confidentiality

A cornerstone of mediation, and one of the major reasons why it is such an appealing and successful form of ADR, is the element of confidentiality. During the caucus sessions, a mediator discusses a party's position privately and confidentially. Information given to the mediator by a party in confidence is not disclosed to the other side without the consent of the disclosing party. Because the law favors the informal resolution of disputes, virtually all states have provisions that provide that a mediator cannot be compelled to disclose any confidential communication made to him or her during the proceedings unless the parties agree to waive confidentiality, and that if the parties fail to reach a settlement, nothing said in the mediation is admissible as evidence in a later trial or arbitration.

Reflecting the general policy in favor of ADR and the recognition that the utility of ADR methods like mediation is founded on the confidentiality of their communications, confidentiality and privilege in mediation have been recognized by nearly all state legislatures as well as many courts.[108] In fact, state legislatures have enacted over 250 mediation privilege statutes.[109] Roughly half of the states have enacted privilege statutes that apply generally to mediations held within

---

107. If a settlement is not reached, the parties may agree to try another round of mediation with the same or a different mediator or to discontinue mediation altogether. It is also notable that parties may agree to waive the confidentiality of mediation discussions by stipulating as such in their written settlement agreement. A confidentiality waiver may be valuable in the event that a dispute arises as to the enforcement of the settlement agreement.

108. *See, e.g.*, Goodyear Tire & Rubber Co. v. Chiles Power Supply, Inc., 332 F.3d 976, 980 (6th Cir. 2003) ("The ability to negotiate and settle a case without trial fosters a more efficient, more cost-effective, and significantly less burdened judicial system. In order for settlement talks to be effective, parties must feel uninhibited in their communications . . . . Without a privilege, parties would more often forego negotiations for the relative formality of trial.").

109. *See* Uniform Mediation Act (UMA), Prefatory Note (amended 2003), http://www.law.upenn.edu/bll/archives/ulc/mediat/2003finaldraft.htm (last visited April 28, 2009). Note that the 250 figure is as of 2001.

the state, while the other half include privileges within the provisions of statutes that establish mediation procedures for specific substantive legal contexts, such as employment.[110] These statutes vary in the definition of mediation, the subject matter of the dispute, the scope of protection, exceptions to the privilege, and the context of the mediation that is subject to the statute. While statutory confidentiality privileges provide the strongest source of protection for mediation communications,[111] few of these statutes confer absolute protection. Indeed, many state mediation privilege statutes exempt certain categories from confidentiality, including admissions of threats to commit some form of physical or bodily harm to another, information pertaining to a crime, where the need for information outweighs confidentiality concerns, or when disclosure is mandated by another statute or court rule.[112]

E. Uniform Mediation Act

1. Overview

One of the statutory sources of a mediation privilege[113] is the Uniform Mediation Act (UMA), which was approved by the National Conference of Commissioners on Uniform State Laws in 2001 and amended in 2003. The UMA was conceived as a model law that would be adopted by states so that, over time, most state mediation laws would be consistent. As of the time of this writing, the UMA has been adopted by 11 states and the District of Columbia.[114] It has also been officially

---

110. *Id.*

111. Representing a statute that provides for a broad privilege, revisions to the California Evidence Code, effective in 1998, were made to protect confidentiality in mediation and mediation consultations. CAL. EVID. CODE §§ 1115–1128 (2009). The protection provided is extremely broad, even including a provision that allows a court to award attorney's fees and costs to a mediator against a party who subpoenas or attempts to compel a mediator to testify regarding protected matters. *Id.* § 1127. *See* Chapter 3 at 259–60.

112. UMA, Prefatory Note, *supra* note 109.

113. This is also discussed in Chapter 3 at 263–64.

114. In addition to the District of Columbia, the states that have adopted the UMA are Idaho, Illinois, Iowa, Nebraska, New Jersey, Ohio, South Dakota, Utah, Vermont, and Washington. *See* http://www.nccusl.org/Update/uniformact_factsheets/uniformacts-fs-uma2001.asp.

endorsed by a number of organizations, such as the American Bar Association, the American Arbitration Association, and the Judicial Arbitration and Mediation Service. The UMA is designed to promote uniformity among the states' mediation laws. It is also intended to "promote candor of parties through confidentiality of the mediation process . . . encourage the policy of fostering prompt, economical, and amicable resolution of disputes . . . [and to] advance the policy that decision-making authority in the mediation process rests with the parties."[115]

2. The UMA Mediation Privilege

The UMA defines mediation broadly as a "process in which a mediator facilitates communication and negotiation between parties to assist them in reaching a voluntary agreement regarding their dispute."[116] The statute covers all mediations, with few exceptions,[117] regardless of whether the parties have signed an agreement to mediate or have been referred by a court or agency. A mediation may be compelled or referred by statute or court or agency ruling, it may be agreed to by the mediating parties in writing (stipulating that mediation communications will have a privilege against disclosure), or it may involve an arrangement in which the parties use as a mediator someone who "holds himself or herself out" as a mediator.[118] The statute defines "mediator" in broad terms, as "an individual who conducts a mediation."[119]

Section 4 of the UMA delineates the parameters of the mediation privilege. This privilege allows a party not only to refuse to disclose the communication, but also to prevent other people from disclosing those communications.[120] Thus, under the UMA, statements made in mediation are treated as inadmissible evidence in much the same way that the law in many states bars the use of statements made to attor-

---

115. UMA, Prefatory Note, *supra* note 109.
116. *Id.* § 1(1).
117. *Id.* § 3 (exceptions include mediations related to labor unions, student peer mediations, and judicial settlement conferences).
118. *Id.*
119. *Id.* § 1(3). To promote the integrity of the mediation process, the UMA also requires the disclosure of conflicts of interest by a mediator and requires the mediator to disclose his or her qualifications when asked. *Id.* § 9.
120. *Id.* § 4.

neys, doctors, and priests.[121] The UMA mediation privilege applies to bar the use of mediation communications in a wide range of post-mediation proceedings, such as civil and criminal trials, arbitrations, administrative hearings, and legislative proceedings.[122] Under the UMA, a "mediation communication" made by a mediating party, a mediator, or a nonparty participant is privileged and is not subject to discovery nor admissible in evidence in a proceeding unless, as provided in Section 5, it is waived by all parties to the mediation and the mediator or nonparty if they are the holders of the privilege.[123] The UMA defines "mediation communication" broadly to include any statements, "whether oral or in a record or verbal or nonverbal, that [occur] during a mediation or [are] made for purposes of considering, conducting, participating in, initiating, continuing, or reconvening a mediation or retaining a mediator."[124]

Section 6 enumerates other limited exceptions to the mediation privilege, such as when a communication is in a written settlement agreement, open to the public under a statutory open records or public meeting provision; contained a threat to inflict bodily harm or commit a violent crime; sought to establish that a mediated settlement agreement was induced by fraud or duress, or the mediator engaged in professional misconduct or malpractice.[125] Also, a judge may—off the

---

121. *See, e.g.*, Jaffee v. Redmond, 518 U.S. 1 (1996) (recognizing a psychotherapist-patient privilege); Trammel v. United States, 445 U.S. 40 (1980) (recognizing a marital privilege).

122. UMA, § 2(7), *supra* note 109.

123. *Id.* § 4–5. To be the "holder" of the privilege is to have the power to raise and waive such privilege. The UMA's commentary provides that the mediating parties are always the holders of the privilege, while the mediator and/or any nonparty may also be a holder of the privilege if such privileged communication is made by them. *Id.*, commentary p. 19–21. This approach differs from many state statutes that fail to identify a holder of the privilege, in which case parties are forced to look to judicial determinations. Mindy D. Rufenacht, *The Concern Over Confidentiality in Mediation—An In-Depth Look at the Protection Provided by the Proposed Uniform Mediation Act*, 2000 J. DISP. RESOL. 113, 118 (2000). Moreover, of the states that do designate a holder, two approaches exist: the first assigns the privilege solely to the parties to share jointly, while the second allows the mediator to be an additional holder. *Id.* at 118–19. The UMA approach combines these latter two approaches. *Id.* at 119.

124. UMA, § 1(2), *supra* note 109.

125. *Id.*, § 6.

record in his or her private chambers—consider evidence that might be needed in a criminal case or in an action involving the enforcement of a mediated settlement agreement, but only if he or she finds that "the evidence is otherwise unavailable, and the need for the evidence outweighs the policies underlying the privilege."[126] However, if a mediator is asked by a court or agency about what transpired in a mediation, he or she may disclose only the fact that a mediation occurred, who attended, and whether a settlement was reached. The mediator cannot be compelled to testify about issues related to the enforcement of the mediation agreement or any alleged professional misconduct by the parties or lawyers present in the mediation.[127] Furthermore, since the mediation privilege draws heavily upon the attorney-client privilege, the mediator's mental impressions based on mediation communications are generally protected.[128]

F. Implications of the Mediation Privilege for Ombuds' Practices

Although there are no state statutes that specifically apply to the confidentiality of organizational ombuds' communications, the statutes that protect the confidentiality of communications made during mediation (or other forms of ADR) may be applicable to ombuds' communications. Much of what ombuds typically do is, in fact, a form of mediation. Protection of discussions in the course of ADR and settlement negotiations has already influenced those courts that have found a privilege for ombuds' communications.[129] The drafters of the UMA recognized that there are many different forms, contexts, and practices of mediation. Accordingly, the UMA defines "mediation" broadly, and includes within its scope a mediation in which "the mediation parties use as a mediator an individual who holds himself or herself out as a media-

---

126. *Id.*, commentary at 34.
127. *Id.* at 31, 35–36.
128. *Id.*, Prefatory Note.
129. *See* discussion in Chapter 3 at 259 and, *e.g.*, Kientzy v. McDonnell Douglas Corp., 133 F.R.D. 570 (E.D. Mo. 1991) (recognizing that a successful ombuds program resolves problems informally and more quickly than court actions, and that the utility of the program is founded on the confidentiality of its communications); Wagner v. The Upjohn Co., No. A91-2156CL (Mich. Cir. Ct., Apr. 22, 1992) (noting that ombuds serve a dispute resolution function, which is preferable to the utilization of judicial proceedings).

tor or the mediation is provided by a person that holds itself out as providing mediation."[130] These arrangements do not require a written mediation agreement between the parties prior to the proceedings to trigger the UMA's protection. The UMA commentary specifically addressed the role of ombuds as mediators:

> *Mediations can be conducted by ombuds practitioners. See* Standards for the Establishment and Operation of Ombuds Offices (August 2001). If such a mediation is conducted pursuant to one of these triggering mechanisms, such as a written agreement under Section 3(a)(2), it will be protected under the terms of the Act. There is no intent by the Drafters to exclude or include mediations conducted by an ombuds a priori. The terms of the Act determine applicability, not a mediator's formal title.[131]

Accordingly, if an organizational ombuds office "holds itself out" as providing mediation to employees, its mediation proceedings may well be covered under the UMA's definition of "mediation." The UMA also defines "mediator" broadly, and its emphasis on neutrality is mirrored in the organizational ombuds's ethical obligation to be impartial.[132] The commentary to the UMA explains, in part, that:

> The mediator's employment situation may present difficult issues regarding impartiality. A mediator who is employed by one of the parties is not typically viewed as impartial, especially if the person who mediates also represents a party. In the representation situation, the mediator's overriding responsibility is toward a single party. For example, the parties' legal counsel would not be an impartial mediator. *Ombuds often are obligated*

---

130. UMA, § 3(3), *supra* note 109. The UMA commentary notes that "holding out" oneself includes "making a representation in a public manner of being in the business or having another person make that representation." *Id.*, commentary, p.11.

131. *Id.*, commentary, p.11 (emphasis added).

132. *See* IOA Standards of Practice 2.1–2.6, Appendix 5 at 264–65 ("The Ombudsman is neutral, impartial, and unaligned . . . . [S]trives for impartiality, fairness and objectivity in the treatment of people and the consideration of issues . . . advocates for fair and equitably administered processes and does not advocate on behalf of any individual within the organization . . . [and] helps develop a range of responsible options to resolve problems and facilitate discussion to identify the best options.").

by ethical standards to be impartial, although they are employed by one of the parties.[133]

Thus, given the broad scope of the UMA, the fact that it has gained passage in a number of states to date, and the fact that it mirrors many other state statutes protecting mediation communications, ombuds who undertake activities that come within the scope of the UMA should describe their role as including mediation so that they may be able assert the protections afforded by this and similar statutes in support of their claim of confidentiality.

---

133. UMA, commentary at 46, *supra* note 109 (emphasis added).

PART III: IMMINENT THREAT OF SERIOUS HARM AS AN EXCEPTION TO CONFIDENTIALITY

A. Background

The Ethical Principles in the IOA Code of Ethics articulate a general rule of confidentiality with only one stated exception (other than being given permission to make disclosure):

> The Ombudsman holds all communications with those seeking assistance in strict confidence, and does not disclose confidential information unless given permission to do so. *The only exception to this privilege of confidentiality is where there appears to be an imminent risk of serious harm.*[134]

The same exception to confidentiality is also contained in the IOA Standards of Practice, but with additional caveats:

> The only exception to this privilege of confidentiality is where there appears to be imminent risk of serious harm, *and where there is no other reasonable option. Whether this risk exists is a determination to be made by the Ombudsman.*[135]

Because ombuds are expected not to disclose confidential communications except in this limited circumstance, they should understand the context in which this exception developed, how the exception was created, and how it has become enmeshed in the law. This exception also has important implications for some ombuds, including attorneys or licensed social workers, who may also be subject to other statutory or ethical standards.

In its most simplified form, the law giving rise to this exception is built on a long tradition of distinguishing what may be perceived as a moral obligation from what the law recognizes as a legal duty. While morally it may be wrong not to assist another in peril if one safely can do so, legally, "'[y]ou don't have to help anybody. That's

---

134. IOA Code of Ethics (emphasis added). *See* Appendix 5 at 460.
135. IOA Standards of Practice 3.1 (emphasis added). *See* Appendix 5 at 465.

what this country's all about.'"[136] More seriously stated, courts have made a sharp distinction in the development of common law between moral obligations and legal duties: "Legal duties are enforceable; moral duties are not."[137] Thus, it is only when there is a legal duty to act that the failure to do so can give rise to liability.

Section 314 of the *Restatement of Torts (Second)* presents a straightforward distillation of the rule on a duty to act for the protection of others: "The fact that the actor realizes or should realize that action on his part is necessary for another's aid or protection does not of itself impose upon him a duty to take such action."[138] The Comments to the Restatement explain the reasoning behind this rule:

> The origin of the rule lay in the early common law distinction between action and inaction, or "misfeasance" and "nonfeasance." In the early law one who injured another by a positive affirmative act was held liable without any great regard even for his fault. But the courts were far too much occupied with the more flagrant forms of misbehavior to be greatly concerned with one who merely did nothing, even though another might suffer serious harm because of his omission to act. Hence liability for non-feasance was slow to receive any recognition in the law. It appeared first in, and still largely confined to, situations in which there was some special relation between the parties, on the basis of which the defendant was found to have a duty to take action for the aid or protection of the plaintiff.[139]

The linchpin of a duty to act in such a situation, therefore, is whether there is a "special relation" that creates such a duty. Because of the conflict between perceived moral obligations and the law, courts

---

136. Philip W. Romohr, *A Right/Duty Perspective on the Legal and Philosphical Foundations of the No-Duty-to-Rescue Rule*, 55 DUKE L.J. 1025 (2006), n.1 (quoting "Seinfeld: The Finale" (NBC television broadcast, May 14, 1998)).
137. *Id.* at 1029.
138. RESTATEMENT (SECOND) OF THE LAW OF TORTS § 314 (1965).
139. *Id.* cmt. c.

have struggled to determine and articulate those circumstances in which a special relation gives rise to a duty to act.[140]

B. Tarasoff v. Regents of University of California

The identification of just such a special relation in the context of this legal tradition is what made the California Supreme Court's 1976 decision in *Tarasoff v. Regents of University of California*[141] such a seminal[142] case on the issue of a duty to warn, notwithstanding a privilege or a promise of confidentiality, where the communication reveals an imminent threat of harm. The court in *Tarasoff* held that once a psychotherapist determines that a patient has made a credible threat of harm, the psychotherapist must warn any identifiable intended third-party victim.[143] The court's holding has been widely followed and is usually credited as the origin of a duty to disclose otherwise confidential communications, such as the rule that is embodied in the IOA Code of Ethics.

Tarasoff, however, was only the second of three important cases decided by the California Supreme Court on the legal duty to warn. Eight years before the ruling in *Tarasoff*, the California Supreme Court recognized, in *Johnson v. California*,[144] a duty to warn potential third-party victims in a somewhat simpler situation. In *Johnson*, the state had requested that the plaintiff and her husband provide a foster home for a 16-year-old boy, whom the plaintiff alleged had homicidal tendencies and a history of violence and cruelty to both animals and people. Within five days of the placement, the youth assaulted the plaintiff.[145] The lawsuit alleged that

---

140. In addition to special relationships, other categories of exceptions to the "no-duty-to-rescue" rule have been categorized: "voluntarily undertaking a rescue of the victim; negligent injury caused by the defendant; innocent injury caused by the defendant; and statutorily created duties." Romohr, *supra* note 136, 1031 n.36.
141. Tarasoff v. Regents of Univ. of Cal., 551 P.2d 334, 340 (1976).
142. Ann Hubbard, *Symposium: The Future of "The Duty to Protect": Scientific and Legal Perspectives on Tarasoff's Thirtieth Anniversary: Symposium Introduction*, 75 U. CIN. L. REV. 429 (2006)
143. *Tarasoff, supra* note 141 at 340.
144. Johnson v. California, 447 P.2d 352 (Cal. 1968).
145. *Id.*

the state of California had been negligent in placing the boy in her home without warning her of his dangerous tendencies.[146] Rejecting a claimed governmental immunity defense, the court held that "this is a classic case for the imposition of tort liability. Defendant failed to warn plaintiff of a foreseeable, latent danger, and this failure led to plaintiff's injury from precisely the expected source."[147] The special relation that gave rise to the duty was thus the state's relation with the foster parents.

In *Tarasoff*, the court was required to resolve a conflict between a duty to warn and a duty to protect the confidentiality of communications between a psychotherapist and his patient. The plaintiffs in *Tarasoff* were the parents of a young woman who was murdered. They alleged that a patient, Poddar, told his therapist at a University of California hospital that he intended to kill a woman, easily identifiable as their daughter, Tatiana Tarasoff. At the time this statement was made, the patient was receiving voluntary outpatient therapy at the hospital. Based on this disclosure, the therapist concluded that the patient may be dangerous and enlisted the help of campus police to have him confined. The police, however, later released Poddar on a promise that he would stay away from Tatiana Tarasoff.[148] The plaintiffs alleged that after Poddar was released, no further action was taken by the defendants to detain him or to warn them of any threat to their daughter. Two months later, when Tatiana returned from a summer abroad, Poddar went to her home and killed her.[149]

On these facts, the Supreme Court of California concluded that "when a therapist determines, or pursuant to the standards of his profession should determine, that his patient presents a serious danger of violence to another, he incurs an obligation to use reasonable care to protect the intended victim against such danger."[150] The court reasoned that this duty may call for a therapist to warn the intended victim, or others likely to inform the victim, of the danger.[151]

The court in *Tarasoff* was sharply divided, and strong dissenting opinions were filed by two of the justices. The court majority concluded

---

146. *Id.*
147. *Id.* at 363.
148. *Id.* at 341.
149. *Id.* at 339.
150. *Id.*
151. *Id.*

that the duty to warn prevailed over the psychotherapist-patient privilege in these circumstances over the strong opposition of the American Psychiatric Association, which argued in an amicus brief (since it was not a party to the case) that "psychiatrists had no standard for predicting dangerousness and that the risks of such a duty could outweigh any protective benefits."[152]

The *Tarasoff* ruling was narrowed and clarified in a subsequent decision by the California Supreme Court two years later. In *Thompson v. County of Alameda*,[153] the court was required to determine whether a duty to warn existed where a juvenile offender who, while being detained in a county institution under a court order, indicated to county officials that he "would, if released, take the life of a young child residing in the neighborhood."[154] When the juvenile offender was eventually released into the custody of his mother, he murdered the plaintiffs' five-year-old son in the garage of their home.[155] In contrast to the ruling in *Tarasoff*, the court in *Thompson* rejected the plaintiffs' claim that the county was liable for its failure to warn the murdered child's mother on the grounds that the threat in *Thompson* had not been specific. The court held that there is no affirmative duty to warn members of the public about individuals who make *"non-specific threats of harm to non-specific victims."*[156] In reaching this conclusion, the court in *Thompson* reiterated the importance of preserving the confidentiality of communications between a therapist and a patient and took pains to explain its rationale in *Tarasoff* and to distinguish the facts in *Thompson* from the facts in those cases:

> Thus, [in *Tarasoff*] we made clear that the therapist has no *general* duty to warn of each threat. Only if he "does in fact determine, or under applicable professional standards reasonably should have determined, that a patient poses a serious danger of violence to others, [does he bear] a duty to exercise reasonable care to protect the *foreseeable victim* of that danger." (17 Cal. 3d at p. 439, italics added.) Although the intended victim as a pre-

---

152. Claudia Kachigian, M.D., J.D & Alan R. Felthous, M.D., *Court Responses to Tarasoff Statutes*, 32 J. AM. ACAD. PSYCHIATRY L. 263 (Nov. 3, 2004).
153. Thompson v. County of Alameda, 614 P.2d 728 (Cal. 1980).
154. *Id.* at 730.
155. *Id.*
156. *Id.* at 735.

condition to liability need not be specifically named, he must be "readily identifiable." (Citations omitted.)

Unlike *Johnson* and *Tarasoff*, plaintiffs here have alleged neither that a direct or continuing relationship between them and the County existed through which County placed plaintiffs' decedent [child] in danger.[157]

As a result of the development of common law in *Johnson*, *Tarasoff*, and *Thompson*, a special relationship giving rise to a duty to warn an identifiable third party has been recognized, despite the protection of confidentiality from a privilege, when a credible threat of harm has been made against that identifiable third party.

C. Adoption of the Tarasoff Rule

The rule articulated in the *Tarasoff* cases has been widely adopted and recognized in other jurisdictions and contexts. The courts of many states have recognized the same principle through court decision.[158] In addition, a number of states have enacted statutes specifically requiring certain categories of health providers—and sometimes others—to warn an identified or identifiable third-party victim when a patient has made a credible threat. Statutes in Illinois,[159] New Jersey,[160] Massachusetts,[161]

---

157. *Id.* at 734.

158. Kachigian & Felthous, *supra* note 152 (listing statutes and court decisions).

159. "There shall be no liability on the part of . . . any person who is a physician, clinical psychologist, or qualified examiner based upon the person's failure to warn . . . except where the [patient] has communicated to the person a serious threat of physical violence against a reasonably identifiable victim or victims." 405 ILL. COMP. STAT. 5/6-103(b) (2008).

160. "A duty to warn and protect is incurred when . . . [t]he patient has communicated to that practitioner [persons licensed by the State of New Jersey in psychology, psychiatry, medicine, nursing, clinical social work or marriage counseling] a threat of imminent, serious physical violence against a readily identifiable individual or against himself and the circumstances are such that a reasonable professional in the practitioner's area of expertise would believe the patient intended to carry out the threat . . . ." N.J. STAT. ANN. § 2A:62A-16(b) (2008).

161. "There shall be no duty owed by a licensed health professional to take reasonable precautions to warn . . . unless: (a) the patient has communicated to the licensed mental health professional an explicit threat to kill or inflict serious bodily injury upon a reasonably indentified victim or victims and the patient has the apparent intent and ability to carry out the threat, and the licensed mental health

and Arizona[162] are but a few examples of such laws. Many of these mandatory reporting laws are much broader than the court's decision in *Tarasoff* in terms of when the duty to report arises and who must do the reporting.[163]

The construct of a "special relation" used in *Tarasoff* and *Thompson* has also found expression as a generally applicable statement of law—not limited to the context of psychotherapist and patient—in the *Restatement (Second) of the Law of Torts*. Section 315 of the Restatement articulates the general principle:

> There is no duty to control the conduct of a third person as to prevent him from causing physical harm to another unless
>
> (a) a special relation exists between the actor and the third person which imposes a duty upon the actor to control the third person's conduct, or
>
> (b) a special relation exists between the actor and the other which gives the other the right to protection.[164]

Thus, the "special relation" creating such a duty can exist between the person with a potential duty to warn and either the person

---

professional fails to take reasonable precautions. . . . ; or (b) the patient has a history of physical violence which is known to the licensed mental health professional and the licensed mental health professional has a reasonable basis to believe that there is a clear and present danger that the patient will attempt to kill or inflict serious bodily injury against a reasonably identified victim or victims and the licensed mental health professional fails to take reasonable precautions . . . ." MASS. GEN. LAWS ch. 123, § 36B(1) (2008).

162. "There shall be no cause of action against a mental health provider nor shall legal liability be imposed for breaching a duty to prevent harm to a person caused by a patient, unless both of the following occur: 1. The patient has communicated to the mental health provider an explicit threat of imminent serious physical harm or death to a clearly identified or identifiable victim or victims, and the patient has the apparent intent and ability to carry out such threat. 2. The mental health provider fails to take reasonable precautions." ARIZ. REV. STAT. § 36-517.02 A. (2008).

163. *See, e.g.,* Maryann Zavez, *The Ethical and Moral Considerations Presented by Lawyer/Social Worker Interdisciplinary Collaborations*, 5 WHITTIER J. CHILD & FAM. ADVOC. 191, 192–95 (2005); Art Hinshaw, *Mediators as Mandatory Reporters of Child Abuse: Preserving Mediation's Core Values*, 34 FLA. ST. U. L. REV. 271, 284–86 (2007).

164. RESTATEMENT (SECOND) OF TORTS § 315 (1965).

whose statements prompted the duty to warn or the person who should be warned.

Even aside from general recognition in common law and legislation dealing specifically with a duty on the part of health-care professionals to report threats, a duty to report has been incorporated into other laws and the codes of conduct for other professions. In some of these situations, the duty is also broader than the standard of a credible threat of violence or harm to an identifiable third party identified in *Tarasoff*. For example, Section 6 of the UMA provides that there is no mediator's privilege under Section 4 for a communication that is "a threat or statement of a plan to inflict bodily injury or commit a crime of violence."[165] Similarly, Rule 1.6 of the Model Rules of Professional Conduct, adopted in many states and articulating the ethical obligations of lawyers, requires a lawyer to "reveal such information to the extent the lawyer reasonably believes necessary to prevent the client from committing a criminal or fraudulent act that the lawyer believes is likely to result in death or substantial bodily harm."[166]

D. Implications for Ombuds

Organizations with ombuds that practice in accordance with the IOA Code of Ethics and Standards of Practice should publicize that there is an exception to confidentiality where there "appears to be an imminent risk of serious harm," and this is a determination made by the ombuds. The practice implications of this provision, however, do not end there, because there are important issues not addressed by the IOA Code of Ethics and Standards of Practice that also should inform an ombuds's practices.

One of the issues that ombuds should address in their practices is the "when there is no other reasonable option" caveat that appears in the IOA Standards of Practice but not in the Code of Ethics. Undoubtedly, looking for options other than breaking confidence is important and should be undertaken in virtually every situation where there appears to be a threat, but the articulation of such a standard also may give rise to a problematic ancillary inquiry: having set a

---

165. UMA § 6(a)(3), *supra* note 109.
166. *See also* Zavez, *supra* note 163, at 195.

standard that states that disclosure would be made only when there is no other reasonable alternative, a party may wish to challenge what other options were considered (and, more important, seek discovery on such matters) as part of the challenge to an ombuds's confidentiality and to determine whether the ombuds complied with that standard. At the very least, the best practices of an ombuds should be to limit any such disclosure to only that needed to prevent or warn of imminent and potentially serious harm.

While the practical risk arising from saying that disclosure will not be made unless there is no other reasonable option may be small, there are two other areas where the potential risk to ombuds may be of more significance. First, regardless of what the IOA Code of Ethics and Standards of Practice state, the courts or the legislature in the jurisdictions in which an ombuds functions likely have articulated a standard giving rise to a *duty* to warn. Ombuds should not assume that the IOA Code of Ethics and the Standards of Practice says it all; they would be well advised to become familiar with both potential statutes and case-law developments in their jurisdictions on the subject of a duty to warn. At the very least, when an ombuds hears a comment that could be considered a threat of violence against an identifiable third party, the ruling from *Tarasoff* and the cases that have followed it counsel an ombuds to understand that, while the IOA Code of Ethics and Standards of Practice indicate that the determination of whether to make a disclosure is made by the ombuds, a court may ultimately rule on whether the duty existed as a matter of law based on those facts.[167]

Second, ombuds should realize that they may be subject to differing standards or ethical obligations if they also have a professional designation or license in another profession. This is particularly true, for example, for attorneys and social workers.[168] While no guidance may be given on this issue in the absence of an analysis of the particular facts involved, ombuds should be mindful that under these circumstances, it is possible that they may have multiple or conflicting duties that will need to be reconciled and should seek the advice of counsel.

---

167. Note that in *Tarasoff*, the court expressly incorporated applicable professional standards. *See* the text accompanying note 141, *supra.*

And finally, some ombuds programs and their organizations, in articulating the standard of "imminent threat of serious harm" as an exception to confidentiality, have taken a view broader of the standard than just credible threats of physical harm to identifiable third parties. While the decision of *when* the circumstances require disclosure should always be left to the determination of the ombuds, the discussion of *what* should prompt disclosure is one that ombuds and their organizations should undertake and agree on with respect to the operative principles and procedures.

PART IV: OMBUDS CONFIDENTIALITY IN CRIMINAL CASES

A. Background

The IOA Code of Ethics and Standards of Practice assert that confidential communications with an ombuds are privileged and state a sole exception to confidentiality for where there is an "imminent threat of serious harm."[169] Not only are the Code of Ethics and Standards of Practice silent on other circumstances in which an ombuds may be forced to disclose confidential communications in civil cases,[170] they also do not address the extent to which confidentiality may be subject to constitutional considerations requiring disclosure in criminal cases. However, even such a well-recognized privilege as the attorney-client privilege is not absolute; courts have determined that in some circumstances attorney-client-privileged communications must be disclosed to ensure that a criminal defendant's constitutional rights are protected. While it may be unlikely that disclosure of confidential communications between an ombuds and an inquirer would be relevant or necessary in a criminal proceeding, ombuds should be aware that if those circumstances arise, the bases for confidentiality and privilege discussed in Chapter 3 may not shield them from compelled disclosure.

B. The Sixth Amendment Right to Confront and Cross-Examine

The Sixth Amendment to the Constitution provides that "[i]n all criminal prosecutions the accused shall enjoy the right . . . to be confronted with the witnesses against him; to have compulsory process for obtaining witnesses in his favor, and to have the assistance of counsel for his defense." This provision, commonly referred to as the Confrontation Clause, applies only to criminal prosecutions, not to lawsuits between parties in civil litigation. The Confrontation Clause, in conjunction with the Due Process Clause of the Fourteenth Amend-

---

168. *See* Zavez, *supra* note 163.
169. *See* Appendix 5 at 460–66.
170. *See* the discussion in the previous section on possible mandatory reporting statutes and ethical standards that may be applicable to ombuds with other professional licenses or designations.

ment, has been construed by the U.S. Supreme Court as including both the right to confront one's accusers and the right to present a complete defense.[171]

The Supreme Court in *Davis v. Alaska*, citing an earlier Supreme Court decision, explained what is meant by "confrontation":

> Confrontation means more than being allowed to confront the witness physically. "Our cases construing the [confrontation] clause hold that a primary interest secured by it is the right of cross-examination." *Douglas v. Alabama*, 380 U.S. 415, 418 (1965). Professor Wigmore stated:
> "The main and essential purpose of confrontation is *to secure for the opponent the opportunity of cross-examination.* The opponent demands confrontation, not for the idle purpose of gazing upon the witness, or being gazed upon by him, but for the purpose of cross-examination, which cannot be had except by the direct and personal putting of questions and obtaining immediate answers." 5 J. Wigmore, Evidence § 1395, p. 123 (3d ed. 1940).

Cross-examination is the principal means by which the believability of a witness and the truth of his testimony are tested.[172] The right to call and cross-examine witnesses is thus fundamental to a criminal defendant's constitutional rights and is a right that dates back to Roman times.[173] The basic premise behind the right to confront stems from the adversarial nature of our judicial system: a person's innocence or guilt should not hinge on the testimony of individuals unavailable or unwilling to submit to questioning, but should result from a clash of opposing interests. The importance of cross-examination to an individual or entity accused of a crime is straightforward: it provides an opportunity to challenge the version of the facts offered by an accuser or adverse witness and to impeach the credibility by demonstrating bias, ulterior motive, or a poor character for telling the truth. Basically, it affords the defendant the chance

---

171. *See* Taylor v. Illinois, 484 U.S. 400 (1988).
172. Davis v. Alaska, 415 U.S. 308, 315–16 (1974) (emphasis in original); Crawford v. Washington, 541 U.S. 36, 43 (2004).
173. 21A AM. JUR 2D *Criminal Law* § 1072 (2008).

to directly confront a witness and say either "you are mistaken" or "you are lying."

Cross-examination is the means by which a defendant can test a witness's perception, memory, narration, and trustworthiness. The first three of these purposes are directed to proving that the witness has a faulty understanding of the facts, enabling the defendant to argue to a jury that they should give less weight to the testimony. For example, if a defendant, through cross-examination, can demonstrate that a prosecution witness failed to accurately perceive or does not accurately remember critical events, dates, or people, then a jury will naturally tend to discredit that witness's testimony. Common sense suggests that jurors will likewise give less weight to a witness's testimony if the witness cannot effectively narrate his or her version of the facts; cross-examination tests whether a witness can tell a believable story.

Another important purpose of cross-examination is that it allows a defendant to test a witness's general trustworthiness or credibility. A defendant may attack a witness's credibility by revealing partiality—that a witness is biased or has some ulterior motive to lie—or by demonstrating that the witness has poor character for honesty and trustworthiness, thereby increasing the likelihood of false testimony in a particular case. Unlike with the first three purposes of cross-examination, effectively undermining a witness's credibility colors the witness's entire testimony. While a jury might understand a witness's failure to remember every single important fact, juries typically do not empathize with biased witnesses or liars. A criminal defendant's most powerful impeaching tactic, therefore, is attacking a witness's credibility. Doing so enables a jury to draw the reasonable inference that a witness is likely to lie about any and all aspects of his or her testimony. Cross-examination also allows a jury not only to hear a witness's substantive responses to questioning but to observe the witness's demeanor—whether the witness shifts or fidgets, speaks with a trembling voice, or in any other manner indicates untruthfulness—to better assess that witness's credibility and to arrive at a clearer picture of the truth. Observing this demeanor necessarily demands that the defendant be able to confront witnesses against him or her.

---

174. Murdoch v. Castro (*Murdoch II*), 489 F.3d 1063, 1069 (9th Cir. 2007).
175. Delaware v. Van Arsdall, 475 U.S. 673, 683 (1986).

A defendant's right to cross-examine a witness is extensive, but not absolute. The Confrontation Clause guarantees defendants the *opportunity* for effective cross-examination, but does not entitle a defendant to cross-examine a witness in whatever way and to whatever extent the defense might wish.[174] Consequently, trial courts have wide latitude to limit the scope of cross-examination for practical considerations.[175] A defendant may not claim a Confrontation Clause violation merely because a court denied a repetitive or irrelevant line of questioning, or because the defendant's attorney, given an opportunity, failed to elicit a desired response from a witness.

A violation of the Confrontation Clause may exist, however, when a trial court prohibits otherwise appropriate cross-examination meant to impeach a witness that, if allowed, would have significantly affected the jury's impression of the witness's credibility.[176] Likewise, if a court precludes cross-examination that would have demonstrated bias, motive, or poor character for truthfulness, then a defendant may state a Confrontation Clause violation. But if the defendant elicits sufficient information from a witness so that a jury can adequately assess the witness's credibility, then no Confrontation Clause problem arises.[177] If the jury undoubtedly would have reached the same result even if the cross-examination had been permitted, a court will usually determine that the error was harmless and did not compromise the defendant's constitutional rights.[178]

C. The Sixth Amendment and Privilege Claims

The right to confront one's accusers through cross-examination is a *constitutional* right. Privileges—even old and established ones, such as the attorney-client privilege—are not found in the Constitution. This critical distinction was the touchstone for the observation by the Seventh Circuit Court of Appeals, in *United States v. Rainone*, that "'[e]ven the attorney-client privilege . . . hallowed as it is, yet not found in the Constitution, might have to yield in a particular case if the right of

---

176. *Id.* at 680.
177. 21A AM. JUR 2D *Criminal Law* § 1075 (2008).
178. *See, e.g., Murdoch II, supra* note 174 (finding that after remand from *Murdoch I*, 365 F. 3d 699 (9th Cir. 2004), exclusion of privileged letter was harmless error where the letter's "intrinsic probative value was low" and other trial testimony through cross-examination effectively made the same points).

confrontation . . . would be violated by enforcing the privilege.'"[179] While the U.S. Supreme Court has not decided the issue directly, the court in *Murdoch I* cited to other circuits[180] and other precedent from the Supreme Court in concluding that the attorney-client privilege would likely yield in the appropriate case to a defendant's constitutional rights:

> [P]recedents, however, clearly provide that evidentiary privileges or other state laws must yield if necessary to ensure the level of cross-examination demanded by the Sixth Amendment. See *Olden v. Kentucky*, 488 U.S. 227, 232 . . . (1988) (holding that the Kentucky court's "speculation as to the effect of jurors' racial biases cannot justify exclusion of cross-examination with such strong potential to demonstrate the falsity of [the government's witness's] testimony"); *Delaware v. Van Arsdall*, 475 U.S. 673,679 . . . (1986) (holding that the trial court's complete prohibition of all inquiry into potential bias resulting from dismissal of government witness's public drunkenness charge violated the Confrontation Clause); *Davis [v. Alaska]*, 415 U.S. 308, 319 . . . (holding that state's policy of keeping juvenile records confidential "is outweighed by petitioner's right to probe into the influence of possible bias in the testimony of a crucial identification witness"). . . .[181]

If the Confrontation Clause can trump such a well-established privilege as the attorney-client privilege, it would undoubtedly be held to trump any privilege claimed by ombuds and any other basis for asserting ombuds confidentiality.[182]

---

179. *Murdoch I, id.* at 703, *quoting* United States v. Rainone, 32 F.3d 1203 (7th Cir. 1994).
180. *Id., also citing to* Mills v. Singletary, 161 F.3d 1273 (11th Cir 1998) *and* United States *ex rel.* Blackwell v. Frazen, 688 F. 2d 496, 501 (7th Cir. 1982).
181. *Murdoch I, supra* note 178, 365 F. 3d at 702–03.
182. The Confrontation Clause has also been held to affect the admissibility of hearsay testimony in criminal cases. In *Crawford v. Washington*, 541 U.S. 36 (2004), the Supreme Court adopted a bright-line test that bars the admission of any prior testimonial statement made by a witness who does not testify at trial, unless the witness is unavailable *and* the defendant had a prior opportunity for cross-examination. 541 U.S. at 69.

D. Implications for Ombuds

Whether expressly stated or not, the Confrontation Clause of the U.S. Constitution limits the confidentiality of communications with an ombuds that may be necessary for a defendant in a criminal case. While this is an important limitation, it is of limited significance in light of the rarity of its occurrence. Moreover, even if an ombuds were called as a witness for the prosecution, the risk of disclosure of confidential communications in cross-examination by the defendant may be mitigated if the direct examination can be limited to non-confidential matters.[183]

There are no known cases dealing with an ombuds's claim of confidentiality in a criminal case, but there are cases involving analogous situations that suggest that in criminal cases, confidentiality similar to that claimed by ombuds has limitations. An early case involving the conflict between a claimed mediation privilege created under a state statute and a federal grand jury subpoena is *Gullo v. United States*.[184] There, the defendant moved to dismiss a grand jury indictment that was based in part on evidence that had been introduced from the mediation of an arbitration proceeding in which the parties had been advised that "the neutral will hold all information received during the hearing as confidential and will not voluntarily divulge that information. [The Parties] agree that the neutral will not be subpoenaed by either party in any subsequent legal proceeding." The court resolved this conflict in favor of protecting the privilege. Although the court recognized the strong public policy in favor of disclosure of information, it also found that the government had not made a showing of a particular need for the evidence at issue.[185] Using a four-part balanc-

---

183. The traditional limits on cross-examination may apply without implicating a Confrontation Clause issue. For example, cross-examination is usually limited to only those matters covered during direct examination. Consequently, if an ombuds testified about *only* non-privileged matters during direct examination, a judge could prohibit questions about privileged information during cross-examination without implicating the Confrontation Clause. The important distinction is that the questions are prohibited because they are beyond the scope of cross-examination altogether, not because they deal with privileged information.

184. United States v. Gullo, 672 F. Supp. 99, 102 (W.D.N.Y. 1987), *as quoted in* Joshua P. Rosenberg, *Keeping the Lid on Confidentiality: Mediation Privilege and Conflict of Laws*, 10 OHIO ST. J. DISP. RES. 157, 175 (1994).

185. United States v. Gullo, 672 F. Supp at 103–04.

ing test (but not the Wigmore test discussed in Chapter 3), the court looked to Federal Rule of Evidence 501 and determined that the balancing of the interests involved favored recognition of a privilege and suppression of the statements made during the mediation proceedings.[186]

Even though the decision in *Gullo* favored preservation of confidentiality, it may be of limited value, in part because it was resolved based on a balancing of the particular facts in that case.[187] Other courts have been less willing to give effect to a claimed mediation privilege in a criminal setting. For example, in *In Re: Grand Jury Proceedings*,[188] the Fifth Circuit Court of Appeals reversed a district court's ruling that documents relating to mediation proceedings were privileged and protected from disclosure to a federal grand jury. In so doing, the court rejected claims that the provisions of a Texas mediation statute, the federal Alternative Dispute Resolution Act, and another federal law (the Agricultural Credit Act) requiring mediation justified not producing the documents. The court found both the Texas statute and the ADRA inapplicable and determined that it was:

> satisfied that Congress did not intend that [the relevant section of the Agricultural Credit Act] be used to shield wrongdoing arising out of the state agricultural loan mediation process. Indeed, even the ADRA provides for disclosure where a court determines that disclosure is necessary to "help establish a violation of law . . . of sufficient magnitude in the particular case to outweigh the integrity of dispute resolution proceedings in general by reducing the confidence of parties in future cases that their communications will remain confidential."[189]

Likewise, the court in *Folb v. Motion Picture Industry Pension & Health Plans*[190] noted that the outer limits of a federal mediation privi-

---

186. *Id.*; Rosenberg, *supra* note 184, at 177.
187. *Id.* at 177.
188. *In re* Grand Jury Proceedings, 148 F.3d 487 (5th Cir. 1998).
189. *Id.* at 493.
190. Folb v. Motion Picture Ind. Pension & Health Plans, 16 F. Supp. 2d 1164, 1178 (C.D. Cal. 1998), *aff'd without published opinion*, 216 F.3d 1082 (9th Cir. 2000).

lege "may be attenuated of necessity in criminal or quasi-criminal cases where the defendant's constitutional rights are at stake."[191]

And finally, the court in *The People v. Scoggins*[192] required prosecutors to turn over to the defendant information, including the police department's ombudsman office records and investigative files[193] relating to discipline of the arresting police officers, to comply with the defendant's constitutional rights.

Because important protections for criminal defendants are embodied in the Constitution, including in the Confrontation Clause of the Sixth Amendment, any claim of confidentiality by ombuds, much like a claim under the attorney-client privilege, may have to yield to constitutional requirements that a defendant be able to confront his accusers and mount a complete defense to the crimes with which he has been charged.

---

191. *Id.* The court cited to a California appellate court decision's discussion of the limits of California Evidence Code § 1119 in juvenile delinquency proceedings.

192. People v. Scoggins, 2003 Cal. App., unpub., LEXIS 2796 (March 24, 2003).

193. It is not clear that the ombudsman office involved in this case operates in accordance with the IOA Code of Ethics and Standards of Practice, as it apparently had investigative files.

PART V: FEDERAL SENTENCING GUIDELINES FOR ORGANIZATIONS

A. Background

The year 1984 marked a turning point in federal criminal law enforcement. Not only did Congress pass the Criminal Fine Enforcement Act of 1984,[194] which greatly increased fine levels for federal crimes, that same year Congress also passed the Sentencing Reform Act of 1984,[195] which, among other things, created the United States Sentencing Commission and has been called "the most dramatic criminal justice reform of the twentieth century."[196] These events coincided with the much-publicized securities fraud and procurement fraud scandals of the 1980s to increase the visibility of corporations as potential criminal targets.

The primary reason for the adoption of the Sentencing Reform Act and the creation of the Sentencing Commission was to "decreas[e] unwarranted sentencing disparity, increas[e] sentencing uniformity and certainty, and for some select offenses, [to] increas[e] sentence severity in order to more effectively deter and more justly punish convicted offenders."[197] Because Congress's principal concern was the disparity in sentencing of individuals convicted of crimes, it was natural that the Sentencing Commission would first direct its efforts to the creation of sentencing guidelines for individuals. By 1987, the Sentencing Commission had developed and issued guidelines for individuals convicted of federal offenses, which dramatically reduced the discretion afforded judges in making sentencing decisions.

---

194. Criminal Fine Enforcement Act of 1984, Pub. L. No. 98-596, 98 Stat. 3134 (1984).

195. Sentencing Reform Act of 1984, Pub. L. No. 98-473, 98 Stat. 1987 (1984).

196. Ilene H. Nagel & Winthrop M. Swenson, *The Federal Sentencing Guidelines for Corporations: Their Development, Theoretical Underpinnings, and Some Thoughts About Their Future*, 71 WASH. U. L.Q.

197. *Id.*, citing to Stephen Breyer, *The Federal Sentencing Guidelines and the Key Compromises upon Which They Rest*, 17 HOFSTRA L. REV. 1, 4–5 (1998); Charles J. Ogletree Jr., *The Death of Discretion? Reflections on the Federal Sentencing Guidelines*, 101 HARV. L. REV. 1938, 1944–51 (1998); *and* Ilene H. Nagel, *Structuring Sentencing Discretion: The New Federal Sentencing Guidelines*, 80 J. CRIM L. & CRIMINOLOGY 883, 892–95 (1990).

Following an intense review and much deliberation, the Sentencing Commission published Sentencing Guidelines for organizations (Guidelines) that Congress accepted and that became effective in November 1991.[198] The impact of these Guidelines on corporations and other organizations has been profound. As mentioned briefly in Chapter 1[199] and Chapter 2,[200] the Guidelines revolutionized sentencing for corporations and other organizations by creating an incentive structure that rewarded certain conduct while heavily punishing corrupt behavior.

After the Sentencing Guidelines (which had the effect of law and were binding on federal judges) had been in place for several years, courts began to grapple with difficult constitutional questions arising out of the application of the federal Sentencing Guidelines and similar state mandatory sentencing schemes. Under these schemes, once a defendant was convicted of a crime, a separate sentencing hearing was held before the judge, who considered, prior to imposing the sentence, evidence of mitigating or aggravating facts or circumstances that might justify an upward or downward departure from the sentencing range provided in the Guidelines.

In 2000, the U.S. Supreme Court held that a criminal defendant had the right to a jury trial under the Sixth Amendment to the Constitution on all facts that might increase the defendant's punishment.[201] This ruling raised doubts about whether a judge's consideration of facts at the time of sentencing (after conviction) not presented to or found by a jury, as was also permitted under various state mandatory sentencing statutes and guidelines, was a violation of the Sixth Amendment. In 2005, the Supreme Court resolved this issue in a case dealing with a state mandatory sentencing scheme by holding that the scheme was unconstitutional in this regard.[202] Because the sentencing scheme in that case was based on the federal Sentencing Guidelines, a challenge to the federal scheme was moved with great haste to the Supreme Court. In its 2005 decision in *United States v. Booker*, the Court

---

198. The Sentencing Commission adopts and forwards to Congress proposed changes to the Guidelines by May 1 of any given year. If Congress does not alter or reject them, they take effect as of the following November 1.
199. *See* Chapter 1 at 17.
200. *See* Chapter 2 at 119–24
201. Apprendi v. New Jersey, 530 U.S. 466 (2000).
202. Blakely v. Washington, 542 U.S. 296 (2004).

declared that, to the extent that the Sentencing Guidelines permitted federal judges to consider facts not found by a jury as part of the sentencing process, the Sentencing Guidelines also violated defendants' constitutional right to a trial by jury.[203] The Court concluded, however, that the appropriate remedy was not to excise or eliminate the Sentencing Guidelines entirely. Instead, the Court ruled that while federal judges must consider the Sentencing Guidelines, they were not binding. Thus, although the *Booker* decision curbed their influence, the Sentencing Guidelines remain important and are considered by federal judges in most cases.

Because the Sentencing Guidelines remain an important consideration in driving compliance programs—and particularly so following the revisions to the Sentencing Guidelines in 2004—ombuds should have a working knowledge of them and how they impact their own work.

B. Basic Structure of the Sentencing Guidelines

As the name suggests, the Organizational Sentencing Guidelines apply to entities other than just corporations. They also apply to "partnerships, associations, joint-stock companies, unions, trusts, pension funds, unincorporated associations, government and political subdivisions thereof, and non-profit organizations."[204] As organizations cannot be incarcerated, designing an effective punishment scheme presented difficult challenges, especially since a fine alone would not likely be a deterrent. For many corporations, fines, even if substantial, amount merely to a cost of doing business.[205]

The Guidelines apply generally to sentencing for convictions of felony and Class A misdemeanor offenses, though the fine levels do not apply to certain types of offenses.[206] This means that the Guidelines apply to crimes such as "fraud, theft, tax violations, antitrust offenses, money laundering, bribery, and kickbacks," while the provi-

---

203. United States v. Booker, 543 U.S. 220 (2005). The *Booker* case was argued within months after *Blakely* had been decided.
204. U.S.S.G. Manual § 8A1.1, Commentary (n.1).
205. *See* Han Hyewon & Nelson Wagner, *Corporate Criminal Liability*, 44 AM. CRIM. L. REV. 337, 338 (2007), noting that prosecutors may also hesitate to punish corporations because of the argument that punishing a corporation punishes its innocent shareholders.
206. U.S.S.G. Manual § 8A1.1, Commentary (n.2).

sions that determine fine levels do not apply to crimes such as "environmental, food and drug, and export control offenses."[207]

In designing the Guidelines, the Sentencing Commission was guided by four basic principles articulated in the Sentencing Reform Act:[208]

(1) *Restitution*—a convicted organization must first remedy any harm caused by its offense;
(2) *Deterrence*—the penalty must be sufficiently high to deter the organization, or other organizations, from engaging in the conduct again, and also to divest the organization operated primarily for criminal purposes or by criminal means of any of its assets;
(3) *Punishment*—the imposition of fines should be based on the seriousness of the crime involved and the organization's culpability; and
(4) *Probation*—as appropriate to ensure compliance with other sanctions.[209]

The Guidelines provide for three different types of punishment for organizations: remediation, probation, and fines. The first is remediation: "As a general principle, the court should require that the organization take all reasonable steps to provide compensation to victims and otherwise remedy the harm caused or threatened by the offenses."[210] Various means of remediation are permitted, including restitution, community service, notice to victims, and other means deemed appropriate.[211] Not intended as punishment, remediation sim-

---

207. Melissa Ku & Lee Pepper, *supra* note 149, at 110. *See also* Report of the Ad Hoc Advisory Group on the Organizational Sentencing Guidelines, *supra* note 149, at 110.

208. *See* Nagel & Swenson, *Corporate Criminal Liability*, 45 AM. CRIM. L. REV. 207 (2008) ("The statute provides that these sentences must be responsive to the goals of just punishment for the offense, deterrence, incapacitation and rehabilitation."); *see also* 18 U.S.C. § 3553(a)(2) (2007)).

209. U.S.S.G. Manual, Introductory Commentary, Chapter 8—Sentencing of Organizations.

210. U.S.S.G. Manual, Introductory Comment, Chapter 8, Part B.1—Remedying Harm from Criminal Conduct.

211. *See generally* U.S.S.G. Manual §§ 8B1.1– 8B1.3.

ply aims to repair the damage done. Probation, similarly, applies as a matter of course to any convicted organization, and a court is authorized to impose conditions that the organization must satisfy.[212] Failure to comply with probation requirements may result in more restrictive conditions or resentencing (imposing higher fines). Judges have wide discretion in setting the conditions of probation, but the probationary term may not exceed five years.[213]

The determination of an appropriate fine is the most significant element of an organization's sentence, and the fine structure itself is the most important way that the Guidelines have changed how organizations are punished for criminal acts.

The Guidelines provide that organizations operated primarily for a criminal purpose must be punished by a fine "sufficient to divest the organization of all its net assets."[214] For other organizations, calculating the fine is a multi-step process that, in broad overview, requires a court to make four determinations: (1) what an appropriate "base fine" should be for a particular offense; (2) what the organization's "culpability score" should be, after consideration of various specified aggravating and mitigating factors; (3) what the penalty range should be, by multiplying the base fine by the "multiplier range" corresponding to the culpability score; and (4) what the maximum and minimum fines to be used for the sentencing should be, from which the court can make upward or downward adjustments provided certain conditions are met.[215] While a detailed study of this process is not possible here, some elaboration of these steps is necessary to understand the incentives in the Guidelines for organizations to minimize exposure to fines.

Step One is to determine the "offense level" for the particular offense on which the conviction is based. The offense level is a number assigned to each crime by the Guidelines, roughly corresponding to the severity of the crime.

Step Two requires a court to take the offense level for the crime and determine the base fine. The amount of the base fine is critical in the calculation of the appropriate sentence, because it is the initial dollar amount from which further adjustments are made to determine

---

212. *Id.*
213. Hyewon & Wagner, *supra* note 205, at 353–54.
214. U.S.S.G. Manual § 8A1.2.(b)(1), § 8C1.1.
215. *See generally* U.S.S.G. Chapter 8, Part C—Fines.

the actual fine. Typically, the base fine is provided by a table in the Guidelines,[216] but if either the pecuniary *gain* to the organization from the offense or the pecuniary *loss* suffered by the victim or victims due to the offense (to the extent that the loss was caused intentionally, knowingly, or recklessly) is greater than the amount provided by the Guidelines, that amount constitutes the "base fine."[217] Thus, the base fine for an offense used in the fine calculation may be substantially higher than the amount provided for in the Guidelines.

Step Three is to determine the organization's culpability score. Each organization starts with a culpability score of five points, which may be adjusted up or down based on various aggravating or mitigating factors. As a general proposition, the lower the culpability score, the lower the ultimate fine will be. Points are added to the culpability score based on: (1) the level of criminal involvement within the organization (zero to five points—the higher the level of criminal involvement within the organization, the greater the number of points); (2) the size of the organization (zero to five points—the more employees in the organization, the greater the number of points); (3) whether the criminal conduct violated a previous court order (one or two additional points); and (4) whether the organization engaged in any activity constituting an obstruction of justice (up to three additional points).[218]

Points are deducted from the culpability score to provide incentives for organizations. For example, points are subtracted if the court finds that the organization "took actions relating to the offense which reduced its culpability, such as self-reporting, cooperating with the investigation, [or] accepting responsibility for its acts."[219] Three points may be deducted from the initial five-point level if the organization had in place, at the time of the violation, an effective compliance and ethics program.[220] The Guidelines provide that an organization can satisfy the "effective compliance and ethics program" requirement— and receive the three-point deduction—by exercising due diligence to prevent and detect criminal conduct, and by otherwise promoting an

---

216. U.S.S.G. Manual § 8C2.3 provides a table indicating each offense and its corresponding base fine.
217. U.S.S.G. Manual § 8C2.4(a)(1–3).
218. U.S.S.G. Manual § 8C2.5.
219. U.S.S.G. Manual § 8C2.5(g); Hyewon & Wagner, *supra* note 205, at 359.
220. U.S.S.G. Manual § 8C2.5(f).

organizational culture that encourages ethical conduct and compliance with the law.[221] This provision, added in the 2004 amendments to the Guidelines, is discussed in more detail below.

Once the aggravating and mitigating factors are considered, Step Four is to determine the appropriate minimum and maximum multipliers from the following table.[222]

Culpability Score	Minimum Multiplier	Maximum Multiplier
10 or more	2.00	4.00
9	1.80	3.60
8	1.60	3.20
7	1.40	2.80
6	1.20	2.40
5	1.00	2.00
4	0.80	1.60
3	0.60	1.20
2	0.40	0.80
1	0.20	0.40
0 or less	0.05	0.20

A court will multiply the amount of the base fine by the minimum and maximum multipliers to determine the minimum and maximum fine that can be imposed, subject to some further upward or downward adjustments. Because the highest maximum multiplier (4.00 for a culpability score of 10 or more) is *80 times higher* than the lowest minimum multiplier (.05 for a culpability score of 0 or less) *for the same offense*, it becomes clear why it is so critically important for organizations to adopt programs that minimize their culpability score. The three-point deduction for an effective compliance and ethics program is thus a powerful incentive. This is particularly true for large organizations with thousands of employees where there is a high likelihood that rogue employees may, sooner or later, engage in conduct for which the organization could be prosecuted.

---

221. U.S.S.G. Manual § 8B2.1.
222. U.S.S.G. Manual § 8C2.6.

The final fine calculation is still subject to upward or downward departure.[223] Before the *Booker* decision, which made the Guidelines advisory, a court could increase or decrease the fine if it found that "there exists an aggravating or mitigating circumstance of a kind, or to a degree, not adequately taken into consideration by the Sentencing Commission in formulating the [Guidelines] that should result in a sentence different from that described."[224] The Guidelines include a non-exhaustive list of factors that may warrant a departure, including if the offense poses a risk of death or bodily injury[225] or threatens national security.[226] After *Booker*, judges still must consult the Guidelines but are not bound by them. Even after *Booker*, however, judges have rarely granted departures for corporate criminal defendants based on mitigating factors that are not listed in the Guidelines.[227]

C. 2004 Amendments to the Sentencing Guidelines

In its original formulation, the Guidelines did not require an "effective compliance and ethics program" to receive the three-point deduction from a culpability score, but rather based this three-point deduction on a determination of whether the organization had an "effective program to prevent and detect violations of law"[228] As mentioned in Chapter 2, the original Commentary to the Guidelines articulated seven factors for a court to review to determine whether this credit should be given.[229] One of these factors required an organization to:

> have taken reasonable steps to achieve compliance with its standards, *e.g.*, by utilizing monitoring and auditing systems

---

223. There are also some other limitations on the fine provisions. For example, if it is reasonably likely that an organization would be unable to pay, no fine calculation need be performed, and the statutory maximum fine will be the maximum fine permitted regardless of the fine calculation under the Guidelines. *See* Report of the Ad Hoc Advisory Group on the Organizational Sentencing Guidelines, *available at* http://www.ussc.gov./corp/advgrgrpt/AG_FINAL_pdf, at 16–17 (last visited April 28, 2009).
224. 18 U.S.C. § 3553(b) (2007).
225. U.S.S.G. Manual § 8C4.2.
226. U.S.S.G. Manual § 8C4.3.
227. Hyewon & Wagner, *supra* note 205, at 359.
228. U.S.S.G. Manual § 8C2.5(f) (1991).
229. *See* Chapter 2 at 122.

reasonably designed to detect criminal conduct by its employees and other agents and by having in place and publicizing a reporting system whereby employees and other agents could report criminal conduct by others within the organization without fear of retribution.[230]

In the 2004 amendments to the Guidelines, the concepts of the original seven factors were retained but expanded, and because the issues addressed in those factors were considered to be significant, they were taken out of the Commentary and formalized in a separate Guideline section, U.S.S.G. § 8B2.1, Effective Compliance and Ethics Program. Though similar, the change from an "effective program to prevent and detect violations of law" to an "effective compliance and ethics program" reflects one of the primary modifications imposed by the Sentencing Commission in the 2004 revisions to the Guidelines.

This change was the result of the recommendations from an Ad Hoc Advisory Group that had been appointed by the Sentencing Commission in 2002 to study and propose changes to Guidelines, if needed, based on the previous decade's experience. In its Report to the Sentencing Commission in 2004, the Advisory Group reported that the record of experience with the Guidelines, especially in light of the criminal conduct by organizations over the previous years, indicated that changes to the Guidelines were necessary to address two problems in particular. First, the "recent revelation of widespread misconduct in some of the nation's largest publicly held companies—misconduct perpetrated at the highest levels of corporate leadership that went undetected despite the existence of compliance programs—required evaluation of whether compliance efforts precipitated by the organizational sentencing guidelines could be made more effective. . . ."[231] The Advisory Group also observed that since the promulgation of the original Guidelines, there had been much development of what were considered "best practices" so that "[i]n short, the Advisory Group believes that the organizational guidelines should be updated to reflect the learning and progress in the compliance field since 1991."[232]

---

230. U.S.S.G. Manual § 8A1.2, Commentary, Application Note 3(k)(5) (1991).
231. Report of the Ad Hoc Advisory Group on the Organizational Sentencing Guidelines, *supra* note 223, at 3.
232. *Id.*

Accordingly, the Advisory Group recommended several changes to the Guidelines, which were substantially reflected in the 2004 Revised Guidelines adopted by the Sentencing Commission and approved by Congress. At the most basic level, the new Guidelines required organizations to "exercise due diligence to prevent and detect criminal conduct" and to "otherwise promote an organizational culture that encourages ethical conduct and a commitment to compliance with the law."[233]

The Guidelines further provided definition of "due diligence": "the establishment of standards and procedures to prevent and detect criminal conduct;" requiring the organization's "governing authority" to exercise reasonable oversight of compliance efforts; making sure that "high-level" personnel are responsible for the compliance program and that the people doing the day-to-day work in compliance have adequate access to those high-level personnel;[234] using reasonable efforts not to give substantial authority to people who previously engaged in illegal or other conduct inconsistent with an effective compliance and ethics program;[235] providing adequate training and dissemination of information about the compliance program;[236] promoting and consistently enforcing the program;[237] and, once criminal conduct has been detected, taking reasonable steps to respond to it and to prevent similar future conduct, including, as necessary, the modification of the compliance and ethics program.[238]

An additional aspect of the due diligence requirement deserves particular mention. In addition to the elements described above, to have an "effective compliance and ethics program," the Guidelines require an organization to take reasonable steps:

(A) to ensure that the organization's compliance and ethics program is followed, including monitoring and auditing to detect criminal conduct;

(B) to evaluate periodically the effectiveness of the organization's compliance and ethics program; and

---

233. U.S.S.G. Manual § 8B2.1(a)
234. U.S.S.G. Manual § 8B2.1(b)(1)–(2).
235. U.S.S.G. Manual § 8B2.1(b)(3).
236. U.S.S.G. Manual § 8B2.1(b)(4).
237. U.S.S.G. Manual § 8B2.1(b)(6).
238. U.S.S.G. Manual § 8B2.1(b)(7).

(C) to have and publicize a system, *which may include mechanisms that allow for anonymity or confidentiality,* whereby the organization's employees and agents may report or *seek guidance* regarding potential or actual criminal conduct without fear of retaliation.[239]

Thus, organizations must engage in monitoring, auditing, and risk assessment; and these aspects of the revisions have received a great deal of publicity.[240] The requirement for periodic risk assessments is separately stated in U.S.S.G. § 8B2.1(c). In addition, the Guidelines require systems that also provide guidance to employees and others on reporting misconduct. Such systems may include "mechanisms that allow for anonymity or confidentiality."

D. Implications for Ombuds

Thus, to have an "effective compliance and ethics program" and be eligible for the three-point deduction for a culpability score, an organization, among other things, *must* take reasonable steps to have a system, *"which may include mechanisms that allow for anonymity or confidentiality,* whereby the organization's employees and agents may report or *seek guidance* regarding potential or actual criminal conduct without fear of retaliation."[241] Ombuds provide just such a confidential or anonymous means of permitting employees and others to seek guidance on how to report misconduct. This was recognized by the Ad Hoc Advisory Group's Report in its explanation of the reasons it was recommending change in the Guidelines' provisions relating to Reporting Systems.[242] Accordingly, this provision of the Guidelines represents an opportunity for ombuds to be identified and to demonstrate that they serve an important supporting role in helping their organization have an effective compliance and ethics program. The Sentencing Guidelines also present an opportunity for ombuds to add references to their supplementary role in documentation relating to

---

239. U.S.S.G. Manual § 8B2.1(b)(5) (emphasis added).
240. *See, e.g.*, Jeffrey M. Kaplan, *The New Corporate Sentencing Guidelines*, 18 ETHIKOS AND CORP. CONDUCT Q. No. 1 at 1 (July/August 2004).
241. U.S.S.G. Manual § 8B2.1(b)(5) (emphasis added).
242. Report of the Ad Hoc Advisory Group on the Organizational Sentencing Guidelines, *supra* note 223, at 78–86.

their programs. Such documentation may then be used as needed in support of the ombuds' claim of confidentiality to show that there is a need for such "confidential and anonymous mechanisms" as a matter of important national public policy.

Another aspect of the Guidelines, and particularly evident in the 2004 revisions, is the requirement of periodic risk assessment. While organizations have begun to engage in this process with respect to compliance programs generally, many of them have not yet focused on the inherent limitations of compliance programs, whistleblower laws and policies, and hotlines presented in Chapter 2. An ongoing risk assessment, however, presents an opportunity for ombuds to encourage their organizations to evaluate whether greater support for an ombuds program can help promote the organizational culture that is widely recognized as so crucial to effective compliance and ethics programs.

PART VI: THE CLERY ACT

A. Background

In 1986, Jeanne Clery, a 19-year-old freshman at Lehigh University, was raped and killed in her dorm room. After her death, her parents learned that the university had not informed its students of 38 violent crimes that had taken place on campus in the three years before Jeanne's death. Her parents, together with the victims of other campus crimes and their relatives, succeeded in obtaining Congress's passage of legislation to require reporting of campus violence. As originally enacted, it was Title II of the Student Right to Know and Campus Security Act[243] and was known as the Crime Awareness and Campus Security Act of 1990. When the act was amended in the Higher Education Amendments Act of 1998,[244] it formally became known as the Jeanne Clery Disclosure of Campus Security and Campus Crime Statistics Act (the Clery Act).[245]

B. Reporting Requirements

The Clery Act applies to institutions of higher education that receive federal funds, which means that virtually all colleges and universities are governed by its provisions. Its principal purpose is to require the collection and dissemination of information on campus crime. The act imposes three basic types of obligations: the development of policies and procedures for dealing with campus sexual assault; the collection and retention of records of crime and reported crime statistics; and the dissemination of this data and related information.[246] In connection with the last of these requirements, the Clery Act mandates that covered institutions undertake very specific reporting obligations, including annual crime reports, timely reports to the campus community on crimes considered to be a threat to other students, and daily logs of criminal occurrences.

---

243. Student Right to Know and Campus Security Act, Pub. L. No. 101-542, 104 Stat. 2381 (1990).

244. Section 486(e) of the Higher Education Amendments Act of 1998, Pub. L. No. 105-244, 112 Stat. 1590 (1998).

245. The provisions of the Clery Act have been codified at 20 U.S.C. § 1092(f) (2007).

Annual Crime Report. The act requires each covered institution to produce a report by September 1 of each year that presents various policies relating to campus security; access to campus facilities; law enforcement policies, including policies for reporting campus crimes and other emergencies; policies dealing with off-campus activities and coordination with local police agencies; and policies relating to the use of alcohol and drugs and enforcement of federal and state laws relating to such use. In addition, the report must disclose various programs that are designed to inform students and employees about campus security practices and procedures and how to prevent crimes. And finally, the annual crime report must contain statistics for various categories of crime occurring on the campus and reported either to campus security officials or the local police for the current calendar year and the two preceding years. Among the categories of offenses that must be included are murder, sex offenses, robbery, aggravated assault, burglary, motor vehicle theft, manslaughter, and arson. Additionally, each institution must disclose liquor law violations, drug law violations, and illegal weapons possessions if the violations resulted in an arrest or disciplinary action.[247]

The annual crime report must be provided to all of the institution's current students and employees. In addition, the institution must make the report available on request to all prospective students and prospective employees.[248]

Threat Reports. In addition to producing an annual crime report, institutions must "make timely reports to the campus community on crimes considered to be a threat to other students and employees."[249] The crimes for which statistics must be disclosed in the annual crime report are the same ones that trigger the obligation for a threat report. There is no mandatory frequency of these reports; they are not required unless there is a determination that a crime poses an ongoing threat to students and employees.

Daily Crime Logs. The act requires schools with a "police or security department of any kind" to maintain daily crime logs that are available to the public during normal business hours.[250] The logs must record

---
246. U.S. DEP'T OF EDUCATION, THE HANDBOOK FOR CAMPUS CRIME REPORTING 3 (2005).
247. 20 U.S.C. § 1092(f)(1) (2007).
248. *Id.*
249. 20 U.S.C. § 1092(f)(3) (2007).
250. 20 U.S.C. § 1092(f)(4) (2007).

all crimes reported to the department within two business days, including the nature, date, time, general location, and disposition of each crime. There are, however, exceptions to the daily reporting requirement. For example, if the disclosure of certain information related to the crime is prohibited by law or will jeopardize the confidentiality of the victim, the information need not be included in the log. Similarly, if there is clear and convincing evidence that the release of criminal information will jeopardize an ongoing investigation, cause a criminal suspect to flee, or result in the destruction of evidence, the information should not be included in the log.

C. Reporting Channels

The Clery Act identifies the channels for providing the information that must be kept and disclosed in the various reports. In particular, 20 U.S.C. § 1092(f)(1)(F) requires that statistics be produced for the enumerated offenses reported to "campus security authorities" or "local police agencies." There is no doubt that a campus ombuds is not a part of a local police agency, but it is less clear from the language of the act whether an ombuds is considered a "campus security authority" for purposes of the act. Regardless of that determination, however, because of concerns over campus security and the potential for violence on campus, some college and university ombuds have experienced pressure to disclose to campus security officials information that may come within the disclosure requirements of the Clery Act.

If the campus ombuds office is created and operated in accordance with the Code of Ethics and Standards of Practice of the International Ombudsman Association (IOA), it should be clear that an ombuds would not be a "campus security authority."[251] Therefore, if campus ombuds were included as campus security authorities—and thus required to record and report confidential information on behalf of the institution—it would be in direct conflict with the standards set forth by the IOA.

---

251. *See* Appendix 5 at 465 (*e.g.,* IOA Standards of Practice, 3.1 (confidentiality provisions generally); 3.5 ("The Ombudsman keeps no records containing identifying information on behalf of the organization."); and 3.8 ("Communications made to the Ombudsman are not notice to the organization. The Ombudsman neither acts as agent for nor accepts notice on behalf of the organization . . . .").

The Department of Education's (DOE) regulations, promulgated pursuant to the Clery Act, provide guidance on the types of positions that are considered to come within the ambit of a campus security authority. This guidance supports the position taken by IOA and campus ombuds that they are not required reporting channels. The regulations define "campus security authority" as: (1) a campus police department or a campus security department of an institution; (2) any individual or individuals who have responsibility for campus security but who do not constitute a campus police department; (3) any individual or organization specified in an institution's statement of campus security policy as an individual or organization to which students and employees should report criminal offenses; and (4) an official of an institution who has significant responsibility for student and campus activities, including, but not limited to, student housing, student discipline, and campus judicial proceedings.[252]

Although it may appear that the category of an official with "significant responsibility for student and campus activities" is sufficiently ambiguous to be problematic, a Final Rule published by DOE regarding the regulations seems to clarify this issue. The Final Rule discusses examples of individuals who are and are not considered as having "significant responsibility for student and campus activities."[253] Individuals such as an institution's dean of students, director of athletics, team coach, and faculty advisor are considered as having significant responsibility.[254] On the other hand, a single teaching faculty member who does not serve as a faculty advisor, a campus physician, or a counselor in a counseling center is not viewed as having "significant responsibility for student and campus activities."[255]

D. Implications for Ombuds

The same concerns that militate against ombuds being thought to have authority to receive notice of claims[256] suggest that ombuds also are not a required reporting channel within the scope of the Clery Act.

---

252. 34 C.F.R. § 668.46 (1999).
253. Student Assistance General Provisions; Final Rule, 64 Fed. Reg. 59,063 (Nov. 1, 1999) (codified at 34 C.F.R. pt. 668).
254. *Id.*
255. *Id.*
256. *See* Chapter 3 at 193–220.

This conclusion, however, does not derive from the title "ombuds"; it is the by-product of a structure and operation that are consistent with the principles of independence, neutrality, confidentiality, and informality on which IOA organizational ombuds programs are based. Some colleges and universities have had administration officials, such as a dean of students, also function as an ombuds. Not only would such a dual role violate the IOA Code of Ethics and Standards of Practice, it likely exposes both the individual involved and the institution to claims that the institution was on notice and had reporting obligations for information that came to the attention of the ombuds. Accordingly, care should be exercised in defining the role and structure of the campus ombuds office to make sure that it is appropriately structured and operated.[257]

In sum, the Clery Act itself, as well as the implementing regulations, suggests that Congress did not intend for individuals serving in roles similar to that of an ombuds to be considered as reporting channels under the act. The standards set forth by the IOA require an ombuds not to have any connection with the institution that would compromise his or her independence or neutrality. Accordingly, the Clery Act should not apply to a proper organizational ombuds program. Nevertheless, both the campus ombuds and the institution itself should clearly state that, in addition to not being a channel for notice, the ombuds is not a reporting channel for matters that would have to be reported under the Clery Act.

---

257. S.S. v. Alexander, 177 P.3d 724 (Wash App. Div. 1, 2008), demonstrates the point that participation of an ombuds in decision-making can lead to exposure in Title IX cases. *See* Chapter 3 at 208–11 for a discussion of *S.S. v. Alexander*. The same risks are also present in this context.

PART VII: PUBLIC SECTOR OMBUDS—RECORDS RETENTION AND FREEDOM OF INFORMATION ACTS

A. Introduction

As described in Chapter 1, ombuds programs of the classical model were established in state and federal governmental entities beginning in the late 1960s. The ombuds concept then spread to universities, and many organizational ombuds programs were established at state universities throughout the country. Also beginning in the late 1960s, a parallel development was under way to promote greater access to the affairs of government—the passage of freedom of information acts, at both federal and state levels. These acts, together with related legislation, such as the Federal Records Act[258] and various state records retention laws, regulate the preservation, access, and destruction of records of governmental agencies. Because ombuds programs in governmental organizations are subject to these laws, it is important for public-sector ombuds to know about them and the extent to which these ombuds are constrained by federal law or the law of their state with respect to the preservation and destruction of any information they create or possess. They should also be mindful of their vulnerability to a demand for access to information maintained by them pursuant to a freedom of information or privacy act request. To the extent that ombuds in the public sector are required to produce records in response to these requests or are restricted in what may be destroyed, their ability to comply with the Standards of Practice of the International Ombudsman Association may be compromised, and they may need to adjust their own policies not only on the preservation and destruction of documents, but also on the creation of records or the possession of other information within the ombuds office.

The laws governing records retention, destruction, and public access vary widely from state to state, so any particularized analysis of the laws of any one state cannot be undertaken here, though a listing of the freedom of information acts or public records laws of each of the states appears at the end of this section. Because many of these laws are modeled after the federal laws, however, it is useful to present a discussion of these issues using federal law as a way of illustrating

---

258. The Federal Records Act, codified at 44 U.S.C. § 3101, *et seq.* (2006).

the challenges facing organizational ombuds in the public sector. While the analysis of these issues under a particular state's laws may be similar, there also may be important differences that should be examined by the ombuds program and its organization with their counsel. Thus, this general discussion may benefit federal agency ombuds most directly, but it should help other public-sector ombuds identify the issues affecting them and assist them and their organizations to obtain appropriate legal advice based on the law applicable to them.

B. Records Preservation, Retention, and Destruction

The Federal Records Act (FRA) creates an obligation on the part of the head of each federal agency to "make and preserve records containing adequate and proper documentation of the organization, functions, policies, decisions, procedures, and essential transactions of the agency . . . ."[259] There is no legislative or interpretive language that specifically exempts ombuds.[260]

The obligation to preserve and retain records thus is applicable to ombuds:

> Records made by an ombud within the course of his or her official duties plainly fall with the [Records Retention] Act. The ombud's actions—just like those of any other agency official—pertain to the "policies, decision, procedures, and essential transactions of the agency . . . ." As the regulations require, an ombud's records are made "in connection with the transaction of agency business . . . ." The matters brought before an ombuds might also concern the rights of "persons directly affected by the agency's activities," whether regulated parties or the agency's employees themselves. As long as records relate to the ombud's official actions—which, after all, are funded by the taxpayer—they must be maintained in accordance with the regulations promulgated under the FRA.[261]

---

259. 44 U.S.C. § 3101 (2006).
260. Harold J. Krent, *Federal Agency Ombuds: The Costs, Benefits, and Countenance of Confidentiality*, 52 ADMIN. L. REV. 17, 26 (2000).
261. *Id.* at 26–27, *citing* regulations for the Federal Records Act at 36 C.F.R. §§ 1222.34 and 1220.14.

Just as there is no provision that would exempt ombuds' records created or held in the performance of their duties from the reach of the FRA, there is no exception based on the type of informal notes they typically create. The FRA has a statutory definition of "records" that is quite broad and appears to apply to virtually any type of record.[262] Although a possible exception may exist for "personal papers, such as calendars or journals of observation about agency work,"[263] this exception is narrow and would not "include any notations or summaries made during the course of agency employment to facilitate agency business."[264]

Once the obligation to preserve a record attaches, it cannot be destroyed except in accordance with the provisions of the FRA.[265] The authority to determine when and if a record may be destroyed has been vested in the federal archivist. Pursuant to the FRA, the archivist has published regulations and records retention schedules to provide retention and destruction policies for the most common form of records.[266] One of these schedules, General Records Schedule 1, refers to ombuds, but only as one of an enumerated list of ADR meth-

---

262. 44 U.S.C. § 3301 (2006) (Definition of records. "As used in this chapter [44 U.S.C. § 3301 (2006) *et seq.*], 'records' includes all books, papers, maps, photographs, machine-readable materials, or other documentary materials, regardless of physical form or characteristics, made or received by an agency of the United States Government under Federal law or in connection with the transaction of public business and preserved or appropriate for preservation by that agency or its legitimate successor as evidence of the organization, functions, policies, decisions, procedures, operations, or other activities of the Government or because of the informational value of data in them. Library and museum material made or acquired and preserved solely for reference or exhibition purposes, extra copies of documents preserved only for convenience of reference, and stocks of publications and of processed documents are not included."). *See* Krent, *supra* note 260, at 27.

263. Krent, *supra* note 260, at 27, *citing* NATIONAL ARCHIVES AND RECORDS ADMIN., DISPOSITION OF FEDERAL RECORDS: A RECORDS MANAGEMENT HANDBOOK (2000 edition *available at* http://www.archives.gov/records-mgmt/pdf/dfr-2000.pdf (last visited April 13, 2009).

264. *Id.*

265. 44 U.S.C. § 3314 (2006).

266. 44 U.S.C. § 3302 (2006); *see* National Archives and Records Admin., *General Records Schedule* 1, Transmittal No. 12, July 2004, *available at* http://www.archives.gov/records-mgmt/ardor/grs01.html (last visited April 13, 2009).

ods, and requires that both general files and case files be maintained for three years.[267]

Alternatively, a federal agency head may submit proposed records retention schedules to the archivist.[268] The archivist is accorded wide discretion to determine whether particular types of records should be retained, based on whether they "have sufficient administrative, legal, research, or other value to warrant continued preservation . . . ."[269] To avoid the application of General Records Schedule 1, the issue of retention policies specifically for ombuds records can be addressed by each ombuds program and its agency by way of a request to the archivist.[270] In the absence of such a determination, the ombuds' records would be covered by the published schedule:

> In short, federal agency ombuds must abide by the FRA. Most materials, no matter how informal, must be retained in accordance with the General Records Schedules. Those schedules, however, may authorize destruction of notes once adequate summaries are created, and there is the chance that the Archivist will find that the preservation value of the records does not eclipse the potential harms of protracted retention.[271]

---

267. *Id.* at 1–15 ("Section 27. Alternative Dispute Resolution (ADR) Files. Alternative Dispute Resolution (ADR) is any procedure, conducted by a neutral third party, that is used to resolve issues in controversy, including, but not limited to, conciliation, facilitation, mediation, fact finding, minitrials, arbitration and use of ombuds. The records covered by this schedule relate to techniques and processes used in an agency's ADR program in resolving disputes with or between its own employees. [**NOTE**: This schedule does not apply to: 1. Administrative grievance files, 2. Adverse action files, 3. Formal and informal equal employment opportunity proceedings, 4. Traditional EEO counseling or other records included in the EEO file when a person chooses to go directly to ADR, or 5. Private-party claims or EEOC involvement with federal sector claims of non-EEOC employees against other federal agencies. These records are covered by other items in CRS1. This schedule does not apply to ADR records that are produced as part of an agency's primary mission.]").

268. 44 U.S.C. § 3303 (2006).

269. 44 U.S.C. § 3303a (2006).

270. Krent, *supra* note 260, at 29–31, *e.g.*, nn.55 & 58 (indicating that the archivist has authorized the FDIC to maintain computerized records of contacts with identities deleted and for shorter periods than other types of agency records).

271. *Id.* at 31.

C. Access to Public Records

There are two principal statutory provisions that require the disclosure of public records. The first, and the most significant, is the federal Freedom of Information Act (FOIA).[272] The second is the Privacy Act.[273]

1. Freedom of Information Act

The FOIA was enacted in 1966 and applies to all records possessed by all agencies of the executive branch[274] of the United States. In essence, it requires the disclosure of all such records to the public in one form or another, unless the records are protected from disclosure by one of the nine exemptions or three exclusions of the FOIA.

Prior to the passage of the FOIA, Section 3 of the Administrative Procedure Act of 1946 (APA)[275] governed public access to the records of federal agencies. The APA was applicable to all agencies of the United States, excluding Congress, the courts, and the governments of the territories, possessions, and the District of Columbia. It required agencies to publish descriptions of their central and field organizations, all final opinions or orders in the adjudication of cases, and matters of official record. By the 1960s there was a general belief that the APA was not sufficient. A 1964 report by the Senate Judiciary Committee in support of the passage of FOIA noted that Section 3 was "of little or no value to the public in gaining access to records of the Federal Government."[276] The committee observed that Section 3:

> is full of loopholes which allow agencies to deny legitimate information to the public. It has been shown innumerable times that withheld information is often withheld only to cover up

---

272. 5 U.S.C. § 552 (2008).
273. 5 U.S.C. § 552a (2008).
274. FOIA does not apply to entities that "are neither chartered by the federal government [n]or controlled by it." *Freedom of Information Act Guide*, May 2004, *available at* http://www.usdoj.gov/oip/introduc.htm#N_14_(last visited April 13, 2009). Therefore, state governments, municipal corporations, the courts, Congress, and private citizens are not subject to the FOIA. *Id.* A listing of state freedom of information or public records laws, however, is provided at the end of this section.
275. 5 U.S.C. § 1002 (1947).
276. S. Rep. No. 1219 (1964).

embarrassing mistakes or irregularities and justified by such phrases in section 3 of the Administrative Procedure Act as—"requiring secrecy in the public interest," "required for good cause to be held confidential," and "properly and directly concerned."[277]

The vague standards of Section 3 allowed government officials to withhold "almost anything" under color of law.[278] The purpose of enacting FOIA, therefore, was to remedy the issues with Section 3 of APA and provide citizens with a court procedure to obtain wrongfully withheld information.[279]

The FOIA became effective in 1967 and has been amended at various times since. Its basic structure includes provisions that describe the type of information that must automatically be disclosed by federal agencies, as well as provisions that create an obligation to respond to particular public requests for information. With respect to this latter category, the FOIA provides both exceptions and exclusions to the obligation to disclose information.

The FOIA's first two subsections—(a)(1) and (a)(2)—specify the type of information that must automatically be disclosed by federal agencies, and, while not overly relevant to issues involving ombuds, they should at least be mentioned. These subsections are sometimes referred to as the "automatic" disclosure provisions of FOIA. Subsection (a)(1) requires certain agency information to be disclosed through publication in the *Federal Register*. This type of information includes descriptions of agency organizations, functions, and procedures; substantive agency rules; and statements of general agency policy.[280] This allows the public to have "automatic access to very basic information regarding the transaction of agency business."[281] Subsection (a)(2), often referred to as the "reading room" provision, requires that certain types of records be routinely made "available for public inspection

---

277. *Id.*
278. *Id.*
279. *Id.*
280. *See* 5 U.S.C. § 552(a)(1) (2008).
281. Freedom of Information Act Guide, May 2004, *available at* http://www.usdoj.gov/oip/introduc.htm#N_14_ (last visited April 13, 2009).

and copying."[282] These records include final agency opinions and orders rendered in the adjudication of cases, specific policy statements, certain administrative staff manuals, and some records previously processed for disclosure under FOIA.[283]

If an agency does not comply with the (a)(1) and (a)(2) disclosure requirements, "any person" may file a complaint to enjoin that agency from withholding its records and to order their production.[284] If a complainant succeeds in an action to order the production of improperly withheld agency records, the court will (1) order the agency to produce the records; (2) assess reasonable attorney fees and other litigation costs against the United States; and (3) issue a written finding on whether the circumstances surrounding the withholding raises questions about whether agency personnel acted arbitrarily or capriciously with respect to the withholding; if so, this will initiate a proceeding to determine whether disciplinary action is warranted against the officer or employee who was primarily responsible for the withholding.[285] Moreover, if an agency does not comply with the orders of the court, the court may punish the responsible employee or member for contempt.[286]

Subsection (a)(3) of the FOIA,[287] its most utilized provision,[288] provides that all records that are not required to be automatically disclosed under the previous subsections, and that are not exempted or excluded from disclosure, are subject to disclosure upon an agency's receipt of a proper FOIA request from any person.[289] Each request must reasonably describe the records being requested. The request must also be made in accordance with published rules stating the time, place, fees (if any), and procedures to be followed.[290] The agency's failure to produce records upon request entitles a member of the pub-

---

282. *See* 5 U.S.C. § 552(a)(2) (2008). *See also* Freedom of Information Act Guide, May 2004, *supra* note 281.
283. 5 U.S.C. § 552(a)(2) (2008).
284. 5 U.S.C. § 552(a)(4)(B) (2008).
285. 5 U.S.C. § 552(a)(4)(F) (2008).
286. 5 U.S.C. § 552(a)(4)(G) (2008).
287. 5 U.S.C. § 552(a)(3)(A) (2008).
288. Freedom of Information Act Guide, *supra* note 281.
289. 5 U.S.C. § 552(a)(3)(A)(i) (2008).
290. 5 U.S.C. § 552(a)(3)(A)(ii) (2008).

lic to go to court to seek relief in the same manner as a violation of subsections (a)(1) and (a)(2).

As with the Federal Records Act, a threshold question under the FOIA is whether ombuds records come within the scope of a statutory definition—in this case, agency records—and the answer is the same: namely, that there is no specific provision that clearly removes any ombuds records from the class of agency records that are subject to disclosure under the FOIA. Ombuds records would satisfy both prongs of a two-pronged test created by the Supreme Court in *U.S. Dep't of Justice v. Tax Analysts* to determine whether disclosure is required: whether the records at issue were either created or obtained by the agency, and whether the records were under agency control at the time of the FOIA request.[291] Moreover, to determine whether an agency had control over the records at the time of the FOIA request, agencies have been directed to consider four factors: (1) the intent of the record's creator to retain or relinquish control over the record; (2) the ability of the agency to use and dispose of the record as it sees fit; (3) the extent to which agency personnel have read or relied upon the record; and (4) the degree to which the record was integrated into the agency's record-keeping system or files.[292]

The use of these factors is illustrated in a recent decision by the U.S. District Court for the District of Columbia. The court, in *In Defense of Animals v. National Institutes of Health*, held that the requested clinical records at the Alamogordo [N.M.] Primate Facility (APF) were agency records within the meaning of FOIA.[293] The case involved an FOIA request seeking documents relating to APF, a government-owned, contractor-operated primate facility, and the chimpanzees kept under a contract with National Institutes of Health (NIH).[294] In determining that the FOIA request should be granted, the court looked at factors such as the fact that NIH owned the facility where the requested documents were kept; NIH personnel could access the chimpanzee medical records; and NIH received a commitment from APF that clini-

---

291. U.S. Dep't of Justice v. Tax Analysts, 492 U.S. 136, 144–45 (1989) (holding that court opinions in agency files are agency records).

292. *See* In Def. of Animals v. NIH, 543 F. Supp. 2d 83, 100 (2008) (citing Burka v. HHS, 87 F.3d 508, 515 (D.C. Cir. 1996)).

293. *Id.*

294. *Id.*

cal files were being created and maintained onsite.[295] The court also noted that the "most important factor . . . is that [NIH had] ownership over the chimpanzees' clinical files."[296]

While an ombuds program at a federal agency created to meet IOA Standards of Practice would be functionally independent and confidential, it is highly unlikely that a court, in applying this four-factor test, would conclude that ombuds records are not agency records subject to the FOIA. Whether any such records would have to be disclosed thus will likely depend on whether any of the FOIA exceptions apply.[297]

Subsection 552(b) of the FOIA specifies nine categories of records that are exempt from disclosure under the FOIA. Several of the categories are not at all relevant to records potentially kept by ombuds programs, but this subsection contains three exemptions that possibly could be applicable: (b)(3)—Information specifically exempted from disclosure by another statute; (b)(5)—Inter-agency and intra-agency memoranda or letters that would not be available to a party in litigation with the agency; and (b)(6)—Personnel, medical and similar files, the disclosure of which would constitute a clearly unwarranted invasion of personal privacy.

Subsection (b)(3), exempting information specifically exempt from disclosure by another statute, implicates the provisions of the Administrative Dispute Resolution Act (ADRA). As discussed in Chapter 3,[298] a new provision was added to the ADRA in 1996 that specifically states that "[a] dispute resolution communication which is between a neutral and a party and which may not be disclosed under this section shall also be exempt from disclosure under section 552(b)(3)."[299] And

---

295. *Id.*
296. *Id.*
297. The FOIA also has categorical exclusions, delineated in 5 U.S.C. § 552 (c). This subsection, which was added as part of the 1986 amendments to FOIA, establishes three special categories of law enforcement–related records that are entirely excluded from the coverage under FOIA. In enacting subsection (c), Congress created a mechanism for protecting certain sensitive law enforcement matters. These provisions, none of which would ordinarily apply to ombuds programs, authorize federal law enforcement agencies to treat especially sensitive records as "not subject to the requirements" of FOIA.
298. *See* Chapter 3 at 264–68.
299. 5 U.S.C. § 574(j) (2007).

while the use of an ombuds is included within the statutory definition of an "alternate means of dispute resolution" under the ADRA,[300] the definition of other terms used in the ADRA suggest that that statute may not cover the whole gamut of ombuds activities.

In particular, a "dispute resolution proceeding" is defined in the ADRA to include any "alternate means of dispute resolution" to resolve an "issue in controversy" in which a "neutral" is appointed and "specified parties" participate.[301] An "issue in controversy" is an "issue which is material to a decision concerning an administrative program of an agency, and to which there is disagreement."[302] A "neutral" is a person who "with respect to an issue in controversy, functions specifically to aid the parties in resolving the controversy."[303] The implication in these definitions is that there is a dispute between different parties and that it relates to an "administrative program of the agency," so it is unclear whether the ADRA would apply to an individual coming to an ombuds in the absence of such a dispute or in connection with a matter that does not implicate an administrative program of the agency.[304] Moreover, the confidentiality section of the ADRA[305] adds further restrictions potentially limiting the applicability of the ADRA, because it provides that a "neutral' in a "dispute resolution proceeding" shall not be required to disclose a "dispute resolution communication" or any communication provided "in confidence" to the neutral, and both "dispute resolution communication" and "in confidence" are defined terms[306] that ultimately tie back to a "dispute resolution proceeding."

In light of the definitional limitations imposed by the ADRA, and despite the amendments to the ADRA in 1996 to specifically include ombuds, it is unclear whether the ADRA provides an exemption for much of the work of an ombuds, particularly when the ombuds provides assistance only to a single inquirer.[307]

---

300. 5 U.S.C. § 571(3) (2007).
301. 5 U.S.C. § 571(6) (2007).
302. 5 U.S.C. § 571(8) (2007).
303. 5 U.S.C. § 571(9) (2007).
304. See Krent, *supra* note 260, at 38–42.
305. 5 U.S.C. § 574 (2007).
306. 5 U.S.C. §§ 571 (5) & (7) (2007).
307. See Krent, *supra* note 260, at 38–42. Note also that while 5 U.S.C. § 574 (2007) creates barriers to disclosure, such as proof of "manifest injustice," no categorical confidentiality is provided.

Subsection (b)(6) of the FOIA provides another possible basis for ombuds records to be exempt. This subsection protects "personnel, medical and similar files" from disclosure if disclosure would "constitute a clearly unwarranted invasion of privacy." In *U. S. Dep't of State v. Washington Post Co.*,[308] the Supreme Court held that Congress intended the term "personnel, medical and similar files" to be interpreted broadly. The Court stated that "Congress' statements that it was creating a 'general exemption' for information contained in great quantities of files suggest that the phrase 'similar files' was to have a broad, rather than a narrow, meaning."[309] The Court noted that files relating to a particular individual meet the threshold requirement for [subsection (b)(6)] protection.[310] Therefore, an ombuds file containing information on a particular agency employee would likely qualify under this exemption.

Protection under subsection (b)(6), however, requires more than meeting the threshold requirement. A balancing test is used to determine whether the public interest in disclosure outweighs the private interest against disclosure. Courts have identified four factors to be balanced: (1) the plaintiff's interest in disclosure; (2) the public interest in disclosure; (3) the degree of invasion of personal privacy; and (4) the availability of any alternative means of obtaining requested information.[311]

Whether an ombuds office's record would satisfy this test will depend on the particular facts involved in the dispute. Courts have, however, given great weight to intimate information that is likely to identify or embarrass an individual. For example, in *Rural Housing Alliance v. U.S. Dep't of Agriculture*,[312] the court noted that a report that contains "information regarding marital status, legitimacy of children, identity of fathers of children, medical condition, welfare payments, alcoholic consumption, family fights, reputation, and so on" was sufficiently intimate to fall under the "similar file" exemption. To the extent that ombuds'

---

308. U.S. Dep't of State v. Wash. Post Co., 456 U.S. 595 (1982).
309. *Id.* at 600.
310. *Id.* at 602.
311. Church of Scientology v. U.S. Dep't of Army, 611 F.2d 738, 746 (1979) (finding that the release of the bulk of the materials requested under FOIA would tend to identify the individual and to reveal details of this individual's life that are clearly exempt under current case law and there was no legitimate public purpose served by the release).
312. Rural Housing Alliance v. U.S. Dep't of Agric., 498 F.2d 73, 77 (1974).

reports and notes on individuals reflect such or similar information, they likely would be protected from disclosure under this subsection.[313]

Subsection (b)(5) of the FOIA may also provide some protection to an ombuds office facing an FOIA request under certain circumstances. This subsection exempts from disclosure "inter-agency or intra-agency memorandums or letters which would not be available by law to a party . . . in litigation with the agency." As construed by the Supreme Court, subsection (b)(5) applies to documents that would be privileged from disclosure to a private party in litigation with an agency.[314] Thus, an ombuds desiring to invoke the provisions of subsection (b)(5) would first have to establish a claim of privilege, an undertaking that has been done, and, as discussed in Chapter 3, may still be available to the ombuds if he or she can meet the burden of proof to show why an ombuds privilege should be recognized. Because such a showing, however, still depends on the exercise of discretion by a trial judge, there are formidable hurdles to invoking a privilege as a basis to claim exemption under the FOIA.

2. The Privacy Act

While the FOIA requires disclosure of agency records to any member of the public who requests them, provided no exclusion or exemption applies, the federal Privacy Act[315] mandates the disclosure to an employee of a federal agency, upon request, certain records maintained by the agency relating to that employee. In this context, "records" are defined to include:

> any item, collection, or grouping of information about an individual that is maintained by an agency, including, but not limited to, his education, financial transactions, medical history, and criminal or employment history and that contains his name, or the identifying number, symbol, or other identifying par-

---

313. This assumes that someone other than the individual whose intimate information is implicated is making the information request. A request for records by the individual implicated would likely be analyzed under the Privacy Act provisions, discussed below, and yield a different result.

314. United States v. Weber Aircraft Corp., 465 U.S. 792, 799–800 (1984); Krent, *supra* note 260, at 36–37.

315. 5 U.S.C. § 552a (2007).

ticular assigned to the individual, such as a finger or voice print or a photograph.[316]

As with the FOIA, the Privacy Act provides a means for requesting access to such records[317] and civil remedies if access is denied.[318] The Privacy Act also mandates procedures for federal agencies to use in maintaining and disclosing such records,[319] as well as both general and specific exemptions.[320]

Although there are no known cases deciding the issue, the provisions of the Privacy Act likely are applicable to an ombuds program in a federal agency, since, as before, there is nothing that clearly removes ombuds from the reach of this act, provided their records would otherwise come within the act's definition of "records." The provisions of the Privacy Act, however, are particularly problematic for ombuds programs, because, at least in the private sector, most of the attempts to obtain records and documents from an ombuds have come from an individual employee who consulted with the ombuds and believed that the ombuds or his records would help substantiate a claim in litigation. If that were the case in a federal agency, the individual would have a right to the record if it could be identified. The implications of this conclusion, however, are not as dire as it may seem, since courts, in construing the requirements of the Privacy Act, have been reluctant to require agencies to search for or produce information if there is not a relatively easy way to identify the individual identified in the records request.[321]

D. Implications for Ombuds

The provisions of the FRA, the FOIA, and the Privacy Act all make life more difficult for federal agency ombuds, assuming that a federal

---

316. 5 U.S.C. § 552a(a)(4) (2007).
317. 5 U.S.C. § 552a(d)(1) (2007).
318. 5 U.S.C. § 552a(g) (2007).
319. 5 U.S.C. § 552a(b), (c) & (e) (2007).
320. 5 U.S.C. § 552a(j) & (k) (2007). None of these exemptions typically would be applicable.
321. Krent, *supra* note 260, *citing* the decisions in Cuccaro v. Sec'y of Labor, 770 F.2d 355, 360 (3d Cir. 1985); Baker v. U.S. Dep't of Navy, 814 F.2d 1381 (9th Cir. 1987); and Carpenter v. IRS, 938 F. Supp 521, 522–23 (S.D. Ind. 1996).

agency ombuds wishes to maintain the confidentiality of communications in the same way that other organizational ombuds do. The FRA and FOIA regulate what information must be preserved and, upon request, disclosed to a member of the public. Because there is nothing that categorically removes ombuds from the broad sweep of these provisions, a federal agency ombuds program, in conjunction with its agency, may wish to seek clarification from the archivist as to what records must be preserved and for how long. They also should be aware that their ability to claim exemption under the FOIA from compelled disclosure may be limited. The exemption provided by the ADRA is good but may have limited applicability. In light of the requirements for the preservation and disclosure of records once they are created, it may be necessary and appropriate for ombuds in the public sector to develop practices to create as few records as possible and to avoid, where possible, identifying people by name. Such an approach would also have benefits under the Privacy Act, since the obligation to produce records under that act stems from the ability to identify a record as pertaining to an individual. Indeed, one commentator has noted that, under the Privacy Act:

> If an agency transcribes summaries of ombuds' discussions or meetings with employees and deletes the names of the employees, no disclosure would be mandated. In addition, if the ombud uses some kind of shorthand abbreviation or code, the file perhaps need not be produced as well. In any event, agencies need not disclose aggregate data drawn from the requestor as well as others.[322]

The challenges presented by these statutes underscore the need for additional legislation to strike the proper balance between the strong public policies served by these federal acts and those served by greater utilization of organizational ombuds programs.

Because there are so many different statutory schemes that address the retention, destruction, and disclosure of public records, one of the purposes of discussing these issues through an analysis of federal law is to provide a paradigm for the analysis of the issues for ombuds programs that are subject to state public records and freedom of information laws. This analysis includes at least the following steps:

---

322. Krent, *supra* note 260, at 42 (citations omitted).

- Are there state or other public records laws or regulations that dictate what records must be maintained by the governmental entity in which the ombuds program operates, and do those laws dictate how long such records must be preserved or the way in which they may be destroyed?
- Are those laws applicable to the types of records kept by the ombuds program?
- Is there a mechanism, akin to a request to the archivist, for a special ruling on the retention obligations, including the type of records that must be retained and the duration of the retention obligation, for ombuds records?
- Is there a state freedom of information law that would apply to ombuds programs that are part of a state or other governmental entity?
- Are there specific exemptions or exclusions to the disclosure obligation under the freedom of information law that are applicable to ombuds records?
- Is there a state privacy law that gives an individual employee of the governmental entity in which the ombuds program operates a right of access to any information about himself or herself?
- Do the provisions of any such privacy act apply to the types of records kept by the ombuds program?
- Are there functional and practical ways that the ombuds in such programs can minimize their exposure to compelled preservation and disclosure by limiting the creation of records or altering the way in which they maintain information?

E. State FOIA Statutes

(Inspection of public records only; does not include public meetings.)

Alabama: ALA. CODE § 41-13-1 through § 41-13-44; § 36-12-40 (rights of citizens to inspect and copy public writings; exceptions)

Alaska: ALASKA STAT. § 40.25.100 through § 40.25.295 (Alaska Public Records Act)

Arizona: ARIZ. REV. STAT. ANN. § 39-101 through § 39-221

Arkansas: ARK. CODE ANN. § 25-19-101 to § 25-19-105

California: Cal. Gov. Code § 6250 through § 6270
Colorado: Colo. Rev. Stat. § 24-72-201 through § 24-72-206
Connecticut: Conn. Gen. Stat. § 1-200 through § 1-242.
Delaware: Del. Code Ann. tit. 29, § 10001 through § 10005
District of Columbia: D.C. Code § 2-531 through § 2-540
Florida: 10 Fla. Stat. § 119.01 through § 119.19
Georgia: Ga. Code Ann. § 50-18-70 through § 50-18-77
Hawaii: Haw. Rev. Stat. § 92F-1 through § 92F-42
Idaho: Idaho Code § 9-337 through § 9-350
Illinois: 5 Ill. Comp. Stat. 140/1.1 through 140/11
Indiana: Ind. Code § 5-14-3-1 through § 5-14-3-10
Iowa: 1 Iowa Code § 22.1 through § 22.14
Kansas: Kan. Stat. Ann. § 45-215 through § 45-223
Kentucky: Ky. Rev. Stat. Ann. § 61-870 through § 61-884
Louisiana: La. Rev. Stat. Ann. § 44:1 through § 44:23.1
Maine: Me. Rev. Stat. Ann. tit. 1, § 401 through § 521
Maryland: Md. Code Ann., State Government § 10-611 through § 10-628
Massachusetts: Mass. Gen. Laws ch. 66, § 1 through §18
Michigan: Mich. Comp. Laws § 15.231 through § 15.246
Minnesota: Minn. Stat. § 13.01- § 13.99
Mississippi: Miss. Code Ann. § 25-61-1 through § 25-61-17
Missouri: 39 Mo. Rev. Stat. § 610.010 through § 610.035
Montana: Mont. Code Ann. § 2-6-101 through § 2-6-112
Nebraska: Neb. Rev. Stat. § 84-712 through § 84-712.09
Nevada: Nev. Rev. Stat. § 239.001 through § 239-330
New Hampshire: 6 N.H. Rev. Stat. Ann. § 91-A:1 through § 91-A:9
New Jersey: N.J. Stat. Ann. § 47:1A-1 through § 47:1A-18
New Mexico: N.M. Stat. § 14-2-1 through § 14-16-19
New York: N.Y. Public Office Law § 84 through § 90
North Carolina: N.C. Gen. Stat. § 132-1 through § 132-10
North Dakota: N.D. Cent. Code § 44-04-17.1 through § 44-04-31

Ohio: 1 OHIO REV. CODE ANN. § 149.43

Oklahoma: OKLA. STAT. ANN. tit. 51, § 24.A1 through § 24.A.24

Oregon: OR. REV. STAT. § 192.001 through § 192.990

Pennsylvania: PENNSYLVANIA'S NEW RIGHT TO KNOW LAW, Act 3 of 2008, effective 1/1/2009 (not codified)

Rhode Island: R.I. GEN. LAWS § 38-2-1 through § 38-2-15

South Carolina: S.C. CODE ANN. § 30-4-10 through § 30-4-165

South Dakota: S.D. CODIFIED LAWS § 1-27-1 through § 1-27-45

Tennessee: TENN. CODE ANN. § 10-7-101 through § 10-7-123

Texas: TEX. GOV'T CODE ANN. § 552.001 through § 552.029

Utah: UTAH CODE ANN. § 63G-2-101 through § 63G-2-207

Vermont: VT. STAT. ANN. tit. 1, § 310 through § 320

Virginia: VA. CODE ANN. § 2.2-3700 through § 2.2-3714

Washington: WASH. REV. CODE § 42.56.001 through § 42.56.904

West Virginia: W. VA. CODE § 29B-1-1 through § 29B-1-7

Wisconsin: WIS. STAT. § 19.31 through § 19.39

Wyoming: WYO. STAT. ANN. § 16-4-201 through § 16-4-205

PART VIII: EUROPEAN UNION DATA PROTECTION DIRECTIVE AND SUBSEQUENT DEVELOPMENTS

A. Introduction

The clash of values and cultural history in international business conduct is nowhere more evident than in the strikingly different legislative and regulatory approaches taken on the issue of whistle-blowing and personal data by the United States and the European Union (EU). In the United States, there are literally hundreds of whistleblower laws that encourage confidential or anonymous reporting of misconduct by others. And while these laws are of questionable effectiveness,[323] the focus of their concern has almost always been on whether the *whistle-blower* will suffer retaliation; there has been little concern that the *subject* of a whistle-blower complaint may be improperly or unfairly implicated in a report. The passage of the Sarbanes-Oxley Act of 2002 (SOX)[324] accelerated the development of whistle-blower mechanisms and policies, including hotlines, by requiring companies listed on national stock exchanges or associations to have anonymous and confidential means by which employees could report accounting or auditing concerns. As a result of these developments, having a hotline and a corporate code of conduct that encourages reporting of misconduct has become a best practice in the United States.

By contrast, the cultural perspective of many countries in Europe on these issues is quite different. The experiences of World War II and the tension brought on by post-war communism in Europe has produced in countries such as the Netherlands, Belgium, France, and Germany a strong and visceral aversion to anonymous reporting and a concomitant concern for the protection of the subject of any such report.[325] These concerns ultimately led to the enactment of the European Union's strict provision limiting the collection, use, and transmission of personal data: the European Union Data Protection Directive

---

323. *See* Chapter 3 at 149–56.
324. Sarbanes-Oxley Act of 2002, Pub. L. No. 107-204, 116 Stat. 745 (2002).
325. Donald C. Dowling, Jr., *Sarbanes-Oxley Whistleblower Hotlines Across Europe: Directions Through the Maze*, 42 INT'L LAW. 12 (2008).

(Data Protection Directive, or Directive).[326] As articulated by the chair of the EU advisory group charged with overseeing implementation of the Directive:

> At any rate, the possibility to file anonymous reports can only increase the risk of frivolous or slanderous reports with the intention of causing the accused damage or distress.
>
> I am personally keen to underline that this assessment must be read in the specific European context. It is certainly useful at this stage to recall that anonymous reporting evokes some of the darkest times of recent history on the European continent, whether during World War II or the more recent dictatorships in Southern and Eastern Europe. This historical specificity makes up for a lot of the reluctance of the EU Data Protection Authorities to allow anonymous schemes being advertised as such in companies as a normal mode of reporting concerns.[327]

The differences between the United States and Europe on the foundations for appropriate public policy on whistle-blowing and data privacy are not merely philosophical; the provisions of the Data Protection Directive impose obligations and restrictions that have been almost incompatible—or at least very hard to reconcile—with legal obligations under U.S. law to provide confidential and anonymous mechanisms to report misconduct and to respond to appropriate discovery motions in litigation.

B. Overview of the EU Data Protection Directive

The Directive was approved by the European Parliament in 1995 and took effect in 1998. It established a regulatory framework to guarantee secure and free movement of data containing personal information

---

326. The Council Directive 95/46/EC of the European Parliament and Council of 24 Oct. 1995 on the Protection of Individuals with Regard to the Processing of Personal Data and on the Free Movement of Such Data, 1995 O.J. (L281) (Nov. 23, 1995) (Directive).

327. Letter from Peter Scharr, Chairman, EU Article 29 Data Protection Working Party, to Ethiopis Tafara, Director, U.S. Securities and Exchange Commission Office of International Affairs (July 3, 2006), *available at* http://ec.europa.eu/justice_home/fsj/privacy/docs/wpdocs/others/2006-07-03-reply_whistleblowing.pdf (last visited April 13, 2009).

across the national borders of the EU member states—of which there are currently 27[328]—and imposed security requirements to protect personal information wherever it is stored, transmitted, or processed. It protects the privacy of all personal information of EU residents and applies to all companies that are established in the EU, do business in the EU, or make use of equipment within the EU, or that are in another jurisdiction where an EU member country's law applies by virtue of private international law. At the same time, it prohibits member states from restricting the "free flow of personal data" within the EU for reasons of protection—that is, the Directive is intended to supersede all national data-protection statutes.

A significant feature of the Directive is the requirement that, in order to achieve adequate and uniform security measures, EU member states are each required to adopt measures to require people or entities that control personal data (controllers) to "implement appropriate technical and organizational measures to protect personal data against accidental or unlawful destruction or accidental loss, alteration, unauthorized disclosure or access, in particular where the processing involves the transmission of data over a network, and against all other unlawful forms of processing."[329] Under the Directive, every EU member state enacts its own national data privacy law and has its own national data enforcement agency, called a Data Protection Authority (DPA). Although each member state's privacy law and DPA are unique, all are harmonized around the common regulatory framework of the Directive. As of 2008, all 27 member states had passed implementing legislation.[330]

The implications of the Directive and the corresponding privacy laws of EU member states are extensive. They affect any company or organization that moves personal data across the national borders of the EU member states and reach into many types of business record-keeping, including human resources personnel files, customer data of

---

328. This figure is as of July 2008. The EU member states are Austria, Belgium, Bulgaria, Cyprus, Czech Republic, Denmark, Estonia, Finland, France, Germany, Greece, Hungary, Republic of Ireland, Italy, Latvia, Lithuania, Luxembourg, Malta, Netherlands, Poland, Portugal, Romania, Slovakia, Slovenia, Spain, Sweden, and the United Kingdom.

329. Directive, *supra* note 326, at art. 17.

330. *See* http://ec.europa.eu/justice_home/fsj/privacy/law/implementation_en.htm (last visited April 13, 2009).

all types, journalism, research, government, and whistle-blower hotlines.[331] These provisions also have implications for ombuds programs located within any multinational organization that may be located in or do business in any of the EU member states. Accordingly, a general working knowledge of and appreciation for European data protection law is important to any such organizational ombuds office.

The goal of this section is to provide some background on the development of the Data Protection Directive, to summarize its critical provisions, and to note some of the subsequent developments that relate to the way in which U.S. corporations satisfy the Directive as well as the way in which the Directive impacts whistle-blower polices and hotlines.

C. History of Data Protection Law in Europe

Data protection legislation in European countries began its development long before the European Parliament approved the Directive in 1995. European countries were "keenly aware of the potential of government misuse of personal data" for two major reasons: the "odious histories" of many of the countries, and because the governments compiled a great deal of data for complicated welfare systems.[332] The United Nations is credited with first raising the issue of data privacy at a 1968 meeting that marked the twentieth anniversary of the signing of the Universal Declaration of Human Rights, when it considered the question of whether limits should be placed on the uses of electronics that may affect the rights of people.[333] Subsequently, the two international organizations that included the advanced industrialized countries within the United Nations—the Organization for Economic Cooperation and Development (OECD) and the Council of Europe (Council)—proposed solutions to problems associated with data protection. The two organizations, which had substantially overlapping membership in 1980, each created data protection expert committees to draft their proposals. That same year, the OECD drafted the voluntary "1980 Guidelines Governing the Protection of Privacy and Transborder Flows of Personal Data"

---

331. For a discussion of the issue of the whistle-blower provisions of SOX, *see* pages 420 to 423.

332. DOROTHEE HEISENBERG, NEGOTIATING PRIVACY: THE EUROPEAN UNION, THE UNITED STATES, AND PERSONAL DATA PROTECTION 52 (2005).

333. *Id.*

(OECD Guidelines) and the Council proposed the binding (upon the signatory states) "Convention for the Protection of Individuals with Regard to Automatic Processing of Personal Data" (Council of Europe Convention).[334] While both proposals subsequently influenced the drafters of the Directive, they were not effective, because by the late 1980s, there was general agreement that they lacked "specificity and enforcement," and that a new approach had to be taken.[335]

To promote uniformity among the EU member states, the European Commission,[336] recognizing that diverging data protection legislation in the EU member states would hinder the free flow of data within the EU, decided that it was necessary to harmonize data protection regulation and proposed the first draft of the Directive in 1990.[337] The draft relied in large part on the German and French data protection laws and placed considerable emphasis on the "fundamental human rights" aspect of the privacy issue.[338] Though the European Parliament made over 200 changes to the first draft, many of which were accepted by the Council and the Commission, most of the draft's central principles were kept intact.[339] Even though European businesses opposed several of the key provisions of the draft, their opposition was largely unsuccessful due in part to the fact that they had not had input into the Commission's proposal at its inception.[340]

The Commission presented its second draft in 1992 in response to challenges from some member states, including the UK and its businesses, which were concerned that harmonizing data privacy laws would result in a stricter standard than what existed in the UK.[341]

---

334. *Id.*
335. *Id.* at 53.
336. The European Commission is the executive branch of the EU.
337. The Council controlled the Directive's legislative path until 1993, when the Treaty of European Union was ratified by all member states, at which time the Directive became subject to the "codecision" procedure, giving the European Parliament more decision-making authority in its development. HEISENBERG, *supra* note 332, at 54.
338. *Id.* at 55.
339. *Id.* at 56–57. *See id.* at 56 ("Except where privacy was in conflict with other fundamental rights, like freedom of the press or freedom of information, Europeans asserted that privacy protection was essential, even if it came at an economic cost.").
340. *Id.* at 57.
341. *Id.* at 65.

After extensive negotiations leading to compromises among the member states, the Council adopted a Common Position on the Directive in February of 1995.[342] The European Parliament reviewed and approved the Common Position in June of that year, the EU's Budget Council passed the Directive in July, and the presidents of the Council and the European Parliament signed the Directive in October, giving the member states (15 at the time) three years to incorporate the Directive into their own law.[343]

D. Summary of the Directive and Key Provisions

The Directive consists of seven chapters and creates a framework that is implemented largely at the member state level. Article 1 sets forth the two objectives of the Directive—"(1) . . . to protect the fundamental rights and freedoms of natural persons, and in particular their right to privacy, with respect to the processing of personal data, [and] (2) . . . [to] neither restrict nor prohibit the free flow of personal data between Member States for reasons connected with the protection afforded under [the first objective]."[344] The content of the Directive is best expressed in terms of the six key principles upon which it is based:

1. *Legitimacy*: personal data may be processed only for limited purposes;
2. *Finality*: personal data may be collected only for specified, explicit, and legitimate purposes and may not be further processed in a manner incompatible with those purposes;
3. *Transparency*: the data subject must be given information regarding data processing that relates to him or her;
4. *Proportionality*: personal data must be adequate, relevant, and not excessive in relation to the purposes for which they are collected and processed;
5. *Confidentiality and security*: technical and organizational measures to ensure confidentiality and security must be taken with regard to the processing of personal data; and

---

342. *Id.* at 65–66.
343. *Id.* at 66.
344. Directive, art. 1.

6. *Control*: supervision of processing by DPAs must be guaranteed.³⁴⁵

At its core, the Directive protects individual privacy in the processing of personal data. Both "personal data" and "processing of personal data" are defined terms. Article 2(a) of the Directive defines "personal data" as "any information relating to an identified or identifiable natural person ('data subject')."³⁴⁶ Article 2(b) defines "processing personal data" as "any operation or set of operations which is performed upon personal data, whether or not by automatic means, such as collection, recording, organization, storage, adaptation or alteration, retrieval, consultation, use, disclosure by transmission, dissemination or otherwise making available, alignment or combination, blocking, erasure, or destruction."³⁴⁷ Another critical term, "controller," is defined in Article 2 to mean "the natural or legal person, public authority, agency or any other body which alone or jointly with others determines the purposes and means of the processing of personal data . . . ."³⁴⁸

These definitions are intended to be interpreted broadly so as to protect a wide range of activities; in fact, any personal information, whether processed manually or automatically (including over the Internet), is within the scope of the Directive.³⁴⁹ In the business context, these sources may include employment applications, employee contracts, and any Web site pages where personal information is collected. Exemptions from the Directive are rare, but include any data collected or processed for any activity outside the scope of Community law or operations concerning public security, defense, state security, and the activities of the state in areas of criminal law.³⁵⁰

Article 6 of the Directive provides that personal data be processed "fairly and lawfully," "collected for specified, explicit, legitimate pur-

---

345. CHRISTOPHER KUNER, EUROPEAN DATA PRIVACY LAW AND ONLINE BUSINESS 17–18 (2003).
346. Directive, art. 2(a).
347. *Id.* art. 2(b).
348. *Id.* art. 2(d). The definition of controller also provides that "where the purposes and means of processing are determined by national or Community laws or regulations, the controller or the specific criteria for his nomination may be designated by national or Community law."
349. *Id.* art. 3(1).
350. *Id.* art. 3(2).

poses," not be "excessive in relation to the purposes" for which they are collected, and not used for further purposes inconsistent with those specified.[351] Article 7 establishes how data controllers may obtain data legitimately and what they may legitimately do with the data.

One of the most important provisions in the entire Directive is the requirement in Article 7 that personal data may be processed only if the data subject has given his or her unambiguous consent or certain other narrow provisions apply.[352] Consent of the data subject is thus required unless the exceptions apply. The exceptions include where the processing is necessary "for the performance of a contract" or to protect the data subject's "vital interests," and where it is "necessary for compliance with a legal obligation to which the controller is subject" or "necessary for the purposes of the legitimate interests pursued by the controller or by the third party or parties to whom the data are disclosed."[353]

Article 8(1) of the Directive generally prohibits the processing of "sensitive data," including data disclosing racial/ethnic origin, religious/philosophical beliefs, political views, membership in a trade union, or information about the subject's health or sexual activity, also subject to limited exceptions.[354] Provided there are adequate safeguards, member states may also add exemptions for reasons of "substantial public interests."[355]

Article 10 specifies that a data controller must provide data subjects at least the following information: (1) the identity of the controller; (2) the purposes of the processing for which the data are intended; and (3) any further information such as the recipients of the data, and the existence of the right of access to, and the right to rectify, the data concerning them (the subjects).[356]

Another critical provision is in Article 11, which provides that if information is collected from a third party (meaning, not from the data subject), the collector must inform the data subject of the third party's

---

351. *Id.* art. 6(1).
352. *Id.* art. 7.
353. *Id.* "Third parties" include outside payroll agencies, marketing firms, and other similar companies to whom functions may be outsourced that require the transfer of personal information.
354. *Id.* art. 8(1).
355. *Id.* art. 8(4).
356. *Id.* art. 10.

identity, the type of information obtained, the purpose for collecting such information, and the identities of those who will receive the information.[357] This is a provision that directly impacts both hotlines and ombuds programs:

> To Americans it is not always obvious how anonymous whistleblowing implicates data protection/privacy laws. . . . Even anonymous whistleblowers generally identify some target individual. For example, if some employee "Horst" calls a hotline, retains his anonymity, but blows the whistle on his coworker "Dieter," and if the company makes a notation about that call, the notation itself instantly becomes regulated personal data, about Dieter. (Horst remains anonymous, so the call is not regulated personal data about *him*).[358]

Furthermore, Article 14 grants a data subject certain rights: to choose not to have the personal data collected; to know how the data will be used and to restrict its use;[359] to know the extent to which the data will be protected;[360] to challenge the accuracy of the data and to provide corrected information; and to seek legal relief through appropriate channels to protect privacy rights.[361] The data subject also has a right to be free from "automated individual decisions," which are defined in Article 15(1) as any decision "which produces legal effects

---

357. *Id.* art. 11(1). These notification requirements are tempered by exemptions for any disclosures that "would involve a disproportionate effort," or are part of historical or statistical studies. *Id.* art. 11(2).

358. Dowling, *supra* note 325, at 19 n.73.

359. Under the Directive, data subjects have the right to request information about the processing of their data. *Id.* art. 12(a). If the subject finds that the Directive is being violated, he or she may request that the processing be brought into conformity with the Directive's requirements or that the data be blocked or erased from the controller's system. Additionally, since the subject is entitled to notice that his or her information is being processed, he or she has a right, on compelling legitimate grounds, to object to the processing of his data. *Id.* art. 14(a).

360. Organizations must "implement appropriate technical and organizational measures to protect personal data." *Id.* art. 17(1). Such measures must be "appropriate to the risks represented by the processing and the nature of the data to be protected." *Id.*

361. *Id.* art. 14.

concerning him or significantly affects him and which is solely based on automated processing of data intended to evaluate certain personal aspects relating to him, such as his performance at work, creditworthiness, reliability, conduct, etc.,"[362] subject to limited exceptions, as long as his or her "legitimate interests" are protected.[363]

Under Articles 16 and 17, data controllers must safeguard the confidentiality and security of personal data through such mechanisms as encrypting data sent over the Internet, as well as implementing other security measures.[364] With few exemptions, under Articles 18 and 19 controllers must also notify the relevant data authorities (including the member state's Data Protection Authority [DPA]) of exactly what data they are processing, and why.[365]

Within the EU, transfers of personal data are generally allowed on a need-to-know basis. The Directive permits this free flow of information by creating standards of protection throughout the EU. However, where the transfer of data is to a non-EU country not subject to the Directive (so-called "third countries"), Article 25 provides that the transfer of data is allowed only if "the third country in question ensures an adequate level of protection."[366] The adequacy of protection is determined by examining "all the circumstances surrounding a data transfer operation," including "the nature of the data, the purpose and duration of the proposed processing operation . . . the country of origin and country of final destination, the rules of law . . . in force in the third country in question and the professional rules and security measures which are complied with in those countries."[367] Article 26 provides exceptions to this standard, including when the data subject has expressly consented to the transfer; the transfer is necessary to further a contract entered into by the data subject; the transfer is necessary or legally required on public interest grounds or to establish or defend legal claims; or contractual provisions are in place under which the data controller has ensured adequate protection of the data.[368] As to the last exception, the EU has approved model contractual clauses for

---

362. *Id.* art. 15(1).
363. *Id.* art. 15(2).
364. *Id.* arts. 16–17.
365. *Id.* arts. 18–19.
366. *Id.* art. 25(1).
367. *Id.* art. 25(2).
368. *Id.* art. 26(1)–(2).

companies to use to aid in compliance. Because the EU has determined that the United States does not ensure an adequate level of protection, companies use other mechanisms to demonstrate that their systems do provide for adequate protections. In particular, the U.S. Department of Commerce offers a "safe harbor" program negotiated with the EU (discussed below) through which participating U.S. companies may be deemed to provide adequate data protection to allow them to receive transfers of personal data from the EU after they self-certify that they are compliant with the Safe Harbor Agreement's provisions.

Articles 22 through 24 of the Directive provide for judicial remedies, liability, and sanctions related to compliance with its provisions. Notably, Article 24 provides that member states shall "lay down the sanctions to be imposed in case of infringement" of the Directive's provisions.[369] Member states' data protection laws therefore specify the sanctions clauses for noncompliant companies and individuals. Companies as well as senior executives and the individuals in firms who control relevant information (such as HR professionals) may face criminal and/or civil penalties for noncompliance.

The member states' Data Protection Authorities monitor the developments and the companies in their respective states, and, therefore, only at the national level can sanctions be imposed for noncompliance.[370] The only EU-level involvement is to provide the setting for the DPAs to meet—the Article 29 "Working Party"—and to officially determine (along with the member state representatives in the Article 31 Committee) whether a third country has adequate data protection laws or mechanisms.[371] The Working Party "considers items placed on its agenda by its chairman, either on his own initiative or at the request of a representative of the supervisory authorities, or at the Commission's request,"[372] and periodically issues policy papers and opinions. This ongoing role serves the Directive's goal of keeping the regulations appropriate to the ever-changing technological environment.

---

369. *Id.* art. 24.
370. *Id.* art. 28.
371. *Id.* arts. 29, 31.
372. *Id.* art. 29(7).

E. Subsequent Developments and Issues Related to European Data Protection Directive

In the years since the Directive's passage, the EU has implemented a number of more specific directives for the telecommunications, banking, and marketing industries, government data collections, and several other sector-specific areas. For instance, Directive 2002/58/EC (Directive on Privacy and Electronic Communications) particularizes and complements the Directive with respect to the processing of personal data in the electronic communication sector, ensuring the free movement of such data and of electronic communication equipment and securities within the EU.[373] The Article 29 Working Party has also addressed such technological matters as e-mail filters, unsolicited communications (spam), and the processing of traffic data for billing purposes or of location data for the purpose of value-added services. Additionally, regular conferences are held to review and improve the implementation of the Directive and the enforcement of data protection more generally. The exchange of best practices and information between national authorities in the area of data protection law has been enhanced by making public on the Commission's Web site a selection of key national policy papers, decisions, and recommendations.[374]

While national legislation and regulations incorporating the Directive exist in all 27 EU member states[375] and these laws are based on the Directive's provisions, they vary in their specific requirements and scope. Thus, an organization seeking to comply with a particular EU country's data protection laws must consult that country's relevant laws and regulations. While many developments have taken place,

---

373. Directive 2002/58/EC of the European Parliament and of the Council of 12 July 2002 concerning the processing of personal data and the protection of privacy in the electronic communications sector (Directive on privacy and electronic communications). This directive was amended in 2006. *See* 2006/24/EC of the European Parliament and of the Council of 15 March 2006 on the retention of data generated or processed in connection with the provision of publicly available electronic communications services or of public communications networks and amending Directive 2002/58/EC.

374. *See* http://ec.europa.eu/justice_home/fsj/privacy/index_en.htm (last visited April 13, 2009).

375. *See* http://ec.europa.eu/justice_home/fsj/privacy/law/implementation _en. htm (last visited April 13, 2009).

and many issues have arisen since the Directive's enactment, this section will mention just two: the Safe Harbor Agreement between the United States and the EU and the implications of the whistle-blower provisions of Sarbanes-Oxley on U.S. companies' compliance with European data protection laws.

1. Safe Harbor Agreement

Article 25 of the Directive allows the transfer of personal data to a non-EU country only if that country "ensures an adequate level of protection."[376] The United States does not meet this standard. Accordingly, in response to the Directive's restrictiveness in the transfer of data to and from non-EU countries, and to help bridge the differences between the United States and the EU in their respective approaches to the issue of privacy,[377] the U.S. Commerce Department negotiated a "safe harbor" program with the EU, which went into effect in 2000. This agreement, approved by both the Council and the Commission, provides requirements that U.S. companies may adhere to in order to participate in the free exchange of personal data with companies in the EU.[378] (Companies that do not choose to use the Safe Harbor Agreement to comply with the Directive may use standard contractual clauses as provided in Article 26(4).) The Commerce Department operates the safe harbor system, and companies that sign up self-certify that they will abide by the safe harbor principles in their dealings with Europeans' personal data.[379] Companies may also utilize independent forms of verification, including the use of trustmark "privacy seal" programs, like BBBOnline or TRUSTe, which oversee a Web site's privacy policy,

---

376. Directive, art. 25. U.S. companies may comply with the Directive's requirement for an "adequate level of protection" either by participating in the Safe Harbor scheme or by the use of intragroup transborder data flow contracts.

377. Indeed, there are "important divisions between EU and US approaches to data protection which reflect cultural and historical differences about the role of government regulation. In general there is a much greater confidence in public institutions and dependence upon administrative law in EU states than is the case in the U.S. where there is far greater esteem for markets and technology." HEISENBERG, *supra* note 322, at 97 (internal quotations omitted).

378. A current list of the U.S. companies that adhere to the Safe Harbor Agreement can be found at http://web.ita.doc.gov/safeharbor/shlist.nsf/webPages/safe+harbor+list (last visited April 13, 2009).

379. HEISENBERG, *supra* note 322, at 74.

and provide an alternative dispute resolution (ADR) mechanism for consumer complaints.[380]

For their European personal data, the companies that sign the Safe Harbor Agreement agree to the following principles:

1. *Notice*: They must inform customers (data subjects) about the purposes for which they collect and use information about them. They must provide information about how individuals can contact them with any inquiries or complaints, the types of third parties to which they disclose the information, and the choices and means they offer for limiting its use and disclosure.
2. *Choice*: They must give individuals the opportunity to opt out before sending their data to a third party or using it for a different purpose. For sensitive data, an affirmative, or opt in, choice must be given if the information is to be disclosed to a third party or used for a different purpose.
3. *Onward Transfer* (transfer to third parties): They must apply the notice and choice principles to disclose information to a third party. Where that third party is acting as an agent, they must make sure that the third party subscribes to the safe harbor principles or is subject to the Directive or another adequacy finding. Alternatively, they can enter into a written agreement with such third party requiring that the third party provide at least the same level of protection as is required by these principles.
4. *Security*: They must take reasonable precautions to protect personal information from loss, misuse, and unauthorized access, disclosure, alteration, and destruction.
5. *Data Integrity*: They should take reasonable steps to ensure that data is reliable for its intended use, accurate, complete, and current.
6. *Access*: They must ensure that individuals have access to the information that the companies have about them and be able to correct, amend, or delete inaccurate information, unless the burden or expense of providing access would be disproportionate to the risks to the individual's privacy, or where the rights of other persons would be violated.

---

380. *Id.*

7. *Enforcement*: They must provide (1) readily available and affordable independent recourse mechanisms for individuals who feel their privacy has been violated, so that each individual's complaints and disputes can be investigated and resolved and damages awarded where appropriate, (2) procedures for verifying that the commitments they make to adhere to the safe harbor principles have been implemented, and (3) obligations to remedy problems arising out of a failure to comply with the principles.[381]

In accordance with these principles, companies must retain their records and make them available upon request in the context of an investigation or complaint about noncompliance. Enforcement of the Safe Harbor Agreement is primarily driven by consumer complaints, which are handled through ADR administered either by the privacy seal programs or the EU Data Protection Authorities. If a Safe Harbor company fails to comply with the ADR's ruling, the Federal Trade Commission (FTC) or the Department of Transportation (DOT) may impose fines to force the company to comply.[382] A company may even be struck from the Safe Harbor Agreement in severe cases of noncompliance.

2. Whistle-blower Provisions of the U.S. Sarbanes-Oxley Act

Actions in France and Germany in the mid-2000s against a number of major U.S. multinational corporations focused attention on conflicts between U.S. legal requirements to establish and manage confidential, anonymous hotlines and other reporting mechanisms and European data protection law. Decisions in May and June 2005 by the DPA in France—the Commission Nationale de l'Informatique et des Libertes (CNIL)—and a German labor court—Arbeitsgericht Wuppertal—invalidated compliance hotlines and other procedures established by

---

381. *See id.* at 74–75. The Safe Harbor Principles are available to any companies that desire to use them. As stated earlier, if a company chooses not to use them, Article 26(4) of the Directive contains a provision for the standard contractual clauses that could be used to come into compliance with the Directive.

382. DOT jurisdiction applies to air carriers and ticket agents, while FTC jurisdiction applies to nearly all remaining sectors.

U.S. multinational companies to comply with SOX.[383] These decisions underscored the tension between European data protection law and compliance under U.S. law, including SOX and other sources, like rules promulgated by the Securities Exchange Commission.

SOX's "whistle-blower provisions" require that companies listed on the U.S. stock exchanges and their subsidiaries set up a method for employees to anonymously report concerns regarding accounting and auditing issues to the audit committee of the board without fear of retaliation.[384] The relevant provisions require companies to develop policies and procedures for receiving, retaining, and responding to accounting, financial reporting, and fraud concerns. This requirement is often addressed through the use of a phone or Internet-based hotline (or helpline). The gathering of information about employees and other persons and the transfer of that data outside the country is a necessary result of such a process. This result, of course, implicates the Directive and the member states' data protection laws that have adopted the Directive's provisions.

In 2005, a German labor court held Wal-Mart Stores, Inc.'s whistle-blower hotline invalid on procedural and data protection grounds.[385] The court refused to allow Wal-Mart to implement part of its company code of conduct that invited employees to report misconduct by means of a company ethics hotline. That same year, the French subsidiaries of two multinational corporations, McDonald's Corp. and Exide Technologies, sought approval from CNIL for whistle-blower initiatives in order to comply with the SOX requirement.[386] However, CNIL rejected

---

383. Deliberation No. 2005-110 of 26 May 2005 on an application of McDonald's France for the implementation of a system of professional integrity (CNIL); Deliberation No. 2005-111 of 26 May 2005 on a request for authorization of the European Company accumulators for the implementation of an ethical line (CNIL); Arbeitsgericht Wuppertal, Lab. Ct., Case 5BV 20/05 (June 15, 2005).

384. Sarbanes-Oxley Act of 2002, Pub. L. No. 107-204, 116 Stat. 745.

385. Arbeitsgericht Wuppertal, Lab. Ct., Case 5BV 20/05 (June 15, 2005). The reasons for this action by the German labor court stemmed from Wal-Mart's procedural failure to engage in "co-determination" with the works counsel. Dowling, *supra* note 325, at 17.

386. *See* Deliberation No. 2005-110 of 26 May 2005 on an application of McDonald's France for the implementation of a system of professional integrity (CNIL); Deliberation No. 2005-111 of 26 May 2005 on a request for authorization of the European Company accumulators for the implementation of an ethical line (CNIL).

both requests on data protection grounds. The CNIL expressed particular concern over anonymous reporting that could lead to slanderous condemnation, disproportionality between the purpose and the risk of malicious reporting, the period of data retention, and the fact that suspected staff would not be informed of a complaint or investigation early in the process.

Because these rulings posed a substantial conflict for U.S. multinational corporations in efforts to comply with both the SOX and European data protection laws, the SEC and the CNIL moved to resolve the issue. In November and December 2005, the CNIL issued guidelines that permit the French operations of multinational corporations to comply with the anonymous-reporting requirements without running afoul of French data protection law.[387] Certain aspects of these

---

387. *See* Dowling, *supra* note 325, *e.g.*, at 20–29 for a thorough discussion of the developments in France. As summarized by Dowling, the 10 requirements for a company to qualify for "blanket-pre-approval" from the CNIL under the December 2005 Guidelines are as follows:

1. Limit the hotline to financial, accounting, banking and anti-bribery whistleblowing only.
2. Get the whistleblower to identify himself, except an anonymous complaint is acceptable if (i) extra "precautions" are taken, and (ii) the employer does not publicize that complaints may be anonymous, and encourages whistleblowers to self-identify.
3. Data collected are strictly limited to necessary information.
4. Data are collected by and communicated to only the circle of those with a need to know. "External Service Providers" must comply with these restrictions.
5. Transfers of whistleblower data outside the EU must comply with the "onward transfer" restrictions of applicable data law ("safe harbor," "model contracts," "binding corporate rules").
6. Report file must be destroyed immediately, or stored longer only as necessary for an active investigation.
7. Strong data security, including "passwords," is necessary for stored and transmitted data.
8. The whistleblowing system must be limited, and communicated according to set rules.
9. The target must be notified of the complaint "as soon as the data is [*sic*] recorded," or as soon as "protective measures" are "implemented" to prevent the destruction of evidence.
10. The target gets access to the report, except the whistleblower's identity remains confidential.

Id. at 25–26 n.108.

requirements (listed in the footnote), such as not publicizing the fact that complaints can be made anonymously, limiting the matters on which the hotline may be used, and notifying the "target" of the whistleblower complaint, seriously undermine the effectiveness of such a mechanism.

In a further effort to find some way to reconcile the requirements under SOX and the Data Protection Directive, the Directive's Working Party undertook a similar exercise. In an opinion issued on February 1, 2006, the EU Working Party concluded that Article 7 of the Directive may justify the establishment of whistle-blower hotlines that require the processing of employee data.[388] In analyzing the issue, the Working Party's opinion followed the approach taken by the French.[389] While the Working Party rejected a proffered justification for whistle-blower hotlines as required by a foreign legal statute or regulation under Article 7(c) on the grounds that doing so would thereby make it "easy for foreign rules to circumvent the EU rules laid down" by the Directive,[390] it opined that compliance with such laws was the pursuit of a "legitimate interest" by the data controller and may justify such processing under Article 7(f), provided that the interest is not "overridden by the interests for fundamental rights and freedoms of the data subject."[391] The Working Party noted that the EU has recognized the importance of good corporate governance to the effective conduct of business, the protection of stakeholders, and the stability of markets. Thus, a corporation's interest in such good corporate governance may also justify the implementation of internal controls, such as the whistle-blower hotlines, that require the involuntary processing of employee data.

F. Implications for Ombuds

There appears to be little doubt that ombuds programs operating globally will on occasion engage in the processing of personal data and may engage in activities regulated by the provisions of the EU Data

---

388. Article 29 Data Protection Working Party, Opinion 1/2006 on the application of EU data protection rules to internal whistleblowing schemes in the fields of accounting, internal accounting controls, auditing matters, fight against bribery, banking and financial crime (adopted on 1 February 2006) (Opinion 1/2006).

389. Dowling, *supra* note 325, at 31.

390. Opinion 1/2006 at 8.

391. *Id.*

Protection Directive. It would be almost impossible for an ombuds program to exist at a multinational program that did not, in some manner, involve the transmission of personal data. However, no cases involving the application of the EU Data Protection Directive to ombuds programs have been identified. Nevertheless, the principles underlying the EU's concerns with whistle-blower hotlines and anonymous and confidential reporting in general would, in all likelihood, cause concerns over ombuds programs. And yet there are important distinctions: organizational ombuds are independent, do not make management decisions, and are not a notice channel for making reports; they are bound by organizational policies and professional standards to protect the confidentiality of information provided to them; and they do not conduct investigations or maintain permanent records with individually identifiable information. Moreover, when an issue is surfaced to a formal channel, the ombuds is typically no longer involved and the formal channel would be required to process the personal data in accordance with the Directive. As a result of these important differences, the risk of harm to the data subject from the potential misuse of personal data by an ombuds is substantially less. Undoubtedly, the law will continue to unfold and, in time, provide more guidance for ombuds and their organizations. In the interim, ombuds and their organizations should heed the lesson of the Wal-Mart case in Germany and make sure that the implementation of ombuds programs be addressed as appropriate with the works councils.

PART IX: EMPLOYMENT LAWS AND CASES

Because so many of the issues raised through a confidential channel such as an ombuds program involve employment-related issues, ombuds should be aware of and have a working knowledge of the relevant laws in this area. Out of necessity, this listing of relevant federal employment statutes, together with a short summary of how they apply, is abbreviated, but should serve as a helpful guide and ready reference.[392] Short summaries are also provided of the decisions in some of the leading employment cases. And finally, a listing of typical areas of state employment statutes is included at the end of this section. It is good practice for ombuds to be aware of relevant state laws in their jurisdictions that may be applicable to employees or others in their organizations.

A. Federal Employment Laws

- **Age Discrimination in Employment Act (ADEA)**

The *Age Discrimination in Employment Act of 1967*[393] protects employees and job applicants who are at least 40 years of age from employment discrimination based on age. The ADEA prohibits such discrimination by employers with 20 or more employees, including state and local governments, as well as employment agencies and labor organizations. Age-based discrimination is proscribed with regard to any term, condition, or privilege of employment. The terms, conditions, and privileges of employment include hiring, firing, promotion, layoff, compensation, benefits, job assignments, and training.

The ADEA also contains an anti-retaliation provision, making it unlawful to retaliate against an individual who has opposed employment practices that discriminate based on age or has filed an age discrimination charge, or who has testified or participated in any way in an investigation, proceeding, or litigation under the ADEA.

---

392. This section was inspired by a similar list prepared by attorney Joan M. Schultz in *Relevant Legal Issues for the Professional Ombudsman* (July 26, 1995). The author wishes to acknowledge the assistance of Leander Dolphin of Shipman & Goodwin LLP in the preparation of this summary.

393. *See* 29 U.S.C. §§ 621–634 (2007).

- **Americans with Disabilities Act (ADA)**

Title I of the *Americans with Disabilities Act of 1990*[394] provides protection for qualified individuals with disabilities from discrimination in employment. The prohibition applies to private employers, state and local governments, employment agencies, and labor organizations with at least 15 employees. Federal employees receive protection from disability discrimination under Section 501 of the Rehabilitation Act, as amended. Discrimination based on disability is unlawful in pre-employment application procedures, hiring, firing, advancement, compensation, and other terms, conditions, and privileges of employment.

Failure to make reasonable accommodations for disabled employees and job applicants constitutes unlawful discrimination under the ADA, unless the employer can show that providing such accommodation is an "undue hardship" on the operation of its business.

The ADA was amended, effective January 1, 2009,[395] to expand and clarify the definition of a disability, and, consequently, the number of employees who may have a disability under the ADA has also increased.

The ADA also contains anti-retaliation and anti-coercion provisions, making it unlawful to: (a) retaliate against an individual who has opposed employment practices that discriminate based on disability, or who has filed a charge alleging disability discrimination, or who has testified or participated in any way in an investigation, proceeding, or litigation under the ADA; or (b) to coerce, intimidate, threaten, or interfere with an individual who enjoyed the protection of the ADA, or who has aided or encouraged any other individual in their enjoyment of the protection of the ADA.

- **Civil Rights Act of 1866 (Section 1981)**

The *Civil Rights Act of 1964*[396] prohibits discrimination in the making and enforcing of employment contracts (i.e., entering into the employment relationship).

---

394. *See* 42 U.S.C. §§ 12101–12213 (2007).
395. *See* Pub. L. No. 110-325, 122 Stat. 3553 (2008).
396. *See* 42 U.S.C. § 1981 (2006).

- **Civil Rights Act of 1964 (Title VII)**

Title VII of the *Civil Rights Act of 1964*[397] prohibits employment discrimination on the bases of race, color, national origin, sex, and religion. Such discrimination is unlawful with respect to recruiting, hiring and promotion, transfer, work assignments, performance measurements, the work environment, job training, discipline and discharge, wages and benefits, or any other term, condition, or privilege of employment. Title VII applies to employers with at least 15 employees, including state and local governments, employment agencies, labor organizations, and the federal government.

Title VII requires that an employee or applicant receive equal opportunity in employment without regard to his/her membership in any protected class (race, color, national origin, sex, or religion). In addition, Title VII bars employment decisions based on stereotypes and assumptions about a particular protected group. Title VII's expansive prohibitions include, but are not limited to, harassment and hostile work environment, accent discrimination, discriminatory English-only rules, sexual harassment or hostile work environment based on sex, and pregnancy discrimination.

Title VII not only applies to intentional discrimination but also prohibits policies that disproportionately impact employees or applicants who are protected by the statute. It is unlawful to retaliate against an individual who opposes a discriminatory compensation decision, or who files, testifies, or participates in any investigation, proceeding, or litigation under Title VII.

- **Civil Rights Act of 1991**

The *Civil Rights Act of 1991*[398] amended the Civil Rights Act of 1964 to "strengthen and improve" federal civil rights laws. The Amendment explicitly provides the right to a trial by jury in employment discrimination cases.

In addition, the Amendment expressly permits the recovery of compensatory and punitive damages in cases of intentional discrimination. The Amendment codifies the disparate impact claim, allowing plaintiffs to allege discrimination when a neutral employer policy has a disparate impact on a particular group.

---

397. *See* 42 U.S.C. § 2000e-2 *et seq.* (2007).
398. *See* 42 U.S.C. §§ 1981–1996(b) (2007).

The Civil Rights Act of 1991 also amended the Civil Rights Act of 1866 to expressly extend Section 1981's prohibition against discrimination to the modification or termination of contracts, i.e., to the post-hire period of employment, up to and including termination.

- **Consolidated Omnibus Budget Reconciliation Act (COBRA)**

The *Consolidated Omnibus Budget Reconciliation Act*[399] protects employees who have lost their health benefits due to a qualifying circumstance, generally including voluntary or involuntary job loss, reduction in the hours worked, transition between jobs, death, or divorce. COBRA requires employers with at least 20 employees who sponsor group health plans to offer eligible employees the opportunity for a temporary extension of health coverage in qualifying circumstances. Protection may also be extended to the families of the employee or recent employee.

- **Consumer Credit Protection Act (CCPA)**

Title III of the *Consumer Credit Protection Act*[400] prohibits employers from terminating employees because of any one debt, and limits the amount that may be garnished in any one week. The CCPA applies to all employers and protects all individuals who receive earnings for personal services.

- **Davis-Bacon Act**

The *Davis Bacon Act*[401] mandates that construction employees working on federally funded contracts (of at least $2,000) be paid no less than the locally prevailing wage. The act applies to both contractors and subcontractors.

- **Drug-Free Workplace Act of 1988**

The *Drug-Free Workplace Act*[402] requires all organizations that contract with the federal government to ensure that their workplace is free of illegal drugs. The act also applies to all individual contractors and grant recipients. The act provides guidance on how the contractor or grant recipient may certify compliance, including publication of a drug-free workplace statement and policy.

---

399. *See* 29 U.S.C. §§ 1161–1169 (2007).
400. *See* 15 U.S.C. §§ 1601–1615 (2007).
401. *See* 40 U.S.C. §§ 3141–3148 (2007).
402. *See* 41 U.S.C. §§ 701–707 (2007).

- **Employee Polygraph Protection Act (EPPA)**

The *Employee Polygraph Protection Act*[403] generally prohibits the use of lie detector tests, either for pre-employment screening or during the course of employment, with certain exemptions. The EPPA applies to most private employers, but does not apply to federal, state, or local governments.

Employers may not discharge, discipline, or discriminate against an employee or job applicant for refusing to take a test or for exercising other rights under the act. However, there are limited exceptions that allow the use of a polygraph in pre-employment screening and investigations of economic misconduct by an employee.

- **Employee Retirement Security Income Act (ERISA)**

The *Employee Retirement Security Income Act*[404] governs non-governmental retirement, health, disability, and other welfare benefit plans. ERISA protects participants in these plans by imposing disclosure and fiduciary responsibilities on plan administrators. ERISA outlines fiduciary obligations and standards of conduct. It also provides participants with grievance and appeals processes to recover benefits under the plan. Participants may also bring a civil action to recover plan benefits.

Section 510 of ERISA makes it unlawful to discharge an employee for the purpose of interfering with the attainment of any entitlement under an ERISA-covered employee benefit plan.

- **Equal Pay Act (EPA)**

The *Equal Pay Act*[405] prohibits discrimination in wage pay based on sex. The EPA requires that equal pay be paid to men and women who work in the same establishment, under similar working conditions, and who perform jobs that require substantially equal skill, effort, and responsibility.

The EPA makes it unlawful for an employer to retaliate against an individual who opposes a discriminatory compensation decision, or who files, testifies, or participates in any investigation, proceeding, or litigation under the EPA.

---

403. *See* 29 U.S.C. §§ 2001–2009 (2007).
404. *See* 29 U.S.C. §§ 1001–1461 (2007).
405. *See* 29 U.S.C. § 206(d) (2007).

- **Executive Order No. 11,246**

Executive Order No. 11,246[406] applies to any federal contractor who receives federal funding (at least $10,000 in one year) and prohibits discrimination in employment decisions on the basis of race, color, national origin, sex, and religion. In addition, all government contractors are required to take affirmative action to ensure equal employment opportunity. Contractors who receive at least $50,000 in federal funds must also develop written affirmative action plans.

- **Fair Credit Reporting Act (FCRA)**

The *Fair Credit Reporting Act*[407] regulates how information on a consumer's credit history is collected and distributed. The FCRA requires employers to notify an individual, in writing, that a consumer report will be used in the employment process. The employer must obtain written authorization from the individual prior to asking for a consumer report. Before taking an adverse employment action based on a consumer report, FCRA requires certain disclosures to the employee or applicant. After taking the adverse action, the employer must also notify the individual of the adverse action and advise the individual of his or her rights to dispute the accuracy or completeness of the report.

- **Fair Labor Standards Act (FLSA)**

The *Fair Labor Standards Act*[408] provides standards for minimum wage, overtime pay, record-keeping, and youth employment.

- **Genetic Information Nondiscrimination Act of 2008 (GINA)** (effective November 21, 2009)

Title II of the *Genetic Information Nondiscrimination Act*[409] prohibits the intentional acquisition of genetic information about applicants and employees, as well as the use of genetic information in employment. GINA also strictly limits disclosure of genetic information, and employers must treat genetic information with the same confidentiality it does with other medical/health information.

Under GINA, it is unlawful to discriminate against any applicant

---

406. *See* 30 Fed. Reg. 12,319 (1964–1965).
407. *See* 15 U.S.C. §§ 1681 *et seq.* (2007).
408. *See* 29 U.S.C. §§ 209–219 (2008).
409. *See* Pub. L. 110-233, 122 Stat. 881 (2008).

or employee on the basis of genetic information in any of the terms and conditions of employment. GINA contains an anti-retaliation provision, which prohibits retaliatory discrimination against an individual who had opposed an unlawful act or practice, or who has assisted or otherwise participated in an investigation, proceeding, or hearing related to this law.

GINA goes into effect on November 21, 2009.

- **Health Insurance Portability and Accountability Act (HIPAA)**

The *Health Insurance Portability and Accountability Act*[410] protects all individually identifiable health information held or transmitted by a covered entity or its business associate in any form or media. With limited exclusions, this so-called "Privacy Rule" prohibits disclosure of such protected health information except when expressly permitted or required by the rule or by written authorization of the individual who is the subject of the information.

HIPAA bars discrimination against employees and their dependents in their enrollment and premiums charged based on health status–related factors, including prior medical conditions, previous claims experience, and genetic information.

- **Family and Medical Leave Act (FMLA)**

The *Family and Medical Leave Act*[411] requires that employers allow eligible employees up to 12 weeks of unpaid leave time during any 12-month period for the birth and care of newborn children of the employee; for placement with the employee of a child for adoption or foster care; for care of an immediate family member with a serious health condition; or for the employee's own serious health condition.

Effective January 16, 2009, the FMLA also provides certain military family leave entitlements, including up to 12 weeks for qualifying exigencies that arise from a covered military member's active duty status, and up to 26 weeks of leave to care for a covered service member recovering from a serious injury or illness suffered in the line of duty.

---

410. *See* Pub. L. 104-191, 110 Stat. 1936 (1996).

411. *See* 29 U.S.C. §§ 2611–2619, as amended by National Defense Authorization Act for Fiscal Year 2008, Pub. L. No. 110-181, 122 Stat. 3 (2008).

- **Immigration Reform and Control Act of 1986 (IRCA)**

The *Immigration Reform and Control Act*[412] makes it unlawful to hire undocumented workers and requires employers to verify all new employees' employment eligibility. In addition, employers are prohibited from discriminating against job applicants on the basis of national origin or citizenship status. The IRCA imposes sanctions on employers who violate the statute's provisions.

- **Labor-Management Relations Act (Taft-Hartley Act)**

The *Taft-Hartley Act*[413] amends the National Labor Relations Act. The Taft-Hartley Act governs the relationship between labor organizations and management. In addition, the act limits a union's right to strike, affords certain rights to individual employees, and enumerates several unfair practices.

- **National Labor Relations Act (NLRA)**

The *National Labor Relations Act*[414] protects an employee's right to organize, join, or support a labor union or organization. The NLRA also protects labor organizations from unfair labor practices by employers and, conversely, protects employers from certain union conduct that interferes with the employer's business. The NLRA encourages collective bargaining between employers and labor organizations.

- **Notification and Federal Employee Anti-discrimination and Retaliation Act of 2002 (No FEAR Act)**

The *Notification and Federal Employee Anti-discrimination and Retaliation Act of 2002*[415] imposes accountability obligations on federal agencies for violations of anti-discrimination and whistle-blower protection laws. The No FEAR Act also requires each federal agency to post statistical information regarding complaints of anti-discrimination and retaliation against the agency.

---

412. *See* 99 Pub. L. 603, 100 Stat. 3359 (1986).
413. *See* 29 U.S.C. §§ 141–144 (2007).
414. *See* 29 U.S.C. §§ 151–169 (2007).
415. *See* Pub. L. No. 107-174, 116 Stat. 566 (2002).

- **Occupational Safety & Health Act (OSHA)**

The *Occupational Safety and Health Act*[416] requires employers to provide a working environment that is healthy and safe. The law compels an employer to take measures to minimize the risk of occupational safety and health hazards in the workplace. OSHA imposes penalties for violations of the act.

- **Patsy Takemoto Mink Equal Opportunity in Education Act (Title IX)**

Title IX of the Education Amendments of 1972, now known as the *Patsy Takemoto Mink Equal Opportunity in Education Act*,[417] prohibits sex discrimination by recipients of federal education funding. Title IX proscribes the exclusion of any person, on the basis of sex, from participating in or receiving the benefits of any education program or activity receiving federal funding. In addition, Title IX prohibits sex discrimination in employment.

- **Pregnancy Discrimination Act (PDA)**

The *Pregnancy Discrimination Act*[418] prohibits employers from discriminating against an employee because of her pregnancy or a condition related to her pregnancy, or because of the prejudices of other employees or customers. In addition, an employer may not discriminate against a pregnant woman in the terms and conditions of her employment, including her entitlement to sick leave or other fringe benefits.

- **Sarbanes-Oxley Act of 2002 (SOX)**

The *Sarbanes-Oxley Act*[419] imposes corporate governance and accountability standards and requires mandatory disclosure of corporate accounting practices on companies listed on national stock exchanges and associations. SOX contains whistle-blower protection provisions, which makes it unlawful to retaliate against an employee who provides information about, or otherwise assists in an investigation of, conduct that violates SOX and other Securities and Exchange Commission regulations.

---

416. *See* 29 U.S.C. §§ 651–678 (2007).
417. *See* 20 U.S.C. §§ 1681 *et seq.* (2007).
418. *See* 42 U.S.C. § 2000e(k) (2006).
419. *See* 15 U.S.C. §§ 7201–7266, Pub. L. No. 107-204, 116 Stat. 745 (2007).

- **Uniformed Services Employment and Reemployment Rights Act of 1994 (USERRA)**

The *Uniformed Services Employment and Reemployment Rights Act of 1994*[420] protects veterans' job rights and benefits. USERRA applies to all employers, regardless of size. Under USERRA, an individual may generally retain reemployment rights if he or she is absent from work for military duty for a cumulative period of up to five years.

USERRA prohibits discrimination against a member of the uniformed services on the basis of that service member's past, present, or future service, regardless of whether the service is voluntary or involuntary. Discrimination is barred in all stages of employment, including hiring, retention, and promotion, and extends to all benefits of employment, including determinations of seniority.

In addition, USERRA requires an employer to make reasonable efforts to assist a veteran returning to employment in becoming qualified for a job, and to make reasonable accommodations if the veteran is disabled.

- **Vietnam-Era Veterans' Readjustment Assistance Act of 1974 (VEVRAA)**

The *Vietnam-Era Veterans' Readjustment Assistance Act of 1974*[421] requires covered federal government contractors and subcontractors to take affirmative action to employ and advance in employment qualified special disabled veterans, disabled veterans, and other eligible veterans.

VEVRAA also prohibits discrimination against such veterans on the basis of veteran status. In addition, covered contractors and subcontractors must make reasonable accommodations for the known disabilities of qualified individuals, unless providing an accommodation would create an undue hardship.

---

420. *See* 38 U.S.C. §§ 4301–4335 (2007).
421. *See* 38 U.S.C. §§ 4211–4215 (2007).

- **Worker Adjustment and Retraining Notification Act (WARN)**

The *Workers Adjustment and Retraining Notification Act*[422] protects employees by requiring that they receive advance notice when there is a covered plant closing or mass layoff. The law requires that covered employees receive, with limited exceptions, at least 60 days' notice in advance of the plant closing or layoff.

B. Selected Landmark Supreme Court Employment Law Cases

The U.S. Supreme Court has developed an extensive body of employment law jurisprudence. Of course, ombuds should be cognizant of not only the landmark Supreme Court cases, but also the state courts' interpretations of relevant state employment laws. This list is not intended to be comprehensive; rather, it is simply intended to briefly highlight some of the seminal cases in the employment area.

- *Griggs v. Duke Power Co.*, 401 U.S. 424 (1971) (facially neutral practices, procedures, or tests that nevertheless have an unjustifiable disparate impact on one group in operation violate Title VII).
- *Cleveland Bd. of Educ. v. LaFleur*, 414 U.S. 632 (1974) (mandatory maternity leave policies violate constitutional guarantee of due process).
- *N. Haven Bd. of Educ. v. Bell*, 456 U.S. 512 (1982) (Title IX prohibits employment discrimination based on sex).
- *Meritor Sav. Bank v. Vinson*, 477 U.S. 57 (1986) (sexual harassment hostile work environment case under Title VII, where Court held that agency principles should guide inquiry of whether an employer is liable for the conduct of its supervisors).
- *Johnson v. Transportation Agency*, 480 U.S. 616 (1987) (consideration of sex of female employee as one factor in her promotion under affirmative action plan does not violate Title VII).
- *Faragher v. City of Boca Raton*, 524 U.S. 775 (1998) (an employer may be vicariously liable for a supervisor's creation of an actionable hostile work environment when there is a tan-

---

422. *See* 29 U.S.C. §§ 2101–2109 (2007).

gible employment action taken by the harasser; such liability is subject to an affirmative defense if the employer exercised reasonable care to prevent and correct sexual harassment and the employee unreasonably failed to take advantage of the employer's preventive or corrective efforts).
- *Burlington Indus. v. Ellerth*, 524 U.S. 742 (1998) (an employer may be vicariously liable even when the harassed employee has not suffered adverse and tangible employment actions, but when there is no such tangible employment action, employer may raise affirmative defense to liability or damages).
- *Oncale v. Sundowner Offshore Serv.*, 523 U.S. 75 (1998) (Title VII bars same-sex sexual harassment).
- *Jackson v. Birmingham Bd. of Educ.*, 544 U.S. 167 (2005) (retaliation against a person because of sex discrimination complaint constitutes intentional discrimination on the basis of sex in violation of Title IX).
- *Smith v. Jackson*, 544 U.S. 228 (2005) (disparate impact claim may be made under the ADEA).
- *Burlington N. & Santa Fe Ry. Co. v. White*, 548 U.S. 53 (2006) (Title VII anti-retaliation provision is not limited to discriminatory actions that affect the terms and conditions of employment, and employer conduct must be reasonably adverse to a reasonable employee or job applicant who may file or assist in filing a charge).
- *Gomez-Perez v. Potter*, 128 S. Ct. 1931 (2008) (ADEA prohibits retaliation against federal employees).
- *CBOCS West v. Humphries*, 128 S. Ct. 1951 (2008) (Section 1981 of the Civil Rights Act of 1866 encompasses claims of retaliation as well as claims of race discrimination).
- *Crawford v. Metro. Gov't of Nashville & Davidson County*, 129 S. Ct. 846 (2009) (an employee who, in an investigation of alleged discriminatory conduct, communicates to her employer a belief that the employer has engaged in a form of employment discrimination has undertaken protected activity under Title VII anti-retaliation provision).

C. Common Areas of State Employment Laws

Most states have enacted laws that are similar to the federal statutes cited here. In some cases, the state law differs from the relevant federal statute in important ways. Because of this, organizational ombuds are encouraged to develop a working knowledge of their state's body of employment law. While a comprehensive listing of state employment laws is beyond the reach of this guide, state laws of relevance to ombuds typically include laws in the following areas:

- *Employment Discrimination*—some state laws prohibit discrimination based on sexual orientation, marital status, or civil union status, while federal laws do not generally provide protection for these classes.
- *Disability Discrimination*—some states may define a disability more expansively than the federal law.
- *Unemployment Insurance*—states administer separate unemployment insurance programs and may impose certain restrictions on employers and employees that are not imposed by the federal law, such as voluntary election of coverage by employers. In addition, certain employment services that are excluded from FUTA coverage must be covered by state law.
- *Wage Laws*—while there are typically many similarities with federal law (FLSA), some states impose different tests for the definition of exempt and nonexempt employees, which will affect application of wages laws, including payment of overtime.
- *Employee Benefit Laws*—states often regulate the payment of fringe benefits, including vacation pay. In addition, many states regulate health and retirement benefits, and may extend benefits to individuals who do not receive such protection under federal law, such as domestic partners and parties to a civil union.
- *Drug-Free Workplace Laws*—states are increasingly enacting state drug-testing laws, with specific procedures for collection and testing conditions, and may also impose additional obligations on an employer when pre-employment test results would bar employment.

- *Workplace Safety*—many states enact laws relating to workplace safety, reporting procedures, and hazardous or otherwise dangerous conditions, including incidences of workplace violence.
- *Employee Privacy Laws*—states may enact privacy laws to regulate employer use of electronic or video surveillance of their employees, or to protect an employee's personally identifiable confidential information (such as Social Security numbers). States also provide protection of employee's medical/health records and information.
- *Whistle-blower Protection Laws*—many states provide protection against retaliation for whistle-blowers.
- *Mini Davis-Bacon Laws*—many states have enacted laws that mandate a prevailing wage for state contractors.
- *Family and Medical Leave*—this is an area of significant diversity among states, which may provide more expansive leave than that provided by the federal FMLA laws.
- *Workers' Compensation Benefits*—workers' compensation benefits are governed by state law, and there is considerable diversity in state laws. Generally, state workers' compensation statutes provide benefits for employees who have suffered job-related injuries. State workers' compensation laws will interact with both state and federal leave, disability, and discrimination laws.
- *Mini WARN Laws*—states are increasingly enacting state-specific advance notification laws, which may be more expansive than the federal WARN Act and may have harsher penalties for violation.

Appendix 1

1969 ABA Resolution and Report

**Midyear Meeting January 1969
American Bar Association
Summary of Actions
House of Delegates**

C. The following sections did not report:
Bar Activities
Criminal Law
Family Law
Labor Relations Law
Patent, Trademark and Copyright Law
Public Utility law

D. Action of the House on Section Recommendations

Administrative Law (Report No. 72)
The resolution which was the first recommendation of the Section was approved with minor amendment in which the Section concurred. As amended, it reads (deletions stricken throughout):

> BE IT RESOLVED, that the American Bar Association recommends:
> 1. That state and local governments of the United States should give consideration to the establishment of an ombudsman authorized to inquire into all administrative actions and to make public criticism.

2. That each statute or ordinance establishing an ombudsman should contain the following twelve essentials: (1) authority of the ombudsman to criticize all agencies, officials, and public employees except courts and their personnel, legislative bodies and their personnel, and the chief executive and his personal staff; (2) independence of the ombudsman from control by any other officer, except for his responsibility to the legislative body; (3) appointment by the executive with confirmation by a designated proper legislative body; (3) appointment by the executive with confirmation by a designated proportion of the legislative body, preferably more than a majority, such as two-thirds; (4) independence of the ombudsman through a long term, not less than five years, with freedom from removal except for cause, determined by more than a majority of the legislative body, such as two-thirds; (5) a high salary equivalent to that of a designated top officer; (6) freedom of the ombudsman to employ his own assistants and to delegate to them, without restraints of civil service and classification acts; (7) freedom of the ombudsman to investigate any act or failure to act by any agency, official, or public employee; (8) access of the ombudsman to all public records he finds relevant to an investigation; (9) authority to inquire into legality, fairness, correctness of findings, motivation, adequacy of reasons, efficiency, and procedural propriety of any action or reaction by any agency, official, or public employee, (10) discretionary power to determine what complaints to investigate and to determine what criticisms to make or to publicize; (11) opportunity for any agency, official, or public employee criticized by the ombudsman to have advance notice of the criticism and to publish with the criticism an answering statement; (12) immunity of the ombudsman and his staff from civil liability on account of official action.
3. That for the purpose of determining the workability of the ombudsman idea within the federal government, the Administrative Conference should (a) experiment by constituting itself an ombudsman for limited areas of federal activity, and (b) encourage and study experimentation by particular agencies with the ombudsman idea.

4. That establishment of a federal government-wide ombudsman system, whether or not designed to assist congressmen in handling constituents' complaints about administration should await findings based upon the experiment recommended.

BE IT FURTHER RESOLVED, that the Section of Administrative law is authorized to present the views of the Association and to encourage the establishment of ombudsmen in accordance with the provisions of this Resolution, by all necessary and appropriate means,

The resolution which was the second recommendation of the Section was approved. It reads:

BE IT RESOLVED, that the American Bar Association initiate and support the founding of a Federal Administrative Justice Center which would have responsibility for developing and supervising the orientation and training of hearing examiners and other lawyers in government service; and

RESOLVED FURTHER, that the Section of Administrative Law be authorized to undertake and further all steps appropriate towards accomplishing these objectives as soon as practicable.

ANNUAL REPORT

of the

AMERICAN BAR ASSOCIATION

Including the proceedings of the

NINETY-SECOND ANNUAL MEETING

Held at

Dallas, Texas

August 11-13, 1969

Volume 94

HEADQUARTERS OFFICE
1155 EAST 60TH STREET
Chicago, Illinois 60637

REPORT OF THE SECTION OF ADMINISTRATIVE LAW

RECOMMENDATION NO. 1*

BE IT RESOLVED, that the American Bar Association recommends:

1. That state and local governments of the United States should give consideration to the establishment of an ombudsman authorized to inquire into all administrative actions and to make public criticism.

2. That each statute or ordinance establishing an ombudsman should contain the following twelve essentials: (1) authority of the ombudsman to criticize all agencies, officials, and public employees except courts and their personnel, legislative bodies and their person-

---

* The recommendation was approved with minor amendment. See page 119.

nel, and the chief executive and his personal staff; (2) independence of the ombudsman from control by any other officer, except for his responsibility to the legislative body; (3) appointment by the executive with confirmation by a designated proper legislative body; (3) appointment by the executive with confirmation by a designated proportion of the legislative body, preferably more than a majority, such as two-thirds; (4) independence of the ombudsman through a long term, not less than five years, with freedom from removal except for cause, determined by more than a majority of the legislative body, such as two-thirds; (5) a high salary equivalent to that of a designated top officer; (6) freedom of the ombudsman to employ his own assistants and to delegate to them, without restraints of civil service and classification acts; (7) freedom of the ombudsman to investigate any act or failure to act by any agency, official, or public employee; (8) access of the ombudsman to all public records he finds relevant to an investigation; (9) authority to inquire into legality, fairness, correctness of findings, motivation, adequacy of reasons, efficiency, and procedural propriety of any action or reaction by any agency, official, or public employee, (10) discretionary power to determine what complaints to investigate and to determine what criticisms to make or to publicize; (11) opportunity for any agency, official, or public employee criticized by the ,ombudsman to have advance notice of the criticism and to publish with the criticism an answering statement; (12) immunity of the ombudsman and his staff from civil liability on account of official action.

3. That for the purpose of determining the workability of the ombudsman idea within the federal government, the Administrative Conference should (a) experiment by constituting itself an ombudsman for limited areas of federal activity, and (b) encourage and study experimentation by particular agencies with the ombudsman idea.

4. That establishment of a federal government-wide ombudsman system, whether or not designed to assist congressmen in handling constituents' complaints about administration should await findings based upon the experiment recommended.

BE IT FURTHER RESOLVED, that the Section of Administrative Law is authorized to present the views of the Association and to encourage the establishment of ombudsmen in accordance with the provisions of this Resolution, by all necessary and appropriate means.

RECOMMENDATION NO.2

BE IT RESOLVED, that the American Bar Association initiate and support the founding of a Federal Administrative Justice Center which would have responsibility for developing and supervising the orientation and training of hearing examiners and other lawyers in government service; and

RESOLVED FURTHER, that the Section of Administrative Law be authorized to undertake and further all steps appropriate towards accomplishing these objectives as soon as practicable.

REPORT NO: 1

REPORT OF THE SECTION OF ADMINISTRATIVE LAW ON THE ESTABLISHMENT OF AN OMBUDSMAN

The ombudsman idea

The basic idea of an independent ombudsman charged solely with the responsibility to investigate and to criticize administration has much appeal. The mere existence of such an officer gives administrators added incentives to avoid injustice and to correct maladministration. An ombudsman's criticisms may provide effective relief to aggrieved citizens when other protections are inadequate, as they usually are when administrative appeal and judicial review are either unavailable or too expensive for the circumstances; yet an ombudsman may withhold criticism when he finds that other remedies are adequate. The Administrative Law Section believes that the ombudsman system can be readily adapted to American state and local governments, in absence of special local reasons to the contrary. At the same time, an ombudsman system cannot be a substitute for competent administration, for conscientious personnel, for adequate supervision of public employees by superiors, for administrative appeals, or for judicial review of administrative action. What is proposed for states and cities is in addition to such protections, not a substitute for them.

The twelve essentials

The twelve essentials the Section recommends for state or local legislation establishing an ombudsman are set forth in the basic resolution.

These principles govern the scope of duties, limitations upon his powers, and the degree of independence necessary for him to carry out his responsibilities. All twelve of these essentials are contained in a widely-circulated model bill prepared by Professor Walter Gellhorn, draft number 3, June 12, 1967, which the Section recommends as a general guide for drafting legislation for states and cities.

The federal government

In the federal government, the Administrative Section believes that experimentation should be the first step. The Administrative Conference Act of 1964, 5 U.S.C. Sections 573-576, authorizes the Chairman of the Conference to "make inquiries into matters he considers important for Conference consideration, including matters proposed by individuals inside or outside the Federal Government." The Section recommends that the Chairman should choose particular governmental functions about which he and his staff will consider complaints from aggrieved parties, for the primary purpose of developing understanding of the potentialities of an ombudsman system for the federal government. It is also recommended that the Administrative Conference should study ombudsman systems already existing within federal agencies and should encourage experimentation with the idea by additional agencies.

The Section believes that experimentation on a limited basis is desirable before moving toward establishment of a government-wide system, because the size of the federal government may change the essential nature of the ombudsman idea. The system of the ombudsman in other countries has been most successful when a single individual of great prestige has won such public confidence that his opinions are highly respected. Although an organization may be capable of doing what an eminent personage can do, an ombudsman's office for the entire federal government might require from 2,000 to 4,000 employees, and such a large bureaucracy may be less effective in checking the bureaucracy than a prestigious individual assisted by a staff.

Congressional Casework

Not only should establishment of a government-wide ombudsman await the experimentation recommended, but so should establishment of a central federal office to assist congressmen in handling constituents' complaints. Congressmen now handle more than 200,000 complaints about administration annually, and the idea of creating an office to help them with their enormous burden is a natural one. A central office would obviously be better organized for handling the vast mass of complaints than are the staff attached to the office of each congressman. But the ombudsman system serves a slightly different purpose It is not linked to service for constituents; the criticism is provided by those who are performing no other function. For this reason, the further development of a system which primarily emphasizes service to constituents should await the development, through actual experience, of better understanding of systems of criticism by independent ombudsmen. The long-term objective should be effective criticism of administrators by independent officers who have no stake, direct or indirect, in any particular result.

The ombudsman system has been in operation in several countries, primarily in Scandinavia. The recommendation here under consideration was first proposed by the Ombudsman Committee of the Administrative Law Section, and the Committee's Chairman, Professor Kenneth Culp Davis. The Section, through unanimous action of its Council, urges the Association to adopt this resolution. No funds need to be specifically appropriated to implement the resolution.

Ben C. Fisher
Chairman

Appendix 2
1971 ABA Resolution and Report

ANNUAL REPORT

of the

AMERICAN BAR ASSOCIATION

Including the proceedings of the

NINETY-FOURTH ANNUAL MEETING

Held at

New York, New York

July 1-7 and 14-20, 1971

Volume 96

HEADQUARTERS OFFICE
1155 EAST 60TH STREET
Chicago, Illinois 60637

REPORT OF THE SECTION OF ADMINISTRATIVE LAW

RECOMMENDATION*

Be It Resolved, That the American Bar Association recommends that the resolution dealing with the establishment of an Ombudsman which was adopted by the House of Delegates at its Midyear meeting in 1969 (94 AIA Rep. 119 [1969]) be amended in the following respects:

A. That Paragraph 2(3) be deleted and that there be substituted in lieu thereof the following Paragraph 2(3);

"2. (3) appointment by the legislative body or appointment by the executive with confirmation by a designated proportion of the legislative body, preferably more than a majority, such as two-thirds;"

B. That Paragraph 3 be deleted and that there be substituted in lieu thereof the following Paragraph 3:

"3. That for the purpose of determining the workability of the ombudsman idea within the Federal government, the Federal government should experiment with the establishment of an ombudsman or ombudsmen for limited geographical area or areas, for a specific agency or agencies or for a limited phase or limited phases of Federal activity."

C. That Paragraph 4 be deleted and that there be substituted in lieu thereof the following Paragraph 4:

"4. That establishment of a Federal government-wide ombudsman program should await findings based upon the experimentation recommended."

REPORT

The proposed amendments constitute minor but nevertheless helpful changes in the resolution adopted by the House of Delegates in 1969. The amendments reflect the experiences of the past two years in implementing the basic resolution. Their approval at this time will permit greater flexibility in further implementation of the basic resolution, particularly at the Federal level.

---

* The recommendation was approved. See page 541.

A. Paragraph 2(3)

Although listed an essential, appointment by the executive is not essential. It may be customary or politic or practical, but not essential. Appointment by the executive with confirmation by the legislature is one of two possible alternatives.

The American Assembly Final Report of the Thirty-Second American Assembly in 1967 on the Ombudsman concluded: "The Ombudsman must be selected in a manner which assures public confidence in his independence, impartiality and professional attainments." Professor Walter Gellhorn in his Unofficial Model draft sets forth appointment by the executive subject to confirmation by two thirds of the members of each chamber of the legislature. However, in his notes, he does point out that some persons favor direct legislative selection without participation by the executive.

The proof of the pudding is in the eating and it should be noted that to date, the only two states that have passed the necessary legislation, Hawaii and Nebraska, both provide for appointment by the legislature. In the case of Nebraska, a two-thirds vote is required and in the case of Hawaii, a majority vote of each house is required.

Reference is made to legislation passed by the Congress of Micronesia. As originally drafted, it was modeled after the Ombudsman Act of the State of Hawaii. It also contained most of the essential features of the American Bar Association resolution, but one essential feature, which was not followed was in the matter of the appointment of the Ombudsman. The bill provided that the appointment be made by the Congress of Micronesia. The High Commissioner, Edward E. Johnson, disapproved of the bill which had passed in the Congress of Micronesia and pointed out the language of the American Bar Association resolution which required that it is essential that a statute establishing an ombudsman office provide that the appointment should be made by the Executive, with the confirmation of the legislature. This is an instance where the American Bar Association resolution represented a barrier in the passage of legislation rather than assistance.

The suggested change gives desired flexibility on appointment.

B. Paragraph 3

As presently worded, this paragraph relies upon the Administrative Conference. The then-Chairman of the Administrative Conference, Jesse Williams, stated in an address to the Western American Assembly on the Ombudsman in September, 1968, that he had "taken the position that the Administrative Conference is not concerned with following an individual citizen's complaint. Our role, rather, is to find out where the trouble spots are." The present Chairman' of the Administrative Conference, Roger C. Cramton, stated in a letter to the Chairman of the Ombudsman Committee that "a thorough study of the workability of the ombudsman approach in the federal government would be a very major undertaking and one which the Conference cannot bite off in one chunk. For this reason, I think it is unfortunate and not in the public interest to have deferred on the question pending the outcome of a Conference study. . . In conclusion, I would urge you to seek modification of resolution No.3 so as to permit your committee to give this subject of tremendous current interest study as you may feel appropriate."

The suggested change eliminates the reliance upon the Administrative Conference and permits experimentation with the concept this time.

C. Paragraph 4

The reason for the proposed change in language is to eliminate the statement "whether or not designed to assist Congressmen in handling constituents' complaints about administration," because such assistance itself might be part of the experiment which might be suggested for the Federal government. The suggested change maintains the principle that a federal-wide Ombudsman system should await the results of experimentation.

Conclusion

The recommendations here under consideration were first proposed by the Ombudsman Committee of the Administrative Law Section. The Section, through action of its Council, urges the Association to adopt this resolution. No funds need be specifically appropriated to implement the Resolution.

INFORMATIONAL REPORT

Submitted herewith is a brief summary of our Section's activities: Probably our major event this year has been the National Institute held under William Ross' able direction in Washington April 16-17 on the Ash Council's recommendations for reorganizing the federal regulatory agencies. President Nixon invited comments from interested bar groups by April 20. We have sent to the White House a transcript or the proceedings, and we will forward the Council's specific comments shortly. About 180 attended our Institute, about half from outside Washington and about a third from the Government and the universities, and the excellent in-depth presentations by the panelists kept the registrants engaged throughout the day and a half.

As you now, our Section was instrumental in the enactment of the Freedom of Information Act which replaced the original Administrative Procedure Act provisions on the availability of public information more than three years ago. It is a significant piece of federal legislation largely because it shifted to the Government the burden of giving good reasons for non-disclosure of information to the press and the public. Because there is some evidence of unwillingness in certain sectors of the Federal bureaucracy to comply with the letter and spirit of the FOIA, our Public Information Committee has conducted a survey to uncover instances of noncompliance and has given the Federal agencies concerned an opportunity to answer. The results of the survey will be published in *Administrative Law Review.*

Last August in St. Louis the House of Delegates approved twelve basic resolutions relating to the revision and improvement of the Administrative Procedure Act. Our Special Committee on revision of the APA is now drafting specific legislation to implement these resolutions.

Along with several other ABA sections we have act up a Committee on Environmental Quality Control to be concerned with the administrative law aspects of this vital problem. Both our New York and London programs will take up the important question of the extent to which there should be public participation in administrative proceedings involving the location and construction of electric power plants and other utilities where environmental and consumer interests desire to be heard—one from the New York State and the other the British point of view.

Another special committee is doing an in-depth study of the status and independence of the HEW Social Security Administration Bearing Examiners. The problem is more complex than one of simply defining the role of the hearing examiner. We are trying to reconcile what appears to be a paternalistic proceeding where the examiner acts as counsel judge at the seine time with the minimum requirements of due process under the APA. We are also dealing with what appears to be a near-impossible statutory standard to administer—which puts great pressure on the examiner to use equitable principles to avoid harsh results, and a government agency which is concerned about inequities to individuals if there is lack of uniformity in decision-making. Finally, there is the problem of an overwhelming volume of cases to be dealt with by a limited number of examiners. In this connection the Supreme Court has just decided *Richardson v Perales*, 39 U.S.L. W. 4497 (May 3,1971), in which it found that the regulations governing hearings and admissibility of evidence under the Social Security Act there in contention were compatible with the APA, thereby effectively overruling a Fifth Circuit decision to which the ABA had objected (in an *amicus curiae* brief) to the effect that the regulations and procedures in question superceded the APA. In its opinion, the Court gave considerable weight to the independence shown by the hearing examiners, as evidenced by the frequency with which they overruled denials of claims under the Social Security Act.

Our Ombudsman Committee is carrying on an intensive program of education and promotion in connection with legislation in states and localities which desire to establish ombudsmen.

Our Division of State Administrative Law is working on a number of important fronts, including collaboration with the American Bar Foundation on a proposed empirical study of state regulation of energy distribution utilities.

Under our special delegation from the Board of Governors, we have filed comments on behalf of the ABA with two federal regulatory agencies in rulemaking proceedings. One involved a new SEC policy to make "no-action-letters" available to the public; several of our suggestions for making the letters more usable and protecting their confidentiality were adopted by the SEC. We have also filed comments with the FCC commenting on their proposed rule permitting "summary decisions" to be made where there are no genuine issues of fact.

Franklin M. Schultz
Chairman

**Annual Meeting, July 1971
American Bar Association
Summary of Action
House of Delegates
American Bar Association
New York, New York
July 5-7, 1971**

D. Action of the House on Section and Division Recommendations

Administrative Law (Report No. 94)
The recommendation presented by the Section was approved. It reads:

Be It Resolved, That the American Bar Association recommends that the resolution dealing with the establishment of an Ombudsman which was adopted by the House of Delegates at its Midyear meeting in 1969 be amended in the following respects:
- A. That Paragraph 2(3) be deleted and that there be substituted in lieu thereof the following Paragraph 2(3);
"2. (3) appointment by the legislative body or appointment by the executive with confirmation by a designated proportion of the legislative body, preferably more than a majority, such as two-thirds;"
- B. That Paragraph 3 be deleted and that there be substituted in lieu thereof the following Paragraph 3:
"3. That for the purpose of determining the workability of the ombudsman idea within the Federal government, the Federal government should experiment with the establishment of an ombudsman or ombudsmen for limited geographical area or areas, for a specific agency or agencies or for a limited phase or limited phases of Federal activity."
- C. That Paragraph 4 be deleted and that there be substituted in lieu thereof the following Paragraph 4:
"4. That establishment of a Federal government-wide ombudsman program should await findings based upon the experimentation recommended."

See NATURAL RESOURCES LAW, Report No. 67. For action on the recommendations submitted jointly by the Sections of Administrative Law and Natural Resources Law.

Appendix 3

The Ombudsman Association Code of Ethics and Standards of Practice (Initial Version)

Code of Ethics

The ombudsman, as a designated neutral, has the responsibility of maintaining strict confidentiality concerning matters that are brought to his/her attention unless given permission to do otherwise. The only exceptions, at the sole discretion of the ombudsman, are where there appears to be imminent threat of serious harm.

The ombudsman must take all reasonable steps to protect any records and files pertaining to confidential discussions from inspection by all other persons, including management.

The ombudsman should not testify' in any formal judicial or administrative hearing about concerns brought to his/her attention.

When making recommendations, the ombudsman has the responsibility to suggest actions or policies that will be equitable to all parties.

Standards of Practice

We adhere to The Ombudsman Association Code of Ethics.

We base our practice on confidentiality.

We assert that there is a privilege with respect to communications with the ombudsman and we resist testifying in any formal process inside or outside the organization.

We exercise discretion whether to act upon a concern of an individual contacting the office. An ombudsman may initiate action on a problem he or she perceives directly.

We are designated neutrals and remain independent of ordinary line and staff structures. We serve no additional role (within an organization where we serve as ombudsman) which would compromise this neutrality.

We remain an informal and off-the-record resource. Formal investigations—for the purpose of adjudication—should be done by others. In the event that an ombudsman accepts a request to conduct a formal investigation, a memo should be written to file noting this action as an exception to the ombudsman role. Such investigations should not be considered privileged.

We foster communication about the philosophy and function of the ombudsman's office with the people we serve.

We provide feedback on trends, issues, policies and practices without breaching confidentiality or anonymity. We identify new problems and we provide support for responsible systems change.

We keep professionally current and competent by pursuing continuing education and training relevant to the ombudsman profession.

We will endeavor to be worthy of the trust placed in us.

Appendix 4

Ethical Principles for University and College Ombudsmen

An ombudsman should be guided by the following principles: objectivity, independence, accessibility, confidentiality and justice; justice is pre-eminent.

An ombudsman should hear and investigate complaints objectively. Objectivity includes impartial attention to all available perspectives on an issue and may or may no entail support of any particular perspective.

An ombudsman should act as independently as possible of all other offices and avoids conflict of interest, external control and either the reality or appearance of being compromised.

An ombudsman should be readily accessible to all members of the constituent community, promotes timely solutions to problems and avoids either the reality or appearance of bias toward any individual or group.

An ombudsman should treat with confidentiality all matters brought to him or her. No action is taken on a complaint without the complainant's permission. Information retained by the ombudsman is kept secure. However, with the verbal or written permission of the complainant, such information may be carried forward by the ombudsman.

If a complainant reports a serious problem but is unwilling to be part of any steps taken to address it, an ombudsman tries to find a way to address the problem that is acceptable to the complainant, or that does not compromise the identity of the complainant.

However, if an individual speaks about intending serious harm to himself or herself or others, or if the complainant confesses to serious misconduct or a crime, an ombudsman must use personal discretion in determining whether or not this information is carried forward. Discretion is likewise required in regard to matters governed by state and federal law.

An ombudsman should consider that confidentiality may preclude complying with requests for information in the context of formal proceedings on or off campus or required by law.

An ombudsman should be guided by a concern for the commitment to justice. Justice requires that an individuals interests be carefully balanced with the consideration of the good of the larger academic community. An ombudsman's commitment to justice includes the understanding of power, identification of the use and misuse of power and authority, and recognition of the need for access to power by the members of the institution.

Other concerns also govern an ombudsman's conduct. While it is the parties who are responsible for choosing a particular resolution, the ombudsman attempts to guide them toward options that are fair, conform with institutional policy, and give clear indication of being in their best interest. An ombudsman remembers, and at all times protects, the right to privacy of all parties, including the alleged offender. An ombudsman generally does not act on third-party complainants.

An ombudsman has a responsibility to maintain and improve professional skills, to assist in the development of new practitioners, and to promote impartial dispute resolution in the institution.

University and College Ombudsman Association

Appendix 5

International Ombudsman Association Code of Ethics and Standards of Practice

A. IOA CODE OF ETHICS
PREAMBLE

The IOA is dedicated to excellence in the practice of Ombudsman work. The IOA Code of Ethics provides a common set of professional ethical principles to which members adhere in their organizational Ombudsman practice.

Based on the traditions and values of Ombudsman practice, the Code of Ethics reflects a commitment to promote ethical conduct in the performance of the Ombudsman role and to maintain the integrity of the Ombudsman profession.

The Ombudsman shall be truthful and act with integrity, shall foster respect for all members of the organization he or she serves, and shall promote procedural fairness in the content and administration of those organizations' practices, processes, and policies.

Ethical Principles

INDEPENDENCE
The Ombudsman is independent in structure, function, and appearance to the highest degree possible within the organization.

NEUTRALITY AND IMPARTIALITY

The Ombudsman, as a designated neutral, remains unaligned and impartial. The Ombudsman does not engage in any situation which could create a conflict of interest.

CONFIDENTIALITY

The Ombudsman holds all communications with those seeking assistance in strict confidence, and does not disclose confidential communications unless given permission to do so. The only exception to this privilege of confidentiality is where there appears to be imminent risk of serious harm.

INFORMALITY

The Ombudsman, as an informal resource, does not participate in any formal adjudicative or administrative procedure related to concerns brought to his/her attention.

B. IOA STANDARDS OF PRACTICE
(in effect prior to October 2009)

Preamble

The IOA Standards of Practice are based upon and derived from the ethical principles stated in the IOA Code of Ethics. Each Ombudsman office should have an organizational Charter or Terms of Reference, approved by senior management, articulating the principles of the Ombudsman function in that organization and their consistency with the IOA Standards of Practice.

Standards of Practice

Independence

1.1 The Ombuds Office and the Ombuds are independent from other organizational entities.

1.2 The Ombuds holds no other position within the organization which might compromise independence.

1.3 The Ombuds exercises sole discretion over whether or how to act regarding an individual's concern, a trend or concerns of multiple individuals over time. The Ombuds may also initiate action on a concern identified through the Ombuds' direct observation.

1.4 The Ombuds has access to all information and all individuals in the organization, as permitted by law.

1.5 The Ombuds has authority to select Ombuds Office staff and manage Ombuds Office budget and operations.

Neutrality and Impartiality

2.1 The Ombuds is neutral, impartial, and unaligned.

2.2 The Ombuds strives for impartiality, fairness and objectivity in the treatment of people and the consideration of issues. The Ombuds advocates for fair and equitably administered processes and does not advocate on behalf of any individual within the organization.

2.3 The Ombuds is a designated neutral reporting to the highest possible level of the organization and operating independent of ordinary line and staff structures. The Ombuds should not report to nor be structurally affiliated with any compliance function of the organization.

2.4 The Ombuds serves in no additional role within the organization which would compromise the Ombuds' neutrality. The Ombuds should not be aligned with any formal or informal associations within the organization in a way that might create actual or perceived conflicts of interest for the Ombuds. The Ombuds should have no personal interest or stake in, and incur no gain or loss from, the outcome of an issue.

2.5 The Ombuds has a responsibility to consider the legitimate concerns and interests of all individuals affected by the matter under consideration.

2.6 The Ombuds helps develop a range of responsible options to resolve problems and facilitate discussion to identify the best options.

Confidentiality

3.1 The Ombuds holds all communications with those seeking assistance in strict confidence and takes all reasonable steps to safeguard confidentiality, including the following:

> The Ombuds does not disclose confidential communications unless given permission to do so in the course of informal discussions with the Ombuds, and even then at the sole discretion of the Ombuds; the Ombuds does not reveal, and must not be required to reveal, the identity of any individual contacting the Ombuds Office, nor does the Ombuds reveal infor-

mation provided in confidence that could lead to the identification of any individual contacting the Ombuds Office, without that individual's express permission; the Ombuds takes specific action related to an individual's issue only with the individual's express permission and only to the extent permitted, unless such action can be taken in a way that safeguards the identity of the individual contacting the Ombuds Office. The only exception to this privilege of confidentiality is where there appears to be imminent risk of serious harm, and where there is no other reasonable option. Whether this risk exists is a determination to be made by the Ombuds.

3.2 Communications between the Ombuds and others (made while the Ombuds is serving in that capacity) are considered privileged. The privilege belongs to the Ombuds and the Ombuds Office, rather than to any party to an issue. Others cannot waive this privilege.

3.3 The Ombuds does not testify in any formal process inside the organization and resists testifying in any formal process outside of the organization, even if given permission or requested to do so.

3.4 If the Ombuds pursues an issue systemically (e.g., provides feedback on trends, issues, policies and practices) the Ombuds does so in a way that safeguards the identity of individuals.

3.5 The Ombuds keeps no records containing identifying information on behalf of the organization.

3.6 The Ombuds maintains information (e.g., notes, phone messages, appointment calendars) in a secure location and manner, protected from inspection by others (including management), and has a consistent and standard practice for the destruction of such information.

3.7 The Ombuds prepares any data and/or reports in a manner that protects confidentiality.

3.8 Communications made to the ombudsman are not notice to the organization. The ombudsman neither acts as agent for, nor accepts notice on behalf of, the organization and shall not serve in a position or role that is designated by the organization as a place to receive notice on behalf of the organization. However, the ombudsman may refer individuals to the appropriate place where formal notice can be made.

Informality and Other Standards

4.1 The Ombuds functions on an informal basis by such means as: listening, providing and receiving information, identifying and reframing issues, developing a range of responsible options, and – with permission and at Ombuds discretion – engaging in informal third-party intervention. When possible, the Ombuds helps people develop new ways to solve problems themselves.

4.2 The Ombuds as an informal and off-the-record resource pursues resolution of concerns and looks into procedural irregularities and/or broader systemic problems when appropriate.

4.3 The Ombuds does not make binding decisions, mandate policies, or formally adjudicate issues for the organization.

4.4 The Ombuds supplements, but does not replace, any formal channels. Use of the Ombuds Office is voluntary, and is not a required step in any grievance process or organizational policy.

4.5 The Ombuds does not participate in any formal investigative or adjudicative procedures. Formal investigations should be conducted by others. When a formal investigation is requested, the Ombuds refers individuals to the appropriate offices or individual.

4.6 The Ombuds identifies trends, issues and concerns about policies and procedures, including potential future issues and concerns, without breaching confidentiality or anonymity, and provides recommendations for responsibly addressing them.

4.7 The Ombuds acts in accordance with the IOA Code of Ethics and Standards of Practice, keeps professionally current by pursuing continuing education, and provides opportunities for staff to pursue professional training.

4.8 The Ombuds endeavors to be worthy of the trust placed in the Ombuds Office.

C. IOA STANDARDS OF PRACTICE
(effective October 2009)

PREAMBLE

The IOA Standards of Practice are based upon and derived from the ethical principles stated in the IOA Code of Ethics.

Each Ombudsman office should have an organizational Charter or Terms of Reference, approved by senior management, articulating the principles of the Ombudsman function in that organization and their consistency with the IOA Standards of Practice.

STANDARDS OF PRACTICE

INDEPENDENCE

1.1 The Ombudsman Office and the Ombudsman are independent from other organizational entities.

1.2 The Ombudsman holds no other position within the organization which might compromise independence.

1.3 The Ombudsman exercises sole discretion over whether or how to act regarding an individual's concern, a trend or concerns of multiple individuals over time. The Ombudsman may also initiate action on a concern identified through the Ombudsman' direct observation,

1.4 The Ombudsman has access to all information and all individuals in the organization, as permitted by law.

1.5 The Ombudsman has authority to select Ombudsman Office staff and manage Ombudsman Office budget and operations.

NEUTRALITY AND IMPARTIALITY

2.1 The Ombudsman is neutral, impartial, and unaligned.

2.2 The Ombudsman strives for impartiality, fairness and objectivity in the treatment of people and the consideration of issues. The Ombudsman advocates for fair and equitably administered processes and does not advocate on behalf of any individual within the organization.

2.3 The Ombudsman is a designated neutral reporting to the highest possible level of the organization and operating independent of ordinary line and staff structures. The Ombudsman should not report to nor be structurally affiliated with any compliance function of the organization.

2.4 The Ombudsman serves in no additional role within the organization which would compromise the Ombudsman' neutrality. The Ombudsman should not be aligned with any formal or informal associations within the organization in a way that might create actual or perceived conflicts of interest for the Ombudsman. The Ombudsman should have no personal interest or stake in, and incur no gain or loss from, the outcome of an issue.

2.5 The Ombudsman has a responsibility to consider the legitimate concerns and interests of all individuals affected by the matter under consideration.

2.6 The Ombudsman helps develop a range of responsible options to resolve problems and facilitate discussion to identify the best options.

CONFIDENTIALITY

3.1 The Ombudsman holds all communications with those seeking assistance in strict confidence and takes all reasonable steps to safeguard confidentiality, including the following: The Ombudsman does not reveal, and must not be required to reveal, the identity of any individual contacting the Ombudsman Office, nor does the Ombudsman reveal information provided in confidence that could lead to the identification of any individual contacting the Ombudsman Office, without that individual's express permission, given in the course of informal discussions with the Ombudsman; the Ombudsman takes specific action related to an individual's issue only with the individual's express permission and only to the extent permitted, and even then at the sole discretion of the Ombudsman, unless such action can be taken in a way that safeguards the identity of the individual contacting the Ombudsman Office. The only exception to this privilege of confidentiality is where there appears to be imminent risk of serious harm, and where there is no other reasonable option. Whether this risk exists is a determination to be made by the Ombudsman.

3.2 Communications between the Ombudsman and others (made while the Ombudsman is serving in that capacity) are considered privileged. The privilege belongs to the Ombudsman and the Ombudsman Office, rather than to any party to an issue. Others cannot waive this privilege.

3.3 The Ombudsman does not testify in any formal process inside the organization and resists testifying in any formal process outside of the organization regarding a visitor's contact with the Ombudsman or confidential information communicated to the Ombudsman, even if given permission or requested to do so. The Ombudsman may, however, provide general, non-confidential information about the Ombudsman Office or the Ombudsman profession.

3.4 If the Ombudsman pursues an issue systemically (e.g., provides feedback on trends, issues, policies and practices) the Ombudsman does so in a way that safeguards the identity of individuals.

3.5 The Ombudsman keeps no records containing identifying information on behalf the organization.

3.6 The Ombudsman maintains information (e.g., notes, phone messages, appointment calendars) in a secure location and manner, protected from inspection by others (including management), and has a consistent and standard practice for the destruction of such information.

3.7 The Ombudsman prepares any data and/or reports in a manner that protects confidentiality.

3.8 Communications made to the ombudsman are not notice to the organization. The ombudsman neither acts as agent for, nor accepts notice on behalf of, the origination and shall not serve in a position or role that is designated by the organization as a place to receive notice on behalf of the organization. However, the ombudsman may refer individuals to the appropriate place where formal notice can be made.

INFORMALITY AND OTHER STANDARDS

4.1 The Ombudsman functions on an informal basis by such means as: listening, providing and receiving information, identifying and reframing issues, developing a range of responsible options, and — with permission and at Ombudsman discretion — engaging in informal third-party intervention. When possible, the Ombudsman helps people develop new ways to solve problems themselves.

4.2 The Ombudsman as an informal and off-the-record resource pursues resolution of concerns and looks into procedural irregularities and/or broader systemic problems when appropriate.

4.3 The Ombudsman does not make binding decisions, mandate policies, or formally adjudicate issues for the organization.

4.4 The Ombudsman supplements, but does not replace, any formal channels. Use of the Ombudsman Office is voluntary, and is not a required step in any grievance process or organizational policy.

4.5 The Ombudsman does not participate in any formal investigative or adjudicative procedures. Formal investigations should be conducted by others. When a formal investigation is requested, the Ombudsman refers individuals to the appropriate offices or individual.

4.6 The Ombudsman identifies trends, issues and concerns about policies and procedures, including potential future issues and concerns, without breaching confidentiality or anonymity, and provides recommendations for responsibly addressing them.

4.7 The Ombudsman acts in accordance with the IOA Code of Ethics and Standards of Practice, keeps professionally current by pursuing continuing education, and provides opportunities for staff to pursue professional training.

4.8 The Ombudsman endeavors to be worthy of the trust placed in the Ombudsman Office.

Appendix 6

Standards for the Establishment and Operation of Ombuds Offices ABA Policy Adopted August 2001

AMERICAN BAR ASSOCIATION

Section of Administrative Law and Regulatory Practice
740 15th Street NW
Washington, DC 20005-1022
(202) 662-1528
Fax: (202) 662-1529
www.abanet.org/adminlaw

January 2002

Re: Recommendation, Standards and Report
For The Establishment and Operation
of Ombuds Offices

Dear Colleague:

Government, academia, and the private sector are answering demands for fairness and responsiveness by establishing ombuds. Ombuds confidentially receive complaints or questions about alleged acts, omissions, improprieties, and broader, systemic problems within the ombuds's jurisdiction and address, investigate, or otherwise examine these issues independently and impartially. There are three basic types of ombuds: a "classical" ombuds receives complaints or inquiries from citizens about the functioning of the government, investigates the matter, and publishes a report making recommendations to resolve the issue. An "organizational" ombuds strives to resolve the multitude of issues that arise in the workplace. An "advocate" ombuds serves a designated vulnerable population and when justified by the facts of a particular case becomes an advocate on behalf of an individual member of that group.

While the basic authorities of these persons called ombuds and the independence, impartiality and confidentiality with which they operate vary markedly, they share essential characteristics which these standards address. To be credible and effective, the office of the ombuds must be independent in structure, form and appearance. The ombuds's structural independence is the foundation upon which the ombuds's impartiality is built. The ombuds must conduct investigations and inquiries in an impartial manner, free from initial bias and conflicts of interest. Confidentiality is a widely accepted characteristic of ombuds,

January, 2002
Page 2

which helps ombuds perform the functions of the office. In addition, these Standards address establishment and operations of ombuds, their qualifications, limitations on their authority, and removal from office.

The Standards for the Establishment and Operation of Ombuds Offices were initially prepared by a joint committee of the Sections of Administrative Law and Regulatory Practice and of Dispute Resolution. The committee consulted with numerous ombuds from Federal, state, and local agencies, academic institutions, companies, and non-profit organizations. Further, it solicited, received and considered comments from the international community of ombuds. The Standards were jointly sponsored by the Section of Administrative Law and Regulatory Practice, the Section of Dispute Resolution, the Commission on Legal Problems of the Elderly, the Section of Business Law, the Senior Lawyer Division, and the Government and Public Sector Lawyers Division. In August, 2001, the American Bar Association's House of Delegates adopted these Standards as Association Policy.

If an ombuds does not adhere to these Standards, individuals may be reluctant to seek the ombuds's assistance because of fear of personal, professional or economic retaliation, loss of privacy, and loss of relationships. The Standards for the Establishment and Operation of Ombuds Offices are appropriate to ensure that ombuds can help protect individual rights and interests against the excesses of public and private bureaucracies.

Ellen Waxman,
Immediate Past Chair
Ombuds Committee
Section of Dispute Resolution

Sharan Lee Levine, Chair
The Ombuds Committee
Section of Administrative
Law and Regulatory Practice

AMERICAN BAR ASSOCIATION
SECTION OF ADMINISTRATIVE LAW AND REGULATORY PRACTICE
SECTION OF BUSINESS LAW
SECTION OF DISPUTE RESOLUTION
SECTION OF STATE AND LOCAL GOVERNMENT LAW
GOVERNMENT LAW AND PUBLIC SECTOR LAWYERS DIVISION
SENIOR LAWYERS DIVISION
COMMISSION ON THE LEGAL PROBLEMS OF THE ELDERLY
NATIONAL CONFERENCE OF ADMINISTRATIVE LAW JUDGES
STANDING COMMITTEE ON ENVIRONMENTAL LAW

REPORT TO THE HOUSE OF DELEGATES

RECOMMENDATION

RESOLVED, that the American Bar Association supports the greater use of "ombuds" to receive, review, and resolve complaints involving public and private entities.

FURTHER RESOLVED, that the American Bar Association endorse the Standards for the Establishment and Operation of Ombuds Offices dated August 2001.

STANDARDS[1] FOR THE ESTABLISHMENT AND OPERATION OF OMBUDS OFFICES

PREAMBLE

Ombuds[2] receive complaints and questions from individuals concerning people within an entity or the functioning of an entity. They work for the resolution of particular issues and, where appropriate, make recommendations for the improvement of the general administration of the entities they serve. Ombuds protect: the legitimate interests and rights of individuals with respect to each other; individual rights against the excesses of public and private bureaucracies; and those who are affected by and those who work within these organizations.

Federal, state and local governments, academic institutions, for profit businesses, non-profit organizations, and sub-units of these entities have established ombuds offices, but with enormous variation in their duties and structures. Ombuds offices so established may be placed in several categories: A Classical Ombuds operates in the public sector addressing issues raised by the general public or internally, usually concerning the actions or policies of government entities or individuals. An Organizational Ombuds may be located in either the public or private sector and ordinarily addresses problems presented by members, employees, or contractors of an entity concerning its actions or policies. Both types may conduct inquiries or investigations and suggest modifications in policies or procedures. An Advocate Ombuds may be located in either the public or private sector and like the others evaluates claims objectively but is authorized or required to advocate on behalf of individuals or groups found to be aggrieved.

As a result of the various types of offices and the proliferation of different processes by which the offices operate, individuals who come to the ombuds office for assistance may not know what to expect, and

---

1. These standards expand on a 1969 ABA resolution to address independence, impartiality, and confidentiality as essential characteristics of ombuds who serve internal constituents, ombuds in the private sector, and ombuds who also serve as advocates for designated populations.

2. The term ombuds in this report is intended to encompass all other forms of the word, such as ombudsperson, ombuds officer, and ombudsman, a Swedish word meaning agent or representative. The use of ombuds here is not intended to discourage others from using other terms.

the offices may be established in ways that compromise their effectiveness. These standards were developed to provide advice and guidance on the structure and operation of ombuds offices so that ombuds may better fulfill their functions and so that individuals who avail themselves of their aid may do so with greater confidence in the integrity of the process. Practical and political considerations may require variations from these Standards, but it is urged that such variations be eliminated over time.

The essential characteristics of an ombuds are:

- independence
- impartiality in conducting inquiries and investigations, and
- confidentiality.

ESTABLISHMENT AND OPERATIONS

A. An entity undertaking to establish an ombuds should do so pursuant to a legislative enactment or a publicly available written policy (the "charter") which clearly sets forth the role and jurisdiction of the ombuds and which authorizes the ombuds to:

(1) receive complaints and questions about alleged acts, omissions, improprieties, and systemic problems within the ombuds' jurisdiction as defined in the charter establishing the office
(2) exercise discretion to accept or decline to act on a complaint or question
(3) act on the ombuds' own initiative to address issues within the ombuds' prescribed jurisdiction
(4) operate by fair and timely procedures to aid in the just resolution of a complaint or problem
(5) gather relevant information
(6) resolve issues at the most appropriate level of the entity
(7) function by such means as:
 (a) conducting an inquiry
 (b) investigating and reporting findings
 (c) developing, evaluating, and discussing options available to affected individuals
 (d) facilitating, negotiating, and mediating

(e) making recommendations for the resolution of an individual complaint or a systemic problem to those persons who have the authority to act upon them
(f) identifying complaint patterns and trends
(g) educating
(h) issuing periodic reports, and
(i) advocating on behalf of affected individuals or groups when specifically authorized by the charter

(8) initiate litigation to enforce or protect the authority of the office as defined by the charter, as otherwise provided by these standards, or as required by law.

QUALIFICATIONS

B. An ombuds should be a person of recognized knowledge, judgment, objectivity, and integrity. The establishing entity should provide the ombuds with relevant education and the periodic updating of the ombuds' qualifications.

INDEPENDENCE, IMPARTIALITY, AND CONFIDENTIALITY

C. To ensure the effective operation of an ombuds, an entity should authorize the ombuds to operate consistently with the following essential characteristics. Entities that have established ombuds offices that lack appropriate safeguards to maintain these characteristics should take prompt steps to remedy any such deficiency.

(1) *Independence*. The ombuds is and appears to be free from interference in the legitimate performance of duties and independent from control, limitation, or a penalty imposed for retaliatory purposes by an official of the appointing entity or by a person who may be the subject of a complaint or inquiry.

In assessing whether an ombuds is independent in structure, function, and appearance, the following factors are important: whether anyone subject to the ombuds' jurisdiction or anyone directly responsible for a person under the ombuds' jurisdiction (a) can control or limit the ombuds' performance of assigned duties or (b) can, for retaliatory purposes, (1) eliminate the office, (2) remove the ombuds, or (3) reduce the budget or resources of the office.

(2) Impartiality in Conducting Inquiries and Investigations. The ombuds conducts inquiries and investigations in an impartial manner, free from initial bias and conflicts of interest. Impartiality does not preclude the ombuds from developing an interest in securing changes that are deemed necessary as a result of the process, nor from otherwise being an advocate on behalf of a designated constituency. The ombuds may become an advocate within the entity for change where the process demonstrates a need for it.

(3) Confidentiality. An ombuds does not disclose and is not required to disclose any information provided in confidence, except to address an imminent risk of serious harm. Records pertaining to a complaint, inquiry, or investigation are confidential and not subject to disclosure outside the ombuds's office. An ombuds does not reveal the identity of a complainant without that person's express consent. An ombuds may, however, at the ombuds's discretion disclose non-confidential information and may disclose confidential information so long as doing so does not reveal its source. An ombuds should discuss any exceptions to the ombuds's maintaining confidentiality with the source of the information.[3]

LIMITATIONS ON THE OMBUDS'S AUTHORITY

D. An ombuds should not, nor should an entity expect or authorize an ombuds to:

(1) make, change or set aside a law, policy, or administrative decision

(2) make binding decisions or determine rights

(3) directly compel an entity or any person to implement the ombuds' recommendations

---

3. A classical ombuds should not be required to discuss confidentiality with government officials and employees when applying this paragraph to the extent that an applicable statute makes clear that such an individual may not withhold information from the ombuds and that such a person has no reasonable expectation of confidentiality with respect to anything that person provides to the ombuds.

(4) conduct an investigation that substitutes for administrative or judicial proceedings

(5) accept jurisdiction over an issue that is currently pending in a legal forum unless all parties and the presiding officer in that action explicitly consent

(6) address any issue arising under a collective bargaining agreement or which falls within the purview of any existing federal, state, or local labor or employment law, rule, or regulation, unless the ombuds is authorized to do so by the collective bargaining agreement or unless the collective bargaining representative and the employing entity jointly agree to allow the ombuds to do so, or if there is no collective bargaining representative, the employer specifically authorizes the ombuds to do so, or

(7) act in a manner inconsistent with the grant of and limitations on the jurisdiction of the office when discharging the duties of the office of ombuds.

REMOVAL FROM OFFICE

E. The charter that establishes the office of the ombuds should also provide for the discipline or removal of the ombuds from office for good cause by means of a fair procedure.

NOTICE

F. These standards do not address the issue whether a communication to the ombuds will be deemed notice to anyone else including any entity in or for which the ombuds acts. Important legal rights and liabilities may be affected by the notice issue.

CLASSICAL OMBUDS

G. A classical ombuds is a public sector ombuds who receives complaints from the general public or internally and addresses actions and failures to act of a government agency, official, or public employee. In addition to and in clarification of the standards contained in Paragraphs A-F, a classical ombuds:

(1) should be authorized to conduct independent and impartial investigations into matters within the prescribed jurisdiction of the office

(2) should have the power to issue subpoenas for testimony and evidence with respect to investigating allegations within the jurisdiction of the office

(3) should be authorized to issue public reports

(4) should be authorized to advocate for change both within the entity and publicly

(5) should, if the ombuds has general jurisdiction over two or more agencies, be established by legislation[4] and be viewed as a part of and report to the legislative branch of government.

ORGANIZATIONAL OMBUDS

H. An organizational ombuds facilitates fair and equitable resolutions of concerns that arise within the entity. In addition to and in clarification of the standards contained in Paragraphs A-F, an organizational ombuds should:

(1) be authorized to undertake inquiries and function by informal processes as specified by the charter

(2) be authorized to conduct independent and impartial inquiries into matters within the prescribed jurisdiction of the office

(3) be authorized to issue reports

(4) be authorized to advocate for change within the entity.

ADVOCATE OMBUDS

I. An advocate ombuds serves as an advocate on behalf of a population that is designated in the charter. In addition to and in clarification of the standards described in Paragraphs A-F, an advocate ombuds should:

---

4. The 1969 ABA Resolution, which remains ABA policy, provided that a classical ombuds should be "appoint[ed] by the legislative body or . . . by the executive with confirmation by the designated proportion of the legislative body, preferably more than a majority, such as two thirds."

(1) have a basic understanding of the nature and role of advocacy

(2) provide information, advice, and assistance to members of the constituency

(3) evaluate the complainant's claim objectively and advocate for change relief when the facts support the claim

(4) be authorized to represent the interests of the designated population with respect to policies implemented or adopted by the establishing entity, government agencies, or other organizations as defined by the charter, and

(5) be authorized to initiate action in an administrative, judicial, or legislative forum when the facts warrant.

REPORT

The American Bar Association (ABA) adopted a resolution in 1969 recommending that state and local governments consider establishing ombuds who would be authorized to inquire into administrative action and to make public criticism. That policy also recommended that the statute or ordinance creating the ombuds contain twelve essential points. The ABA then adopted a resolution in 1971 recommending that the Federal government experiment with the establishment of ombudsmen for certain geographical areas, specific agencies, or for limited phases of Federal activities.

Over the past three decades, and particularly recently, an extraordinary growth in the number and type of ombuds[5] has taken place. Congress has established several ombuds in various programs. In addition to specific legislation concerning ombuds, the Administrative Dispute Resolution Act authorizes Federal agencies to use "ombuds."

Federal, state and local governments, academic institutions, for profit businesses, non-profit organizations, and sub-units of these entities have established ombuds offices, but with enormous variation in their duties and structures. Ombuds offices so established may be placed in several categories. A Classical Ombuds operates in the public sector addressing issues raised by the general public or internally, usually concerning the actions or policies of government entities or individuals. An Organizational Ombuds may be located in either the public or private sector and ordinarily addresses problems presented by members, employees, or contractors of an entity concerning its actions or policies. Both types may conduct inquiries or investigations and suggest modifications in policies or procedures. An Advocate Ombuds may be located in either the public or private sector, and like the others evaluates claims objectively but is authorized or required to advocate on behalf of individuals or groups found to be aggrieved.

As a result of the various types of offices and the proliferation of different processes by which the offices operate, individuals who come

---

5. The term ombuds in this report is intended to encompass all other forms of the word such as ombudsperson, ombuds officers, and ombudsman, a Swedish word meaning agent or representative. The use of ombuds here is not intended to discourage others from using other terms.

to the ombuds's office for assistance may not know what to expect, and the offices may be established in ways that compromise their effectiveness. These standards were developed to provide advice and guidance on the structure and operation of ombuds offices to the end that ombuds may better fulfill their functions and so that individuals who avail themselves of their aid may do so with greater confidence in the integrity of the process.

The ABA's Board of Governors establishes legislative and governmental priorities annually. Based on its importance to society, to the practice of law, and in the administration of justice, one of the year 2001 priorities is alternative dispute resolution. The ABA supports the greater use of alternative dispute resolution by private parties, government agencies, and the courts "as a necessary and welcome component of America's civil justice system, so long as all parties' legal rights and remedies are protected." As a protector of individual rights against the excesses of public and private bureaucracies, an ombuds receives complaints and questions from individuals concerning the functioning of an entity, works for the resolution of particular issues, and where necessary, makes recommendations for the improvement of the general administration of the entity. As an independent, impartial, and confidential complaint handler, an ombuds serves as an alternative means of dispute resolution—a means by which issues may be raised, considered, and resolved.

Consistent with ABA priorities, the Sections of Administrative Law and Regulatory Practice and of Dispute Resolution have worked together and appointed a steering committee consisting of representatives from the Coalition of Federal Ombudsmen, the National Association of State Ombudsman Programs, the International Ombudsman Institute (IOI subsequently withdrew), The Ombudsman Association, the United States Ombudsman Association, and the University and College Ombuds Association, as well as other experts in the field. The committee consulted with numerous ombuds from Federal, state, and local agencies, academic institutions, companies, and non-profit organizations. Further, it solicited, received, and considered comments from the international community of ombuds. Based on the steering committee's work and following extensive consultation with the Commission on Legal Problems of the Elderly, the Section of Business

Law, and the Section of Labor and Employment Law, the Sections of Administrative Law and Regulatory Practice and Dispute Resolution have developed a resolution encouraging the use of ombuds in the public and private sectors that adhere to the Standards for the Establishment and Operation of the Ombudsman Offices (Standards).

The Resolution and Standards broaden the ABA's existing policy to address ombuds who are appointed within government, academia, and the private sector, and who respond to complaints from individuals from within and outside the entity. Further, they clarify the means by which various types of ombuds operate.

For Federal, state, and local governments that want to create a Classical ombuds who would be authorized to address, investigate or inquire into administrative action and to criticize agencies, officials, and public employees, the ABA's 1969 policy continue to serve as a model.[6]

---

6. The twelve essential characteristics that were identified in the original ABA resolution continue to have vitality and remain ABA policy. They are: (1) authority of the ombudsman to criticize all agencies, officials, and public employees except courts and their personnel, legislative bodies and their personnel, and the chief executive and his personal staff; (2) independence of the ombudsman from control by any other officer, except for his responsibility to the legislative body; (3) appointment by the legislative body or appointment by the executive with confirmation by the designated proportion of the legislative body, preferably more than a majority of the legislative body, such as two thirds; (4) independence of the ombudsman through a long term, not less than five years, with freedom from removal except for cause, determined by more than a majority of the legislative body; (5) a high salary equivalent to that of a designated top officer; (6) freedom of the ombudsman to employ his own assistants and to delegate to them, without restrictions of civil service and classifications acts; (7) freedom of the ombudsman to investigate any act or failure to act by any agency, official, or public employee; (8) access of the ombudsman to all public records he finds relevant to an investigation; (9) authority to inquire into fairness, correctness of findings, motivation, adequacy of reasons, efficiency, and procedural propriety of any action or inaction by any agency, official, or public employee; (10) discretionary power to determine what complaints to investigate and to determine what criticisms to make or to publicize; (11) opportunity for any agency, official, or public employee criticized by the ombudsman to have advance notice of the criticism and to publish with the criticism an answering statement; and, (12) immunity of the ombudsman and his staff from civil liability on account of official action.

This Resolution and the Standards clarify that independence, impartiality in conducting inquiries and investigations, and confidentiality are essential characteristics of all ombuds. Ombuds must operate consistently with these essential characteristics to discharge the duties of the office effectively. Practical and political considerations may require variations from these Standards, but it is urged that such variations be eliminated over time.

THE RESOLUTION

The resolution recognizes the value of the ombuds in the public and private sectors. For example, the Organizational Ombuds in one prominent company resolves several hundred workplace matters every year; that experience is echoed by other companies and increasingly by government agencies and academic institutions. Classical Ombuds have investigated and issued reports on important issues that need to be addressed by the body politic; a recent prominent example concerned prison conditions. Advocate Ombuds have been successful in protecting vulnerable populations, such as children and residents of nursing homes. As a result, the Resolution recognizes the contribution these offices make in providing a means by which complaints are received, the underlying facts developed through an informal inquiry or a more formal investigation, and those complaints found to have merit are suitably addressed in a means that fits the situation. The Resolution, therefore, supports the greater use of ombuds.

The Resolution also recognizes that entities that create ombuds offices should adhere to the Standards for the establishment and operations of the ombuds offices. The fundamental underlying premise of this resolution is that all ombuds must operate with certain basic authorities and essential characteristics. The effort here is to provide practical advice and guidance on the structure and operation of ombuds offices so that ombuds may better fulfill their functions and so that individuals who avail themselves of their aid may do so with greater confidence in the integrity of the process.

STANDARDS

Section A. Establishment and Operations

An ombuds is a person who is authorized to receive complaints or questions confidentially about alleged acts, omissions, improprieties, and broader, systemic problems within the ombuds's defined jurisdiction and to address, investigate, or otherwise examine these issues independently and impartially.

Importantly, the ombuds's jurisdiction—who complains and who or what are complained about—needs to be defined in advance, setting out the scope of the duties and authority. The ombuds's jurisdiction must be defined in an official act that establishes the office, which is appropriately called the "charter" in the standards. The charter may be a legislative enactment[7] or a publicly available written policy. The jurisdiction may be limited to a defined constituency or population. For example, a state ombuds may receive complaints or questions from any person, while a university student ombuds may receive complaints or questions only from students at that university, and a long-term care ombuds has jurisdiction only to resolve complaints initiated by or on behalf of residents receiving long-term care.

The ombuds determines whether to accept or to act on a particular complaint or question. The ombuds also has the discretion to initiate action without receiving a complaint or question. An ombuds may determine that the complaint is without merit. Or, an ombuds may receive a complaint or question on a specific topic and conduct an inquiry on a broader or different scope.

Appropriate subjects for an ombuds to review include allegations of unfairness, maladministration, abuse of power, abuse of discretion, discourteous behavior or incivility, inappropriate application of law or policy, inefficiency, decision unsupported by fact, and illegal or inappropriate behavior. It is essential that the ombuds operate by fair procedures to aid in the just resolution of the matter. Ombuds need access to all information relevant to a complaint or a question so that the review is fair and credible, and the charter should authorize access to all relevant information. The entity must be responsible for protecting those seeking assistance from or providing information to the ombuds from personal, professional, or economic retaliation, loss of privacy, or loss of relationships.

---

7. The "legislative enactment" might be in a constitution, statute, local government charter, or local ordinance depending on the establishing jurisdiction.

An ombuds may make a formal or informal report of results and recommendations stemming from a review or investigation. If such a report is issued, the ombuds should generally consult with an individual or group prior to issuing a report critical of that individual or group, and include their comments with the report. Moreover, the ombuds should communicate the outcome, conclusion or resolution of a complaint or an inquiry to the complainant and may also communicate with other concerned entities or individuals.

In addition, to ensure the office's accountability, an ombuds should issue and publish periodic reports summarizing the ombuds's findings and activities. This may include statistical information about the number of contacts with the ombuds, subjects that the ombuds addressed, evaluation by complainants, etc. These reports may be done annually, biannually, or more frequently.

In receiving complaints or questions and examining problems, the ombuds may use a variety of dispute resolution and other techniques. These processes include: conducting an inquiry; investigating and reporting findings; developing, evaluating, and discussing the options which may be available for remedies or redress; facilitating, negotiating, and mediating; making recommendations for the resolution of an individual complaint or a systemic problem to those persons who have authority to act on them; identifying complaint patterns and trends; and educating.

As necessary, the ombuds may advocate on behalf of affected individuals or groups when authorized by the charter and the situation warrants that action. An ombuds may initiate litigation to enforce or protect the authority of the office. For example, if an ombuds issues a subpoena and the subpoena is ignored, the ombuds should be able to initiate litigation to compel a response. In addition, an ombuds may initiate litigation as otherwise provided by these standards or as required by law. For example, an advocate ombuds should be authorized to initiate action in an administrative, judicial, or legislative forum when the facts warrant.

An ombuds uses the powers of reason and persuasion to help resolve matters. The goal of the ombuds's efforts is to provide a path to fairness and justice. Therefore, the ombuds's quest is to seek the fair and just resolution of the matter.

Section B. Qualifications

An ombuds should be a person of recognized knowledge, judgment, objectivity, and integrity. The establishing entity should provide the ombuds with relevant education and the periodic updating of the ombuds's qualifications.

Section C. The Essential Characteristics

The original 1969 resolution contained twelve essentials for the ombuds described in it. These have been distilled and expanded in the Standards. The core qualities are independence, impartiality in conducting inquiries and investigations, and confidentiality. Without them, an ombuds cannot discharge the duties of the office effectively. The Standards therefore provide that an entity should authorize an ombuds it establishes to operate consistently with these essential characteristics to ensure the effective operation of the duties of the office. The Standards also recognize, however, that some entities may have already established offices that lack appropriate safeguards to comply fully with the characteristics. The Standards then provide that such entities should take prompt steps to remedy any such deficiency.

1. Independence in structure, function, and appearance

To be credible and effective, the office of the ombuds is independent in its structure, function, and appearance. Independence means that the ombuds is free from interference in the legitimate performance of duties and independent from control, limitation, or a penalty imposed for retaliatory purposes by an official of the appointing entity or by a person who may be the subject of a complaint or inquiry. In assessing whether an ombuds is independent, the following factors are important: whether anyone subject to the ombuds's jurisdiction or anyone directly responsible for a person under the ombuds's jurisdiction (a) can control or limit the ombuds's performance of duties, or (b) can, for retaliatory purposes, (1) eliminate the office, (2) remove the ombuds, or (3) reduce the office's budget or resources.

Historically, ombuds were created in parliamentary systems and were established in the constitution or by statute, appointed by the legislative body, and had a guarantee of independence from the control of any other officer, except for responsibility to the legislative body. This structure remains a model for ensuring independence, and a number of states have followed it. In more recent times, however, ombuds have been created by public officials without legislation, by regulation or decree, and by private entities. Ensuring the independence of the ombuds is equally important in these instances, but will require other measures.[8]

Great care has to be exercised in establishing the ombuds structure to ensure that the independence described in the resolution is, in fact, achieved. Choosing which of these approaches are appropriate will depend on the environment. The instrument used to establish independence should be the strongest available and should guarantee the independence of the ombuds from control by any other person.

The twelve essential characteristics of the 1969 ABA Resolution continue to serve as the model for an ombuds reporting to the legislative branch of government who is authorized to investigate administrative action, help provide legislative oversight, and offer criticism of agencies from an external perspective. While there are a number of potential avenues of achieving independence, experience on the state and local level has demonstrated rather consistently that unless there is a

---

8. In the United States since the late 1960s, a number of other ways have been developed to ensure independence. Examples of approaches that contribute to an ombuds's independence include: establishment of the office through a formal act of a legislature or official governing body of an organization; establishment outside the entity over which the ombuds has jurisdiction; a direct reporting relationship to a legislative body, the official governing body of an organization or the chief executive; designation as a neutral who is unaligned and objective; a broadly defined jurisdiction not limited to one part of the entity or one subject matter; appointment or removal of the ombuds free of influence from potential subjects of a complaint or inquiry; a set term of office; no reporting relationship to someone with assigned duties that conflict with the ombuds's role; no assignment of duties other than that of the ombuds function; specifically allocated budget and sufficient resources to perform the function; freedom to appoint, direct, and remove staff; sufficient stature in the organization to be taken seriously by senior officials; placement in an organization at the highest possible level and at least above the heads of units likely to generate the most complaints; discretion to initiate and pursue complaints and inquiries; access to and resources for independent legal advice and counsel; prohibition of disciplinary actions against the ombuds for performing the duties of the office; removal only for cause; provision of an employment contract that the ombuds will receive a significant severance provision if terminated without good cause.

structural independence for these ombuds akin to the 1969 ABA Resolution that independence will not be accomplished and the office will not be able to function as envisioned in this resolution and the accompanying standards.

Structuring independence for ombuds who serve inside organizations and classical ombuds who address issues within a single program or agency require similar care. These elements should be in the charter. The ombuds position should be explicitly defined and established as a matter of organizational policy, authorized at the highest levels of the organization; the ombuds should have access to the chief executive officer, senior officers and the oversight body or board of directors of the organization; the ombuds should also have access to all information within the organization, except as restricted by law; and the ombuds should have access to resources for independent legal advice and counsel.

The Standards recognize that at this time there are ombuds who have not achieved this goal. The Standards urge and anticipate that these variations will be eliminated over time.

2. Impartiality in conducting inquiries and investigations

The ombuds's structural independence is the foundation upon which the ombuds's impartiality is built. If the ombuds is independent from line management and does not have administrative or other obligations or functions, the ombuds can act in an impartial manner.

Acting in an impartial manner, as a threshold matter, means that the ombuds is free from initial bias and conflicts of interest in conducting inquiries and investigations. Acting in an impartial manner also requires that the ombuds be authorized to gather facts from relevant sources and apply relevant policies, guidelines, and laws, considering the rights and interests of all affected parties within the jurisdiction, to identify appropriate actions to address or resolve the issue.

The ombuds conducts inquiries and investigations in an impartial manner. An ombuds may determine that a complaint is without merit and close the inquiry or investigation without further action. If the ombuds finds that the complaint has merit, the ombuds makes recommendations to the entity and/or seeks resolution for a fair outcome. Impartiality does not, however, preclude the ombuds from developing an interest in securing the changes that are deemed necessary where the process demonstrates a need for change nor from otherwise being an advocate on behalf of a designated constituency. The ombuds therefore has the authority to become an advocate for change where the results of the inquiry or investigation demonstrate the need for such change. For example, when an ombuds identifies a systemic problem, it would be appropriate for the ombuds to advocate for changes to correct the problem. An advocate ombuds may initiate action and therefore serve as an advocate on behalf of a designated population with respect to a broad range of issues and on specific matters when the individual or group is found to be aggrieved. But, when determining the facts, the ombuds must act impartially.

3. Confidentiality

Confidentiality is an essential characteristic of ombuds that permits the process to work effectively. Confidentiality promotes disclosure from reluctant complainants, elicits candid discussions by all parties, and provides an increased level of protection against retaliation to or by any party. Confidentiality is a further factor that distinguishes ombuds from others who receive and consider complaints such as elected officials, human resource personnel, government officials, and ethics officers.

Confidentiality extends to all communications with the ombuds[9] and to all notes and records maintained by the ombuds in the performance of assigned duties. It begins when a communication is initiated with the ombuds to schedule an appointment or make a complaint or inquiry. Confidentiality may apply to the source of the communications and to the content of the communications. Individuals may not want the ombuds to disclose their identity but may want the ombuds to act on the information presented. Therefore, an ombuds does not reveal the identity of a complainant without that person's consent. The

---

9. For example, the Model Ombudsman Statute for State Governments that was developed by the Ombudsman Committee of the Section of Administrative Law and Regulatory Practice in 1974 directs the ombudsman to "maintain secrecy in respect to all matters and the identities of the complainants or witnesses coming before him." See, Bernard Frank, *State Ombudsman Legislation in the United States,* 29 U. Miami L.R. 379 (1975).

ombuds may, however, disclose confidential information so long as doing so does not compromise the identity of the person who supplied it. It should be emphasized that the decision whether or not to disclose this information belongs to the ombuds, and it would not be appropriate for anyone to demand that the ombuds disclose such information, except as required by statute. To the extent that an ombuds may not maintain confidentiality, the ombuds should discuss those exceptions with individuals who communicate with the office.

The authorizing entity should allow the ombuds to provide confidentiality of the identity of persons who communicate with the ombuds and of information provided in confidence. The authorizing entity should not seek information relating to the identity of complainants nor seek access to the ombuds's notes and records.

Providing for confidentiality and protection from subpoena in a statute is particularly important because, where statutes have not provided confidentiality, state courts have not consistently recognized an ombuds privilege nor granted protective orders to preserve the confidentiality of communication made to ombuds. One Federal district court, *Shabazz v. Scurr*, 662 F. Supp. 90 (S.D. Iowa 1987), recognized a limited privilege under Federal law for an ombuds with a state statutory privilege. The only Federal circuit court to have addressed the issue, *Carman v. McDonnell Douglas Corp.*, 114 F. 3d 790 (8th Cir. 1997), failed to recognize an ombuds privilege.

Short of explicit statutory authority, ombuds offices should adopt written policies that provide the fullest confidentiality within the law. These policies should be publicly available, broadly disseminated, and widely publicized. Several existing model ombuds acts and policies of ombuds organizations address confidentiality.

An ombuds will rarely, if ever, be privy to something that no one else knows. Therefore, providing confidentiality protection to the ombuds allows the ombuds to perform assigned duties while at the same time, society continues to have access to the underlying facts. As evidenced by the statutes and policies that have been developed, there may be instances in which other, competing societal interests dictate that the ombuds must disclose some information. If an individual speaks about intending harm to himself or herself or others, an entity may require an ombuds to disclose this information. Moreover, an ombuds may be compelled by protective service laws or professional reporting requirements to report suspected abuse.

Section D. Limitations on the ombuds' authority

An ombuds works outside of line management structures and has no direct power to compel any decision. The office is established by the charter with the stature to engender trust and to help resolve complaints at the most appropriate level of the entity. To ensure the ombuds' independence, impartiality, and confidentiality, it is necessary to establish certain limitations on the ombuds' authority.

An ombuds should not, nor should an entity expect or authorize an ombuds to make, change, or set aside a law, policy or administrative/managerial decision, nor to directly compel an entity or any person to make those changes. While an ombuds may expedite and facilitate the resolution of a complaint and recommend individual and systemic changes, an ombuds cannot compel an entity to implement the recommendations.

It is essential that an ombuds operate by fair procedures which means that the actions taken will likely vary with the nature of the concern, and that care must be taken to protect the rights of those who may be affected by the actions of an ombuds. Furthermore, since due process rights could well be implicated, it would not be appropriate for the ombuds's review to serve as the final determination for any disciplinary activity or civil action, nor as a determination of a violation of law or policy. An ombuds's inquiry or investigation does not substitute for an administrative or judicial proceeding. In an administrative or judicial proceeding, the deciding official should not consider the ombuds's review or recommendations to be controlling. Rather, the deciding official must conduct a de novo examination of the matter.

Moreover, it would not be appropriate for the ombuds to act as an appellate forum when a complainant is dissatisfied with the results in a formal adjudicatory or administrative proceeding. Thus, an ombuds should not take up a specific issue that is pending in a legal forum without the concurrence of the parties and the presiding officer. It may, however, be fully appropriate for an ombuds to inquire into matters that are related to a controversy that is in litigation so long as they are not the subject of the suit.

Further, an ombuds should not address, nor should an entity expect or authorize an ombuds to address, any issue that is the subject of a collective bargaining agreement. There are two potential exceptions to this general prohibition: An ombuds may address issues concerning employees who have a lawfully designated collective bargaining agreement if: (1) the ombuds is authorized to do so by the collective bargaining agreement covering the employees or (2) the collective bargaining representative and the employing entity jointly agree to allow the ombuds to do so.

Even where there is no collective bargaining agreement, the involvement of an ombuds in matters that fall within the purview of labor or employment laws raises sensitive issues that may implicate the rights and liabilities of the parties under those laws, such as the issue of notice mentioned in Section F of the Standards. Accordingly, the Standards contemplate that an employer, in establishing an ombuds office, should consider its overall policies for maintaining compliance with those laws, and determine in that light whether to authorize the ombuds to address those matters. That recommendation is in no way intended to suggest, however, that a policy of authorizing an ombuds to address labor- or employment-related matters should be a suspect or disfavored practice. On the contrary, involvement in such matters is a role typically performed by Organizational Ombuds, and the growing reliance on ombuds at institutions across the country is largely attributable to the broad satisfaction with ombuds' fulfillment of that role on the part of both management and the affected employees. Thus, the language in the Standards indicating that an employer should specifically authorize an ombuds to address labor- or employment-related matters does not require any detailed or ponderous recitals. Rather, it should be read as simply a particularized application of the generalized expectation in Section A of the Standards that the jurisdiction of an ombuds office should be identified in its charter.

Finally, an ombuds should not act in a manner inconsistent with the grant and limitations on the jurisdiction of the office when discharging the duties of the office of ombuds.

Section E. Removal from office

Entities which establish ombuds offices need to ensure their accountability. Therefore, the charter that establishes the office of ombuds should also provide for the discipline or removal of the ombuds for good cause by means of a fair procedure.

Section F. Notice

When meeting with an ombuds, people discuss allegations of unfairness, maladministration, abuse of power, and other sensitive subjects. They may fear personal, professional, or economic retaliation, loss of privacy, and loss of relationships. Faced with sexual or racial harassment, for example, many people will quit, get sick, or suffer in silence. People often need help in developing ways to report or act so that these matters will be considered and resolved.

Communications must be protected if people are to be willing to visit and speak candidly with the ombuds. As noted above, some ombuds have confidentiality protected by law. Under these Standards, entities that establish an ombuds should authorize the ombuds to operate with confidentiality and independence. If an ombuds functions in accordance with these Standards by operating with confidentiality and independence, it can be strongly argued that management lacks the control over day to day operations that is essential for someone to be deemed an agent. Likewise, there would be a strong argument that any communication to the ombuds should not be imputed to any other person, including the entity. Rather, the ombuds would be deemed independent of the entity itself for these purposes. Thus, it would not be appropriate for the ombuds to accept notice on the entity's behalf with respect to any alleged grievance.

However, some ombuds offices that have been instituted outside the framework of these Standards do not operate with confidentiality or independence. In some cases, management's control over the ombuds may be so extensive as to weaken substantially the argument that the office cannot be deemed to be an agent of management. This circumstance would, in turn, give force to the argument that a communication to the ombuds should be imputed to management.

Because the law in this area is continuing to evolve, it is unclear what a court might decide with regard to notice in the wide range of circumstances that may arise. These Standards, therefore, do not address the issue of whether a communication to the ombuds will be deemed notice to anyone, including any entity in or for which the ombuds acts.

Important legal rights and liabilities may, however, be affected by the resolution of that issue. Accordingly, an ombuds should, in appropriate circumstances, advise an individual that, unless the individual authorizes the ombuds to inform the management of an entity about a matter, the entity may not be deemed to have notice of the matter and such failure to give notice to the entity about the matter might impair the individual's legal rights.

Section G. Classical Ombuds

A Classical Ombuds operates in the public sector addressing issues raised by the general public or internally, usually concerning the actions or policies of government entities or individuals. A Classical Ombuds may conduct inquiries or investigations and suggest modifications in policies or procedures. To ensure access to all pertinent facts, a Classical Ombuds should be granted subpoena power for testimony and evidence relevant to an investigation. In addition, a Classical Ombuds should be authorized to issues public reports and to advocate for change both within the entity and publicly. To ensure the essential independence, the standards provide that whenever a classical ombuds has general jurisdiction over two or more agencies, that position should be established by legislative action and the ombuds should be regarded as part of the legislative branch of government. Thus, for example, it would be appropriate for an agency to establish an ombuds who has jurisdiction over a single program, but the agency should provide the essential independence in the charter establishing the program. To the extent that an agency has established ombuds offices with jurisdiction over a single agency or program but that do not comply with the essential characteristics as described in Paragraph C of the Standards, it should take prompt steps to remedy any deficiency and to provide the requisite independence. If, however, the ombuds has jurisdiction over multiple agencies, experience has shown that it is extraordinarily difficult to provide independence if the ombuds reports to someone in the executive branch.

Section H. Organizational Ombuds

An Organizational Ombuds ordinarily addresses problems presented by members, employees or contractors of an entity concerning its actions or policies. An Organizational Ombuds may undertake inquiries and advocate for modifications in policies or procedures.

Section I. Advocate Ombuds

The Advocate Ombuds may be located in either the public or private sectors, and like the Classical and Organizational Ombuds, also evaluates claims objectively. However, unlike other ombuds, the Advocate Ombuds is authorized or required to advocate on behalf of individuals or groups found to be aggrieved. Because of the unique role, the Advocate Ombuds must have a basic understanding of the nature and role of advocacy. In addition, the Advocate Ombuds should provide information, advice, and assistance to members of the population identified in the law or publicly available written policy. Further, the Advocate Ombuds represents the interests of a designated population with respect to policies implemented or adopted by the establishing entity and government agencies.

CONCLUSION

Government, academia, and the private sector are answering demands for fairness and responsiveness by establishing ombuds. Ombuds receive complaints and questions concerning the administration of the establishing entity. However, the basic authorities of these persons called ombuds and the independence, impartiality, and confidentiality with which they operate vary markedly. An ombuds works for the resolution of a particular issue, and where necessary, makes recommendations for the improvement of the general administration of the entity. To be credible and effective, the office of the ombuds must be independent in structure, form, and appearance. The ombuds's structural independence is the foundation upon which the ombuds's impartiality is built. The ombuds must conduct investigations and inquiries in an impartial manner, free from initial bias and conflicts of interest. Confidentiality is a widely accepted characteristic of ombuds, which helps ombuds perform the functions of the office. Without these Standards, individuals may be reluctant to seek the ombuds's assistance because of fear of personal, professional, or economic retaliation, loss of privacy, and loss of relationships. This Resolution and the Standards for the Establishment and Operation of Ombuds Offices are appropriate now to ensure that ombuds can protect individual rights against the excesses of public and private bureaucracies.

Appendix 7

Standards for the Establishment and Operation of Ombuds Offices
ABA Policy Adopted February 2004

AMERICAN BAR ASSOCIATION

ADOPTED BY THE HOUSE OF DELEGATES

February 9, 2004

RESOLVED, That the American Bar Association endorses the revised Standards for the Establishment and Operation of Ombuds Offices dated February, 2004.

STANDARDS[1] FOR THE ESTABLISHMENT AND OPERATION OF OMBUDS OFFICES

REVISED FEBRUARY, 2004

PREAMBLE

Ombuds[2] receive complaints and questions from individuals concerning people within an entity or the functioning of an entity. They work for the resolution of particular issues and, where appropriate, make recommendations for the improvement of the general administration of the entities they serve. Ombuds protect: the legitimate interests and rights of individuals with respect to each other; individual rights against the excesses of public and private bureaucracies; and those who are affected by and those who work within these organizations.

Federal, state and local governments, academic institutions, for profit businesses, non-profit organizations, and sub-units of these entities have established ombuds offices, but with enormous variation in their duties and structures. Ombuds offices so established may be placed in several categories: A Legislative Ombuds is a part of the legislative branch of government and addresses issues raised by the general public or internally, usually concerning the actions or policies of government entities, individuals or contractors with respect to holding agencies

---

1. The ABA adopted a resolution in August, 2001, that supported "the greater use of 'ombuds' to receive, review, and resolve complaints involving public and private entities" and endorsed Standards for the Establishment and Operation of Ombuds Offices. These standards modify those Standards in four regards. First, they clarify the issue of notice in Paragraph F; secondly, they modify the limitations on the ombud's authority; third, they provide for a new category of executive ombuds that is described in Paragraph H; and, fourth, they modify the definition of legislative ombuds and the standards applicable to them to make them conform to the new category of executive ombuds. The 2001 Standards, in turn, expanded on a 1969 ABA resolution to address independence, impartiality, and confidentiality as essential characteristics of ombuds who serve internal constituents, ombuds in the private sector, and ombuds who also serve as advocates for designated populations.

2. The term ombuds in this report is intended to encompass all other forms of the word, such as ombudsperson, ombuds officer, and ombudsman, a Swedish word meaning agent or representative. The use of ombuds here is not intended to discourage others from using other terms.

accountable to the public. An Executive Ombuds may be located in either the public or private sector and receives complaints concerning actions and failures to act of the entity, its officials, employees and contractors; an Executive Ombuds may either work to hold the entity or one of its programs accountable or work with entity officials to improve the performance of a program. An Organizational Ombuds may be located in either the public or private sector and ordinarily addresses problems presented by members, employees, or contractors of an entity concerning its actions or policies. An Advocate Ombuds may be located in either the public or private sector and like the others evaluates claims objectively but is authorized or required to advocate on behalf of individuals or groups found to be aggrieved.

As a result of the various types of offices and the proliferation of different processes by which the offices operate, individuals who come to the ombuds office for assistance may not know what to expect, and the offices may be established in ways that compromise their effectiveness. These standards were developed to provide advice and guidance on the structure and operation of ombuds offices so that ombuds may better fulfill their functions and so that individuals who avail themselves of their aid may do so with greater confidence in the integrity of the process. Practical and political considerations may require variations from these Standards, but it is urged that such variations be eliminated over time.

The essential characteristics of an ombuds are:

- independence
- impartiality in conducting inquiries and investigations, and
- confidentiality.

ESTABLISHMENT AND OPERATIONS

A. An entity undertaking to establish an ombuds should do so pursuant to a legislative enactment or a publicly available written policy (the "charter") which clearly sets forth the role and jurisdiction of the ombuds and which authorizes the ombuds to:

(1) receive complaints and questions about alleged acts, omissions, improprieties, and systemic problems within the

ombuds's jurisdiction as defined in the charter establishing the office

(2) exercise discretion to accept or decline to act on a complaint or question

(3) act on the ombuds's own initiative to address issues within the ombuds's prescribed jurisdiction

(4) operate by fair and timely procedures to aid in the just resolution of a complaint or problem

(5) gather relevant information and require the full cooperation of the program over which the ombuds has jurisdiction

(6) resolve issues at the most appropriate level of the entity

(7) function by such means as:

(a) conducting an inquiry

(b) investigating and reporting findings

(c) developing, evaluating, and discussing options available to affected individuals

(d) facilitating, negotiating, and mediating

(e) making recommendations for the resolution of an individual complaint or a systemic problem to those persons who have the authority to act upon them

(f) identifying complaint patterns and trends

(g) educating

(h) issuing periodic reports, and

(i) advocating on behalf of affected individuals or groups when specifically authorized by the charter

(8) initiate litigation to enforce or protect the authority of the office as defined by the charter, as otherwise provided by these standards, or as required by law.

QUALIFICATIONS

B. An ombuds should be a person of recognized knowledge, judgment, objectivity, and integrity. The establishing entity should provide the ombuds with relevant education and the periodic updating of the ombuds's qualifications.

INDEPENDENCE, IMPARTIALITY, AND CONFIDENTIALITY

C. To ensure the effective operation of an ombuds, an entity should authorize the ombuds to operate consistently with the following essential characteristics. Entities that have established ombuds offices that lack appropriate safeguards to maintain these characteristics should take prompt steps to remedy any such deficiency.

(1) <u>Independence</u>. The ombuds is and appears to be free from interference in the legitimate performance of duties and independent from control, limitation, or a penalty imposed for retaliatory purposes by an official of the appointing entity or by a person who may be the subject of a complaint or inquiry.

In assessing whether an ombuds is independent in structure, function, and appearance, the following factors are important: whether anyone subject to the ombuds's jurisdiction or anyone directly responsible for a person under the ombuds's jurisdiction (a) can control or limit the ombuds's performance of assigned duties or (b) can, for retaliatory purposes, (1) eliminate the office, (2) remove the ombuds, or (3) reduce the budget or resources of the office.

(2) <u>Impartiality in Conducting Inquiries and Investigations</u>. The ombuds conducts inquiries and investigations in an impartial manner, free from initial bias and conflicts of interest. Impartiality does not preclude the ombuds from developing an interest in securing changes that are deemed necessary as a result of the process, nor from otherwise being an advocate on behalf of a designated constituency. The

ombuds may become an advocate within the entity for change where the process demonstrates a need for it.

(3) <u>Confidentiality</u>. An ombuds does not disclose and is not required to disclose any information provided in confidence, except to address an imminent risk of serious harm. Records pertaining to a complaint, inquiry, or investigation are confidential and not subject to disclosure outside the ombuds's office. An ombuds does not reveal the identity of a complainant without that person's express consent. An ombuds may, however, at the ombuds's discretion disclose non-confidential information and may disclose confidential information so long as doing so does not reveal its source. An ombuds should discuss any exceptions to the ombuds's maintaining confidentiality with the source of the information.[3]

LIMITATIONS ON THE OMBUDS'S AUTHORITY

D. An ombuds should not, nor should an entity expect or authorize an ombuds to:

(1) make, change or set aside a law, policy, or administrative decision

(2) make binding decisions or determine rights

(3) directly compel an entity or any person to implement the ombuds's recommendations

(4) conduct an investigation that substitutes for administrative or judicial proceedings

(5) accept jurisdiction over an issue that is currently pending in a legal forum unless all parties and the presiding officer in that action explicitly consent

---

3. A legislative ombuds should not be required to discuss confidentiality with government officials and employees when applying this paragraph to the extent that an applicable statute makes clear that such an individual may not withhold information from the ombuds and that such a person has no reasonable expectation of confidentiality with respect to anything that person provides to the ombuds.

(6) address any issue arising under a collective bargaining agreement or which falls within the purview of any federal, state, or local labor or employment law, rule, or regulation, unless there is no collective bargaining representative and the employer specifically authorizes the ombuds to do so,[4] or

(7) act in a manner inconsistent with the grant of and limitations on the jurisdiction of the office when discharging the duties of the office of ombuds.

REMOVAL FROM OFFICE

E. The charter that establishes the office of the ombuds should also provide for the discipline or removal of the ombuds from office for good cause by means of a fair procedure.

NOTICE

F. An ombuds is intended to supplement, not replace, formal procedures.[5] Therefore:

(1) An ombuds should provide the following information in a general and publicly available manner and inform people who contact the ombuds for help or advice that—

(a) the ombuds will not voluntarily disclose to anyone outside the ombuds office, including the entity in which the ombuds acts, any information the person provides in confidence or the person's identity unless necessary to address an imminent risk of serious harm or with the person's express consent

---

4. Under these Standards, the employer may authorize an ombuds to address issues of labor or employment law only if the entity has expressly provided the ombuds with the confidentiality specified in Paragraph C(3). An ombuds program as envisioned by these Standards supplements and does not substitute for other procedures and remedies necessary to meet the duty of employers to protect the legal rights of both employers and employees.

5. An ombuds program as envisioned by these Standards supplements and does not substitute for the need of an entity to establish formal procedures that may be necessary to *protect legal rights and to* address allegedly inappropriate or wrongful behavior or conduct.

(b) important rights may be affected by when formal action is initiated and by and when the entity is informed of the allegedly inappropriate or wrongful behavior or conduct

(c) communications to the ombuds may not constitute notice to the entity unless the ombuds communicates with representatives of the entity as described in Paragraph 2

(d) working with the ombuds may address the problem or concern effectively, but may not protect the rights of either the person contacting the office or the entity in which the ombuds operates[6]

(e) the ombuds is not, and is not a substitute for, anyone's lawyer, representative or counselor, and

(f) the person may wish to consult a lawyer or other appropriate resource with respect to those rights.

(2) If the ombuds communicates[7] with representatives of the entity concerning an allegation of a violation, then —

(a) a communication that reveals the facts of

(i) a specific allegation and the identity of the complainant or

(ii) allegations by multiple complainants that may reflect related behavior or conduct that is either inappropriate or wrongful should be regarded as providing notice to the entity of the alleged violation and the complainants should be advised that the ombuds communicated their allegations to the entity; but otherwise,

(b) whether or not the communication constitutes notice to the entity is a question that should be determined by the facts of the communication.

---

6. The notice requirements of Paragraph F do not supercede or change the advocacy responsibilities of an Advocate Ombuds.

7. Under these standards, any such communication is subject to Paragraph C(3).

(3) If an ombuds functions in accordance with Paragraph C, "Independence, Impartiality, and Confidentiality," of these standards, then —

(a) no one, including the entity in which the ombuds operates, should deem the ombuds to be an agent of any person or entity, other than the office of the ombuds, for purposes of receiving notice of alleged violations, and (b) communications made to the ombuds should not be imputed to anyone else, including the entity in which the ombuds acts unless the ombuds communicates with representatives of the entity in which case Paragraph 2 applies.

LEGISLATIVE OMBUDS

G. A legislative ombuds is established by the legislature as part of the legislative branch who receives complaints from the general public or internally and addresses actions and failures to act of a government agency, official, public employee, or contractor. In addition to and in clarification of the standards contained in Paragraphs A-F, a legislative ombuds should:

(1) be appointed by the legislative body or by the executive with confirmation by the legislative body[8]

(2) be authorized to work to hold agencies within the jurisdiction of the office accountable to the public and to assist in legislative oversight of those agencies

(3) be authorized to conduct independent and impartial investigations into matters within the prescribed jurisdiction of the office

(4) have the power to issue subpoenas for testimony and evidence with respect to investigating allegations within the jurisdiction of the office

---

8. This restates the 1969 ABA Resolution, which remains ABA policy, that a legislative ombuds should be "appoint[ed] by the legislative body or . . . by the executive with confirmation by the designated proportion of the legislative body, preferably more than a majority, such as two thirds."

(5) be authorized to issue public reports, and

(6) be authorized to advocate for change both within the entity and publicly.

EXECUTIVE OMBUDS

H. An executive ombuds may be located in either the public or private sector and receives complaints from the general public or internally and addresses actions and failures to act of the entity, its officials, employees, and contractors. An executive ombuds may either work to hold the entity or specific programs accountable or work with officials to improve the performance of a program. In addition to and in clarification of the standards contained in Paragraphs A-F, an executive ombuds:

(1) should be authorized to conduct investigations and inquiries

(2) should be authorized to issue reports on the results of the investigations and inquires, and

(3) if located in government, should not have general jurisdiction over more than one agency, but may have jurisdiction over a subject matter that involves multiple agencies.

ORGANIZATIONAL OMBUDS

I. An organizational ombuds facilitates fair and equitable resolutions of concerns that arise within the entity. In addition to and in clarification of the standards contained in Paragraphs A-F, an organizational ombuds should:

(1) be authorized to undertake inquiries and function by informal processes as specified by the charter

(2) be authorized to conduct independent and impartial inquiries into matters within the prescribed jurisdiction of the office

(3) be authorized to issue reports, and

(4) be authorized to advocate for change within the entity.

ADVOCATE OMBUDS

J. An advocate ombuds serves as an advocate on behalf of a population that is designated in the charter. In addition to and in clarification of the standards described in Paragraphs A-F, an advocate ombuds should:

(1) have a basic understanding of the nature and role of advocacy

(2) provide information, advice, and assistance to members of the constituency

(3) evaluate the complainant's claim objectively and advocate for change or relief when the facts support the claim

(4) be authorized to represent the interests of the designated population with respect to policies implemented or adopted by the establishing entity, government agencies, or other organizations as defined by the charter

(5) be authorized to initiate action in an administrative, judicial, or legislative forum when the facts warrant, and

(6) the notice requirements of Paragraph F do not supersede or change the advocacy responsibilities of an Advocate Ombuds.

REPORT

The American Bar Association (ABA) adopted a resolution in 1969 recommending that state and local governments consider establishing ombudsmen who would be authorized to inquire into administrative action and to make public criticism. That policy also recommended that the statute or ordinance creating the ombudsmen contain twelve essential points. The ABA then adopted a resolution in 1971 recommending that the Federal government experiment with the establishment of ombudsmen for certain geographical areas, specific agencies, or for limited phases of Federal activities. In 2001, ABA the adopted a resolution supporting the greater use of "ombuds"[9] to receive, review, and resolve complaints involving public and private entities. That policy also endorsed Standards for the Establishment and Operations of Ombuds Offices (Standards). The 2001 Resolution and Standards broadened the ABA's existing policy to address ombuds who are appointed within government, academia, and the private sector, and who respond to complaints from individuals from within and outside the entity. The 2001 Resolution and the Standards also clarified that independence, impartiality in conducting inquiries and investigations, and confidentiality are essential characteristics of all ombuds. Ombuds must operate consistently with these essential characteristics to discharge the duties of the office effectively.

This Resolution recognizes that entities that create ombuds offices should adhere to the Standards for the Establishment and Operations of Ombuds Offices, dated February, 2004. The fundamental underlying premise of this resolution is that all ombuds must operate with certain basic authorities and essential characteristics. The effort here is to provide practical advice and guidance on the structure and operation of ombuds offices so that ombuds may better fulfill their functions and so that individuals who avail themselves of their aid may do so with greater confidence in the integrity of the process. These Standards modify the Standards for the Establishment and Operation of Ombuds Offices that were adopted by the ABA in August, 2001, in

---

9. The term ombuds in this report is intended to encompass all other forms of the word such as ombudsperson, ombuds officers, and ombudsman, a Swedish word meaning agent or representative. The use of ombuds here is not intended to discourage others from using other terms.

four regards. First, they clarify the issue of notice in Paragraph F; secondly, they modify the limitations on the ombud's authority in Paragraph D; third, they provide for a new category of executive ombuds that is described in Paragraph H; and, fourth, they modify the definition of legislative ombuds and the standards applicable to them to make them conform to the new category of executive ombuds.

INTRODUCTION

Over the past three decades, and particularly recently, an extraordinary growth in the number and type of ombuds has taken place. Congress has established several ombuds in various programs. In addition to specific legislation concerning ombuds, the Administrative Dispute Resolution Act authorizes Federal agencies to use "ombuds." As a protector of individual rights against the excesses of public and private bureaucracies, an ombuds receives complaints and questions from individuals concerning the functioning of an entity, works for the resolution of particular issues, and where necessary, makes recommendations for the improvement of the general administration of the entity.

As an independent, impartial, and confidential complaint handler, an ombuds serves as an alternative means of dispute resolution—a means by which issues may be raised, considered, and resolved. Federal, state and local governments, academic institutions, for profit businesses, non-profit organizations, and sub-units of these entities have established ombuds offices, but with enormous variation in their duties and structures. Ombuds offices so established may be placed in several categories. A Legislative Ombuds is established by the legislature as part of the legislative branch and addresses issues raised by the general public or internally, usually concerning the actions or policies of a government agency, official, public employee, or contractor. An Executive Ombuds may be located in either the public or private sector and receives complaints from the general public or internally and addresses actions or failures to act of the entity, its officials, employees, or contractors; an Executive Ombuds may either work to hold the entity or specific programs accountable or work with officials to improve the performance of a program. An Organizational Ombuds may be located in either the public or private sector and ordinarily addresses problems presented by members, employees, or contractors of an entity concerning its actions or policies. An Advocate Ombuds may be located in either the public or private sector, and like the others evaluates claims objectively but is authorized or required to advocate on behalf of individuals or groups found to be aggrieved.

As a result of the various types of offices and the proliferation of different processes by which the offices operate, individuals who come to the ombuds' office for assistance may not know what to expect, and the offices may be established in ways that compromise their effectiveness. The ABA endorsed Standards that were developed to provide advice and guidance on the structure and operation of ombuds offices to the end that ombuds may better fulfill their functions and so that individuals who avail themselves of their aid may do so with greater confidence in the integrity of the process. The ABA action was based on the collaborative efforts of the Sections of Administrative Law and Regulatory Practice and of Dispute Resolution who worked together and appointed a steering committee consisting of representatives from the Coalition of Federal Ombudsmen, the National Association of State Ombudsman Programs, the International Ombudsman Institute (IOI subsequently withdrew), The Ombudsman Association, the United States Ombudsman Association,[10] and the University and College Ombuds Association, as well as other experts in the field. The committee consulted with numerous ombuds from Federal, state, and local agencies, academic institutions, companies, and non-profit organizations. Further, it solicited, received, and considered comments from the international community of ombuds. Within the ABA, the Commission on Law and Aging, based on its experience with advocate ombuds, was instrumental in distinguishing among the types of ombuds. The Section of Business Law collaborated extensively with the committee to further the understanding and appreciation of the role of the ombuds in the business environment. Consultations with the Section of Labor and Employment Law resulted in refining the limitations on the ombuds' jurisdiction.

The Standards for the Establishment and Operation of Ombuds Offices dated August 2001 have been widely distributed and utilized

---

10. The United States Ombudsman Association did not endorse the Standards that were adopted in 2001 and was not involved in the subsequent revisions to the Standards.

by Federal, state and local governments, academic institutions, for profit businesses, non-profit organizations, and sub-units of these entities. For example, Congress is currently considering legislation to reauthorize an ombuds at the U.S. Environmental Protection Agency and has relied upon the ABA's Standards in defining the position.

To ensure that ombuds can protect individual rights against the excesses of public and private bureaucracies, now, again, the Sections of Administrative Law and Regulatory Practice, Business Law, Dispute Resolution, and Individual Rights and Responsibilities have worked together and with the ombuds community and other ABA entities to develop a resolution to support amendments to the Standards for the Establishment and Operations of Ombuds Offices.

STANDARDS

Section A. Establishment and Operations

An ombuds is a person who is authorized to receive complaints or questions confidentially about alleged acts, omissions, improprieties, and broader, systemic problems within the ombuds's defined jurisdiction and to address, investigate, or otherwise examine these issues independently and impartially.

Importantly, the ombuds' jurisdiction—who complains and who or what are complained about—needs to be defined in advance, setting out the scope of the duties and authority. The ombuds's jurisdiction must be defined in an official act that establishes the office, which is appropriately called the "charter" in the Standards. The charter may be a legislative enactment or a publicly available written policy. The jurisdiction may be limited to a defined constituency or population. For example, a state ombuds may receive complaints or questions from any person, while a university student ombuds may receive complaints or questions only from students at that university, and a long-term care ombuds has jurisdiction only to resolve complaints initiated by or on behalf of residents receiving long-term care.

The ombuds determines whether to accept or to act on a particular complaint or question. The ombuds also has the discretion to initiate action without receiving a complaint or question. An ombuds may determine that the complaint is without merit. Or, an ombuds may receive a complaint or question on a specific topic and conduct an inquiry on a broader or different scope.

Appropriate subjects for an ombuds to review include allegations of unfairness, maladministration, abuse of power, abuse of discretion, discourteous behavior or incivility, inappropriate application of law or policy, inefficiency, decision unsupported by fact, and illegal or inappropriate behavior. It is essential that the ombuds operate by fair procedures to aid in the just resolution of the matter. Ombuds need access to all information relevant to a complaint or a question so that the review is fair and credible, and the charter should authorize access to all relevant information and require the full cooperation of the program over which the ombuds has jurisdiction. The entity must be responsible for protecting those seeking assistance from or providing information to the ombuds from personal, professional, or economic retaliation, loss of privacy, or loss of relationships.

An ombuds may make a formal or informal report of results and recommendations stemming from a review or investigation. If such a report is issued, the ombuds should generally consult with an individual or group prior to issuing a report critical of that individual or group, and include their comments with the report. Moreover, the ombuds should communicate the outcome, conclusion or resolution of a complaint or an inquiry to the complainant and may also communicate with other concerned entities or individuals.

In addition, to ensure the office's accountability, an ombuds should issue and publish periodic reports summarizing the ombuds's findings and activities. This may include statistical information about the number of contacts with the ombuds, subjects that the ombuds addressed evaluation by complainants, etc. These reports may be done annually, biannually, or more frequently.

In receiving complaints or questions and examining problems, the ombuds may use a variety of dispute resolution and other techniques. These processes include: conducting an inquiry; investigating and reporting findings; developing, evaluating, and discussing the options which may be available for remedies or redress; facilitating, negotiating, and mediating; making recommendations for the resolution of an individual complaint or a systemic problem to those persons who have authority to act on them; identifying complaint patterns and trends; and educating.

As necessary, the ombuds may advocate on behalf of affected individuals or groups when authorized by the charter and the situation warrants that action. An ombuds may initiate litigation to enforce or protect the authority of the office. For example, if an ombuds issues a subpoena and the subpoena is ignored, the ombuds should be able to initiate litigation to compel a response. In addition, an ombuds may initiate litigation as otherwise provided by these standards or as required by law. For example, an advocate ombuds should be authorized to initiate action in an administrative, judicial, or legislative forum when the facts warrant.

An ombuds uses the powers of reason and persuasion to help resolve matters. The goal of the ombuds's efforts is to provide a path to fairness and justice. Therefore, the ombuds' quest is to seek the fair and just resolution of the matter.

Section B. Qualifications

An ombuds should be a person of recognized knowledge, judgment, objectivity, and integrity. The establishing entity should provide the ombuds with relevant education and the periodic updating of the ombuds's qualifications.

Section C. The Essential Characteristics

The original 1969 resolution contained twelve essentials for the ombuds described in it. These have been distilled and expanded in the Standards. The core qualities are independence, impartiality in conducting inquiries and investigations, and confidentiality. Without them, an ombuds cannot discharge the duties of the office effectively. The Standards therefore provide that an entity should authorize an ombuds it establishes to operate consistently with these essential characteristics to ensure the effective operation of the duties of the office. The Standards also recognize, however, that some entities may have already established offices that lack appropriate safeguards to comply fully with the characteristics. The Standards then provide that such entities should take prompt steps to remedy any such deficiency.

1. Independence in structure, function, and appearance

To be credible and effective, the office of the ombuds is independent in its structure, function, and appearance. Independence means that the ombuds is free from interference in the legitimate performance of duties and independent from control, limitation, or a penalty imposed for retaliatory purposes by an official of the appointing entity or by a person who may be the subject of a complaint or inquiry. In assessing whether an ombuds is independent, the following factors are important: whether anyone subject to the ombuds's jurisdiction or anyone directly responsible for a person under the ombuds's jurisdiction (a) can control or limit the ombuds's performance of duties, or (b) can, for retaliatory purposes, (1) eliminate the office, (2) remove the ombuds, or (3) reduce the office's budget or resources.

Historically, ombuds were created in parliamentary systems and were established in the constitution or by statute, appointed by the legislative body, and had a guarantee of independence from the control of any other officer, except for responsibility to the legislative body. This structure remains a model for ensuring independence for Legislative Ombuds, and a number of states have followed it. In more recent times, however, Executive Ombuds have been created by public officials without legislation, by regulation or decree, and by private entities. Ensuring the independence of the ombuds is equally important in these instances, but will require other measures.[11]

Great care has to be exercised in establishing the ombuds structure to ensure that the independence described in the resolution is, in fact, achieved. Choosing which of these approaches are appropriate will depend on the environment. The instrument used to establish independence should be the strongest available and should guarantee the independence of the ombuds from control by any other person.

The twelve essential characteristics of the 1969 ABA Resolution continue to serve as the model for an ombuds reporting to the legisla-

---

11. In the United States since the late 1960s, a number of other ways have been developed to ensure independence. Examples of approaches that contribute to an ombuds's independence include: establishment of the office through a formal act of a legislature or official governing body of an organization; establishment outside the entity over which the ombuds has jurisdiction; a direct reporting relationship to a legislative body, the official governing body of an organization or the chief executive; designation as a neutral who is unaligned and objective; a broadly defined jurisdiction not limited to one part of the entity or one subject matter; appointment or removal of the ombuds free of influence from potential subjects of a complaint or inquiry; a set term of office; no reporting relationship to someone with assigned duties that conflict with the ombuds's role; no assignment of duties other than that of the ombuds function; specifically allocated budget and sufficient resources to perform the function; freedom to appoint, direct, and remove staff; sufficient stature in the organization to be taken seriously by senior officials; placement in an organization at the highest possible level and at least above the heads of units likely to generate the most complaints; discretion to initiate and pursue complaints and inquiries; access to and resources for independent legal advice and counsel; prohibition of disciplinary actions against the ombuds for performing the duties of the office; removal only for cause; provision of an employment contract that the ombuds will receive a significant severance provision if terminated without good cause.

tive branch of government who is authorized to investigate administrative action, help provide legislative oversight, and offer criticism of agencies from an external perspective. While there are a number of potential avenues of achieving independence, experience on the state and local level has demonstrated rather consistently that unless there is a structural independence for these ombuds akin to the 1969 ABA Resolution that independence will not be accomplished and the office will not be able to function as envisioned in this resolution and the accompanying standards.

Structuring independence for ombuds who serve inside organizations require similar care. These elements should be in the charter. The ombuds position should be explicitly defined and established as a matter of organizational policy, authorized at the highest levels of the organization; the ombuds should have access to the chief executive officer, senior officers and the oversight body or board of directors of the organization; the ombuds should also have access to all information within the organization, except as restricted by law; and the ombuds should have access to resources for independent legal advice and counsel.

The Standards recognize that at this time there are ombuds who have not achieved this goal. The Standards urge and anticipate that these variations will be eliminated over time.

2. Impartiality in conducting inquiries and investigations

The ombuds' structural independence is the foundation upon which the ombuds' impartiality is built. If the ombuds is independent from line management and does not have administrative or other obligations or functions, the ombuds can act in an impartial manner.

Acting in an impartial manner, as a threshold matter, means that the ombuds is free from initial bias and conflicts of interest in conducting inquiries and investigations. Acting in an impartial manner also requires that the ombuds be authorized to gather facts from relevant sources and apply relevant policies, guidelines, and laws, considering the rights and interests of all affected parties within the jurisdiction, to identify appropriate actions to address or resolve the issue.

The ombuds conducts inquiries and investigations in an impartial manner. An ombuds may determine that a complaint is without merit and close the inquiry or investigation without further action. If the ombuds finds that the complaint has merit, the ombuds makes recommendations to the entity and/or seeks resolution for a fair outcome. Impartiality does not, however, preclude the ombuds from developing an interest in securing the changes that are deemed necessary where the process demonstrates a need for change nor from otherwise being an advocate on behalf of a designated constituency. The ombuds therefore has the authority to become an advocate for change where the results of the inquiry or investigation demonstrate the need for such change. For example, when an ombuds identifies a systemic problem, it would be appropriate for the ombuds to advocate for changes to correct the problem. An advocate ombuds may initiate action and therefore serve as an advocate on behalf of a designated population with respect to a broad range of issues and on specific matters when the individual or group is found to be aggrieved. But, when determining the facts, the ombuds must act impartially.

3. Confidentiality

Confidentiality is an essential characteristic of ombuds that permits the process to work effectively. Confidentiality promotes disclosure from reluctant complainants, elicits candid discussions by all parties, and provides an increased level of protection against retaliation to or by any party. Confidentiality is a further factor that distinguishes ombuds from others who receive and consider complaints such as elected officials, human resource personnel, government officials, and ethics officers.

Confidentiality extends to all communications with the ombuds and to all notes and records maintained by the ombuds in the performance of assigned duties. It begins when a communication is initiated with the ombuds to schedule an appointment or make a complaint or inquiry. Confidentiality may apply to the source of the communications and to the content of the communications. Individuals may not want the ombuds to disclose their identity but may want the ombuds to act on the information presented. Therefore, an ombuds does not reveal the identity of a complainant without that person's consent. The ombuds may, however, disclose confidential 15 information so long as doing so does not compromise the identity of the person who supplied it. It should be emphasized that the decision whether or not to disclose this information belongs to the ombuds, and it would not be appropriate for anyone to demand that the ombuds disclose such information, except as required by statute. To the extent that an ombuds may not maintain confidentiality, the ombuds should discuss those exceptions with individuals who communicate with the office.

The authorizing entity should allow the ombuds to provide confidentiality of the identity of persons who communicate with the ombuds and of information provided in confidence. The authorizing entity should not seek information relating to the identity of complainants nor seek access to the ombuds's notes and records.

Providing for confidentiality and protection from subpoena in a statute is particularly important because, where statutes have not provided confidentiality, state courts have not consistently recognized an ombuds privilege nor granted protective orders to preserve the confidentiality of communication made to ombuds. One Federal district court, *Shabazz v. Scurr*, 662 F. Supp. 90 (S.D. Iowa 1987), recognized a limited privilege under Federal law for an ombuds with a state statutory privilege. The only Federal circuit court to have addressed the issue, *Carman v. McDonnell Douglas Corp.*, 114 F.3d 790 (8th Cir. 1997), failed to recognize an ombuds privilege.

Short of explicit statutory authority, ombuds offices should adopt written policies that provide the fullest confidentiality within the law, and the entities that establish ombuds offices should expressly provide the ombuds with fullest confidentiality specified in the standards. These policies should be publicly available, broadly disseminated, and widely publicized. Several existing model ombuds acts and policies of ombuds organizations address confidentiality.

An ombuds will rarely, if ever, be privy to something that no one else knows. Therefore, providing confidentiality protection to the ombuds allows the ombuds to perform assigned duties while at the same time, society continues to have access to the underlying facts. As evidenced by the statutes and policies that have been developed, there may be instances in which other, competing societal interests dictate that the ombuds must disclose some information. If an individual speaks about intending harm to himself or herself or others, an entity may require an ombuds to disclose this information. Moreover, an ombuds may be compelled by protective service laws or professional reporting requirements to report suspected abuse.

Section D. Limitations on the ombuds' authority

An ombuds works outside of line management structures and has no direct power to compel any decision. The office is established by the charter with the stature to engender trust and to help resolve complaints at the most appropriate level of the entity. To ensure the ombuds's independence, impartiality, and confidentiality, it is necessary to establish certain limitations on the ombuds's authority.

An ombuds should not, nor should an entity expect or authorize an ombuds to make, change, or set aside a law, policy or administrative/managerial decision, nor to directly compel an entity or any person to make those changes. While an ombuds may expedite and facilitate the resolution of a complaint and recommend individual and systemic changes, an ombuds cannot compel an entity to implement the recommendations.

It is essential that an ombuds operate by fair procedures which means that the actions taken will likely vary with the nature of the concern, and that care must be taken to protect the rights of those who may be affected by the actions of an ombuds. Furthermore, since due process rights could well be implicated, it would not be appropriate for the ombuds's review to serve as the final determination for any disciplinary activity or civil action, nor as a determination of a violation of law or policy. An ombuds's inquiry or investigation does not substitute for an administrative or judicial proceeding. In an administrative or judicial proceeding, the deciding official should not consider the ombuds's review or recommendations to be controlling. Rather, the deciding official must conduct a de novo examination of the matter.

Moreover, it would not be appropriate for the ombuds to act as an appellate forum when a complainant is dissatisfied with the results in a formal adjudicatory or administrative proceeding. Thus, an ombuds should not take up a specific issue that is pending in a legal forum without the concurrence of the parties and the presiding officer. It may, however, be fully appropriate for an ombuds to inquire into matters that are related to a controversy that is in litigation so long as they are not the subject of the suit.

Further, an ombuds should not address, nor should an entity expect or authorize an ombuds to address, any issue that is the subject of a collective bargaining agreement or that arises under labor or employment law. Even where an employee is not covered by a collective bargaining agreement, the involvement of an ombuds in matters that fall within the purview of labor or employment laws raises sensitive issues that may implicate the rights and liabilities of the parties under those laws, such as the issue of notice mentioned in Section F of the Standards. Accordingly, the Standards contemplate that an employer, in establishing an ombuds office, should consider its overall policies for maintaining compliance with those laws, and determine in that light whether to authorize the ombuds to address those matters. The entity should do so only if the ombuds office meets the three essential characteristics of Independence, Impartiality, and Confidentiality. This recommendation is in no way intended to suggest, however, that a policy of authorizing an ombuds to address labor or employment-related matters should be a suspect or disfavored practice. Involvement in such matters is a role typically performed by Organizational Ombuds, and the growing reliance on ombuds at institutions across the country is largely attributable to the broad satisfaction with ombuds' fulfillment of that role on the part of both management and the affected employees. Thus, the language in the Standards indicating that an employer should specifically authorize an ombuds to address labor or employment related matters does not require any detailed or ponderous recitals. Rather, it should be read as simply a particularized application of the generalized expectation in Section A of the Standards that the jurisdiction of an ombuds office should be identified in its charter.

Finally, an ombuds should not act in a manner inconsistent with the grant and limitations on the jurisdiction of the office when discharging the duties of the office of ombuds.

Section E. Removal from office

Entities which establish ombuds offices need to ensure their accountability. Therefore, the charter that establishes the office of ombuds should also provide for the discipline or removal of the ombuds for good cause by means of a fair procedure.

Section F. Notice

When meeting with an ombuds, people discuss allegations of unfairness, maladministration, abuse of power, and other sensitive subjects. They may fear personal, professional, or economic retaliation, loss of privacy, and loss of relationships. Faced with sexual or racial harassment, for example, many will quit, get sick, or suffer in silence. People often need help in developing ways to report or act so that these matters will be considered and resolved. Because an ombuds is intended to supplement, not replace, formal procedures, the Standards recognize that the person contacting the ombuds for assistance needs to understand the difference between working with an ombuds and seeking formal redress. It may be that the ombuds informs people coming to the ombuds office of the issues identified in the Standards; it may be that the ombuds office has a brochure or web page that explains the functioning of the office, working with the ombuds office, and the items listed in Section F(1); or, it may be that the entity itself includes similar information in a manual, other information provided to affected people, or as part of the charter for the ombuds office. But the standards recognize that responsibility needs to be allocated in a way that ensures the communication will actually be made in the relevant circumstances, so it places it at the point of contact with the individual: the ombuds office.

Communications must be protected if people are to be willing to visit and speak candidly with the ombuds. As noted above, some ombuds have confidentiality protected by law. Under these Standards, entities that establish an ombuds should authorize the ombuds to operate with confidentiality and independence, and an ombuds should inform anyone who contacts the ombuds offices, that the ombuds will not voluntarily disclose to anyone outside the ombuds office, including the entity in which the ombuds operates, any information the person provides in confidence or the person's identity, unless necessary to address the imminent risk of serious harm or with the person's express consent. The standards recognize, however, that in some limited circumstances an ombuds may be compelled by a court to divulge confidential information.

The standards are designed to make sure that a person coming to the ombuds will be aware that legal rights might well be at stake and that the person may have to take action beyond working with the ombuds to protect those rights. This is to ensure that the person approaching the ombuds office to redress some particular problem understands that protecting rights may depend on just when formal action is initiated and whether notice is given to the entity. Working with the ombuds does not change that requirement or the specific time when the action must be started. In addition, the ombuds should advise persons that communications to the ombuds may not constitute notice to the entity unless the ombuds contacts the entity.

Further, the ombuds should describe to visitors that working with the ombuds is an informal process that may well address the person's concern effectively, but doing so may not protect that person's legal right or indeed, those of the entity for whom the ombuds functions. Moreover, the ombuds needs to make clear that the ombuds is not serving as anyone's lawyer, representative or counselor — not for the complainant nor for the entity. Thus, the ombuds is not the person's lawyer or labor representative nor a human resources or social work counselor. So that the person is not lulled into putting off checking what legal rights may be affected, the Standards provide that the ombuds should inform the person that he or she may wish to consult a lawyer or other appropriate resource with respect to preserving and protecting those rights. The standards do not contemplate the ombuds providing any sort of legal advice as to what the legal rights and procedures are, only that they may exist and that the person coming to the office may wish to consult with a lawyer or other resource to determine them.

If an ombuds functions in accordance with these Standards by operating with confidentiality and independence, the details of what is told to the ombuds will not be told to anyone in the entity itself, and hence it would not be appropriate or accurate to impute it to the entity — that is, holding the entity responsible for knowing something it cannot know. Further, the Standards provide that the ombuds should not be deemed an agent of any person or entity, other than the Office of the Ombuds, for purposes of receiving notice of alleged violations. Rather, the ombuds would be deemed independent of the entity itself for these purposes. Thus, it would not be appropriate for the ombuds to accept notice on the entity's behalf with respect to any alleged grievance.

When an ombuds works to address an issue, he or she may need to work with those in the entity. An ombuds may therefore communicate with representatives of an entity which, under the standards, the ombuds has the discretion but not the requirement to do. Any such communication would be subject to the confidentiality provisions of Paragraph C(3). If the communication reveals the facts of a specific allegation and the identity of the complainant, then the entity should be regarded as having notice of the alleged violation. Similarly, if the ombuds communicates allegations of multiple complainants that may reflect related behavior or conduct that is either inappropriate or wrongful then here too the entity should be regarded as having notice of the alleged violation since the multiple complainants makes up for the lack of specific identity. In these cases, the complainants should be informed that the ombuds has communicated their allegations to the entity so they may decide whether or not to take formal action. In both instances, the information provided would need to be sufficiently detailed that the entity could conduct its own investigation with respect to the allegations. Furthermore, the ombuds may provide enough information—even though confidentiality is maintained—that the entity in fact is on notice that a potential offense has occurred. The Standards provide, therefore, that when an ombuds communicates with representatives of the entity concerning an allegation by an individual, whether or not that communication constitutes "notice" to the entity is a question that should be determined by the facts of the communication.

Thus, the Standards draw a clear distinction between communications to an ombuds when the ombuds makes no further communication to the entity and those situations where the ombuds communicates with agents of the entity. In the former case, the Standards would provide that it is not appropriate to impute the communication to the entity in the form of notice since it has no way of learning what was communicated. But in the second instance, whether or not the entity has notice depends on the facts relayed and the applicable law.

Section G. Legislative Ombuds

A Legislative Ombuds is established by the legislature as part of the legislative branch and receives complaints from the general public or internally and addresses actions and failures to act of a government agency, official, public employee, or contractor. For Federal, state, and local governments that want to create a Legislative ombuds who would be authorized to address, investigate or inquire into administrative action and to criticize agencies, officials, and public employees, the ABA's 1969 policy continue to serve as a model.[12] A Legislative Ombuds should be appointed by the legislative body or by the executive with confirmation by the legislative body.[13] A Legislative Ombuds should be authorized to work to hold agencies within the jurisdiction

---

12. The twelve essential characteristics that were identified in the original ABA resolution continue to have vitality and remain ABA policy. They are: (1) authority of the ombudsman to criticize all agencies, officials, and public employees except courts and their personnel, legislative bodies and their personnel, and the chief executive and his personal staff; (2) independence of the ombudsman from control by any other officer, except for his responsibility to the legislative body; (3) appointment by the legislative body or appointment by the executive with confirmation by the designated proportion of the legislative body, preferably more than a majority of the legislative body, such as two thirds; (4) independence of the ombudsman through a long term, not less than five years, with freedom from removal except for cause, determined by more than a majority of the legislative body; (5) a high salary equivalent to that of a designated top officer; (6) freedom of the ombudsman to employ his own assistants and to delegate to them, without restrictions of civil service and classifications acts; (7) freedom of the ombudsman to investigate any act or failure to act by any agency, official, or public employee; (8) access of the ombudsman to all public records he finds relevant to an investigation; (9) authority to inquire into fairness, correctness of findings, motivation, adequacy of reasons, efficiency, and procedural propriety of any action or inaction by any agency, official, or public employee; (10) discretionary power to determine what complaints to investigate and to determine what criticisms to make or to publicize; (11) opportunity for any agency, official, or public employee criticized by the ombudsman to have advance notice of the criticism and to publish with the criticism an answering statement; and, (12) immunity of the ombudsman and his staff from civil liability on account of official action.

13 This restates the 1969 ABA Resolution, which remains ABA policy, that a legislative ombuds should be "appoint[ed] by the legislative body or . . . by the executive with confirmation by the designated proportion of the legislative body, preferably more than a majority, such as two thirds."

of the office accountable to the public and to assist in legislative oversight of those agencies. A Legislative Ombuds may conduct inquiries or investigations and suggest modifications in policies or procedures. To ensure access to all pertinent facts, a Legislative Ombuds should be granted subpoena power for testimony and evidence relevant to an investigation. In addition, a Legislative Ombuds should be authorized to issues public reports and to advocate for change both within the entity and publicly.

Section H. Executive Ombuds

An Executive Ombuds may be located in either the public or private sector and receives complaints from the general public or internally and addresses actions and failures to act of the entity, its officials, employees, and contractors. An Executive Ombuds may either work to hold the entity or specific programs accountable or work with officials to improve the performance of a program. In addition, an Executive Ombuds should be authorized to conduct investigations and inquiries. An Executive Ombuds should also be authorized to require the full cooperation of the program over which the ombuds has jurisdiction, including, where appropriate, subpoena power. It may not be appropriate, however, to authorize subpoena power where an Executive Ombuds has been established to receive complaints from regulated entities with regard to an agency's regulatory or enforcement activities. An Executive Ombuds should be authorized to issue reports on the results of the investigations and inquiries. Finally, if located in government, an Executive Ombuds should not have general jurisdiction over more than one agency, but may have jurisdiction over a subject matter that involves multiple agencies. For example, an Executive Ombuds may oversee a variety of governmental agencies having jurisdiction over child welfare, crime victims, or mental health issues.

Section I. Organizational Ombuds

An Organizational Ombuds ordinarily addresses problems presented by members, employees or contractors of an entity concerning its actions or policies. An Organizational Ombuds may undertake inquiries and advocate for modifications in policies or procedures.

Section J. Advocate Ombuds

The Advocate Ombuds may be located in either the public or private sectors, and like the Legislative and Organizational Ombuds, also evaluates claims objectively. However, unlike other ombuds, the Advocate Ombuds is authorized or required to advocate on behalf of individuals or groups found to be aggrieved. Because of the unique role, the Advocate Ombuds must have a basic understanding of the nature and role of advocacy. In addition, the Advocate Ombuds should provide information, advice, and assistance to members of the population identified in the law or publicly available written policy. Further, the Advocate Ombuds represents the interests of a designated population with respect to policies implemented or adopted by the establishing entity and government agencies. The notice requirements of Paragraph F do not supersede or change the advocacy responsibilities of an Advocate Ombuds.

CONCLUSION

Government, academia, and the private sector are answering demands for fairness and responsiveness by establishing ombuds. Ombuds receive complaints and questions concerning the administration of the establishing entity. However, the basic authorities of these persons called ombuds and the independence, impartiality, and confidentiality with which they operate vary markedly. An ombuds works for the resolution of a particular issue, and where necessary, makes recommendations for the improvement of the general administration of the entity. To be credible and effective, the office of the ombuds must be independent in structure, form, and appearance. The ombuds's structural independence is the foundation upon which the ombuds's impartiality is built. The ombuds must conduct investigations and inquiries in an impartial manner, free from initial bias and conflicts of interest. Confidentiality is a widely accepted characteristic of ombuds, which helps ombuds perform the functions of the office. Without these Standards, individuals may be reluctant to seek the ombuds's assistance because of fear of personal, professional, or economic retaliation, loss of privacy, and loss of relationships. This Resolution and the Standards for the Establishment and Operation of Ombuds Offices are appropriate now to ensure that ombuds can protect individual rights against the excesses of public and private bureaucracies. Practical and political considerations may require variations from these Standards, but it is urged that such variations be eliminated over time.

Respectfully submitted,

William F. Funk
Chair, Section of Administrative Law and Regulatory Practice

Steven O. Weise
Chair, Section of Business Law

Richard Chernick
Chair, Section of Dispute Resolution

Joan Kessler
Chair, Section of Individual Rights and Responsibilities

February, 2004

Appendix 8

The Ombudsman Association Standards of Practice, 1995

STANDARDS OF PRACTICE

The mission of the organizational ombudsman is to provide a confidential, neutral and informal process which facilitates fair and equitable resolutions to concerns that arise in the organization. In performing this mission, the ombudsman serves as an information and communication resource, upward feedback channel, advisor, dispute resolution expert and change agent.

While serving in this role:

1. We adhere to The Ombudsman Association Code of Ethics.

2. We base our practice on confidentiality.

2.1 An ombudsman should not 'use the names of individuals or mention their employers without express permission.

2.2 During the problem-solving process an ombudsman may make known information as long as the identity of the individual contacting the office is not compromised.

2.3 Any data that we prepare should be scrutinized carefully to safeguard the identity of each individual whose concerns are represented.

2.4 Publicity about our office conveys the confidential nature of our work.

3. We assert that there is a privilege with respect to communications with the ombudsman and we resist testifying in any formal process inside or outside the organization.

3.1 Communications between an ombudsman and others (made while the ombudsman is serving in that capacity) are considered privileged. Others cannot waive this privilege.

3.2 We do not serve in any additional function in the organization which would undermine the privileged nature of our work (such as compliance of officer, arbitrator, etc.).

3.3 An ombudsman keeps no case records on behalf of the organization. If an ombudsman finds case notes necessary to manage the work, the ombudsman should establish and follow a consistent and standard practice for the destruction of any such written notes.

3.4 When necessary, the ombudsman's office will seek judicial protection for staff and records of the office. It may be necessary to seek representation by separate legal counsel to protect the privilege of the office.

4. We exercise discretion whether to act upon a concern of an individual contacting the office. An ombudsman may initiate action on a problem he or she perceives directly.

5. We are designated neutrals and remain independent of ordinary line and staff structures. We serve no additional role (within an organization where we serve as ombudsman) which would compromise this neutrality.

5.1 An ombudsman strives for objectivity and impartiality.

5.2 The ombudsman has a responsibility to consider the concerns of all parties known to be involved in a dispute.

5.3 We do not serve as advocates for any person in a dispute within an organization; however, we do advocate for fair processes and their fair administration.

5.4 We help develop a range of responsible options to resolve problems and facilitate discussion to identify the best options. When possible, we help people develop new ways to solve problems themselves.

5.5 An ombudsman should exercise discretion before entering into any additional affiliations, roles or actions that may impact the neutrality of the function within the organization.

5.6 We do not make binding decisions, mandate policies or adjudicate issues for the organization.

6. We remain an informal and off-the-record resource. Formal investigations—for the purpose of adjudication—should be done by others. In the event that an ombudsman accepts a request to conduct a formal investigation, a memo should be written to file noting this action as an exception to the ombudsman role. Such investigations should not be considered privileged.

6.1 We do not act as agent for the organization and we do not accept notice on behalf of the organization. We do always refer individuals to the appropriate place where formal notice can be made.

6.2 Individuals should not be required to meet with an ombudsman. All interactions with the ombudsman should be voluntary.

7. We foster communication about the philosophy and function of the ombudsman's office with the people we serve.

8. We provide feedback on trends, issues, policies and practices without breaching confidentiality or anonymity. We identify new problems and we provide support for responsible systems change.

9. We keep professionally current and competent by pursuing con-

tinuing education and training relevant to the ombudsman profession.

10. We will endeavor to be worthy of the trust placed inns.

GLOSSARY

Confidential
Confidential describes communications, or a source of communications, which are intended to be held in secret. In an ombudsman's work confidentiality is often accomplished by providing anonymity to the source of communications. When the source of a communication is kept secret or private, this is known as an anonymous communication.

Independent
An ombudsman functions independent of line management. The ombudsman reporting relationship is with highest authority in an organization.

Neutrality
We do not serve as advocates for any person in a dispute within an organization; however, we do advocate for fair processes and their fair administration.

When making recommendations, the ombudsman has the responsibility to suggest actions or policies that will be equitable to all parties.

Privilege
Privilege is a legal term which describes a relationship which the law protects from forced disclosure. Traditional privileges are client/lawyer, doctor/patient, priest/penitent, husband/wife. An ombudsman privilege differs from these other forms of privilege because the office holds the privilege and it cannot be waived by others. The privilege is necessary to preserve the process that allows people to come forward to resolve their concerns in a confidential setting without the risk of reprisal.

Appendix 9

The University and College Ombuds Association Standards of Practice, 2000

Standards of Practice

INTRODUCTION

The University and College Ombuds Association has developed the following standards of practice to provide a model for individual practice and for the establishment of office policies and procedures. These standards were developed in accordance with commonly understood principles within the Ombuds profession and reflect the core values of the University and College Ombuds Association. Standards of Practice help guide members in making responsible choices and further, they are intended to promote constituents' understanding of and confidence in Ombuds Offices and their services.

DEFINITION

A college or university ombudsman* is authorized by an institution of higher education to confidentially receive complaints, concerns or inquiries about alleged acts, omissions, improprieties, and/or broader systemic problems within the ombudsman's defined jurisdiction and to listen, offer options, facilitate resolutions, informally investigate or otherwise examine these issues independently and impartially.

---

* The term Ombudsman is used in this definition in order to communicate with the widest possible community and is not intended to discourage others from using more gender neutral terms. In accordance with UCOA practice adopted in 1991, the document uses the term Ombuds throughout. UCOA acknowledges, with respect, that many practitioners use alternative forms of this word, such as ombudsperson, ombuds officer and the like.

Members of the University and College Ombuds Association strive to practice according to the following standards:

1. Independence
The Ombuds Office must be independent in its structure, function and appearance.

1.1 The Ombuds institutional reporting relationship to her/his supervisor is for administrative and budgetary purposes only.

1.2 The Ombuds should be placed at the highest possible level.

1.3 The Ombuds should have no assignment of duties that would present a conflict of interest to her/his duties as ombuds.

1.4 The Ombuds is independent of the units which the office informally investigates or examines.

1.5 The Ombuds has the sole power to appoint and remove Ombuds Office staff and is directly involved in staff supervision.

1.6 The Ombuds acts on issues, concerns, inquiries, complaints, or on her or his own initiative.

1.7 The Ombuds should issue periodic reports summarizing the ombuds' activities.

1.8 The Ombuds should have a set and renewable term or should be removable only for cause.

1.9 The Ombuds should have a specific allocated budget and sufficient resources to perform the function.

1.10 The Ombuds Office should be established through an act of the organization's official governing body, or in written policies, such as terms of reference or resolution.

1.11 The Ombuds has access to all relevant sources of information.

2. Impartiality/Neutrality
The Ombuds is neutral, impartial, unaligned and objective.

2.1 The Ombuds has no personal interest or stake in and incurs no personal gain or loss from the outcome of an issue.

2.2 The Ombuds avoids situations which may cause or result in conflicts of interest for the Ombuds.

2.3 The Ombuds is an advocate for good and fair process, not an advocate on behalf of individuals or the institution.

2.4 The Ombuds acts in consideration of and with respect for the legitimate interests and concerns of all affected parties.

2.5 The Ombuds should recommend and advocate for responsible and appropriate systems change.

2.6 The Ombuds should bring to the attention of appropriate parties policies, programs, personnel matters, or institutional practices or decisions which affect persons' health, safety or rights.

3. Confidentiality

The Ombuds must not disclose and must not be required to disclose any information provided in confidence, except to address an imminent risk of serious harm where there is no other responsible option.

3.1 The Ombuds safeguards the identity of individuals and their issues and does not disclose having met or talked with a party or parties, without permission of the party or parties.

3.2 The Ombuds does not disclose without permission communications received from any or all parties in the course of performing her/his duties.

3.3 The privilege of confidentiality of communications and records belongs to the Ombuds and the Ombuds Office, rather than to any party to an issue.

3.4 The Ombuds does not comply with requests for information about individual cases.

3.5 The Ombuds takes specific action related to an individual's issues only with the individual's permission and only to the extent permitted.

3.6 If the Ombuds pursues an issue systemically, the Ombuds does so without revealing the identity of a complainant or a singular situation that could be associated with a particular individual(s).

3.7 The Ombuds does not violate institutional standards of privacy or confidentiality in the pursuit or provision of information.

3.8 The Ombuds maintains information (e.g., notes, phone messages, appointment calendars) in a secure location and manner.

3.9 The Ombuds carefully prepares data and/or reports in anonymous and aggregate form to preserve confidentiality and prohibit identification of individuals.

3.10 Communication with the Ombuds is not notice to the organization.

3.11 The Ombuds publicizes the confidential nature of Ombuds work.

4. Informality

The Ombuds functions on an informal basis by such means as: listening, providing and receiving information, reframing issues, developing options, referral, third party intervention, shuttle diplomacy, mediation, and systems change.

4.1 The Ombuds does not take an active role in any formal institutional investigative or adjudicative procedures. The Ombuds may informally investigate or otherwise examine alleged procedural irregularities of a formal process and allegations about alleged acts, omissions, improprieties and/or broader systemic problems.

4.2 The Ombuds supplements, but does not replace, any steps required in formal internal or external procedures. Use of the Ombuds office is not a required step in any grievance process or organizational policy.

4.3 The Ombuds hears, considers, and as appropriate, pursues resolution of the concerns, issues, perceptions, interpretations, facts, and/or allegations of inappropriate acts, omissions, or improprieties presented by individuals.

4.4 The Ombuds may conduct informal fact finding when appropriate.

4.5 When a formal investigation is requested, the Ombuds refers individuals to the appropriate offices or persons.

5. Access to Services

All members of the specified community may voluntarily seek services and will be treated with respect and dignity.

5.1 The Ombuds exercises discretion in response to requests for service.

6. Professional Competence

The Ombuds acts in accordance with professional standards of practice and pursues and provides opportunities for staff to pursue continuing education and training.

8/30/00

Copyright, 2000 University and College Ombuds Association

Appendix 10

The International Ombudsman Association Guidance for Best Practices and Commentary on the American Bar Association Standards for the Establishment and Operation of Ombuds Offices Revised February 2004

March 14, 2006

I. INTRODUCTION 535

II. OMBUDS OFFICE CHARTER 539
    IOA Recommendation

III. LIMITATIONS ON THE OMBUDS'S AUTHORITY 540
  a. Quotation of Section D(6) of the ABA Standards
  b. IOA Commentary and Recommendations
     i. Issues arising under a Collective Bargaining Agreement
        IOA Recommendations
     ii. Issues that fall within the purview of federal, state or local labor or employment laws
        IOA Recommendations

IV. NOTICE 545
  a. Quotation of Section F of the ABA Standards
  b. IOA Commentary and Recommendations on Sections F (2) and F (3)
    IOA Recommendations
  c. IOA Commentary and Recommendations on Section F (1) (a- f)
     i. Communication of the Six Items in Section F (1) (a- f)
        IOA Recommendations
     ii. Voluntary Disclosure of Any Information- Section F (1) (a)
        IOA Recommendations

V. CONCLUSIONS AND FUTURE PLANNING 555

THE INTERNATIONAL OMBUDSMAN ASSOCIATION

GUIDANCE FOR BEST PRACTICES AND COMMENTARY ON THE AMERICAN BAR ASSOCIATION STANDARDS FOR THE ESTABLISHMENT AND OPERATION OF OMBUDS OFFICES, REVISED FEBRUARY 2004

March 14, 2006

The International Ombudsman Association (IOA) wishes to clarify its own guidance on best practices for organizational ombuds in light of the 2004 modifications to the American Bar Association (ABA) Standards for the Establishment and Operations of Ombuds Offices as revised in February 2004 (hereafter, the "ABA Standards").

I. INTRODUCTION

Until recently, organizational ombuds standards have been asserted, without challenge, as a set of ideals for a role that was principally self-regulated. In the United States, there have been no laws or rules that define necessary credentials for declaring oneself an ombudsman, no training path required to be entitled to use the name, and no criteria for certifying any ombuds programs as legitimate. As the organizational role became more widely established, during the 1990s, the two United States organizational ombuds organizations, The Ombudsman Association (TOA) and The University and College Ombuds Association (UCOA), ratified their own Standards of Practice and criteria for professional association membership. These two organizations merged in July of 2005 to form The International Ombudsman Association, which developed its own IOA Standards of Practice and criteria for membership. Members of the ombuds profession hoped that the standards they defined for themselves would set the parameters for other efforts to define formal or legal terms of reference for the role. The ABA Standards for the Establishment and Operation of Ombuds Offices and accompanying Report, initially created in 2001, constituted the first time that another profession has fully examined the ombuds role in the light of its own perspectives and interests and offered its interpretation of the role. The ABA Standards were revised in February 2004. (In 1969 the ABA adopted a resolution "recommending that state and local governments consider establishing ombudsmen who would be authorized to inquire into administrative action and to make public criticism." That Report was written in reference to classical ombudsmen and did not address the organizational ombudsman role which was, at that time, in its infancy.)

The 2004 ABA Standards modified the Standards passed by the ABA in 2001. The 2001 document represented a partially successful compromise document as the result of the joint efforts of the Administrative Law and Alternative Dispute Resolution (ADR) sections of the ABA working with representatives of several ombuds organizations. They guided a group proposing Standards that attempted to reflect the central concerns of the ombuds community while working closely and intensely with the various sectors of the ABA. The United States Ombudsman Association (USOA), which largely represents classical ombudsmen, was unhappy with the results and withdrew its support and disavowed the proposed report and recommendations.

In addition, certain issues, such as notice and the relation of organizational ombuds to unions, were not fully addressed in the 2001 Standards because it was not possible to reach a formulation satisfactory to all parties. The 2004 Standards represent a second compromise—that between the key ABA drafters of the earlier report and representatives of additional ABA sections who had voiced a variety of new concerns that emerged as different sections reacted to the first report. Because of internal dynamics within the ABA, representatives of the different ombuds organizations were not able to play as active a role in the development of the 2004 Standards as they had in the first process, and a number of the objections and critical changes offered by ombuds organizations were ultimately not included in the second report.

In August of 2004, the Boards of Directors of TOA and UCOA approved the following Resolution in response to the ABA Standards of 2004:

RESOLVED: The Ombudsman Association and The University and College Ombuds Association note the Resolution adopted by the American Bar Association House of Delegates on February 9, 2004, on Standards for the Establishment and Operation of Ombuds Offices. The ABA Resolution significantly departs—in provisions including but not limited to confidentiality and notice—from the Standards of Practice adopted by The Ombudsman Association and The University and College Ombuds Association, which were derived from the best practices of organizational ombuds based on many years of collective experience. The Ombudsman Association and The University and College Ombuds Association therefore reaffirm their Standards of Practice.

The ABA Standards approved by the ABA Board of Delegates in February of 2004 include several changes that require the serious consideration of all practicing organizational ombuds and IOA members. Many of the principles stated in the ABA Standards are helpful to organizational ombuds, particularly the ABA's support for the essential ombuds characteristics of independence, impartiality, and confidentiality. Part II of this document (hereafter referred to as "IOA Guidance"), endorses the ABA's recommendation that the scope and authority of every organizational ombuds office be defined by a written charter.

Other areas of ombuds practice addressed in the 2004 ABA Standards raise serious concerns among the organizational ombuds community either because their implications are ambiguous or because they seem to constrain or undermine certain key aspects of the ombuds role. Key among these is Section D of the ABA Standards, entitled "Limitations on the Ombuds's Authority," which refers to the extent to which it is appropriate for an organizational ombuds to address issues arising under a collective bargaining agreement or within the purview of federal, state, or local labor or employment laws. The third part of this IOA Guidance comments on Section D of the ABA Standards.

The language of Section F of the ABA Standards, entitled "Notice," also raises concerns for ombuds practitioners. The fourth part of this IOA Guidance therefore comments on issues regarding notice. The first half of the fourth section deals with general principles for ombuds practice to clarify that a visitor's communication to only the ombuds office does not constitute notice to the organization, but that under certain circumstances it is possible for the ombuds to put the entity on notice. The second half of the fourth section addresses how the ombuds should advise the visitor about the issues of confidentiality, notice to the organization and other aspects of the visitor's rights.

Sections D and F of the ABA Standards are quoted in full at the beginning of Parts III and IV below. The complete text of the ABA Standards is available at www.abanet.org/adminlaw/omb uds/115.pdf.

This IOA Guidance document, originally drafted by TOA and UCOA, was presented online to the members of those organizations in February 2005, and distributed and discussed in sessions of the annual conferences April 9-13, 2005; the memberships' open comment period extended from February through the end of April 2005. All comments received were carefully evaluated and many were incorporated into the document and/or will be integrated into ombuds training programs. The final revised version, presented to IOA members in March 2006 through the IOA Legal and Legislative Affairs Committee of IOA, is intended to provide:

1. Guidance for IOA members in interpreting the ABA Standards document, including recommendations for best practices in their offices and guidance when having discussions with their own organizations' management, counsel and other relevant parties about charter or terms of reference, job descriptions and related matters;
2. Guidance for instructors in IOA training courses regarding the implications of the ABA document for how IOA defines and explains the ombuds role;
3. Guidance for organizations considering the establishment of new ombuds programs or the review of existing programs;
4. Greater clarity regarding the key areas where the view expressed by ombuds professionals of their role and functions may vary somewhat from the view of the ABA.

It is important to emphasize that there are many elements of the ABA Standards that are supported by the ombuds community. In many ways the IOA Standards of Practice are consistent with the ABA Standards. In some of the commentary in this IOA Guidance document, the perspective may be different from that of the ABA, but the ultimate definition of the ombuds function may be similar. Some of our recommendations may be compatible or even identical with the intentions of the ABA.

We recognize that both the ABA and the IOA are committed to creating greater uniformity in the formulation and practice of the ombuds role while simultaneously recognizing the value to society of informal, interest-based conflict resolution programs. It is to this end that we offer the following guidance and commentary.

II. OMBUDS OFFICE CHARTER

Most prominent among the helpful components of the ABA Standards is the stipulation that every organization with an ombuds should have a charter (also sometimes known as "terms of reference") that specifies the functions, roles, limitations and protections of that ombuds office, especially the essential characteristics of independence, impartiality, and confidentiality. The charter will help each organization's ombuds practice to maintain the highest standards and will help the organization and the individuals who use the office have a better understanding of its functions and confidence in the integrity of the process.

The ABA Standards includes a 12-page "Report" that includes a detailed description of the duties and authorities of the ombuds that should be defined in a written and publicly available charter. The recommendation for best practice below is a summary of the discussion of the ombuds office charter as found in the Report appended to the ABA Standards.

IOA Recommendation

- **Each entity that establishes an organizational ombuds office should ensure that the office has a charter that affirms the essential characteristics of the ombuds function—independence, impartiality, and confidentiality—that govern the** role in which the ombuds receives complaints, works to resolve particular issues informally, and makes recommendations for the general improvement of the organization. The charter should also specify and define the ombuds' scope of practice and limitations on the ombuds' authority; qualifications to be an ombuds; office structure; procedures; confidentiality; and an understanding about the ombuds office not accepting notice on behalf of the entity.

III. LIMITATIONS ON THE OMBUDS'S AUTHORITY

This part of the IOA Guidance for organizational ombuds responds to Section D (6) of the ABA Standards which presents limitations on the ombuds' authority to "address any issue arising under a collective bargaining agreement or which fall within the purview of any federal, state, or local labor or employment law, rule or regulation. . ."

We first quote from the relevant section of the ABA Standards:

a. Quotation

LIMITATIONS ON THE OMBUDS'S AUTHORITY
D. An ombuds should not, nor should an entity expect or authorize an ombuds to:
   (1) make, change, or set aside a law, policy, or administrative decision
   (2) make binding decisions or determine rights
   (3) directly compel an entity or any person to implement the ombuds's recommendations
   (4) conduct an investigation that substitutes for administrative or judicial proceedings
   (5) accept jurisdiction over an issue that is currently pending in a legal forum unless all parties and the presiding officer in that action explicitly consent
   (6) address any issue arising under a collective bargaining agreement or which falls within the purview of any federal, state, or local labor or employment law, rule, or regulation, unless there is no collective bargaining representative

and the employer specifically authorizes the ombuds to do so,[1] or

(7) act in a manner inconsistent with the grant of and limitations on the jurisdiction of the office when discharging the duties of the office of ombuds.

(ABA Standards, Section D)

We believe this section of the ABA Standards generally reinforces an important and long-standing principle of ombuds practice, namely to provide an informal, impartial and confidential resource for resolution of various workplace issues. Items (1) – (5) and item (7) are compatible with IOA Standards of Practice. Only item (6) raises concerns, which are discussed below.

b. IOA Commentary and Recommendations

i. Issues arising under a Collective Bargaining Agreement (CBA)

Ombuds generally have great respect for the principles and goals of organized labor's advocacy for fair and just treatment of workers, and many ombuds are routinely called upon to provide informal assistance to union members. These requests for assistance, or referrals, which may come from union representatives, managers, or the union members involved, normally do not involve issues arising under a collective bargaining agreement (for example, union members may seek the assistance of an ombuds to address concerns about the entity or workplace in general, or conflict between members of the same union or with a non-union co-worker). Ombuds do not participate in formal grievances or substitute for existing grievance procedures. Thus, if an issue *does* fall under a CBA, the ombuds must first consider whether it would be appropriate to listen to the concern or accept the referral. If the union representatives, management, and union member(s) all agree to refer the problem for informal resolution, the referral may be appropriate for the ombuds. Typically, these kinds of

---

1. Under these Standards, the employer may authorize an ombuds to address issues of labor or employment law only if the entity has expressly provided the ombuds with the confidentiality specified in Paragraph C(3). An ombuds program as envisioned by these Standards supplements and does not substitute for other procedures and remedies necessary to meet the duty of employers to protect the legal rights of both employers and employees.

referrals are made in the spirit of cooperation and with the goal of benefiting union and non-union employees, management, and the workplace and entity as a whole. Moreover, ombuds intervention under these kinds of circumstances is consistent with the spirit of many workplace policies and CBAs that recommend that, where possible, problems should be addressed through means of alternative dispute resolution.

When an ombuds assists a union employee, he or she should discuss generally known and applicable union options and resources with the union employee, and should defer to the union process any issue covered by the CBA contract unless otherwise agreed to by the visitor, the organization, and the union. An ombuds is not expected to be a substitute for a union representative in terms of providing advice about formal union processes or available union benefits or services.

This practice is consistent with the role of the ombuds to supplement existing resources available to their constituents, rather than to circumvent, duplicate, or create alternative grievance mechanisms. We agree with the statement in the ABA Report that an entity's policy of allowing an ombuds to address labor or employment-related matters should not be considered a suspect or disfavored practice.

IOA Recommendations

- **The ombuds charter, and, where possible, any relevant collective bargaining agreement, should define the involvement of an ombuds with union employees and with issues that arise under the collective bargaining agreement. For those ombuds whose scope of services includes union employees, the ombuds should defer to the union process any issue covered by the CBA unless otherwise agreed to by the union, the entity, and the persons involved.**

- **The ombuds should always inform covered employees about the union process when providing assistance on an issue that might be covered by the CBA.**

ii. Issues that fall within the purview of federal, state, or local labor or employment laws

In addition to issues arising under a CBA, Section D(6) also raises questions about whether the involvement of an ombuds, in matters of labor and employment-related laws, could raise sensitive issues that may affect the rights and liabilities of the parties under those laws. Our longstanding position has been and continues to be that unless specifically excluded from involvement in labor or employment law issues, the organizational ombuds may address these issues. The IOA believes that the ABA's position in this area is inconsistent with the sound principles of alternative dispute resolution.

We recognize that visitors to the ombuds office may discuss a wide range of workplace concerns, some of which may relate to federal, state, or local law, and we respect the ABA's concern for preserving visitors' legal rights. As clearly stated above, our position is that an ombuds may address issues that fall within the purview of federal, state or local labor and employment laws. The ombuds should adopt important safeguards and considerations when dealing with cases concerning rights arising under a CBA or potentially relevant employment law. This recommended practice enhances the ability of an ombuds to effectively and appropriately address certain cases. We believe the safeguards and considerations recommended by the ABA Standards mirror existing ombuds ethics, values and best practices. For example, the ABA Standards suggest that an entity authorize its ombuds office to address matters related to labor and employment law only if the office meets the three essential characteristics of independence, impartiality and confidentiality (ABA Standards, Section D (6), Footnote 4). These characteristics are of equal importance to the ombuds profession and are the foundation of ombuds standards, values and ethics.

For most entities, it is the combination of informal services and formal grievance procedures, embodied in a conflict management system, that provides the appropriate range of options and that allow for early identification and resolution of potential legal issues or concerns. Central to ombuds practice is the principle that an ombuds program supplements, but does not replace or seek to duplicate existing formal grievance procedures, and that it is the role and obligation of the ombuds to refer visitors to the entity's formal procedures and remedies whenever appropriate. Nevertheless, visitors will often choose to explore informal options for a wide variety of reasons.

We believe the recommended safeguards reaffirm this important principle, and that they afford an opportunity for ombuds to demonstrate support for the provision of equitable and adequate formal grievance procedures as well as informal ombuds conflict resolution options. We note that the ABA positions stated in the ABA Standards and the ABA Report are internally inconsistent. We, therefore, want to draw special attention to, and express our concurrence with, the statement in the ABA Report that an entity's policy of allowing an ombuds to address labor or employment-related matters should not be considered a suspect or disfavored practice.

IOA Recommendations
- Ombuds should function in a way that addresses concern for preserving the legal rights of visitors. An ombuds should present and if appropriate discuss an appropriate range of options available to the visitor from the very informal to the most formal. Formal options may include ways to put management on notice of an issue, referrals to rights-based elements of the organization's conflict resolution system, or the provision of information about seeking external legal advice (for example, providing contact information to the local bar association's attorney referral service).
- When the ombuds works with the visitor to address issues that may involve other formal alternatives (under law, rules, or regulations), it should be made clear to the visitor that an informal approach does not automatically exclude the visitor's later participation in more formal options. The ombuds should remind the visitor to keep in mind possible time limits and their potential impact on the visitor's more formal options. The ombuds should not provide legal advice, but should suggest alternatives that make the visitor aware of the possible need to seek legal advice.

IV. NOTICE

This part of the IOA Guidance discusses the concept of legal notice in general, and responds to the ABA Standards for notice as set forth in Section (F) of the 2004 revised Standards. We first quote the relevant section of the ABA Standards:

a. Quotation

NOTICE

F. An ombuds is intended to supplement, not replace, formal procedures.[2] Therefore:

(1) An ombuds should provide the following information in a general and publicly available manner and inform people who contact the ombuds for help or advice that—
  (a) the ombuds will not voluntarily disclose to anyone outside the ombuds office, including the person provides in confidence or the person's identity unless necessary to address an imminent risk of serious harm or with the person's express consent
  (b) important rights may be affected by when formal action is initiated and by and when the entity is informed of the allegedly inappropriate or wrongful behavior or conduct
  (c) communications to the ombuds may not constitute notice to the entity unless the ombuds communicates with representatives of the entity as described in Paragraph 2
  (d) working with the ombuds may address the problem or concern effectively, but may not protect the rights of either the person contacting the office or the entity in which the ombuds operates[3]

---

2. An ombuds program as envisioned by these Standards supplements and does not substitute for the need of an entity to establish formal procedures that my be necessary *to protect legal rights and to* address allegedly inappropriate or wrongful behavior or conduct

3. The notice requirements of Paragraph F do not supersede or change the advocacy responsibilities of an Advocate Ombuds.

(e) the ombuds is not, and is not a substitute for, anyone's lawyer, representative or counselor, and
(f) the person may wish to consult a lawyer or other appropriate resource with respect to those rights.

(2) If the ombuds communicates[4] with representatives of the entity concerning an allegation of a violation, then—
   (a) a communication that reveals the facts of
       (i) a specific allegation and the identity of the complainant or
       (ii) allegations by multiple complainants that may reflect related behavior or conduct that is either inappropriate or wrongful should be regarded as providing notice to the entity of the alleged violation and the complainants should be advised that the ombuds communicated their allegations to the entity; but otherwise,
   (b) whether or not the communication constitutes notice to the entity is a question that should be determined by the facts of the communication.

(3) If an ombuds functions in accordance with Paragraph C, "Independence, Impartiality, and Confidentiality," of these standards, then—
   (a) no one, including the entity in which the ombuds operates, should deem the ombuds to be an agent of any person or entity, other than the office of the ombuds, for purposes of receiving notice of alleged violations, and
   (b) communications made to the ombuds should not be imputed to anyone else, including the entity in which the ombuds acts unless the ombuds communicates with representatives of the entity in which case Paragraph 2 applies.

---

4. Under these standards, any such communication is subject to Paragraph C(3).

b. IOA Commentary and Recommendations on Sections F (2) and F (3)

Certain federal and state laws require an organization to take action when placed on "notice" of an alleged violation of the law. Therefore, there are situations where conversations within the workplace can place the organization "on notice," thus requiring the organization to act, whether or not that is the wish of the person involved. Typically, the organization establishes official reporting channels designated as points of contact for reporting certain concerns such as sexual harassment (e.g., the human resources office, the sexual harassment prevention office, women's resource center, or similar office) or fraud, waste and abuse of government/public/company resources (e.g., the ethics office, internal audit, or similar office). In addition, an organization may be placed on notice when information becomes known to certain organizational managers by virtue of the management level or seniority of their positions.

The ombuds office asserts that communications made to the ombuds are confidential, the office will assert a privilege to protect those communications, and therefore communications made to the ombuds are never notice to the organization.

The ombuds office's claim of confidentiality is based upon and supported by its founding tenets, in particular, by its establishment as an independent, neutral, informal and alternate channel for people to seek guidance on how to resolve workplace disputes or raise issues of concern. The ombuds' confidentiality is based upon many values, including prompt, informal resolution of workplace disputes; organizational critical self-examination and continuous improvement; and enhanced risk management in providing a safe, off-the-record channel for people who otherwise would not come forward to seek guidance or learn how they can resolve workplace disputes or report concerns. The sense of safety created by the ombuds as a confidential channel enhances the communication and articulation of concerns and thus the organization's ability to effectively respond to those concerns. The need to protect confidentiality of communications with the ombuds office is thus premised on "best practice" principles for organizational governance, including such important federal policies as those embodied in The Sarbanes-Oxley Act of 2002 and the U.S. Sentencing Guidelines for Organizations.

The ombuds office thus asserts a privilege, which is held by the office, that communications with the ombuds are confidential. This privilege is critical to making the ombuds office a place where people can raise any issue, including a violation of statute, regulation, or ethical standard. Only by offering the security of confidentiality can the ombuds facilitate organizational responsibility and accountability, which are at the heart of provisions contained in the U.S. Sentencing Guidelines and the Sarbanes-Oxley Act that call for mechanisms of confidential reporting and/or guidance. Where issues cannot be confidentially raised, they may not be raised at all, thereby depriving the organization of an opportunity to address issues and rectify misconduct that has not yet surfaced through other channels. The ability to have confidential communications that do not constitute "notice" to the organization is essential to the effective functioning of an ombuds office and distinguishes the ombuds from other reporting channels also generally available. It is the "off- the-record" aspects of the office that lead people who use the ombuds to do so before taking any official or formal action. The ombuds office enables people to come forward with an issue when they would otherwise be afraid to do so or when they fear retaliation from managers or peers.

Given the confidential nature of communications made to the ombuds office, and the privilege which should attach to those communications, IOA asserts, and the ABA agrees, that communications made to the ombuds do not constitute notice to the organization. Both the IOA and ABA assert as a part of their standards that no one, including the organization that employs the ombuds, should consider the ombuds office to be an agent of notice and no one, including the entity, should seek information about communications to the ombuds office. The IOA and ABA also agree that the nature and role of confidentiality should be explained to the visitor, who should understand that the ombuds claims the privilege for the office and that it is not the visitor's privilege to waive. Visitors should understand that as a condition for accepting and benefiting from the services, they have the obligation to support the ombuds claim of privilege and not to attempt to breach this claim.

While the IOA and ABA agree on many important principles for establishing and operating an ombuds program, the IOA believes that some of the provisions in the ABA Standards with respect to when an ombuds places an organization on notice are not well founded or legally supported. The ABA resolution suggests that circumstances may exist in which an Ombuds places an organization on notice other than by disclosing a specific allegation and the identity of the complainant or allegations by multiple complainants reflecting a pattern of "wrongful" conduct. In particular, the ABA addresses this possibility by noting that whether or not an ombuds communication constitutes notice to the entity is a question that should be determined by the "facts of the communication." We are concerned that this language does not capture accurately what may be a very limited number of peculiar situations, and instead offers an imprecise catch-all provision that could inadvertently invite courts to more closely examine communications to the ombuds as context for understanding communications by the ombuds to the entity. The ABA language, then, could jeopardize ombuds confidentiality and effectiveness.

The IOA takes the position that a communication to the ombuds *never constitutes notice to the organization.* As ombuds office administrative manager, the lead ombuds may be responsible for receiving notice about wrongful behavior of any ombuds office staff member whom the lead ombuds supervises. Except in this ombuds' administrative capacity as the manager of the ombuds office, the ombuds is never an agent of notice or a designated point of contact to accept formal claims or concerns. A communication between an ombuds and an organization's point of contact may serve as notice under some circumstances, as explained below, but the scope of that notice is limited strictly to the substance of the communication between the ombuds and the point of contact, and *never* includes any communications between the visitor and the ombuds. In most situations where notice to the organization may be appropriate, the ombuds helps direct the visitor to the proper point of contact. It is only in rare instances that the ombuds may choose to take action directly to place the organization on notice, such as in the unlikely event that the visitor to the ombuds office is not able or not willing to do so themselves.

Communications of a visitor to the ombuds are confidential, except in cases where the ombuds receives permission from the individual to share certain information or where the ombuds determines that there is an imminent risk of serious harm. An ombuds may place the organization on "notice" when the ombuds evaluates the circumstances and specifically elects to place the organization on notice by identifying an appropriate point of contact within the organization and communicating to that point of contact specific information which the ombuds expressly intends to share for the purpose of placing the organization on notice of a specific concern or specific situation. If an ombuds makes such an intentional notice communication, confidentiality is waived only with regard to the specific communication made with the point of contact for purposes of the notice communication. It is the conversation between the ombuds and the appropriate point of contact within the organization that constitutes notice and not the conversation between the ombuds and the visitor. Thus, under no circumstances, is the original communication to the ombuds part of the notice communication.

All ombuds offices should have a well-defined and generally available procedure detailing the limited circumstances and the processes under which the ombuds may provide notice. If the ombuds elects to place the organization on notice under the conditions above, the ombuds should follow the protocol of the particular ombuds office regarding this unusual action. The protocols should include specific steps so that is clear that the ombuds made an intentional decision to make a notice disclosure. The steps may include, for example:

- Identify the appropriate office of notice;
- Articulate the ombuds' intention of placing that agent of the organization on notice to take action;
- Give narrow and specific information (such as names and dates) regarding the allegations or concerns, sufficient to allow the organization to act on the notice;
- Provide the information in a way that preserves the maximum

confidentiality possible, while providing information adequate for the organization's required response;
- Provide the recipient with narrow, carefully screened written information and instruct the recipient of the information to keep a record of the communication;
- Clarify that if called later to testify or to participate in a formal procedure that testimony is limited narrowly to questions pertaining directly to the ombuds' original notice communication to the organization and nothing more;
- Expressly state that limited disclosure of information necessary to provide notice does not act as a waiver to other information or conversations relevant to the matter.
- Remind the agent receiving the notice communication the he or she may not want to take specific adverse action based solely upon the notice of the communication, but instead may now be required to *investigate* the allegation, and then may want to consider whether any action is warranted based upon the results of his or her investigation.

In circumstances where the ombuds places the organization on notice, it may or may not be appropriate to seek permission from or to inform the original source(s) of the information. For example, in some circumstances the ombuds may determine that there is an imminent risk of serious harm to others besides the original source and seeking permission of the source could actually compromise otherwise protected information. In other situations the ombuds may determine that seeking permission of the visitor could actually cause the visitor harm. However, if it is appropriate and practical, the ombuds should advise complainants that the entity has been put on notice.

IOA Recommendations
- **Except in the administrative capacity as manager of the ombuds office, the ombuds is never an agent of notice, and communications to the ombuds office never constitute notice to the organization.**
- **The nature and role of confidentiality should be explained to the visitor, who should understand that the ombuds claims the privilege for the office and that it is not the visitor's privilege to waive.**

- **In most situations where notice to the organization may be appropriate, the ombuds helps direct the visitor to the proper point of contact. It is only in rare instances that the ombuds may take action, at his or her discretion, directly to place the organization on notice of an allegation of wrongdoing, such as in the rare event that the visitor to the ombuds office is not able or not willing to do so himself or herself.**
- **An ombuds may also place the organization on notice in the unusual situation in which the ombuds perceives there to be an imminent risk of serious harm. However, even in this instance, the original communication to the ombuds is not part of the notice communication.**
- **Every ombuds office should have a well-defined and generally available procedure detailing the limited circumstances and processes under which the ombuds may provide notice, and this protocol should be strictly followed when the ombuds takes the unusual action of placing the organization on notice.**
- **In circumstances where the ombuds places the organization on notice, it may or may not be appropriate to seek permission from or to inform the original source(s) of the information.**

c. **IOA Commentary and Recommendations on Section F (1) (a) – (f)**
   i. Communication of the Six Items in Section F (1) (a-f)

Section F (1)(a) - Section F (1)(f) of the ABA Standards discusses the issue of "notice," and proposes six subjects the ABA believes an ombuds "should" communicate to persons who contact the ombuds. We will first comment on these six items in general, and then add specific comments on the voluntary disclosure of information in trend reporting and the "imminent risk of serious harm" language of Section F (1)(a).

We believe it is unnecessarily burdensome to ombuds practitioners, and potentially awkward and problematic for the building of rapport with those who contact the ombuds for assistance, to tell each and every person, whether by phone or in person, all six of the items recommended by the ABA. For example, part of the ombuds role is referral to appropriate resources. It may be immediately obvious to an ombuds that the caller seeks only an answer to a simple policy question or a referral to another office, such as an employee assistance program or human resources. As another example, the person may simply want coaching on communication skills, in which case telling the visitor about potentially contacting a lawyer regarding their rights could be unnecessarily alarming and irrelevant. It would not be appropriate to recite all six items to someone for whom some or all of these items are irrelevant.

IOA Recommendations
- **It is extremely important for the ombuds to demonstrate consistent practice when discussing with visitors the potential impact and limits of "notice" to the organization. The ombuds should ensure that all visitors, at the very least, have access to materials that explain the ombuds role and limits in relation to notice in detail. In addition, the ombuds should develop criteria (specific to the environment and needs of the ombuds' own organization) for a consistent approach to providing information about notice, where and when relevant. Failure to demonstrate consistency of practice in this regard may expose the ombuds to the need to discuss ombuds conversations on a case-by-case basis relevant to determining whether the visitor adequately understood the options and the notice implications.**
- **The six items listed in the ABA Standards Section F (1) (a) – (f) as appropriate communications to persons who contact the ombuds office should be published on the ombuds office website, in the ombuds office brochures and other explanatory information, as well as in the entity's charter for the ombuds office, so that this information is generally and publicly available.**
- **The decision as to which, if any, of the six items should be communicated directly to the visitor should be left to the discretion of the ombuds, who will make the decision based on the overall circumstances and the criteria developed**

within the ombuds' own organization (consistent with these guidelines).
- When necessary or appropriate, the ombuds should clarify how an ombuds program "fits" with other systems and services by explaining to visitors that:
  a. The visitor may have important legal rights that may be involved with the visitor's issue, and important time limits and other factors may be involved.
  b. The ombuds program is not a substitute for a lawyer or other professional who might represent the visitor's rights, and the visitor may wish to consult with these other services separately from their conversation with the ombuds.
  c. The visitor may wish to consult with additional resources and services (e.g., an employee assistance program) which the ombuds may describe if they might be appropriate given the visitor's presenting circumstances.

ii. Voluntary Disclosure of Any Information – Section F (1) (a)

Section F (1) (a) recommends that ombuds inform users of services that "the ombuds will not voluntarily disclose to anyone outside the ombuds office, including the entity in which the ombuds acts, any information the person provides in confidence or the person's identity unless necessary to address an imminent risk of serious harm or with the person's express consent." This recommendation raises two concerns: trend reporting and "imminent risk of serious harm."

First, as part of trend reporting and advocacy for systemic change, both of which are appropriate ombuds roles, an ombuds may decide to disclose information to people outside the office even without a person's consent — but only when this can be accomplished in a way that protects the person's confidentiality and/or identity. For example, if an ombuds is informed of a problem by many people, the ombuds may let someone higher up in the organization know that "several" people have communicated the problem.

We note that the ABA Standards are internally inconsistent on this topic. Other sections of the document encourage ombuds reporting:

the ABA Standards identify ombuds roles as "making recommendations for the resolution of . . . a systemic problem to those persons who have the authority to act upon them," "identifying complaint patterns and trends," and "issuing periodic reports" [ABA Standards, Section A (7)]; the ABA Report states that the ombuds may "disclose confidential information so long as doing so does not compromise the identity of the person who supplied it" (ABA Report, Section 3). Taken together, these statements seem inconsistent with the requirement in Section F (1) (a) that an ombuds not disclose "any" information provided in confidence without "the person's express consent."

Second, the reference to ombuds disclosure when there is "an imminent risk of serious harm" should include a proviso that the decision to make such a disclosure rests solely in the discretion of the ombuds.

IOA Recommendations
- **Ombuds materials (websites, brochures, etc.) should state that ombuds do report trends, and advocate for systemic change when appropriate, but that they do so in a manner that protects the identity of individuals.**
- **Ombuds materials that make reference to ombuds disclosure when there is "an imminent risk of serious harm" should always state that the decision to make such disclosure rests solely at the discretion of the ombuds.**

V. CONCLUSIONS AND FUTURE PLANNING

As stated in the introduction, the intent of this document is to provide guidance to IOA members in interpreting the ABA document and to make recommendations for best practices for organizational ombuds offices. IOA does not intend for this to be the end of the discussion about professional standards, but instead views this as a further step in understanding the application of our standards of practice to our daily professional activities. The road ahead should include consideration of the evolution of some of the legal and other issues raised here, as well as how to strengthen our legal standing in the future.

Specific next steps for our professional association include further clarification of our ethics, standards, and best practices, and enhancement of training programs to include these recommendations for best practices, with attention to giving practitioners greater awareness of the ABA Standards and other legal issues that may impact our practices.

The IOA looks forward to collaborations forging greater partnerships with the ABA and other organizations as we further define our profession and our professional standards.

— Respectfully submitted by members of the task force that developed and revised this document, under the auspices of TOA, UCOA, and IOA: John Barkat, Judy Bruner, Howard Gadlin, Kevin Jessar, Bruce MacAllister, Martha McKee, Francine Montemurro, David Talbot, Marsha Wagner (chair), and Margo Wesley.

Appendix 11
IOA Best Practices

A Supplement to IOA's Standards of Practice[1]
Version 3, October 13, 2009

The Best Practices guide is intended to provide guidance to Organizational Ombudsmen[2] in practicing according to IOA Standards of Practice to the highest level of professionalism possible. Any questions or suggested revisions are welcome and should be sent to the Chair of the Professional Ethics, Standards, and Best Practices Committee.

PREAMBLE

> The IOA Standards of Practice are based upon and derived from the ethical principles stated in the IOA Code of Ethics.
>
> Each Ombudsman Office should have an organizational Charter or Terms of Reference, approved by senior management, articulating the principles of the Ombudsman function in that organization and their consistency with the IOA Standards of Practice.

Before implementing an Ombudsman program, an organization should educate all affected constituencies about the nature and scope of the program, including the role of the Ombudsman within the organization and the Standards of Practice that will govern the activities of the office.

Each entity that establishes an organizational Ombudsman Office should make certain that the office has a Charter that ensures that the Ombudsman will function according to the Standards of Practices and the core values of independence, impartiality/neutrality, confidentiality, and informality. These Standards of Practice will govern the way in

---

1. IOA Standards of Practice are indicated by text boxes; recommended Best Practices follow each text box. IOA Code of Ethics, Standards of Practice, and Best Practices are designed to guide "Organizational Ombudsmen" as distinguished from "Classical", "Advocate", "Executive" or other types of Ombudsmen.

2. The term Ombudsman is used to communicate to the widest possible community and is not intended to discourage others from using alternatives. IOA respectfully acknowledges that many practitioners use alternative forms of this word.

which the Ombudsman receives complaints, works to resolve issues, and makes recommendations for the general improvement of the organization. The Charter should also specify the Ombudsman's scope of practice, limitations on Ombudsman authority, and qualifications to be an Ombudsman.

IOA asserts that communications with an ombudsman are confidential and strives to protect confidentiality for all protected communications.

One basis for protecting confidentiality is a claim of privilege. The law on this issue is still evolving and the determination of whether such a privilege is applicable is made by courts on a case-by-case basis since there is no statute creating such a privilege. In addition, ombudsman offices have been able to protect the confidentiality of communications where program materials adequately state that people who use the office agree to abide by expressed confidentiality principles or where statutes dealing with alternative dispute resolution or mediation are applicable to ombudsman communications.

STANDARDS OF PRACTICE

INDEPENDENCE

1.1 The Ombudsman Office and the Ombudsman are independent from other organizational entities.

The director of the Ombudsman Office should report directly to the highest level of the organization (such as board of directors, CEO, agency head, etc.) in a manner independent of ordinary line and staff functions.

The director of the Ombudsman Office should have terms of employment that indicate that his or her stature in the organization is not subordinate to senior officials.

The Ombudsman should be able to function independently from control, limitation, or interference imposed by any official in the entity.

The Ombudsman should be protected from retaliation (such as of elimination of the office or the Ombudsman, or reduction of the Ombudsman budget or other resources) by any person who may be the subject of a complaint or inquiry.

The Ombudsman should have a set and renewable term, or should be removable only for neglect of duty, misconduct, or medical incapacity, and only by means of a fair process and procedure.

The Ombudsman should obtain assurance from the organization at the outset, and apart from any particular dispute, of access to outside legal counsel at his or her own discretion.

The expense of outside counsel should be covered by the organization and included in the overall budget for the Ombudsman Office. The Ombudsman should have an understanding with the organization that the Ombudsman is not required to inform the organization when it communicates with or accesses outside counsel.

The purpose of outside legal counsel should be to enhance the Ombudsman's ability to practice according to the Standards of Practice. The Ombudsman should consider how outside counsel may assist in a variety of situations, including when the entity and the Ombudsman need to strategize how best to handle a discovery request made of the Ombudsman, or when the Ombudsman and the entity could benefit from consultation with outside counsel regarding how best to establish and operate the office so as to ensure the integrity of function, and to protect the Ombudsman.

> 1.2 The Ombudsman holds no other position within the organization which might compromise independence.

See Sections 2.3 and 2.4.

> 1.3 The Ombudsman exercises sole discretion over whether or how to act regarding an individual's concern, a trend or concerns of multiple individuals over time. The Ombudsman may also initiate action on a concern identified through the Ombudsman's direct observation.

The Ombudsman should bring to the attention of the appropriate office those policies, programs, procedures or practices which may be problematic for the organization or which negatively affect people's health, safety or rights.

The Ombudsman should issue periodic reports summarizing activities, problem areas identified, and recommendations for systemic change.

Ombudsman Office materials (websites, brochures, etc.) should state that all such reporting is conducted in a manner that protects the identity of individuals and does not place the organization on notice.

1.4 The Ombudsman has access to all information and all individuals in the organization, permitted by law.

1.5 The Ombudsman has authority to select Ombudsman Office staff and manage Ombudsman Office budget and operations.

The Ombudsman Office must be provided with sufficient resources to operate an independent and effective program. These resources include adequate space, equipment, staffing, staff development, and the production and distribution of informational materials.

The independence of the Ombudsman Office may be supported by having the selection and evaluation of the Ombudsman, as well as the establishment of an appropriate level of funding, be determined by or in consultation with committees representative of various institutional constituencies.

NEUTRALITY AND IMPARTIALITY

2.1 The Ombudsman is neutral, impartial, and unaligned.

See Section 1.2.

2.2 The Ombudsman strives for impartiality, fairness and objectivity in the treatment of people and the consideration of issues. The Ombudsman advocates for fair and equitably administered processes and does not advocate on behalf of any individual within the organization.

All members of the specified community served by the Ombudsman may voluntarily seek services from the Ombudsman Office and will be treated with respect and dignity. The Ombudsman should assure access impartially, including to people with disabilities, people who need language interpreters, or people whose work hours require flexibility in scheduling appointment times.

The organization should assure that all specified members of the organization have the right to consult with the Ombudsman, and retaliation for exercising that right will not be tolerated.

2.3 The Ombudsman is a designated neutral reporting to the highest possible level of the organization and operating independently of ordinary line and staff structures. The Ombudsman should not report to nor be structurally affiliated with any compliance function of the organization.

The Ombudsman should have direct access to the board of directors (or other oversight body as appropriate). See Sections 1.1 and 1.2.

While the Ombudsman should be an internal position, it should not report to, nor have the appearance of reporting to, any compliance office or function or the organization.

The Charter or Terms of Reference for the Ombudsman Office should state specifically that the Ombudsman does not serve as an agent of notice for the organization.

2.4 The Ombudsman serves in no additional role within the organization which would compromise the Ombudsman's neutrality. The Ombudsman should not be aligned with any formal or informal associations within the organization in a way that might create actual or perceived conflicts of interest for the Ombudsman. The Ombudsman should have no personal interest or stake in, and incur no gain or loss from, the outcome of an issue.

See Sections 1.2, 4.4, and 4.5.

Except in the administrative capacity as manager of the Ombudsman Office, the Ombudsman should not participate in formal management functions or serve in any other role that poses an actual conflict of interest or creates the perception of one. For example, an Ombudsman ought not conduct formal investigations; serve in a position or role that is designated by the organization as a place to receive notice on behalf of the organization; serve as a voting member on a search committee (other than for Ombudsman staff); handle formal appeals of management actions; keep case records on behalf of the organization; or be charged in any way to make, change, enforce or set aside a law, rule or management decision.

If possible, the Ombudsman should hold only one position in the organization.

If the Ombudsman does hold another role within the organization, the different roles should be structured so that they are as separate and distinct as possible. The Ombudsman should not provide Ombudsman services to people whom the Ombudsman—in the other role—serves, manages, reports to, teaches, advises, or evaluates, in order to avoid partiality or perceptions of conflict of interest. The Ombudsman should provide Ombudsman services in a location that is different from the location in which the Ombudsman, in the other role, works, teaches, counsels, etc., to clarify the distinctions between roles, and to assure confidentiality and off-the-record informality of the Ombudsman communications. The Ombudsman's support staff (people who take messages or receive visitors, for example) for the Ombudsman role should be separate and distinct from the support staff in any other role. The Ombudsman should continually call attention to the role in which he or she is acting at any given time, and repeatedly educate members of the organization about the principles in the Ombudsman Office's Charter. The Ombudsman should attempt to provide alternatives for people and situations in which the Ombudsman cannot serve as Ombudsman due to actual or perceived conflicts of interest.

2.5 The Ombudsman has a responsibility to consider the legitimate concerns and interests of all individuals affected by the matter under consideration.

2.6 The Ombudsman helps develop a range of responsible options to resolve problems and facilitate discussion to identify the best options.

An Ombudsman should help the visitor explore and assess an appropriate range of options, from the very informal to the most formal. Formal options may include ways to put management on notice of an issue, referrals to rights-based elements of the organization's conflict resolution system, or the provision of information about the possibility of seeking external resources or assistance. The Ombudsman should never provide legal advice.

When the Ombudsman works with the visitor to address issues that may involve formal alternatives (under laws, policies, rules, or regulations), the Ombudsman should make clear to the visitor that an informal approach does not automatically exclude the visitor's later participation in more formal options, but that the visitor should keep in mind possible time limits and their potential impact on the visitor's formal options. See Section 4.4.

The impartiality of the Ombudsman Office may be supported by consultation with various organizational constituencies regarding the Ombudsman Office's effectiveness.

CONFIDENTIALITY

3.1 The Ombudsman holds all communications with those seeking assistance in strict confidence and takes all reasonable steps to safeguard confidentiality, including the following: The Ombudsman does not reveal, and must not be required to reveal, the identity of any individual contacting the Ombudsman Office, nor does the Ombudsman reveal information provided in confidence that could lead to the identification of any individual contacting the Ombudsman Office, without that individual's express permission, given in the course of informal discussions with the Ombudsman; the Ombudsman takes specific action related to an individual's issue only with the individual's express permission and only to the extent permitted, and even then at the sole discretion of the Ombudsman, unless such action can be taken in a way that safeguards the identity of the individual contacting the Ombudsman Office. The only exception to this privilege of confidentiality is where there appears to be imminent risk of serious harm, and where there is no other reasonable option. Whether this risk exists is a determination to be made by the Ombudsman.

The Ombudsman publicizes the confidential nature of Ombudsman work.

The Ombudsman Office should be situated in an appropriate location to protect the privacy of visitors to the office.

When an individual gives the Ombudsman permission to reveal his or her identity, disclose information, or act on his or her concerns, such permission must be given at the time that the Ombudsman is engaged in the informal conflict resolution process, not as part of a formal process.

The Ombudsman Office Charter for each organization should specify what types of events rise to the level of "imminent risk of serious harm." The Ombudsman may negotiate with the organization to be exempt, based on Ombudsman confidentiality, from some mandates that require reporting by other employees. Best practice is to interpret "imminent risk of serious harm" as narrowly as possible—for example, imminent risk to human life.

> 3.2 Communications between the Ombudsman and others (made while the Ombudsman is serving in that capacity) are considered privileged. The privilege belongs to the Ombudsman and the Ombudsman Office, rather than to any party to an issue. Others cannot waive this privilege.

The confidentiality privilege is critical to making the Ombudsman Office a place where people can raise any issue, including an alleged violation of statute, regulation, rule, policy, or ethical standard.

IOA asserts that communications made to the Ombudsman do not constitute "notice" to the organization. No one, including the employing entity, should consider the Ombudsman Office to be agent of notice (that is, an office that receives formal notice on behalf of the organization) and no one, including the entity, should seek information about communications to the Ombudsman Office.

The nature and role of confidentiality should be explained to the visitor, who should understand that the Ombudsman claims the privilege for the office and that it is not the visitor's privilege to waive. Whenever possible, this information should be communicated prior to discussing the concerns brought by the visitor.

Visitors should understand that as a condition for accepting and benefiting from the Ombudsman Office services, they have the obligation to support the Ombudsman claim of privilege and not to attempt to breach this claim.

The Ombudsman should emphasize in office materials and with the management of the organization:

- that the ability to have confidential communications that do not constitute "notice" to the organization is essential to the effective functioning of an Ombudsman Office and distinguishes the Ombudsman from formal reporting channels;

- that it is the "off-the-record" aspects of the office that lead people who use the Ombudsman to do so before taking any official or formal action;

- that the Ombudsman Office enables people to come forward with an issue when they might otherwise be afraid to do so or when they fear retaliation from managers or peers;

- that only by offering the security of confidentiality can the Ombudsman facilitate organizational responsibility and accountability, which are at the heart of provisions contained in the U.S. Sentencing Guidelines and the Sarbanes-Oxley Act that call for mechanisms of confidential reporting and/or guidance;

- that where issues cannot be confidentially raised, they may not be raised at all, thereby depriving the organization of an opportunity to address issues and rectify misconduct that has not yet surfaced through other channels.

3.3 The Ombudsman does not testify in any formal process inside the organization and resists testifying in any formal process outside of the organization regarding a visitor's contact with or confidential information communicated to the Ombudsman, even if given permission or requested to do so. The Ombudsman may, however, provide general, non-confidential information about the Ombudsman Office or the Ombudsman profession.

The IOA Board has asked the IOA Standing Committee on Professional Ethics, Standards, and Best Practices to review the language and interpretation of 3.3. Please look for updates in the near future.

See Section 4 on informality.

3.4 If the Ombudsman pursues an issue systemically (e.g., provides feedback on trends, issues, policies and practices) the Ombudsman does so in a way that safeguards the identity of individuals.

Ombudsman materials should state that any Ombudsman reporting of trends, or communication of recommendations for systemic change, is done in a manner that protects the identity of individuals.

3.5 The Ombudsman keeps no records containing identifying information on behalf of the organization.

3.6 The Ombudsman maintains information (e.g., notes, phone messages, appointment calendars) in a secure location and manner, protected from inspection by others (including management), and has a consistent and standard practice for the destruction of such information.

The Ombudsman record-keeping systems and/or database should be independent of the organization's technology system, with access allowed only to Ombudsman Office personnel. The Ombudsman Office should also be secure to protect private information and records. The office should develop and implement processes and procedures to regularly purge information that could identify individual visitors to the office. Records such as phone bills, which may indicate with whom the office has communicated, should be made available only to the Ombudsman Office staff. The Ombudsman should take all reasonable steps to protect the confidentiality of any temporary notes or documents, such as locking file drawers and offices, and exercising extreme vigilance if any notes are carried from one place to another.

3.7 The Ombudsman prepares any data in a manner that protects confidentiality.

3.8 Communications made to the Ombudsman are not notice to the organization. The Ombudsman neither acts as agent for, nor accepts notice on behalf of, the organization and shall not serve in a position or role that is designated by the organization as a place to receive notice on behalf of the organization. However, the Ombudsman may refer individuals to the appropriate place where formal notice can be made.

Except in the administrative capacity as manager of the Ombudsman Office, the Ombudsman is never an agent of notice (that is, an officer who receives notice for the organization), and communications to the Ombudsman Office never constitute notice to the organization.

If a visitor wishes to make a record, or put the organization "on notice," the Ombudsman can provide information about how to do so.

Best practice is for the organization to receive allegations of wrongdoing directly from a complainant or witness, and not indirectly through the Ombudsman.

If the visitor is reluctant to make a formal report to the organization, the Ombudsman can work with the visitor to address the reasons the visitor resists reporting, or to work with the organization to make formal reporting channels more accessible.

If the visitor gives the Ombudsman permission to discuss a concern with a manager, and if the concern may involve some allegation of wrongdoing, the Ombudsman should pass on information only in general terms (without specifying names, dates, or events). If the Ombudsman does pass on allegations of wrongdoing, the Ombudsman should emphasize the he or she has not confirmed the accuracy of the allegations. It is not appropriate for the organization to take any adverse action on the basis of information reported informally through the Ombudsman. The Ombudsman may coach the manager on how to make reporting channels more accessible or how to gather information himself or herself

An ombudsman may place the organization on "notice" when the ombudsman evaluates the circumstances and specifically elects to place the organization on notice by identifying an appropriate point of contact within the organization and communicating to that point of contact specific information which the ombudsman expressly intends to share for the purpose of placing the organization on notice of a specific concern or specific situation. If an ombudsman makes such an intentional notice communication, confidentiality is waived only with regard to the specific communication made with the point of contact for purposes of the notice communication. It is the conversation between the ombudsman and the appropriate point of contact within the organization that constitutes notice and not the conversation between the ombudsman and the visitor. Thus, under no circumstances, is the original communication to the ombudsman part of the notice communication.

All ombudsman offices should have a well-defined and generally available procedure detailing the limited circumstances and the processes under which the ombudsman may provide notice. If the ombudsman elects to place the organization on notice under the conditions above, the ombudsman should follow the protocol of the particular ombudsman office regarding this unusual action. The protocols should include specific steps so that is clear that the ombudsman made an intentional decision to make a notice disclosure.

INFORMALITY AND OTHER STANDARDS

4.1 The Ombudsman functions on an informal basis by such means as: listening, providing and receiving information, identifying and reframing issues, developing a range of responsible options, and—with permission and at Ombudsman discretion—engaging in informal third-party intervention. When possible, the Ombudsman helps people develop new ways to solve problems themselves.

The Ombudsman should work with the organization to encourage it to provide its constituents with a variety of effective formal (rights-based) and informal (confidential and interest-based) options for surfacing and resolving concerns. All options should be well established and clearly and regularly communicated to the entire organization.

As the visitor may wish to consult with additional resources and services, such as the employee assistance program, human resources, or the benefits office, the Ombudsman should describe resources that might be appropriate to the visitor's presenting circumstances. See Section 2.6

The Ombudsman may consider issues, perceptions, interpretations, information, and concerns about inappropriate acts, omissions, or improprieties presented by individuals or groups.

Ombudsman functions include informal third-party intervention, such as shuttle diplomacy, facilitating communication, and informal mediation, which is voluntary and may or may not produce a written agreement.

Any documents or written agreements resulting from informal processes should not be maintained by or within the Ombudsman Office.

The Ombudsman uses a flexible approach with regard to concerns brought to the Ombudsman Office; options are tailored to individual circumstances.

4.2 The Ombudsman as an informal and off-the-record resource pursues resolution of concerns and looks into procedural irregularities and/or broader systemic problems when appropriate.

4.3 The Ombudsman does not make binding decisions, mandate policies, or formally adjudicate issues for the organization.

The Ombudsman should not participate in formal management functions. See Section 2.4.

4.4 The Ombudsman supplements, but does not replace, any formal channels. Use of the Ombudsman Office is voluntary, and is not a required step in any grievance process or organizational policy.

For most entities, it is the combination of informal services and formal grievance procedures, embodied in a conflict management system, that provides the appropriate range of options to allow for early identification and resolution of potential legal issues or concerns. The Ombudsman should give visitors information about the entity's formal procedures and remedies whenever appropriate. While a visitor may choose to explore informal options for a wide variety of reasons, the Ombudsman should remind the visitor to keep in mind possible time limits and their potential impact on the visitor's formal options. See Section 2.6.

The Ombudsman Charter or Terms of Reference should define the role, if any, of the Ombudsman in relation to employees and issues covered by collective bargaining agreements (CBAs). This role definition should also, where possible, be incorporated in CBAs, and should include a statement that although the CBA permits the Ombudsman to function in these defined ways, the Ombudsman nevertheless retains the authority to decline to be involved. (See Section 1.3.) The union and management may also enter into an ad hoc agreement permitting an Ombudsman to handle an issue.

4.5 The Ombudsman does not participate in any formal investigative or adjudicative procedures. Formal investigations should be conducted by others. When a formal investigation is requested, the Ombudsman refers individuals to the appropriate offices or individual.

The Ombudsman may be requested or required to speak with public officials, in a private or public setting, about the functions of the Ombudsman Office, or about trends published in a written report. If so, the Ombudsman should still observe the confidentiality standards as stated in 3.1 and 3.3.

    4.6 The Ombudsman identifies trends, issues and concerns about policies and procedures, including potential future issues and concerns, without breaching confidentiality or anonymity, and provides recommendations for responsibly addressing them.

The Ombudsman should be particularly careful to maintain neutrality when making recommendations for system change.

    4.7 The Ombudsman acts in accordance with the IOA Code of Ethics and Standards of Practice, keeps professionally current by pursuing continuing education, and provides opportunities for staff to pursue professional training.

    4.8 The Ombudsman endeavors to be worthy of the trust placed in the Ombudsman Office.

Appendix 12

American Recovery and Reinvestment Act of 2009

Section 1553
Protecting State and Local Government and Contractor Whistleblowers

One Hundred Eleventh Congress of the United States of America

AT THE FIRST SESSION

Begun and held at the City of Washington on Tuesday, the sixth day of January, two thousand and nine

An Act

Making supplemental appropriations for job preservation and creation, infrastructure investment, energy efficiency and science, assistance to the unemployed, and State and local fiscal stabilization, for the fiscal year ending September 30, 2009, and for other purposes.

Be it enacted by the Senate and House of Representatives of the United States of America in Congress assembled,

SECTION 1. SHORT TITLE.

This Act may be cited as the "American Recovery and Reinvestment Act of 2009".

SEC. 2. TABLE OF CONTENTS.

The table of contents for this Act is as follows:

DIVISION A—APPROPRIATIONS PROVISIONS
TITLE I—AGRICULTURE, RURAL DEVELOPMENT, FOOD AND DRUG ADMINISTRATION, AND RELATED AGENCIES
TITLE II—COMMERCE, JUSTICE, SCIENCE, AND RELATED AGENCIES
TITLE III—DEPARTMENT OF DEFENSE
TITLE IV—ENERGY AND WATER DEVELOPMENT
TITLE V—FINANCIAL SERVICES AND GENERAL GOVERNMENT
TITLE VI—DEPARTMENT OF HOMELAND SECURITY
TITLE VII—INTERIOR, ENVIRONMENT, AND RELATED AGENCIES
TITLE VIII—DEPARTMENTS OF LABOR, HEALTH AND HUMAN SERVICES, AND EDUCATION, AND RELATED AGENCIES
TITLE IX—LEGISLATIVE BRANCH
TITLE X—MILITARY CONSTRUCTION AND VETERANS AFFAIRS AND RELATED AGENCIES
TITLE XI—STATE, FOREIGN OPERATIONS, AND RELATED PROGRAMS
TITLE XII—TRANSPORTATION, HOUSING AND URBAN DEVELOPMENT, AND RELATED AGENCIES
TITLE XIII—HEALTH INFORMATION TECHNOLOGY
TITLE XIV—STATE FISCAL STABILIZATION FUND
TITLE XV—ACCOUNTABILITY AND TRANSPARENCY
TITLE XVI—GENERAL PROVISIONS—THIS ACT

DIVISION B—TAX, UNEMPLOYMENT, HEALTH, STATE FISCAL RELIEF, AND OTHER PROVISIONS
TITLE I—TAX PROVISIONS
TITLE II—ASSISTANCE FOR UNEMPLOYED WORKERS AND STRUGGLING FAMILIES
TITLE III—PREMIUM ASSISTANCE FOR COBRA BENEFITS
TITLE IV—MEDICARE AND MEDICAID HEALTH INFORMATION TECHNOLOGY; MISCELLANEOUS MEDICARE PROVISIONS
TITLE V—STATE FISCAL RELIEF
TITLE VI—BROADBAND TECHNOLOGY OPPORTUNITIES PROGRAM
TITLE VII—LIMITS ON EXECUTIVE COMPENSATION

SEC. 3. PURPOSES AND PRINCIPLES.

(a) STATEMENT OF PURPOSES.—The purposes of this Act include the following:

SEC. 1553. PROTECTING STATE AND LOCAL GOVERNMENT AND CONTRACTOR WHISTLEBLOWERS

(a) PROHIBITION OF REPRISALS.—An employee of any non-Federal employer receiving covered funds may not be discharged, demoted, or otherwise discriminated against as a reprisal for disclosing , including a disclosure made in the ordinary course of an employee's duties, to the Board, an inspector general, the Comptroller General, a member of Congress, a State or Federal regulatory or law enforcement agency, a person with supervisory authority over the employee (or such other person working for the employer who has the authority to investigate, discover, or terminate misconduct), a court or grand jury, the head of a Federal agency, or their representatives, information that the employee reasonably believes is evidence of—

(1) gross mismanagement of an agency contract or grant relating to covered funds;

(2) a gross waste of covered funds;

(3) a substantial and specific danger to public health or safety related to the implementation or use of covered funds;

(4) an abuse of authority related to the implementation or use of covered funds; or

(5) a violation of law, rule, or regulation related to an agency contract (including the competition for or negotiation of a contract) or grant, awarded or issued relating to covered funds.

(b) INVESTIGATION OF COMPLAINTS.—

(1) IN GENERAL.—A person who believes that the person has been subjected to a reprisal prohibited by subsection (a) may submit a complaint regarding the reprisal to the appropriate inspector general. Except as provided under paragraph (3), unless the inspector general determines that the complaint is frivolous, does not relate to covered funds, or another Federal or State judicial or administrative proceeding has previously been invoked to resolve such complaint, the inspector general shall investigate the complaint and, upon completion of such investigation, submit a report of the findings of the investigation to the person, the person's employer, the head of the appropriate agency, and the Board.

(2) TIME LIMITATIONS FOR ACTIONS.—

(A) IN GENERAL.—Except as provided under subparagraph (B), the inspector general shall, not later than 180 days after receiving a complaint under paragraph (1)—

(i) make a determination that the complaint is frivolous, does not relate to covered funds, or another Federal or State judicial or administrative proceeding has previously been invoked to resolve such complaint; or

(ii) submit a report under paragraph (1).

(B) EXTENSIONS.—

(i) VOLUNTARY EXTENSION AGREED TO BETWEEN INSPECTOR GENERAL AND COMPLAINANT.—If the inspector general is unable to complete an investigation under this section in time to submit a report within the 180-day period specified under subparagraph (A) and the person submitting the complaint agrees to an extension of time, the inspector general shall submit a report under paragraph (1) within such additional period of time as shall be agreed upon between the inspector general and the person submitting the complaint.

(ii) EXTENSION GRANTED BY INSPECTOR GENERAL.—If the inspector general is unable to complete an investigation under this section in time to submit a report within the 180-day period specified under subparagraph (A), the inspector general may extend the period for not more than 180 days without agreeing with the person submitting the complaint to such extension, provided that the inspector general provides a written explanation (subject to the authority to exclude information under paragraph (4)(C)) for the decision, which shall be provided to both the person submitting the complaint and the non-Federal employer.

(iii) SEMI-ANNUAL REPORT ON EXTENSIONS.—The inspector general shall include in semi-annual reports to Congress a list of those investigations for which the inspector general received an extension.

(3) DISCRETION NOT TO INVESTIGATE COMPLAINTS.—

(A) IN GENERAL.—The inspector general may decide not to conduct or continue an investigation under this section upon providing to the person submitting the complaint and the non-Federal employer a written explanation (subject to the authority to exclude information under paragraph (4)(C)) for such decision.

(B) ASSUMPTION OF RIGHTS TO CIVIL REMEDY.—Upon receipt of an explanation of a decision not to conduct or continue an investigation under subparagraph (A), the person submitting a complaint shall immediately assume the right to a civil remedy under subsection (c)(3) as if the 210-day period specified under such subsection has already passed.

(C) SEMI-ANNUAL REPORT.—The inspector general shall include in semi-annual reports to Congress a list of those investigations the inspector general decided not to conduct or continue under this paragraph.

(4) ACCESS TO INVESTIGATIVE FILE OF INSPECTOR GENERAL.—

(A) IN GENERAL.—The person alleging a reprisal under this section shall have access to the investigation file of the appropriate inspector general in accordance with section 552a of title 5, United States Code (commonly referred to as the "Privacy Act"). The investigation of the inspector general shall be deemed closed for purposes of disclosure under such section when an employee files an appeal to an agency head or a court of competent jurisdiction.

(B) CIVIL ACTION.—In the event the person alleging the reprisal brings suit under subsection (c)(3), the person alleging the reprisal and the non-Federal employer shall have access to the investigative file of the inspector general in accordance with the Privacy Act.

(C) EXCEPTION.—The inspector general may exclude from disclosure—

(i) information protected from disclosure by a provision of law; and

(ii) any additional information the inspector general determines disclosure of which would impede a continuing investigation, provided that such information is disclosed once such disclosure would no longer impede such investigation, unless the inspector general determines that disclosure of law enforcement techniques, procedures, or information could reasonably be expected to risk circumvention of the law or disclose the identity of a confidential source.

(5) PRIVACY OF INFORMATION.—An inspector general investigat-

ing an alleged reprisal under this section may not respond to any inquiry or disclose any information from or about any person alleging such reprisal, except in accordance with the provisions of section 552a of title 5, United States Code, or as required by any other applicable Federal law.

(c) REMEDY AND ENFORCEMENT AUTHORITY.—

(1) Burden of Proof.—

(A) DISCLOSURE AS CONTRIBUTING FACTOR IN REPRISAL.—

(i) IN GENERAL.—A person alleging a reprisal under this section shall be deemed to have affirmatively established the occurrence of the reprisal if the person demonstrates that a disclosure described in subsection (a) was a contributing factor in the reprisal.

(ii) USE OF CIRCUMSTANTIAL EVIDENCE.—A disclosure may be demonstrated as a contributing factor in a reprisal for purposes of this paragraph by circumstantial evidence, including—

(I) evidence that the official undertaking the reprisal knew of the disclosure; or

(II) evidence that the reprisal occurred within a period of time after the disclosure such that a reasonable person could conclude that the disclosure was a contributing factor in the reprisal.

(B) OPPORTUNITY FOR REBUTTAL.—The head of an agency may not find the occurrence of a reprisal with respect to a reprisal that is affirmatively established under subparagraph (A) if the non-Federal employer demonstrates by clear and convincing evidence that the non- Federal employer would have taken the action constituting the reprisal in the absence of the disclosure.

(2) AGENCY ACTION.—Not later than 30 days after receiving an inspector general report under subsection (b), the head of the agency concerned shall determine whether there is sufficient basis to conclude that the non-Federal employer has subjected the complainant to a reprisal prohibited by subsection (a) and shall either issue an order denying relief in whole or in part or shall take 1 or more of the following actions:

(A) Order the employer to take affirmative action to abate the reprisal.

(B) Order the employer to reinstate the person to the position that the person held before the reprisal, together with the compensation (including back pay), compensatory damages, employment benefits, and other terms and conditions of employment that would apply to the person in that position if the reprisal had not been taken.

(C) Order the employer to pay the complainant an amount equal to the aggregate amount of all costs and expenses (including attorneys' fees and expert witnesses' fees) that were reasonably incurred by the complainant for, or in connection with, bringing the complaint regarding the reprisal, as determined by the head of the agency or a court of competent jurisdiction.

(3) CIVIL ACTION.—If the head of an agency issues an order denying relief in whole or in part under paragraph (1), has not issued an order within 210 days after the submission of a complaint under subsection (b), or in the case of an extension of time under subsection (b)(2)(B)(i), within 30 days after the expiration of the extension of time, or decides under subsection (b)(3) not to investigate or to discontinue an investigation, and there is no showing that such delay or decision is due to the bad faith of the complainant, the complainant shall be deemed to have exhausted all administrative remedies with respect to the complaint, and the complainant may bring a de novo action at law or equity against the employer to seek compensatory damages and other relief available under this section in the appropriate district court of the United States, which shall have jurisdiction over such an action without regard to the amount in controversy. Such an action shall, at the request of either party to the action, be tried by the court with a jury.

(4) JUDICIAL ENFORCEMENT OF ORDER.—Whenever a person fails to comply with an order issued under paragraph (2), the head of the agency shall file an action for enforcement of such order in the United States district court for a district in which the reprisal was found to have occurred. In any action brought under this paragraph, the court may grant appropriate relief, including injunctive

relief, compensatory and exemplary damages, and attorneys' fees and costs.

(5) JUDICIAL REVIEW.—Any person adversely affected or aggrieved by an order issued under paragraph (2) may obtain review of the order's conformance with this subsection, and any regulations issued to carry out this section, in the United States court of appeals for a circuit in which the reprisal is alleged in the order to have occurred. No petition seeking such review may be filed more than 60 days after issuance of the order by the head of the agency. Review shall conform to chapter 7 of title 5, United States Code.

(d) NONENFORCEABILITY OF CERTAIN PROVISIONS WAIVING RIGHTS AND REMEDIES OR REQUIRING ARBITRATION OF DISPUTES.—

(1) WAIVER OF RIGHTS AND REMEDIES.—Except as provided under paragraph (3), the rights and remedies provided for in this section may not be waived by any agreement, policy, form, or condition of employment, including by any predispute arbitration agreement.

(2) PREDISPUTE ARBITRATION AGREEMENTS.—Except as provided under paragraph (3), no predispute arbitration agreement shall be valid or enforceable if it requires arbitration of a dispute arising under this section.

(3) EXCEPTION FOR COLLECTIVE BARGAINING AGREEMENTS.— Notwithstanding paragraphs (1) and (2), an arbitration provision in a collective bargaining agreement shall be enforceable as to disputes arising under the collective bargaining agreement.

(e) REQUIREMENT TO POST NOTICE OF RIGHTS AND REMEDIES.—Any employer receiving covered funds shall post notice of the rights and remedies provided under this section.

(f) RULES OF CONSTRUCTION.—

(1) NO IMPLIED AUTHORITY TO RETALIATE FOR NON-PROTECTED DISCLOSURES.—Nothing in this section may be construed to authorize the discharge of, demotion of, or discrimination against an employee for a disclosure other than a disclosure protected by subsection (a) or to modify or derogate from a right or remedy otherwise available to the employee.

(2) RELATIONSHIP TO STATE LAWS.—Nothing in this section may be construed to preempt, preclude, or limit the protections provided for public or private employees under State whistleblower laws.

(g) DEFINITIONS.—IN THIS SECTION:

(1) ABUSE OF AUTHORITY.—The term "abuse of authority" means an arbitrary and capricious exercise of authority by a contracting official or employee that adversely affects the rights of any person, or that results in personal gain or advantage to the official or employee or to preferred other persons.

(2) COVERED FUNDS.—The term "covered funds" means any contract, grant, or other payment received by any non-Federal employer if—

(A) the Federal Government provides any portion of the money or property that is provided, requested, or demanded; and

(B) at least some of the funds are appropriated or otherwise made available by this Act.

(3) EMPLOYEE.—The term "employee"—

(A) except as provided under subparagraph (B), means an individual performing services on behalf of an employer; and

(B) does not include any Federal employee or member of the uniformed services (as that term is defined in section 101(a)(5) of title 10, United States Code).

(4) NON-FEDERAL EMPLOYER.—The term "non-Federal employer"—

(A) means any employer—

(i) with respect to covered funds—

(I) the contractor, subcontractor, grantee, or recipient, as the case may be, if the contractor and

(II) any professional membership organization, certification or other professional body, any agent or licensee of the Federal government, or any person acting directly or indirectly in the interest of an employer receiving covered funds; or

(ii) with respect to covered funds received by a State or local government, the State or local government receiving the funds and any contractor or subcontractor of the State or local government; and

(B) does not mean any department, agency, or other entity of the Federal Government.

(5) STATE OR LOCAL GOVERNMENT.—The term "State or local government" means—

(A) the government of each of the several States, the District of Columbia, the Commonwealth of Puerto Rico, Guam, American Samoa, the Virgin Islands, the Commonwealth of the Northern Mariana Islands, or any other territory or possession of the United States; or

(B) the government of any political subdivision of a government listed in subparagraph (A).

Appendix 13

H.B. 3578
Introduced in Texas Legislature, 2007

By: Rose, et al.   H.B. No. 3578

A BILL TO BE ENTITLED

AN ACT

relating to the confidentiality of certain communications involving an ombudsman program established by an employer as an alternative dispute resolution service.

BE IT ENACTED BY THE LEGISLATURE OF THE STATE OF TEXAS:

SECTION 1. Title 7, Civil Practice and Remedies Code, is amended by adding Chapter 160 to read as follows:

CHAPTER 160. OMBUDSMAN PROGRAM ESTABLISHED BY EMPLOYER

Sec. 160.001. DEFINITIONS. In this chapter:

(1) "Employee" means a person employed by an employer.

(2) "Employer" means a person who employs at least one employee.

(3) "Investigation" means an inquiry conducted for an employer, the purpose of which is to make an official factual determination or an official disposition or decision.

Sec. 160.002. ESTABLISHMENT OF OMBUDSMAN PROGRAM.

(a) An employer may establish an ombudsman program to provide an alternative dispute resolution service. The program may provide information, facilitation, mediation, and conciliation guidance and assistance to:

(1) help employees and others resolve workplace disputes; and

(2) permit employees and other persons to have confidential communications on issues of concern or conflict, including allegations of misconduct.

(b) An ombudsman program established under this chapter by an employer:

(1) must be neutral and functionally independent;

(2) may not have the authority to make managerial decisions with regard to any issue brought to the program;

(3) may not be responsible for any essential business function of the employer, including operations, compliance, human resources, or equal employment opportunity;

(4) may not be staffed by employees who hold other positions with responsibility for any essential business function of the employer, including operations, compliance, human resources, or equal employment opportunity;

(5) may be staffed by employees of the employer but not by an officer or director of the employer; and

(6) must have direct access to the employer's senior management.

(c) An ombudsman program may not have authority to receive notice of claims against the employer.

(d) An ombudsman program may not have authority to collect, assemble, or maintain permanent information or records relating to confidential communications for the employer.

(e) An ombudsman program may not have the authority to conduct a formal investigation for the employer.

(f) An ombudsman program and the employer establishing the program shall adequately publicize the existence, purpose, and limitation of the program and inform employees that communications with the program are confidential.

(g) An employer that establishes an ombudsman program under this chapter shall ensure that the program has procedures and facilities adequate to permit confidential access to the program's office and to preserve confidential communications. The program shall adhere to generally accepted standards for organizational ombudsman programs to preserve confidentiality of communications.

Sec. 160.003. CONFIDENTIALITY PROVISIONS. (a) This section applies only to an ombudsman program that meets the requirements of Section 160.002.

(b) The following oral and written communications are confidential, privileged, not subject to discovery, and may not be used as evidence in any judicial or administrative proceeding:

(1) communications between a staff member of the program and an employee or other person for the purpose of assisting with the informal and expeditious resolution of a concern or complaint; and

(2) communications between staff members of the program for the purpose of assisting with the informal and expeditious resolution of a concern or complaint.

(c) Notwithstanding Subsection (b), a staff member of an ombudsman program may voluntarily disclose confidential information if the staff member determines that disclosure is necessary to prevent an imminent threat of serious harm.

(d) Information discovered or disclosed in violation of this chapter is not admissible as evidence in any proceeding or for any other purpose.

Sec. 160.004. APPLICATION OF OTHER LAW. The confidentiality provisions of this chapter are in addition to any privilege or protection under statutory or common law, including Section 154.073, the attorney-client privilege, and the attorney work product privilege.

Sec. 160.005. ADMISSIBILITY OF OTHER INFORMATION. This chapter does not prevent:

(1) the discovery or admissibility of information that is otherwise discoverable;

(2) the disclosure of information for research or educational purposes in connection with a training or educational program of an ombudsman program if the identity of the parties and the specific issues from the confidential communication are not identifiable; or

(3) the preparation and disclosure of statistical summary reports organized by category of the issues presented if the summary is based on a sufficiently large number of issues so that the identity of the parties and the specific issues from the confidential communication are not identifiable.

Sec. 160.004. APPLICATION OF CHAPTER. (a) This chapter does not apply to an ombudsman program or other alternative dispute resolution service established by an employer unless the program or service provides expressly in writing that this chapter applies to the program or service.

(b) This chapter does not prevent an employer from establishing an ombudsman program or other alternative dispute resolution service that is not subject to this chapter.

SECTION 2. The change in law made by this Act with regard to the confidentiality of communications applies only to a suit or administrative proceeding commenced on or after the effective date of this Act. A suit or administrative proceeding commenced before the effective date of this Act is governed by the law in effect on the date the suit or proceeding was commenced, and the former law is continued in effect for that purpose.

SECTION 3. This Act takes effect September 1, 2007.

Appendix 14
Additional Ombuds Examples

Coaching and trend reports help both an individual and the organization

An employee had seen an online posting for a job in another department that he thought he would be a good fit for him, in light of his qualifications and experience. He applied for the job and thought the interview went well. He was excited about the prospect of the new job, but there was no follow-up after the interview. Some weeks later, he met the new person who had been hired for the job.

The employee was bothered that he had never received any feedback on the interview and had not even been informed that the position was filled by someone else. He did not want to complain to HR or the other department, however, out of fear that he would be seen as a troublemaker or get a reputation that would hurt his chances for a transfer in the future. He contacted the ombuds to discuss how best to handle the situation.

After discussion, the employee decided that the best option was to approach HR for a candid conversation about his qualifications. The ombuds coached him on how to handle the discussion so that it would be positively received and help him identify ways to improve so that he could be in a better position if there were future openings.

The ombuds also knew that other employees had also raised the issue of not receiving feedback after an interview or hearing of the final decision, and without disclosing the names or any of the circumstances of the people who had come to the ombuds office, noted this in a trend report to higher-level management as an issue that should be addressed throughout the organization.

Use of the ombuds office by vendors permitted ombuds to identify a trend that resulted in improved vendor communication

The organization's external Web site or Internet site prominently listed the ombuds office as one of four organizational contacts. As a result, the ombuds office was used by a wide variety of non-employees as an initial point of contact when they were seeking assistance in dealing with the organization.

Although the ombuds office had been established as an internal employee resource, it quickly became clear to the ombuds office that it was being contacted by many external parties, including customers, who were not sure who to contact for even such things as machine repair or replacement. The ombuds thought that management could do a better job in communicating to customers the appropriate parties to contact for specific business needs.

This point was included in one of the trend reports made by the ombuds office to management. Management reviewed the situation and decided to make improvements in its communication materials provided to customers. Management later reported that the changes resulted in more efficient customer service and higher customer satisfaction and retention.

Personal coaching improves the workplace

A long-tenured senior employee had been the subject of numerous complaints to the ombuds over a period of time. One day, that employee himself came to the ombuds, and when asked how he hoped the ombuds could be of assistance, he responded with "I don't want to be an a_ _h_ _ _ anymore."

Over the course of several meetings, the ombuds provided coaching around stress, conflict, and anger management. The ombuds also provided the employee with resources for additional self-learning.

Two years have elapsed since this episode, and no further issues dealing with this employee have been brought to the ombuds.

How does a new senior manager deal with a lack of support from above and below?

A senior manager scheduled a meeting after a lengthy phone conversation about how the ombuds office conducts its business (confidentiality, neutrality, informality, and independence). When he met with the ombuds, he disclosed that he was new to the organization and had been hired after a national search. He said that both during the search process and after his accepting the position, he had had many discussions with the people above him about how his unit had not been performing well for many years. He said that he was told that his predecessor had been in the position for many years and was popular with employees but regarded as entrenched and resistant to change. The new manager believed he was given a "mandate" to make systemic changes within his unit.

After he accepted the job and began work, the manager experienced a great deal of resistance (covertly and overtly) from employees at various levels in the organization. Not fully appreciating the culture of the unit or the broader organization, he admitted to having made some tactical missteps that compromised his legitimacy and the respect of the employees. He felt unsupported by those above him and undermined by those below. Though given a mandate to make significant systemic changes because of the unit's history of poor performance, that mandate was never articulated to the employees in the unit. Rather, senior officials in public speeches praised the "wonderful work" that previously had been done by his unit. This created a perception that changes were unnecessary. As a result, his initiatives were perceived by the employees in his unit as being motivated by his need to "reinvent the wheel" and to put his stamp on the unit. He felt very isolated and was seriously considering resigning. He said that he felt he could not discuss these issues either with those to whom he reported or those who reported to him (directly or indirectly).

During the course of many meetings to discuss options, strategy, and implementation, he and the ombuds also addressed the organization's culture, how to develop "buy-in," how to rebuild his reputation, and how to nudge those to whom he reported. While there continue to be challenges with his position, the manager did not resign and has reported that his situation has improved immensely.

Ombuds helps employees and management address a potentially destructive rumor

Several employees at a facility called the ombuds office, all within a few days of each other, with concerns about losing their jobs based on rumors they had heard about the company having lost a large contract that could affect their facility. One of the employees who met with the ombuds permitted the ombuds to make inquiries to the local management to find out if the rumor was true, provided that management not be informed of her identity.

When the ombuds spoke with the facility manager about the rumor, he was surprised to hear that a rumor had been circulating among employees. He indicated that losing the contract was a possibility but that a final decision had not been made. Based on this discussion, the manager decided to hold a meeting the next day with employees to address their questions. At the town hall–type meeting, employees were able to ask their questions, and the manager was able to give an accurate status report to dispel the rumors.

The manager and the ombuds subsequently also met with representatives from the company's communications group and HR to discuss communication recommendations for this type of situation in the future.

Local management misconduct and the fear of retaliation

Employees at one unit of the company had been using company products and equipment to create their own personal business, resulting in a loss of customers and revenues for the company. Some of the people involved in the scheme were members of the local management. As a result, employees who knew about this misconduct felt that they could not report it to local management and were afraid to raise it through formal channels. They were not sure how to contact or approach higher levels of management or if higher management might also be involved.

Some of the employees who knew about the scheme came to the ombuds office because they understood that it was independent and confidential. After discussing the issue with the ombuds, the ombuds at their request facilitated a contact with the compliance office, which investigated and eventually terminated the employment of those involved in the scheme. The employees who came to the ombuds office stated that the experience made them more comfortable raising issues with the company's compliance office.

A probationary employee clarifies a policy without hurting his career

The organization president issued a policy statement to all employees mandating a furlough. The policy stated that all employees had to take a certain amount of time off without pay and that they could do so when they chose—in partial-day increments, one day at a time, or in multiple-day blocks up to five consecutive days.

An employee still in probationary status (having worked for the organization for less than one year) contacted the ombuds office because, contrary to the directive from the president, his supervisor had dictated when employees had to take the unpaid days off. Because he was still in his probationary period, the employee was unwilling to raise the issue directly out of fear that doing so would hurt his chances for employment when his probationary period ended.

After discussing various options, the employee gave the ombuds permission to contact the HR office to raise the issue generically. Once HR became aware of the issue, it revised the FAQs on its Web site to address the issue with a question on whether a department or division could mandate when furlough is taken. The answer to this question given by HR was "No. A department should not dictate when the required furlough days must be taken by an employee or a department." This information was disseminated to all departments, including the department in which the employee worked, and the problem was eliminated.

A department chair wants to obtain information confidentially to figure out how to correct a mistake

The chair of an academic department came to the ombuds office and disclosed that he had had a challenging relationship with another senior faculty member in the same department for a number of years. Over the years, the two of them had had very public heated disagreements, and he admitted that their disdain for each other was well known.

The issue that brought the department chair to the ombuds office involved a dispute over the leadership of a national project, during which the chair made some decisions in haste and anger that adversely affected the other senior faculty member. The department chair conceded to the ombuds that he had made a mistake in judgment and needed additional information to decide how best to manage "damage control," but he was not willing to seek the information himself or disclose his mistake without considering this additional information. He requested the ombuds to approach HR, the general counsel's office, and the provost's office to request both general and specific information but to do so in a way that would not disclose who was asking for the information, identify the department involved, or reveal why the information was being sought. The ombuds was able to obtain the information sought and then to discuss options with the department chair about what to do. In gathering the data, the ombuds also gained insight on the best way for the department chair to speak with someone in each of those areas, which he eventually did.

Concern over both practices and lack of all the facts results in policy reform

An employee came to the ombuds office with concerns that his manager might be using company funds to pay for personal expenses and possibly expenses related to the board of directors of another company on which the manager served. It was not against his employer's policy for the manager to serve on that board, but the inquirer said that he had noticed that trips taken by his manager on company business often appeared to have been arranged to coincide with board meetings for the other company. The inquirer said that he thought he was the only person who was aware of these patterns and felt uncertain about reporting them because he was not sure if what the manager was doing was wrong, or if he (the inquirer) knew all the facts. He was also worried about what would happen if he made an accusation and was wrong.

After discussing various options with the ombuds, the inquirer agreed that he would like the ombuds to raise the issue anonymously with the compliance office. The ombuds did this, and compliance's examination of the manager's travel patterns revealed no wrongdoing but suggested that the manager may have created the risk of a conflict of interest. As a result, the company changed its ethics rules to prohibit managers in the position of this manager from serving on boards of companies like the one involved in this case, and the manager subsequently resigned from the board of the other company.

The employee expressed his appreciation to the ombuds that the company was able to address his concerns anonymously and for the way in which it addressed the policy issue involved.

Organizational culture can be a barrier to new employees

An organization reorganized its sales force and brought in several new employees with no background or understanding of the organizational culture, terminology, and philosophy. They were also not given any background on the reasons for the reorganization. Unfortunately, the prevailing culture in this organization was to let new employees learn on the job and not to provide them with training or orientation.

The new employees' excitement at being a new and reenergized part of the organization soon gave way to confusion and frustration, as management and the new employees were not communicating effectively with each other. Some of the new employees reached out to the ombuds and were coached on various aspects of the organization and the history of the reorganization that led to their hiring. The ombuds also presented them with options for how to raise the issue of the need for better communications going forward.

The employees chose the option of requesting an opportunity to sit down with management and discuss their frustration over the lack of training and communication. The ombuds was given permission to make this request to management. Management agreed to the meeting, and as a result, management recognized that it needed to provide a better understanding of the organization and reorganization to these new employees. Roles were clarified, training implemented, and the employees gained a better understanding of the organization's needs, style, and expectations.

Cross-cultural conflict resolved with facilitated conversations

The visitor to the ombuds office was an African-American woman employee in her late thirties whose job required her to coordinate with a counterpart in another department: a white woman who was not comfortable with the expression of strong emotions. The visitor said that she had exhausted all other options to try to address what she perceived as a lack of communication between them and that it was affecting her work performance. She requested the ombuds office to facilitate an informal conversation to address the communication problem. When the ombuds spoke with the colleague, the colleague expressed her view that there was no problem and that she preferred to communicate by e-mail.

The visitor gave the ombuds permission to speak with her own supervisor and to see if the supervisor of the colleague (they reported to different supervisors) might agree to participate in a facilitated conversation with all four people. All four agreed to participate in a facilitated conversation in this setting. The two workers and their supervisors met on several occasions in facilitated sessions with the ombuds, during which they identified issues, decided on issues to work on, brainstormed options, agreed on next steps toward resolution, and established activities to improve communication and teamwork. The process appeared to be successful, as the participants agreed on a plan of actions they would take.

When the ombuds followed up with the visitor a couple of months later to see how the group was doing, the visitor indicated that the initial issues had been addressed but that were other issues involving her and her supervisor that had not been fully addressed in the group facilitation. In particular, she expressed frustration that she had been unable to get her supervisor, who had been born and raised in a former British colony and who had came to America via Britain, to address issues she brought to him. She requested another facilitated conversation with just her supervisor. When approached by the ombuds with this request, he agreed to participate.

The facilitated conversation between the visitor and her supervisor lasted over three hours and revealed very different styles of interaction and that each clearly was frustrated by the other person's style. The visitor had a direct communication style and embraced conflict. Her approach was to say exactly what was on her mind. The supervisor was conflict-avoidant and preferred a more indirect approach. The facilitated conversation allowed each person to better understand his or her own and the other person's approach to conflict and communication, and gave them both insight into the source of their continued difficulty in working together. The ombuds also assisted them in developing mutually acceptable strategies for addressing future problems and conflict.

Confidential request leads to better explanation by management

The support function had suddenly implemented an alternative work arrangement in which all team members were required to work twice a week from home. Many employees expressed their belief that this change should have been implemented only after discussion and acceptance by everyone. Several employees had limited or no space at home from which to work. A senior team member approached the ombuds and wanted to use the channel to provide feedback to the functional leader and change agent. The ombuds conveyed the message as requested. The leader was surprised that team members did not have the trust to come forward directly. The leader appreciated the feedback and agreed to communicate with the team that the rationale for change was primarily to save jobs despite the inconvenience it caused. A month later, the inquirer informed the ombuds that he was satisfied that confidentiality was maintained. He then raised another situation about his leader's diversity and inclusion. That concern also was raised to the senior leader to address.

Shuttle diplomacy results in an equitable settlement

The ombuds received a call from an employee who had left the company a few weeks earlier. The caller claimed that the company owed her for overtime for which she had not been compensated. The ombuds received permission from the caller to talk with the human resources manager about the situation. After some discussion, the HR manager told the ombuds that it was possible that the caller's claims could be correct. The manager recognized, however, that the organization's relationship with the former employee had broken down to the point that a discussion between HR and the former employee would not be productive. He asked the ombuds to assist in trying to resolve the dispute and referred the matter to his supervisor, the director of human resources for the division.

The ombuds went back to the caller and asked for and received the information on overtime hours for which she claimed she was owed. The ombuds then shuttled back and forth between the director of human resources and the caller until they reached agreement on the number of overtime hours. Each side was satisfied with this resolution to an issue that could have resulted in a civil lawsuit or a claim with the Department of Labor.

Departing employee finally discloses his concerns

Two weeks after the announcement of a major layoff, the ombuds was contacted by an employee who was included in the layoff and who would be leaving the organization at the end of the month. Given his imminent departure, the employee had decided to share concerns about expense voucher abuse on the part of his supervisor. Although the employee had been aware of the abuse for over a year, he had only now decided to talk about it because he was leaving the organization and his fear of retribution was diminished. He also expressed concern for the organization because the supervisor, who was also being laid off, was being considered for another position in the organization.

The employee provided the ombuds with multiple examples of expense voucher misconduct by the supervisor and authorized the ombuds to forward the information to the formal channels of the organization. When the ombuds forwarded the information to the formal channels, an investigation by the formal channels validated the allegations. The supervisor was dropped from consideration for another position in the organization.

Help for a new manager

A newly promoted manager came to the ombuds with a concern about an employee who was described as volatile and intemperate but also a good friend and former peer and co-worker of the new manager. The manager expressed the desire to preserve the friendship but also that he wanted to do a good job as manager. Because he was so new in the job, the manager was unwilling to reveal to higher management that he needed help in resolving this issue. Being able to have a confidential discussion of the problem was critical to him.

After exploring various options, the manager had the ombuds coach him on how to speak directly with the employee. The ombuds and the manager engaged in role-playing, and the ombuds helped the manager craft language about the impact of the employee's problematic behavior and the manager's predicament as the "boss." The ombuds helped the manager find ways to articulate his desire both to preserve the friendship and to be a good boss, but that he would have to be a good manager if the two roles conflicted and could not be reconciled.

In a follow-up discussion much later, the manager reported that he had had the conversation and that it had been a very difficult one, but that there had been no more incidents of volatility. The manager also expressed more comfort in being able to impose discipline if it became necessary.

Trend report helps management address workplace civility

Based on conversations with inquirers over an extended period, the ombuds raised the issue of workplace civility in an annual trend report. The ombuds also had extended discussions with management about how it might address the issue globally.

Two main options were chosen by management to address this issue. First, management found various occasions to write messages to all employees defining management's expectation of respectful treatment in the workplace. In addition, they clarified expectations by setting performance objectives for their direct reports that stated that they would be held accountable in their performance reviews for setting a respectful example and tone in the workplace and for dealing with instances of incivility in their respective areas.

There has been no scientific measurement of the impact of management's approach, but after these actions were taken, fewer inquirers came to the ombuds with issues of disrespect.

Extended mediation helps transition of leadership in physician practice

A very successful physician practice was stuck in a leadership transition between the founding physician, who would not or could not relinquish control over the practice, and some of the remaining members of the practice who felt stifled and ready to leave if the founding physician did not let go. The practice was extremely successful, however, and everyone in the practice was fearful that public disclosure of the discord could hurt the practice and its reputation. They also were adamant that no one at the hospital where they had privileges should know about the problem. As a result, they approached the ombuds to see if she might be able to mediate the impasse.

The ombuds met with each of the physicians and then with the entire group. She was also invited to attend meetings of the physicians in the practice over an extended period where she could observe the way they handled the administrative business of the practice. At the end of each of these sessions, the ombuds gave observations on the interaction and made suggestions on how the process might be improved. The ombuds was gradually able to lead the founding physician to the realization that he could trust the other physicians to carry on with the practice and turn the business over to them. Had this type of mediation not have been available, a very highly regarded practice (and a very beneficial one from the standpoint of the hospital) likely would have disintegrated.

An ombuds helps an employee use the hotline

An employee came to the ombuds because she was concerned that a colleague in her office was tampering with time sheets. She said that she would normally have reported this to her supervisor but could not do so in this situation, because she was one of the few people who knew that the colleague and their supervisor were having an affair. She felt that under the circumstances, the supervisor would not be an appropriate person to whom to make the report, and she was afraid that if she tried to report this to someone else, she would be asked why she had not reported it to the supervisor. She did not want to have to lie or answer that question.

The employee and the ombuds discussed various options to surface the issue, including speaking with her supervisor's supervisor, an anonymous letter sent through intraoffice mail, and an anonymous call to the organization's hotline. She still was uncomfortable raising the issue with a formal channel or the supervisor's supervisor directly. Because hotline calls were received by an off-site, independent company, she felt that was a better option than sending an anonymous letter to someone at the company. She decided to raise the issue that way. The ombuds worked with her to explain how to include in the hotline call sufficient hard facts to adequately describe the problem for the investigators.

Help in enforcement of global policies

An employee from a location outside of the United States contacted the ombuds to say that her boss had called her into his office to tell her that he noticed that she was pregnant and that he knew she was unmarried. She said that the boss had told her that if she were not married by the time the baby was delivered, she would be fired. Such conduct was not illegal in the country where she worked but violated the company's policies. She was uncertain what to do, afraid of losing her job, and feared retaliation by management of the company in her country, who she felt would support her manager.

The ombuds discussed various options on how to proceed and assured her that such action would violate company policy. With her permission, the ombuds forwarded her issue to a formal channel at the company headquarters, which intervened with local management to reinforce the company's policies and reiterated to local management that retaliation against her for bringing this issue to the attention of the company would not be tolerated.

Contact by a concerned spouse

Not knowing where else to go, the spouse of an employee contacted the ombuds with concerns that her husband had a drug addiction problem and needed help. The problem was affecting both the employee's home life and his job performance. The spouse was uncertain where else she could go to discuss what to do. After discussions with the ombuds, she was able to get the employee to agree to speak with the ombuds office.

The ombuds explored with both the employee and his spouse various options to deal with the addiction and the resulting family problems. The ombuds provided the employee and spouse with information that helped the employee obtain medical attention for the addiction, and both he and his family received counseling for the other issues. The employee also gave the ombuds permission to contact HR and the employee's supervisor with his request for a medical leave in order for the employee to undergo further treatment. The request for leave was granted and the employee did get additional treatment.

These actions enabled the employee to overcome the addiction problem and keep both his family and his job.

An ombuds helps the organization avoid a potential class-action lawsuit

A female professional staff member contacted the ombuds office with concerns over actions by the predominantly male staff in her group. She had only been with the organization for a few years but was highly educated and at the cutting edge of her scientific field. She had also received high ratings as an employee. She related that she and other women in her group had experienced demeaning, disrespectful, and dishonest treatment by the male professional staff. She thought one of the worst offenders was her former mentor, who was also a highly valued staff member responsible for bringing in millions of dollars of new business. She and the other female scientists and technical staff had been ignoring the demeaning behavior by him and the other male colleagues because they needed his skill and research projects.

The female staff member also mentioned an episode six months earlier in which a male staff member had created a dangerous condition in the lab with only women present. While the incident had been investigated and the male staff member transferred to another group, a verbal threat on her life had been made to prevent her from speaking about the episode. That event clearly had traumatized her, and she had not reported the threat. Since that time, however, she had been keeping a record of the incidents and comments. In addition, the women in the group had been advising potential new recruits to the organization that they could not recommend working at the organization.

The ombuds discussed various options with her on several occasions. During this time, the staff member urged other women in her group also to speak with the ombuds. The ombuds thought that the facts outlined by the women created a real possibility of a class-action lawsuit against the organization, and he was trying to find a way to help get the issue to senior management. While most of the women insisted on anonymity, two of the women with whom the ombuds spoke were willing to speak about their concerns with management.

The ombuds helped coordinate a meeting between those two women and the CEO. As a result of those conversations, an investigation was undertaken to deal with the issues in that group. In addition, senior management engaged workplace consultants to work with staff throughout the organization to raise awareness and deal with gender-related communication and interaction.

The need for a truly confidential discussion and helpful suggestions from the ombuds

An employee contacted the ombuds, relying on the promise of confidentiality, to discuss possible implications of a serious health problem that the employee had involving a chronic and deteriorating (but non-communicable) disease. He wanted to know the benefits that would be available to his wife when he died. The employee indicated that he was able to function well at present but did not trust HR to keep such an inquiry confidential. He also did not want to inform his supervisor because he did not believe he would be incapacitated any time soon and was afraid that he would not be taken seriously for promotions or new responsibilities if others knew about his life-threatening illness.

The ombuds helped him research all of the applicable company policies to answer his questions on death benefit policies. The ombuds also expressed concern over the fact that because no one else in the organization knew about his condition, it could be a problem for the organization if he were to be incapacitated or die suddenly. The ombuds and the employee discussed several options, and the employee decided to prepare a sealed envelope with instructions that it only be opened in the event that there were a medical crisis while he is at work.

Suspicions of misconduct but a fear of reporting

An employee believed his supervisor had a falsified resume, including advanced degrees that the supervisor never earned. He thought this was wrong and wanted it reported, but only if his name could be separated from the report. The employee was not willing to allow any action to be taken unless he could be assured that his identity would be protected.

After hearing various options explained by the ombuds, the employee decided that he would use the organization's hotline option, as he now understood that information communicated to the hotline was passed directly to the chief of HR, who had responsibility for conducting an investigation. The ombuds coached the employee on the process of calling the organization's hotline and advised the employee how to include enough information in the report to allow the investigators to assess and investigate the allegation. Once the information was disclosed, the investigation revealed that the information was correct and the supervisor was disciplined.

Confidential coaching for faculty members

A department chair came to the ombuds with a concern over a mentoring relationship between a minority female junior faculty member that the chair had recruited and a senior white male faculty member who was assigned to mentor her. The chair had a high regard for both faculty members and thought that it would be good for each of them to be in this mentoring relationship, but perceived that both parties were having problems with it. The chair was concerned about losing the junior woman, since the department had experienced difficulties in recruiting and retaining good minority and female faculty members. The chair did not want to go to the dean with this issue or involve anyone else out of concern that it could affect everyone's reputation and career.

The ombuds discussed mentoring guidelines and successful practices with the department chair. They considered various options, including coaching by the ombuds of one or both faculty members; coaching the department chair and then having the chair conduct separate and joint conversations with the faculty members; having the ombuds conduct a facilitated conversation between the faculty members with a view toward developing an agreed-upon action plan; hiring external coaches for one or both faculty members; and having the ombuds sit in on several mentoring activities to help assess the situation and make further recommendations.

The department chair chose a combination of these options. The ombuds provided individual coaching to the department chair and the junior female faculty member. The chair had a private conversation with the male faculty member and provided funds for an external coach for him for a reasonable period. The chair then followed up periodically with each of the faculty members to provide support. As a result, the department chair believes that the issues were addressed without blemishing anyone's career, and the junior faculty member continues to make good progress in her career on a tenure track.

A vendor uses the ombuds office to get a bill paid by a valued customer

An outside vendor contacted the ombuds office because it had not been paid for a service it had provided to the organization. The vendor had tried repeatedly for over eight months to get the bill paid, but had not been successful. The organization was a very big client of the vendor, and it did not want to sue or take formal action that could jeopardize its other business with the organization. At the same time, the vendor needed to be paid and felt that the unit of the organization involved was giving it the red-tape "runaround." The vendor expressed a desire for the ombuds to help resolve the matter informally and off the record.

After discussing various options with the vendor, the ombuds was given permission to speak with the business manager of the unit involved. It became clear to the ombuds as a result of this discussion that the business manager was relatively new to the organization and was experiencing a shortage of staff, but he had been unwilling to ask for help. The business manager appreciated the informal way in which the issue had been raised. The vendor was paid and the matter resolved in a way that allowed the vendor to remain on good terms with the organization.

Only after extended conversations does an employee decide to come forward

A long-term employee close to retirement contacted the ombuds office anonymously to discuss concerns over possible ethics violations by management in vendor contracts. Being so close to retirement and fearing retaliation, the employee refused to reveal his name, location, or anything else that he felt could reveal his identity. The employee, however, was willing to generically discuss the behaviors that he felt were unethical.

The ombuds presented various options to the employee. The ombuds and the employee then discussed and considered the possible ramifications of each option to the employee if he were to reveal his identity. After several conversations, the employee agreed to let the ombuds contact HR with a scenario that he and the ombuds had developed to ascertain what HR's response and process would be if he chose to reveal his identity and participate in an investigation.

The ombuds spoke with HR and then with the employee on several occasions thereafter as they tried to work through how to proceed. Although it took some time, the employee gradually came to trust both the ombuds and HR. Finally, he agreed to meet with HR based on the repeated promise that retaliation would not be tolerated.

As a result of the information that the employee provided, an investigation was conducted, resulting in the termination of high-level personnel. The employee felt supported not only by the ombuds office, but also by HR and the organization. He retired soon thereafter and expressed his appreciation to the ombuds for helping him work through the decision to come forward on the ethical violations that had bothered him.

An ombuds can sometimes help with bureaucratic obstacles

The wife of a former 29-year employee who had retired due to a job injury called the ombuds office because they had not received his retirement check for the months of November and December, even though they usually received his check every month "like clockwork." She said that she had made numerous frustrating calls and left messages at local and national organization levels, during which she reported being given the runaround.

After hearing what she had tried to do to address the issue and understanding the importance of two months' pay to a retiree (especially with Christmas approaching), the ombuds asked for and was given permission to make inquiries to the head of retiree benefits. Although he was unavailable, the ombuds was able to speak with a retiree analyst who explained the process for getting the checks reinstated. With a couple of additional phone calls and e-mails, the ombuds was able to get assurance that the December check would be forthcoming.

In regard to the November check, however, the organization claimed that the retiree had not responded in a timely manner to paperwork that had been sent, so the only avenue was an administrative appeal to an overseeing board. The board was scheduled to meet that week but then not again until the first quarter of the next year, so a regular appeal would be considered then. The ombuds explored whether the paperwork could be submitted by fax and considered by the board at the meeting scheduled for that week and learned shortly thereafter that it would be permitted.

The paperwork was faxed and approved by the board, and the checks were issued before Christmas.

Sometimes it is necessary to take an issue to the CEO

Several employees and leaders expressed concern to the ombuds about a very senior leader's bad temper. His behavior was intimidating and caused his direct reports to be afraid to approach him, provide information, or seek guidance from him. Nevertheless, there was an imminent possibility that this leader would be elevated to the next level despite such behavior. The employees who came to the ombuds office were afraid to be identified, but some of them asked the ombuds to raise the issue with higher management without identifying them as the source.

The ombuds met with the CEO of the organization and indicated that concerns had been expressed about the conduct of this senior manager, and provided some examples of his conduct that could have been easily observed by many people but did not reveal the identity of any person who had come to the ombuds. The CEO expressed appreciation for the information and arranged for an executive coach to assist the leader.

A different perspective results in a win-win

An employee's progress toward his goals and his managerial competencies were below expectations for his position. The HR representative brought the issue to the attention of the ombuds, indicating that the employee's supervisor had coached and counseled the employee on these issues several times but there had been no improvement to date. As a result, the employee's supervisor recommended termination of employment. After further discussions with the local HR manager, organization decided to offer the employee a Mutual Agreement (a very common practice in China to release the employee with terms/conditions to which both parties agree).

After a few sessions to negotiate this with the employee, however, the parties had been unable to reach an agreement. In addition, the employee was starting to complain to others within the organization about being treated unfairly and had started sending e-mails to senior management. It was at this point that the HR manager asked the ombuds if he would be willing to speak with the employee.

The ombuds agreed to contact the employee but made it clear to the HR manager, and then to the employee, that any discussions between the employee and the ombuds would be voluntary and confidential. The employee requested a face-to-face meeting with the ombuds. During the meeting, the employee described the situation from his point of view and explained why he felt he had been treated unfairly. The ombuds asked a few clarifying questions to make sure he understood the employee's concerns. The ombuds also asked the employee to examine the situation from other perspectives, including the perspective of managing the business and responsibilities of a manager within the organization. In the course of this discussion, the employee gained a better understanding of the situation and inquired if he might fit better in a different role in the organization. The employee asked the ombuds if it would be possible for him to change roles. The ombuds explained that he was not part of management and did not have the authority to make such decisions, but if the employee requested, the ombuds would forward the request to the management team. The employee requested the ombuds to do so.

The ombuds presented the proposed move to the management team, and they allowed the employee to move from a manager's role to one of individual contributor. The organization was able to fill the manager's role with a more qualified person, and the employee was allowed to remain employed but in a role that better fit his skills and abilities. This was a win-win for both the organization and the employee.

A visit to the ombuds results in a repaired relationship and cleaner workspace

An employee in a represented bargaining unit contacted the ombuds to discuss issues he was having with a co-worker. The caller was a second-shift employee in a manufacturing location. The first shift worker who operated the same machinery as the caller was leaving the machinery dirty, causing the caller to have to clean up the mess on his shift. Sometimes the first shift employee would purposely put grease on the operating handles of the machinery. The caller was becoming fed up with this conduct but did not want to report it to management for fear of causing discipline to a fellow represented employee.

The ombuds discussed options with the caller as to how to approach his fellow worker to resolve the issues and to "air out" their differences. The ombuds suggested that the caller consider utilizing the services of the shop steward or another union official to serve as a mediator or conduit for the discussion. The caller stated that he had contacted the shop steward and, in fact, the shop steward suggested that he contact the ombuds for resolution suggestions.

The caller went back to the steward and discussed the situation and the steward helped to arrange a truce between the co-workers.

Cooperation between audit and the ombuds office

Internal audit received a report that a member of the research and development staff of 20 had been conducting a personal real estate business from his office computer. Two auditors arrived at the department one morning. They announced to the entire department that they were there to conduct an audit and then began at the office at the south end of the corridor.

An employee in the department, who or may not have been the whistle-blower, realized that the office of the person with the personal business was on the north end and that the auditors would not get there for several hours, giving the employee plenty of time to erase files. He immediately called the ombuds to describe the situation and gave only the office number of the suspected employee. He never disclosed who he was or any other individual information. It then took the ombuds less than a minute to reach the chief of audit to relay the information. The chief of audit then immediately called the auditors in the field to inform them that they should begin in office number 20 at the north end of the corridor.

The audit discovered evidence of the employee's personal business on the company computer. Both the audit chief and the ombuds felt that the cooperation between the ombuds and audit worked well. Doubtless the employee making the call to the ombuds would agree.

Facilitation of an awareness of different cultural perspectives

Two employees came to the ombuds office because they were concerned about what they perceived to be a threat made by another person who worked for the company. The two visitors, a man and a woman, were both from an Asian country and were at the company's U.S. headquarters on a one-year temporary permit.

They reported that they returned to their building late one night after a break for dinner. The security guard had left, so they used their electronic employee badges to enter the building. As they entered, they noticed that an African-American man slipped into the building behind them. Concerned about security, especially post-9/11, they decided to follow the man. They said that they tried to be discreet as they followed him up the internal staircase in the building. When the man entered an office they became very alarmed and stood in the hallway, discussing what to do next. They noticed an office directory on the wall by the staircase and checked the name associated with office the man had entered. At that point, the man suddenly burst forth from the office and shouted at the visitors. Startled and tremendously frightened, they ran down the stairs, retreating to the office they shared. They considered reporting the incident to their superiors but did not because they were unsure of themselves and because they did not know if the man in the office was actually the same person listed on the directory. They decided to come to the ombuds office to ask for confidential guidance on what they should do.

After discussing various options, the visitors gave the ombuds permission to contact the person listed in the directory. The ombuds did so and learned that he was the African-American man whom they had seen enter the office. The man told the ombuds that he had been very disturbed and offended by the two visitors' behavior and that he had questioned their motives.

The ombuds presented all three people with an option to have a mediation in which to discuss their concerns, and they agreed. The African-American man explained that he found the behavior by the other two to be both threatening and racist. He described experiences in being followed and harassed by police and explained how insulting he found it to be that the others assumed that he did not belong in the building. He also explained that he had felt threatened by their actions in following him and that he actually feared for his own safety. It had occurred to him that *they* might be terrorists, as they looked vaguely Middle-Eastern or South Asian. The visitors explained to him that they were not familiar with issues of race in the United States and had no idea that their actions would be interpreted as they had been. They assured the man they had they had not intended to cause him alarm, and that that they would have done the same no matter who had slipped in behind them. They stated that they appreciated the cultural lesson and had learned much from it. They also were glad that the ombuds was available for them to talk about their concerns.

Breach of confidentiality because of personal safety concerns

An employee learned that a supervisor was going to be attacked at work the next day by other employees. Concerned that her own safety would be at risk if she reported this to anyone, she felt that she could tell the ombuds about it confidentially and that the ombuds could take the issue from there.

With such a short time to act and no other reasonable option, the ombuds determined that the situation justified invoking the exception to confidentiality and notified security of the allegation and the identity of the employees who allegedly were involved.

Security responded quickly and defused the immediate threat to personal safety. A broader investigation was also commenced that revealed extensive drug trafficking at this location. Local police were informed and several arrests were made, resulting in a safer and more productive work environment. The person initially reporting the incident was satisfied that her identity was never revealed.

Sensitivity to cultural issues gives an inquirer more options

A female doctoral student from a Muslim country came to the ombuds only after carefully checking out the documentation available about the program's confidentiality. After the initial conversation about the office and how it operates, the visitor engaged in a somewhat extended conversation about her home country during which the ombuds demonstrated a sensitivity to her culture and customs. Only after this extended conversation, during which the ombuds perceived that the visitor was trying to determine whether or not to trust the ombuds, did the visitor reveal her principal concern: she had become sexually active while at the university but she was going to be completing her program soon and her family expected her to return home to an arranged marriage. She was terrified of the potential ramifications for her and her family and for the planned marriage. While there were other places that the visitor could have gone to discuss the personal and cultural issues involved, her desire for confidentiality and the ability to explore options were paramount and led her to the ombuds office.

The ombuds reaffirmed the principle of neutrality and, without making value judgments, indicated a willingness to discuss a full range of potential options with the visitor, from going home to the arranged marriage as planned to rejecting the arranged marriage and not going home. The option selected by the visitor, and one she had not previously considered, was to pursue a position in a post-doctoral program, which would give her more time to assess the situation and decide how she wanted to proceed.

New call center employee has concerns and wants a safe place to discuss her options

A call center employee for a multinational organization who had started work only five months earlier became suspicious about a co-worker who started at the same time as she and who had been in the same training class. The inquirer said that her co-worker was frequently using her cell phone at her workstation, particularly when the supervisor was not in the area, even though this was prohibited. The inquirer also had noticed that on weekends, when there was no supervisor close to their work area, the co-worker would read off numerous account numbers while on her cell phone. The event prompting the call to the ombuds occurred when the co-worker offered to go buy dinner for their eight-person team and said, "Don't worry . . . it's my treat!" The inquirer accompanied her co-worker to help her carry the food back to the office and noticed that when the co-worker brought out her wallet to pay the bill, she had at least 10 different credit cards in her wallet, all with different names.

The inquirer was worried and at a loss about what she could do, particularly since she was such a new employee. She and the ombuds discussed several options to raise the concern. The employee was fearful and wanted to remain anonymous, but she gave the ombuds permission to communicate the identity of the co-worker and the general nature of her concern to HR and Security. Once alerted, they conducted an investigation and determined that fraudulent charges had been incurred on some of the accounts on which the co-worker had worked. The co-worker was terminated and criminal charges were filed against her. In addition, further fraudulent activity was stopped.

Job protection and fear at all costs

The ombuds received an anonymous call from an employee in a multinational organization through an overseas operating center. The caller was extremely nervous about calling but was put at ease by the ombuds first explaining how the ombuds office works (confirming confidentiality, neutrality, informality, and independence) and by being able to speak in the person's first language. The caller explained that he worked in a unit that had high security, separate badge access, and security cameras because the unit dealt with valuable assets and financial information. He explained that his supervisor had been harassing his unit for over a year, making veiled threats about employees losing their jobs, asking for personal errands, bullying them, and instigating rough-play games (such as hitting, boxing, wearing blindfolds, tying people with a rope, etc.). The so-called "games" were played in an area with no security camera coverage and supposedly were to have "fun" and break the monotony in the work area. Even though there were at least 20 employees in the unit who had been subjected to these practices and an HR office and higher supervisors were located in the same building, there was so much fear of potential job loss that no one spoke up for a year. Finally, when a co-worker had to leave work discreetly to go to the hospital because he broke several ribs in one of the "games" and did not report the incident, the caller decided to call the ombuds office in the United States, because he had heard that it was confidential and had seen announcements about the office when the ombuds visited his location several months earlier.

The ombuds and the caller discussed various ways that the issue could be raised. The caller decided to give the ombuds permission to contact HR and Security, but he was too fearful to give permission for the ombuds to contact the higher-up supervisor (a vice president of the organization) because he believed that the immediate supervisor was extremely well regarded by that person. The ombuds, without revealing the identity of the employee who had made the call, passed along information to HR and Security concerning the type of activity that had apparently had been occurring. They then investigated the matter by interviewing many of the employees separately at an outside location. The investigation corroborated the allegations, and the supervisor and a higher-ranking supervisor were terminated from the organization.

A sense of vulnerability and fear too great even for an ombuds

A female medical resident came to the ombuds with concerns over conflict with her (older male) attending physician. The attending physician enjoyed a great deal of respect at the institution and had a national reputation in his field. She reported what she perceived to be sexist behavior in his decision-making in dealing with patients and in his evaluation of other residents. She indicated that medical errors made by male residents were laughed off, but errors made by female residents were discussed openly at meetings. She said that other female colleagues had told her that they agreed with her observations, and even some male residents had said privately that they saw the same problem and sympathized but were not willing to come forward about the attending physician's conduct. She told the ombuds that she felt vulnerable and a great deal of pressure to remain silent, because the attending physician could destroy her career if she were to cross him. She said that she was having difficulty sleeping and constant stomach problems.

The ombuds discussed with the resident a variety of avenues to try to raise the issue. The resident also was fully aware of her options for legal recourse if she chose to go that route. Despite several discussions over an extended period of time, the resident, while fully aware of her formal and informal options, was too afraid of the consequences to her career to raise the issue in any fashion. She endured the treatment, finished her residency program, and tried to move on with her life.

Persistent retaliation

An employee came to the ombuds with concerns over retaliation by her manager for a complaint that the employee had made to HR about the manager. In the course of her discussion with the ombuds, it came out that the employee had been at the company for only one year and that the manager was hired from another company by the next-level manager, a vice president and a long-time friend. The employee, the manager, and the vice president were all women.

The employee had first complained to HR about her manager making negative comments in front of other employees about the employee's looks and the fact that she was from another country. She had also informed HR about other encounters with her manager and the manager's behavior in meetings at which the employee was present and tried to speak. HR had brought the issue to the attention of the manager and the vice president, but the manager responded by later confronting the employee about the complaint made to HR. The employee also felt that once HR had become involved, the manager was reducing the employee's work without justification. The employee believed that HR had not handled the matter confidentially and she was most concerned about further retaliation. She wanted to speak to the ombuds confidentially about what could be done.

In the course of the discussions with the ombuds, the employee indicated that she thought that the manager had violated the company's code of conduct but was afraid to report it out of fear of further retaliation. With coaching from the ombuds and after discussing various options, the employee filed an anonymous report on the possible violation. Once she did so, however, she came back to the ombuds to share the latest experiences of retaliation, because although the report was anonymous, the manager and the vice president had assumed that she had filed it and were making her life very difficult. After receiving permission from the employee, the ombuds spoke with a senior person about the investigation that had been undertaken with respect to the code of conduct allegation and the persistent retaliation.

By escalating the issue in this manner, both the code of conduct issue and the retaliation were fully investigated. This enabled the employee to express her concern directly in connection with the investigation. The company found that the manager had, in fact, been retaliating against the employee, and the manager's employment was terminated. The vice president was reprimanded for her involvement in the matter. The employee was able to retain her position and report to a new manager.

Breach of confidentiality because of risk of harm to others

The ombuds was contacted separately by five different individuals. Each one reported concern about the unusual or troubling behavior of a high-status female employee. Each of the odd behaviors—including sharing a risqué photograph, finding an "accidental" fire in a trash can, keeping a knife in a desk drawer to slice fruit at lunchtime, making what might be interpreted as veiled threats in an e-mail—had been investigated by a compliance office, but in each case there was insufficient evidence for a sanction harsher than a warning. However, when the bystanders discussed their concerns with the ombuds, they were able to provide more context and explain why they felt afraid of this employee. Moreover, the ombuds was the only person in the organization who had enough information to "connect the dots" and see a pattern.

In light of the number and type of complaints about serious and inappropriate conduct that had been raised, the ombuds approached the female employee and encouraged her to seek psychiatric help. When she refused, but demonstrated anger, despair, and fascination with violence, the ombuds was concerned that this person may pose an imminent threat of serious harm to herself or to others and that confidentiality could not be maintained. The ombuds disclosed to the HR director and the general counsel some of the information that suggested the seemingly disparate instances might reflect a pattern and that several other employees felt concerns for their personal safety. While the ombuds does not know what the HR director and the general counsel then did to evaluate this information, they subsequently developed a plan to remove the female employee from the organization's premises until a satisfactory psychological evaluation had been completed.

Extended communications with the ombuds allows an employee to become comfortable with reporting

The ombuds received a call from a compliance officer at an unrelated but affiliated organization about possible financial misconduct by the president of that organization. The inquirer was so concerned about her identity being compromised that she made the call from a public telephone at a mall. She was the compliance officer of her organization, but it was a relatively small organization and she was afraid that she could not successfully accuse or investigate the president of the organization without being victimized herself.

After discussing various options to surface the issue, the inquirer remained uncomfortable with her identity being disclosed and was unwilling to select any of the options suggested by the ombuds. The conversation ended with the caller remaining anonymous and with the ombuds encouraging her to call back later so that they could continue to discuss how to raise the issue. Similar conversations took place several times over the next few months—the inquirer calling from a mall to avoid Caller ID and continuing to remain anonymous. The inquirer also continued to be unwilling to select an option to permit the issue to be raised. At the end of each conversation, the ombuds encouraged a further call from the inquirer after they each had more time for reflection. After several such calls, however, the inquirer began to appreciate the fact that significant misconduct could be involved and that it needed to be reported. As she began to trust the ombuds to preserve her confidentiality (especially since no word had leaked out about her calls), she grew more comfortable with the idea of initiating an investigation. She finally gave the ombuds permission to reveal basic information, including the identity of her organization and the nature of her concerns, to other formal channels that could conduct an investigation. With this permission, the ombuds then made the authorized disclosure, and an investigation and audit were commenced. The investigation revealed a multimillion-dollar fraud that ultimately sent the organization's president to prison. Throughout all of this, the inquirer insisted on remaining anonymous, even to the ombuds.

Improving the organizational culture

An employee with less than a year of service came to the ombuds to discuss what she should do with information she had learned during one of her assignments. She had been asked to create a new work guide for her department, and in so doing, she had spoken with individuals and work teams about what work instructions had already been created, what was useful, and what else might be needed. In the course of these meetings, she heard many concerns from employees about management and vice-versa. She knew that she was not in a position to "fix" the problems but felt obligated to inform management. At the same time, she was in distress because she still was a relatively new employee and uncertain what the impact on her would be if she were to raise the unfavorable issues with management.

After a discussion of various options and some role-playing, the employee decided to speak directly with her boss by indicating that in the course of her work, various concerns had been expressed to her and then inquiring of her boss if he wanted to hear about them. Depending on his reaction, she was prepared to distance herself from the comments by indicating that she was only the messenger and reporting what she had heard.

She had the conversation with her boss, and informed the ombuds that it went well. She was later selected to sit on a staff/management panel to brainstorm possible resolution options.

Confidential group assessment by the ombuds

The management of a unit perceived that there were problems with the unit and that the employees in it appeared alienated from the organization. They wanted to get a better sense of the problems and believed that they could do this only by having the employees in the unit speak honestly. They knew, however, that employees would be reluctant to do this unless they were able to speak with a third party confidentially. Consequently, management contacted the ombuds office to ask them to speak with employees with the understanding that the ombuds would not disclose identities or confidential communications but would share conclusions from the interviews.

The ombuds agreed to meet with employees and speak with them with that understanding. The ombuds explained to employees that the communications would be confidential and that only summary conclusions would be shared with local management. After speaking with employees and focus groups, the ombuds shared observations and conclusions with the local management. This allowed management to address some of the systemic problems and employees to feel confident that they had been able to express their concerns, but the identities of those who had made specific comments would still be kept confidential.

Effective counseling avoids a lawsuit

An employee came to the ombuds with concerns that his boss was discriminating against him because of his sexual orientation. He was adamant that he did not want to raise this issue with anyone in HR or with his boss out of fear of further retaliation. He was fully aware of his legal rights and was close to a decision to quit and bring a lawsuit against the company and his boss for retaliation.

The ombuds worked with the employee for an extended period to try to identify options that the employee could feel comfortable with to deal with the issue. Finally, the employee and the ombuds were able to identify a manager in another area who was willing to work with the employee to help him look for another job both inside the company and elsewhere.

The employee was very grateful to have had help in finding a manager with whom he could discuss his concerns and from whom he could seek advice. The employee ultimately found another job outside of the company, and a lawsuit was avoided.

Where does a compliance investigator go for help?

A compliance investigator contacted the ombuds asking for guidance on how to deal with what he saw as a recurrent problem: he would investigate allegations of violations and then draft a report with recommended sanctions, but the director of compliance would frequently tone down the report and lighten the recommended sanctions. The director had told the investigator that he was too straightforward and lacked "political savvy." The investigator felt that the director's reluctance to take a stand often amounted to a "whitewash" or a cover-up of the issues.

The investigator did not know how to raise this issue and was fearful of retaliation if he were to complain about the actions of the director. After discussing the situation, the investigator was not comfortable with any of the options they discussed and nothing further was done at that time.

Many months later, the director fired the investigator for insubordination because of the employee's outspoken complaints about and to the director. The investigator again contacted the ombuds to discuss whether there were any options for him to get the job back and to discuss his concerns over the previous actions of the director. The ombuds was not able to assist in overturning the termination from employment but was able to arrange a meeting between the investigator and senior management to give the investigator an opportunity to share his perspective on the differences between his draft reports and the director's revisions of them. The employee was relieved to have had the opportunity to report his concerns to senior management, and senior management felt that he had given them information that alerted them to the need to be more mindful of the reports from the director.

Local management ethical issues raised safely through ombuds office

Some employees at one unit of the company were aware that key contract terms were being changed by their local management after a contract had been agreed to and signed by the customer but prior to being submitted to the company's corporate offices. This practice resulted in larger bonuses to local management than they should have received. Corporate Audit was generally aware there had been problems with certain types of contracts in the field but had been unable to pinpoint the specifics or the people involved.

The employees who knew about this practice feared that they would be retaliated against if they raised this issue through formal channels, especially since it involved their local management. Some of these employees contacted the ombuds office because they thought it would be a safe way to obtain guidance on how to deal with the problem.

The ombuds, with permission of the employees, was able to facilitate the involvement of formal resources in a way that maintained the anonymity of the employees raising the issue and resulted in an investigation, eventual discipline of those involved in the fraudulent contracts, and a change in policy to prevent similar problems in the future.

Effective mediation blocks abusive tactic against foreign student

A foreign national graduate student contacted the ombuds because his thesis advisor had failed or refused to read the corrected version of his thesis for over six months.

The ombuds explained various options the student could use to resolve the impasse. At the student's request, the ombuds conducted mediation sessions with the faculty member thesis advisor. In the course of these mediation sessions, the advisor's comments suggested that he was planning to claim authorship of the student's work and publish it as his own. The ombuds believed that the professor had been intimidating the student by causing the student to fear that he would not graduate so that the student would, in fact, return to his country of origin without graduating. The ombuds asked the advisor if that was his intention. Once the issue was articulated, the advisor signed off on the student's thesis, and the student was able to graduate.

If the ombuds had not been there as a confidential resource for the student to provide guidance on what he could do, the student would have given up his career and returned home.

Checking out the process can be very involved

The ombuds office was contacted by a woman who said that she was employed by the organization but who disclosed neither her name nor the area in which she worked. She said that she was gathering information about what the ombuds office did and did not do, but she was quite thorough: the initial call lasted 45 minutes. This is a fairly typical action by some people who, before doing anything, want to "check out the process."

A few weeks later, the same woman called again, although the ombuds knew this only by recognizing her voice (and later confirmed it); she made no reference to having spoken to the office before. She scheduled an appointment with the ombuds office but used an assumed name. When she met with the ombuds, she did not disclose either her position or where she worked in the organization. Her concerns focused on a number of issues she said she had been having with colleagues and her supervisor, including a general lack of civility (basic rudeness) and the need for clarification of responsibilities. She said that her issue with the supervisor was that he was not engaged as a manager and not managing staffing problems. The ombuds provided coaching for her and gave her options on how she could address the issues.

Approximately a month later, she returned for another discussion with the ombuds. They discussed how things had been going and strategized other options for her. More coaching was provided, and she left again to address her issues on her own. When she returned again approximately a month later, the ombuds assumed it was for another debriefing and further guidance, but at this point the woman revealed that all of the prior discussions had not been on the "real issue" and that she had resolved all of the other matters. Not until this discussion did she disclose that she was a post-doctoral graduate student working in a lab under the direction of a primary investigator (PI), who was well known both in their particular specialized field and at the organization as a major researcher and senior faculty member. Only at this point did she disclose that from the beginning, the true issue was this PI's sexual harassment of her. She admitted that she had raised all the other issues to see if the ombuds really knew what he was talking about, appreciated the political realities of her position, and was "truly confidential."

She said that she had gone through the extended "checking out the process" period because she was extremely concerned at how vulnerable her position was. The PI was eminent in his field and had the power to make or break her career. She was clear that she did not want to engage any formal process, but she wanted the harassment to stop. After long discussions on a few occasions about various options, she finally decided that she would attempt to leave his lab and find another one. In the research world, this approach can be very be problematic on many levels, especially if the PI of the lab being left attempts to prevent someone from transitioning to another lab or poisons the person's reputation. To address this issue, she asked the ombuds to speak with the PI to see if he would consent to her departure. The ombuds then had a confidential, informal, neutral, and frank conversation with the PI and helped him realize that it was in everyone's best interest for him to embrace her leaving his lab as a great opportunity for her "intellectual and professional development." He agreed and she found a new lab where she has flourished.

The fear of retaliation is so great the employee will trust only the ombuds

An employee was concerned that a supervisor was misappropriating funds by submitting false entertainment vouchers. The employee was extremely concerned about possible retaliation and the consequences of raising these issues about her supervisor. She said that she was not prepared to submit any documents or to speak to anyone other than the ombuds because the ombuds communications were confidential.

After several rounds of conversation with the ombuds during which the ombuds and she discussed options for raising the issue, she finally agreed to speak with an internal auditor but only on an anonymous basis. The ombuds arranged for an anonymous call between her and internal audit. The employee, communicating through the ombuds as an intermediary, was also able to provide internal audit with other information they needed to commence the investigation, but the employee's identity was never disclosed. The audit revealed misconduct and the supervisor was terminated.

Ombuds delivers message that leads to improved air quality

A union employee called the ombuds office because he was concerned that co-workers were turning off the exhaust fan when it was cold outside to keep the plant warm. The employee was concerned that this was not in compliance with both plant environmental standards and the law, as this practice resulted in smoke in the plant on very cold days. He did not want to report this to the union or HR because it could get other employees in trouble. The employee asked the ombuds to contact the HR manager to alert him to the situation.

The ombuds notified the HR manager of the issue but not the identity of the person who had raised it. The HR manager had not been aware of the situation, but once it was brought to his attention, he was able to see the problem. He notified plant maintenance area, and working together they found there was a problem with the plant's exhaust system. The plant maintenance department brought in experts who were able to fix the exhaust system and the problem was resolved.

Bankruptcy fears with the employer as a debtor

As the economic decline worsened, several employees contacted the ombuds to inquire about the organization's policy related to filing for personal bankruptcy. They were especially concerned about its effect on their employment status because their debts included money owed to the organization. The employees did not want to ask their supervisors for fear of being cast in a negative light. They also were reluctant to consult HR because they thought HR would advise their supervisors anyway. The employees came to the ombuds because they saw it as a confidential option to help them assess the likely consequences before making a personal decision about how to proceed.

Without revealing any information about any employee who had spoken with the ombuds office, the ombuds made an inquiry generically to the organization's formal channels to confirm the policy that an employee's employment status would not be negatively affected if he or she filed for personal bankruptcy, even if the organization were listed as a creditor. The ombuds was then able to convey this information back to the employees who had raised the issue.

Systemic management problem but fear of retaliation

Several inquirers came to the ombuds over many months with concerns about the director of their department. He was variously described as a bully and a taskmaster, and he reportedly retaliated against those he perceived as challenging him. At first, none of the inquirers were willing to speak directly with him or even participate in facilitated discussions with the ombuds as a third-party mediator. After a while, a few became willing to permit their concerns to be expressed to higher management, but only if their names were not revealed for fear that disclosure of their identities would come back to haunt them—both from retaliation by the director and because higher management might see them as whiners and disloyal.

When the ombuds raised the issue with an executive in higher management generically, the executive communicated to the ombuds that he wanted to encourage the employees to speak with him directly. After numerous follow-up discussions with the employees and with the executive, two employees told the ombuds that they would be willing to speak with the executive directly. Other employees agreed to write out their concerns for the ombuds to give to the executive but would not agree to be identified.

The executive met with the two employees, received the written comments, and subsequently undertook his own analysis of the situation. Ultimately, the executive determined that management had enough information to relieve the director of his duties. A new director was installed, and the previous inquirers reported much improved functioning and morale.

Trend report results in policy change

Company policies required employees to notify the company of any change in the number of dependents covered under benefits provided by the company. The policy required that an employee furnish the necessary documentation within 30 days of the event giving rise to the change. Several employees contacted the ombuds office for guidance in dealing with difficulties they had experienced in complying with this policy when they had a child. Thirty days frequently appeared to be insufficient time to obtain a birth certificate, resulting in a number of otherwise qualified dependents not being covered by important benefits such as health insurance. This trend was quickly spotted and reported to the corporate benefits office. As a result, the policy was changed to allow employees up to six months to furnish the necessary documentation.

Testing the ombuds first

An employee came to the ombuds to inquire confidentially whether a supervisor who had insisted that the employees in his unit be at their desks at 8:30 could discipline an employee who arrived later than that but still before 9:00, which is the standard time work begins at the company. The ombuds provided the employee with information on the issue and coaching on how the employee could deal with the supervisor.

A month later, the employee again came to the ombuds office with another concern and mentioned that no one had found out about the first contact. On this occasion, however, the employee explained that for the past year, the supervisor had been offering the employee gifts, bonuses, and perks, and that the employee believed that these were an attempt by the supervisor to give the employee "hush money" because of the employee's awareness of false claims on the supervisor's expense reports.

After discussing various options, the employee indicated a willingness to speak with a very senior person in the ethics office. The ombuds helped the employee understand the type of documentation that the ethics officer would look for to document the allegation.

An ombuds helps an employee receive medical help and use the organization's dispute resolution process

An employee with a previous exceptional performance record came to the ombuds with concerns over treatment by his new boss. His former boss had been promoted, resulting in the employee being reassigned to another director who had not been consulted or given any say in the reassignment. The employee said that his new boss had indicated that there were problems with his work and work ethic and had given him a poor performance rating.

At the same time, the employee told the ombuds that a terminally ill parent was living with him and had to be cared for daily, including being delivered to and from an adult care facility while the employee worked. The employee had used vacation time and sick leave for the extra time that this required, but he had recently learned that he might be eligible under FMLA for additional time off. His director, however, had told him that he could not leave early or arrive late; and when he did apply for FMLA leave, the director denied his request without explanation. The employee was distraught by this situation and did not know where else to go. He himself was also experiencing stress and other health-related concerns as a result of the situation.

In the course of consultations with the ombuds, the ombuds was able to help the employee first consult with medical services to attend to his own health problems while they worked on the other issues. They discussed various options to try to address the continuing issues with the director. The option selected by the employee was to use the organization's dispute resolution process to appeal the performance rating that he had been given by the director. As a result of the dispute resolution process, the employee's performance rating was changed, the FMLA request was granted, and the director was reprimanded for his actions.

A need for information without revealing who asked for it

An employee came to the ombuds office because he was concerned that with several job functions being outsourced, he could be displaced or offered a job at another location. Because this was a result of a company-wide reengineering initiative, any such displaced employee would be eligible for severance benefits. The employee was unwilling, for obvious reasons, to go through formal channels to find out "what constituted a comparable job" and asked the ombuds if that inquiry could be made without revealing his identity.

The ombuds was able to speak with HR on a generic basis without revealing the identity of the employee and then provide the employee with the information requested. The ombuds was also able to direct the employee to the company's Web site for additional helpful information.

A systemic issue identified by the ombuds leads to better policies

Several employees reported in separate communications with the ombuds that they were confused by various written and oral warnings they had received. Often employees were surprised when they were told that the verbal warning stage was over and a written warning had been issued.

In its mid-year trend report, the ombuds identified this confusion by employees over the various levels of oral and written warnings as an issue. As a result of this feedback, HR reviewed its warning policies and how they were being implemented. The review resulted in HR revising the applicable procedures to simplify the process and to more clearly define and articulate when each type of warning should be given. As a result, significantly fewer instances of confusion over the meaning of a warning were presented to the ombuds.

Use of the ombuds office by vendors permitted ombuds to identify a trend that resulted in improved vendor communication

The organization's external Web site or Internet site prominently listed the ombuds office as one of four organizational contacts. As a result, the ombuds office was used by a wide variety of non-employees as an initial point of contact when they were seeking assistance in dealing with the organization.

Although the ombuds office had been established as an internal employee resource, it quickly became clear to the office that it was being contacted by many external parties, including customers, who were not sure who to contact for even such things as machine repair or replacement. The ombuds thought that management could do a better job in communicating with customers for specific business needs.

This point was included in one of the trend reports made by the ombuds office to management. Management reviewed the situation and decided to make improvements in its communication materials provided to customers. Management later reported that the changes resulted in more efficient customer service and higher customer satisfaction and retention.

Index

A

AMA/HRI Business Ethics Survey 108
American Bar Association
  2001 Report
    confidentiality 59
    impartiality 54
  2004 Report
    confidentiality 59
    impartiality 54
    independence, assessment of 48
    ombuds authority, limitations on 67
  Commission on Legal Problems of the Elderly 38
  Government and Public Sector Division 38
  House of Delegates 38
  Ombuds Committee 37
  ombuds resolutions
    See ABA ombuds resolutions 24–27
  recommendation on federal ombuds programs 22
  resolution identifying ombudsman characteristics 7
  Section of Administrative Law and Regulatory Practice 38
  Section of Business Law 38
  Section of Dispute Resolution 38
  Section of Individual Rights and Responsibilities 42
  Senior Lawyer Division 38
American Bar Association ombuds resolutions
  1969 ABA Resolution 35
    essential characteristics of organizational ombuds 27–29
    failure to address neutrality 28
  2001 ABA Resolution 38–41
    confidentiality, issue of 39, 59
    criteria for program establishment 25
    essential characteristics 28
    impartiality, issue of 39, 53
    independence, issue of 39, 47
    investigations 53
    issues not addressed 39
    limitations on ombuds authority 40
    ombuds authority, limitations on 66
    organizational ombuds, defined 25
    preamble to 24
    types of ombuds programs, framework for 38
    written policy provision 38
  2004 ABA Resolution 26, 42–44, 212–18, 279, 287–89
    classification of ombuds programs 26, 42
    collective-bargaining agreement 42
    confidentiality 59
    independence, issue of 47
    International Ombudsman Association (IOA) response to 45, 50
    investigations 53
    notice, issue of 43
    ombuds as agent of notice 212
    ombuds authority, limitations on 66
    Section of Individual Rights and Responsibilities 42

627

Acord v. Alyeska Pipeline Service Co. 232
Administrative Conference of the United States 22
  recommendation on creation of ombuds programs 22
Administrative Dispute Resolution Act 23, 264–68. 397–98
  confidentiality provisions of 264–68
Administrative Procedure Act 393
admission, requests for 320–21
Age Discrimination in Employment Act 274, 425
alternative dispute resolution 23, 180, 264, 340–43
American Law Institute 195
American Recovery and Reinvestment Act of 2009 156–58
  whistle-blower protections 140
American Red Cross Governance Modernization Act 171
Americans with Disabilities Act 426
Anderson, Stanley 6
arbitration 273–76, 340–43
  Age Discrimination in Employment Act 274
  as threat to confidentiality 273
  Circuit City Stores v. Adams 274
  Federal Arbitration Act 343
  Gilmer v. Interstate/Johnson Lane Corp. 274

B

Bendersky, Corinne 145
best practices
  International Ombudsman Association
    adoption of 55, 61, 70
    recommendations 72–75
best practices, necessity for 142–44
  management practices 142
Browne, John 109

Burlington Indus. v. Ellerth 133, 436
Burlington N. & Santa Fe Ry. Co. v. White 135, 436

C

Caiden, Gerald 2
California Caucus of College and University Ombuds 14
California Constitutional Right of Privacy 256–59
California Evidence Code 260–61
Carman v. McDonnell Douglas Corp. 221, 233
CBOCS West v. Humphries 136, 436
Chambers v. Wal-Mart Stores, Inc. 201
charters establishing ombuds offices 278–83
Circuit City Stores v. Adams 274
Civil Rights Act of 1866 426
Civil Rights Act of 1964 427
Civil Rights Act of 1991 427
Civil Service Reform Act 150
  whistle-blower protections 139
Clery Act 384–88
  reporting channels 386–87
  reporting requirements of 386
    annual crime report 386
    daily crime logs 387
    threat reports 387
Cleveland Bd. of Educ. v. LaFleur 435
Coalition of Federal Ombudsmen 24
codes of ethics 30–37
  Corporate Ombudsman Association 30
  International Ombudsman Association
    confidentiality 57
    informality 65
    revised code 46
  The Ombudsman Association 31

Index **629**

collective bargaining
  International Ombudsman Association Guidance and Commentary 45, 69
Commission on Campus Unrest
  reform of university governance, need for 12
Commission on Defense Management 18
Commission on Higher Education 13
common-law privilege 221–49
  federal testimonial privileges 221–27
    Federal Rule of Evidence 501 221
    Trammel v. United States 222
    United States v. Bryan 224
    United States v. Nixon 223–24
    Upjohn v. United States 225
communications, organizational ombuds role in 75
compliance programs
  confidentiality, limits on 144
  ethics officer responsibility for 144
  favorable impact in workplace 168
  growth in 145
  hotlines for reporting misconduct. *See also.*
  human resources responsibility for 144
  reporting, inhibiting of 145
  strict enforcement
    risks of 147
  zero tolerance policies 146
confidentiality
  2001 ABA Resolution 59
    defined 59
  2004 ABA Resolution 59
  ABA 2001 Report 59
  ABA 2004 Report 59
  Administrative Dispute Resolution Act 264–68
  arbitration as threat to confidentiality. *See also.*

California Constitutional Right of Privacy 256
criminal cases, confidentiality in. *See also.*
discovery, court regulation of. *See also.*
documentation, importance in claims of confidentiality. *See also.*
federal mediation privilege 269
Garstang v. The Superior Court of Los Angeles County 256
imminent threat exception. *See also.*
implied contract of 249–55
  implied in fact 250, 252
  implied in law 250, 253
importance in ombuds programs 28, 173
  expressing concerns about misconduct 29
  influence on ombuds conduct 29
  IOA Code of Ethics 57
  IOA Standards of Practice 57
  limits on promise of 144
  legal bases for 220–77
    Carman v. McDonnell Douglas Corp. 221
  means for protecting
    imputed notice. *See also.* 193
  retribution, protection from 29
  state statutes 259–62
  The Ombudsman Association Standards of Practice 34
  Uniform Mediation Act provisions 263–64
confidentiality in litigation, protecting 300–09
  claim of ombuds confidentiality, understanding of 302
  depositions, considerations for 303
  discovery considerations for 300
  documentation, preservation of 303

independent counsel for ombuds 305–07
motions 307–09
ombuds consultation with counsel 302
privilege. *See also.*
Consolidated Omnibus Budget Reconciliation Act 428
Consumer Credit Protection Act 428
contracts, third-party ombuds 283
corporate ethics, global 108–11
  AMA/HRI Business Ethics Survey 108
  corruption, prevention of 110
  employee recruitment and retention, impact on 110
  failures of 109
  integrity issues, impact on management 109
  need for 108
  public perceptions, importance of 110
  scandals, prevention of 110
  World Economic Forum opinion poll 110
corporate governance and government regulation
  federal agency reporting incentives 128
  In re Caremark 126–27
  prosecution guidelines 125–26
    McNulty Memo 125
  Securities Exchange Commission 129–30
  Stone v. Ritter 127
  U.S. sentencing guidelines 119–22
    Sentencing Reform Act 120
  USA Patriot Act 128
Corporate Ombudsman Association 20
  Code of Ethics 30
  formation of 17
  name change to Ombudsman Association 21
Cotrone v. Marquette University 205

Crawford v. Metro. Gov't of Nashville & Davidson County 136, 436
criminal cases, confidentiality in 364–71
  right to confront and cross-examine 364–37
    Davis v. Alaska 364
    Douglas v. Alabama 365
  Sixth Amendment privilege claims 367–68
    United States v. Rainone 367
Criminal Fine Enforcement Act 372
criminal liability for organizations 119–26
  criminal sentencing 121, 129
    culpability score, assignment of 121
  early development of 117–19
    Foreign Corrupt Practices Act 118
    New York Central & Hudson Railroad v. United States 117
    Insider Trading and Securities Fraud Enforcement A 128
    investigations, increase in 118
  NASDAQ 130
  New York Stock Exchange 130
  penalties for, increase in 119
  prosecution guidelines 125–26
    Holder Memo 125
    McNulty Memo 125
    "Principles of Federal Prosecution of Business Organizations" 125
    Thompson Memo 125
  Sarbanes-Oxley Act 124, 129
  Securities Exchange Commission 124
  sentencing guidelines
    2004 revisions to 122–24
    ethics and compliance programs, development of 122
    federal agency reporting incentives 128

U.S. Sentencing Commission 120
United States v. Booker 123
U.S. sentencing guidelines 119–22
Sentencing Reform Act 120
USA Patriot Act 128

D

Davis, Kenneth Culp 6, 9
Davis v. Alaska 365
Davis-Bacon Act 428
defense industry 17–20
    Commission on Defense Management, purpose of 18
    defense contractors, investigations of 18
    Defense Industry Initiative. *See also.*
    misconduct in 18
Defense Industry Initiative 18–19, 29, 231
    adoption of 19
    Commission on Defense Management 18
    defense contractors, investigations of 18
        ombudsman programs, creation of 19
    principles of 19
demographics, shift in 86–95
    educational institutions, impact on 89
    ethnic diversity, increase in 86
    generational changes 93–94
    growth rate of workforce, decrease in 93
    immigration 87–88
        Immigration and Nationality Act 87
        impact of 88
    impact of
        conflict, increase in 94
        misunderstandings, increase in 94

    international, impact on 91–92
    women, increased role in workplace 92
depositions 316–17
devaluation, protection from
    importance in ombuds programs 9
Devine, Thomas 156
discovery
    admission, requests for 320–21
    confidentiality, harm in breaching 271
    court regulation of 271–73
    depositions 316–17
    electronically stored information. *See also.*
    expenses for failure to admit 327
    inspection, requests for 319–20
    information, determination of relevancy 271
    interrogatories 317–19
    ombuds' practice, implications for 338
    production, requests for 319–20
    remedies 324–27
        motion for protective order 308
        motion in limine 308
        motion to compel discovery 308, 325
        protective orders 324
    rules in civil actions 315–16
    sanctions for failure to comply 326
    scope of 321–24
        privileges 322–24
diversity as force for change 89
documentation for ombuds offices
    charters 278–83
        articulating features of the office 279
        framework for 280
        governing principles 282
        independence, support for 280
        need for 278
        public policies, importance to 281

usefulness as court document 280
confidentiality, importance in establishing 277–300
imputed notice, establishment of 277
necessary provisions 277
position descriptions 285
publicizing availability of ombuds programs. *See also.*
Dolan, Peter 109
Douglas v. Alabama 365
Drug-Free Workplace Act of 1988 428
Dudley Thompson v. The Coca Cola Co. 205

E

Eastern Montana College 10
educational institutions
changing demographics, impact on 89
Edwards, Gary 165
electronically stored information
discovery of 327–38
duty to preserve 329–32
preservation 329–36
duty, triggering of 329–32
materials covered 332
noncompliance, consequences of 336
obligation, satisfying 335
Elezovic v. Ford Motor Co. 202, 218
Employee Polygraph Protection Act 429
Employee Retirement Security Income Act 429
employment law 132–42, 425–38
Age Discrimination in Employment Act 425
Americans with Disabilities Act 426
anti-harassment policies, need for 134

Civil Rights Act of 1866 426
Civil Rights Act of 1964 427
Civil Rights Act of 1991 427
complaint mechanisms, need for 134
Consolidated Omnibus Budget Reconciliation Act 428
Consumer Credit Protection Act 428
Davis-Bacon Act 428
discrimination training programs, need for 139
Drug-Free Workplace Act of 1988 428
Employee Polygraph Protection Act 429
Employee Retirement Income Security Act 429
Equal Pay Act 429
Executive Order No. 11,246 430
Fair Credit Reporting Act 430
Fair Labor Standards Act 430
Family and Medical Leave Act 431
Genetic Information Nondiscrimination Act of 2008 430
harassment training programs, need for 139
Health Insurance Portability and Accountability Act 431
Immigration Reform and Control Act of 1986 432
Labor-Management Relations Act 432
National Labor Relations Act 432
Notification and Federal Employee Anti-discrimination and Retaliation Act 432
Occupational Safety & Health Act 433
Patsy Takemoto Mink Equal Opportunity in Education Act 433
Pregnancy Discrimination Act 433

Sarbanes-Oxley Act 433
state legislation 437–38
Taft-Hartley Act 432
Title IX cases 137–38
   Gebster v. Lago Vista Independent School District 137
   Jackson v. Birmingham Board of Education 138
Title VII cases 133–37
   Burlington Industries, Inc. v. Ellerth 133
   Burlington Northern & Santa Fe Railway Co. v. White 135
   CBOCS West v. Humphries 136
   Crawford v. Metropolitan Government of Nashville and Davidson County 136
   Farragher v. City of Boca Raton 133
   Garcetti v. Ceballos 137
   hostile environment discrimination 133
   Kolstad v. American Dental Association 135
   Meritor Savings Bank v. Vinson 133
   quid pro quo discrimination 133
   sexual discrimination 133
U.S. Equal Employment Opportunity Commission 135, 194, 218
Uniformed Services Employment and Reemployment Rights Act 434
Vietnam-Era Veterans' Readjustment Assistance Act 434
whistle-blower laws 139–44
   American Recovery and Reinvestment Act 140
   Civil Service Reform Act of 1978 139
   False Claims Act 139
   Notification and Federal Employee Anti-discrimination and Retaliation Act 140
   Sarbanes-Oxley Act 139
   state laws 140
   Worker Adjustment and Retraining Notification Act 435
employment litigation, ombuds programs' role in reducing 180–83
Equal Pay Act 429
essential characteristics, organizational ombuds 27–72
   ABA 1969 Resolution 27
   ABA resolutions regarding 27–29
   confidentiality, influence on ombuds conduct 29
   impartiality. *See also.*
   independence. *See also.*
   neutrality. *See also.*
   Ombuds Association, The Standards of Practice 33–35
   confidentiality. *See also.*
   retribution
      need to address fears about 29
Ethics Resource Center 159
   National Business Ethics Survey 159, 165–67, 170
ethics officers 144–47
   compliance programs, administration of 144
   confidentiality, preserving request for 145
   ethics survey data 157–71
   hotlines, administration of 157–71
   National Government Ethics Survey 166
   role of 145
   whistle-blowers, protection of 147–57
ethics survey data 157–71
European Union
   Data Protection Directive 406–24

history of 409–11
provisions of 407–09, 411–16
Safe Harbor Agreement 418–20
whistle-blower provisions 420
Executive Order No. 11,246 430

F

Fair Credit Reporting Act 430
Fair Labor Standards Act 430
False Claims Act 139, 149
 whistle-blower protections 139
Family and Medical Leave Act 431
Faragher v. City of Boca Raton 133, 199, 435
Federal Arbitration Act 343–45
federal government, adoption of ombuds programs 21–78
 Administrative Conference of the United States 22
  recommendation on creation of ombuds programs 22
 Administrative Dispute Resolution Act 23, 180, 264–68, 340
  ombuds role, defining of 23
 American Bar Association recommendation 22
 Coalition of Federal Ombudsmen 24
 federal agency programs, functioning of 22
 Federal Interagency ADR Working Group 24
Federal Interagency ADR Working Group 24
Federal Records Act 389–92
Federal Rule of Evidence 501 221–27, 230–33
Foegen, J.H. 17
Folb v. Motion Picture Industry Pension & Health Plans 269
forces of change 86–115
 demographics. *See also.*
 globalization. *See also.*
 impact on the workplace 113–17

multinational corporations. *See also.*
technology. *See also.*
Foreign Corrupt Practices Act 118
Freedom of Information Act 393–400
 amendments to 394
 exemptions from 397
 noncompliance 395
 provisions of 394
 state statutes 403
Friedman, Thomas 86

G

Garcetti v. Ceballos 137
Garstang v. The Superior Court of Los Angeles County 256
Gebster v. Lago Vista Independent School District 137
Gellhorn, Walter 6,, 9
generational changes, impact on workplace 93
Genetic Information Nondiscrimination Act of 2008 430
Gilmer v. Interstate/Johnson Lane Corp. 274
global workforce, emergence of 101–02
 economic impact of 101
 outsourcing, increase in 101
Gnazzo, Patrick 144, 173
Gomez-Perez v. Potter 436
Greenberg, Hank 109
Griggs v. Duke Power Co. 435
Grother v. Union Pacific Railroad Co. 203

H

Heineman Jr. ,Ben W. 108, 119
Health Insurance Portability and Accountability Act 431
Hooker v. United Parcel Services 201
Hoffman, Michael 113
Holder, Eric 126

hotlines for reporting misconduct 157–87
  employee reluctance to use 165
  features of 160–61
  ineffectiveness of 179
  limitations on effectiveness of 161–87
    formal reporting channels 161
    outsourcing of the service 162
  reasons for creating 158–60
    employee pressures 158
    Ethics Resource Center surveys 159, 165–68
    Sarbanes-Oxley Act provisions for 159

I

Immigration and Nationality Act 87
immigration as force for change 87–88
  Immigration and Nationality Act 87
  Immigration Reform and Control Act of 1986 432
imminent threat exception to confidentiality 354
  Tarasoff v. Regents of University of California 356
    Tarasoff rule, adoption of 359
impartiality 28
  ABA 2001 Report 54
    defined 54
  ABA 2001 Resolution 53
  ABA 2004 Report 54
  ABA 2004 Resolution 53
  IOA Code of Ethics 52
implied contract of confidentiality 249–55
  implied in fact 250
  implied in law 250, 253
imputed notice 193–220
  ABA 2004 Resolution
    ombuds as agent of notice 212
  basic principles of 193–95

Chambers v. Wal-Mart Stores, Inc. 201
confidentiality, relation to 277
Cotrone v. Marquette University 205
decision to impute, considerations for 195–97
Dudley Thompson v. The Coca Cola Co. 205
Elezovic v. Ford Motor Co. 202, 218
Faragher v. City of Boca Raton 199
Grother v. Union Pacific Railroad Co. 203
Hooker v. United Parcel Services 201
IOA Standards of Practice
  ombuds as agent of notice 212
Karibian v. Columbia University 198
Norden v. Samper 207
Palomo v. The Trustees of Columbia Univ. 202
S.S. v. Alexander 208
Sims v. Med. Ctr. of Baton Rouge, Inc. 200
Torres v. Pisano 200
Webb v. Merck & Co., Inc. 204
In Defense of Animals v. National Institutes of Health 396
In re Caremark 126–27
In re Doe 230–32
independence 28
  2004 ABA Report 48
  ABA 2001 Resolution 47
    defined 47
  ABA 2004 Resolution 47
  assessment of 47
  establishing in ombuds charters 280
  importance in ombuds programs 9
  International Ombudsman Association
    Code of Ethics 47

Standards of Practice 47
The Ombuds Association, Standards
of Practice 34
informality
   IOA Code of Ethics 65
   IOA Standards of Practice 65
   UCOA standards of practice
     provision 36
inquiries
   ABA 2001 Resolution 53
   ABA 2004 Resolution 53
Insider Trading and Securities Fraud
   Enforcement Act 128
inspection, requests for 319–20
International Ombudsman Association
   36
   2004 ABA Resolution, response to
     50
   2009 Best Practices 51, 55, 61, 70
     recommendations 72–75
   Code of Ethics 172
     impartiality, issue of 52
     independence, issue of 47
     neutrality, issue of 52
     revised 46
   Guidance and Commentary 45
     collective bargaining 45, 69
     notice, issue of 46
   Standards of Practice
     independence, issue of 47
     ombuds as agent of notice 212
     revised 46
interrogatories 317–19
investigations
   ABA 2001 Resolution 53
   ABA 2004 Resolution 53
   conduct of
     UCOA standards of practice 36
   importance in ombuds programs 9
issue resolution
   organizational ombuds role in 75

J

Jackson v. Birmingham Bd. of Educ.
   138, 436
Jeanne Clery Act 311, 284–88
Johnson v. Transportation Agency
   435

K

Kaplan, Jeffrey M. 123
Karibian v. Columbia University 198
Kent State University 12
Kientzy v. McDonnell Douglas Corp.
   231
Kleinfeld, Klaus 109
knowledge workers, increased need
   for 98
Kolstad v. American Dental Association 135
KPMG Integrity Survey 166, 168–70

L

Labor-Management Relations Act
   432
Lawlor III, Edward E. 111
Leslie v. United Technologies Corp.
   243

M

Maassarani, Tarek 156
Madoff, Bernard 117, 155
Manley, Mark 187
Markopolos, Harry 153
Mazlish, Bruce 82
McNulty, Paul J. 126
mediation 345–48
   confidentiality 347–48
   privilege 347–48
Meltzer, D. Leah 22
Meritor Sav. Bank v. Vinson 133, 435
Michigan State University 10
Miller v. Regents of the Univ. of Colo.
   240, 242
multinational corporations 104–17

corporate ethics, global. *See also.*
globalization, impact of
Budweiser 106
Halliburton 106
IBM 106–08
increase in corporations outside U.S. 106
Lenovo 106
growth of 105–06
power and influence of 105
world recession, impact on 112–13
decrease in employee security 114
decrease in spending on ethics programs 113

N

N. Haven Bd. of Educ. v. Bell 435
NASDAQ
criminal liability for organizations 130
National Institutes of Health 396
National Labor Relations Act 432
neutrality 28
importance in ombuds programs 176
IOA Code of Ethics 52
The Ombuds Association, Standards of Practice 34
New York Central & Hudson Railroad v. United States 117
New York Stock Exchange
criminal liability for organizations 130
Norden v. Samper 207
notice
addressed in ABA 2004 Resolution 43
imputed. *See* imputed notice.
issue of
International Ombudsman Association Guidance and Commentary 46
ombuds as agent of 212
Notification and Federal Employee Anti-discrimination and Retaliation Act 432
whistle-blower protections of 140

O

Occupational Safety & Health Act 433
The Ombuds Association
Code of Ethics 31
Standards of Practice
confidentiality 34
independence 34
neutrality 34
survey of hotline usage 177
ombuds authority, limitations on
2004 ABA Report 67
ABA 2001 Resolution 66
ABA 2004 Resolution 66
ombuds, public sector
records retention requirements 389–405
ombudsman, history of 1–27
Canadian adoption of 5
corporate adoption of 15–17
Corporate Ombudsman Association 17
defense industry. *See also.*
federal government, adoption of ombuds programs. *See also.*
German adoption of 5
New Zealand adoption of 5
ombudsman offices, structure of 9
Scandinavian expansion of 4–5
Swedish origins 2–4
United States, introduction in 6–9
American Bar Association resolution 7
congressional consideration of 7
municipal ombudsman offices, creation of 9

state ombudsman offices, creation of 9
university adoption of ombuds programs. *See also.*
Oncale v. Sundowner Offshore Serv., 436
organizational ombuds
   areas of concern 75–78
      communications and outreach 75
      identification of areas for systemic change 75
      issue resolution 75
   charters establishing 278–83
   defined 25
   discovery, implications for 338–39
   effectiveness of, measuring 297
   essential characteristics. *See* essential characteristics, organizational ombuds.
   privilege. *See* privilege, ombuds.
   publicizing the office 286
   third-party provider
      contract for 283
organizational ombuds programs
   effectiveness of 178, 184–87
   reasons for creating 79–86
      checks and balances, need for 79, 81
      criminal liability for organizations. *See also.*
      effectiveness in uncovering misconduct 179
      ethical conduct, need for 81
      forces of change. *See also,*
      means for resolving personnel issues 183
      proper behavior, need for 80
      reduction of employment litigation 180–83
      societal challenges 81
      usefulness to upper management 183
   structure of. *See* structure of ombuds programs

success of, reasons for 80
   freedom from management responsibility 80
O'Toole, James 111
outreach, organizational ombuds' role in 75
outsourcing, increase in 101

P

Packard Commission (President's Blue Ribbon Commission on Defense Management) 18–19, 235
Packard, David 18
Palomo v. The Trustees of Columbia Univ. 202
Patsy Takemoto Mink Equal Opportunity in Education Act 433
personnel issues
   ombuds programs as means for resolving 183
Pfeffer, Jeffrey 111
Phillips, John B. 187
Pregnancy Discrimination Act 433
Privacy Act 400–18
privilege
   common law. *See* common-law privilege.
   federal mediation 269–71
      Federal Rule of Evidence 408 269
      Folb v. Motion Picture Industry Pension & Health Plans 269
   Uniform Mediation Act
      exception to privilege 361
      implications for ombuds offices 263–64, 351
privilege, ombuds 227–39
   Acord v. Alyeska Pipeline Service Co. 232
   Carman v. McDonnell Douglas Corp. 233, 239–43
   claim, invocation of 244–45
   In re Doe 230, 232
   Kientzy v. McDonnell Douglas Corp. 231

Miller v. Regents of the Univ. of Colo. 240–42
recognition of 245–56
    Leslie v. United Technologies Corp. 243
    Van Martin v. United Technologies Corp. 243
    Roy v. United Technologies Corp. 229
    Shabazz v. Scurr 227, 240
production, requests for 319–20
public records, access to 393–401
    Administrative Dispute Resolution Act 397
    Administrative Procedure Act 393
    Freedom of Information Act 393–400
        amendments to 394
        exemptions from 397
        noncompliance 395
        provisions of 394
        scope of 396
        state statutes 403
    In Defense of Animals v. National Institutes of Health 396
    Privacy Act 400–18
    Rural Housing Alliance v. U.S. Dep't of Agriculture 399
    U.S. Dep't of State v. Washington Post Co. 399
    U.S. Dep't of Justice v. Tax Analysts 396
publicizing availability of ombuds programs 286–90
    ABA resolution provisions 287
    core principles of office 289
    effectiveness of office, measuring 297–301
    methods for
        annual reports 289
        brochures 286
        bulletin board posters 289
        internal communications media 289
        training presentations 289
        web sites 286
    notice assumption 287
    operation of office 290–95
        case files, handling of 292
        policies and procedures 291–92
    organizational information, need to review 290
    trend reports to management 295–97
        considerations in preparing 296

R

Raines, Frank 109
Reagan, Ronald 18
records retention 389–405
    Federal Records Act 389–92
removal from office, ombuds 48
Restatement of Torts (Second) 355, 360
Restatement (Second) of the Law of Agency 195–97
Restatement (Second) of the Law of Contracts 251–54
retribution
    need to address in ombuds programs 29
    protection from, importance in ombuds programs 9
Robbins, Lee 17
Roosevelt, Theodore 116
Rowat, Donald 5, 6
Rowe, Mary 14–17, 29, 145
Roy v. United Technologies Corp. 229
Rural Housing Alliance v. U.S. Dep't of Agriculture 399

S

S.S. v. Alexander 208
Sarbanes-Oxley Act 150, 406, 420–38, 433

criminal liability for organizations 124, 129
hotline provisions 159
whistle-blower laws 139
Securities Exchange Commission
criminal liability for organizations 124, 129
stock exchange and association requirements 129–30
sentencing guidelines
criminal liability for organizations 119–22
U.S. Sentencing Commission 120
federal guidelines for organizations 372–83
2004 amendments to 379
basic principles of 375
basic structure of 374
Criminal Fine Enforcement Act 372
Sentencing Reform Act 372
U.S. Sentencing Commission 372
ongoing risk assessment 143
Sentencing Reform Act 120, 372
Shabazz v. Scurr 227, 240
Sims v. Med. Ctr. of Baton Rouge, Inc. 200
Sixth Amendment to the Constitution 364–71
Smith v. Jackson 436
Solorzano v. Shell Chemical Co. 241
Souter, David 136
standards of practice 30–37
International Ombudsman Association
confidentiality 57
informality 65
revised standards 46
Ombuds Association, The 31–37
essential characteristics of organizational ombuds 35

Stone v. Ritter 127
structure of ombuds programs 171–76
confidentiality, importance of 173
information, reporting of 175
management functions, freedom from 175
neutrality, importance of 176
supplementing traditional channels 172
voluntary nature of 173
structure of ombudsman offices 9
systemic change, need for
organizational ombuds role in identifying 75

T

Taft-Hartley Act 432
Tarasoff v. Regents of University of California 356
technology as force for change 95–104
global workforce, emergence of 101–02
economic impact of 101
outsourcing, increase in 101
information technology sector, growth of 98
interconnectivity of information systems, physical separation, problems of 95
knowledge workers, increased need for 98
United States lagging behind other countries 97
universities, globalization of 102–05
foreign students studying in U.S. 104
Open Doors study 102
study-abroad programs 103
virtual workspace, prevalence of 99
Thompson, Larry D. 126
Torres v. Pisano 200
Trammel v. United States 222
trend reports 295

U

U.S. Dep't of Justice v. Tax Analysts 396
U.S. Dep't of State v. Washington Post Co. 399
U.S. Equal Employment Opportunity Commission 135, 181, 173–74, 194, 218
U.S. Sentencing Commission 120, 372
U.S. Sentencing Guidelines 119–22, 141, 372–83
   2004 Revision to the Organizational Sentencing Guidelines 122–24
Uniform Mediation Act 263–64, 348–51
   confidentiality provisions of 263–64
   privilege provisions 349
      exception to privilege 361
      ombuds offices, implications for 351
   purpose of 348
Uniformed Services Employment and Reemployment Rights Act 434
United States v. Booker 123
United States v. Bryan 224
United States v. Nixon 223–24
United States v. Rainone 367
universities, globalization of 102–05
   foreign students studying in the U.S. 104
   Open Doors study 102
   study-abroad programs 103
university adoption of ombuds programs 10–15
   California Caucus of College and University Ombuds 14
   California public universities 13
   Commission on Campus Unrest 12
      reform of university governance, need for 12
   Commission on Higher Education report recommending adoption of ombuds programs 13
   Eastern Montana College 10
   Kent State University 12
   Massachusetts Institute of Technology 14
   Michigan State University 10
   national conference on 12
   purpose of college programs 14
   reform of university governance, need for 12
   University and College Ombuds Association. *See also.*
University and College Ombuds Association 14, 21, 36
   formation of 14
   standards of practice 36
      informality provision 36
      investigations, conduct of 36
   Statement of Ethical Principles 36
Upjohn v. United States 225
USA Patriot Act 128

V

Van Martin v. United Technologies Corp. 243
Vietnam-Era Veterans' Readjustment Assistance Act 434
virtual workspace, prevalence of 99–101
   impact of 99

W

Webb v. Merck & Co., Inc. 204
whistle-blower laws 139–44
   American Recovery and Reinvestment Act 140. 156–58
   Civil Service Reform Act of 1978 139
   effectiveness of 149–50
      Civil Service Reform Act 150
      False Claims Act 149
      Sarbanes-Oxley Act 150

False Claims Act 139
Notification and Federal Employee Anti-discrimination and Retaliation Act 140
retaliation, forms of 148
Sarbanes-Oxley Act 139
whistle-blowers 147–57
  personal consequences for 148
  policies governing, limitations of 147
  policies on, failures of 151–56
    accusations not taken seriously 153
    cultural aversion to the concept 152
    lack of protection for accuser 153
    peer or co-worker retaliation 151
    reporting time constraints 154
    the boss as a factor 151
  retaliation against 148
  supervisors of, effects on 149
women, increased role in workplace 92
Worker Adjustment and Retraining Notification Act 435
world recession, multinational corporations, impact on 112–13
Wratney, George R. 144

Y

Yuanqing, Yang 107

Z

Zakaria, Fareed 82
Zinsser, John 180